AF689251

ALL WERE NOT HEROES

A study of the list of U.S. soldiers executed by U.S. military authorities during the late war.

by
Edward C. Johnson
Gail R. Johnson
Melissa Johnson Williams

To Douglas Howard
Best wishes on your Program
cordially yours
LTC Edward C Johnson
USAR (Ret)

©1997 by Edward C. Johnson

All rights reserved. Except for appropriate use in critical reviews or works of scholarship, the reproduction or use of this work in any form or by any electronic, mechanical, or other means now known or hereafter invented, including photocopying and recording, and in any information storage and retrieval system, is forbidden without written permission of the author, Edward C. Johnson, 5033 W. Gunnison, Chicago, Illinois 60630. Permission is never granted for commercial purposes.

Printed in Canada

10 9 8 7 6 5 4 3 2 1

ISBN: 1-886094-74-8

CONTENTS

FORWARD

The title, "ALL WERE NOT HEROES," was selected from various quotations of memories of events occurring during the Civil War as related by Private Wilhelm Frederick Graef, Wisconsin Volunteer Infantry, grandfather of Edward C. Johnson. Graef, of German birth, often had "old comrades" of his Regiment as visitors in his home after the war. Speaking in German, they discussed events of the late war. Catherine Barbara Graef, mother of Edward C. Johnson, often related events of the Civil War overheard in her childhood during such gatherings. One such event was the viewing of an execution by her father either as a casual spectator or as a member of his Regiment ordered to attend. Private Graef commented, "Alle Wahren Nicht Helden," (All Were Not Heroes), an appropriate title for this book.

PREFACE

Our interest in Civil War executions, which culminated in the production of *"Study of the List of U.S. Soldiers Executed by the United States Military Authorities during the Late War,"* grew out of our earlier interest in studies of the Embalming Surgeons and casualty treatment of the Civil War dead. In 1965, we acquired copies of the case book of a Civil War Embalming Surgeon, William J. Bunnell, which contained among other notations a curious reference to Privates Geary and Gordon of the 72nd New York Volunteer Infantry. Bunnell had written across the entry list of the case book of these consecutive cases, "these two men was hung for the rape of a lady" and the fact that the bill for his services and merchandise (coffins, etc.) were to be billed to the Provost Marshall General Marsena Rudolph Patrick.

We made further inquiry concerning Civil War Military executions and were told by the late Don Russell and the late E. B. (Pete) Long that there existed a "List of U.S. soldiers executed by United States Military authorities during the late war." The list, when obtained from National Archives, was found to be imprinted with, "For Official Use Only" and a penciled warning "Confidential." The list is arranged by states, special Military units such as U.S. Colored Troops, Regulars, U.S. Volunteers ("galvanized Yankees or Penitent Rebels"), Veteran Reserve Corps and miscellaneous.

The total number of listings were for 267 men alleged to have been executed. Our interest was whetted and we began the time consuming and often frustrating collection of all available Military Records, copies of the Court Martial Proceedings, newspaper and contemporary book accounts from Regiment histories, State Adjutant General Reports, and similar sources for each man listed. E. C. Johnson was a Lieutenant Colonel in the USAR QM Corps and was transferred, in 1965, as a Military Historian assigned to the U.S. Army, Office of the Chief of Military History, Washington, D.C. where further sources of information were located.

In the 1980s, we recommended, to Michael E. Pilgrim of National Archives, that the collection of all available proceedings (trial records) of court martials of the 267 men listed as executed, be assembled onto microfilm. Mr. Pilgrim and associates did reproduce same onto eight reels of microfilm which is now available to interested parties. In addition, we searched for and located illustrations of executions by hanging and by firing squads, newspaper ads for substitutes and have incorporated as an appendix to our study a large variety of Military correspondence forms, many of which have not previously been given wide exposure.

While we feel the present volume is reasonably complete, we look forward with considerable anticipation to the possibility of securing more documentation concerning existing listed individuals, and of examining other similar cases not on the list, hidden by error and time.

ACKNOWLEDGEMENTS

We are indebted to so many people and institutions for assistance and guidance on this project. What we at first conceived as a brief study, insidiously enlarged to a search and study extending for over twenty years.

First and foremost, we must acknowledge the two individuals who provided us with material, assistance and encouragement, the late Don Russell, authority on western history and aspects of the Civil War, and the late great E. B. (Pete) Long, authority par excellence on Civil War history, author of "Civil War Day by Day" and researcher for Bruce Catton.

Obviously, the people at National Archives, Washington, D.C. made the documentation of all the individual records possible. Among whom were Michael Pilgrim, William A. Lind and their many associates to whom we owe so much. To the Library of Congress, Manuscript Division, and the Photo-Duplication Service of the Library of Congress. To Peter Aimone, of the Library at the U.S. Military Academy at Westpoint, New York. To Roger Long, the authority on the Johnson's Island Prisoner of War Camp for Confederate Prisoners near Sandusky, Ohio. To Charles L. Sullivan of Mississippi for data on Military Crimes committed in Mississippi. To Dr. Lawrence A. Frost, authority on General Custer. To Daniel Weinberger and Abraham Lincoln book shop. To Eugene Murdock, authority on Civil War Draft Laws. To Theodore Cook, descendent of Mrs. Minerva Cook, murdered near Vicksburg, Mississippi. And to the premier out-of-state researcher we consulted, Katy Matthews of Topeka, Kansas, another top researcher was Jean Collier of Columbus, Ohio. To John Y. Simon, authority on General Grant. To Dee Brown, authority on "Galvanized Yankees." To John M. Carroll, authority on Custer in Texas. To Kenneth Krah, assistant researcher. To Roy Kiplinger, acting Curator of Manuscripts of the William L. Clements Library. To William L. Clements Library, Ann Arbor, Michigan. To Robert Torrey of the New Mexico State Records and Archives Center, Sante Fe. To the Rhode Island Secretary of State, Archives Division. To the Pentagon Library, U.S. Department of Defense at the Pentagon, Washington, D.C. To the Office of the U.S. Army, Department of Military History, Washington, D.C. To all the Librarians at the Chicago Public Library, Special Collections Center. To the Chicago Historical Society. To the Ohio Historical Society. To the Kansas State Historical Society. To the Oliveira Library at Brownsville, Texas. To the Texas State Library. To the University of Texas Archives. To the Massachusetts Historical Society. To the Kentucky Public Records Division and Archives. To the Florida State Library. To the Florida State Archives. To the Illinois Archives Division. To the Indiana State Library and Archives. To the Louisiana Secretary of State, Archives and Records Division. To the Michigan Department of State, History Division, State Archives Unit. To the Mississippi Department of Archives and History. To the New York State Archives. To the North Carolina State Archives. To the Oregon Secretary of State, Archives Division. To the State Historical Society of Wisconsin. To the West Virginia Department of Archives and History. To the University of Oregon Library. To the U.S. Army Military History Institute (Carlisle, Pennsylvania). To the U.S. Department of the Interior, National Park Service, Gettysburg. To the National Military Park and Andersonville National Cemetery. To the U.S. Army Judge Advocate General's School. To the California State Archives and last but not least, our deep gratitude to Ralph G. Newman, Civil War/President Lincoln authority par excellence, who from early on, advised and encouraged us on this project.

The cover was designed by Paula Johnson DeSmet.

To all others not mentioned, our deep gratitude for their advice and assistance in this protracted study.

E. C. Johnson
G. R. Johnson
M. Johnson-Williams

INTRODUCTION

The reader of this study must keep ever in mind that the events herein related occurred between 135-140 years ago. It is difficult for the contemporary reader to realize that the original records were all handwritten and hand copied (as carbon paper was not then in use). The copies of records obtained in this study contain varying degrees of legibility as well as obvious discrepancies particularly as to spelling of names, dates, physical description data as to age, height, hair, skin and eye color and occupation. Some documents pertaining to the soldier's service record are absent from the individual file whether by loss, deterioration or misfiling. We have attempted to determine the literacy of the individual soldier using as the criteria, his ability to sign his name. However, in a number of cases, since signed enlistment papers were not in the file, such determination was impossible. Another means of estimating literacy was by occupation. Thus, if the soldier was a bookkeeper, school teacher, bank clerk, or similar occupation, it was not unreasonable to assume the individual could be classified as literate. There are not, however, sufficient sets of documents bearing such proof to be able to present any useful estimate of the literacy of the enlisted men in this study of the Union Army personnel during the Civil War.

Our study of the 267 men listed as executed, yielded a variety of unusual and interesting facts. Private Jeremiah Richards, Company D, 55 Pennsylvania Volunteer Infantry was actually listed as Private Jeremiah Roberts, Company D, 55 Pennsylvania Volunteer Infantry and our report of same to National Archives made possible the correction of the Court Martial Proceedings records as there was such a record for a Richards but none for Roberts. We also learned that death sentences for a number of convicted soldiers were commuted after they had been executed. These cases included Private David Geer, Company D, 28th Illinois Volunteer Infantry and Pvt. Jacob Morgan, Company D, 8th Connecticut Volunteer Infantry. Several convicted soldiers named as executed on the official list were not actually executed. Private Samuel Mapp, Company D, 10th Infantry, U. S. Colored Troops and Private Benjamin McCloud, Company E, 37th Infantry, U. S. Colored Troops, both managed to escape execution. The records also indicate a number of family relationships. Privates William and George A. Blowers, Company A, 2nd Vermont Veteran Volunteer Infantry, deserted together but only George was executed. Privates John W. and Christopher Coffey, Company C, 27th Kentucky Volunteer Infantry deserted together and were executed together. Privates James and John W. Hardup, Company A, 43rd Ohio Volunteer Infantry were brothers who fled the Army after John committed murder. Both were apprehended but only John was executed.

Two soldiers, Private Alexander Driscoll, Company H, 7th Kansas Volunteer Cavalry and Private Thomas R. Dawson, Company I, 20th Massachusetts Volunteer Infantry, were said to have been in the British Army during the Crimean War.

While over one half of all the crimes for which the executed soldiers were convicted were for desertion, the overwhelming number of such executions for desertion were committed by 137 white soldiers. The U. S. Colored troops had only one such listed execution for desertion.

There are several detailed accounts of autopsies and embalmings performed following execution.

One soldier, Private Reuben Stout, Company K, 60th Indiana Voluntary Infantry was convicted of murder while absent without leave. He was, by his own confession, influenced by his membership in the subversive organization known as "The Knights of the Golden Circle." He was tried, convicted, sentenced to death and transported to the Johnson's Island (off the coast of Sandusky, Ohio) Prisoner of War Camp for Confederate soldiers, where he was recorded and held as a Confederate prisoner before he was executed and buried there. Two of the executed solders were in the U. S. Volunteers

Regiments of the Union Army whose ranks were composed of Confederate prisoners who had forsaken the Rebel cause, taken an oath of allegiance to the Union, released from Union Army Prisoner of War Camps and sworn into the service of the Union Army. These regiments of ex-Confederates, were dubbed "Galvanized Yankees" or "penitent rebels" and were to be sent to the west to fight indians, maintain order, and were specifically not to be used against Confederate troops.

One soldier, tried, convicted and sentenced to be executed, Private H. M. Carabajol, Company D, 1st New Mexico Cavalry was never executed. He was pronounced insane, therefore unfit for execution, and sent to a government mental hospital in Washington D.C. for treatment. He was discharged as cured and seemingly never executed.

The entire list of the 267 alleged to have been executed were enlisted men and non-commissioned officers, no Union officer was known to have been officially executed during the Civil War.

We did locate a number of executions not on the "Official List" and they will be dealt with separately from the listed executions.

One set of Union Army executions not borne on the "Official List" are the "6 Andersonville Raiders" convicted by a fellow prisoner imposed court martial and hung within the prison compound at the infamous Confederate Andersonville Prisoner of War Camp in Georgia. We did, we believe, solve the mystery as to the correct identity of the six executed raiders, concerning which there has been much controversy.

And finally, we discovered the answer to the basic question as to the origin of the "Official List." On June 2, 1884, Brigadier General Richard C. Drum, Adjutant General of the U. S. Army, ordered Joseph W. Kirkley, statistician in the Adjutant General's office, to prepare a statistical report of deaths in the United States Army during the late War (Civil War). Kirkley completed the voluminous and detailed report and presented it to the Adjutant General on May 22, 1885. The report covered every state's military units and special units, listing deaths occurring from causes such as killed in action, suicide, drowned, murdered, sunstroke, and those executed by U. S. Military authorities. The latter listing totaled 267, the same number as the "Official List."

Kirkley's report and the "Official List" differs in that he listed only the numbers of executed soldiers for each state and separate Military Unit, while the "Official List" provides the name, rank, date of execution, crime, mode of execution and authority for same (court martial order number, etc.). On the last page of the "Official List" is a penciled notation, "AGO, Wash. Aug 1, 1885" thus chronologically linking the two documents.

The format of our study includes the basic information concerning the laws governing military justice, the Articles of War and Court Martials and trial procedures. An introduction to military forces recruitment, volunteering, draft laws and the bounty system, which contributed a most substantial part of the desertion problem, as well as copies of many form letters in use during the Civil War which may be unfamiliar to the reader in a companion volume now in preparation.

The main body of the study consists of an exposition of the biography, military and civilian, as available, and the circumstances of the crime, trial and execution of each soldier on the "Official List" taken in chronological order. Some of the individual biographies are extensive and detailed while others contain little more than the most meager facts. These differences reflect the amount of basic military biographical data available at National Archives or from similar sources. This section is followed by a similar treatment for men executed but not placed on the "Official List".

INTRODUCTION TO THE CASE STUDIES

Individual Case Record Studies of the Union Army Soldies Executed During the Civil War

There are two separate sets of records studied:

A -comprises the 267 men listed on "The Official Records"
B -a much smaller group of cases studied which, for one reason or another, do not appear on "The Official Records" list.

Some, discussed in this latter section, were executed under unique situations, in less than normal circumstances. Two such examples are the "6 Andersonville Raiders," executed within the Andersonville P.O.W. camp after a court martial trial by their peers. Another example is the three members of the 11th Ohio Cavalry Regiment who were shot for mutiny while on the march in Indian territory. Included here, too, are some examples of fate intervening to provide justice without the ritual execution. In one such case, the condemned prisoner developed smallpox and died before execution. In another case, the condemned prisoner escaped from the guardhouse at the Fort where he was confined awaiting execution only to drown during the attempted escape in the moat surrounding the walls of the Fort.

It may well be that other cases of executions, unreported in the original compilation to Kirkely and his aides, will be uncovered in the future. All such cases, however, must be documentable, and not vague allusions by some diarist or letter written about some unidentified person being executed.

We have arranged each case individually to provide, insofar as possible, a biography of the person executed and the events of the crime, trial and execution. Some individuals have, for whatever reason, many sources of information available and thus we were able to produce more detailed accounts of such cases. In other instances only the most meager information was discovered after exhausting all known sources of information.

We have departed from the customary system of using references in several particulars. First, whenever possible, we have reproduced the *entire* pertinent quoted source in the body of the relevant case study and we have listed the reference source for each such case study at the end of each individual study. We have far too long wrestled with references that quoted a few words ostensibly from a larger quotation and wondered what the entire quoted section might have said. The reader will probably reply that all we had to do was to use the reference title and source and read it in the original text. Alas, it seems that many of such desired quoted sources are contained in rare book or manuscript collections, in newspapers or books in libraries at some distant point or are restricted to use at the library having custody of the item. We, therefore, decided to depart from the traditional format and proceeded as outlined above in order to permit the reader immediate access to the material quoted in our text.

The source of our data base is about 95% from the National Archives Old Military Records (Washington, D.C.) - Personnel, Court Martial Proceedings, and Military Pension Records and the various State individual Military Personnel Record centers. Additional Federal records include the Official Records of the War of the Rebellion, lists of telegraph messages sent and received and official correspondence of the War Department, various armies and their commanders, Judge Advocate's Department,

General and Special Orders of all Military Units. Newspaper and Journal accounts were most useful when available as were individual diaries and letters. Some regimental histories ignore mentioning executions entirely as though it were a stain on the record of the Regiment as well as on the record of each surviving veteran member. We had the good fortune to locate some descendants of the principals involved, in one way or another, with the original events.

It must be noted that while most of crimes for which the subjects of this study were executed were crimes individually perpetrated and the convicted criminal being individually executed, there are numerous instances where two or more individuals carried out a crime resulting in guilty verdicts, death sentences and multiple executions. In these cases, we have described the full details, insofar as available, of the crime, trial and execution in only one of the related case studies, the others containing only a minimum of pertinent data with a statement referring the reader to the location of the full description in the text. Individuals involved in a common crime are grouped together in consecutive order providing simple access to such facts.

The basic data, the Military Personnel Records, from National Archives or the State Military Record sections were reasonably complete and available. In some few cases no such records exist or are possible to be located. There are twenty-six (26) Court Martial Proceedings (trial records) missing, but most difficult to understand are the very meager and inadequate records originally collected for the men in the Regular Army Military Units. Far better records were available for the Civil War Volunteers, drafted men and substitutes. The very earliest records encountered (1861) often did not contain a description of the soldier. This was later added to the Personnel Record data and physical descriptions are noted in most later enlisted individual's file. One item not on the list was the marital status of the soldier, although if he entered a hospital the name of the next of kin was recorded and occasionally the company clerk would indicate on the margin of a muster roll card that the individual soldier listed was married. The term "literate" as used in this study is based on the ability of the soldier to write his name. Unfortunately, there are only a few documents, enlistment papers, which require a signature and many of those missing from the record file. Some documents in the personnel files were missing, strayed or whatever! From time to time, we noted contradictory data concerning an individual in his individual personnel file. Ages sometimes were recorded on separate documents varying as much as ten (10) years. All ages quoted in our case studies are the ages given upon entering military service. Similar discrepancies are noted from time to time regarding height, place of birth, and occupation.

One most commonly encountered problem was that of a number of individuals in the same Company sharing an identical name. The Civil War Company clerks, however, overcame the problem by identifying each such individual with a number. For example, if there were three John Smith's in one Company, they would appear listed on the records as John Smith #1, John Smith #2, and John Smith #3. A person unaware of the problem could (and we did) order and receive records of a person with the requested name, but with an entirely different personal and military biography. Another problem encountered with names was the variant spelling. In some records, the spelling of a name such as Smith might be spelled as Schmidt, Smidt, Schmitt. These variants are listed in the case study with the initials NV (Name Variant). When the individual used an alias in an endeavor to conceal his identity, such aliases are prefixed with the initials AKA (also known as). Some of the misspelling resulted from the attempt by the original recording clerk to translate the name as spoken to a written version. Most of these errors occurred when foreign born inductees used the foreign pronunciation of the name and the clerk recorded an anglicized version. Other errors contributing to the problem included poor handwriting which made for difficulty in copying the records. Copyists were also frequently overworked and made errors as a result of fatigue. One of the most frequent changes involved the title or designation of a particular Military Unit. Early in the war, it was common for Companies or Regiments to carry their leader's name such as Smith's Company or Regiment. In a similar case of change, the Negro Regiments were originally listed in various ways by states, incorporating the term Corps d'Afrique, or the initials A.D. (African Descent) in the designation. The changes were to eliminate duplications and promote uniformity in designations.

The individual cases that follow are listed and consecutively numbered chronologically, thus *Case #1* is the first soldier executed during the Civil War and *Case #267* is the last soldier executed. We have also provided a separate index of the names arranged alphabetically. "List B" composed of men executed, but not on the Official List, is not numbered as it is lacking in quantity, but each case described has more substance than some of those on the "Official List."

The result of our study is uneven. Some individual case studies are only slightly expanded accounts beyond the "Official List." Others have abundant reference sources and are filled with details of the case. All in all, we feel that we have found and presented a reasonably accurate and fair account of the deeds and deaths of the 267 men of the Union Army executed for crimes committed during the Civil War.

To understand the enormous amount of research employed in this study, the reader is referred to the bare bones of the work, "The List of U.S. Soldiers Executed...etc.". As one can see, the list consists of the listing of the name, rank, company, regiment, date of execution, method of execution, crime and authority for execution (order # - date - Headquarters or other). From this list we had to obtain Military Personnel Records which detailed, in later years of the War, a physical description of the soldier, his dates of enlistment, transfers, promotions, demotions, pay record, bonus payments, money owned the government, Sutler's or Laundress and any desertions, illness, wounds or Court Martial. Many of the details of a crime were unstated in those records but were generally well revealed in the Court Martial Records. Most of the 267 cases, to be exact are contained on the Micro Film Reels available from National Archives. In a study of this type, use of Micro film is a futile pursuit of knowledge. We had to have the Micro Film converted to printed pages for more efficient study. Here problems were additionally encountered as the paper and the ink of the period either faded or darkened. Some pages were virtually blank while others were nearly totally black. Magnification and special lighting assisted in exposing much of what was illegible. Handwriting had variants, although most was readily legible. A minor problem was the use of an older system of written alphabet, for example, employing a different form of the T at the end of the word and a different form of S in the middle of a word.

Some records were nearly devoid of information necessitating the search for other sources. The obvious source was the innumerable Regimental Histories. Examination of many apparently relevant volumes disclosed first - a failure to mention the execution of a member of the Company or Regiment whether from collective embarrassment or outright shame. In other cases we noted that there were variant's from documented irrefutable facts which we attributed to the fading of memory in the passing of time to the writing about events occurring up to 50 years earlier.

We then turned to and relied more on contemporary reports from Newspapers and the Court Martial Proceedings (trial records). Some newspapers - particularly in the South, were not in continuous publication due to shortage of paper, ink and outright prohibition by the occupying army. In some cases the Court Martial records were not enlightening, particularly where the accused plead guilty as no testimony was called for from witnesses.

By contrast with the foregoing complaint of meager information is the staggering amount of data generated in the Military Commission Trial of Hiram Oliver and John W. Hardup for Murder in Ohio in 1865. The trial proceedings generated over 5,000 pages of testimony, the trial extending about three months, some 200 witnesses were called and about 100 exhibits were filed. Reading this 11 inch stack of material and reducing it to the basic relevant facts nearly created blindness for the authors.

1861
"The War Begins"

Cases #1 - #7
(7 Executions)

Case # 1
Pvt. John W. Cole
Co. G, 1st Kansas Vol Inf Regt
NV: Joseph N., Joseph W.
Executed for Murder
July 14, 1861

The first Union's army soldier to be executed, according to "The Official List." "The Official List" has Private Cole's given name recorded as John whereas his Military Personnel record records it as Joseph. Kansas State Military Archives also record the name as Joseph W. while an account of the incident in the Leavenworth Times of July 23, 1861 gives his middle initial as N.

DESCRIPTION:

21 years of age, the usual physical description is missing from his records. He was said to have been born in Pennsylvania, not married, a Teamster by occupation, literacy undetermined. Enlisted on May 29, 1861 at Leavenworth, Kansas in Company B, 1st Kansas Volunteer Infantry Regiment. This organization subsequently became designated at Company G, 1st Kansas Volunteer Infantry Regiment. The Regiment was moved into Missouri to form part of Brig. General Lyon's command and maneuvered within Henry County, Missouri.

On July 8, 1861, Private Cole stabbed to death his friend and tent mate, Private Michael E. Stein of the same Company and Regiment. The murder apparently took place within or near the Company tent area. Private Stein is described from the meager Military records extant as 30 years of age, born in Ireland, not married, and a laborer by occupation, literacy undetermined. Both murderer and victim enlisted at the same time, both were residents of Leavenworth and may have been acquainted prior to enlistment.

No court martial proceedings or military personnel records have been found and the only accounts located are contained in newspapers of the period.

Cole was arrested, placed in the guardhouse, court martialed, found guilty and ordered to be shot by G.O. #8, Army of the West, dated July 12, 1861.

Several newspapers related the details of the execution which took place on July 14, 1861. The Leavenworth Times of July 23 mentioned the fact that Cole led a life centered in saloons, brothels and gambling dens and that he would be neither mourned nor long remembered.

The New York Times of 22 July described the execution, "A file of 27 men with muskets loaded, some with ball and some with blank cartridges, were in line, the victim facing them, blindfolded, kneeling on one knee; the order given to fire and Cole fell, pierced by 6 bullets. Such is war."

REFERENCES:

New York Times, July 22, 1861
Leavenworth Times, July 19 to 23, 1861
Military Personnel Records, RG-#94
Kansas State Historical Society Records
Lawrence Republican, July 25, 1861

Case # 2
Pvt. William F. Murray
Co. F, 2nd N.H. Inf Regt
Executed for Murder
August 2, 1861

DESCRIPTION:

18 years of age, no other description located.

Murray enlisted on May 27, 1861 and was mustered into service on June 4, 1861 at

Portsmouth, New Hampshire in Company F, 2nd New Hampshire Infantry Regiment. The Regiment was on duty, stationed in the Washington, D.C. area.

A Military Commission was convened at Alexandria, Virginia and on July 30, 1861, tried Private William F. Murray, Company F, 2nd New Hampshire Infantry Regiment on a charge of Murder.

Testimony of witnesses divulged that on July 27, 1861 at Alexandria, D.C., Murray called out to a Mary Butler, as she was crossing an alley, to halt. She looked over her left shoulder at him and said, "I will be back in a moment," and continued on. Murray thereupon again told her to halt and drew his rifle up and shot her down. Mary Butler fell in the alley near to Murray and exclaimed, "Help me! Help me! Goodbye Ellen!" Her dress began to burn as a result of the firing of the rifle. John Dooley, a Zouave (Union soldier) ran up and put the fire out by tearing off burning areas of cloth. Dooley chased Murray who fled the scene of the shooting. Murray, finally caught by Dooley, resisted being subdued. Dooley asked for and received the assistance of several bystanders and finally the rifle with a still warm barrel, was wrested from Murray and he was taken to the Provost Marshall's office where an order was obtained to lodge Murray in the City Jail. Dooley testified that he asked Murray why he shot her and the reply was, "she robbed me."

Mary Butler, the deceased, had been living with Ellen McCarthy for a period of only four days since her release from the "Work House," a "jail" for those convicted of minor offenses such as prostitution. Ellen McCarthy, by her own admission was a "working proprietress" of a "House of Ill-Repute" and Mary Butler was in her temporary employ. John Dooley was a Private in Company E, 11th New York Infantry Regiment (Zovaves) the Regiment recruited and led by the famous Colonel E. E. Ellsworth, whose ranks were at its inception almost entirely filled from volunteers of the New York City Fire Department. Dooley apparently was residing in the home of Ellen McCarthy and as she expressed it, "he had been assisting me by protecting me." The implication is that Dooley was her pimp.

Murray apparently lived only a few houses from the McCarthy house and made use of its "facilities" sampling Mary Butler's offerings. Murray later claimed she stole his money while he was recovering from his exertions and she refused to discuss the matter or return a portion of the money. Murray was declared to be sober when he shot Mary Butler by Dooley and other witnesses.

McCarthy and Dooley told of placing Butler in her coffin in the McCarthy house. They mentioned the large wound in her left side from which a firearm ball (rifle? pistol?) fell out during the coffining of the body. The ball was given to the court as evidence by Dooley and was described as about two-thirds the size of an Army Musket ball.

A local physician, Dr. D. M. French, testified that he was called to attend the Coroner's inquest and examine the body, but did not perform a Post Mortem examination. Her dress was burned as though the weapon with which she was shot was very close to her body when fired. The wound was described as entering the back, near the spine and passing out through the region of the heart. The exit wound was described by Dr. French as large enough to admit two fingers. Both Dooley and McCarthy described it as considerably larger. Dr. French offered his opinion that the ball would not have remained in the body, even if it were a popular load called "Buck and Ball." This cartridge consisted of a musket ball and two or three buckshot and a powder charge all enclosed in a paper wrapper. The only other explanation of the ball remaining in the body where there was a well defined exit wound, was that the weapon may have been loaded with two bullets, one behind the other. Such occurrences were not infrequent in Civil War battles.

Murray had no witnesses to testify in his behalf, but did offer a statement for the defense.

Statement:

"When I got up Saturday morning I took three drinks right in the house. The woman in whose house I stopped brought it to me in a bottle, and her husband drank just as I did. I don't know how much he drank. I then told the woman, Mrs. Whelan that I was going to Head Quarters to secure a pass to go to Washington. I was unable to get a pass. I came back and went to mary Butler's house. It was just on my way as I came back. I asked Ellen McCarthy if she had got any liquor in the house. She replied that there was no liquor in the house, that she could not buy any, that she could not get any, in any place. I have nothing more to say."

The commission then deliberated, found Murray guilty and sentenced him to be hung by the neck until dead.

The execution took place on August 2, 1861 at Fort Ellsworth, in the District of Columbia.

There are two interesting items in this file, one an excerpt from the report of the Military Commission proceedings which is a single sentence on page 2 thereof, reading as follows: "The Commission will act in accordance with the usages of the American Army in the Mexican War." This seems to indicate the Military authorities were uncertain as to exactly how a Military Commission was to function as this was the first Military Commission convened. The other item is a photo copy of a Military telegram sent on August 1, 1861 by a Major Wood to Captain Fry, Assistant Adjutant General. The message read, "In the case of Murray, Nine (9) members voted for the sentence One (1) against." Divulging the number of votes, pro or con of a General Court Martial was forbidden. As a consequence, the method of reporting a guilty verdict was standardized as follows: two-thirds of the members of the court concurring in the verdict."

A letter to a Colonel Davies, dated August 1, 1861, commanding in Alexandria advised him: "You will take the most effectual means to render the rescue or escape of this man impossible and to carry out the sentence promptly. Make some officer or officers responsible (with ample guards) for the security of the man tonight and until he is executed. Let there be no hesitation or failure in carrying out the sentence."

Your obt. Svt.
James B. Fry
A.A.G.

REFERENCES:
Military Personnel Records, RG-#94
Court Martial Proceedings, RG-#153 II 523

Case # 3 Pvt.
Robert Dickman
Co G, 18th Illinois Inf Regt
NV: Dickerman
Executed for Murder
October 2, 1861

DESCRIPTION:

27 years of age, 5 feet 10 inches tall, brown hair, hazel eyes, fair complexion, born in England, occupation farmer.

Dickman enlisted and was mustered into service on May 28, 1861 at Anna, Illinois in Captain Cooper's Company, 18th Regiment Illinois Infantry. The unit designation was later changed to Company G, 18th Illinois Infantry Regiment. On September 30, 1861, Dickman murdered Private William Evans, originally in Company G, 18th Illinois Infantry Regiment. Evans was 28 years of age, a farmer from the same Illinois area as Dickman, both born in England, and they both enlisted at the same place and time. The murder occurred at Mound City, Illinois. Military Pension applications on behalf of Evans' heirs provide a slight explanation of the circumstances of the murder. Evans was transferred on September 13, 1861 to Captain Schwartz' battery, 1st Regiment Illinois Artillery. A brief statement by 2nd Lt. Joseph M. Campbell, Company G, 18th Illinois Infantry Regiment quotes him as saying that Dickman was drunk when he shot Evans who was on sentry duty and gave no offense whatsoever to the murderer.

The mentioned pension documents date from December 12, 1870 to March 26, 1885. General Logan, later Senator from Illinois, interested himself in behalf of Evans' heirs in the pension application.

A Regimental Court Martial was immediately convened and Dickman was found guilty and sentenced to death by hanging on October 2, 1861 at Mound City, Illinois.

No Court Martial Proceedings have been located at the National Archives.

REFERENCES:
Military Personnel Records, RG-#94
Military Pension Records, RG-#115

Case # 4
Pvt. Joseph Raymond
NV: Raymon, Ramon
Co. C, 7th Kansas Vol Cavalry Regt
Executed for Theft
November 24, 1861

DESCRIPTION:

23 years of age, 5 feet 7 inches tall, black eyes, black hair, dark complexion, born in Santa Fe, New Mexico of Spanish decent, occupation Teamster, not married, literacy undetermined.

Raymond enlisted in Company C, 1st Kansas Volunteer Cavalry Regiment on September 19, 1861 at Leavenworth, Kansas. The designation of the unit was later permanently changed to Company C, 7th Kansas Volunteer Cavalry Regiment.

A punitive expedition, by some eight Companies of the 7th Kansas Cavalry, to the area of Pleasant Hill, Cass County, southwest of Kansas City, was completed on November 22, 1861 with the return of the units to their Kansas City area camp. On the evening of the 22nd of November about 40 of the members of "C" and "H" Companies broke into a store in Kansas City and stole thousands of dollars worth of merchandise and cash. The following night, the 23rd of November, Raymond and two companions went to a Kansas City German boarding house and Saloon called "The Garden City House." The proprietress, a Mrs. Geiger, whose husband was away as a member of a Kansas military unit, refused them admission and locked the doors. They responded by firing their revolvers into the premises and gained entrance by breaking windows. Upon entering, they confronted the barkeeper and demanded liquor. Upon the reply by the barkeeper that they sold no liquor to anyone, they pointed their revolvers at him and two daughters of Mrs. Geiger, who had blundered in upon the scene. They searched for and found some liquor, then placed their revolvers over the girls' hearts and forced them toward the upstairs rooms. In the meantime, the barkeeper, free of surveillance, ran out to locate the police or military patrol for assistance, while Mrs. Geiger managed to prevent the forcing of her daughters up the stairs to the bedrooms. The soldiers then ransacked the entire premises and stole a small quantity of silverware and a silver watch and compelled the women to drink some wine. When they left, they entered a private dwelling and repeated the insults to the woman of the home. Both older women identified Raymond as the principal culprit and pointed out positive identification of Raymond as the soldier who had cut and bleeding hands from smashing windows. He also was missing a finger of his right hand.

Raymond was arrested, tried and convicted of the crimes and sentenced to be shot. No military order or trial proceedings were located or cited.

At 9:00 a.m. on November 24, 1861, the Commander of the 7th Kansas Volunteer Cavalry Regiment, Colonel Jennison, had the regiment drawn up into a square with the troops on three sides facing inward with Raymond and firing party occupying the fourth side. Colonel Jennison stated in his address to the regiment that he regretted the need for this extreme penalty, but "if such a crime went unpunished no man's life was safe, the honor of no woman secure, all property was in danger." The firing squad readied for action, the Chaplain offered an impressive prayer, then retired. Raymond refused to have his eyes blindfolded and freely confessed his guilt to all the charges. The commands were given, the squad fired and Raymond fell pierced by many bullets. He was buried in the afternoon.

REFERENCES:
"The Weekly Conservative," 28 November 1861
"Jennison's Jayhawkers," see prior citation
State of Kansas Descriptive Roll, Company C, 7th Kansas Volunteer Cavalry Regiment, CW
U.S. Military Personnel Records, RG-#94

Case # 5 Pvt.
William H. Johnston
NV: Johnson
Co. D, 1st New York Vol. Cav. Regt.
Executed for Desertion
December 13, 1861

DESCRIPTION:
No physical description has been located.

Johnston apparently enlisted and was mustered into service at New York City, New York about August 31, 1861 in Company D, 1st New York Cavalry Regiment. The Regiment was stationed in Virginia at Camp Williams. On December 2, 1861, Johnston while on picket duty near Benton's Tavern, Virginia deserted his post and rode away toward Burke's Station, where en route he encountered Colonel G. W. Taylor, 3rd New Jersey Regiment who was in command of a small scouting party. Johnston mistook the scouting party for Rebels, galloped toward them and proceeded to provide Colonel Taylor with all the details in his possession of the location and distribution of the Union Pickets in the area. He was promptly arrested and placed in irons under confinement.

On December 6, 1861 a letter from W. B. Franklin, Brigadier General, to General S. Williams, Adjt. General Army of the Potomac, containing the charges of desertion filed against Johnston was sent. It recommended "the severest and speediest punishment." It further recommended giving first priority to Johnston's trial, holding other cases in abeyance, and if convicted "to be executed as soon as possible."A lengthy reply by the Assistant Adjt. General to Brigadier General W. B. Franklin, Division Commander, dated December 7, 1861:

Sir: Your letter accompanying the charge against Private William H. Johnston, Co. D, 1st NY V. Cavalry is received. In as much as this is a very flagrant case the utmost exactness is necessary and the offence must be described in the *very words* of the Articles of War, or the record will not support a capital sentence. No one can be punished for desertion from the service of the United States (#20 article of War) unless *he has received pay in the service of the United States* or has *been duly enlisted* in it. It is necessary that the deserter should be described as having done the one or the other of these acts. The *proof* of his having been duly enlisted or of having received pay, in the service of the U. S. is another matter. His own admission or conduct inexplicable upon any other hypothesis than that of regular enlistment, *may*, in the absence of regular evidence be resorted to: but it is supposed that at any rate there will be no difficulty in proving that he has *received pay* in that service. This can be proved by anyone who saw him receive such pay as well as by the Paymaster, though if that officer be accessible, resort had better be made to him among others. Without some such proof a Capital sentence will in all probability fail of execution.

"I have taken the liberty of framing a charge and specifications against Johnston. I have so drawn it as to admit of proof either that he was duly enlisted or that he received pay. The Court will, if he be not proved to have been duly enlisted; negative so much of the specification. If he be not proved to have received pay they will negative that averment: but of the averment to prove that he was received pay I can scarcely conceive. If the reporting officer adopts the form I send the charge can be tried without any preliminary return to this office.
I have the honor to be
Very Respectfully, Your Obt Svt
Asst Adjt. General"

A Court Martial was convened at the Camp of Franklin's Division and on December 10, 1861 tried Private William H. Johnston, Company D, 1st New York Cavalry Regiment on a charge of desertion.

Testimony was presented that Johnston revealed he had deserted for the purpose of going to New Orleans to see his mother who resided there. He further stated that New Orleans was his birthplace, but he did not record it on his enlistment papers as he had been told he would not have been accepted for enlistment. Johnston admitted he had enlisted with the intention of going to New Orleans.

About six and one-half miles from Fairfax Courthouse, Virginia, on the old Braddock Road on the right bank of the Accotink River on the night of December 14, 1861, Johnston having deserted his picket post approached a Union Cavalry scouting party, believing them to be Confederates. He engaged the Commander of the scouts in conversation stating he wanted to join the rebels and go to New Orleans and visit his mother. He offered some details of the positions of the union lines and picket posts before he was arrested.

The accused offered no witnesses and presented no statement of his defense.

The court deliberated, found the accused Guilty and sentenced him to be shot to death by musketry at Camp Kearney, Virginia on December 13, 1861.

A letter from a Civil War soldier L. G. Martin, describes witnessing the execution of Johnston at Camp Franklin, Virginia, December 17, 1861:

Dear Folks at Home,

"On Friday of last week Gen Franklin's Division were all drawn up in line, and of course among them was Col. Oakes 96th Penn Vol. We were not drawn up in line for the purpose of resisting an expected attack from the enemy but for the purpose of witnessing the shooting of a deserter named Johnson (sic) who had deserted while on picket duty and attempted to betray our position to the enemies Pickets but was caught in the act, secured, tried, condemned and shot."

The execution of Johnston was followed by an autopsy, one of only two we have found reported in such detail.

"Notes of *Autopsy* made on the body of *Private W. H. Johnston, 1st NY Cavalry* shot by order of a General Court Martial, For desertion, Franklin Division, Virginia.

The detachment for Executing the sentence of death on the prisoner, named above, consisted of twelve men, one from each company in his Regiment, they were divided into two firing parties; of which the first consisted of eight men; four being held in reserve. The arms used were Sharps carbines; all carefully loaded with conical ball cartridges; with the exception of one as is usual in such cases. After the first volley it was discovered that two of the party had reserved their fire; and as the officer in charge of the execution, believed none of the wounds to be mortal, the reserve were ordered up, and the corpse received the contents of their carbines. The whole number of balls discharged was nine, seven of which took effect.

At the autopsy, held Six hours after death, there were found four penetrating wounds of the chest and three about the head and face.

The Thorax and Abdomen were first examined. The first round noticed, was a little below the coracoid process of the left scapula and had a course downwards and inwards; on inspection the ball was found to have comminuated the fourth and fifth ribs of the left side, a short distance in front of their angles, causing several spicules of bone to project into the pleural cavity.

The second wound was about two inches below the right sterno-clavicular articulation; the cartilage was found to have been detached from its attachments to the third rib; and fractured near that place. There was a wound of the Anterior and inner edge of the right lung and the Aorta was discovered to present a large wound near its origin.

The *third wound*, was directly to the inside of the left nipple; the lower edge of the fifth rib was found to have been injured by this ball; which probably cased a large jagged opening into the left Ventricle of the heart.

The *fourth ball* was found to have caused a wound to the right of the upper border of the Xiphoid cartilage and to have detached the cartilages of the sixth and seventh ribs of the right side at their junction with the Sternum. Some portions of clothing were found in this wound; corresponding with this, there was a wound of the lower part of the pericardium and an opening into the right ventricle. There was no aperture found between the two sides of the heart, which organ was strongly contracted, and empty.

The cavity of the chest was found filled with blood. A small button from the jacket was found in the left Pleural cavity; the upper portion detached from (missing words) and much rent. There was an opening in the diaphragm close to that for the Aorta and a portion of intestine and Omentum protruding through it into the chest. Immediately below this was a large jagged hole through the left lobe of the liver; a loop belonging to a button was found here. The stomach was perforated through both its sides below (about ½ inch) the middle of the lesser curvature.

The spleen was found much lacerated; the left kidney was wounded both at the upper and lower parts of its outer border. The small intestine was pierced about the commencement of the Ilium. The bladder was distended with urine and an Examination proved the absence of any stricture of the Urethra.

About the head and face there were three wounds. One ball entered below the middle of the lower lip and passed outward through the buccal muscles of the left side, having an orifice of Exit opposite to the second molar tooth of the lower jaw.

The Second wound showed the ball to have passed obliquely from within outwards, carrying away the bridge of the nose; the left superciliary ridge and the roof of the orbit and to have caused a rupture of the left eyeball. Spicules of bone were found penetrating the Meninges near this point, but no wounds here or elsewhere of the Cerebrum.

The third hole entered behind and below the right ear and passed obliquely from right to left and from before backwards, through the Cerebellum; the right lobe of which was lacerated and passed out at a point to the left of the External Occipital protuberance.

In examining the back an orifice of exit was found about three inches to the left of the spines of the middle dorsal Vertebra, and two balls just under the integuments, one about two inches below the inferior angle of the right Scapula, the other about three inches to the left of the median line in the lower part of the dorsal region.

REFERENCES:

Military Personnel Records, RG-#94

Court Martial Proceedings, RG-#153 II 746

Manuscript Division, Civil War Soldiers letters, Schoff Collection, Clements Library, University of Michigan, Ann Arbor Michigan, letter of L. J. Martin.

Story and illustrations of execution of Traitor Johnson in Frank Leslie's Illustrated News, January 1, 1862.

Case # *6*
Pvt. Richard Gatewood
Co C, 1st Kentucky Infantry Regiment
Executed for Desertion
December 20, 1861

DESCRIPTION:

21 years of age, 5 feet 10 inches tall, dark hair, gray eyes, fair complexion, born in Indiana, occupation steamboat cook, literacy not determined.

Gatewood was enlisted and mustered into service at Camp Clay, Ohio on June 7, 1861 in Company C, 1st Kentucky Infantry Regiment. Gatewood deserted on August 3, 1861 and was arrested in Charleston, Virginia (West Virginia) on or about August 10, 1861. He was charged with desertion and with using abusive and threatening language to officers and men in whose charge he was placed during September 1861. The list included Colonel Lowe, C.O. of 12th Ohio Regiment and his own officers and guards. He also assaulted one of his guards, Private Joseph Bankland, on October 8, 1861 during an attempt to escape from the guardhouse.

A General Court Martial was convened at Tompkins Farm, Virginia and on October 26, 1861 proceeded to the trial of Pvt. Richard Gatewood, Company C, 1st Kentucky Infantry Regiment on charges of violation of the 20th and 49th Articles of War.

Testimony offered disclosed that Gatewood left the regiment on August 3, 1861, ostensibly to visit some men of the 2nd Kentucky Infantry Regiment camped nearby. Inquiry as to his presence at the 2nd Kentucky instigated upon his failure to return to his own regiment, revealed he had never been there. Gatewood was arrested four or five days later at Charleston, West Virginia and returned to his Regiment. He offered the excuse that he had become intoxicated and was persuaded to "leave" or he never would have done so. When taken to the guardhouse of his regiment he was drunk and disorderly there. Major Leiper tried to quiet Gatewood and when unable to do so "tied the prisoner up" (apparently bucked and gagged) as Gatewood complained at his trial "Major Leiper had me tied by the hands and a stick put in my mouth." The prisoner verbally abused Major Leiper with unprintable obscenities and repeatedly threatened his life.

During Gatewood's stay in the guardhouse, he attacked another prisoner with a knife in a quarrel over Sutler's Tokens.

On another occasion, Gatewood was out of the guardhouse and near the Commissary Tent which was guarded by a sentinel. It seems that Gatewood approached the provision tent so close that the guard lowered his bayoneted rifle from his shoulder and poked it at Gatewood, who however continued his approach, whereupon the sentinel cocked the hammer on his loaded rifle. Gatewood took personal offense at these maneuvers and retreated about 15 or 20 feet where he found a large stone, described by witnesses at the trial to weigh 3½ - 4 lbs. Gatewood picked up the stone and threw it at the sentry, striking him in the small of the back.

Somehow during his stay at the guardhouse under confinement, Gatewood received liquor, daily.

The accused declined to offer testimony in his defense but did offer a verbal statement, as follows:

"The evening I left I stayed with the 2nd Kentucky. Boyer begged me to go with him - I was drunk and went with him. I left him below Charleston (West Virginia) and returned - intending to rejoin my regiment when I got to Charleston. I was arrested and brought back - we were drawing rations when the difficulty occurred which lead to my striking the sentinel. I picked up a piece of meat, and said I wanted that - the sentinel pointed his bayonet towards me - and spoke a few words. Then he cocked his gun at me. I threw the stone and hit him on the side and arm - as to abusing Major Leiper. I got into a quarrel with another prisoner about some Sutler's tokens. They reproached us and Maj. Leiper had me tied up by the hands and a stick put in my mouth - I hardly know what I said to him. I suppose I used hard language."

The court deliberated, found the accused guilty and sentenced him to death by musketry.

Gatewood was tried by court martial in late October 1861, the Judge Advocate of his trial was a Major Rutherford B. Hayes of the 23rd Ohio Volunteer Infantry Regiment, later to become the 19th President of the United States. Of Gatewood's case, he wrote in his diary, "One (Richard Gatewood) conviction for desertion and other aggravated offenses, punished with the sentence of death. I trust the General will mitigate this." General Rosecrans, however, approved the death sentence. The execution was delayed by a movement of troops from Gauley Bridge to Charleston, Virginia (West Virginia) to set up winter Quarters.

Gatewood was shot by a six-man firing squad on December 20, 1861 in what is today Charleston, West Virginia's west side. A meadow near the Elk River between present day Pennsylvania and Delaware Avenues was the actual site of the execution.

(There were another set of circumstances which provoked a high level of tension at the time of the Gatewood execution. For those details, see List B, (not on official list, Sergeant Joyce.)

A rare practice occurred after Gatewood's execution, an autopsy was performed by the 1st Kentucky regimental surgeon. His report stated:

"Camp Cox, 20th December, 1861

Report of Post Mortem examination of the body of Richard Gatewood, P. Co C, 1st Reg K. V. executed by order court martial.

There was three wounds any of which was mortal, one passing through the right lung shattering it to pieces. A second wound tore the stomach, perforating it completely. The third, passing between 5th & 6th ribs, entered and tore to pieces a portion of the left lung. He died in less than one minute.

S. G. Menzies, Surg, 1st Regt K.V. USA
Acting Brig. Surg.
Pro. tem."

Brigadier General Cox issued a General Order #38 dated at Charleston, Virginia (West Virginia) on December 20, 1861, "The troops of this command have to day witnessed the execution of Richard Gatewood, late a private in the 1st Kentucky regiment for the crime of desertion, mutinous conduct and a murderous assault upon a sentinel on duty. The painful duty of his execution devolved upon a detail of his fellow soldiers chosen by lot from the ranks and who had performed the stern duty with soldierly firmness though they would most gladly have been excused from this necessity.

"The Commanding General hopes the example thus given of the end which awaits the violent and insubordinate will not be lost upon the troops but that each officer and private will so exert himself to secure good order, discipline, sobriety and cheerful obedience that there may no more arise a necessity for a similar scene. In every officer he expects a kind and careful attention to the good of his soldiers combined with firm military discipline, and in everyone, he expects such earnestness and good spirit - in his performance of duty, that severe discipline may not be needed.

By order of Brig Genl J. D. Cox
Commdg"

Gatewood's father sent the following telegram:
"Madison, Ind, Dec. 23d
Gen Rosecrans,

Richard B. Gatewood of Co. C, 1st Ky Regt my son has been sentenced by a court-martial up the Kanawah to suffer death Has the sentence been executed if not will you ask its suspension until I can reach your camp there are mighty reasons that can be presented for respite please answer

Silas Gatewood

Genl, The whole family await ans. in Madison."

Gatewood had been dead for three days when the message was sent.

REFERENCES:

Military Personnel Records, RG-#94
Court Martial Proceedings, RG-#153 II 531
"Military Execution at Charleston's West Side," by Boyd Suter, January 28, 1962, Education Foundation, Inc., Charleston, West Virginia.
Diary, Rutherford B. Hayes.
Military Reminiscences, Major General J. B. Cox.

Case # 7 Pvt.
John Lanahan
NV: Lannagan, Lannagin
Co I, 46th Penn Inf Regt
Executed for Murder
December 23, 1861

DESCRIPTION:

25 years of age, no further description is located amongst Lanahan's Military documents.

Lanahan enlisted at Scranton, Pennsylvania on August 26, 1861 and was mustered into service near Muddy Branch, Maryland, on October 31, 1861. Lanahan murdered a Major Lewis on or about September 22, 1861 and was arrested and confined pending a trial by court martial.

A General Court Martial was convened at headquarters of General Banks Division near Damestown, Maryland and on September 24, 1861 tried Private John Lanahan, Company I, 46th Pennsylvania Infantry Regiment on a charge of murder.

Lanahan pleaded guilty to the charge.

The crime was committed while the 46th Pennsylvania Infantry Regiment was marching from Rockville, Maryland to Damestown, Maryland on September 23, 1861. Lanahan is said to have loaded his musket and taking deliberate aim at Major Arnold Lewis of the 46th Pennsylvania Infantry Regiment, fired the weapon. The ball striking Major Lewis in the body, caused his immediate death. No reason was ever advanced for the crime.

Lanahan was seized, arrested and confined until brought before the General Court Martial on the 24th of September, 1861.

When asked by the Judge Advocate if he had any statement to make to the court, Lanahan replied, "All I ask is that I may have the benefit of my church, that I may see a priest before I die."

The court deliberated and confirmed the accused plea of guilty and sentenced him to be hung.

Memoranda in the Court Martial file seems to indicate some official dissatisfaction with certain legal aspects of Lanahan's trial. The notation reads as follows: "The Secretary (of War) is of opinion that the Gen. Court Martial in this case should have been appointed by the *"General Commanding the Army"* of the Potomac under the Articles of War, and that the proceedings of the court appointed by Genl. Banks were merely a Division of that army and are null and void.

As the act is murder, the Secretary of War states it should be tried as such capital crime, under "the laws of the land" in the ordinary courts. (see the 33rd article of War) and the Secretary directs that the military deliver him to the proper civil authority for trial.

J.F. Lee"

No further correspondence has been located concerning the matter. It must be noted that at the time there had been less than ten (10) General Court Martials convened and legal procedures had not been well coordinated. The time between the date of trial, September 24, 1861 and Lanahan's execution on December 23, 1861 would seem to indicate that there was some correspondence and/or debate on the matter and that eventually the Secretary of War and the President must have considered the matter legally concluded.

The execution was carried out near Damestown, Maryland.

REFERENCES:

Military Personnel Records, RG-#94

Court Martial Proceedings, RG-#153 LL 2924

1862
"Year Twos"

Cases #8 - #21
(14 Executions)

Case #8
Pvt. Michael Lanahan
Co. A, 2nd Inf. Regt, US Army Regulars
Executed for Murder
January 6, 1862

DESCRIPTION:

A letter from National Archives dated in 1987 states that neither enlistment records nor physical description of Private Michael Lanahan are located in the regular Army records of the 2nd U.S. Infantry Regiment.

A General Court Martial was convened at Washington, D.C. and on November 25, 1861 tried Private Michael Lanahan, Company A, 2nd U.S. Infantry Regiment (regulars) on a charge of Violation of the 9th Article of War.

Witnesses testified that on or about half past two A.M. on the early morning of October 29, 1861, Company A of the 2nd U.S. Infantry was performing guard duty in Washington, D.C. and was forming a relief for the posted sentinels. At the guardhouse, Sergeant Brennan of Company A was forming up the relief and all were present but the man who was to relieve post #2, Private Michael Lanahan. Sergeant Brennan began relieving the posted sentinels with the next group scheduled for duty. As Sergeant Brennan started from the guardhouse, he saw Lanahan coming across the street toward the guardhouse. Brennan told him to get his musket in a hurry. Then Brennan slapped Lanahan across the face and told him, "he was never there when he was wanted to be put on post." Lanahan said to the Sergeant, "Don't hit me again." Brennan informed Lanahan that he was assigning him an extra half hour of duty. The two men were said to have been quarreling as they proceeded toward Post #2 where Lanahan was assigned to duty. No one seemed to have heard the substance of their bickering. Moments after, Brennan and Lanahan arrived at Post #2, a shot was heard, Brennan fell to the street mortally wounded by a gunshot fired by Lanahan.

Several soldiers ran to the post and found Brennan moribund, motionless and speechless. Lanahan was arrested and taken to the guardhouse. His weapon was examined some time later and believed to have been fired. Sergeant Brennan's body was examined in the Company quarters about half past seven on the morning of October 29, 1861. A musket ball had entered on the right side of the chest, nearly opposite the heart. On the opposite side of the chest, the musket ball was detected under the skin broken into small fragments. Blood had accumulated in the chest which seemed to indicate the ball severed the aorta. Lanahan was described on the late morning of the 29th of October as having a blood shot eye, blood around his mouth, nose and cheeks. Witnesses stated Brennan had a violent temper and was known to have struck and beaten Company members in the past.

The accused was described as a good soldier who only infrequently gave any problems and then only if had imbibed too freely of liquor.

The accused asked permission of the Court to introduce additional evidence on his behalf which the Court granted. All were character witnesses.

The accused then offered the following statement in his defense.

"I throw myself upon the mercy of the Court for justice. I am going on my 9th year in the service. I proved myself a soldier under Col. Sumner at Pike's Peak on the Cheyenne expedition. I belonged to the 6th Infantry at that time. Sgt. Brennan always slighted me previous to this, he used disrespectful language to me several times. That night I was taken prisoner, the Orderly Sergeant proposed to Lynch me, in the presence of the Officer of the Day. The Officer of the Day replied, 'I shouldn't.' I should be tried by a Court Martial. I am going on my 18th year in America, the 3rd of July. I hope the court will give me as much justice as if I was a Sergeant."

The Court then deliberated, found Lanahan guilty and sentenced him to be hanged by the neck until dead.

The execution took place in Washington, D.C. on January 6, 1862.

Lanahan killed his Sergeant and received the death penalty from the court martial. The sentence was carried out on a snowy January 6, 1862 in the City of Washington. A scaffold newly erected between O and P Streets, near Vermont Avenue, was surrounded by troops and about an estimated 1,000 spectators, soldiers and citizens gathered to view the proceedings. Lanahan, his arms in irons, was conveyed to the scaffold in a curtained carriage accompanied by guards and a Catholic Priest. Before he mounted the stairs to the scaffold, Lanahan is said to have cried out, "Goodbye, Soldiers, goodbye!" After the execution was completed and the corpse removed, souvenir hunters cut up the rope into one inch segments and hacked pieces of wood from the scaffold.

REFERENCES:
Military Personnel Records, RG-#94
Court Marital Proceedings, RG-#153 II 443
Frank Leslies Illustrated News, January 1862
"Reveille in Washington" by Margaret Leech 1940

Case #9
Private Samuel H. Calhoun
Co. A, 2nd KY Vol. Inf. Regt.
Executed for Murder
February 5, 1862

DESCRIPTION:
26 years of age, no further physical description:

Calhoun enlisted on May 10, 1861 at Pendleton, Ohio, and was mustered into service on June 5, 1861 at Pendleton, Ohio, and assigned to Company A, 2nd Kentucky Volunteer Infantry Regiment. Calhoun committed murder in early 1862. A letter in his personnel file dated February 2, 1862 at Bardstown, Kentucky (where the court martial trial was held) states that since the adjournment of the court martial trial of Calhoun, the prisoner has again fully confessed to the crime and that the writer had ordered the confession to be reduced to writing.

A General Court Martial was convened at Bardstown, Kentucky On January 30, 1862 to try the case of Private Samuel H. Calhoun, Company A, 2nd Kentucky Infantry Regiment, charged with violation of the 9th Article of War.

Calhoun pleaded not guilty.

Testimony of witnesses described the events and nature of the offense.

Calhoun left the camp of the 2nd Kentucky Regiment located near Bardstown, Kentucky on the 23rd of January without a written pass, a violation of standing orders.

Private Robert B. Besnick of Company A, 2nd Kentucky Infantry Regiment testified that he and Calhoun were arrested one week after a Mr. William Sutherland, a citizen residing near the camp, was shot to death. They were taken to Bardstown, handcuffed, and confined in a cell in the County Jail. Besnick was mystified as to the reason for his arrest and in conversation, in jail, with Calhoun was told that he, Calhoun, had murdered Sutherland. The circumstances he related were as follows: Calhoun left the regiment camp before daylight carrying his rifle and revolver and went to the home of Sutherland, and sent a negro man to the door to ask Sutherland to come out. Sutherland did not respond and Calhoun then went to the door, which was opened by Sutherland. Calhoun then told him that he was searching for the men who had killed one of Sutherland's beef cattle and would see that they were arrested and punished when apprehended. Sutherland was so delighted with the news that he asked Calhoun into his home to share breakfast. During the partaking of the breakfast, Calhoun told Sutherland that the regimental Commander, Colonel Sedgewick, had sent him to inform Sutherland that he wanted him to come to Regimental Headquarters as the Colonel wished to reimburse Sutherland for the cost of the beef which had been stolen. During the discussion Sutherland expressed some doubts that the beef cattle, found by the regiment, was his lost cattle. Calhoun offered to take him to the spot so that he might be satisfied as to the certainty of his claim. Calhoun led Sutherland to a heavily wooded area about 300 yards from his home where they then halted. Calhoun backed away from Sutherland and then shouted, `You are the damned old son of a bitch, who had me arrested yesterday' and that he intended to kill him. Sutherland began to tremble and begged, for heaven's sake don't shoot me! (or words to that effect). Calhoun replied `dry up', and then shot him. Calhoun then returned to camp."

The day following Calhoun's confession to Besnick in the jail, Calhoun displayed great uneasiness and told Besnick not to repeat what he had been told about the murder. Besnick was further advised by Calhoun that he was in no danger at all and if they were both condemned to death, he (Calhoun) would confess the true state of affairs and clear Besnick before the firing squad could fire.

Dr. A. K. Core, a practicing physician of Bardstown stated that Sutherland was killed by a mini ball which left powder burns indicating it was fired only a short distance from the victim. The missile entered his back at about the height of the 8th rib, near the spine and exited at the height of the 4th rib near the sternum.

Chaplain William Price of the 2nd Kentucky Infantry Regiment testified concerning his prison visit to Calhoun, during which time the prisoner indicated that he was guilty of the charges lodged against him.

A number of Company A members testified as to the time of Calhoun's presence on the morning of the 23rd.

There being no further testimony, the court permitted Calhoun to make a verbal statement: "

Defense"

"I am surprised at some of the testimony given here yesterday. I was arrested on the 22nd instance (January) and that evening my Captain sent over for me and I was brought back to camp and set at liberty. I helped to skin the shoat (all other reference is to a beef) we were arrested for killing, and then eat my supper and went to bed after roll call in the evening. I got up the next morning just as the drums commenced beating, just at break of day, I went to the fire, stood there a few minutes and then went into ranks and answered to my name. I knocked about the company after that, talked with one or two men until breakfast, I then eat my breakfast and commenced *writing* to some of my friends. I wrote till after guard mounting and then got my gun. I then commenced cleaning my gun, and worked on it until near dinner time. I then went out and voted for the Major, got my dinner, and then worked on my gun again till about 2 o'clock and then came to town, I got back a few minutes before retreat. I did not leave camp again, until I was arrested the same night, I have nothing more to say."

The Court adjourned, deliberated, and found the accused guilty. He was sentenced to death by hanging at a camp near Bardstown on February 5, 1862.

REFERENCES:

Military Personnel Records, RG-#94
Court Martial Proceedings, RG-#153 II 71

Case #10
Pvt. Michael Connel
NV: Connal
Co. E, 24th Ohio Vol Inf Regt
Executed for Unknown Crime
March 5, 1862

DESCRIPTION:

24 years of age, 5 feet 6-¼ inches tall, blue eyes, black hair, fair complexion, born in County Kerry, Ireland, occupation laborer, literacy not determined.

Connel was enlisted for a three months service period beginning on April 28th 1861 but ended on May 29, 1861 at which time records indicate he then re-enlisted for three years service at Camp Jackson, Columbus, Ohio. His regiment went on duty in West Virginia and fought in the Cheat Mountain and Greenbriar Battles and was heading toward the Shiloh battle (April 6-7, 1862) when Connel committed an offense for which he was executed on March 5, 1862 at Camp Andrew Jackson, Tennessee. There is no existing record located which divulges the crime, the method of execution or the specific G.O.# or C.M.O.# authorizing his execution. There is repeated mention of execution ordered by General Court Martial without mention of the date or Order #. "The Official List" is silent on the matter as is the roster of Ohio Troops, Company E, 24th Regiment Ohio Volunteer Infantry. Attempts to locate newspaper or journal accounts of his execution have all been fruitless.

REFERENCES:

Military Personnel Records, RG-#94
State of Ohio, Roster of 24th Regiment Ohio Volunteer Infantry
Tennessee State Library and Archives, Nashville, Tennessee

Case #11
Private Joseph Kuhnes
Co. I, 2nd Maryland Inf. Regt.
Executed for Murder
March 7, 1862

DESCRIPTION:

35 years of age, no other physical description located, literacy undetermined.

Kuhnes enlisted and was apparently mustered into service on September 5, 1861 at Baltimore, Maryland into Company I, 2nd Maryland Independent Infantry Regiment. The Regiment remained on duty at Camp Carroll in the Baltimore area and on December 10, 1861, Kuhnes shot and killed 2nd Lieutenant David Whitson of Company I, 2nd Regiment Maryland Volunteers.

A General Court Martial was convened at Camp Carroll, Baltimore, Maryland and on January 20, 1862 tried Private Joseph Kuhnes, Company I, 2nd Maryland Infantry Regiment on a charge of Violation of the 9th Article of War. Kuhnes requested a postponement of the trial in order to secure counsel. The Court deliberated and denied the request.

Kuhnes had apparently been permitted later to retain as his counsels J. Morrison Harris and William H. Young esq.

The testimony presented stated that about three P. M. on December 10, 1861 in Camp Carroll, Baltimore, Maryland, Kuhnes was seated on a bench before his tent on the Company street, his loaded musket beside him. Lieutenant David Whitson, having been asked to take charge of the company during the afternoon Battalion drill because of the temporary indisposition of the Company Commander, walked up to Kuhnes and said "fall in with the Company," turned and walked away. Kuhnes got up, picked up his loaded musket and raised it to his hip and fired a shot into the Lieutenant's back. The Lieutenant turned partially around, exclaimed, "Oh my God!" and fell to the ground.

The Company Commander, Captain Robert Kains was in his tent when he heard the shot fired. He ran out of the tent into the Company street and saw Lieutenant Whitson fall and Kuhnes standing, musket in hand, facing the fallen Lieutenant. As Captain Kains ran up toward the accused, Kuhnes dropped his gun and when asked why he had done this replied, "I am satisfied, Captain, I will go with you." Lieutenant Davis, the officer of the day, then came up and took charge of the accused and the Captain examined Lieutenant Whitson. The Lieutenant was barely alive. Assistant Regimental Surgeon, Joseph E. Beattie, examined the Lieutenant as he lay on the Company street minutes after he was shot. "He was covered with a cold sweat and pulseless at the wrist. He was still breathing and gasping about twice per minute. The wound entered his back between the 4th and 5th ribs near the spine and emerged below the right breast." The surgeon surmised the wound was produced by a ball and three buckshot (Buck and ball charge). Death ensued in about 15 minutes after the wound was inflicted.

Testimony revealed that Kuhnes had, as late as the week prior to the shooting of Lieutenant Whitson, threatened, before witnesses, to kill him. Kuhnes reportedly said that if Lieutenant Whitson ever entered his house again, he would kill him." It was rumored that Lieutenant Whitson was "overly friendly" with Kuhnes wife. She visited both Kuhnes and Lieutenant Whitson at the camp. Both Kuhnes and Whitson had been friendly. A few weeks prior to Whitson's murder, however, Whitson was observed leaving Kuhnes house about 8:30 A. M., Kuhnes being in confinement at the guardhouse.

Lieutenant Whitson was informed of Kuhnes threats to kill him but dismissed them as mere braggadoccio. Other officers had been told by Kuhnes that he suspected Whitson of having relations with his wife, but all believed it overly apprehensive and imaginative on Kuhnes part.

Witnesses testifying for the accused stated that he had been in Nicaragua about 1858, possibly as a mercenary with the American Walker attempting to overthrow Spanish rule. Kuhnes apparently acquired some disease during his sojourn there. Kuhnes was perceived as one "not in his right mind," or feeble minded, as well as an alcoholic. Kuhnes was arrested for disturbing the peace, and breaking up his own furniture. Kuhnes home was regarded in the neighborhood as a "house of assignation" and a Mrs. Kline was his "house keeper." Kuhnes later married Eliza Kline who then became the "femme fatale."

The defense ended it's presentation of witnesses and offered a lengthy statement for the defense of the accused.

"The prisoner Joseph Kuhnes is arraigned for the violation of the 9th Article of War, which reads as follows.

`Any Officer or soldier who shall strike his Superior Officer, or draw, or lift up any weapon, or offer any violence against him, being in the execution of his office, on any pretence whatever, or shall disobey any lawful command of his Superior Officer shall suffer death, or such other punishment as shall according to the nature of his offense be inflicted upon him by the sentence of a Court Martial.'

The defense has made no effort to evade the responsibility the *prisoner* has incurred for the actual violation of the Article of War. The fact of the homicide is proved, and the defence rests upon the circumstance surrounding the act, for such consideration as is deemed to be properly within the purview of the Court. While it is not denied that the simplicity and directness of the Military Law regrets those distractions of pleading and grades of crime which characterize the administration of justice in the Civil Courts, yet it is to be assumed that in Military as in other courts, *human life* has it's grave and inappreciable value, and that in adjudicating the punishment to be inflicted for a committed offence the ordinary plea of the weakness of our Common nature, and the pertinent argument of great provocation are not excluded from the consideration of a Military Tribunal. To these the prisoner will ask only that fair consideration that is warranted by the proof, and while he will not seek to influence a decision in his case by any appeal to the feelings of his judges, he suggests at the threshold of his defence that his is a case in which mercy may well be asked to temper justice because the proof conclusively shows him to have acted upon an instinct which the most honorable natures are the most prompt to recognize. Dull and unrefined and of feeble mind as he is shown to be, there was clearly something in his nature that vibration to the consciousness of what he held to be a personal dishonor, and if it is proved, that when he struck, it was at one he believed had abused the friendly relations that had existed between them to outrage him by cohabitation with his wife.

The man who under so much excitement, and with tears complained to the witness

Hoover at the conduct of the deceased, appealing to him to know if he too would not kill a man who thus behaved with his wife is clearly shown to have been actuated by a sentiment that would undoubtedly have raised the arms of his superiors in social position, for it is to be borne in mind that she was his wife, and, while her character is not, apart from him, assailed; in this case it is certain that the case of the deceased was the only one of any infidelity of hers brought home to his knowledge and his appreciation of that act is legibly written upon the record.

It is urged that the Article of War in question opens up to the Court all these considerations as part of the *Res Gestae* in the case and attention is now asked to them more in detail.

The testimony for the Prosecution shows *the* prisoner to have gone to camp upon the morning of the homicide with a certificate from a Physician showing that he had been ill. His Physician, Dr. Healy, proves the fact of that previous sickness which left him convalescent but suffering from nervous excitement. Sergeant Loudes testifies that the deceased came to his tent where he was lying upon a bench and ordered him upon duty, that he said `Am I to fall in Lieutenant?' and that as the Lieutenant left him he walked to the front of his tent, and raising his musket to his thigh, fired the fatal shot, saying as Capt Kains arrested him, `I am satisfied' or as Sergeant Loudes swears `That is what he wanted, now I am satisfied' then dropping the gun, he yields without resistance to the arrest.

The exclamation `Now I am satisfied' is the key to the tragedy. He told the witness Hoover a week before the act, that he had learned that the deceased had been too familiar with his wife. He asked Hoover `If he would not kill a man who fooled with his wife.' He told Hoover then, that he would kill the deceased the first opportunity, he got. He told Lieutenant Register, a week before the act that he would kill the deceased. And more important than all, *he told the deceased himself* in the presence of Sergeant Buckingham a week before the act `That if he ever came to his house again he would kill him.' And then about the same time prior to the killing Hoover testifies to seeing the deceased coming out of the House of the Prisoner at an early hour of the morning, when the prisoner had been confined in the Guard House at the Camp by the deceased. The Prisoner then, in open Camp with no attempt whatever at concealment; his gun loaded beside him on the bench, contrary to the usage of the Camp, kills the deceased, quietly drops his gun, and exclaimed, `now I am satisfied.' He has got what he wanted (doubtless meaning deserved) and gives himself up to arrest.

Now this act, committed under such circumstances must be explained under one of two theories. Either it was the act of a man of imbecile if not unsound mind or it is one of those cases in which a man believing himself to have been wronged by improper intercourse with his wife takes the administration of criminal justice into his own hands. It is not sought in this case to set up any strained or ficticious defense of insanity. Those who have been asked to act as Counsel of the Prisoner are very far from wishing to bring to his aid even in the grave emergency in which he stands any defenses not fairly warranted by the proof in the case: and it is only thought necessary to suggest to the Court in this connection, whether there is not testimony in the case sufficient to warrant an inquiry by a proper board into the real mental condition of the Prisoner, for it would be a sad thing, that the ultimate punishment of the law should be adjudged against one in whose case any reasonable doubt existed upon such a point.

Doctor Healy, his medical attendant, while he has never examined him as to his mental condition and therefore is not willing definately to pronounce him of unsound mind yet does swear distinctly that he is a person `of feeble mind,' while the other witnesses on this point, men of his own class of life, not nice or very descriminating observers yet men whose opportunities of observing him have run through years, do not hesitate to swear that they do not consider him to be of sound mind.

It may be that they do not instance decisive Acts of mental alienation nor give such clear definitions of an unsound state as more educated witnesses would have adduced, yet they certainly do suggest a doubt, and the existence of that doubt raises a question which is respectfully suggested to the consideration of a Court called upon to decide the great issue of a human life.If the killing in open day, without the ordinary concomitants of attempted concealment or covert execution does not of itself suggest a doubt of his sanity, it surely does establish the other theory and the case while it presents a violation of the Article of War, is surrounded by circumstances which, would under ordinary administration of Criminal Law, make it easy to assign to it, it's proper grade of offence and it's reduced measure of punishment to the Justice of the Court it is now committed.

Regarded as a case in which the penalty of death might be adjudged, it is elevated above all the uninteresting surroundings of the prisoner, and it is invested with that serious dignity inseperable from every exercise of the high perogative of decreeing the death of a fellow man, and it is confidently hoped that it will receive that merciful consideration to which the peculiarity of it's attendant circumstances would seem to entitle it."

The Court then deliberated, found Kuhnes guilty and sentenced him to be hung by the neck until dead.

On February 4, 1862 Major General George B. McClellan, Commanding the Army of the Potomac, addressed the following letter to the President of the United States, Washington, D. C.

"Sir, I have carefully read and examined the proceedings of the courtmartial of which Lieut/Col. Thos S. Clark is President in the case of Private Joseph Kuhnes, Co. A, 2nd Regt. Md. Vols. The proceedings are unexpungable in point of form. The killing of Lieut. Whitson by the prisoner at the moment when the deceased in the execution of his office gave him the order to `fall in' for Battalion drill is not contested. It appears that the intention of the prisoner to commit the homicide had been entertained for several days. The defense set up was two-fold and consisted of 1) a suggestion of *insanity* on the part of the accused, This may be at once dismissed for it is entirely unsupported by evidence. The second ground of defence was the supposed criminal connection of the deceased with the wife of the prisoner. I am forced to the conclusion that the accused has not made out the least excuse either for the Act of Mutiny or the Crime of Murder by showing the adultery of his wife with the deceased.

In order to express my views in the strongest manner I will enquire whether there are here any circumstances which in an ordinary Criminal Court would reduce this Homicide to the degree of Manslaughter.

The ruled law on this subject is believed to be well settled. An innocent and injured husband finding an adulterer with his wife may kill him *on the spot*, and such killing will not be murder. If however he allows an interval to pass in which the blood may cool, and then kills him, without fresh provocation, *it is murder*.

A Civil Action for damages is given to the husband against the adulterer. These damages may be exemplary and they may also be nominal. If the defendant had invaded a happy home and corrupted the fidelity of a wife the damages are exemplary. If the home were a house of assignation, the wife a bawd and a strumpet, and the husband a pimp, a jury would regret to give him by way of amends, the smallest coin known to the law.

In the case under consideration, the proof that the prisoner married this woman from a house of ill fame is from wholly his own witnesses. He knew her to be a strumpet and a bawd. The evidence of his connivance at her familiarity with the deceased is persuasive, but need not be dwelt upon for the provocation to the killing of Lt. Whitson occurred (see p. 383) `A week or two previous to the killing.' The killing is moreover marked by every circumstance of premeditation. The prisoner exhibits himself in the character of one who commits a murder on calculation, quite as much for the sake of *e'clat* as of revenge.

In a *military* point of view this offence is wholly unpardonable without the most serious injury to discipline.

I have felt it *my duty* when transmitting the record to you excellency in obediance to the enclosed case to accompany it with a statement of my views.
I have the honor to be
Very respectfully,
your most obt. Svt.
George B. McClellan
Maj. Genl Comdg."

On February 8, 1862, E. W. Bates, Attorney General of the United States sent the following letter to President Lincoln."Sir: I have the honor to acknowledge the receipt of your note of the 6th Inst. enclosing for my examination and opinion, the proceedings of the General Court Martial convened at Baltimore, Md. for the trial of Private Joseph Kuhnes of Co. I, 2nd Md. Volunteer.

I have examined these proceedings with the care and attention which their momentous import to the prisoner demands, and I am compelled to say that in my opinion they are regular in form, and the finding and sentence of the court are warranted by the facts.

The communication of General McClellan to you of the 4th Inst. on the subject, makes an accurate statement of the principles applicable to the case, and I can do no better than to express my approval of his reasoning and of the conclusions at which he arrives.

I am, Sir, with great respect
Your Obedient Servant
E. W. Bates,
Attorney General"

The execution took place on March 7, 1862 at Camp Carroll, Baltimore, Maryland.

In a commentary appended to the Court Martial sentence appears the following: "The Major General Commanding perceives no palliation of the offense committed. It was not merely the highest Military Crime of which, short of deserting to the enemy the accused could have been guilty, but it was a cold blooded assassination for which a false pretext was with perverse ingenuity elaborated before hand. It is plain that the prisoner imagined that he had taken all precautions necessary to secure impunity to his crime.Let the fall of this self deluded felon be a warning to all who are tempted to follow his example. Pvt Joseph Kuhnes, Co. I, 2nd Regiment of Maryland Volunteers will be hanged by the neck within the camp of the Division of Major General Dix at such spot and at such hour of the seventh day of March, 1862 as Major General Dix shall designate.
(signed) S. Williams, Asst Adjt Genl."

A soldier spectator commented on the execution in a letter dated March 9, 1862 to the "homefolks." "there was a man hung by Martial Law at Fort McHenry yesterday for shooting his second lieutenant and a General Order from Major General Dix ordering the troops in the division to be at the fort to witnes the execution at noon and so our regiment went and i along with it it is about four miles from our Camp. We found seven regiments of infantry and one of cavalry and one battery of light artilery and two companys of heavy artilery and some two thousand citizens the prisoner apeared firm and cool and was game to the last he was said to die easy it was the first hanging i ever saw and i hope it will be the last"

REFERENCES:

Military Personnel Records, RG-#94
Court Martial Proceedings, RG-#153 II 726
Manuscript Division, Civil War Soldiers Letters, Schoff Collection (Letter of James T. Miller). Clements Library, University of Michigan, Ann Arbor, Michigan.

Case #12
Pvt. Alexander Driscol
NV: Driscoll
Co. H, 7th Kansas Vol Cav Regt
Executed for Desertion
March 18, 1862

DESCRIPTION:

27 years of age, 5 foot 10 inches tall, blue eyes, dark hair complexion, born in Ireland, shoemaker by occupation, literacy undetermined, enlisted in Company H, 1st Kansas Volunteer Cavalry Regiment on October 10, 1861. This unit was redesignated Company H, 7th Kansas Regiment.

The 7th Kansas Volunteer Cavalry Regiment was recruited from elements in a number of areas outside Kansas where abolitionist sentiment was strong. For example, recruiting in Illinois areas such as Wyanet County for Company D, Chicago for Company E and Christian County for Company F produced substantial numbers of enlistments. The regiment, in its early stages, developed a reputation as a loosely disciplined mob with fierce and zealous fighting ability. One member of Company H, 7th Kansas Volunteer Cavalry Regiment was William F. Cody, later to gain fame as "Buffalo Bill" and in 1872 to be awarded the Congressional Medal of Honor as an army scout during the Indian Campaigns. The award was revoked in 1914, along with nearly 1,000 others. The medal was restored by Congress in mid 1989.

Driscol is said to have been a member of the British Army in the Crimean War (1853-1856) and that he deserted from the service. He is also alleged to have served in General Price's rebel force at Lexington, Missouri. Neither of these reports have been substantiated by documentation.

By March of 1862, Driscol was confined in the guardhouse for a robbery committed in Missouri and the stabbing of a member of the 7th Regiment. Somehow he managed to break out of the guardhouse, seize an officer's horse and escape the confines of the camp. It is conjectured that he was seeking to escape to and resume sanctuary within the Confederate forces lines. His capture was effected, however, after he sprained an ankle and became virtually immobile. He was returned to captivity and charged with desertion.

A court martial trial on March 8, 1862 convicted him and sentenced him to be executed by a firing squad, which is said to have taken place at Humboldt, Kansas on March 18, 1862. No record of the court martial or Execution Order is cited in "The Official List."

REFERENCES:

"Jennison's Jayhawkers," a civil war cavalry regiment and its commander, Stephen Z. Starr, 1973 Louisiana State University Press, Baton Rouge, Louisiana.
"Early History of the 7th Kansas Cavalry," Simon M. Fox, Kansas State Historical Society.
"The Daily Conservative," Leavenworth, Kansas, 27, March, 1862.
Military Record G-#94, Personnel Records, CW

Case #13
Pvt. John Tansey
Co. K, 3rd Cavalry Regt., US Regulars
Executed for Murder
April 6, 1862

DESCRIPTION:

(First Enlistment) 22 years of age (on 15, June, 1855) 5 feet 11 inches tall, brown hair, hazel eyes, ruddy complexion, born in Roscommon, Ireland, occupation laborer, illiterate.

Tansey has records of two enlistments. The first occurred at Louisville, Kentucky on June 15, 1855 when he enlisted for five years in the 2nd Cavalry Regiment US Army Regulars. Tansey's records indicate he deserted on June 24, 1855. His next enlistment occurred on February 17, 1861 at Fort Union, Territory of New Mexico. He stated that he "voluntarily reenlisted—as a soldier in the Army of the United States of America for a period of five years"—and that he last served in Company K—Regiment of Mounted Riflemen and was discharged February 16, 1861. He was presented with a bounty of $36.00 (3 months extra pay) for reenlisting for five more years.

His last set of records indicate service in Company K, 3rd Cavalry Regiment, US Army regulars. His career was ended on April 6, 1862 when executed in New Mexico Territory for murder.

A General Court Martial was convened at Camp near La Jolla, New Mexico and on April 4, 1862 tried Private John Tansey, Company K, 3rd Cavalry Regiment (regulars) on a charge of violation of the 9th Article of War.

Testimony described the following sequence of events which occurred on or about April 4, 1862. Witnesses state that Tansey shot Sergeant Edward Cullinan of Company K, 3rd Cavalry Regiment (regulars) sometime between 9-12AM about three miles outside of La Jolla, New Mexico while the sergeant was in the performance of his duty. Tansey was observed on foot closely followed by the sergeant who was mounted, the impression to other soldier witnesses was that Tansey was in custody of the Sergeant. Captain Tilford, 3rd Cavalry Regiment, a witness, testified that he had placed Tansey, a prisoner, in the Sergeant's charge that morning with orders to bring him to La Jolla. One witness stated he had heard the Sergeant order Tansey to get up, before the shooting and Tansey replied, "he would fix him off." The presumption was that Tansey had been walking for a long distance and had fallen down. All in the area were startled by a pistol shot and their attention was drawn to the Sergeant who fell next to his horse and to Tansey who was standing near the head of the horse, his pistol drawn and pointing at the Sergeant. The Sergeant rolled on his right side and struggled to draw his own pistol and fired one or two shots wildly and harmlessly at Tansey, then collapsed on the ground.

Dr. B. A. Clements, U.S. Army stated that the Sergeant was shot in the lower part of the left chest and was in a dangerous condition and Dr. Clements advised against the Court questioning the Sergeant as it might be injurious to his health.

The prisoner had no evidence to offer or remarks to make to the Court.

The Court deliberated, found the prisoner quilty and sentenced him to be shot to death in the Camp of the Column on April 6, 1862.

REFERENCES:

Military Personnel Records, RG-#94
Court Martial Proceedings, RG-#153 II 964

Case #14
Darius A. Philbrook
1st Sgt., Co. K, 1st Colorado Cavalry
Executed for Murder
April 8, 1862

DESCRIPTION:

29 years of age, 5 feet 7 inches tall, brown eyes, black hair, dark complexion, born in Yates County, New York, which lies in the beautiful finger lake county between Lakes Seneca and Canandaigua where his family operated a farm. He listed his occupation, upon enlistment, as a farmer. Sgt. Philbrook had first enlisted in the 3rd Regular Army Infantry in 1850 and had been continuously in military service since. He had enlisted in the 1st Colorado Cavalry at Denver on September 1, 1861 and had been appointed 1st Sgt. on October 5, 1861.

The court martial proceedings described the events leading to his arrest and eventual conviction. On 13th March (1862) the accused was drinking in the Sutler's Shop at Camp Slough (near Ft. Union) and became quite boisterous and unruly. A Lt. Isaac Gray, of the 1st Colorado Volunteers, was Officer of the Guard and either being present in the Sutler's Shop or being summoned thereto, was asked to quiet Sgt. Philbrook. Lt. Gray remonstrated unsuccessfully with Philbrook and was attempting to physically remove him from the premises, whilst he was verbally abusive and resisted the effort. Finally, Lt. Gray stated that he would have to call for members of the Guard to take the Sgt. in charge, and walked away, the Sgt. slowly following. At a point about 10 yards from the door of the Sutler's Shop, Sgt. Philbrook, several yards behind the Lieutenant, drew his Colt revolver and fired two shots at the back of Lt. Gray. Both shots missed and the Lieutenant turned about facing the Sergeant, drew his sword and struck him twice. The Sergeant fired a third shot which struck Lt. Gray at the apex of the nose, between the eyes. The Lieutenant fell to the ground and the Sergeant took five or six strides toward the camp and then fell to the ground, where he was seized and taken uninjured to the guardhouse.

Lt. Gray, at the time of the court martial, was alive and the medical prognosis was most hopeful for his eventual complete recovery. No further medical report was found. He was listed, for a number of years, on duty in the Army, apparently completely recovered.

A General Court Martial was convened at Camp Slough, New Mexico and on March 17, 1862 tried 1st Sergeant Darius A. Philbrook, Company K, 1st Colorado Cavalry Regiment on a charge of violation of the 9th Article of War. When Philbrook was asked if he had any objection to any of the members of the Court assigned to his trial, he replied that he objected to Captain James H. Ford, 4th New Mexico Volunteers and 2nd Lt. Edward A. Jacobs, 1st Colorado Volunteers as having heard that these two officers had expressed an opinion in his case. The Court was closed and after deliberation sustained Philbrook's objection. Two other officers were appointed to replace those objected to.

Witnesses described the events that transpired on March 13, 1862.

Sgt. Philbrook's defense was based almost entirely on character references by former officers, under whom he had served and a plea to the court for mercy blaming the incident on the fact of his inebriation, he not intending any harm to an officer he respected as a friend.

The verdict of guilty as charged was rendered, reviewed and approved by Col. Edward R. S. Canby, 19th Infantry, Commanding the Department of New Mexico. Col. Canby was to be treacherously murdered on April 11, 1873 at a peace conference in Northern California by "Captain Jack," a leader of the Modoc Indians.

The execution of Sgt. Philbrook, by firing squad, took place at Ft. Union, which was about 30 miles North East of present day Las Vegas.

The writers have been unable to locate any other contemporary witness accounts or comments.

REFERENCES:

Military Personnel Records, RG-#94
Court Martial Proceedings, RG-#153 II 953

Case #15
Pvt. John McMahon
Co. F, 99th NY Infantry Regt
Executed for Murder
June 13, 1862

DESCRIPTION:

24 years of age, 5 feet 6 inches tall, black hair, hazel eyes, fair complexion, born in County Mayo, Ireland, occupation laborer, literacy undetermined.

McMahon enlisted and was mustered into service on December 11, 1861 at New York City, New York in Company F, Union Coast Guard, New York Infantry. The Unit designation was later changed to Company F, 99th New York Infantry Regiment.

On January 29, 1862 McMahon committed murder by shooting Michael Dolan. He was arrested and sent to Fort Calhoun and then to Fort Monroe. He was finally transferred to and confined at Fort Wool, Rip Raps, Virginia.

A General Court Martial was convened at Fort Monroe, Virginia and on May 7, 1862 tried

Private John McMahon, Company F, 99th New York Infantry Regiment on a charge of wilful murder.

The accused pleaded guilty to the charge and specification. The crime of the accused was described as having been committed at Camp Hamilton, Virginia on January 29, 1862. The accused confronted Private Michael Dolan, of his own Company on the Company street, and raised his musket to his shoulder, aiming at Dolan and said, in a calm and deliberate manner, "Dolan, God have mercy on your soul!" and fired a shot into the body of Dolan, who died within fifteen or twenty minutes.

The Court began the trial but was interrupted by an order for all troops stationed at Fort Hamilton to hold themselves in readiness to move at moments notice. This caused problems with the court roster as most of the officers were from Fort Hamilton. On May 20th, the Court was reconvened in Norfolk, Virginia. Two of the accused defense witnesses were unavailable despite being sent for by the trial Court Judge Advocate. It was found that the two witnesses had been sent in error to Fort Monroe rather than to Norfolk and a further postponement of the trial was made. The two witnesses arrived and Court resumed the trial on May 21, 1862 at Norfolk, Virginia.

Questioning of the first defense witness as to how long he had known the accused elicited the reply, "three or four weeks prior to the murder." The next question asked was "Have you ever heard that the deceased had sexual intercourse with the mother of the accused?" Answer: "No sir, not previous to his (Dolan) being shot."

Q: "When did you first hear of the story of Dolan's (the deceased) having had connexion (sexual intercourse) with the accused's mother?"

A: "The same day, after Dolan was shot."

Q: "Did Dolan (the deceased) ever unbutton his pantaloons in your presence and illustrate the manner in which he had connexion with the accused's mother?"

A: "No sir, never."

The testimony of the accused second witness followed the preceding in answering narrowly directed questions relative to possible sexual relations between the deceased and the mother of the accused.

The accused had no more witnesses to bring before the Court nor any statement to make, the Court deliberated. McMahon was found guilty as he had plead. The Court sentenced him to be hung by the neck until he be dead.

The execution took place at Fort Wool on June 13, 1862.

A comment on the case of Private McMahon was made by Major General Wool.

"In reviewing the evidence the Commanding General has sought in vain for some mitigating circumstance some cause which, in the eyes of the world, might excuse the commission of a crime so dreadful, and which can only be expiated by the highest penalty known to the laws of the land, and that is death. It only remains for the reviewing officer to confirm the sentence, and Private John McMahon, Company F, 99th Regiment New York Volunteers will be hanged by the neck until he be dead at twelve M on Friday, the 13th of June 1862 at Fort Wool."

REFERENCES:

Military Personnel Records, RG #94
Court Martial Proceedings, RG #153 II 903

Case #16
Pvt. Frank L. Newton
Co. F, 13th Conn. Infantry Regt.
Executed for Burglary
June 16, 1862

DESCRIPTION:

22 years of age, no further description located.

Newton enlisted on February 3, 1862 in Company F, 13th Connecticut Infantry

Regiment. The Regiment was in service at New Orleans, Louisiana under Major General Benjamin Butler. On May 20, 1862, Newton was given a disability discharge. Shortly after Newton's discharge, a band of robbers made their appearance in the New Orleans area. They wore Union Army uniforms and presented forged warrants giving them authority to search private homes for weapons and other contraband of war. They generally, however, removed valuables such as jewelry, watches, money and silver objects, leaving a statement that stipulated all in the residence were loyal and so forth. Sprague, in his history of the 13th Connecticut, relates how Butler was enraged at the reports of these depredations and how by good fortune received a clue to the location of the gang. A resident of New Orleans reporting such a theft noted the horse carriage cab number as it carried the search party of robbers away from his home.

Butler's men located the cab driver and persuaded him to reveal the destination of the cab, which was a popular coffee shop. Butler's men arrested all patrons at the coffee shop and brought them before the General. Looking over the detainees, Butler, a former judge in Boston, recognized Frank Newton a convicted burglar.

Butler threatened to hang Newton immediately and the threat persuaded Newton to confess the entire operation details. In addition to Newton, there were arrested Stanislaus Roy and Theodore Leib of New Orleans. George W. Craig, ex-first officer of SS City of New York, W.M. Clary, ex-second officer of the Transport Saxon.

All five were tried, convicted and sentenced to be hung. The mother of Leib interceded with Butler who commuted the death sentence to a prison term.

Special Order - #108 - issued by headquarters of the Gulf, New Orleans, Louisiana, June 14, 1862.

Theodore Leib of New Orleans, George William Craig, late 1st Officer of the ship "City of New York" and *PRIVATE FRANK NEWTON, COMPANY F, 13TH CONNECTICUT INFANTRY REGIMENT* upon their own confession and clear proof, after a full hearing were convicted of being members of an organized gang of thieves consisting of seven or more of which William Clary and Stanislaus Roy mentioned in Special Order #98, and now under sentence of death were principals, bound together by an oath or obligation, engaged by means of a forged authority and false uniforms in robbing the houses of divers peaceable citizens of their monies, watches, jewelry and valuables under pretence of searching for arms and articles contraband of war must suffer the proper penalty.

At least eight houses, as appears by their confession were plundered by three or more of their gang, while others were watching without at various times, and a large amount of property carried off, a large portion has been since recovered.

The heinousness of their offence is heightened by the contempt and disgrace brought upon the uniform, authority and flag of the United States by their fraudulent acts in making it cover their nefarious practices, render them peculiarly the subjects of prompt and condign punishment.

It is therefore ordered that George William Craig and *FRANK NEWTON*, for their offenses as aforesaid be hanged by the neck until they and each of them are dead, and that this sentence be executed upon them at or near the Parish Prison in the City of New Orleans on Monday, the sixteenth day of June, instant, between the hours of six AM and 12 M under the direction of the Provost Marshall, and for so doing this shall be his sufficient warrant.

Theodore Leib being a youth of eighteen years has his punishment commuted to confinement at hard labor on the fortifications at Ship Island, or nearest military Post during the pleasure of the President of the United States.

By command of Major General Butler
(signed) R. S. Davis
Captain and A. A. Adjt."

Craig, Roy and Clary were *not* members of the union Army. They were said to have also been excuted by hanging.

REFERENCES:
Military Personnel Records, RG-#94
Court Martial Proceedings, RG-#153 3130 A(EB) 1874
"History of the 13th Regiment of Connecticut Volunteers during the Great Rebellion," H. B. Sprague.

Case #17
Private John Bell
Company I, 2nd Kansas Volunteer Cav. Regt.
Executed for Rape
July 11, 1862

DESCRIPTION:
23 years of age, 5 feet 10½ inches tall, hair light, eyes blue, complexion light, born in Preston, Virginia, occupation farmer, literacy undetermined.

Bell enlisted and was mustered into service at Fort Riley, Kansas on June 6, 1862 in Company G, 2nd Kansas Cavalry Regiment. On July 2, 1862 he was transferred to Company I, same Regiment. A few days thereafter on July 4th he committed the crime of Rape.

Private John Bell of Company I, 2nd Kansas Cavalry Regiment was tried for the crime of rape before a "Drumhead Court martial." on July 8, 1862 at the encampment of the 2nd Kansas Cavalry Regiment near Iola, Kansas.

The Drumhead Court Martial proceeded much like a General Court Martial with 12 commissioned officers involved as members of the court, Judge Advocate, Recorder and President and full recorded, detailed testimony.

Bell was charged with attempted rape and committing a rape.

Testimony at the trial disclosed that on the night of July fourth, Bell and several companions secured passes, left the camp of the regiment and rode toward Humboldt, Kansas ostensibly to attend a dance. As they rode along the trail south of Rock Creek, toward Humboldt, they came to a two story home, where they stopped and inquired of the woman of the house, a Mrs. Elizabeth Haywood, for directions to the place where the dance was being held. Mrs. Haywood (wife of Private H. H. Haywood, 9th Regiment Kansas Volunteers on Duty) replied that she was unaware of such an event. The men remounted their horses and turned back riding on the trail toward their Camp and Iola. After riding about one mile, the men noted Bell absent from their group and they saw no more of him until he joined them, very drunk, at the hotel in Iola, well after midnight.

Bell, after departing from his companions, returned to the Haywood home in the company of Private John Cummins of company K, 2nd Kansas Cavalry Regiment. Cummins, known as "Uncle Johnny", was apparently nearly unconscious from imbibing liquor. No testimony states just where he and Bell met, but both entered the Haywood home and demanded water of Mrs. Haywood which she provided. They then both remounted their horses and rode off, but soon returned and asked for something to eat. Mrs. Haywood provided food, and the men sat at the table in the kitchen only one of them eating. The other man, Bell, proceeded to cover the kitchen windows and Mrs. Haywood left the kitchen to go into another room with Bell following her. Bell pushed her away from the door which he closed and ordered her to put out the lamp. Mrs. Haywood told Bell to leave and not to bother her. He replied that his companion, Cummins, was so drunk he could not mount his horse, and that they could not leave. Mrs. Haywood stated that if they could not leave she would go upstairs to bed. Bell replied that he would carry the drunken Cummins upstairs to bed, and she should carry the lamp to light the way. Upstairs, Bell pulled off Cummins' boots and left him lying on the floor. They then returned to the first floor where she attempted to elude Bell, begging him to leave her alone. Bell extinguished the lamp and seizing her, threw her upon the floor and attacked her. Bell warned her if she made any outcry or resistance he would blow her brains out, as he carried two revolvers. Moments after the consummation, four men came to the front of the house and "hallowed the house." Bell got up and went out saying he was returning to camp. Mrs. Haywood went into an adjoining room and awakened her little boy and told him to run to their neighbor Abrams house and tell them two men were in his home and threatening to kill his mother. Bell returned to the room after convincing the men who had halted in front of the house that nothing was amiss. They were one officer and three enlisted men from his own Regiment who then rode off toward their camp and Iola.

When Bell returned to the room he ravished Mrs. Haywood twice more, then demanded that she prepare a meal for him. She told him to make it himself.

Two of the Abrams boys returned to the Haywood home with the Haywood boy. Bell asked if they were her sons and she replied one is. Bell went upstairs and carried the drunken Cummins down the stairs and then Mr. Abrams appeared. Bell began beating the drunk with his hat to waken him in order to ride back to camp.

As they were leaving Mrs. Haywood told Abrams to especially note the appearance of Bell for future identification purposes. She also urged Abrams to follow them, but this was impossible as Abrams had no horse.

Bell rode into Iola and met some of his regiment at the hotel and later returned to camp.

On the morning of July 5, 1862, two citizens went to the 2nd Kansas Cavalry Regiment Commander and reported the rape stating it was perpetrated by a member of his Regiment.

On the morning of July 7th, Bell was arrested and Mrs. Haywood, her son, Mr. Abrams, and his sons each positively identified Bell from a lineup. In addition to this Bell had confessed his guilt to Private Thomas Leach, of Company G, 2nd Kansas Cavalry Regiment who made a deposition which was filed with the court.

Bell had three cavalrymen testify in his behalf but they contributed no value to his cause.

The Court found Bell guilty as charged and sentenced him "to be hung until he was dead, dead, dead." His execution was scheduled to take place on the 9th of July but as an item in a newspaper states, same was delayed until July 11th when Bell became the first person legally hanged in Kansas.

"The Manhattan Express", Manhattan, Kansas July 22, 1862 describes the execution of Bell.

"Communication, Camp #9 near Iola, July 11, 1862:

Today capital punishment has been resorted to for the second time in Kansas. Private John Bell, of Company I, was arrested for an offense (rape) committed on the fourth Inst. tried by a drumhead court martial, found guilty and sentenced to be hanged by the neck until he was dead. It was intended to hang him at sunset on the 9th inst., but the citizens heard of it, and men, women and children flocked in and around the camp, as though there was to be some great show. The Colonel wisely decided, that though John Bell should die, to pay the penalty of his crime, he should not die for the amusement of the citizens, so there was no parade or execution that day. The next day the citizens hovered around camp all day like so many fools. Last night commanders of companies were ordered to have their companies ready for parade at sunrise. This morning our companies were formed and marched to the place prepared for the execution; as soon as we arrived there several citizens could be seen poking their heads out of the grass. Our duty has been performed, the criminal has been executed, and the citizens of Iola have made fools of themselves. Several men laid all night in the wet grass to see a soldier hung."

REFERENCES:

Military Personnel Records, RG-#94 CMSR

"Legal Hangings in Kansas" by Louise Barry, in the Kansas Historical Quarterly, August, 1950, Topeka, Kansas.

Manhattan Express, As above cited.

Case #18
Pvt. Lewis Stivers
NV: Stevers, Stevens, Stephens
Co. B, 7th Kentucky Vol Inf Regt
Executed for Murder
September 21, 1862

DESCRIPTION:

41 (42) years of age, no other description located.

Enlisted August 19, 1861 in Captain Lucas Company 3rd Kentucky Volunteer Infantry Regiment which later was redesignated Company B, 7th Kentucky Volunteer Infantry Regiment.

The Regiment was formed at Camp Dick Robinson and was quickly ordered into service near Wild Cat, Kentucky which lies beyond Mt. Vernon, Kentucky, to blunt the advances of Rebel forces under General Zollicoffer. They fought one of the first battles in Kentucky having four men killed and eighteen wounded. The Regiment retired to Wild Cat and then advanced toward Cumberland Gap at Mt. Vernon where it went into winter quarters. In the Spring of 1862, the Regiment together with other Kentucky and Union Regiments advanced to Cumberland Gap and occupied the area. They held possession of the area until September of 1862 when the Union force in the area withdrew to the north.

Stivers, on September 18, 1862 in the vicinity of Manchester, Kentucky, engaged another member of his Company in an argument as stated in the victim's record file, and shot him. The shooting resulting in death, Stivers was arrested and charged with murder. A statement in his Military Record file dated August 16, 1884 states, "The records of the court martial before which this man was tried for the murder of James Cundiff is not on file in this office (Adjutant General's Office, War Dept, Wash. D.C.) nor in the office of the Judge Advocate General."

Stivers was found guilty of murder and sentenced to death before a firing squad on September 21, 1862 at or near Manchester, Kentucky. Examination of the roll of members of the 7th Kentucky Volunteer Infantry Regiment indicate a number of its members named Stivers.

The victim, Private James Cundiff (Candiff), was also a member of Company B, 7th Kentucky Volunteer Infantry Regiment having enrolled and served at the same time and place as Stivers.

REFERENCES:

Union Regiments of Kentucky, Thomas Speed
Adjutant General's Report, State of Kentucky
Muster Roll of Captain John Lucas, Company B, 7th Regiment Kentucky Volunteer Infantry Volunteers
National Archives, Military Service Records, RG-#94

Case #19
Cpl. Charles Smith
Co. K, 1st CA Vol. Infantry Regt.
Executed for Mutiny
November 26, 1862

DESCRIPTION:

28 years of age, 5 feet 4½ inches tall, gray eyes, brown hair, fair complexion, born in Pennsylvania, occupation shoemaker, literacy undetermined.

Smith enlisted in Company K, 1st California Volunteer Infantry Regiment on January 28, 1862 at San Francisco, California. The Regiment was on duty in the Arizona Territory at Camp Lathorn, Fort Craig and Mesilla.

On September 1, 1862, Smith was appointed a Corporal in Company K, 1st California Volunteer Infantry Regiment. On November 26, 1862, Smith engaged in Mutinous Conduct and was shot at Mesilla by order of Colonel J. R. West commanding officer of the 1st California Regiment. The details of this incident are contained in several letters.

"Headquarters District of Arizona
Mesilla - November 27, 1862
Captain

I have to report, for the information of the General Commanding the following serious occurrence at this post. Corporal Clifton of Company B, 2 Cavalry Col. Volunteers, a prisoner in irons awaiting sentence for desertion, escaped from the guardhouse on the evening of the 25th Inst. under such circumstances as to induce the belief that the sergeant of the guard and sentinels on post connived at his escape. I ordered the sergeant and three sentinels (all of K Company-1st Infantry C.V) to be placed in irons until some account could be given for such dereliction of duty. Members of the guard have heretofore done such things here, and it is difficult to decide whom to trust.

Yesterday morning all the privates of K Company refused duty, a corporal Smith acting as spokesman. The long roll was beat, Company K appearing, by orders, without arms: Corporal Smith was called to the front and asked by myself "Will you do your duty sir?" His reply was "I will do as my Company does." On my repeating the question he answered "Not until Sergeant Miller is released." Corporal Smith was then shot by my orders: he died within an hour.

Company A, 5th Infantry and D of my regiment were on duty: the latter executed my orders to shoot the mutineer, but missed him entirely the first volley, and fired the second so wild as to wound a soldier of A company 5th who was acting as Captain Smith's servant and standing at the door of his quarters. The Captain supposes that the man, being hard of hearing, did not hear the long roll beats: he is seriously wounded and may not recover. It was the evident intention of the men of D Company to avoid shooting the prisoner by firing wild, and so this circumstance is to be attributed the shooting of Captain Smith's man.

The men of Company K were then separably called to the front and all answered that they would resume duty. The escaped prisoner was recaptured the same day, and as by his examination it is proved that the members of the guard were no way cognizant of his escape, the latter have been released.

No one can regret more than myself the painful necessity of taking the life of one of our own soldiers: this course had to be pursued or all authority to command ceased. The command has become somewhat demoralized by desertion, and remaining in a town where whiskey, gambling and women are plentiful. The course that I have taken, was, in my judgement, unavoidable, and I trust that the General Commanding may see nothing in it to disapprove of.

I am Captain, Very respectfully your obedient servant,
J.R. West, Colonel 1st Infantry Cavalry Volunteers Commander"
To: Captain Ben C. Cutler
Assistant Adjutant General, Santa Fe

"Headquarters, Department of New Mexico, Sante Fe, New Mexico, December 3, 1862.

To: Brigadier General Joseph R. West , Commanding District of Arizona, Mesilla.

General: I have the honor to acknowledge the receipt of your letter of the 27th Ultimo, wherein you report the death of Corporal Smith of Company K 1st Infantry California Volunteers.

It would be well for you to ask that a court of inquiry be ordered to investigate the matter to report the facts and its opinion in the case.

The whole affair is deeply to be regretted, I am General,
Very respectfully,
James H. Carleton, Brigadier General Commander"

"Headquarters, District of Arizona, Mesilla, December 9, 1862
Captain:
I have respectfully to ask for a court of inquiry to examine into the facts and circumstances connected with the shooting for Mutiny by my orders of Corporal Smith, Company K, 1st Infantry California Volunteers at Mesilla, November 26, 1862.
The officers present at the post on the day named were:
Lieutenant Colonel Rigg; Major McMullen; Captain Mitchell; Lieutenants Pettis, Wood, Rynerson and Phelan; 1st Infantry California Volunteers, Surgeon Prentiss, and Lieutenant James 1st Cavalry California Volunteers. Captain Joseph Smith and Lieutenant Higdon, 5th Infantry California Volunteers.
If the General Commander, in ordering the court will be good enough to instruct them to enquire into the accidental shooting of Private Edward Trobitz of Company A, 5th Infantry California Volunteers on the same day and occasion, it will be esteemed a favor by your obedient servant.
J.R. West, Brigadeer General-Commander"

A Court of Inquiry was convened at Mesilla, Arizona and on February 2, 1863 met to examine the facts of the execution of Corporal Charles Smith, Company K, 1st California Infantry Regiment by order of Genl J. R. West former C.O. of 1st California Infantry Regiment for mutiny. The court was also directed to examine the circumstances of the accidental shooting of Private Edward Trobitz, Company A, 5th California Infantry Regiment.

Testimony of witnesses provided the information from the Commander of the post of Hart's Mills, Franklin, Texas, which is adjacent to El Paso, Texas, that large numbers of "secessionists" were in El Paso in late 1862 as well as numbers of deserters from the California military regiments. These two groups collaborated to oppose the U. S. Government. Several 1st California Infantry Regiment members were "assisted" in escaping from the Guard house by the aforementioned cooperating groups. In late November, 1862 a plan was conceived by the Confederate forces to attack and capture the post at Hart's Mills. One report was that some 6000 confederate troops were leaving San Antonio, Texas to attack the post at Hart's Mill's and that another 100-200 rebels would arrive from Presidio del Norte to join some 65-70 local rebels and deserters from California regiments already in El Paso. Credibility to these reports was provided by the movement of substantial portions of the Mexican population in the Hart's Mills, El Paso district to the Mexican side of the Rio Grande to avoid being caught in an anticipated Military Conflict. There also existed a peculiar ability of inmates of the Guard House at the Mesilla Post to escape with some degree of regularity. Investigation of the security measures at the guard house revealed gross carelessness as well as connivance on the part of the guards. A Corporal Clifton, Company B, 2nd California Cavalry Regiment made his escape by simply walking out of the guard house into the street unimpeded by the guards and thence continued his unhindered flight. Sergeant Miller of the guard and his three sentinels were arrested, ironed and confined to the guard house, being deemed responsible for the escape of Corporal Clifton.

On the 26th of November, 1862 after morning roll call, Corporal Smith, Company K, 1st California Infantry Regiment stepped forward from his place in the company formation and said "Lieutenant I will not do duty until the irons are removed from Sergeant Miller and he be released from the guardhouse." He then laid his musket on the ground. His action was followed by all but three men of the formation. All the mutineers were moved into number 1 squad room. The long roll was beat (a drum call for all troops to assemble as a military emergency exists) and the troops assembled on the Plaza. Company K troops assembled without arms. When the entire garrison was assembled, Colonel West called Corporal Smith to "front and center." Colonel West asked Corporal Smith if he were ready to do his duty. Smith replied "only if Sergeant Miller were released from the Guard House." The question was asked a second and a third time and in each case the same reply was made by Smith. Colonel West then ordered Corporal Smith to be shot. Smith was marched to the wall of a church on the Plaza and an execution squad was formed. Two volleys were fired at Smith but not a bullet struck him. He waved his cap over his head as a sign of victory and appreciation. A third firing squad was brought up and a volley was fired which struck Smith, who died within a half hour thereafter.

The men of Company K were then questioned individually as to whether they were prepared to do their duty. All agreed. They then marched to where their weapons had been deposited, took them up and proceeded to perform the drill they had previously refused to do.

It was stated that if the mutiny had not been quickly suppressed by Colonel West, the whole command would have been demoralized, and that discipline could not otherwise have been enforced. The mutiny also strongly jeopardized the security of Colonel West's command.

The Court Then deliberated

"The Court of Inquiry, after a careful investigation of the questions at issue find from the evidence adduced that Corporal Charles Smith of Company K, 1st California Infantry Regiment was shot to death on the Plaza at Mesilla, Arizona on the 26th day of November, 1862, by order of the District Commander Brigadier General Joseph R. West, then Colonel of the 1st California Infantry Regiment for repeated disobedience of orders and mutinous conduct: and the Court is unanimously of opinion that the shooting of Corporal Charles Smith, Company K, 1st California Infantry Regiment by the orders of the District Commander was for the safety of his command, the best interests of the public service, the preservation of discipline and in strict accordance with his duties as an Officer and Soldier."

The Court of Inquiry then moved to examine the circumstances connected with the shooting of Private Edward Trobitz, Company A, 5th California Infantry Regiment.

Trobitz was shot by accident by the execution squad that shot Corporal Smith. Smith was in front of a Church wall on the Plaza. The firing squad fired wildly. Despite Colonel West's efforts to clear the plaza and warn stragglers in both English and Spanish of the danger of wild shots or ricocheting bullets, Trobitz stood near the doorway of Captain Smith's quarters on the Plaza to the right of the line of fire. Trobitz was "hard of hearing" and was in Captain Smith's quarters when the first volley was fired at Smith. He ran outside to ascertain the reason for the shooting and arrived on the Plaza just as the second volley was fired by which he was mortally wounded. "No blame whatsoever should be attached to Brigadier General Joseph R. West, then Colonel of the 1st Infantry California, for the accidental death of Private Trobitz."

REFERENCES:

Militry Personnel Records, RG-#94

Records of Court of Inquiry, February 2, 1863, at Mesilla, Arizona. RG 153 LL 861

Case #20

Private (Corporal) William W. Lunt

Co. I, 9th Maine Infantry Regiment

Executed for Robbery

December 1, 1862

DESCRIPTION:

22 years of age, 6 feet 4½ inches tall, brown hair, hazel eyes, light complexion, born in Orono, Maine, occupation agent, not married, literate.

Lunt enlisted, and was mustered into Captain Cumming's Company, 9th Maine Volunteers as a corporal on September 22, 1861. The designation of this unit was later changed to Company I, 9th Regiment Maine Infantry. In January, 1862, he was detailed to duty in the Quartermaster Department, and was returned to his Company in March 1862.

The 9th Maine was sent to Florida, and stationed at Fernandina. On April 7, 1862, Lunt deserted to the enemy, without arms or accouterments. On April 8, 1862, committed highway robbery near the Lofton railroad bridge of the railroad line running from Fernandina to Baldwin, Florida.

Lunt was arrested, confined and tried by Court Martial.

A General Court Martial was convened at St. Augustine, Florida, and on April 28, 1862 tried Private William W. Lunt, Company I, 9th Maine Infantry Regiment charged with desertion and highway robbery.

Lieutenant I. W. Hobbs, 4th New Hampshire Infantry Regiment, was appointed by the court as counsel to Lunt.

The defense moved for a delay of the trial to permit several witnesses to testify. The request, after mature deliberation, was denied.

Testimony showed that Lunt, on April 7, 1862 requested permission from his 1st Lieutenant to leave the Company area to purchase some eggs. Permission was granted with the admonition to be gone no longer than one hour. The Lieutenant never saw Lunt until some 10 to 12 days later in jail in Fernandina, Florida.

A member of Company I stated that he was approached by Lunt toward the end of March (1862), to join Lunt and another Company member in desertion.

A woman resident near the Camp of the 9th Maine stated that, on April 7th, Lunt entered her home and asked if anyone else was in the building. The woman replied that a Sergeant Webster and Private Chase of his Regiment were there, and the prisoner became agitated, stating he didn't want them to see him there, and he left.

Ellen Manning testified that she first met Lunt at the railroad tracks on the outskirts of Fernandina, Florida while she was accompanied by another man. Lunt asked her if she had seen any Rebels, as he was out scouting. She replied, not since Baldwin. Lunt advised the man with her to turn back, as picket guards were only 1/2 mile away. The man left them, and abandoned the bundle he was carrying as well. Lunt then picked up the abandoned bundle, and accompanied Manning for a short distance then stopped. Manning urged him to continue which he did for another short distance. Manning tried to take the bundle from Lunt and continue the journey alone, but he would not surrender it. Manning asked what money was "good" in Fernandina, and Lunt showed her a federal five dollar bill. She showed him a twenty dollar confederate bill which he returned to her, and then took her pocket book out of her skirt pocket so violently that the pocket was torn. He refused to return it saying the confederate money was more useful to him in "Secesh" country than where she was going in Fernandina. Lunt counted the money in the pocket book, and it tallied $275.00. She begged for the return of the pocket book, and the money it contained, but Lunt refused and told her to stop following him. Lunt entered a wooded area and then got onto the railroad line and headed toward Baldwin within the Rebel lines. Manning indicated under questioning that Lunt was armed only with a penknife and no firearms or other equipment. Manning was said to have been known as "Big Ellen."

Testimony was presented that Lunt was captured by Rebel forces and brought to the Head Quarters of a Colonel Davis, Commanding Rebel forces in East Florida. Davis communicated with the commander of the 9th Maine Regiment and advised him of his capture of Lunt and the fact of Lunt's admission of desertion, and further that he was returning Lunt and the money he stole to the Union forces as he did not wish to have such men under his jurisdiction. Lunt was apparently delivered to Jacksonville, Florida, and brought from there to the Regiment by the gunboat "Ottawa."

The defense and prosecution ended their presentations. The defense asked for a one day postponement to prepare their defense statement, which was granted.

Statement of the Defense

"Gentlemen: You have now before you a fellow soldier who has been put upon his trial for a violation of a known law of the land, to wit - desertion and Highway Robbery. When I look at all the circumstances with which he is surrounded, that he is now many miles from his place of nativity in the land of strangers, which he visits for the purpose of quelling one of the greatest Rebellions that ever existed in the known world, that he is engaged in the cause of his country. Yet he is called upon to answer a charge against the magisty of that law for which he has staked his life. Still more than all of this, were I to judge from the evidence and the manner in which it was delivered I would say that the prisoner has much more to fear from the crimes of others than his own, viz: that bane of hell, prejudice. However careful a man may be or however pure his motive may be yet prejudice will cause him to see things darkly on one side and lightly on the other. Many a spirit if you could hear their cries from the Spirit Land would say in thunder-tone - "prejudice sent no hero." It may be the case with Lunt, yet I hope not. I am happy to say that he is not to be tried (by) the witnesses who testified against him, if he was he would be already convicted. You are today trying Private Lunt on the charges preferred against him and not on his past character be that good or bad. You have nothing to do with that neither can you allow what you have heard outside of this room to bias your judgement. Men ought to be more particular to give a man against whom so much is said a fair trial than he who has a strong character.

Now let us examine the charges against him. Viz: Desertion, there is not one particle of legal evidence against him under that charge. None of the witnesses know anything and their thoughts about the matter is not entitled to anymore credit than mine, and I would not say today for my arm that Private Lunt intended to leave his service. What the emaculate Colonel Davis of the Rebel Service has said is all. And that was said by a man who could not today be a witness in this court if he were here having committed one of those offences which render him incapable of testifying in any court viz: Treason.

Lt. Col. Bisbee's testimony is illegal see 1, "Greenleaf on Evidence," 124 and note which prohibits any such testimony being introduced. The Lt. Col. has stated an affirmative it is necessary for him to establish his charge by positive testimony, it is not for the prisoner to show he is not guilty, he must first be proven guilty before he is called upon to show by his evidence that he is not. Point your finger to one sylable of testimony that show that Private Lunt ever had the most remote idea of leaving the service of his country. I emphatically say that you can not do so. Then condemn a man on the prejudiced idle thoughts: is not a man's liberty, life and good name worth more than that to himself and his posterity. Here you commence to travel on dangerous ground, once establish the precedent that a man may be convicted of any offence however trivial without evidence you then open a door to a dangerous landing. The `*Bane of Hell'* prejudice does not select it's victims, it may tomorrow morning glow around your ears, and the next wind that sweeps from the south may convey the sad intelligence to the loved ones at home that you have fallen a victim of prejudice and forever ruined and sent to account to that God who does all things well. I ask nothing in God's name for the prisoner but justice. Give him that and he is clear of the first charge. Do that and you will have shown yourselves worthy of the trust placed in you by your countrymen and discharge a more Honorable duty to *God*. Highway robbery is the next charge and stands upon the solitary statements of one witness, that witness acknowledging herself an enemy of the prisoner. Could she assert more she would say she is your enemy and mine too and is only peaceable because she fears to be otherwise. Examine all the facts and show to me where the robbery lies, I may be dull of comprehension but I can not see it. Lunt must be convicted by evidence in accordance with the Laws of the Land.

There can be no crime committed on an individual who is known as an alien enemy or in Rebellion against the Government, and all persons residing in a territory of alien enemies or persons in Rebellion are *all* considered enemies or Rebels until they prove themselves otherwise. (Blackstone, Chap. IV, 198-151)

Let us now take a cursory view of this *Remarkable Witness* (Big Ellen) testimony. She says I was a coming along the Railroad and I met the prisoner and after a conversation with him he started back with me to go to Fernandina after going with him a little distance, and sat down I wanted him to go on and he went on again, I wanted to take the bundle myself and he would not give it to me. A conversation then about good and bad money. She gave him a $20.00 Confederate note, he returns it to her, and then afterwards takes her pocketbook from her pocket, all this time they appear from the testimony to be on the best of terms for a short acquaintance. Then comes the tug of war with the poor little beautiful creature met thus alone in the woods. He wouldn't give it back. There was no force used to gain possession of the stolen property so it could not be Highway Robbery [see Blackstone, Chapter IV side page 243] which explicitly declares that money obtained in this manner is not Highway Robbery. Then I ask in the name of common sense how will you condemn him for a crime which the law declares he cannot commit.

It is misfortune to the feelings of this poor little innocent woman met in the woods alone and lost her money and more too if it were possible. (The court objected to the previous paragraph.)

It is necessary if the witness had have succeeded in showing that she was dreadfully frightened and thereby lost all her worldly chattles that she must prove a value, which she failed to do as fast a witness as she was. I say that no man, woman or child can be convicted for stealing Confederate Notes for no such an institution exists known to the laws of the U.S. or in force within the territory. They are not of much value in Fernandina.We have disposed of Jeff Davis traveling swindles. Thus far nothing is proved and no body harmed. Now comes the St. John's money and the other amount in Georgia and South Carolina. It is not proven anywhere that there ever was such a bank as either of those named. In order to convict a man of larceny when he steals a bank note it must be proved that such a bank existed at that time and that the notes were genuine, and not forgeries [see Greenleaf on Evidence, 153] Nothing of this kind has been done. Then I ask with astonishment where is the evidence against the prisoner, echo answers *where?*

Are you here for the purpose of punishing a fellow citizen without the sanction of law and without testimony, Nay that is not your business. it cannot be. There are other features connected with the case which I must notice. While I in all cases dislike to discredit any personal statements though he may be the largest story teller of the country. Yet I am driven to question the statements of this poor little beautiful creature met in the woods by a soldier. Where did she get the money to buy that box of goods, I ask where? Did she get it by working around, if so she must have worked around a great while. It is impossible she could not have done it. How did she come in the possession of those goods? She did not buy them. She had not been a sea merchant, then answer me how did she get them?

Oh I can answer the interrogation by letting my imagination work a little, me thinks I can see a little Jew with his Roman nose agoing from depot to depot on the Railroad ejaculating, `where is mine pox', could I speak to him I would say, alas poor fellow your pox is gone. Big Ellen sold the goods and pocketed the cash and made her way to Fernandina and on the way she met a man who from his appearance would do to make her banker and another thought ran through her head viz: that this same money might be found on me and I would then be in a fix. She says to the prisoner here keep that and let me have a `V' until you come back. After a good hearty kiss they part to meet again ere long on Fernandina shore each one passes on his way rejoicing. But poor Lunt he soon falls into the hands of the Rebels and is by them carried far away from his lady love. She woman like waits along time for the return of her valiant swain *alas* too long and then gets angry, what a pity, and sets her wicked head to work to punish the person who had thus proved false to her, forgetting in her anger that her poor banker had fallen into the hands of the Phillistines, and *could not* return.

(The previous entire paragraph was objected to by the Court)

In evidence that this is true I must ask why did she not give some alarm of this crime at the time it was committed? It is in evidence that she was in a half mile of a house and that the house had a man in it for she saw him go in it. Judging from her size, she could have been heard by just giving a holler. Or why did she not make known to the neighborhood that there was a live Yankee in the woods and he would have been hunted down like the bear of the forest. She quietly pursues her way and in due time arrives in Fernandina, and says nothing of the money until she becomes angry with her errant lover. Gentlemen there is `something rotten in Denmark', I repeat it, `there is something rotten in Denmark'.

Gentlemen, are you prepared to convict a man on such flimsy testimony? It cannot be possible that a body of intelligent men can act thus. You have the passage between the prisoner and degradation. I ask then in God's name give him that justice which is due from a Judge to the adjudged. If there is a doubt in your mind, the prisoner is entitled to it's benefit by the Laws of the Land, Laws of God and simple naked justice.

I now submit his case to you feeling satisfied that you will give him that justice which his case deserves and merits at your hands. I have discharged my duty to an erring Brother. It now but remains for you to discharge yours and say to the accused you are henceforthly discharged, you will have discharged that duty which you owe to your fellow man and to that being who rules the universe."

The Court then deliberated and found the defendant guilty of desertion and sentenced him to be executed by a firing squad.

The execution took place on December 1, 1862.

Following the then required review of the legal proceedings by the President, who approved the sentence, orders of October 29, 1862 promulgated his execution. Lunt was transferred to Hilton Head Island, South Carolina where the sentence was carried out on December 1, 1862.

REFERENCES:
Military Personnel Records, RG-#94
Court Martial Proceedings, RG-#153 KK 287

Case #21
Pvt. John Kessler
Co. K, 103rd, NY Infantry Regt.
Executed for Murder
December 5, 1862

DESCRIPTION:

36 years of age, 5 feet 8 inches tall, brown hair, gray eyes, dark complexion, born in Germany, occupation farmer, literacy undetermined.

Kessler enlisted and was mustered into service on February 24, 1862 at New York City, New York in Company K, 103rd New York Infantry Regiment. The 103rd Regiment was stationed in the Washington, D.C. area and on May 15th, 1862 Kessler was reported to be a jailed prisoner. On September 17, 1862, Kessler, had been returned to his Company for duty and during a quarrel used a bayoneted rifle to stab First Lieutenant Fernando Linzy of Company K, 103rd New York Infantry Regiment. The stabbing, which caused Lt. Linzy's death, occurred at the foot of 6th street in Washington, D.C.

Kessler was arrested, and confined awaiting trial by Court martial.

A General Court Martial was convened at the headquarters of the Military District of Washington, D. C. and on September 20, 1862 tried Private John Kessler, Company K, 103rd New York Infantry Regiment for murder.

Sergeant B. Zimmerman, Company K, 103rd New York Infantry Regiment was sworn in as an interpreter as the accused had little if any knowledge of English, communicating only in German.

The charges and specifications being read in the presence of the accused, he was asked how he plead. Viz: "When asked to plead to the charge and specification he answered foriegn to the purpose." The court therefore ordered the plea of *Not Guilty* to be entered to both the charge and the specification.

"Prisoner was asked if he desired counsel to which he replied in the negative, he being willing to trust his case to the Court without special counsel."

Witnesses were then called and offered the following statements.

On or about September 17, 1862 at the camp of the 103rd New York Infantry Regiment in Washington City at about 1 AM in the morning, Private Kessler was heard "swearing, cursing and quarrelling with another private of Company K, Conrad Finger. The noise awoke Sergeant Bernard Zimmerman of Company K who shared a tent with 1st Lieutenant Fernando Linzy also of Company K. Sergeant Zimmerman got out of bed barefoot, and went to the place where the two were arguing and ordered them both to go to their tents and keep quiet. Kessler refused to obey the order and Sergeant Zimmerman returned to his tent to put on his shoes. While so occupied, Lieutenant Linzy raised up in bed and inquired what was going on. Sergeant Zimmerman explained and said he would take care of it. Lieutenant Linzy, however, got out of bed, left the tent, and went to Kessler who still was arguing with Finger. Zimmerman followed Linzy by a few minutes. Kessler, now armed with a bayoneted rifle, was told by Lieutenant Linzy, who took out his watch, noted the time, then said, "It is near 2 o'clock. Everybody ought to be quiet at this time. You ought to be in your tent long ago." Kessler said his tent mates wouldn't let him in. Linzy replied, "that if he behaved himself he could get in a tent well enough." Kessler responded, "I don't want to go in no tent! You haven't got no sentries here and I want to be sentry." Linzy said, "he did not want a sentry." Then Finger and Kessler argued again and Kessler moved towards Finger and told him to get his rifle and he would fight him. Finger replied he would not fight with a rifle but if Kessler would lay his rifle aside he (Finger) would fight him with his fists. Sergeant Zimmerman ordered Kessler to lay down his rifle to which Kessler responded by moving towards the Sergeant who said, "What are you doing? Do you charge bayonet against your Sergeant?" Kessler replied, "No I won't do it. I respect you too much and you are the best man in the company." Sergeant Zimmerman told Kessler, "If you respect me you should go in a tent or into a vacant barracks nearby" but he refused. At this point, Lieutenant Linzy again ordered Kessler, "Kessler lay down your piece, if you don't I'll have you tied and sent to the guard house." Kessler did not obey and Lieutenant Linzy ordered Sergeant Zimmerman and a Corporal Wolf to carry out his threat. At this, Kessler ran toward the Lieutenant in the position of charge bayonet and stabbed the Lieutenant in the right breast saying, "then I have to defend myself." The Lieutenant groaned and fell to the ground. Kessler was seized and disarmed while the sergeant and other soldiers sought the services of a doctor, none were immediately found. The Lieutenant was moved to a tent and was believed dead within ten minutes after being stabbed. A Doctor Frederic Miller testified that he viewed Lieutenant Linzy shortly after he died, that the Lieutenant was a healthy man and finally that, in Dr. Miller's opinion, the Lieutenant had died as a result of the bayonet wound in the chest.

Dr. Frederic Schafhirt, assistant surgeon in the Surgeon General's Office, Washington, D. C. was called and testified as follows:

Q: "Do you sometimes practice embalming dead bodies?

A: I do.

Q: Did you embalm the body of Lieutenant Fernando Linzy?

A: I did.

Q: What day of the month was it?

A: I do not remember the date, but it was one day last week, near the 18th or 19th of September.

Q: How did you know it was the body of Lieutenant Linzy?

A: That was the name given me.

Q: Where was the wound, if any, on that body?

A: I found a triangular wound on the right side of the sternum, between the 7th and 8th ribs.

Q: How far from the point of the rib?

A: Near the junction with the breast bone.

Q: Did you *examine** that wound after the death of the party? (*Autopsy - editor)
A: I did. I was obliged to.
Q: Describe the wound as clearly as possible.
A: The wound went upwards in an oblique direction backward toward the spine. It separated the upper lining membrane, the serous membrane of the diaphragm. And so it passed through the lower portion of the pericardium, toward the spine where it divided the artery. I found the left thoracic cavity filled up with coagulated blood. So in the same manner the pericardium. The left lung was not injured but compressed by the blood.
Q: Did you find any other cause of death?
A: I found all the system in perfect order, washing off the heart and lungs. I had also to open the abdomen to embalm the lower portion of the body and found all the intestines in a perfect healthy condition.
Q: At what point did you embalm the body?
A: Those who have been wounded in the thorax I embalm from the arch of the aorta. If I had taken the femoral artery and the wound being inflicted in one of the thoracic vessels, the solution would have run in the thoracic cavities and not in the vascular system.
Q: Is it your opinion that this wound caused the death of Lieutenant Linzy?
A: It is my opinion. I think I could safely swear that that killed him.-Bayonet was here shown to the witness-
Q: Was the wound such as a bayonet like this would inflict?
A: It was."
Witness excused.

The accused presented no witnesses to the Court but offered the Court a statement on his behalf.

"Prisoner's Statement"

"He (Conrad Finger) enraged me. After that he wanted to fight with me. I then picked up a musket which was lying there, to ward him off. Then the sergeant ordered me back to my tent. It was impossible for me to go in there because they would beat me when I went back. I then said to sergeant, I would rather stay as guard here as there is none. Then the sergeant told me to lay down my musket. I said I will hold the musket to hold the persons off who want to strike me. Then Lieutenant Linzy commanded that they should bind me. Then they tried to take the musket from me. Sergeant Zimmerman said to me `Kessler, what are you doing? Are you going to stick me?' `No I won't, I respect you as being the best man in the Co.' They again tried to take away the musket from me. Then it is possible that the Lt. may have rushed against the bayonet. Then the Lt. groaned loud. Then they threw me down upon the ground and bound me. They bound my feet and struck me on the head. Then they took me to a Watch House."

The Court deliberated, found Kessler guilty and sentenced him to be hanged by the neck until dead.

On October 30, 1862 an order was issued to reconvene the Court which tried Private John Kessler, Company K, 103rd New York Infantry Regiment to amend the proceedings of his trial.

On November 7, 1862 the Court reconvened in accordance with the order and amended the proceedings of the original trial of Private Kessler to wit, "two thirds of the members of the court concured in the sentence embraced in the foregoing proceedings of said Court Martial." The amendment was certified by the President and Judge Advocate of the Court.

Kessler was executed at Washington, D. C. on December 5, 1862.

REFERENCES:

Military Personnel Records, RG-#94
Court Martial Proceedings, RG-#153 KK 316

1863
"Desertions Increase"

First Member of the
U.S. Colored Troops executed
Cases #22 - #88
(67 Executions)

Case #22
Pvt. Charles Clark
NV: Clarke
Battery H, 1st Penn. Lt. Arty. Regt.
Executed for Murder
March 2, 1863

DESCRIPTION:

No description is present in Clark's Military Records file.

Clark's records are confusing as there are some important documents missing from his military file. In one remaining document, Clark is recorded as enlisting at Harrisburg, Pennsylvania on September 1, 1861 while another identical document states he entered service in July, 1861 also at Harrisburg, Pennsylvania. On another document, a memorandum states that Clark was transferred to Battery H from Battery E both in 1st Pennsylvania Light Artillery Regiment. On September 5, 1862 near Yorktown, Virginia, Clark, in company of Private William Dormady Case #23 also of Battery H, 1st Pennsylvania Light Artillery Regiment, did quit his post to plunder and pillage.

A military commission was convened at Yorktown, Virginia proceeded, on October 12, 1862 to the trial of Private Charles Clark, Company H, 1st Battery of Pennsylvania Artillery on the following charges: Quitting his post to plunder and pillage, assault with intent to kill, murder.

Testimony of witnesses was offered as follows. A Mrs. Dawson, a citizen of York County related that Clark had come to her home on September 5, 1862 and stated he was sent by "Authority" to search for and arrest certain persons (dead or alive) who had whipped two of his men the day before. Stated he would enter and search the Dawson home and Mrs. Dawson asked him for his authority to do this. Clark drew his pistol and pointed it at Mrs. Dawson saying, "This is my authority." Clark then left and joined a group of 13 to 14 other soldiers waiting on the road. This occurred around noon, prior to the assault on Mr. Stokes. The entire party of soldiers, led by Clark then continued on down the road in the direction of the Stokes house. Clark claimed in court that Mrs. Dawson threatened to shoot or kill him if he did not leave her premises, that she was a secessionist with two sons in the Rebel service, that he Clark was like many northerners, the offscouring of the human race all of which Mrs. Dawson denied. As the party led by Clark walked down the road they encountered a Mr. Hezekiah Stokes, a citizen of York County, Virginia, who was seated in a cart pulled by a mule. One of the soldiers in the group noting Stokes said, "there is one of the men that whipped us!" Two soldiers of the group grabbed the reins and bridle of the mule and halted him. One addressed Stokes saying, "Now God damn you we are going to kick you, get out of your cart." With that said, they lead the mule to the side of the road and tied him to a tree and the cart was somehow over turned precipitating Stokes on the road. Some of the soldiers in the party began beating Stokes about the head and body with clubs. Stokes cried out for help and crawled into bushes on the side of the road hoping for some protection from the attackers. The beating continued, some soldiers in a frenzy shouting, "Damn him, kill him, kill him." Another soldier drew his revolver and cocked it saying, "God damn you if you open your jaws I'll shoot you." As Stokes lay prostrate on his right side, he was stabbed in the left chest area, the assailant crying, "Damn him that's good enough for him." Stokes managed to get to his feet and tried to escape by running. He was overtaken and knocked down again, one attacker saying, "keep still or I'll kill you." At this point, Stokes became unconscious and when he regained consciousness he found himself alone. He managed to unhitch the mule from the tree where it had been tethered and drive the mule and cart toward his home which he reached about 3 PM.

His first words upon being carried into his house were, "The Lord have mercy upon me, I have been murdered." About an hour after his arrival an army surgeon arrived and provided medical care which extended over a period of nearly two weeks when a civilian doctor, Robert Powers, took over his case. All the 13 attackers were arrested at

the scene and delivered to the custody of the Provost Marshall. The 13 assailants in custody were brought into the presence of Stokes and he made a *"death bed"* statement which is dated September 7, 1862 and sworn to and witnessed by a number of Union Army officers. In the statement he described his assault, identifying specifically those who stabbed and struck him. He firmly believed he was dying and concluded the statement with the following words. "I assert that I am and always have been a loyal citizen of the United States and that I have taken the oath of Allegiance to the United States and that I have not at any time interfered with or molested in any way the parties in my presence or any other of the forces of the United States Government"
"Hezekiah (X) Stokes" (his mark)

Dr. Powers, in examining Stokes on September 14th observed that the stab wound in the chest was suppurating (generating pus formation as a result of infection) and his prognosis was very poor. Stokes died on October 7th and was buried on October 8, 1862.

The testimony being concluded the accused secured consent to address the court before it deliberated.

The prisoner addressed the court, hoping that the fact of his confinement in the guard house would mitigate his sentence and justify his acts and expressed the thought that the murdered man was a secessionist and a mail carrier to Richmond and that he had a pistol (the day previous to his assault) in beating a Union Soldier.

The trial then concluded and the commission deliberated finding the accused guilty and sentenced him to death by hanging.

Clark was confined at Fort Norfolk, Virginia to await the review of his trial and the fixing of the date of his execution. On February 23, 1863, he addressed a letter to the Judge Advocate General.

"Fort Norfolk, Va. Feb. 23, 1863:

Judge Advocate General, Dear Sir: Hopeing you will pardon me for intruding on you I would kindly call your attention to my case. I was tried by a board of Commissioners at Yorktown, Va. on the 14th of October 1862 consisting of Brig. Generals McNagle & Van Allen and Lieut. Col. Flood of the 1st Penn. Lite Artillery and have received no returns as yet. Gen. Dix says he has sent to Washington some time ago for my release but has got no answer. I have been confined here for nearly six months and have received no returns from my trial. I would like to have you forward to me here at this place a coppy of the proceedings of my court martial and oblige.
Your obedient Servant,
Charles Clark
Battery H, 1st Penn. Lite Artillery"

Clark was hung on March 2, 1863.

REFERENCES:
Military Personnel Records, RG-#94
Court Martial Proceedings, RG-#153   LL 3

Case #23
Pvt. William Dormady
NV: Dormody
Batty H, 1st Penn Reserve Light Artillery
Executed for Murder
March 2, 1863

DESCRIPTION:

19 years of age, no other details found.

Enlisted and enrolled July 20, 1861 at Harrisburg, Pennsylvania, mustered in for duty

August 5, 1861 in Captain Brady's Battery, 1st Regiment Pennsylvania Artillery. This organization subsequently designated Battery H, 1st Regiment Pennsylvania Reserve Light Artillery. He was absent March and April of 1862 in the General Hospital (not geographically identified). By late August - early September, Dormady's Battery was situated at Yorktown, Virginia. On September 5, 1862, Dormady left his post to "plunder and pillage" citizens of York County, Virginia. Dormady did attack a civilian, Hezekiah Stokes, a citizen of York County and did strike, beat and stab Stokes with intent to kill. Stokes died as a result of this attack.

Dormady was tried by a Military Commission convened at Yorktown, Virginia October 18, 1862 and charged with quiting his post to plunder and pillage, assault with intent to kill, murder. He was convicted of the major charge of murder and sentenced to be hung. He was executed on March 2, 1863 at Fort Yorktown, Virginia.

REFERENCES
Military Peronnel Records-RG-#94
Court Martial Proceedings-RG-#153

Case #24
Pvt. Robert Gay
Co D, 6th Indiana Cavalry Regiment
and Co D, 71st Indiana Inf Regt
Executed for Desertion
March 27, 1863

DESCRIPTION:
27 years of age, about 6 feet tall, dark brown hair, blue eyes, clear complexion, born Marietta, Ohio, resided at Bowling Green, Indiana, not married, occupation school teacher, literate, no further information available.

Gay enlisted August 6, 1862 at Camp Thomson, Indiana and was mustered into service on August 18, 1862 at Indianapolis, Indiana in Captain Conover's Company, 71st Indiana Infantry Regiment. The unit designation was changed to Company D, 71st Indiana Infantry Regiment and on February 23, 1863 was mounted and changed to Cavalry and again redesignated as Company D, 6th Indiana Cavalry Regiment. The 71st Indiana Infantry Regiment had the misfortune to be captured twice; first at Richmond, Kentucky August 30, 1862 and at Muldraugh's Hill, Kentucky December 28, 1862. It is difficult to place Gay as one of those captured with the Regiment at one or both catastrophes. His personnel records indicate that he was sick and absent with leave from August 18th to October 31, 1862. This, if accurate, would prove his absence from the Richmond debacle. Further examination of his records seem to indicate that he was in confinement (under arrest) during the attendance reporting periods of November/December 1862 and January/February 1863.

Contemporary accounts of his desertion and spy activities, arrest, trial and execution are fairly numerous. One report, in the "Indianapolis Daily Gazette" March 28, 1863 states that, "Gay was sick in a hospital in Kentucky last fall and that he was captured and paroled by the Rebels." It is further stated that "Gay asked for and received permission to take the Oath of Allegiance to the Confederacy." He also, apparently, agreed to act as a spy for the Rebel forces. After his return to his Indiana Regiment following release as a prisoner of the Rebels, he secured a sick leave and when it expired was given an extension of leave time. He was arrested before the expiration of his leave time and accused of deserting to the enemy. He denied the accusation until his clothing was searched and a copy of the Oath of Allegiance was found folded up and secured into a pant leg of his trousers. He then confessed the entire truth.

A General Court Martial was convened at Indianapolis, Indiana and proceeded to the trial of Pvt. Robert Gay, Company D, 71st Ind. Infantry Regiment on December 27, 1862, on charge of desertion. Gay pleaded guilty to the charge.

Gay deserted his regiment on September 5, 1862, where it was in service in the field, near Richmond, Kentucky. Gay deserted to the enemy and took their oath of allegiance to serve the Confederacy "faithfully against all enemies who oppose them whomsoever."

The court deliberated, confirmed the plea of the accused by a finding of guilty and sentenced him to be shot to death.

The execution was scheduled to take place at Camp Morton, Indianapolis, near Burnside's Barracks on Friday, March 27, 1863 at 3 p.m.

The usual procedure for an execution was followed. The troops witnessing the execution formed on three sides of the square. The prisoner, seated upon his coffin, faced the firing squad on the open side of the square. Gay's clothing was opened to display his breast, his feet and hands were bound, his eyes blindfolded. Some reports indicate he made an impassioned speech to the assembled troops urging them to adopt and obey a more religious life, stated he was not a spy and finally urged the firing squad to aim for his heart. All of the nine rifles containing ball ammunition fired at Gay, struck a vital area. Eight pierced the area of his heart and the ninth struck the base of his throat.

REFERENCES:

Military Personnel Records, RG-#94
Court Martial Proceedings, RG-#153 LL 106
"History of Greater Indianapolis," Volume I, Dunn.
"Indianapolis News," March 27, 1903.
"Daily State Sentinel," Indianapolis, March 28, 1863.
Address of Dr. James A. Ramage to CWRT (Chicago), November 13, 1989
Letter of September 14, 1987, L. G. Meldum, Assistant Archivist Indiana Commission on Public Records, Indianapolis, Indiana.
Indianapolis Daily Gazette, March 28, 1863.
Indianapolis Star, February 1, 1944.
"A Little Fifer's War Diary," C. W. Bardeen, Syracuse, New York, 1910.

Case #25
Pvt. Henry Hamill
NV: Hammill
Co. D, 131st NY Vol Inf Regt
Executed for Straggling and Pillage
April 25, 1863

DESCRIPTION:

39 years of age, 5 feet 8 inches tall, gray eyes, brown hair, dark complexion, born in Ireland, occupation laborer, illiterate.

Hamill enlisted at Brooklyn, New York on August 28, 1862 and was mustered into service on September 9, 1862 and served with the 19th Army Corps in the Department of the Gulf.

There are two letters in his file, one, Special Order 106, May 2, 1863 and one, seemingly a draft of a letter as it is not addressed nor signed.

The draft letter reads as follows:

"The soldiers of this Brigade have been warned so often against straggling and pillaging that any further orders on that subject would be silly and demoralizing. The soldier knows that the penalty of straggling and pillaging is death. The regulations of the army decree it — the Commanding Genl. of this department has said that soldiers guilty of this offense 'fight a fools fight and deserve a dog's death' — In spite of every warning soldiers of this brigade in the face of the enemy, have straggled and pillaged. Private Henry Hammill has this day been taken with his plunder on his person — he has confessed his crime — He entered the house of a citizen, he terrified women and children, he stole clothing and shot guns — It is hereby ordered that Private Henry Hammill, Co. F, 131st NY Vol Inf Regt be shot to death in front of this command at sundown tonight — the fate of Hammill shall be the fate of soldiers who disobey orders in this command. The Genl. Comdg. this Brigade regrets the necessity for this act, but the command is too much exposed to the blows of the enemy to permit demoralization — the duty is a trying one but it will be performed.

"The Genl. Comdg. thanks the soldiers of this Brigade for their general good conduct; he urges them to continue their good conduct and enjoy the satisfaction of worthy and good soldiers."

The Special Order #106 states:

"Headquarters Department of the Gulf, 19th Army Corps, Opelousas (Louisiana) May 2, 1863.

Special Order #106 [extract]

#4 — The action of Brigadier General William Dwight commanding 1st Brigade, 4th Division in causing Private Henry Hammill, Co. F, 131st NY Vol Inf Regt., to be shot to death in front of the Brigade, at sunset on the 25th of April for quiting his colors to plunder and pillage, while the Brigade was on detached service, in exposed position and in presence of the enemy, is fully approved by the General Commanding the Army. The last warning against straggling and pillage has been exhausted. It has become necessary to prevent demoralization, that the fate of this wretched man should be measured out to all who follow his example. The safety of the Army is more important than the life of any man in it from the humblest private to the Commanding General.
By command of Major General Banks"

No record of a trial or court martial has been located.

REFERENCES:
Military Personnel Records, RG-#94

Case #26
Pvt. Julius Milika
Co. E, 10th Michigan Vol Inf Regt
Executed for Desertion
May 15, 1863

DESCRIPTION:

30 years of age, 5 feet 7¼ inches tall, dark eyes, dark hair, dark complexion, born in Prussia, not married, literacy undetermined.

Milika enrolled in Captain Hartsuff's Company 10th Michigan Volunteer Infantry Regiment at Flint, Michigan on February 6, 1862. The Company designation was later changed to Company E, same Regiment. He apparently served satisfactorily until sometime in April 1863 when he deserted his unit. He was captured and court martialed on May 4, 1863 at Nashville, Tennessee. He was found guilty of desertion and ordered to be shot at Noon on Friday, May 15, 1863 on the Commons west of Granny White Pike near the City of Nashville, Tennessee.

While languishing in jail, prior to his execution, Milika addressed a letter appealing for mercy to General Morgan who was addressed as the Post Commander. It is not known if Milika himself wrote the letter or whether it was written by a clerk as he dictated the contents. This latter procedure was common in an army with a substantial percentage of illiterates.

The letter itself, dated May 12, 1863 at the Nashville Jail, is very faded and rambling. The authors have managed to read most of the letter, although some words remain nearly invisible.

"Nashville Jail, May 12, To Genl Morgan, Comdg Post, Sir I am sentenced to be shot on the 15th Inst and before that time arrives, I would say a few words to you hoping that they may be of aid. In my trial, the witness for me did not appear in court my forgetting his name therefore I was left in the lurch. his name is August Wald belonging to the first Tenn Infantry Company K I saw him today. he was present when his Lieutt persuaded me to join his Company, his (the Lieutt) told me that the pay coming to me from my Reg he would get for me and that I would not be harmed all this, this man Wald was present and heard. how sir can you not assist me in this hour of great need I do not wish to have it said that I was shot for deserting the flag of my adopted country Then I have no one left to support the declining years of my poor old mother. Please sir exert your energy in behalf of a soldier who has erred but who is repentant and you shall command the lasting gratitude of a fellow mortal. And can you say that I may have a prospect in that my case may be petitioned as life is very sweet — especially when one is not prepared. And in conclusion can you let me know today what you can do for me. I have been a soldier now for some 10 years and never thought for once that it would come to this for I hve always tried to do my duty (illegible) ever since this war I have been in the army.
Yours most Respfly
Julius Milika
10th Reg Mic Vol"

"I should like to have the Art of War read to me here as I do not fully comprehend it. Yours J. M."

His letter was duly forwarded without recommendation. Milika was reported as buried in Nashville City Cemetery in grave #4553 on May 15th 1863, the day of his execution.

One other document of interest is a U.S. Military Telegraph Message dated May 15, 1863 reporting Milika's execution sent to Brig. General James A. Garfield, Chief of Staff.

REFERENCES:
Military Personnel Records, RG-#94

Case #27
Private John P. Wood
Co. F, 19th, IND. Infantry Regt.
Executed for Desertion
June 12, 1863

DESCRIPTION:

19 years of age, 5 feet 6 inches tall, dark hair, gray eyes, dark complexion, born in Brown County, Ohio, occupation farmer.

Wood enlisted and was mustered into service on July 29, 1861 at Indianapolis, Indiana in Company F, 19th Indiana Infantry Regiment. He first deserted his Regiment on August 20, 1862 at Rappahanock Station, Virginia and was apprehended on November 17, 1862 at Fayetteville, Virginia and was returned to duty. He again deserted at Fredericksburg, Maryland on December 13, 1862 and was arrested and returned to his Regiment on January 1, 1863. He was released from arrest and returned to duty without a fine or other punishment. In late April of 1863, on the 29th as recorded, Wood made his third attempt to desert. There are several different versions of the event which occurred during the Chancellorsville Battle. The plan for his desertion was apparently aimed at securing a rebel uniform, and masquerading as such. By surrendering and being sent to a Union Army Prisoner of War/Provost Marshall holding area, where he would swear allegiance to the USA and be given his "parole" freedom to go north, he would be free of any further military service responsibility.

In one version of his desertion, he entered the Confederate lines and secured an enemy uniform, returned to the Union lines and claimed to be a deserter from a Tennessee Rebel Regiment. Under interrogation he was unable to name his Company or Regimental Officers and finally confessed his true identity. Another version has him acquiring a Confederate uniform from one of a group of captured rebels he was escorting to a Union Army Provost Marshall stockade and at the last possible moment discarded his rifle and accouterments, donned the rebel clothing and attempted to march into captivity with the prisoners he was escorting. In this version he also was detected and arrested.

A General Court Martial was convened at the Headquarters of the 1st Division, 1st Army Corps and on May 29, 1863 tried Private John P. Wood, Company F, 19th Indiana Infantry Regiment on charge of desertion to which charge he pleaded guilty. Wood deserted the service on April 29, 1863 while his Regiment was marching to meet the enemy and when apprehended by the Provost Marshall on May 16, 1863, Wood was dressed in a black slouch hat, butternut colored trousers, and a short cavalry jacket. Under arrest he had made the following statement.

"I am a deserter from the 19th Tennessee under command of Gen'l A.P. Hill. It was never brigaded. Col. Eager of the 19th had command of the Brigade when I left. It was over to Fredericksburg when I left on the night. The regt. was never together, always detached, different companies standing about guard. I am not acquainted with much of the Regiment. I was raised and born in Brown Co., Ohio. I have been in service a year and nine months. I enlisted in Memphis, Tennessee. I know the 7th and 9th Tennessee of the Brigade. The 7th is in Jackson's Corps. We were encamped about 3 miles from Fredericksburg. I was here the first fight. We were never in any particular brigade. I had been in Memphis 4 months before the war broke out. I was overseeing about 30 niggers when I enlisted. Our Regt. went to Richmond from Memphis, then to the James river. I know Genl's Lee, Longstreet, Jackson, Breckenbridge and most of them on the other side of the river," or words to that effect!

Testimony was offered to establish Wood's time of desertion and apprehension. Wood offered no defense but did make a statement to the Court.

"The reason I left the Regiment before crossing the river near Fredericksburg was because I did not want to go in a fight. I can't fight, I cannot stand it to fight. I am ashamed to make the statement, but I may as well do it now as at any other time. I never could stand a fight. I never could bear to shoot anybody. I have done my duty in every way but fight. I have tried to do it but cannot. I am perfectly willing to work all my lifetime for the United States in any other way but fight. I have tried to do it but cannot. I went to my doctor when I left the Regiment and wanted him to give me a pass and I would go and work and wait on the wounded in the Hospital. He told me that he guessed he had heard enough. I had better go on and try to do my duty. He said he would see about it. I could not find out where the hospital was. He had not stationed it. Then after awhile I came to the conclusion I would try to go home. I started to go to Aquia Creek Landing and got lost on my way and got outside of our picket lines, out by Stafford Court House. I met the pickets there and came on to our own pickets and gave myself up. I had been acquainted in Tennessee and I gave myself up as a rebel. I made the statement for fear they would think I was a bushwacker. Then I was sent on under arrest, until they received me here. I am willing to do all I could for my country. I like it as much as anybody does. I was always willing to try to fight for my country, but I never could. I am willing to try to fight for it again. I am ashamed of my conduct and will always try to do better hereafter."

The Court deliberated and confirmed Wood's guilty plea and sentenced him to death by musketry on June 12, 1863.

A rude coffin was constructed and a firing squad, it's members selected from each of the five Regiments of the Brigade was assigned. On the night of June 11, 1863, the 1st Corps was ordered to move north toward Pennsylvania. Woods, handcuffed and shackled, seated upon his coffin in an ambulance wagon, was conveyed with his Regiment in the long marching column moving north. His Regiment halted for supper on the 12th of June, 1863 near Harwood Church (another version states Berea Church) and preparations were made for Wood's execution. A grave was dug, his coffin placed beside it. The troops to witness the execution assembled, the firing squad moved into position and Wood was seated upon his coffin. Some reports state that Wood made some last, remarks others say he remained mute. The squad fired and Wood fell back on his coffin, by one version, quite dead. By another version, another single rifle ball was needed to extinguish the flickering flame of his life. The troops marched by the body to a lively tune and Wood was placed in his coffin and buried. The troops continued their march north to a place called Gettysburg.

REFERENCES:

Military Personnel Records, RG-#94
Court Martial Proceedings, RG-#153 LL 434
"The Skirmish Line," The Journal of the North/South Skirmish Assn. May/June 1988. W.J.K. Beaudot.
"In the Bloody Railroad Cut at Gettysburg," Herdegen and Beaudot, 1990, Morningside Press, Dayton, Ohio.
Milwaukee Sunday Telegraph, 1880, 11 part serial, August 6, 1882, March 1, 1885, April 12, 1885, May 24, 1885.

Case #28
Pvt. William Lynch
Co. G, 2nd Mass. Calvary Regt.
Executed for Mutiny
June 16, 1863

DESCRIPTION:

26 years of age, apparently of foreign birth, no further description available.

Lynch apparently enlisted on March 20, 1863 at Rowe, Massachusetts and was mustered into service at Camp Quincy, Boston, Massachusetts on April 9, 1863 in Company G, 2nd Massachusetts Cavalry Regiment. He was charged with Mutiny by a court martial on April 16, 1863.

A General Court Martial was convened at Fort Independence, Boston Harbor, Massachusetts and on May 11, 1863 tried Private William Lynch, Company G, 2nd Massachusetts Cavalry Regiment on charges of Mutinous Conduct and violations of the 6th and 9th Articles of War.

Testimony revealed the following events. The second Massachusetts Cavalry Regiment was still in the organizing stage. Company G of the 2nd Massachusetts was stationed in a large building at #2, City Hall Avenue, in Boston, Massachusetts. The place was named Camp Quinzy after the building owner George H. Quinzy, Justice of the Peace who was the Recruiting Officer for the Regiment. The basement area was used as drill quarters, the first floor as Offices for the Officers and Non-Commissioned Officers Quarters and the enlisted men occupied other floors as barracks.

Nearby Camp Quinzy was a barber shop and bath house owned by a James Burns. Burns had been contracted by Mr. Quinzy to provide shaving, barbering, bathing and shampooing for the men of Company G. Mr. Burns stated that anywhere from one to fifty men were in his shop each day except Saturdays and Sundays. As with his contemporary counterpart, Burns both over heard and directly conversed with members of Company G and became aware of their problems. The principal immediate concern of the men was the receipt of their enlistment bounty of twenty five dollars and a period of leave prior to their transfer to Camp Readville, Massachusetts. Some men believed that they would receive the bounty payment before going to Camp Readville and others thought the payment would be made after they arrived at Camp Readville. Some men advocated refusing to go to Readville unless they received the bounty payment and leave. Burns testified that two men, Lynch and another Private Pendegast, were the unappointed leaders and most influential men amongst the enlisted men. Lynch is perceived as an unschooled individual with strong ambitions and desires for military leadership and rank. He was voluble, outspoken and dramatic. Pendegast, his companion, was a planner and manipulator. Lynch and Pendegast, Burns related, had developed a plan which called for the men to be mustered into service but not go out to Camp Readville until they had received their bounty and been given liberty. Pendegast stated "him and Lynch controlled the majority of the men in that company and as they went the majority of the men would go." Pendegast further stated "he did not care a damn how he got out of it, they would get out of it either by fair means or by foul. He was willing to lead the men on with their sabres. If they got into any trouble that Lynch would do their talking for them to the Colonel. Lynch was opposed to handling a sabre himself and told Pendegast to be on his guard as to what they said. The officers, if they knew of the plans, would commence ironing the ringleaders and that the moment they began to iron the men was the moment to strike the blow. Pendegast said he would be the first one to lead them on and he did not care a damned if he was the first one to fall. If he was unfortunate enough to be shot that Lynch and others would avenge his death." Lynch stated "he would do the talking for them and he did not care a damned how much talk the officers had they could not talk him down. They must have their Bounty money and Liberty before they went to Camp. If they insisted they would have it and the officers could not get rid of it." Burns considered the plan one for fomenting mutiny.

When asked why he did not advise the Officers of the Company of the matter, he replied, "I mentioned some details of the plan to a newly commissioned officer who told me that most of the men were half full of rum and did not know what they said and it did not make any difference what they did say."

On the morning of April 9, 1863, 1st Sergeant, H. G. Burlingham of Company G, 2nd Massachusetts Cavalry Regiment was in the basement drill hall at Camp Quinzy attempting to iron Private Joseph Darwin of Company G and place him in arrest on a charge of drunkenness. The accused saw the attempted ironing and rushed up to the 1st Sergeant, shouting "What in the hell are you ironing that man for?" "None of your business" was the reply. Lynch angrily retorted "Damn you, you have ironed men enough in this camp!" and then struck the 1st Sergeant in the face with his fist, the 1st Sergeant left for the upper floor pursued by Lynch who struck him again. The 1st Sergeant returned to the basement drill hall accompanied by Captain McKindrey the Company Commander. The Captain ordered Lynch to be ironed. Lynch replied "I will not submit to being ironed." The Captain said "Lynch be a man and submit to being ironed." Lynch replied "Sir you nor no other damned Officer can iron me!" The Captain ordered non-commissioned officers to iron Lynch. Lynch strongly resisted, seized the handcuffs and threw them across the room while kicking and striking at the men trying to subdue him. The enlisted men of Company G gathered around shouting encouragement to Lynch and interfering with the attempt to seize Lynch. At this point the Regimental Commander, Colonel Charles R. Lowell arrived on the scene and had the men fall in to ranks. He asked the 1st Sergeant for a revolver. Called for Lynch to front and center. Directed Captain McKindrey to iron him and admonished the men not to resist his order as he will shoot the first one who does so. The Captain and a non-commissioned officer seized Lynch and threw him on the floor and ironed him while the enlisted men broke ranks again. A pistol shot was heard, and the rioting ceased. Pendegast lay on the floor, dead, shot by the Colonel. Lynch was pulled to his feet and he walked over to the corpse, and saw it was Pendegast, he turned to the Colonel and said, "You have killed my best friend" raising his ironed hands above his head he exclaimed, "I swear before God and man to avenge that man's blood." At this point a City of Boston detective, Frank E. Scott arrived on the scene to take Lynch to "the toombs", the city jail. Lynch would not permit any non-commissioned officer of Company G to touch him, kicking at 1st Sergeant Burlingham saying "God damn you I will have your heart's blood!" Lynch was confined at "the toombs" while awaiting Court Martial.

There were reports that some of the mutinous mob had been drinking and that some had seized sabres from the racks during the height of the mutiny and one non-commissioned officer reported he received a cut on his head by a sabre wielder.

Witnesses for the accused tended to testify that he acted as a sabre drill coach for the "awkward squad" and was most popular with the other enlisted men. Lynch tried to convey the impression that he was "appointed" as a drillmaster and that only he could control the men as they had respect and confidence in him.

The accused presented a long statement to the court on his behalf.

"Mr. President, and gentlemen of the court, I do not wish you to understand that the witnesses that I have here are the only men that I can obtain if I felt so inclined. To establish my innocence, as far as participating in the Mutiny may be concerned; but my extreme desire to put the Court to as little trouble as possible and at the same time keeping in view the Welfare of the Company, I might call upon at least four times that number who could testify to those facts that I hope are already established but if I'm to be brought to trial for the misconduct of other men I wanted no one. But If I am brought to trial for what I have done I will be satisfied with the result. I do not make this defence in order to deny anything which I have done but merely to state the facts of the case for my love of truth will not permit me to assert anything to the contrary. I have never attempted to deny that I struck the man and I was provoked into doing it yet this seems to be the least of my charges. Mutiny is preferred as a charge against me and to confute this I have proven by several witnesses that so far was I from participating in the said mutiny that I did endeavor to the utmost of my power to stop said mutiny by telling the men to fall into line and not to draw sabres and not to attempt to strike or insult an Officer. My conduct here gentlemen may seem somewhat strange that I a private of the company should thus command them to do so and succeed as I did. But it will not appear so strange when I tell you the fact that I was acting in the capacity of Drillmaster and had the drilling of 23 men and the Lieutenant had the rest of them under his charge for they could not all be drilled in one room. And we had no non-commissioned capable of drilling them. And furthermore when Sergeant Burlingham found he could not teach the sabre drill himself he took no pains to conceal his aversion of me and never omitted an opportunity of making me the object of his insults and which my proficiency in that particular was the cause. Being the drillmaster of part of my company I did not think it improper to intercede for a man who belonged to my squad. That he was about to put in irons and tied to a post and my request was more urgent when I knew that he had no orders to do so, I spoke to him with civility and he insulted me and repelled me with contempt and after he had ironed the man I struck him with my clenched fist fully assured that he would repay me for my presumption as he often said he would do to any man that said anything to him, but what was my surprise to see him turn away. This was what he was waiting for since first I took charge of this squad and he my superior in strength and stature resolved sooner or later that I would be provoked into some overt act in order to have me out of the company. This case gentlemen is not without it's precedent. Doubtless each of you know or have heard of some case similar to this where ambitious men have had recourse to such detestable intrigues as this, only on a larger scale, but the smaller the scale, the meaner the act, and thus to have a man removed whose only crime was that he knew more than himself and consequently dreaded his being elevated above himself. Often had I guarded myself against this snare so sytematically set for me. And almost all the men said that I should not be ironed they were aware of his malice against me, I did not ask them to interfere in the matter and I did not expect that they would. On the contrary I told them to keep back and not insult the officers. This was the last I saw of the matter for I was thrown down and ironed and held until the man was shot. Then I was sent to prison where five more were sent sometime after they were mustered into the service of the U. S. It was then I learned that I was about to be tried for mutiny and if I had told the men to do anything contrary to law and order I might with justice be tried for that crime. But I did not do so and therefore I leave it to the better judgement of the court to decide this, holding me responsible for my conduct or for the conduct of the other parties herein concerned. It may be said that I was the cause of all this but there is a great difference in the cause and the result of such cause. For if I said to a man, I have dropped my purse in the river and he should go to find it and in the attempt get drowned would I be to blame and could I be tried for that man's life? I may have been the cause of this sad affair but I had no hand in it. Perhaps some of the men had been ill treated by the sergeant and took this opportunity of showing their dislike of him. He had treated a great many men in the company as something akin to slaves and animals but I cannot answer for their conduct in his particular for he made scruple of cuffing or shaking a man called Hurley. To the great detriment of said individual, J. Neck, who he knew was not able to resent it, said recruit not being in the company three days. No man feels more sensitive of his character than myself and more, no man could be more willing to obey the orders of his officers for I have served in the English Army for 9 years and obtained a good name and character as drill master which is my profession and since I have been in this country I have followed it. My Captain can form some idea of my abilities in that capacity and my willingness to do all in my power for the welfare of the company. But gentlemen what surprised me the most was that I was charged with drawing a sabre on my superior officer but I have I think successfully confuted this charge and again I have been charged with mutiny and I have confuted that also and proven to the court that I had no part in it. And gentlemen although a stranger to most persons in this country my best abilities would have been put to task to do them and the country a service in the hour of need. There are a great many of my countrymen in the field that are doing and daring for their adopted country and believe me I meant to emulate the example thus showed me. When I enlisted in this company I resolved to do my best to have it second to none in the regiment so far as my abilities were concerned. But all too often has a noble ambition been thwarted by a person whose only purpose seemed to be the ruin of another that he might despite himself and satisfy his craven appetite for power and at the same secrete his actions in the seeming guise of duty. Now gentlemen the fact that the balance of the men were recruits and I myself an entire stranger to the Articles which govern the Army of the U. S. would at least excuse in part our fault. Hoping that you in justice will consider our cases and give us a chance to retrieve our character in the face of the foe, and in defense of the National Banner. I entirely submit myself to your consideration and leniency. William Lynch"

The Court then deliberated, found the accused guilty and sentenced him to be shot to death with musketry.

The execution was carried out at Fort Independence, Boston Harbor, Massachusetts on June 16, 1863. No record has been found of any Court of Inquiry into the circumstances of the shooting of Private Pendegast by Colonel Lowell.

REFERENCES:
Military Personnel Records, RG-#94
Court Martial Procedings, RG-#153 LL 472

Case #29
Private William Minix
Co. A, 9th Ky. Infantry Regt.
Executed for Desertion
June 16, 1863

DESCRIPTION:

25 years of age, no further physical description located.

Minix enlisted and mustered into service on September 25, 1861 at Allen County, Kentucky in Company A, 9th Kentucky Infantry Regiment. He deserted at Bowling Green, Kentucky on September 10, 1862. Sometime in April 1863, he was apprehended and taken to Murfeesboro, Tennessee.

A General Court Martial was convened at Headquarters of the 3rd Division Left Wing, Murfreesboro, Tennessee and on May 7, 1863, tried Private William Minix, Company A, 9th Kentucky Infantry Regiment on a charge of desertion.

Testimony of the Company Commander of the accused stated that Minix was his cook. The Regiment was to move from Nashville, Tennessee, to Bowling Green, Kentucky and was ordered to leave all baggage and wagons behind. The accused was left with the company baggage and wagons and ordered not to leave it under any circumstances. The baggage and wagon trains, however, preceded the marching column to Bowling Green. When Company A arrived the Company Commander learned that the accused had left the train about September 10, 1862 despite his strict orders not to do so. He was not seen again until he was arrested by the Provost Marshalls Guard and returned to his Regiment between the 1 - 14 of April, 1863.

The accused offered neither defense witnesses nor statement in his behalf to the court.

The Court then deliberated, found the accused guilty and sentenced him to be shot to death with musketry.

The execution was carried out at Murfreesboro, Tennessee on June 16, 1863.

Minix wrote from "the Camp Guard House, 3rd Division, June 14, 1863, Col. Cram, Sir as you are doubtless aware I am sentenced to be shot on Tuesday next, others have also been sentenced the same as my self who have done much worse than my self and yet have been reprieved and I feel shure if you would interest your self in my behalf my life mite be saved And I will promase no swear if I escape that, awful degrading death I will hence forth be a true and loyal and a law abiding soldier May God help me for I cannot help my self Yours with respect, William Minix."

Minix was executed on June 16, 1863 as ordered.

REFERENCES:

Military Personnel Records, RG-#94
Court Martial Proceedings, RG-#153 LL 595

Case #30
Pvt. William Grover
NV: Groves, Gruver
Co. A, 46th Pennsylvania Infantry Regt.
Executed for Desertion
June 19, 1863

DESCRIPTION:

18 years of age, no further description is located amongst Grover's military records.

Grover enlisted at Lewistown, Pennsylvania on August 24, 1861 and was mustered into service on September 2, 1861 in Captain Mathew's Company 46th Pennsylvania Infantry Regiment. The unit designation was changed to Company A, 46th Pennsylvania Infantry Regiment. Grover deserted from the camp of the 46th Pennsylvania near Stafford Court House, Virginia on June 5, 1863 and was arrested June 6, 1863 and confined.

A General Court Martial was convened at Headquarters, 1st Division, 2nd Corps near Stafford Court House and on June 8, 1863 tried Private William Grover (Gruver), Company A, 46th Pennsylvania Infantry Regiment on the charge of desertion.

It was charged that Grover deserted his company while it was drawn up in line preparatory to movement. He did not return until arrested.

No testimony was offered by either the prosecution or defense. The accused made a brief simple statement; "I intended to go home and come back again."

The Court deliberated and found the accused guilty, sentenced him to death by musketry.

Grover was executed on June 19, 1863.

A description of the execution is contained in the diary of Private Weethmiller (a copy furnished through the courtesy of Colonel F. A. Lord). The entry in the diary for Friday, June 19, 1863 states that three members of the 46th Pennsylvania Volunteers were to be executed by a firing squad at the same time. In addition to Grover case #30, Lanahan case #7 and McKee case #32 were executed. The account records the standard execution ceremony. The troops to witness the execution were formed about three sides of a square, the unoccupied side reserved for the condemned, the graves for the condemned having been previously dug there. At 1:00PM the party arrived, led by the wagon containing the coffins, which were unloaded and placed in front of each grave. Another wagon followed carrying the three condemned men, their hands pinioned behind them. The "shooting party" of thirty men from the 46th Pennsylvania Volunteers, who were arranged in position before the prisoners who were blindfolded and seated upon their coffins.

The Provost Marshall stepped forward and read the order of execution and gave way to the chaplain who asked for divine mercy for the souls of those about to die. The Commander of the "shooting party" commanded "Ready-aim-fire" and the volley of musketry heralded that the law had been appeased and the souls of the victims winged their way to the throne of the Almighty. May God have mercy on their souls.

REFERENCES:

Military Personnel Records, RG-#94

Court Martial Proceedings, RG-#153 LL 445

"Diary of August G. Werthmiller, Company G, 5th Ohio Infantry Regiment" now in possession of Colonel F. A. Lord and used by his kind permission.

Case #31

Pvt. Christopher Krubart

Co. B, 13th NJ Infantry Regt.

Executed for Desertion

June 19, 1863

DESCRIPTION:

36 years of age, 5 feet 5 inches tall, brown hair, blue eyes, dark complexion, born in Germany, occupation shoemaker, literate.

Krubart enlisted on August 16, 1862 at Jersey City, New Jersey and was mustered into service at Camp Frelinghuysen, Newark, New Jersey on August 25, 1862 in Company B, 13th New Jersey Infantry Regiment. Krubart deserted from his Regiment at Wolf Run Shoal, Virginia on January 18, 1863. There are several notations in his military records concerning his desertion. One such reads, "Returned from desertion, May 12, 1863" but does not stipulate whether the return was voluntary or under arrest. A second notation states that Krubart had "returned from desertion prior to December 1, 1863."

A General Court Martial was convened at the Camp of the 1st Division, 12th Army Corps near Stafford Court House, Virginia and on June 5, 1863 tried Private Christopher Krubart, Company B, 13th New Jersey Infantry Regiment on a charge of Desertion.

Evidence was presented to the Court veerifying that Krubart had been enlisted and served in the 13th New Jersey Infantry Regiment by means of signed original enlistment papers and so forth. Witnesses testified that Krubart was present with his Company on the morning of the 19th of January 1863 at Wolf Run Shoals, Virginia but was absent thereafter until arrested in Trenton, New Jersey and returned in arrest to his Regiment near Stafford Court House, Virginia on or about May 14, 1863.

The accused offered no witnesses in his behalf but did offer a statement to the Court.

"Statement of the Accused"

"I was a coming from the country the 11th of May and was a going to report myself when I was taken. I told the man who took me that I was a going to report myself under the proclamation (of Presidental Amnesty for Deserters). I can not read English and there is no German paper where I was working."

The Court deliberated, found the accused guilty and sentenced hiim to be shot to death with musketry. The execution was carried out on June 19, 1863 near Stafford Court House, Virginia.

REFERENCES:
Military Personnel Records, RG-#94
Court Martial Proceedings, RG-#153 LL 445

Case #32
Pvt. William McKee
NV: Frank, Meeker, McKey
Co. A, 46th Penn. Inf. Regt.
Executed for Desertion
June 19, 1863

DESCRIPTION:
19 years of age, no further description of McKee was located amongst his Military Records.

McKee enlisted at Lewistown, Pennsylvania on August 26, 1861 and was mustered into service on September 2, 1861 at Harrisburg, Pennsylvania. McKee was captured at Winchester, Virginia on May 25, 1862 and was imprisoned at Richmond, Virginia until September 17, 1862 when he was sent to Camp Parole, Maryland (Fort Delaware). He was hospitalized at Fort Delaware (Camp Parole, near Annapolis). Records indicate he was assigned to the 1st Battalion Paroled Prisoners in early 1863 at Camp Parole, Maryland . This organization was formed from paroled prisoners of war for duty compatible with their parole by G.O. #72, A.G.O., June 28, 1862 and the members were returned to their original commands from time to time. McKee was returned to his old Regiment on January 5, 1863 where he served until June 5, 1863 when he deserted the Regiment encamped near Stafford Court House, Virginia. He was arrested the following day, confined and tried by Court Martial.

A General Court Martial was convened at the Camp of the 1st Division, 12th Army Corps near Stafford Court House and on June 8, 1863 tried Private William McKee, Company A, 46th Pennsylvania Infantry Regiment on a charge of desertion.

Testimony offered disclosed that the accused deserted from the ranks of his Company and Regiment while it was formed preparatory to moving from it's station on or about June 4, 1863. Captain Bentley of the 9th New York Cavalry testified that he arrested the prisoner at a house near his camp. The prisoner was dressed in citizen's clothes consisting of a linen coat and dark blue pants. The prisoner stated when questioned that he was an independent Sutler named Samuel Johnson and was stationed at Falmouth, Virginia, had never been a soldier and that he was on his way to Washington. His father had preceded him with the wagons by way of Dumfries while the accused and a companion named Harry Smith were going there by way of the mail boat. The Provost Marshall remarked that he was glad to know they were independent Sutlers as General Hooker had ordered them all to be arrested and either sent home to be drafted or kept in confinement. Captain Weber, commander of Company A, 46th Pennsylvania Regiment related that after McKee was reported missing he and the Commander of the 46th, Colonel Selfridge went to Stafford Court House where the Provost commander told them, his men had arrested two men the previous evening. Upon viewing them, Captain Weber immediately identified McKee and his companion as members of his Company. They were taken to the Provost Guard of the 1st Division where they were confined awaiting filing of charges and trial.

The prisoner had no witnesses to call before the Court on his behalf but did made a brief statement to the Court.

Statement of the Accused

"I intended going home a little while and intended coming back again."

The Court deliberated, found the accused guilty and sentenced him to be shot to death with musketry.

The sentence was carried out on June 19, 1863 near Stafford Court House, Virginia.

REFERENCES:

Military Personnel Records, RG-#94
Court Martial Proceedings, RG-#153 LL 445

Case #33
Pvt. David Blazer
4th Battery, Ind. L. Artillery
Executed for Desertion
June 20, 1863

DESCRIPTION:

22 years of age, 5 feet 8 inches tall, dark hair, gray eyes, dark complexion, born in Columbus, Delaware County, Ohio, occupation farmer, literacy undetermined.

Blazer enlisted and was mustered into service at Nashville, Tennessee on February 15, 1863 in the 4th Battery of Indiana Light Artillery.

Private David Blazer, 4th Indiana Battery was the subject of a General Court Martial on May 6, 1863 at Murfreesboro, Tennessee for Desertion in the face of the enemy.

Testimony revealed Blazer deserted his Battery, on April 24, 1863 at Liberty, Tennessee which was waiting to engage the enemy. He was arrested by a Union Cavalry unit near Alexandria, Tennessee on April 27, 1863. Blazer was dressed in gray pants and a checked coat and an altered black brimmed hat. When he deserted, he had worn the standard Union Army Uniform.

Under questioning by Union Army Officers, Blazer stated his name was Whitlock and that he was a rebel cavalry man of General Floyd's Confederate Command and that he was a citizen of Northern Tennessee. A few of those who interviewed him at Headquarters and at the Provost Marshall's Office believed he was a deserter from the 4th Indiana Battery.Blazer made the following statement to the court on his own behalf:

"When I went from the Battery, it was not my intention to desert the Army at all. When I went out with the train, (the horse drawn supply wagons) I went to get some eggs. I went a little too far from the camp, between three and four miles, I got captured out there. They thought I had so much better clothes on than they had, they would take mine off and give me a different suit."

Blazer was found guilty and was sentenced to be shot to death on June 20, 1863 near the Battery Camp.

Blazer died at 10 minutes before 12 o'clock A.M. on that day.

REFERENCES:

Military Personnel Records, RG-#94
Court Martial Proceedings, RG-#153 LL 643

Case #34
Private John Shockman
Co. I, 1st Kentucky Infantry Regiment
Executed for Desertion
June 23, 1863

DESCRIPTION:

20 years of age, no further physical description is listed.

Shockman enlisted on May 10, 1861, and was mustered into service on June 5, 1861 at Pendleton, Ohio. He was enrolled in Company I, 1st Kentucky Infantry Regiment.

On December 4, 1861, while with his Regiment on the march from Camp Gauley to Charlestown, Virginia (West Virginia), he deserted. During his period of desertion, Shockman enlisted in Company M, 4th Ohio Volunteer Cavalry Regiment. On the 25th of August, 1862, Shockman physically assaulted his former Company Commander (Company I, 1st Kentucky Infantry Regiment), and resisted efforts to arrest him for desertion at Cincinnati, Ohio. He was eventually arrested on May 11, 1863 and returned for court martial.

A General Court Martial was convened at the Headquarters of the 2nd Division, 1st Army Corps, on the 7th of May, 1863, and on May 23, 1863 tried Private John Shockman, Company I, 1st Kentucky Infantry Regiment on the charge of desertion and offering violence to his superior officer while in the execution of his office.

Shockman was mustered into the military service at Camp Pendleton, Ohio, in Company I, 1st Kentucky Infantry Regiment on June 5, 1861. Shockman deserted his Company and Regiment at or near Camp Gauley, West Virginia on or about December 1, 1861 without obtaining a discharge therefrom. He subsequently enlisted in Company M, 4th Ohio Cavalry Regiment and when seen and recognized by his former company Commander, Captain A. J. Hogan, Company I, 1st Kentucky Infantry Regiment, in Cincinnati, Ohio on August 25, 1862, did successfully resist Captain Hogan's attempt to arrest him on a charge of desertion. He disappeared until captured and was returned under arrest to his Regiment then in Tennessee on May 11, 1863.

There were no records of the actual testimony offered at the trial except that the Court after due deliberation found Shockman guilty and sentenced him to be shot to death.

He was found guilty and sentenced to be executed by a firing squad on June 23, 1863 at the Camp of the 2nd Division at Cripple Creek, Tennessee.

The execution, took place within the limits of the camp of the 2nd Division at Cripple Creek, Tennessee on June 23, 1863. The report of the execution signed by Brigadier General Charles Craft, carries the date as July 23, 1863.

REFERENCES:
Military Personnel Records, RG-#94
Court Martial Proceedings, RG-#153 CMSR

Case #35
Private William H. Laird
Co. G, 17th ME Inf. Regt.
Executed for Desertion
July 15, 1863

DESCRIPTION:

27 years of age, 5 feet 10 inches tall, brown hair, blue eyes, dark complexion, born in Maine, occupation farmer, married, literacy undetermined.

Laird enlisted on August 7, 1862 at Ruxton, Maine, and was mustered into service on August 18, 1862 at Portland, Maine in Company G, 17th Maine Infantry Regiment. According to available records, Laird was detailed (sent on temporary duty) to Livingstons Battery of Artillery, by one record, on September 3, 1862. He deserted while on detached service from Fort Picket, Maryland on or about October 11, 1862. He was arrested on May 23, 1863, jailed, and held for Court Martial.

A General Court Martial was convened at Augusta, Maine, and on July 2, 1863 tried Private William H. Laird, Company G, 17th Maine Infantry Regiment on charges of Desertion and Violation of the 9th Article of War.

Laird requested that he be allowed the privilege of counsel (counselor not named) and the Court granted the request.

Testimony of witnesses revealed that Laird had deserted his Regiment on or about October 15, 1862 and after a diligent search over many months, was located, on a farm near Berwick, Maine about the 23rd of May, 1863. 1st Lieutenant Nathan Walker of the 5th Maine Infantry Regiment was sent from Headquarters in Augusta, Maine to arrest Laird and bring him into confinement. Between 11 and 12 o'clock, Lieutenant Walker, from a point of concealment, carefully observed Laird working on the farm of a man named Gowell. Laird was driving a team, hauling manure. Lieutenant Walker approached Laird and advised him that he was an Army Officer assigned to arrest him as a deserter. Laird had a manure fork in his hands as he was engaged in shoveling manure into a cart. Lieutenant Walker told him to lay the manure fork aside and Laird instead presented the forked tines at him. Walker then grasped hold of the fork with one hand and drew his revolver with the other and managed to jerk the fork from Laird's hands. Walker ironed (handcuffed) Laird and was requested by the prisoner for the privilege of seeing the lady of the house as the man of the house had gone away. Laird entered the house followed closely by Lieutenant Walker. Laird tried to leave the first room they had entered to go into another room. Walker advised him that if he wished to see the lady, he had to see her there, not in any other room. Lieutenant Walker, meanwhile having moved to another room while keeping Laird under observation, was talking with a member of the 10th Maine Infantry named Waterhouse who accompanied him as an aide, and a man named Hanson who assisted in investigations. Suddenly the woman of the house entered, pale and gasping. Lieutenant Walker followed her into the room where the prisoner was waiting. As Walker entered he saw Laird with a revolver in his hands pointed at him, Laird trying frantically to cock the hammer but unable to accomplish his purpose being prevented by the hand cuffs. As Walker rushed at the prisoner, Laird threw the pistol on a chair.

Laird was immediately removed from the house and taken by railroad to Augusta, Maine for confinement and trial.

The accused having nothing to offer, the Court retired and deliberated, finding the accused guilty. Laird was sentenced to be shot to death with musketry.

Laird was transferred to Fort Preble, Maine for custody and execution, arriving there on July 9, 1863.

A Letter from the Commandant of Fort Preble, Maine explains the problem existing at that Post.

"Headquarters Fort Preble, Maine
July 9, 1863

Major: I have the honor to report the arrival this P.M. of Private William H. Laird of Company G, 17th Regiment Ma. Vols. now under sentence of death and to be executed on the 15th inst.

As the Maj. Genl. commanding desires the proceedings to be as private as possible, I wish to place before him the situation of this post and other evidence tending to show the impossibility of anything being kept private here. The security of the Rebel prisoners now here requires one half my force for guard each day. The engineers at work on the Fort have 150 men employed. The post now has as many entrances to the parade as there are individuals desiring to enter and nothing but a chain of sentinels encircling the whole grounds can keep them out and my whole garrison is not large enough for such a purpose.

I enclose slips from two newspapers to illustrate how news circulates here. The evening paper from which I cut is published in Portland at 5 o'clock P.M. while the prisoner Hutchison did not arrive at the post until after 4 o'clock P.M. yesterday.

Should the Maj. Genl. Commanding in view of these facts decide to sent the prisoners to Fort Independence or some other isolated or enclosed post, I respectfully request a guard may be detailed from such post and sent here for the prisoners as I have neither Officers or men sufficient to admit of my furnishing such a guard as would be required without jeopardizing the safe keeping of the prisoners of war.

I am sir, very respfy your obt. svt.
Geo. S. Andrew
Maj. 17th Inf.
Comdg. Post."

Major Andrew's letter was not acted upon and on July 15, 1863 he wrote that "Private William H. Laird, Co. G, 17th Regt. Maine Volunteers was not at this place (Fort Preble, Maine) at 2:58 o'clock this P.M."

The execution took place at Fort Preble, Maine on July 15, 1863.

REFERENCES:
Military Personnel Records, RG-#94
Court Martial Proceedings, RG-#153 NN 45

Case #36
Pvt. Peter Kleinkopf
NV: Kleinkoff
Co E, 4th Calif Vol Inf Regt
Executed for Desertion
July 17, 1863

DESCRIPTION:
25 years of age, 5 feet 8 inches tall, light blue eyes, light hair, fair complexion, born in Germany, occupation shoemaker, literate.

Kleinkopf enlisted at Benicia Barracks, California in Company E, 4th California Volunteer Infantry Regiment on January 10, 1863. Kleinkopf deserted after committing an assault with a deadly weapon and robbery of one of his fellow soldiers, Pvt. John Williams, Company E, 4th California Volunteer Infantry Regiment on the night of February 12th at or near Benicia, California. On March 22, 1863, Kleinkopf while clad in civilian clothes, surrendered to Col. Ferris Forman, 4th California Volunteer Infantry at Benicia Barracks, California and stated he was Charles Smith, a deserter from Company I, 3rd Artillery, U.S. Army. He was confined in the guardhouse.

A General Court Martial was convened at the Benicia Barracks, California and on March 30, 1863 tried Private Peter Kleinkopf, Company E, 4th California Infantry Regiment on the following charges Desertion, assault with intent to commit robbery, and assault with intent to commit murder.

The prisoner being asked if he desired counsel replied, "none other than the Judge Advocate."

Testimony given by witnesses disclosed the following facts: Kleinkopf deserted from his Company on or about the night of February 10, 1863 and returned on March 22, 1863.

Private John Williams, Company E, 4th California Infantry Regiment testified that about 8:00 PM on the night of February 10, 1863, he started to the town of Benicia accompanied by Privates White and Baker of his Company and Regiment. On their way they stopped at a saloon called the "Snug." Williams' two companions began playing cards and remained at the "Snug." Kleinkopf was present and came up to Williams and asked if he was going on into town. williams said he was and he and Kleinkopf started off. At the steam boat wharf they entered a saloon and Williams bought Kleinkopf a drink. Kleinkopf smoked a cigar during the hour or so they remained in the saloon. They watched the Stockton Steamboat arrive and depart then continued their walk to town. As they trudged along, Williams heard footsteps of several persons approaching them from the rear. He halted and told Kleinkopf who continued on a few steps past him to wait until the followers arrived or past them. Williams turned to the two men coming up and noted that they were in civilian dress. He received a terrific blow on the head which knocked him to his knees and then the two men assaulted him and were joined in their attack by Kleinkopf. One of the attackers he remembered later, was named Wilson who had been in the Guard House and was later sent to jail for his part in the attack. The attackers continued bludgeoning

Williams said he attempted to draw a pocket pistol he carried but it was knocked away. He was cut and stabbed with a bowie knife. Williams heard Kleinkopf distinctly shout, "kill the son of a bitch, kill him!" Williams then began screaming, "Murder, Murder, Murder!" which startled his assailants so that they ran away. Williams, bleeding profusely, stumbled up to a nearby house and sought assistance but no one responded to his knocking on the door. He stopped at a second house and a man come out but offered no assistance not even the drink of water Williams begged for. At that moment Sergeant Chapman of Company A, 4th California Infantry Regiment happened to pass by and Williams related his travail. The man he had begged for water then came with a pitcher of water which Williams consumed hastily and gratefully. Sergeant Chapman took him to the hospital where his wounds were treated and where he convalesced for nearly a month. The stab wounds in his back were blunted by the scapula but the knife wounds on his hands were most serious as they had severed tendons on the back of his hand.

Investigation disclosed that the assailant Wilson had been in daily touch with Kleinkopf at the Reynolds Hotel where he stayed for about a week. Wilson left bloody clothing behind and was positively identified as the man Kleinkopf visited.

Kleinkopf was established as the owner of the Bowie knife used in the attack on Williams. The knife was found at the scene and identified by several soldiers, one testified that Kleinkopf tried to sell it to him while another said Kleinkopf threatened him with it.

During the trial it was brought out that Kleinkopf had been serving a long prison term at a California State Prison and had escaped after six years of incarceration, just prior to his enlistment in the California Regiment.

Kleinkopf offered no witnesses on his behalf before the Court, but did offer a statement of defense.

Statement of Defense

"Adjutant Dear Sir, Please copy this for your unfortunate client, Peter Kleinkopf. Benicia Barracks, California, 28th March, 1863 to the honorable members of the Court Martial at Benicia Barracks! Gentlemen and honorable, (1) Benicia Barracks California, March 28, 1863, gentlemen and honorable members of the court, the accused, Peter Kleinkopf begs most sincerely the pardon and the permission of the to make this statement in behalf of my defense and at the same time the reason of me having deserted from the camp to which I formerly belonged to, I Peter Kleinkopf the unfortunate now in your presence some of these gentlemen that is now here if not all of them, are aware of my former situation before I joined the army at this post. That being a prisoner in the state Prison of this state and got my liberty after having suffered for the term (6) six years and at the time I escape but not possess the means of leaving the country when I found that some of their camp at Benicia would soon go away from here so I went and enlisted thinking that the Company would be leaving in a few days which was the general talk at that time in and about the garrison. Where I have remained for some time undisturbed and was in hopes of remaining so, when misfortune happened to me by meeting one of the men from states prison and soon another in the Town of Benicia both of which know my unhappy and unpleasant state after the meeting of these two persons, it was not but a few days when some of the men of my respected company found out that I had formerly been an inmate of the States prison and I had it thrown up to me in the Quarters and I was scared to look any man in the face after that. I bore it as long as I was able to bear it. I was liable to be taken at any moment out of the Quarters by the Civil Authorities and taken to that miserable Police cell again and to have that happen to me to be taken away under these circumstances would have been most horrible to me. A man in my place, in fact I did not know what to do I was about to tell the Captain of my company the circumstances and ask his advice but on account of me being or having escaped from the most horrible place that a man could be in and did not wish to disgust the Camp. Why I kept from doing so and in the moment of the deranged state of the mind deserted and committed a crime for which God alone can pardon me that is of forfeiting the solemn obligation and oath that I had taken in regard to serve the United State, but it was as I said before it was the miserable condition that I was in made me do it. Now as nothing in this world but to await and endure the sentence that will be passed upon me I have no hope whatever to receive one favorable spark of mercy on my sins, but as there is one poor creature in this world which is my sister and the only person that remains of my family and who perhaps is looking to her unfortunate brother if not for support but for protection maybe at some coming day. And gentlemen it is for her, not for my sake to spare my life even I shall be imprisoned for any number of years and be deprived of seeing her again she won't be for to come and see her unfortunate brother who is the unworthy subject now in your presence at this honorable court. Now gentlemen take these circumstances in consideration and have a little mercy upon me and shall I ever be able to breathe the free air again in the World it will be from a new made man and from the reformed sinner and an grateful person before you.

"I hope to be pardoned for making this statement, I sign my dishonored name.

Peter Kleinkopf"

The Court deliberated, found Kleinkopf guilty and sentenced him to be shot to death with musketry on July 17, 1863 at Benicia Barracks, California.

On May 13, 1863 Major General Holt the Adjutant General wrote from his office in Washington D.C. to President Abraham Lincoln:

"No reason appears from the within record why the approval of the proceedings of the Court Martial by the General Cmdg. the Department should not be approved. The prisoner is not only found guilty of desertion, but of an aggravated assault with intent to rob and murder, committed at the same time upon a fellow soldier and comrade; and the facts proved justify the finding. The assault was in the night, and consisted in the infliction of dangerous wounds with a knife upon the breast, back and hand; and with a club upon the head. The prisoner had been but a month in service, and had, previous to his enlistment, escaped form State's Prison, where he had been confined for six years. The arrest and conviction took place in March last. The prisoner did not voluntarily return. The desertion appears to have been a flight from the anticipated consequences of the assault.

Holt
Judge Advocate General

Sentence approved, A. Lincoln, May 20, 1863"

On May 21st, 1863, a letter was written concerning the status of Kleinkopf as his Company was ordered to another area. The question was whether Kleinkopf was to accompany his Company. The answer was no.

Order #83, July 16, 1863, Headquarters Benicia Barracks, Col. Black commanding read in part, "The Comdg Officer indulges in the hope that the execution may prove a warning and admonition to all soldiers against the great crime of desertion, the punishment for which in these times by the 20th Article of War is death."

The report of the execution and death of Kleinkopf dated July 17, 1863, stated "was carried into execution at 11½ O'clock AM today. 12 men composed the party for the execution, 11 with ball and 1 with blank cartridge & 11 balls went through his breast, his heart was literally riddled & he died instantly (after the first discharge)."

REFERENCES:

Military Personnel Records, RG-#94

Military Court Martial Proceedings, RG-#153 MM 93

Case #37
Private Bradford Butler
Co. I, 157th, NY Infantry Regt.
Executed for Desertion
August 1, 1863

DESCRIPTION:

26 years of age, 5 feet 5 inches tall, brown hair, gray eyes, light complexion, born in Ontario County, New York, occupation farmer, literacy undetermined.

Butler enlisted on August 13, 1862 at Sullivan, New York and was mustered in to service on September 19, 1862 at Hamilton, New York in Company I, 157th New York Infantry Regiment. Butler served with his Regiment in Virginia until April 27/28, 1863 when he deserted at or near Stafford C. H., Virginia. He was captured, placed in arrest, and confined on May 20, 1863.

Private Bradford Butler, Company I, 157th New York Infantry Regiment was tried before a General Court Martial convened on May 29, 1863 at the Headquarters of the 3rd Division, 11th Army Corps, Virginia. Butler was charged with desertion.

Butler pleaded guilty and no testimony was offered by either the prosecution or the defense.

Butler had enlisted in August 1862 and by April 1863, the Regiment was encamped near Stafford, Court House, Virginia. On April 28, 1863, Butler deserted as the Regiment was preparing to march and engage the enemy in battle. Butler was described in G.O. #72, July 28, 1863, Head Quarters, Army of the Potomac at Warrenton, Virginia "as a bad soldier and largely instrumental in urging others to desert." He is specifically named as persuading five members of the 157th New York Infantry Regiment and one member of the 45th New York Infantry Regiment to desert. They were all captured, tried, and sentenced to death which sentences were later commuted.

Butler was arrested on May 20, 1863 and brought for trial as mentioned above.

The Court confirmed the prisoner's plea of guilty and sentenced him to death by a firing squad on August 1, 1863 at Warrenton, Virginia.

REFERENCES:
Military Personnel Records, RG-#94
Court Martial Proceedings, RG-#153 LL 652

Case #38
Private Thomas Jewett
Co. D, 5th Maine Infantry Regiment
Executed for Desertion
August 14, 1863

DESCRIPTION:

33 years of age, 5 feet 8½ inches tall, brown hair, hazel eyes, light complexion, born in England, occupation laborer, not married.

Jewett enlisted and was mustered into service at Camp Preble, Portland, Maine on June 24, 1861 in Captain Thompson's Company, 5th Regiment, Maine Volunteers. The unit designation was later changed to Company D, 5th Regiment Maine Infantry. The Regiment was serving in the Maryland/Virginia area when on or about May 3, 1863, Jewett deserted from Fredericksburg, Maryland. A notation on the deserter file dated June 1, 1863 states: "said to be arrested and lodged in jail at Washington."

A General Court Martial was convened at the headquarters of the 2nd Brigade, 1st Division, 6th Army Corps, and on August 3, 1863 tried Private Thomas Jewett,

Company D, 5th Maine Infantry Regiment on a charge of desertion.

Testimony disclosed that the Regiment had marched from Fredericksburg, Maryland, and was resting prior to the engagement at Salem Church, Virginia. A roll call after the Regiment formed up for battle showed Jewett absent. He was not seen again by any member of his Regiment until he was returned to his Company under arrest, from Washington D. C. on July 17, 1863.

Witnesses stated the prisoner had been a good soldier, and had participated with the Regiment in the battles of Gaines Mill, and Antietam, and one other engagement. He also was reported to have been afflicted with diarrhea just prior to his desertion.

Another memorandum dated May 26, 1863 from the headquarters Provost Marshall's office Wash, D. C. stated, "Thomas Jewett says he went to Belle Plaine to peddle; boat left and could not get back. Belongs in Rockland, Maine. is a deserter from the 5th Maine, Co. D." Written across this notation is "Escaped from Forrest Hall Prison, Georgetown, D C." Jewett was mentioned as a prisoner in the Central Guard House, Washington, D. C. in a June 1, 1863 memorandum from a Judge Advocate in Washington, D. C.

Having no defense witnesses to present before the Court, Jewett offered a statement in his defense.

"Statement"

"I was in the fight at Salem Church, after the fight I started to Fredericksburg and got as far as a house about half a mile from the city. There I stayed overnight, and the next morning, May 4th, I was in the fortifications and fought about an hour against rebel skirmishers advancing on our left flank, we were obliged to fall back and I was obliged, in order to save myself to throw my rifle and accouterments into the river and to swim across as the bridges having been taken up. I met two men of the 90th Penn, John (illegible) and Mike(illegible) who persuaded me to desert with them, they (illegible) were saying that there was in Pennsylvania (illegible_____) and they could (illegible_____) I should be responsible for throwing away my things, if I went back to the regiment and I was therefore induced to go with them."

The Court deliberated, found Jewett guilty, and sentenced him to be shot to death with musketry.

The execution was carried out on the 14th of August, 1863.

REFERENCES:

Military Personnel Records, RG-#94
Court Martial Proceedings, RG-#153 MM 588

Case #39

Pvt. (Cpl.) Francis Scott
Co. F, 1st Louisiana Vol Inf Regt
Executed for Murder
August 14, 1863

DESCRIPTION:

29 years of age, born in County Monahan, Ireland.

Scott is said to have five years honorable service in the U.S. Regular Army before the Civil War, was in New Orleans at the time war was declared and said to have re-enlisted in the 1st Louisiana Heavy Artillery (Confederate) and served at Fort Jackson when it was captured by Admiral Farragut's (USN) forces in April 1862. He was paroled and enlisted in the 1st Louisiana Infantry Regiment (U.S. Army) on August 19, 1862 and was mustered into service on August 31, 1862. Scott was stationed at Fort Butler, Donaldsonville, Louisiana when he shot the Post Commander, Major Bullen, on July 5, 1863. He was arrested, confined, and tried by Court Martial.

A General Court Martial was convened at New Orleans, Louisiana and on July 24, 1863 tried Private Francis Scott, Company F, 1st Louisiana Infantry Regiment on the charges of violations of the 7th and 9th Articles of War.

Testimony provided by witnesses related that Major J. D. Bullen, 28th Maine Infantry Regiment was shot to death by Scott about 9:30PM on the night of the 5th of July, 1863 at Fort Butler, Donaldsonville, Louisiana.

Events occurring previous to the shooting were the movements of two companies of Infantry ordered to occupy positions outside the stockade of the Fort. One Company having moved into its designated position was ordered to move, by Major Bullen, so as to permit another Company, Company F, 1st Louisiana Infantry Regiment, to take up its assigned position. As Company F maneuvered into place, loud grumbling was heard from one soldier in the front rank of Company F. Major Bullen asked the grumbler if he was directing his remarks at him. The soldier replied that Major Bullen was ordering his Captain about when he didn't know how to drill himself or words to that effect. The Major said, "What do you mean? Are you talking to me?" Scott replied, "No sir, I am talking to my Captain." Bullen then exclaimed, "you rascal!" The Major moved toward the soldier, some witnesses claiming he drew his pistol and pointed it at the soldier, while others swore the Major was unarmed. In any case, the soldier pointed his musket at the Major and fired. The ball struck Major Bullen in the left wrist passing through and entered his left side. The major fell upon being shot, exclaiming, "Oh my father! Oh father I'm dying!" Soldiers immediately carried the Major off to the guard house as well as the soldier who shot the Major. Scott was arrested, placed in irons, and taken aboard the U. S. Gun Boat Princess Royal, tied up at dockside, and questioned. Scott was described as having been drinking but not drunk, and clearly aware of what he had done. He was impudent, belligerent and making profane statements about the knowledge of Military Matters possessed by Major Bullen. He stated, "I have shot the Major and am willing to die for it." Scott was unremorseful.

Major Bullen only lived about two hours after he was shot, insensible the entire time.

Scott presented witnesses in his defense who emphasized in their testimony that Major Bullen was armed or was in the act of drawing his pistol or was actually pointing the pistol at Scott.

Scott offered a statement in his defense.

"I have a few words which I wish to offer, in explanation of my conduct. I am charged with the shooting of Major Bullen, with malice aforethought. Now I wish to state that I bore him no malice. The act of my firing at him was an impulsive movement, made, as I then believed, and now believe, in my own defense: It was the instinct of self-preservation, and not a wilfull and deliberate murder. I have always borne a good character and have enjoyed the good will of all my officers, as any of them will testify. I trust my crime, may not be considered, so much a crime, as a misfortune: and hope you who sit in judgement on my case, will be lenient in your sentence."

Respectfully submitted to the consideration of the Court
(signed) Francis A. Scott
Company F, 1st Louisiana Infantry Volunteers

The Court deliberated, found Scott guilty, and sentenced him to be shot to death by musketry on August 14, 1863 in the New Orleans, Louisiana area.

On August 12th, 1863, the New Orleans City Provost Marshall wrote a memorandum inquiring whether "he shall inform the prisoner of the fact (time and date of execution) previous to that time in order to give him a chance to prepare himself to meet his fate." No reply is found.

The *Daily True Delta* newspaper of New Orleans, dated August 15, 1863, carried an account of the execution of Private Francis Scott under the title of "Military Execution."

"A soldier shot for killing his superior officer, at 8 p'clock yesterday morning (Aug. 14, 1863) a military execution took place on the levee between the Vicksburg and Reading cotton presses. There was no previous announcement of the event except the cortege which we mentioned in yesterday's Evening True Delta. Our confrere of the Picaynne was there, and we give part of his account:

'Among the regiments present were the 26th Mass., the 9th Conn. and the 91st N.Y., together with a considerable force of Cavalry and Artillery. A covered wagon drove up containing the prisoner with his arms pinioned, seated on his coffin. He was accompanied by his spiritual adviser, Father Dufau, and some members of the Provost Guard.

'The prisoner, Francis Scott, was a man in the very prime of life, having just completed his thirtieth year. He was a native of County Monahan, Ireland and had spent five years in service as a soldier in the Regular United States Army. Being in this city when the war broke out, he joined the First Louisiana Heavy Artillery (confederate) and was in service at Ft. Jackson when it surrendered to Admiral Farragut in April of last year. He then was paroled with other prisoners, but finally he rejoined the United States service, attaching himself to the 1st Louisiana Regiment.

'The offense for which he was tried and convicted by a courtmartial was committed on the 5th of July last, at Ft. Butler, Donaldsonville. It appears that a difficulty arose between him and Major Bullen of the 28th Mass. Regiment, then in command of that point, when Scott, being on duty at the time, raised his musket and shot the Major through the body, thereby causing his death.

'He surveyed the preparations that were being made for his execution with a calm, unflinching gaze.

'The sentence of the courtmartial was read to him by Capt. Pickering, Provost Marshall of the defenses of the city, and copies of it were read to the various regiments which lined the square, after which the prisoner was led to his coffin, and Father Dufau addressed a prayer for mercy to the Throne of Grace. The solemn ceremony of preparation being ended, the priest bade farewell to the prisoner, and the latter, turning to his late comrades in arms, said: 'Soldiers, I came here to die. I shot Major Bullen on the 5th of July last and would do so again under like circumstances.' He then went on to give a detail of some of the duties he had performed at Donaldson and elsewhere, when he repeated: 'I shot the Major through the wrist and body, and am willing to die for it. I made a reply which I should not have done, when he called me a rascal and drew his revolver. I thought he intended to shoot me, and I shot him and must die for it. If he had shot me. There would have been nothing of it. My Colonel, last year, shot a man at Camp Williams, and nothing was done to him. He said the men were in mutiny, but it was no such thing. But I forgive every one, as I hope to be forgiven. I die as a soldier. If General Banks had a thousand such soldiers as I am, they would be worth all the conscripts that ever came from Maine.' He then said, 'Farewell' and kneeling down, observed calmly, 'I am ready.'

A handkerchief was then bound over his eyes, and the order to fire was given. At the word, twelve muskets were discharged, and the convict fell over and died without a struggle. Seven Bullets struck him, two passing through his heart, four through his body and one through his wrist."

REFERENCES:

Military Personnel Records, RG-#94
Court Martial Proceedings, RG-#153 MM 697
Daily True Delta (Newspaper, New Orleans), August 15, 1863
Daily Picayune (Newspaper, New Orleans), August 15, 1863

Case #40
Private Hiram Reynolds
NV: Ruynolds
Co. H, 82nd, IN Infantry Regt.
Executed for Murder
August 17, 1863

DESCRIPTION:

33 (42) years of age, 6 feet 1½ inches tall, gray hair, black eyes, fair complexion, born in Lincoln County, Tennessee, occupation gambler, married.

Reynolds had enlisted in September 1861 in Company G, 27th Indiana Infantry Regiment at Indianapolis, Indiana. No further record has been located although he states he was discharged for disability.

Reynolds later enlisted on August 9, 1862 at Nashville, Indiana and was mustered into service on August 30, 1862 at Madison, Indiana in Company H, 82nd Indiana Infantry Regiment. On May 19, 1863, in the camp of the 82nd Regiment near Triume, Tennessee, Reynolds did feloniously, willfully, maliciously and of his own malice shoot Washington Moser, also of Company H, 82nd Indiana Infantry Regiment. He shot Moser in the head, the bullet striking him on the left temple. On June 1, 1863, Reynolds was transferred to Nashville prison.

A General Court Martial was convened at the 3rd Division, 14th Army Corps, Department of the Cumberland and on May 25, 1863 tried Private Hiram Reynolds, Company H, 82nd Indiana Infantry Regiment on charges of murder in the 1st degree. Reynolds requested admission of Captain William W. Browning, 82nd Indiana Infantry as his counsel, which the Court granted.

The accused then offered the following: "I, Hiram Reynolds charged with murder before this Court, plead in Bar of Trial, that there is not sufficient charge against me for violaton of any Article of War or any General Orders, and wholly fails to set out the Law of the State which has been violated. I therefore move the Court to dismiss the case."

The Court withdrew to deliberate the motion and the Court overruled the motion.

The testimony offered stated that on May 19, 1863 in the camp of the 82nd Indiana Infantry Regiment near Triume, Tennessee, Reynolds shot Private Washington Moser, Company H, 82nd Indiana Infantry Regiment, thereby causing his death.

Captain John W. Matheney, commanding Company H, 82nd Indiana Infantry Regiment stated that some few days previous to the death of Moser, he had taken Reynolds' rifle and accouterments away from him after he threatened fellow members of his Company with the rifle. He kept the rifle in his own tent and a pistol Reynolds carried was turned over to the Lieutenant who owned it.

On the day of the shooting, Moser was an assistant to the cook and was in the Cook Shanty. Moser was searching for a large serving pan to carry beans to the tables to serve the men. He could not locate it anywhere and one of the men said that Reynolds had taken it out of the kitchen. Reynolds, being present in the dining area, was approached by Moser and asked about the whereabouts of the pan. Reynolds denied any knowledge of the pan and a quarrel developed between him and Moser. Reynolds said if "Jesus Christ came down from Heaven and swore (he had taken it) to it, it was a lie." Reynolds quarreled with several other soldiers at the same time and place. He said I know what is the matter, you are all afraid of me, afraid I will steal something. Moser then spoke up and said I am not afraid of you, but go off and behave yourself. Reynolds got up, started to walk away, halted, turned around and said, "Mr. Moser, are you in earnest?" Moser replied, "You fool around and I will show you." Reynolds muttered, "I know what I have got to fight" and left the Cook Shanty.

The question was asked of the witness, "Did the accused appear to be cool or was he excited when he left the Cook Shanty?" The answer, "He was mad as fire. I know that for a man that would talk as he did. I knew he was mad."

Reynolds, at some time previous to the shooting had retaken custody of his rifle, without the knowledge or permission of his Captain.

Reynolds went to his tent and minutes later, Moser fired his rifle from the Cook shed, apparently at Reynolds. Reynolds then emerged from his tent and, while aiming his rifle, shouted, "Boys look out" or "Boys get out of the way." "Some of the boys crawled under the mess tables while others scooted in all directions." Then Reynolds fired his rifle. Moser was struck in the head and fell on the floor of the Cook shed.

Captain Matheney was walking near Reynolds' tent when the first shot was fired and he hurried in the direction of the report. He saw Reynolds leave his tent, enter the

Company street, aim and fire. Matheney feared Reynolds would reload and continue firing so he ran between the tents and approached Reynolds as he was in the act of reloading his rifle and seized the weapon from his hands. He then escorted Reynolds to the Regimental Colonel who had Reynolds placed under guard.

Moser was shot in the head by a cal. 58 ball from a Springfield Rifle. The ball entered the left temporal area above and lateral to the left eye, severing a major branch of the Temporal Artery and in passing through the brain, severed the Internal Carotid Artery and exited through the center of the back of the head. Moser lived for some fifteen minutes, totally insensible.

The defense offered no witnesses to the Court but did offer a statement on behalf of the defense.

"To the Court Martial now in session
Triume, Tennessee, May 26, 1863

I, Hiram Reynolds, charged with the murder of Washington Moser, a private soldier of Co. H, 82nd Ind. Inf. Regt. for final statement say that I deny that the present Court Martial has jurisdiction in my case. The Charge being Murder. Ques. Should you have jurisdiction. I contend that the evidence clearly shows I was acting in self defense. It shows that Moser and I were quarelling, that Moser got his gun in about a minute and fired the first shot and I supposed he had fired at me. I therefore contend that I was justified in the eyes of the law. I regret the death of Moser very much and would to God it was otherwise. All I ask at your hands is that you examine all the testimony carefully and ask yourself what witness proved my premeditation or malice on my part thereby making me guilty of Murder. After you have done this and made your decision, I shall cheerfully submit to my fate be that as how it may.
Hiram Reynolds

The Court deliberated, found Reynolds guilty and sentenced him to be executed by hanging at Nashville, Tennessee on August 14, 1863.*

*Original Date, apparently Reynolds was granted, upon his request, a few days respite until the 17th of August 1863.

On August 13, 1863, Reynolds addressed a letter to Major General Rosecrans. It read as follows:

"Provost Jail or Military Prison
Nashville, Tennessee, August 13, 1863.

Maj. Genl. Rosecrans. Dear Sir, My sentence of execution has been read to me this night about the hour of 9 o'clock, to take place to morrow between the hours of 10 A.M. and 2 P.M. I confess of not being the cause, as my opponent has fired the first shot which had been proved the day of my trial. I also inform you that I have two Honorable Discharges from the United States service, and had been faithful to our government in doing what was right during my services for which I can get good character, If I only got time to send for it. I fought under Colonel James Lane, 3rd Ind. Infantry at the time of the Mexican war, and was in the 27th Ind. Infty. At the commencement of this Rebellion under Col. Colgrove and transferred to the Naval Service under Commodore Foot, and had been discharged by reason of Disability, and, when capable of doing duty, enlisted again. I am now to be executed for self defence, I confess not to be in the fault, I think it very hard to be hung, so sudden after my sentence had been read to me and not giving me chance to prepare myself. I wish, if not reprieved to be granted a few days to prepare for death. I hope you will enquire of my Col. about my character since I joined his Regt.

Sir, I am a widower and have two children. I hope you will take compassion on them and not have them orphans under the mercy of the world.
I remain your obediant servant until death,
Hiram Reynolds,
82nd Ind. Inf."

There are no Indiana State Military Records to verify or disprove Reynold's claim to service in the Mexican War. It is within the realm of possibility that he could have served considering the different ages listed for him, 42 and 33 years. If 42 years old in 1863, he would have been 25 years of age in 1846 and if 33 years of age, he would have been 16 years of age and possibly could have passed for 18 years. There is no record of his service in the Navy as claimed, but the Navy had a rather lax record system at this time so his Naval service claim may have been valid. His service in the 27th Indiana Regiment is on record in Indiana State Archives.

Reynolds made one last plea for clemency in a letter dated August 15, 1863.

"Nashville August 15/63
To Major Gen. Rosecrans.

Hiram Reynolds of Comp. H. Eighty second (82) Indiana Condemned to be executed on Monday (17th) makes this *last request*.

If it is possible that my life may be *spared* my punishment be *imprisonment for life*.
Hiram Reynolds"

He was hung at Nashville, Tennessee on August 17, 1863.

REFERENCES:
Military Personnel Records, RG-#94
Court Martial Proceedings, RG-#153 NN 188
Indiana State Military Records

Case #41
Pvt. Henry McLean
NV: McClain
Battery C, 2nd ILL. Artillery Regt
Executed for Desertion
August 25, 1863

DESCRIPTION:

18 years of age, occupation farmer, home Sparta, Illinois, no further description located.

McLean enlisted and was mustered into service on July 10, 1862 at Paducah, Kentucky in Battery. C, 2nd Illinois Regiment Light Artillery. He deserted the service on December 26, 1862, was apprehended and confined.

A General Court Martial was convened at Fort Heiman, Kentucky and on January 22, 1863 tried Private Henry McLean, Battery C, 2nd Illinois Light Artillery Regiment on charges of stealing and desertion.

On an expedition in Tennessee on or about December 22, 1862 near the village of Bucksnort, Tennessee the accused entered a house of a citizen. McLean saw a locked trunk and was attempting to stamp and kick it open. A soldier identified only as "Red," came in and said, "stop that!" The accused stopped and "Red" came over to the trunk, took a pair of tweezers out of his pocket and unlocked the trunk with them. McLean took away a tin seidlitz powder box said to contain a gold locket and chain, a masonic breast pin, pencil and some other small articles and a reputed $600.00 in U.S. currency. McLean's Captain saw him display the locket boasting, "look what I've got." The captain took it away from him saying he would locate the owner and the accused requested to have it back if unclaimed. McLean was also seen carrying out of the house quantities of bed clothing, wearing apparel, and meat. The accused was arrested at Camden, Tennessee on or about December 24, 1862 and charged with robbery particularly the stealing of the $600.00 which was never found. When arrested, McLean was tied up by his thumbs when he refused to discuss the $600.00 matter. The accused, according to one witness, admitted the theft of the money but said they could keep him tied up until his thumbs fell off and he would not tell about its whereabouts. After an hour and a half of such suspension, however, he agreed to tell all he knew. He said the money was rolled up in one of his shirts on one of the artillery caissons. He led them to the caisson and two shirts were found but the one he had described as containing the currency was gone. The money was never located or accounted for.

During his interrogation McLean stated that he had stolen money before, had been in a state's prison for two years and had belonged to a gang of horse thieves in Iowa. He had once killed a man with a knife and complained he was only 19 years of age and had no parents to guide him.

While confined at Fort Heiman, Kentucky awaiting the Court Martial trial, the accused managed to escape from a guard on or about December 27, 1862. He was recaptured in Paducah, Kentucky and returned for his trial.

The prisoner called no witnesses in his defense nor did he offer a statement to the Court.

The Court deliberated, found the accused guilty and sentenced him to be *publicly* shot to death.

The execution actually took place at Fort Donelson, Tennessee on August 25, 1863.

On June 9, 1863, the new commander of Fort Donelson, Colonel William Lyon, wrote the following letter to C. Goddard, Assistant Adjutant General, Department of the Cumberland.

"I have the honor to ask instruction of the General Commanding the Department as to the case of Private Henry McLean Battery C, 2nd Ill. Light Artillery. When assuming the command of this post as permanent commander on the 7th June instant, I found at these Hd. Qrs. the orders (No., 105 a copy of which is herewith enclosed) publishing the sentence in the case with the direction of the General Commanding as to it's execution, The Order of the General Commanding being that the sentence "be carried into effect on the 22nd of May under the direction of Colonel W.W. Lowe commanding Fort Donelson Tennessee. I do not feel authorized to act in the matter, without further orders of the General Commanding.
Very Resp'y Your Obt. Servt
Wm. Lyon, Colonel, 13th Wis. Infty Vols.
Commanding Post."

Colonel Lyon received the following reply.

"Head Qtrs Dept of Cumberland, June 25, 1863,

Colonel: In reply to your communication of the 9th inst. the Comdg. Genl. directs you to carry out the sentence passed on Private Henry McLean, Battery C, 2nd Ill Light Artillery, on the second day after receipt of this letter.
I am Colonel, Very Respectfully
Your Obt. Servt.
C. Thall, Capt, and A.A.G."

There would seem to be some further delays which occurred as the letter of the June 25th date above and the August 25th actual date of execution proved a longer span of time than directed in the preceding letter referred to.

REFERENCES:

Military Personnel Records, RG-#94
Court Martial Proceedings, RG-#153s LL 526

Case #42
Pvt. William F. Hill
Co. K, 20th Mass. Infantry Regt.
Executed for Desertion
August 28, 1863

DESCRIPTION:

21 years of age, 5 feet 5 inches tall, light hair, blue eyes, fair complexion, born in Brookfield, Massachusetts, occupation laborer, illiterate.

Hill enlisted at Boston, Massachusetts on August 6, 1862 and was mustered into service at Cambridge, Massachusetts on August 26, 1862 and assigned to Company K, 20th Massachusetts Infantry Regiment. Hill deserted his Regiment November 6, 1862 near Paris, Virginia.

On June 5, 1863 a letter from North Brookfield, Massachusetts, Hill's birthplace, stated as follows: "There is in this town at our Almshouse a lad by the name of William F. Hill between 17 and 18 years old. Both he and his father, Moses Hill, are inmates. Some two years ago the old man took this boy and went to Randolph (Mass.) where he had formerly resided with the intention of not being further chargeable to us. Something more than a year ago the old man came back and settled down in the poor house again (for life as he said) leaving William in the vicinity of Randolph to shirk for himself, during last summer the old man received a letter from some selectman in R. (Randolph) stating that William had enlisted and was to have a bounty and wished the old man to secure it if he could. He came to me with the letter (as an overseer of the poor) to consult respecting it. Sometime last winter, William came back to us in a destitute and filthy condition having the appearance of a *Deserter*. I wrote to the S. Men (select men) of Canton (where the letter above alluded to said he enlisted) and received a reply that a young man by that name did enlist in a Canton Quota and got his bounty - $100.00. The writer believed he enlisted in the 20th Regiment. William (to me) denies ever being in the service or securing the bounty; says he went to camp and waited on the captain some three months but was never sworn in or moved from the camp with the Regiment which he says was the 33rd.

I think I have good reason to believe that he was in the Battle of Antietam that he deserted at or about that time threw away his arms and equipments and changed clothing with some Confederate and found his way back to us. He is a stout hearty but shiftless fellow, has ever since his return complained of one knee but gives no satisfactory answer how he was injured. We have supposed he was older than the age I have given but I have found in a house where the family lived some years ago, an old Bible containing a family record which I doubt not is true made by the mother (a smart woman) now deceased. He is there entered as born September 12, 1845.
Respectfully yours, Hiram Knight
Enrolling Officer."

William Hill was on August 9, 1862 only 16 years, 10 months and 27 days old when he enlisted, if the above bible record is correct. If age is correct Hill is the youngest soldier executed by the Union Army.

On June 11, 1863 Charles M. Ruggles, Special Officer, was sent the following from the Worcester, Massachusetts office of the Provost Marshall.

"Sir: you are directed to arrest William F. Hill, lately of Canton, Massachusetts, a deserter from the 20th Regiment Massachusetts Volunteers and report with him to this office, with accompanying papers, he is now at the Alms House in the town of North Brookfield."

Special Officer Charles M. Ruggles, reported, "I have arrested the within named William F. Hill. I have this day delivered him to the custody of the Provost Marshall.

Expenses

Use of horse to Brookfield	3.50
Aid to J. Kane	2.00
Subsistence	*.75*
	$ 6.25

Hill made a statement concerning his brief Military experiences. "Enlisted 33rd,

Colonel Maggi, last spring from Canton, Received bounty in Boston for 33rd Captain Richards took it away and put it in bank, School st, Boston, in his own name, got about $30.00 myself. The Captain and S. Wentworth of Canton the rest. Was not passed by the examining Surg. 33rd and Colonel Maggi had me passed previously in Boston. In July 1862 went into the 20th in Boston, recruiting office, left the regiment soon after the battle of Antietam."

A General Court Martial was convened at the Headquarters of the 2nd Division, 2nd Corps, near Morrisville, Virginia, and on August 17, 1863 tried Private William H. Hill, Company K, 20th Massachusetts Infantry Regiment on a charge of desertion in the face of the enemy.

Hill deserted on or about November 6, 1862 in Virginia as his regiment prepared to meet the enemy. He was not seen again until returned to his regiment in arrest on July 17, 1863.

Hill pleaded guilty and neither he nor the prosecution offered testimony before the court. Hill did offer a brief statement in his defense: "I was sick and my feet were done and I could not keep up. That was all the cause to fall out. I went to a farmer's house and the farmer urged me to desert. My father was very sick and I thought I must go home."

The Court deliberated, confirmed his plea of guilty and sentenced Hill to be shot to death with musketry.Hill was executed August 28, 1863.

Reading the documents would lead one to believe William Hill was (perhaps) mentally retarded and certainly, if the accounts be true, was not only cheated of his bounty, but for any further proof of his minority, deprived of his life.

REFERENCES:
Military Personnel Records, RG-#94
Court Martial Proceedings, RG-#153 NN 1831

Case #43
Pvt. John Smith
1st Co., (Andrew) Sharpshooters
Mass. Vols.
Executed for Desertion
August 28/30, 1863

DESCRIPTION:

35 years of age, 5 feet 5 inches tall, light hair, blue eyes, sandy complexion, born in Philadelphia, Pennsylvania, occupation mechanic.

Smith enlisted and was mustered into service on November 29, 1862 at Cambridge, Massachusetts in Captain Plumers Company, Andrew sharpshooters, attached to 15th Regiment of Massachusetts Infantry. This organization designation was changed to 1st Company Andrew Sharp Shooters, Massachusetts Volunteers. He deserted on January 11, 1863 from camp near Falmouth, Virginia. He was apprehended, confined and tried by court martial for desertion.

A General Court Martial was convened at the headquarters of the 2nd division, 2nd Army Corps camp near Morrisville, Virginia and on August 19, 1863 tried Private John Smith, 1st Company Andrew's Sharpshooters, Massachusetts Infantry on a charge of desertion.

Testimony was offered to the court which revealed that Smith duly enlisted and entered the sharpshooters on December 10, 1862 in the service of the United States, deserted the service on January 15, 1863 at Falmouth, Virginia and remained absent until he was arrested near Morrisville, Virginia on August 15, 1863.

Smith had again enlisted in the 19th Massachusetts Infantry Regiment and was sent as an unassigned recruit to the Regiment near Morrisville, Virginia. He was recognized among the replacements sent to the 19th Massachusetts by an officer of his former Company of Sharpshooters, arrested and confined pending charges and trial.

Smith offered no witnesses for the defense but did prepare a statement for the Court.

Statement in Defense

"I went away and intended to come back and did not get a chance until the present. I did not think of going away until I got out from camp with some men, and got to drinking, and I concluded to go home and come back again. I had no chance until I met a friend who was drafted and he said he would give me a chance to get back and would pay me for it. I thought if I would come into the service again it would be all right and I knew where I was coming to."

The Court then deliberated, found the prisoner guilty and sentenced him to be shot to death with musketry.

The execution took place on August 28, 1863 near Moundsville, Virginia.

REFERENCES:

Military Personnel Records, RG-#94
Court Martial Proceedings, RG-#153 NN 149

Case #44
Private John Folancy
NV: Follaney, Falling
AKA: Giancinto Verchzie
Co. I, 118th PA Inf. Regt.
Executed for Desertion
August 29, 1863

DESCRIPTION:

24 years of age, 5 feet 4 inches tall, black hair, gray eyes, dark complexion, born in Italy, occupation shoemaker, literacy not determined.

Folancy was drafted into the military and mustered in on July 15, 1863 and assigned to Company I, 118th Pennsylvania Infantry Regiment encamped near Beverly Ford, Virginia. He deserted the camp on August 8, 1863 and was captured on August 10, 1863 and returned to the Regimental camp under arrest where he was confined.

A General Court Martial was convened on August 19, 1863 at the Headquarters of the 2nd Brigade, 1st Division, 5th Corps near Beverly Ford, Virginia and proceeded to the trial of Private John Folancy, Company I, 118th Pennsylvania Infantry Regiment on the charge of desertion.

Testimony at the trial disclosed that Folancy was identified as a regularly enrolled member of the Army who did desert his Regiment on August 8, 1863 and was not apprehended until August 13, 1863 (some stated this date as August 18th). Folancy, a substitute, was one of 109 recruit replacements delivered to the 118th Pennsylvania Regiment on August 6, 1863.

Folancy offered no defense testimony but did present a written statement in his behalf which the Court accepted:

"The night I left camp I was going to get a wash, about six o'clock at night, he slept in the woods and lost his way in the dark, the next morning I was hungry and I went to a house to get something to eat, I inquired the way back to camp, after I get in the road I met three soldiers who ask me if I had a pass. I said I had no pass, he asked me where I was going, I told him that I was going to my Regiment, he says, if you have got no pass, you must come along with me, he sent me to the Provost Marshall, and the Provost Marshall kept me three or four days, when he sent me to my Regt. If I had wanted to desert I had plenty of chances in Philadelphia, I did not want to desert."

Folancy, of Italian birth, used the "alias" of Giacento Lerchize.

The Court deliberated, found Folancy guilty and sentenced him to death by musketry.

Folancy was one of five deserters executed at the same time by firing squads on August 29, 1863.

His Court Martial Proceedings contain relevant documents, not only to Folancy's case but to the other four deserters.

"Head Quarters, 11th Army Corps,
Provost Marshalls Office
Near Catletts Station, Va., Aug. 12, 1863
General Patrick
Provost Marshall Gen
General,

I have the honor to forward you under guard the following prisoners.

G. Weik, (enrolled name, George Kuhn), C. Zeis, (enrolled name, Charles Walter), and E. Duffie, (enrolled name, Emil Lai). The same were arrested near Kettle Rein Bridge, *G. Weik* says he was going to Alexandria to buy salt, for some citizens around here in this neighborhood but seemed not in the least to be acquainted in this country.

C. Zeis and E. Duffie say they are from New York City and came to this part of the Country to sell Wine, Cheese and Cigars, that they left the city of New York some ten days ago, came through Washington, D. C. and Alexandria without a pass. They stated also by giving a person Five Dollars, the party brought them on the steamer which runs between the two above named cities. The same person giving them instructions to get out of Alexandria, to get on one of the Sutlers wagons which they did.

Also two prisoners:

Giacento Lerchize (enrolled name John Folancy), and *Gio Rionese* (enrolled name, John Rionese), Deserters from the 118th Penn. Vols. You will find also a translation of an italian letter, which they intended to post by the first opportunity.

Gio Rionese has $200 Dollars in Greenbacks on him.

Giacinto Lerchize has about $22.00 dollars in his possession. These prisoners were arrested at Bristows Station, Va. making for Alexandria without any passes or papers showing permission to be within our lines.
I am sir
Your Obediant servant
W. E. Schofield
Captain & Asst. Provost Marshall"

The orderly in charge of the prisoners has a package containing a pocket book and $222 dollars belonging to the prisoners.
"W. E. Schofield"
"Capt. & Asst."

Head Quarters, 1st Brigade
August 12, 1863
Sir:

I have the honor to send you under guard, the following persons, deserters from your Regt., G. Weik, C. Zene, E. Duffie, Giacento Lerchize, Geo. Rionese, Chas. Lyons, and Augustus Facado, also a pocket book containing $222.15. The pocket book belongs to Geo. Rionese with $200 in Greenbacks the other package of money $22.15 belongs to Giacento Lerchize. Enclosed are the papers forwarded with them.
Very Respectfully
Your obt. Servt.,
Fred T. Docke
A. A. A. G.

The Reverend Constantine L. Egan, O. P. writes of his experiences in a chapter within the

Very Reverend Corby's book, "Memoirs of Chaplain Life," three years Chaplain in the famous Irish Brigade, Army of the Potomac, 1894, Notre Dame Scholastic Press, South Bend, Indiana which has an excellent description of the execution as does the sketches of it by *Alfred Waud*, Civil War Newspaper artist. The illustrations he made appeared in the September 26, 1863 issue of *"Frank Leslie's Illustrated Newspaper."* Two sketches appear illustrating the march to the place of execution and the actual execution itself.

The procession was led by the Provost Marshall, followed by the band playing a funeral dirge, followed in turn by the firing squads (5 squads of 12 men each), then came the coffins carried by four soldiers, a handcuffed prisoner following his own coffin and followed by his clergyman. Surgeons, pioneers with picks and shovels, and an armed infantry escort brought up the rear. At the grave sites, the coffins were placed in front of each grave and the blindfolded prisoners seated on the foot of each coffin.

Father Eagen, previously referred to, relates that he was asked to come from Washington, D. C. to the camp of the 118th Pennsylvania Infantry Regiment at the request of General Meade to provide religious solace to Folancy and Rionese who were Roman Catholic. A Rabbi, Dr. Zould, was obtained for Kuhn, and a Protestant Chaplain performed religious services and prayers for Walter and Lai. Henry Blake relates, in his "Three Years in the Army of the Potomac" Boston, 1865, Lee and Shepard, that Father Eagen and Rabbi Zould had a disagreement about precedence, which was quickly settled by the Provost Marshall who used the issue of seniority, the Jewish religion antedating the Christian, to settle the dispute.

Henry T. Peck, "a Historical Sketch of the 118th Infantry Regiment Pennsylvania Volunteers, Corn Exchange Regiment," September 8, 1884, (no publisher listed) wrote that General Griffin, present at the execution, grew restive of delays which diminished the legal time allotted for the execution. He finally irritably shouted, "Shoot these men or after 10 minutes it will be murder!" An officer issued the commands and the execution squads fired. As the smoke cleared away, four bodies were observed to have fallen back over their coffins, while one remained seated upright. The surgeon pronounced all five dead.

As was the custom, all assembled troops marched past the dead, following the band playing a lively march. The dead were coffined and buried in the previously dug graves which were to remain unmarked.

Also see case #46 Lai, Case #48 Walter, Case #45 Kuhn, Case #47 Rionese.

REFERENCES:

Military Personnel Records, RG-#94

Court Martial Proceedings, RG-#153 MM 687

"Memoirs of Chaplain Life, 3 Years Chaplain in the Famous Irish Brigade, Army of the Potomac," Very Reverend William Corbey, C. S. C., Notre Dame Scholastic Press, South Bend, Indiana, 1894.

"Three Years in the Army of the Potomac," Henry T. Blake, 1865, Boston.

"A Historical Sketch of the 118th Regiment Pennsylvania Volunteers, Corn Exchange Regiment," Henry T. Peck, 1884.

"Bucktailed Wildcats, A Regiment of Civil War Volunteers," Edwin A. Glover, New York City, Thomas Yoseloff, 1960.

Case #45

Private George Kuhn
NV: Kuhne
AKA: George Weik
Unassigned, 118th PA Inf. Regt.
Executed for Desertion
August 29, 1863

DESCRIPTION:

22 years of age, 5 feet 6½ inches tall, brown hair, blue eyes, light complexion, born in Prussia, occupation barber, literacy undetermined.

Kuhn was drafted and mustered into service on July 15, 1863 at Philadelphia, Pennsylvania and was forwarded in a draft of men as replacements assigned to the 118th Pennsylvania Infantry Regiment. Kuhn deserted en route to the assigned Regiment and, eluding his escort, remained a fugitive from military service until August 13, 1863 when he was captured and taken as a prisoner to his Regiment's camp near Beverly Ford, Virginia where he was confined.

A General Court Martial was convened at the Headquarters of the 2nd Brigade, 1st Division, 5th Army Corps, Beverly Ford, Virginia, and on August 20, 1863 tried Recruit George Kuhn (alias G. Weik) 118th Pennsylvania Infantry Regiment.

Testimony offered stated that the name Kuhn was an assumed name while the accused's real name was Weik. It was said that Kuhn/Weik said he changed his name because he wanted to conceal his entrance into the Army from his parents. Kuhn/Weik, a substitute, deserted on August 6, 1863 during his journey to his assignment to the 118th Pennsylvania Infantry Regiment even though he and about eight others were traveling under an armed escort. The accused was wearing a gray civilian suit at the time of his desertion and was still so garbed when he was returned to the 118th Regiment under arrest. The accused was identified by another recruit replacement assigned to the 118th Pennsylvania Regiment as having been seen on board the Steamboat carrying about 200 replacements from Philadelphia, Pennsylvania to Alexandria, Virginia and further that Kuhn/Weik was the only one not wearing a uniform. He wore the gray civilian suit previously mentioned.

The accused offered no witnesses on his behalf, but did present a statement to the Court.

The statement of the accused was made in German and interpreted by Surgeon Thomas of the 118th Pennsylvania Infantry Regiment having been first sworn to make a true interpretation.

Translation of the statement of the accused:

"I went to bring water and I went some distance off and was arrested. Three soldiers came and arrested him, he went with them without any opposition, it was not my object to desert, I have nothing further to say. George Kuhn"

The Court deliberated, found Kuhn/Weik guilty and sentenced him to be shot to death with musketry.

Kuhn was executed together with Privates John Folancy, George Rionese, Emil Lai, and Charles Walter on August 29, 1863 near Beverly Ford, Virginia. All the condemned men were substitutes and either unassigned recruits or recently arrived replacements for the 118th Pennsylvania Infantry Regiment. Their execution was depicted in graphic detail by Civil War Newspaper Artist *A. Waud*. For full details of the entire affair see the account of Case #44 *Private John Folancy*, as well as case #'s *46,47 and 48*.

Also see Case #44 Folancy, Case #47 Rionese, Case #48 Walter, and Case #46 Lai.)

REFERENCES:

Military Personnel Records, RG-#94
Court Martial Proceedings, RG-#153 MM 687
"Memoirs of Chaplain Life," three years Chaplain in the famous Irish Brigade, Army of the Potomac, 1894, Very Reverend Father William Corby.

Case #46
Private Emile Lai
AKA: E. Duffe
Unassigned, 118th PA Inf. Regt.
Executed for Desertion
August 29, 1863

DESCRIPTION:

30 years of age, 5 feet 6¾ inches tall, brown hair, gray eyes, light complexion, born in Germany, occupation clerk, possibly literate.

Lai was drafted and mustered into military service at Philadelphia, Pennsylvania on July 30, 1863. He was assigned to the 118th Pennsylvania Infantry Regiment. He deserted en route to his Regiment, eluding the escort of the replacement party, on August 6, 1863 and was arrested and delivered to the Camp of the 118th Pennsylvania Infantry Regiment near Beverly Ford, Virginia on August 13, 1863 where he was confined.

A General Court Martial was convened at the Headquarters 2nd Brigade, 1st Division, 5th Army Corps near Beverly Ford, Virginia, and on August 20, 1863 tried Emile Lai, a recruit for the 118th Pennsylvania Infantry Regiment on a charge of desertion. Emile Lai was "also known as" E. Duffe.

Testimony offered indicated that Lai deserted on August 6, 1863 while en route to the 118th Pennsylvania Regiment by evading the escort taking the party of nine or ten men substitutes to their assigned Regiment. He was delivered in arrest to the Camp of the 118th near Beverly Ford, Virginia, on August 13, 1863. It was further stated that he was wearing an Army uniform when he boarded the Steamship in Philadelphia, Pennsylvania. During the trip, aboard ship, from Philadelphia, Pennsylvania to Alexandria, Virginia he slept next to a recruit who did join the 118th. Major Henning of the 118th Pennsylvania Infantry Regiment stated that he received a draft of 109 men but Lai was not present with the group although his name appeared on the roster of replacements.

When brought to Regiment in civilian clothes under arrest Lai insisted his name was E. Duffe, but after questioning he admitted he was Emile Lai, the name carried on the replacement roster.

The accused offered no witnesses to the Court on his behalf but did present a statement of defense to the Court written in German. Surgeon Thomas of 118th Pennsylvania was duly sworn in as an interpreter pledging to provide a true interpretation of the statement.

Translation of Prisoner's statement given in German.

"I was informed in Philadelphia, where I was sworn in, that on reaching Alexandria, I could enter the Cavalry service, I was in the Cavalry service in Germany, when we reached Alexandria, we were placed in the cars, and I discovered that I could not enter the kind of service that I wished, and so on reaching a stoping place, I concluded that there would be no harm in leaving, and going where I should be likely to join the Cavalry, I intended going to Alexandria at once, and connect myself with the cavalry, I have more to say. I wish to add, that I did not intend to desert and did not think it was desertion to leave one branch of service and go to another, that in Germany until a man joins a Co. and Regt. he is not considered as belonging to it. I changed my clothes, that I might be better able to reach Alexandria."
Emil Lai

The Court deliberated, found Lai guilty and sentenced him to be shot to death with musketry. Lai was executed together with Privates John Folancy, George Rionese, George Kuhne and Charles Walter. All of the condemned men were substitutes, either unassigned recruits or recently arrived replacements for the 118th Pennsylvania Infantry Regiment. For more details of the entire affair see the account of Private John Folancy, Case *#44* as well as cases *#45, 47, 48*.

Also see Case #47 Rionese, Case #44 Folancy, Case #48 Walter, and Case #45 Kuhn.

REFERENCES:

Military Personnel Records, RG-#94
Court Martial Proceedings, RG-#153 MM 687

"Memoirs of Chaplain Life," three years Champlain in the famous Irish Brigade, Army of the Potomac, 1894, the very Reverend Father William Corby.

Case #47
Private John Rionese
NV: George, Rainese, Rainnesi
Executed for Desertion
August 29, 1863

DESCRIPTION:
23 years of age, 5 feet 9½ inches tall, dark hair, blue eyes, florid complexion, born in Italy, occupation barber, literacy undetermined.

Rionese enlisted and was mustered into service on July 29, 1863 at Philadelphia, Pennsylvania and assigned to Company I, 118th Pennsylvania Infantry Regiment. While with the Regiment near Beverly Ford, Virginia, Rionese deserted the service on August 8, 1863. He was apprehended and confined.

A General Court Martial was convened at the Headquarters of the 2nd Brigade, 1st Division, 5th Army Corps near Beverly Ford, Virginia and on August 13, 1863 tried Private John Rionese, Company I, 118th Pennsylvania Infantry Regiment on a charge of desertion.

Testimony was offered that stated Rionese arrived with 100 other recruits for duty on August 6, 1863 and deserted about mid-day on August 8, 1863. The Articles of War had not been read to him but he and the other recruits were expressly forbidden to leave camp and could only go to the "sink" (toilet) under guard. Rionese apparently eluded his guard on an excursion to the "sink." Rionese was arrested on August 8, 1863 by Provost Marshalls and returned to his Regiment.

One letter, written in Italian by Rionese, was taken from him as well as some $200.00 in Greenbacks contained in a pocketbook. For more information on the Rionese case, see Case #46 *Emil Lai.*

The translation of the Rionese letter stated:

"Dear Friend, I received you letter some days ago but as I had been in Philadelphia, I could not answer it immediately. At present I send you the sum of ten dollars. You will do me the favor to get my trunks at No. 8, Goward (?) Street, Jersey City or demand it from Mr. Asmeio (?), where I used to board, and get 4 razors, 1 pair of scissors, 1 stone, 1 comb and sponge, and then do as directed. (Rionese was a barber by trade). I am in the 118th Regt. corner of Exchange place (probably in the recruiting office) can therefore not let you know when I will come. Let Eresbino (?) know that I am in the south without letting him know that I am a soldier. I hope very soon to be able to come, if I do not die before, as I am near the rebels and have been this day morning in the first fight without being hurt. I laid my gun and myself on the ground and put five dead bodies upon me so that I could see what they did around me. You will please answer me immediately as I will send you some money before I leave here. The letter you send to me you can put in New Jersey in the Post Office and let me know everything. I have nothing more to write. I embrace you as my friend. My name is the following.
Geo. Rionese
Co. I, 118th Regt. Penn. Vols.
Washington, D. C. (or elsewhere)"

Rionese offered no witnesses, but did present a statement to the Court on his behalf.

Rionese wrote his letter to the Court, but there is no indication whether this was the original written letter or a translation from one written in Italian.

"I went away from camp to find some water, no guard stopped me, I lost the way and could not find the camp, then I went to find the railroad and found a guard that asked me if I had a pass, and I said no, then they asked me where I belonged and I told them

the truth, that I belonged to the 118th Penn. Vols., Co. I. They asked me what Corps I belonged to, and I told them that I did not know, having been out to the Regiment but one day, I told the Provost Marshall that I wanted to come under my Officer, I asked the Lieutenant the first day I joined my Co. that if I did my duty well if I could be a Corporal, I had no intention of deserting the Co.
Jian Rainese"

The Court deliberated, found Rionese guilty and sentenced him to be shot to death with musketry.

The execution took place on August 29, 1863.

Also see Case #45 Kuhn, Case #48 Walter, Case #44 Folancy, and Case #46 Lai.

REFERENCES:

Military Personnel Records, RG-#94
Court Martial Proceedings, RG-#153 MM 687
"Memoirs of Chaplain Life," three years in the famous Irish Brigade, Army of the Potomac, 1894, the very Reverend Father William Corby.

Case #48
Private Charles Walter
AKA: C. Zene
Unassigned, 118th PA Inf. Regt.
Executed for Desertion
August 29, 1863

DESCRIPTION:

29 years of age, 5 feet 5¾ inches tall, dark hair, dark eyes, dark complexion, born in Germany, occupation bookkeeper, literate.

Walter was drafted and mustered into service on July 31, 1863 at Philadelphia, Pennsylvania and was assigned to the 118th Pennsylvania Infantry Regiment which was stationed in the Beverley Ford area of Virginia. Walter deserted from his replacement draft enroute to the camp of the 118th Pennsylvania Infantry Regiment on August 13, 1863 and was captured and confined.

A General Court Martial was convened at Headquarters 2nd Brigade, 1st Division 5th Army Corps Camp at Beverly Ford, Virginia, and on August 20, 1863 tried recruit Charles Walter, unassigned, 118th Pennsylvania Infantry Regiment on a charge of desertion.

Testimony of witnesses positively identified Walter as having seen him in the barracks at Philadelphia, Pennsylvania and on the boat, carrying 200 substitutes, from Philadelphia to Alexandria, Virginia. Walter deserted on August 6, 1863 about a day after his arrival at Alexandria, Virginia while being escorted, with other replacement recruits, to the 118th Pennsylvania Infantry Regiment. He was arrested, in Citizens clothing on August 19, 1863.

Walter called no witnesses but did offer a statement, written in German and translated by Surgeon Thomas of the 118th Pennsylvania Infantry Regiment after being sworn as a translator by the Court.

Statement of the Prisoner

"The Officer of the Day in Philadelphia informed me, that we would be sent to camp at Alexandria and that each man would have an opportunity to choose *what* branch of service he preferred entering, what regiment and what Company. My wish was not to enter the Infantry service, instead of stopping at Alexandria, we were brought on the cars, and I discovered we were deceived, my wish was to enter the Cavalry service. This is the sum and substance of what I have to say.

Charles Walter"

The Court deliberated, found the accused guilty and sentenced him to be shot to death with musketry.

The execution took place on August 29, 1863 near to Beverly Ford, Virginia.

For a more detailed description of Walter's desertion see Case #44 John Folancy, Case #45 George Kuhne, Case #46 Emil Lai, and Case #47 John Rionese. All five deserters were executed together.

REFERENCES:
Military Personnel Records, RG-#94
Court Martial Proceedings, RG-#153 MM 687
Also see references listed in Case #44 John Folancy.

Case #49
Pvt. William Davis
Co. G, 2nd R.I. Cavalry Regt.
Executed for Mutiny
August 30, 1863

DESCRIPTION:

23 years of age.

Davis enlisted in Company G, 2nd Rhode Island Cavalry Regiment at Providence, Rhode Island on January 7, 1863. The unit, by August 1863, was on duty in the New Orleans, Louisiana area where it became understrength by personnel losses resulting from disease and combat. On August 24, 1863, S.O. #209-HQS., Department of the Gulf, transferred the men of the 2nd Rhode Island Cavalry Regiment to the 1st Louisiana Cavalry Regiment and all but nine officers were mustered out of service or resigned.

A Military Commission was convened at Thibadeaux, Louisiana on September 5, 1863 to inquire into the cause of the mutiny, it's course and suppression in the 1st Louisiana Cavalry.

Lieutenant Colonel H. Robinson, commander of the 1st Louisiana Cavalry Regiment testified that S. O. #209 Paragraph 8 Department of the Gulf, dated August 24, 1863 ordered the consolidation of the 2nd Rhode Island Cavalry Regiment and the 1st Louisiana Cavalry Regiment by dissolving the 2nd Rhode Island and transferring all of it's enlisted personnel to the 1st Louisiana and all 2nd Rhode Island officers were to be mustered out of the service unless they desired to apply for a commission and go before a board for certification.

On August 29, 1863 the 1st Louisiana Cavalry Regiment assembled for dress parade and was formed in line and the 2nd Rhode Island Cavalry Regiment was to form a parallel line facing the Louisiana Regiment at about a 40 yard interval. The lines being formed, the Adjutant of the 1st Louisiana read S.O.l #204 Paragraph 8. When he finished reading the order, the Rhode Island Troopers shouted "No-No!" and other mutinous statements of refusal to obey the lawful order. Lieutenant Colonel Robinson then ordered "Present Sabers" and return sabers. The Rhode Islanders were ordered to dismount and form as to fight on foot. Louisiana Regiment soldiers then led the horses of the dismounted men away, and the men of the Rhode Island Cavalry were assigned to companies of the Louisiana Cavalry and marched away.

On the morning of the 30th of August, the officers of the 1st Louisiana Cavalry were told the Rhode Island assigned to them had left, returning to the original Rhode Island Campsite. Lieutenant Colonel Robinson, accompanied by his adjutant rode to the former Rhode Island camp and found the Rhode Islanders lying or sitting on the ground. Lieutenant Colonel Robinson ordered them to take their knapsacks and join their new respective companies to which some responded "Colonel we have made up our minds that as we enlisted in the 2nd Rhode Island Cavalry we will, by God, serve in no other! We will not go. Do as you like, but, by God, we won't serve." and a murmur of assent ran through the crowd as no one moved.

Lieutenant Colonel Robinson then called for one company of Mounted Troopers and three companies of dismounted troopers of the 1st Louisiana Cavalry to come to the camp. The mounted troop surrounded the camp and the dismounted troops faced the Rhode Islanders on foot in a line. Lieutenant Colonel Robinson then had S. O. #209 read to them again in Spanish, French, English, and German and ordered them to join their Louisiana Cavalry Regiment companies and none of them obeyed. He then told them if they did not immediately obey his order, he would order them to be fired on. This convinced the Rhode Islanders that Robinson meant business and they arose and fell into their proper places. Lieutenant Colonel Robinson then picked out what he felt were the two ringleaders of the mutiny, Private Richard Murphy alias Richard Smith and Private Frederick Freeman alias William Davis and ordered them shot. He wrote out the order for execution while astride his horse. The order read:

"1st Lieutenant Hall, adjutant of the 1st Louisiana Cavalry is hereby appointed Provost Marshall of the Day, and is charged, as such, with the execution of Private Richard Murphy, alias Richard Smith and of Private Frederick Freeman alias William Davis, Mutineers, a military neccessity.
Signed, H. Robinson,
Lieutenant Colonel Commanding 1st Louisiana Cavalry"

(The names of the two Rhode Islanders were actually Richard Smith and William Davis as shown on the 2nd Rhode Island Cavalry Regiment Rolls.)

The Louisiana Cavalry was formed into position on three sides of a square and the prisoners Smith and Davis had their hands bound and eyes blindfolded and escorted to the fourth or open side of the square. The adjutant asked if either man had any last requests and granted them time to pray. Company F of the Louisiana Regiment was brought up and formed two execution squads, they fired on command and Smith and Davis fell dead.

Robinson contended that what action he took was a military neccessity to preserve discipline and order otherwise the 1st Louisiana Cavalry Regiment would have been destroyed. He further stated that the Rhode Islanders all were a dirty lot who failed to maintain their equipment and rifles in a usable condition but since their consolidation into his regiment they have become good well disciplined soldiers.

The findings of the Military Commission were:
I The origin of the Mutiny was the reading of the order of consolidation.
II The course of the mutiny began with the reading of S.O. 209 Paragraph 8, ordering the consolidation of the 2nd Rhode Island and 1st Louisiana Cavalry Regiments on August 29th and continued until the execution of Privates Smith and Davis on the 30th of August, 1863.
III The suppression of the Mutiny was in the prompt and efficient manner in which the ringleaders were executed by order of Lieutenant Colonel H. Robinson 1st Louisiana Cavalry.

Major General N. P. Banks Commanding the Department of the Gulf at New Orleans, Louisiana commented in a letter written on October 22, 1863 as follows:

"It is probable that order could have been maintained in the regiment without the application of Capital Punishment to the two men executed; but the conduct of the 2nd Rhode Island Cavalry was such that it was impossible to say how soon the Mutiny would have been repeated. Severe measures were required with them. The commanding General regrets the neccessity for the execution, but is unable, with his knowledge of the facts, to say that it was not justifiable in consideration of the circumstances of the case."

REFERENCES:

Military Personnel Records, RG-#94
Record of Military Commission MM 1080
Military Records of State of Rhode Island

Case #50
Pvt. Richard Smith
Co. F, 2nd R.I. Cavalry Regt.
Executed for Mutiny
August 30, 1863

DESCRIPTION:

26 years of age, no other description location.

Smith enlisted in Company F, 2nd Rhode Island on December 30, 1862 at Providence, Rhode Island and was mustered in on January 19, 1863. His military history is identical to that of Private Davis previously cited. When the remaining officers and men of the 2nd Rhode Island saw the order for the transfer to the 1st Louisiana Cavalry Regiment, with the consequent loss of identity of their Rhode Island origin, they decided at a meeting to protest the consolidation.

On the morning of September 1, 1863, Lieutenant Colonel H. Robinson, Commander of the 1st Louisiana Cavalry Regiment, sent an order to the 2nd Rhode Island Cavalry to move from their quarters to the camp of the 1st Louisiana Cavalry Regiment. This was completely ignored and so reported to Robinson. He immediately mounted his horse and rode to the encampment of the Rhode Islanders and repeated the order in person. The men are said to have replied that, "We belong to Rhode Island, and not to Louisiana," and continued to refuse to obey the order. Robinson left and returned within 15 minutes with his Louisiana Regiment on foot and armed with sabres, revolvers and carbines and formed them on two sides of the Rhode Island encampment facing the recalcitrant Rhode Islanders. Robinson again repeated his order for the Rhode Islanders to move to the camp of the 1st Louisiana Regiment and added, "Hurry up or I will fire into you!" The Rhode Islanders realized further resistance was fruitless and slowly formed ranks to march to their new camp.

Angered by the very evident reluctance to comply with his order, Robinson had his troopers seize the last two men forming up in ranks, Davis and Smith. They were marched under guard to a field in the front of the camp, hands tied, eyes bandaged and two firing squads were assembled. The order to fire was given and Davis fell dead, killed by the first volley. Smith was not so fortunate, being only wounded in the legs. The Louisiana Regiment Adjutant and the Firing Squad Commander, a Sergeant, dispatched Smith with revolver shots.

Robinson is reported to have addressed the remaining Rhode Islanders, after the executions, in most threatening terms. Lt. Colonel Robinson acted contrary to Military Law in not having Davis and Smith arrested, tried by Court Martial, having any guilty verdict reviewed and so forth. This execution was essentially murder.

The entire affair was protested at a high level of governmental authority with the result that on January 14, 1864 an order was issued transferring the recalcitrant Rhode Islanders from the 1st Louisiana Regiment to the 3rd Rhode Island Cavalry Regiment.

The reader will notice a discrepancy between the dates of death listed on "The Official List" (August 30, 1863) and in the account cited above (September 1, 1863).

Such details are, from time to time, encountered in Civil War Military Records.

REFERENCES:

State of Rhode Island Adjutant General's Report 1865, Volume III, Rhode Island

Volunteers 1861-1865.
State of Rhode Island Record of the 2nd Rhode Island Cavalry Regiment.
Records of the 1st Louisiana Cavalry Regiment State of Louisiana Archives.
Military Personnel Records, NA, RG-#94 MM 1080

Case #51
Private James Anderson
Co. H, 27th KY Inf. Regt.
Executed for Desertion
September 4, 1863

DESCRIPTION:

36 years of age, no further description available.

Anderson enlisted on November 27, 1861 at Camp Nevin, Kentucky, and was mustered into service on March 21, 1862 at Rochester, Butler County, Kentucky, and was assigned to Company H, 27th Kentucky Infantry Regiment. Anderson was detailed as a cook on May 25, 1862 at a U. S. Military Hospital in Corinth, Mississippi. he nursed his sick brother there, but deserted from his assignment at the Hospital after his brother's death. He seems to have found a position in a hospital in Louisville, Kentucky as his personnel record states he deserted from a hospital there in October, 1862. He returned to his home in Kentucky and was known to be living with his wife and small child. He was seized and arrested at his farm on Young's Creek, Hardin County, Kentucky around midnight of May 31, 1863 while asleep in a corn crib, about 50 yards from his farm house. Cradled in his arms was his loaded squirrel rifle. He was tried in Munfordville, Kentucky in August, 1863, by a General Court Martial, found guilty and was sentenced to be executed by a firing squad on September 4, 1863.

A number of petitions requesting mercy were sent to the Commanding General of the Department. One was signed by 25 officers and men of the Regiment.

One letter requesting mercy read, "Mercy without reason founded in truth is all that can be asked for this man." Colonel C. S. Penneypacker. August 27, 1863, Brigadier General J. T. Boyle of the Headquarters District of Kentucky at Louisville, Kentucky forwarded the Colonel's request for mercy with the comment—"The endorsement of Colonel Penneypacker is not understood, but suppose it means mercy is all that can be urged as a plea for the reprieval of the prisoner."

Anderson was executed as scheduled.

REFERENCES:
Military Personnel Records, RG-#94
Court Martial Proceedings, RG-#153 NN 152

Case #52
Private Frazier Carmen
NV: Carmon, Carman
Co. F, 27th KY Volunteer Inf. Regt.
Executed for Desertion
September 4, 1863

DESCRIPTION:

22 years of age, no further information as to his physical description has been located.

Carmen was enlisted and mustered into the service at Breckenbridge, Kentucky on October 20, 1861, and was assigned to Company F, 27th Kentucky Volunteer Infantry Regiment. He deserted on October 9, 1862 at Perryville, Kentucky. He was apprehended and confined.

A General Court Martial was convened at Munfordville, Kentucky on June 26, 1863 for the trial of Private Frazier Carmen, Company F, 27th Kentucky Infantry Regiment accused of Desertion.

The testimony divulged that Carmen, in October, 1862, was one of a squad of ten men detailed from Camp Wild Cat, Kentucky to Lebanon, Kentucky to protect a regimental Wagon train. On the 20th of October, 1862 Carmen was given verbal consent by his Sergeant to be absent for a short time, about an hour or so, to secure provisions. He never returned voluntarily. He was arrested at a house in Breckenridge County, Kentucky, and returned to the Camp of the 27th Regiment at Munfordville, Kentucky on or about May 23, 1863.

The accused offered no defense and the court adjourned to deliberate. The court found Carmen guilty and sentenced him to be executed by a firing squad at Munfordville, Kentucky. The execution took place on September 4, 1863.

He was shot at the same time as the Coffey brothers, John and Christopher, also of the 27th Kentucky Volunteer Infantry Regiment. (See Cases #53 and #54).

REFERENCES:

Military Personnel Records, RG #94
Court Martial Proceedings, RG #153   LL 749

Case #53
Private Christopher Coffey
Co. C, 27th KY Infantry Regt.
Executed for Desertion
September 4, 1863

DESCRIPTION:

22 years of age, no further description located.

Christopher Coffey enlisted at Campbellsville, Kentucky on October 12, 1861, and was mustered into service on March 21, 1862 at Rochester, Kentucky and assigned to Company C, 27th Kentucky Infantry Regiment. Christopher and his brother, John W. Coffey, enlisted, were mustered in and assigned to the same Company and Regiment. They both deserted on October 9, 1862 and were apprehended.

A General Court Martial was convened at the Courthouse in Munfordville, Kentucky on July 8, 1863 for the trial of Christopher Coffey, Company C, 27th Kentucky Infantry Regiment who was charged with desertion.

Testimony presented during the trial revealed that Christopher Coffey and a Sergeant Lyon of Company C, 27th Kentucky Infantry were left at Bowling Green, Kentucky while sick, to remain with the Regimental Wagon train and to stay with same until the wagon train reached the Regiment. The balance of the Regiment then moved rapidly to a new position. On or about October 1, 1862 near Litchfield, Grayson County, Kentucky, Christopher Coffey (brother of John Coffey) left the Wagon train without authority, and was not seen until arrested about June 30, 1863.

His Company commander, Captain Bailey went to Coffey's mother's home, after a futile search for Coffey, and told her to have both boys (Christopher and John) report to his Company and Regiment before April 1, 1863 to be eligible for the Presidential Amnesty but neither reported.

Christopher Coffey was eventually found in Russell County, Kentucky cutting wheat for a farmer. He was handcuffed and brought to Munfordville, Kentucky on July 3, 1863 where his regiment was then stationed, to be confined while awaiting trial.

Christopher Coffey presented no defense or final statement. The court deliberated and found Christopher Coffey guilty and sentenced him to be shot by a firing squad at Munfordville, Kentucky on September 4, 1863.

The Coffey brothers were shot to death together with Private Carmen on September 4, 1863.

(See Case #52 and Case #54)

REFERENCES:
Military Personnel Records, RG-#94
Court Martial Proceedings, RG-#153 LL 749
Military Records, State of Kentucky, Adjutant Generals Report.
Census Report State of Kentucky East 1860.

Case #54
Private John W. Coffey
Co. C, 27th KY Volunteer Infantry Regt.
Executed for Desertion
September 4, 1863

DESCRIPTION:
24 years of age, no further physical description has been found.

J. W. Coffey enlisted at Campbellsville, Kentucky on October 12, 1861 and was mustered into service on march 21, 1862 at Rochester, Kentucky. He was assigned to Captain Bailey's Company 27th Kentucky Infantry Regiment whose designation was later changed to Company C, 27th Kentucky Infantry Regiment. He deserted on March 21, 1862 and was apprehended and confined.

A General Court Martial was convened at the Courthouse in Munfordville, Kentucky on July 8, 1863 for the trial of Private John W. Coffey, Company C, 27th Kentucky Infantry on the charge of desertion.

Testimony was presented that John Coffey deserted his Company on October 9, 1862 near Perryville, Kentucky. Captain Bailey, Commanding Officer of Coffey's Company did actually locate Coffey in his home in Russell County, Kentucky in March, 1863 and told John Coffey (brother of Christopher) of the President's Proclamation granting amnesty to deserters who returned voluntarily. He (Coffey) promised to come to Captain Bailey's home in Adair County, Kentucky in March and they would go to the Regiment together to clear Coffey of the charge. He never came to Captain Bailey's home or to the Regiment until he was arrested at his home after a prolonged period of searching. he was brought to Munfordville, Kentucky, and confinement on July 3, 1863. The defense offered no testimony and the accused is said to have made a brief oral statement in his defense, which is not recorded in the Court proceedings.

The Court deliberated and found John Coffey guilty and sentenced him to death by a firing squad. Same was carried out at Munfordville, Kentucky on September 4, 1863.

J. W. Coffey was executed at the same time and place as his brother Christopher Coffey, and a Private Frazier Carmen.

(See Cases #53 and #52)

REFERENCES:
Military Personnel Records, RG-#94
Court Martial Proceedings, RG-#153 NN 152
Kentucky State Military Records, Adjutant Generals Report.
Union Regiments of Kentucky, 27th Kentucky Volunteer Infantry, by Colonel John H. Ward.

Case #55
Private James A. Pointer
Co. H, 27th KY Inf. Regt.
Executed for Desertion
September 4, 1863

DESCRIPTION:
19 years of age, no further physical description appears in his Personnel document file.

James A. Pointer is noted to have enlisted at Metcalf County, Kentucky on October 12, 1861. His records are not well time coordinated as his muster in date is not shown nor is his date of desertion, which is noted elsewhere as March 20, 1863, nor is there documentation as to the place of desertion. He was eventually apprehended and tried.

A General Court Martial was convened at Munfordville, Kentucky, and on July 1, 1863 tried Private James A. Pointer, Company H, 27th Kentucky Infantry Regiment on a charge of desertion.

The testimony of witnesses revealed the following course of events. Pointer enlisted in October, 1861 and in November of 1861 obtained a leave of absence for a 5-6 day period to return to his home in Metcalf County, Kentucky.

A Sergeant Craddock, of Company H, was sent to find Pointer, after he failed to return from leave, and tell him to return to his Regiment and every effort would be made to give him a minimum sentence. Pointer agreed to surrender himself and named a place and a day to meet Sergeant Craddock. The sergeant arrived at the agreed upon place and date but Pointer failed to appear. Several days after Pointer failed to appear to surrender himself, Sergeant Craddock searched for him, found and arrested him about December 25, 1862. Craddock was prevented from returning Pointer immediately to the Regimental Camp in Munfordsville, as Confederate General Morgan was conducting a raid through Kentucky and his forces were between Craddock and his destination. Craddock was compelled to remain stationary and retain custody of Pointer. Pointer, however, managed to escape from the Sergeant about December 27, 1862 and was not seen again until the end of April, 1863. At that time, Pointer was under arrest at the Military Prison for an unnamed offense. Sergeant Craddock again took charge of Pointer and escorted him under arrest from the Military Prison to the Guard House of the 27th Kentucky Infantry Regiment where he again escaped from custody.

A detail of soldiers was sent to the Pointer home in Metcalf County, Kentucky in the latter part of May, 1863, and surrounded the house. Pointer suddenly emerged from a door of the house and ran toward a wooded area. He was ordered to halt, and was fired at, to no avail. He continued his flight and ran into the midst of another squad of soldiers, who arrested him and took him under heavy guard to the camp of the 27th Regiment, then near Woodsonville, Kentucky.

No further evidence being introduced, Pointer apparently made a few unrecorded remarks to the Court.

The Court deliberated, found Pointer guilty, and sentenced him to be "shot until he is dead."

The execution took place at the Regimental Camp near Munfordville, Kentucky on September 4, 1863.

The sentence pronounced on Pointer was in sharp contrast to sentences for similar offenses meted out in the 22nd Kentucky Infantry Regiment. The 22nd Kentucky listed 145 known deserters who were apprehended and court martialed, *not one of whom was sentenced to death.* Sentences were limited to fines and extensions of the period of their military service equal to the period of their absence from service.

James A. Pointer apparently had a brother, Private James H. Pointer, Company E, 27th Kentucky Infantry Regiment. He also enlisted on October 12, 1861 at Campbellsville, Kentucky, no other place or date of muster, into service is recorded. His date of desertion is listed as January 28, 1862 at Elizabethtown, Kentucky. He was said to have been arrested and tried for desertion November 17, 1862. He was in confinement awaiting the decision of the Court as to his sentence until January 1863. The verdict was a sentence of death which was not carried out as he died of disease on February 24, 1863 at Woodsonville, Kentucky while awaiting announcement of the date of execution. (The records in his case are few and contradictory.)

REFERENCES:

Military Personnel Records, RG-#94
Court Martial Proceedings, RG-#153 NN 152

Case #56
Private (Cpl) Jacob Aierdan
NV: Aierdain, Aierdam
Co. G, 119th Regt, NY Infantry
Executed for Desertion

September 17, 1863

DESCRIPTION:

29 years of age, 5 feet 7 inches tall, blond hair, blue eyes, fair complexion, born in Munchen, Bavaria, Germany, occupation farmer, literate.

Aierdan enlisted and was mustered into service on September 5, 1862 at New York City in Company G, 119th New York Infantry Regiment. The Regiment was operating in Virginia when Aierdan deserted. He was apprehended, and confined awaiting court martial.

A General Court Martial was convened at the Headquarters, 3rd Division, 11th Army Corps, at Weaverville, Virginia on August 29, 1863 for the trial of Corporal Jacob Aierdan, Company G, 119th New York Infantry Regiment on a charge of desertion.

Testimony was presented that Aierdan deserted his Regiment on August 12, 1863 from it's camp at Brentsville, Virginia and was absent until apprehended near the Potomac River and returned on the 19th of August 1863 in arrest.

Witnesses characterized Aierdan as a grumbler and drinker who refused to go on picket duty. Another witness stated Aierdan was a good soldier who had taken to drinking and acting like he was half crazy. Aierdan claimed he was "hazed and berated" by the orderly Sergeant and refused his rightful clothing allotment and further he was ordered on picket duty when it was not his turn.

The Court deliberated and found the accused guilty and sentenced him to be executed before a firing squad.

"The Genl. Commdg. Division, in view of the fact that this case is not of the worst character of desertion, respectfully recommends that the sentence of death be commuted to imprisonment, laboring, forfeiture of pay and wearing a ball and chain for the unexpired term of service, or such other punishment as may be deemed best."
Hector Tyndale
Brigadier Genl, Commdg. Div."

Major General George C. Meade denied the request and the execution took place on September 18, 1863.

REFERENCES:

Military Personnel Records, RG-#94
Court Martial Proceedings, RG-#153 LL 759

Case #57
Private John T. Barnett
NV: Barret
Co. A, 11th Penn Cav. Regt.
Executed for Highway Robbery
September 17, 1863

DESCRIPTION:

20 years of age, 5 foot 11 inches tall, blue eyes, light hair, light complexion, born in Georgia, occupation, laborer, literacy undetermined.

Barnett entered U.S. military service on April 19, 1863 at Camp Suffolk, Virginia in Company A, 11th Pennsylvania Cavalry Regiment.

On July 1, 1863, the 11th Cavalry Regiment was on the march from King William courthouse to Brandywine, Virginia on the road leading to the Aylete Ferry. En route, the Regiment encountered four southerners, Samuel Hoffhermer, Ben Adler, Louis Hamburger and Sam Mann who made a living by following Union Army raids, and taking advantage of the frightened farmers, bought their slaves at low rates and shipped them south. The four business men were examined and allowed to pass on. After the Cavalry column had left the scene, two men, Barnett (said to have been a deserter from the 63rd Georgia Confederate Volunteers) and a Private Hiram Evans of Company A, 11th Pennsylvania Cavalry left the cavalry ranks without leave and returned in search of the four business men. Finding them, they held them up and robbed them of about $16,000 in state bank bills, two gold and one silver watch, one diamond breast pin and a gold headed cane. They then threatened Hoffhermer with death if he ever mentioned the robbery. Hoffhermer managed to effect his escape into adjoining fields and both Barnett and Evans fired their revolvers at him as he successfully escaped unscathed.

The Regiment was resting at Brandywine, Virginia when Hoffhermer caught up with them and reported the robbery. The Commanding Officer had the Regiment fall in formation and Hoffhermer scanned their faces but failed to note Barnett or Evans in their ranks. The Commanding Officer, taking note of the absence of Company A at the formation, as they had been sent ahead to guard Nelson's Bridge, ordered Lt. Butts and an escort detachment to convoy Hoffhermer to Company A duty point. Hoffhermer there recognized both his assailants, Barnett and Evans and they were immediately arrested. Only $6,970.00, two watches and the diamond pin seems to have been recovered and turned over to Hoffhermer and his associates. Barnett and Evans were being taken to be turned over to the Provost Marshall pending trial. En route, Evans cut the ropes that bound him to his horse and escaped never to be heard from again. Two men not further identified from Company I, 11th Pennsylvania Cavalry Regiment who were said to have shared the stolen money deserted.

Barnett was tried by a Military Commission on July 3, 1863 for highway robbery and assault with intent to commit murder, was found guilty and sentenced to death before a firing squad. Barnett was confined in Norfolk, Virginia jail pending his execution and on August 28, 1863, escaped from jail.

"On the 9th (also stated as September 6th) of September 1863, while on a raid around Dismal Swamp, Barnett, the thief, was captured by Major Wetherill's Command. He was in a wagon, a prisoner, in charge of a Confederate Corporal and four men. Barnett had escaped from Norfolk jail, had gone *back* to the Confederates; but having been recognized as one of the Eleventh, had been arrested as a spy and was en route to Raleigh to be tried. (He was returned to the Union Army jail.)

By the order of President Lincoln, Barnett was shot on the 17th of September 1863 (near Portsmouth, Virigina) and the Chapter of his misconduct closed."

REFERENCES:

Military Personnel Records, RG-#94
Court Martial Proceedings, RG-#153 MM 460
"The History of the 11th Pennsylvania Voluntary Cavalry Regiment," Philadelphia, Pennsylvania, 1902.

Case #58
Pvt. Edward Elliott
Co. I, 14th Conn. Infantry Regt.
Executed for Desertion
September 18, 1863

DESCRIPTION:

22 years of age, 5 feet 6⅛ inches tall, light hair, blue eyes, light complexion, born in Massachusetts, occupation bookkeeper, substitute, literate.

Elliott was drafted and mustered in as a substitute on July 18, 1863 at New Haven, Connecticut and assigned to Company I, 14th Connecticut Infantry Regiment. Elliott deserted his Regiment in camp near Elk Run, Virginia on August 18, 1863. He was captured on August 24, 1863 in 'Citizen's dress and claiming to be a deserter from the rebel army". He surrendered his pocket book which contained $103.00 which was recorded on the inventory of his effects.

A General Court Martial was convened at Camp near Morrisville, Virginia and proceeded on August 26, 1863 to the trial of Private Edward Elliott, Company B, 14th Connecticut Infantry Regiment, charged with desertion.

Elliott deserted on August 18, 1863 from his Regimental camp near Elk Run, Virginia and was apprehended in civilian attire claiming to be a deserter from the rebels.

Elliott pleaded guilty, offered no defense, but did offer a statement. "In entering the service of the United States I expressed my willingness to join the service stating I wished to join a Cavalry Regiment. I was told I would have my choice what else I have to say is that upon coming here I was put into service without having anything to say or any choice whatsoever given. Our treatment from the time of starting was very stringent, having hardly sufficient to eat. My reasons for deserting after being placed in my Regiment was the influence of others, that is all I have to say."

The Court deliberated, confirmed Elliott's guilty plea and sentenced him to death by musketry.

He was executed on September 18, 1863 near the Rapidan River, Virginia.

REFERENCES:
Military Personnel Records, RG-#94
Court Martial Proceedings, RG-#153 LL 757

Case #59
Pvt. Albert Jones
Co. K, 3rd MD Infantry Regt.
Executed for Desertion
September 18, 1863

DESCRIPTION:

22 years of age, 5 feet 8 inches tall, dark hair, hazel eyes, dark complexion, born in Baltimore, Maryland, occupation boatman, literacy undetermined.

Jones enlisted and was mustered into service on December 3, 1861 at Baltimore, Maryland in Dix's Baltimore Light Infantry Regiment which in May of 1862 were transferred to form the 3rd Maryland Infantry Regiment and Jones was assigned to Company K. Jones deserted the Regiment on or about July 27, 1862 and "rejoined" the Regiment on or about January 1, 1863, apparently "without prejudice." he deserted a second time, while on the march with his Regiment at or near Frederick, Maryland on June 29, 1863. He was arrested in Baltimore, Maryland on July 9, 1863 and confined and tried by court marital.

A General Court Martial was convened at Kelly's Ford, Virginia on August 17, 1863 tried Private Albert Jones, Company K, 3rd Maryland Infantry Regiment on a charge of desertion (second time).

Witnesses testified that Jones was a regularly enlisted member of his Company and Regiment and that he did, without permission, absent himself from said Company and Regiment on June 29th 1863 near Frederick, Maryland. He was arrested in Baltimore, Maryland about July 5, 1863 and a $10.00 reward was paid for his capture. He is said to have left Baltimore and reported back voluntarily to his Company and Regiment on July 9, 1863.

A Lieutenant Gove testified that Jones had a previous conviction on a charge of desertion in January 1863 near Fairfax Station, Virginia. He was sentenced to three months hard labor under supervision of the Division Provost Guard and the loss of all pay and allowances.

Several witnesses stated that Jones had maintained a good character in the Regiment. Jones offered a statement in his behalf.

"Statement of Prisoner"

"On the 29th of June, coming through Frederick some of us got hold of some liquor, and got pretty heavy under it, and stopped there. I heard there that the 3rd Maryland had been ordered to Baltimore. I stayed at Frederick twenty four hours and then went on to Middleburgh. There they told us that the regiment had gone to Baltimore. We then went to Westminster, got on the cars there and went to Baltimore. That was on the fourth of July and before we could find out whether it was our Regiment or the 3rd Maryland Home Brigade I was arrested on the fifth. Had no time to report myself or anything. The Colonel told us that he expected the regiment would go home every day. I didn't know but what it was so and that's the way I came to go to Baltimore. I had my belt and full uniform on when I was arrested."

The Court deliberated, found Jones guilty and sentenced him to be shot to death with musketry.

The execution took place on September 18, 1863 in the 1st division area.

Apparently an appeal for executive clemency was addressed to President Lincoln on behalf of Jones, as on September 17, 1863 Major General George G. Meade, Commanding the Army of the Potomac wrote in reply to Pres. Lincoln's request as to the details of the case.

"The President-"

Private Albert Jones, Company K, 3rd Maryland Volunteers is ordered to be shot on Friday next. Charge desertion second time. His second desertion, for which he is now sentenced to be shot occured about the 29th of June at Frederick, Maryland. He was arrested at Baltimore on or about the 9th of July. This being his second desertion and it having occured after your proclamation and solemn warning to the army. I do not consider him a fit subject for executive clemency."

Jones was executed on September 18, 1863 at the same time and place as Case #61 William Smith, Case #64 Cornelius Treese, and Case #62 George Van.

REFERENCES:

Military Personnel Records, RG-#94
Court Martial Proceedings, RG-#153 MM 650

Case #60
Pvt. George Layton
NV: Charles Eastman, George Laton
Co K, 14th Conn. Infantry Regt.
Executed for Desertion
September 18, 1863

DESCRIPTION:

20 years of age, 5 feet 3¼ inches tall, brown hair, gray eyes, dark complexion, born in Maine, occupation farmer-miller, substitute.

Layton enlisted and was mustered in as a substitute on July 18, 1863 at New Haven, Connecticut. He was forwarded to Virginia and assigned to Company K, 14th Connecticut Infantry Regiment where he deserted on August 18, 1863 near Elkton, Virginia and was apprehended in civilian dress.

A General Court Martial was convened at Camp near Morrisville, Virginia and on August 29, 1863 tried Private George Layton alias Charles Eastman, Company K, 14th Connecticut Infantry Regiment charged with desertion.

The prisoner having no testimony to offer submitted the following statement:

"When we came the understanding was that we could have our choice of going into Cavalry or Infantry. When we got here I could not have the choice of that. I was sick when we were coming on and could get nothing to eat in the boat, we had nothing. If my punishment is not to be shot I am willing to stay and be as good a soldier as I can. I am willing to go anywhere I am told to go. Others urged me to go; and I would not have gone had it not been for being urged. I have been sorry ever since I went."

No further testimony being offered the Court deliberated and found the accused guilty. He was sentenced to be shot to death by musketry. The execution took place on September 18, 1863 near the headquarters of the 2nd Army Corps. near to Morrisville, Virginia.

REFERENCES:
Military Personnel Records, RG-#94
Court Martial Proceedings, RG-#153 LL 757

Case #61
Pvt. William Smith
Co. E, 78th NY Infantry Regt.
Executed for Desertion
September 18, 1863

DESCRIPTION:

35 years of age, 5 feet 9 inches tall, light hair, gray eyes, light complexion, born in Boston, Massachusetts, occupation farmer.

Smith enlisted January 2, 1862 at Alden, New York and was mustered into service on January 25, 1862 at Buffalo, New York in Captain Randall's Company, 4th Regiment Eagle Brigade. This unit designation was subsequently changed to Company E, 78th New York Infantry Regiment. In June 1862, Smith was listed on his Company rolls as a cook. Smith deserted the Regiment about July 25, 1862 from Camp Goodrich, near Middleton, Virginia. He was arrested in his hometown of Alden, Erie County, New York on July 10, 1863. The expense of his arrest is listed as $3.96. Smith was sent to Fort Columbus, New York Harbor arriving there on July 29, 1863 and was transferred from there back to custody of his Regiment in Virginia.

A General Court Martial was convened at the headquarters of the 2nd Division, 12 Army Corps, at New Ellis Ford, Virginia, and on September 5, 1863, tried Private William W. Smith, Company E, 78th New York Infantry Regiment on a charge of Desertion.

Testimony given disclosed that the Regiment left Camp Goodrich for Front Royal, Virginia and several men were left behind to guard supplies, ordnance and excess baggage of the Regiment until transportation could be provided to forward materials to the new regimental position. Smith apparently dropped out of the marching ranks of the Regiment very soon after it left, and made his way back to Camp Goodrich. He explained that he had a sore foot which prevented his maintaining the pace of the Regiment. He was never given permission, official or unofficial, to leave his place in the marching column.

The supply wagons were then, a day or so later, ordered to Winchester, Virginia and Smith went with them. The supply wagons and soldiers remained in Winchester for two days and two nights and then set out again, this time to Warrenton, Virginia. Smith got on a wagon to ride, but was ordered off by a Captain Chappell while the convoy was still in Winchester, Virginia and he was not seen again until his arrest and return in citizens clothes.

Members of the Regiment learned that Smith had deserted to his home in Erie County, New York by letters from people in Erie County who had seen him.

Smith offered no witnesses on his behalf but did present a statement in his defense.

Prisoners Statement

"I asked for conveyance of Captain Chappell to the Regiment, at the time we left Winchester and his answer was `that I should go as far as I could, and when I could go no farther to lay down and rest,' so I lay down beside a shade tree; I lay there all night, the wagon never came near me, right aside of the road; and in the morning I went back to Winchester - there were soldiers there, but no guards ever asked me where I belonged as lame and sick as I was, I made out to go home and lay sick a long time after I got home, I never wanted to desert from my regiment, I was not able to come back, if I hadn't got home as I did I wouldn't have been here now, for after I got there I had the inflamation on the brain. When I was at Camp Goodrich I showed my feet to the doctor who said they were pretty `hard looking feet,' and who went by me and never did a thing for me. My soldier's clothes were burned in my knapsack; another lot of articles also were destroyed by Captain Chappell belonging to the companies by being burned up. I was obliged to put on citizens clothes when I got home to keep from being naked. I wanted to come back and would have come back if they had not taken me, as quick as they did, though I did not write to my Regiment that I wanted to come back."

The court deliberated, found the prisoner guilty and sentenced him to be shot to death with musketry. The execution took place at the Divisional encampment on September 18, 1863.

REFERENCES:
Military Personnel Records, RG-#94
Court Martial Proceedings, RG-#153 LL 760

Case #62
Pvt. George Van
NV: Vann, Vane
Co. D, 12th NY Infantry Regt.
Executed for Desertion
September 18, 1863

DESCRIPTION:
22 years of age, 5 feet 4 inches tall, light hair, blue eyes, light complexion, born in USA, occupation farmer.

Van enlisted and was mustered into service on November 26, 1861 at Buffalo, New York in Company D, 12th New York Infantry Regiment. Van deserted May 13, 1862 at White House on the Pamunkey, Virginia. He was apprehended, arrested and returned to his Regiment near Culpeper, Virginia in irons, under heavy guard on August 15, 1863.

A General Court Martial was convened at headquarters of 2nd Brigade, 1st Division, 5th Army Corps at Beverly Ford, Virginia and on August 22, 1863 tried Private George Van, Company D, 12th New York Infantry Regiment on a charge of desertion.

Testimony was offered which showed that Van deserted his Regiment while on the march from West Point, Virginia to White House, Virginia on or about May 15, 1862. He was arrested near Rhinebeck, New York and returned to his Regiment on August 14, 1863.

The accused tried to show that, *when present* with his Company, he always answered roll calls and did his duty. He offered neither defense witnesses nor statement.

The court deliberated, found the prisoner guilty and sentenced him to be shot to death with musketry.

A dispute arose as to which command should have the responsibility for carrying out the execution. Brigadier General Griffin, 1st Division Commanding states in a letter of September 15, 1863 that Van is not from his Command and his Division should not be imposed upon with the details of the execution. Major General Sykes replies September 15, 1863 that the order to take the responsibility for the execution of Van was made by the General Commanding the Army and that the order stands as issued.

On September 13, 1863 Chaplain O. B. Clark, of the 83rd Pennsylvania Volunteers wrote a letter to Major General Meade, Commanding the Army of the Potomac, asking for executive clemency for Van. The reply, in part, was that, "the case is not considered a proper one for the exercize of executive clemency: the request cannot therefore be considered."

Van was executed as directed by the sentence of the Court Martial on September 18, 1863 near Culpeper, Virginia.

REFERENCES:

Military Personnel Records, RG-#94
Court Martial Proceedings, RG-#153 LL 758

Case #63
Pvt. John Timlin
Co. D, 145th NY Infantry Regt.
Executed for Desertion
September 25, 1863

DESCRIPTION:

19 years of age, 5 feet 6 inches tall, brown hair, blue eyes, light complexion, born in Ireland, occupation newsman, literate.

Timlin enlisted on July 20, 1862 at New York City and was assigned to Company D, 145th New York Infantry Regiment in Virginia. Timlin's records state that he deserted on or about September 20, 1862 and was apprehended on April 19, 1863 at New York City arrested and confined at Fort Columbus, New York Harbor where he was forwarded under guard to Washington D.C. April 28, 1863.

Timlin was forwarded to custody of his Regiment, charged with desertion.

A General Court Martial was convened at the headquarters of the 1st Division, 12th Army Corps at Kelly's Ford, Virginia and on August 28, 1863 tried Private John Timlin, Company D, 145th New York Infantry Regiment on a charge of Desertion.

The accused applied to the Court to introduce Lt. E. W. Pattison as his counsel, which was granted.

Testimony of witnesses revealed the following events. The prisoner was a duly enlisted member of the 145th New York Regiment encamped at New Dorp, Staten Island, New York and deserted there from on September 21, 1862 just days before the Regiment moved south to Frederick City. He was captured, arrested and returned to the Regiment, then encamped at Stafford Court House, Virginia. This was just a short time before the Regiment moved towards Gettysburg. Timlin's desertion at New Dorp was possibly a double desertion. A witness related that Timlin left Staten Island and arrived in New York City where he was inadvertently seen by a Lt. Poole of his own Company on the "cars" without a pass. The Lieutenant took him in charge and turned him over to Private B. Lorridge, Company D, 145th Regiment New York, a clerk in the Adjutant's Office of New York City. The clerk was to return Timlin to the Regiment on Staten Island. On Staten Island, Timlin begged Lorridge to let him visit his relatives who lived one half mile from the station on Staten Island and he would faithfully report to the Regiment in the morning. The clerk consented and Timlin did not again appear until he was returned in arrest to the Regiment then at Stafford Court House on June 11, 1863. On June 16, 1863, the prisoner again escaped from a guard assigned to him personally. Timlin was recaptured in a wooded area about 1/2 mile away by members of the 2nd Massachusetts Regiment.

The prisoner had also attempted to escape on June 15, 1863 while his unit halted awaiting a bridge over a creek to be completed. The accused simply walked rapidly back down the road the Regiment had advanced over. Needless to say, he was quickly captured again.

Testimony as to the mental state of Timlin was provided by Surgeon John J. H. Love, M.D., 13th New Jersey Infantry Regiment who stated that in his opinion Timlin was fully capable of distinguishing right from wrong, displayed no evidence of mental derangement or imbecility. He characterized Timlin as sharp, keen and one who simulates imbecility.

No other evidence or statement was provided by the accused.

The court deliberated, found the accused guilty and sentenced him to be shot to death with musketry. On September 25, 1863 at a point one half mile north and west of Brandy Station, Virginia. The prisoner was dead within two minutes after the fatal volley was fired.

REFERENCES:
Military Personnel Records, RG-#94
Court Martial Proceedings, RG-#153 MM 737

Case #64
Pvt. Cornelius Treece
Co. K, 78th NY Infantry Regt.
Executed for Desertion
September 25, 1863

DESCRIPTION:

23 years of age, 5 feet 8 inches tall, brown hair, blue eyes, light complexion, born in La Grange, Indiana, occupation mason.

Treece enlisted at La Grange, Indiana on February 7, 1862 and was mustered into service at New York City on April 7th, 1862. A notation on his personnel file states, "sharpshooter." Treece deserted his Regiment, while on the march, near Front Royal, Virginia on July 5/6, 1863 and was arrested in Kendallville, Indiana on July 8, 1863, which seems incredible. The report also indicates he was sent to the headquarters of the Military Commander at Indianapolis, Indiana on July 8, 1863. The records seem to be contradictory as one dated Indianapolis, Indiana, July 24, 1863 states Treece was furnished transportation to Washington, D.C. at a cost of $14.72. Another record, dated August 6, 1863, indicates that Treece was arrested on August 5, 1863 at Kendallville, Indiana for which $10.00 in expenses was paid. The report concludes with the statement that Treece was received at Camp Douglas, Chicago, Illinois on August 6, 1863.

A General Court Martial was convened at headquarters of the 2nd Division, 12th Army corps and on September 2, 1863 tried Private Cornelius Treece, Company K, 78th New York Infantry Regiment on a charge of Desertion.

The accused, before making his plea, had the 20th Article of War "earnestly read" to him by the Trial Judge Advocate. He then pleaded guilty to the charge and requested substitution of the words "5th or 6th of July" for the words "21st of June" in the specification to which he also pleaded guilty.

In brief, Treece was on the march with his Regiment from Front Royal, Virginia to Washington, D.C. when on the 5th or 6th of July, 1863 he deserted. He was arrested in Kendallville, Indiana, his native state, on or about July 8, 1863 and was returned to his Regiment for trial.

A single defense witness was called who testified as a character witness, stating "he was with the Regiment only a few months, was a little inclined to shirk duty but otherwise good."

The prisoner offered a statement to the court.

Prisoner's Statement

I never received any pay from the government, nothing but a half suit of clothes; I was with them from the 7th of February until I left, without pay; I was sick then, was sick while away, and am now, this was my cause for going. I sent my arms back to the Regiment, I never took them away!

The court then deliberated, confirmed the defendant's plea of guilty and sentenced him. The court, being unable to discover a single mitigating circumstance, do, therefore, sentence Private Cornelius Treece, Company K, 78th New York Infantry Regiment to be shot to death by musketry.

The execution took place at Racoon Ford, Virginia on September 25, 1863.

REFERENCES:
Military Personnel Records, RG-#94
Court Martial Proceedings, RG-#153 LL 760

Case #65
Pvt. Charles Williams
NV: Charles Smith
Co. D, 4th MD Infantry Regt. (New)
Executed for Desertion
September 25, 1863

DESCRIPTION:
24 (26) years of age, 5 feet 11 inches tall, dark hair, dark eyes, fresh complexion, born in Brooklyn, New York, occupation none.

Williams enlisted on June 10, 1862 at Baltimore, Maryland and was mustered into service at Camp Hoffman, near Baltimore, Maryland on July 24, 1862 in Company D, 4th Maryland Infantry Regiment (new). On the 20th of September 1862, he deserted his Regiment near Hagerstown, Maryland as it was drawn up in line of battle to meet the enemy. He was arrested on August 5, 1863 amongst a detail of substitutes being forwarded to the 90th Pennsylvania Infantry Regiment using the alias of Charles Smith. He was confined and charged with desertion and inciting to mutiny.

A General Court Martial was convened at the headquarters of the 1st division, 1st Army Corps and on August 25, 1863 tried Private Charles Williams, Company D, 4th Maryland Infantry Regiment on charges of desertion and inciting to mutiny.

Williams deserted his Regiment on September 20, 1862 while it was formed in line for battle between Hagerstown and Williamsport, Maryland. He and another private of his company named Murray left the ranks ostensibly to seek water. They were intercepted by a Captain Bishop and ordered to return to their battle positions. Murray refused and Captain Bishop drew his sword and struck Murray a sharp blow on the head and Murray then left. Captain Bishop then threatened Williams with his sword and Williams also turned back. Williams apparently deserted the same day. Conflicting testimony was offered as to the state of sobriety of Murray and Williams.

On August 5, 1863, about one year later, on the south side of the Rappahanock River, near Rappahanock Station, Williams was seen amongst a group of recruits reporting to the 90th Pennsylvania Infantry Regiment. His former Company Commander, being notified of Williams' presence, went to the 90th Pennsylvania Regimental area and requested the arrest and surrender of Williams who was using the name of Charles Smith, as a substitute from Philadelphia (for which he had received a $300.00 bounty). Williams was surrendered to his former Regiment and while on the regimental camp ground managed to harangue the members of Company B, 4th Maryland Infantry Regiment on August 15, 1863 by telling them, "If I were you men, I'd be damned if I would do any duty."

Charges were then filed leading to his trial. The defense offered witnesses and Williams questioned both the prosecution and defense witnesses.

Williams offered a statement to the Court. "When I was laying at Hagerstown, about 2 miles from Hagerstown, We stacked Muskets and I went up to a farm house to get some water, me and a man by the name of Murray, and while we were up there, there was a man had been in the garden getting things and they throwed a suspicion unto me and Murray, which I told to Captain Bishop. I showed him the man and with that he drew his sword which he struck Murray with over the head inflicting a bad wound and he undertook to draw it on me which he did, and I told if he would strike me, I would go home, and as soon as that I went to Col. Bowermann and stated my case, which he laughed at me, while sitting on the fence. I told him I would leave and go home if I didn't get satisfaction."

The Court deliberated and found Williams guilty on the charge of desertion. He was sentenced to death by musketry. The execution was to take place on September 25, 1863, however, on September 21, 1863, a telegram from President A. Lincoln stating that an appeal for clemency had been received based upon the assumption of "unsoundness of mind." Judge Advocate General Holt carefully examined all records pertinent to the case and stated there was no evidence of "Mental infirmity" or any other extenuating circumstances.

On September 23, 1863, the Provost Marshall General wrote a recommendation for commutation of the sentence of execution by reason of "the condition of the Man's mind." Major General Meade replying to an inquiry from President Lincoln in the matter replied that he deserted as the Regiment was prepared to meet the enemy and did not return until he enlisted again under a false name as a substitute for a bounty. There was no reason to believe he would not repeat the process. In short, he was not a fit subject for executive clemency.

Attached to the Court Martial proceedings is a memorandum.

"Executive Office - August 22, 1865

Respectfully referred to the Honorable Secretary of War. If this case has not otherwise been disposed of the sentence will be commuted to Dishonorable Discharge with loss of all pay, allowances, bounty and one years imprisonment at hard labor in a penitentiary to be selected by the Secretary of War."
Andrew Johnson,
Pres. U. S."

Williams was executed at Fort McHenry, Baltimore, Maryland on September 25, 1863.

REFERENCES:
Military Personnel Records, RG-#94
Court Martial Proceedings, RG-#153 MM 945

Case #66
Pvt. Adam Smalz
NV: Maltz, Small, Shmalz, Schmalz
Co. E, 66th N.Y. Inf. Regt.
Executed for Desertion
October 2, 1863

DESCRIPTION:

18 years of age, 5 feet 6 inches tall, brown hair, blue eyes, light complexion, born in New York City, occupation laborer.

Smalz enlisted on October 23 and was mustered into service on November 4, 1861 at New York City, New York in Company E, 66th New York Infantry Regiment. The many variations of the spelling of Smalz' name create confusion. Records seem to indicate that SMALL is an alias as the name is usually identified with membership in Company G, 66th Regiment. It could, of course, indicate a clerical error of filing Small's documents in SMALZ file. There is, however, some common factors existing between the SMALL and SMALZ records. Adam SMALZ, Company E, 66th Regiment is reported "Absent Without Leave" in July, 1863. The charges filed against Smalz, Company E, 66th Regiment for desertion on August 22, 1863 state that he did desert on July 1, 1863 and remained absent until returned to his Regiment by the Provost Marshall on August 21, 1863. Records of Deserters included in the Smalz file state that Adam Small, Company G, 66th Regiment, who deserted in July 1863 near Gettysburg, Pennsylvania was arrested on July 27, 1863 at Hanover, Pennsylvania and delivered to the Provost Marshall at Carlisle Barracks, Carlisle, Pennsylvania on July 31, 1863. (A reward of $10.00 was paid for the capture). Smalz was then delivered by the Provost Marshall to his Regiment on August 21, 1863. It is a reasonable assumption that Small and Smalz are one and the same person, that Small is an alias identity adopted by Smalz. Smalz was tried by Court Martial for desertion after charges were preferred on August 22, 1863.

A General Court Martial was convened at the Headquarters of the 1st Division, 2nd Army Corps and on August 14, 1863, tried Private Adam Smalz, Company E, 66th New York Infantry Regiment on a charge of Desertion.

When the accused was asked, as routinely done in all military trials, if he had an objection to any officer nominated to serve on the Court, Smalz objected to the presence of Captain John F. Bartholf of the 66th New York Infantry Regiment on the ground that he was the Commander of his Company and would testify against him and make it harder for him. The Court then deliberated and found the "Challenge is sustained as sufficient and Capt. John F. Bartholf 66th NY Inf Regt is excused from serving as a member of the Court." The accused had no objections to other Court members. The Court was then (as in all other cases) sworn in his presence. The trial then began.

Testimony revealed that Smalz deserted on or about July 1, 1863 and was returned under arrest on August 21, 1863.

The prisoner pleaded guilty to the charge and did not wish to call any witnesses but did present a statement to the Court.

"Statement"

"I was sick about the time and staid with a farmer, Henry Wolf, Abbot Town, Penn. and went to work for him. He gave me citizens clothes."

The Court deliberated, confirmed the accused plea of guilty and sentenced him to be shot to death with musketry.

The execution took place on October 2, 1863.

Father William Corby, a Roman Catholic Army Chaplain mentions the final hours of Smalz in his book, "Memoirs of Chaplain Life." He does not mention Smalz by name, nor does he ever mention other condemned prisoners in his book by name, however, his description of the prisoner as a young man, not yet 19 years of age, American born of German descent and the general description of the circumstances seem to clearly indicate the condemned man to be Smalz.

Reverend Corby describes his hasty baptism of Smalz one half hour before the execution and in company with Smalz' protestant Chaplain, accompanied him to the place of execution. The execution was routine except for the fact that Smalz did not die immediately although struck by eleven bullets. He was dispatched by a final coup de grace from the Provost Marshall's revolver.

REFERENCES:

Military Personnel Records, RG-#94
Court Martial Proceedings, RG-#153   LL 861
"Memoirs of Chaplain Life: Three years Chaplain in the Famous "Irish Brigade" Army of the Potomac," Notre Dame Scholastic Press, South Bend, Indiana, 1894, Very Reverend William Corley, C.S.C.

Case #67
Pvt. William Smitz
Co. F, 90th Pennsylvania Infantry
Executed for Desertion
October 2, 1863

DESCRIPTION:

21 years of age, 5 feet 6½ inches tall, brown hair, hazel eyes, dark complexion, born in Germany, occupation farmer.

Smitz was drafted and mustered into service on July 27, 1863 at West Chester, Pennsylvania. He was forwarded to the 90th Pennsylvania Infantry Regiment, Company F near Rappahanock Station, Virginia where he deserted on August 13, 1863. He was arrested on August 19, 1863.

A General Court Martial was convened at Headquarters of the 1st Division, 1st Army Corps near Rappahannock Station, Virginia and on August 28, 1863 tried Private William Smitz, Company F, 90th Pennsylvania Infantry Regiment on a charge of desertion.

"The accused being German, Sergeant A. Stillnight, Company I 90th Pennsylvania Infantry Regiment was duly sworn in as Interpreter by the Judge Advocate in the presence of the prisoner."

Testimony was offered showing that Smitz deserted the Company and Regiment on or about August 13, 1863 without authorization and was arrested and returned on August 19, 1863.

Smitz, when arrested in civilian clothes, was taken to the headquarters of Brigadier General H. Baxter, Commander of the 2nd Brigade, 2nd Division, 1st Army Corps, where he was questioned by the General. Smitz stated he left because he did not like soldiering. Asked why he went into the army, Smitz said, "for the money." As to the civilian clothing, Smitz said "he brought them with him from home, expecting to wear them to get away with." The General indicated that Smitz spoke broken English but seemed to understand questions put to him in English.

Further testimony revealed that Smitz arrived in a detachment of replacements at the Regiment on August 3rd and was assigned to his Company on August 4th.

When Smitz deserted, he left all arms, accouterments and extra clothing behind. At his capture he was clad in a citizen's suit, white shirt, unbleached linen pants and citizen's hat.

Smitz abandoned knapsack contained a black frock coat, a blanket, writing paper, under clothing, and a furlough pass. His gun and accouterments were with the knapsack. The furlough pass referred to was made out in the name of a Private Miller of the 91st Pennsylvania Infantry Regiment. It was believed to have been a forgery. Smitz testified that he found it in the woods near the camp.

A Corporal James Sanford, Company F, 90th Pennsylvania Infantry Regiment testified to a conversation he had with Smitz while Smitz was under guard. "I said hello Smitz! Why didn't you use your furlough, instead of getting caught? Says I, where was you going? He said, to Washington. I said that is a pretty place to be going, to Washington. There was some other conversation that passed between us of no consequence either way." Smitz stated he had brought the citizen's clothes from Philadelphia to get away in and that he took off his uniform and left it in a wooded area, donned the citizen's clothes and began his trek.

Smitz had no witnesses to offer before the Court but made an oral statement in German which was translated into English by the court sworn interpreter and reduced to writing by the Judge Advocate.

Prisoner's Statement

"There was a man in the Regiment by the name of Herman, I don't know what Company. Either H, or G, and he persuaded me by giving me money to leave. He gave me ten dollars, and told me to leave on the morning of the 13th and he would meet me on this side of the River. Herman didn't come. I waited half a day for him. so I walked to Bealton Station and he didn't come there, and after that I walked, I didn't know where, and was caught by the Provost Guard. Herman told me I could get away, and if I came back in four months afterwards, nothing would be done. Herman has gone from the Regiment.

When the General asked me what I came out for I didn't mean to say I came out for the money for myself, but to relieve a drafted man."

The court then deliberated, found the prisoner guilty and sentenced him to be shot to death with musketry.

The execution took place on October 2, 1863 near the Regimental Camp of the 90th Pennsylvania.

REFERENCES:
Military Personnel Records, RG-#94
Court Martial Proceedings, RG-#153 LL 862

Case #68
Pvt. John Connelly
NV: Conley
Co. H, 4th NJ Infantry Regt.
Executed for Desertion
October 9, 1863

DESCRIPTION:
22 years of age, no other description found among his military records.

Connelly enlisted and was mustered into service on August 23, 1861 at Trenton, New Jersey in Company H, 4th New Jersey Infantry Regiment. On June 21, 1862, Connelly was sick and was left at Mechanicsville, Virginia while the Regiment continued it's march. He was evacuated to a hospital (not specifically identified) in Philadelphia, Pennsylvania for treatment. On August 29, 1862, Connelly deserted the hospital and was apprehended and returned to his Regiment under arrest on March 31, 1863. He was tried by court martial, convicted of desertion and sentenced to forfeit all pay up to April 14, 1863 and returned to duty. On July 2, 1863, while on the march to Gettysburg, Pennsylvania Connelly again deserted. He was returned from desertion on September 5, 1863 under arrest for which a reward was authorized and paid.

A General Court Martial convened at Headquarters of the 1st Division, 6th Army Corps at Warrenton, Virginia on September 21, 1863 for the trial of Private Joseph H. Connelly, Company H, 4th New Jersey Infantry Regiment on the charge of Desertion.

Witnesses testified that Connelly deserted his Company and Regiment on the march toward Gettysburg, Pennsylvania on July 2, 1863. He was listed as a deserter and remained absent until apprehended by Provost guards and returned to his Regiment on September 5, 1863. Further testimony disclosed that Connelly had been sent to a hospital in Philadelphia, Pennsylvania on June 21, 1862 from which he deserted.

Testimony was offered that Connelly's first desertion was occasioned by his two brothers who were members of the 12th New York Infantry Regiment as they persuaded him to join their Regiment.

The accused offered no defense but presented a brief written statement.

"This last time I was coaxed away from the Regiment I went down home in Gloucester County, New Jersey. The day I was taken up, I was going to give myself up to the Marshall. I have now two brothers in the 12th N.Y. Regiment."

The Court then considered the evidence, found Connelly guilty and sentenced him to be executed by musketry. The execution took place on October 9, 1863 near the camp of his Regiment near Culpeper, on the Rapidan River, Virginia.

REFERENCES:
Military Personnel Records, RG-#94
Court Martial Proceedings, RG-#153 LL 897

Case #69
Pvt. James Haley
NV: James T. Smith
Co. B, 116th Penn. Infy Regt
Executed for Desertion
October 16, 1863

DESCRIPTION:

23 years of age, 5 feet 6 inches tall, light hair, gray eyes, sandy complexion, born in Chester, Pennsylvania, occupation farmer.

Haley enlisted and was mustered into service on June 11, 1862 at Philadelphia, Pennsylvania in Company I, 116th Pennsylvania Infantry Regiment. This unit designation was changed by S.O. #23, A.G.O., January 26, 1863 to Company B, 116 Pennsylvania Infantry.

Haley was ill in the camp hospital sometime between his entrance into service and August 31, 1862 and again during the November/December 1862 period when the Regiment was near Falmouth, Virginia.

A General Court Martial was convened at the headquarters of the 1st Division, 2nd Corps and on September 30, 1863 tried Private James Haley, Company B, 116th Pennsylvania Infantry Regiment on a charge of desertion.

Witnesses testified that Haley deserted on or about July 8, 1863 near Gettysburg, Pennsylvania. Haley went to Philadelphia, Pennsylvania and enlisted as a substitute in the 143rd Pennsylvania Infantry Regiment for which he received a bounty of $250.00, enlisting under the assumed name of James T. Smith on August 24, 1863. Haley's new Regiment was stationed at Brailton, Virginia and a Private Allman of his old Company, Company B, 116th Pennsylvania Infantry Regiment saw Haley at a newspaper stand in Brailton and notified a Sergeant of Company B who in turn sent two men to arrest him on September 14, 1863. They were asking for James Haley unaware of his alias James T. Smith and the records of the 143rd showed no such person. They returned on September 15, 1863 and by chance saw Haley in the Camp of the 143rd and promptly arrested him under the direction of an officer of the 143rd. Haley was returned to the 116th Pennsylvania Infantry Regiment under arrest and was confined awaiting charges and trial.

The prisoner made the following statement:

"The time I left the Regiment I was starving. I went to the Doctor and asked him for a leave to fall out, I did not get it. I went on with the Regiment as far as I was able to go. I had no intention when I fell out to leave at that time. I staid in Maryland at a German's house for three or four days, I was not able to go. When I got better the Army had crossed back into Virginia. So I thought I could go home and see my folks and return again. I was home about three weeks. I left then and went to Little York, Penn. to see a cousin of mine. I got to drinking, it was about the time the drafting commenced, one of those substitute agents came and encouraged me to go as a substitute. I was so much in liquor I did not know what I was about, so I went. I did not know what I was going for at the time, or anything else, when I came to my senses I was at Carlisle, Penn. That is all I wish to say. I do not have any other testimony for the defense."

The Court deliberated and found the accused guilty. Haley was sentenced to make good the time lost by desertion, to forfeit all pay and allowances due him to the first day of October, 1863 and ten dollars of his monthly pay for the balance of his enlistment, and to carry a log weighing 25 pounds attached to his leg for a period of three months. The court then adjourned until the next morning.

The Court resumed hearings on October 1, 1863. The Judge Advocate requested the court to reconsider the sentence in the case of Private Haley and the court agreed to do so.

The Court duly reconsidered all the evidence in the case of Private Haley's charge of desertion. The court then did substitute the following sentence:

That Private James Haley, Company B, 116th Pennsylvania Infantry Regiment be shot to death with musketry. Haley was executed on October 16, 1863.

REFERENCES:

Military Personnel Records, RG-#94
Court Martial Proceedings, RG-#153 NN 391

Case #70

Pvt. Henry C. Beardsley
Co. G, 5th Michigan Vol Inf Regt

Executed for Desertion
October 16/17, 1863

DESCRIPTION:

26 years of age, 5 feet 11 inches tall, blue eyes, brown hair, fair complexion, born at St. Clair, Michigan, occupation sailor, literacy undetermined.

Beardsley enlisted on September 4, 1861 and was mustered into service at Fort Wayne (near Detroit), Michigan on September 6, 1861. He apparently deserted on or about August 22, 1862 at or near Alexandria, Virginia. He is reported to have been apprehended on June 1, 1863 and charged with Desertion.

Private Henry C. Beardsley, Company G, 5th Michigan Infantry Regiment was tried by General Court Martial on September 29, 1863 charged with desertion. The Court was convened at Headquarters of the 3rd Brigade, 1st Division, 3rd Army Corps.

Beardsley applied to the Court for permission to retain a Captain Stuart as his counsel and the application was granted, however, counsel later withdrew from the case.

The testimony stated that on the 23rd of August, 1862, the Regiment returned from the peninsula and landed at Alexandria, Virginia and halted outside the town. Beardsley and other soldiers of the Company requested and received permission to visit in the area but were to remain within hearing range of calls for assembly. Beardsley did not return with the others upon the assembly and command of Fall-In. It was stated that Beardsley traveled by boat to Massachusetts and then to Canada. He was arrested in his home town, St. Clair, Michigan, on June 1, 1863 and returned to his Regiment for trial.

The Court found him guilty as charged and sentenced him to death by firing squad at Fairfax Station, Virginia on October 16, or 17, 1863 as some records indicate.

REFERENCES:

Military Personnel Records, RG-#94
Court Martial Proceedings, RG-#153 NN 391

Case #71
Pvt. Reuben Stout
Co. K, 60th Indiana Infantry Regiment
Executed for Desertion/Murder
October 23, 1863

DESCRIPTION:

28 years of age, 5 feet 6 inches tall, blue eyes, auburn hair, fair complexion, born in Berks County, Pennsylvania, occupation farmer, illiterate, married with children.

Stout's records show he enlisted in Delphi, Indiana on January 1, 1862 and was mustered into service at Indianapolis, Indiana on February 25 (March 11), 1862. (Stout states that he "enlisted in December 1861 in a Cavalry Company but the Regiment failed to secure enough volunteers and was never mustered into service.") He was told by "an officer" that his enlistment in the unborn cavalry regiment required him to enter the military service in any regiment available though he maintained he was never sworn into service, and he was enrolled in the 60th Indiana Infantry Regiment, Company K.

The 60th Indiana Infantry Regiment was captured at Cranes River, Kentucky in November, 1862 and the men were paroled and sent to Indianapolis, where they were furloughed. Stout said he went home, stayed out the furlough, and started the return to report to his Regiment, accompanied by his wife and sister to Dayton where Stout went on alone. However, he became ill at Lafayette, Indiana remaining there for five days, at which time Stout was taken to his father-in-law's home for further recuperation. Two weeks after arrival at his father-in-law's home, he was approached by various individuals who later proved to be members of the "Knights of the Golden Circle" organization sympathetic and supportive of the southern cause. This organization was said to have strong support in Ohio, Indiana and Illinois. The members of the K.G.C. as it was abbreviated, persuaded Stout that he should never return to service with his Regiment as it was solely an "abolitionist war." He attended meetings of the K.G.C. and eventually became a full fledged member of the order. The purposes of the order, as explained to Stout, were to work against the war by resisting a draft if one should be enacted, to resist and oppose all confiscation or emancipation measures in every possible way by not giving another dollar or man to the Federal Government. In his lengthy statement and confession, Stout describes identification passwords and hand grips as well as other methods of identification, some rather complicated, when in combat. The members of the K.G.C. instructed Stout on how to defend himself against capture even advising him to kill such government marshals or soldiers if there were no more than one or two in the arresting party. All members of the K.G.C. were expected to be constantly armed. Arms were available through gunsmiths, such as a Mr. Bixler of Lafayette, Indiana. Stout named all members of K.G.C. he could remember. Clinton County, Indiana had the largest number of members, with a few being resident in Mulberry and Lafayette, Indiana. After about four months of residence with his father-in-law Stout journeyed to Delphi, Indiana to visit his brother. On the evening of his second day of visit, March 14, 1863, two men, Soloman Huffman, later identified as a Special Marshall and another man named McAfee came to the house and inquired for Stout. He being on the second story of the house at the stairwell, overheard the conversation between Huffman and Stout's brother and wife. In exasperation Huffman finally said "You are all a set of damned copperheads, and if we get him, this will be the last time for him." Stout, alarmed by the turn of the conversation, drew his revolver and stepped to the head of the stairs as Huffman began his ascent with a lighted candle in his hand. Stout shouted that he would come down if Huffman halted, but if he took one more step he would shoot him. Huffman shifted the candle from one hand to the other apparently in preparation to draw his own pistol and Stout shot him. Huffman, in falling, is said to have exclaimed "Oh God! I'm killed!" Huffman was carried out of the house and Stout says he never saw him again.

A General Court Martial was convened at Camp Morton, near Indianapolis, Indiana, on November 6, 1862. On November 18, 1862 they changed it's location to the City of Indianapolis, Indiana "Owing to inefficient accommodations at Camp Morton." and on May 14, 1863, tried Private Reuben Stout, Company K, 60th Indiana Infantry Regiment on charges of Killing in violation of the Laws of War and desertion.

Stout asked permission of the Court to introduce as his counsels John Colerick and Jonathan C. Applegate esqrs., to which request the Court consented.

Testimony was introduced by witnesses to show that Stout was a member of his Regiment and had been paid and had a history of deserting while being treated with great leniency on a previous violation. He deserted April 1, 1862 and was returned on or about April 22, 1862. He again deserted on November 24, 1862 and remained absent until on or about March 24, 1863.

It was during an attempted capture while in hiding on his second desertion that Stout committed murder on March 14, 1863.

When Stout deserted on November 24, 1862, he moved about from place to place but by March 14, 1863 he was, with his wife and child, at the residence of his brother, Daniel Stout, in Carroll County, near Delphi, Indiana. Benjamin J. McAfee, town Marshall of Delphi, Indiana, was asked on March 14, 1863 to arrest Reuben Stout who was reported as staying at his brother's residence. McAfee secured the assistance of Soloman Huffman to accompany him to arrest Reuben Stout. Huffman was reputed to be a drinking man and quarrelsome when intoxicated. Some trial witnesses believed Huffman to have been drinking prior to his murder. The two men rode out to Daniel Stout's home, knocked on the door and were admitted. They talked with Daniel Stout and Reuben's wife, Reuben having retreated to the second floor when they arrived.

All denied knowing of Reuben's whereabouts. Permission was sought to search the house and was granted. Huffman, provided with a candle, approached the foot of a narrow staircase leading to the second floor. As Huffman prepared to ascend the stairs to the second floor, he muttered, "By God it's death on him this time" and reached his right hand under his coat toward his left breast, as though he were attempting to draw a weapon. As he stepped on the first step, a voice from the second floor called out, "Step back! step back!" which was followed by the report of a pistol shot. Huffman staggered back exclaiming "I am killed." McAfee hastened to his side and assisted him out of the house. McAfee testified that he heard the same voice from upstairs saying, after Huffman was shot, "Let the other son-of-a-bitch come and I'll kill him too!" McAfee held Huffman's head in his lap until he died after Huffman fell to the ground outside the Stout home. McAfee stated there were two wounds in Huffman's chest, one entering near the right nipple and the other entering about four inches away. (This was later explained by the fact that Reuben Stout had double -shotted the pistol) McAfee, after Huffman died, mounted his horse and went for assistance. Reuben Stout, after McAfee left, went to the nearby home of William Bugher and stated he had gotten in a row at his brother Daniels house, and had shot a man, and wanted him to come over to the house. Bugher accompanied Reuben Stout to his brother's house and saw Huffman's dead body.

Reuben Stout surrendered on either the 15th or the 16th of March, 1863. Nor is it clear from the testimony as to exactly where he was surrendered. A prosecution statement to the court indicates that Reuben Stout went into hiding following the shooting, that a reward of $200.00 was offered for his capture and a day or two thereafter he was brought in by a relative and surrendered to a Justice of the Peace. He was then bound over for civil trial on a charge of murder. On May 9, 1863 Reuben Stout was indicted by the Grand Jury of Carroll County, Indiana and held on a charge of murder with bail set at $20,000.00. The Military authorities took the prisoner under their jurisdiction and the General Court Martial trial revealed the facts as previously described. Stouts defense labored unsuccessfully to portray the entire Court Martial trial as lacking in jurisdiction, arguing that Civil Courts should have jurisdiction.

Stout was found guilty and sentenced to forfeit all pay that may be due him and that he be shot to death with musketry.

On June 3, 1863, General Burnside, approved and confirmed the proceedings, findings and sentence and ordered the prisoner, Reuben Stout, to be sent under proper guard to Johnson's Island, Depot of Prisoner's of War off Sandusky, Ohio, where his sentence was to be executed on June 26, 1863.

On July 8, 1863, Stout's legal counsel, J. C. Applegate, addressed an Appeal to President A. Lincoln.

"Delphi - Ind. July 8 - 1863 -
His Excellency - Abraham Lincoln -

Reuben Stout, was tried at Indianapolis, by Court Martial and sentenced to be shot at Johnson's Island, June 26th Ult. General Burnside granted a respite for thirty days. His punishment is too severe. The homicide is excusable and the charge of desertion wrong. He left his Regiment on furlough and stayed over the time limits and before he could comply with your proclamation, he was arrested, so that he could not return on the 1st of April as you directed. He was charged with killing an officer who went to arrest him before the 1st of April. The arrest was attempted at an improper hour in the night time. His wife and child ask for his life to be spared and any other punishment substituted. If you can't decide immediately, can't you grant a respite until you can examine the papers now in the War Department. His Captain tells me Reuben Stout was a *good* soldier. Now that Victory has crowned our arms at Gettysburg and Vicksburg can't you save a *good* soldier's life. You alone can do it. It is true I am his atty. Yet I *truly* feel in my heart that his punishment is too severe, and that he should be relieved from the death penalty. *Perjury* produced the severity of the punishment.
I am - Your Excellencies
Obt. Servt.
John C. Applegate.'

As a result of the appeal, President Lincoln suspended execution of the death sentence until the record of the Court Martial Proceedings could be examined.

On July 29, 1863, the Judge Advocate General Holt, presented an eight page meticulous and detailed analysis and study of the Court Martial Proceedings of the trial of Reuben Stout and in his conclusion wrote: *"To the President"*

"If the President shall concur in the opinion here expressed that the Court Martial had the right to try the case not withstanding trial proceedings, in it's (*illegible*) first been commenced by the State Courts that there brings nothing in the (*illegible*) of evidence to the case to show why the sentence of the Court Martial should not be carried into execution.
I have the honor to be - Your Obt. Servt.
Holt —
Judge Advocate General

The President Replied:

"Without deciding the general question raised as to the right of the Court Martial, under the circumstances, to try the prisoner for the homicide committed, there can be no doubt of it's right to try and convict him of desertion, which has been done and in as much as this crime is punishable with death, the prisoner's guilt of it as declared supports the death sentence - which is therefore approved."
August 1, 1863 A. Lincoln'

On the afternoon of August 1, 1863, General Holt replied to President Lincoln "Judge Advocate General's office, August 1, 1863 His Excellency, A. Lincoln, President U.S.
Sir:

In the case of Reuben Stout, where the death sentence was approved by you this morning, a question arises, which I omitted to bring to your notice, but which deserves consideration.

The prisoner deserted in April, 1862, and at the expiration of three weeks, was arrested. He deserted again in November, 1862, and does not seem to have been re-arrested. On the 14th of March, 1863, he killed the Assistant of the Officer who was endeavoring to arrest him, and on the 26th of that month was taken into custody under a state warrant for murder, and on the same day he was regularly committed to close jail for this crime by a state Justice of the Peace. In consequence of this proceeding, he was in prison, when the limitation fixed by the proclamation for the return of deserters, 1st April, expired. Could he, under these circumstances, be held to be entitled to the benefit of the amnesty promised by the proclamation?

You have constantly decided where a deserter is debarred from voluntarily returning to his regiment in consequence of his having been arrested and held for his offense by the U. S. Military Authorities, that he should be treated, as though he had returned, in as much as it could not be certainly known that he would not have done so, had not the action of the government prevented him. Does Stout's case fall within this category? It is to be remarked that he was in prison, not from the action of the U. S. authorities, but of the authorities of the State of Indiana. Further, this imprisonment was the result of his own conduct, of an atrocious murder committed by him. It is a fundamental principle that a man shall not take advantage of his own wrong, shall he be permitted to take advantage of his own crime? When it is remembered that this murder was perpetrated in resisting a return to the service which he had deserted, would it not be hazardous to hold that the imprisonment consequent upon such a crime, committed for such a purpose, should excuse from the responsibility of a failure to return in obedience to the proclamation?"
Very Respectfully
Your obedient Servt.
Holt
Judge Advocate General"

On August 3, 1863, John Hay, President Lincoln's personal secretary replied to General Holt.

"The President directs me to say that he still approves the Death Sentence of Stout as by the Memorandum of August 1."

From this point on a rare procedure was followed. Stout was treated as a member of the Confederate forces as disclosed in "General Order #89, Headquarters, Department of the Ohio, Cincinnati, Ohio, June 3rd, 1863, Page 3, II ... the Prisoner will be sent under proper guard and delivered into the custody of the Commanding Officer on Johnson's Island (camp for Confederate P.O.W., an island located in Sandusky Bay, about three miles offshore of the city of Sandusky, Ohio) Depot of Prisoners of War, near Sandusky, Ohio. The commander of that post will see that the sentence is duly executed between the hours of 12 o'clock, noon, and 3 o'clock PM on Friday, June 26, 1863." Appeals for clemency were made but only resulted in deferring the execution until October 23, 1863. On the Roll of Prisoners of War at the Depot Prisoners of War, near Sandusky, Ohio (Johnson's Island, Ohio, Register #1, Page 144) and on the Register of Prisoners of War who died at Johnson's Island, Ohio is the name Reuben Stout (Confederate) (Register #3, Page 38).

The execution of Stout is mentioned in a number of diaries kept by prisoners of war at Johnson's Island at the time.

Edmund D. Patterson in his diary makes mention of Stout's execution. "Friday, 23rd. The day is cold, and dark and cheerless, a fit day for the scene I have just witnessed, the execution of a deserter. It is said that he first deserted our army and joined the Federals. Soon after that he deserted them and killed the Provost Marshall who was attempting to arrest him. ... The convict was led out, heavily ironed ... seated on his coffin ... The command was given to fire ... the convict fell back on his coffin, a corpse" ...

The Rev. Robert M. Thrasher, of the 18th Arkansas Infantry wrote "Reuben Stout of Company K, 60th Indiana Regiment, charged with murder and desertion from the federal army was shot at 2 PM. He had a wife and 2 children."

The Arkansas Gazette, of Little Rock, Arkansas published on October 25, 1936 and continued weekly in Sunday editions extracts of the Diary of Johnson Island P.O.W. Captain R. W. Bingham, Company G, 44th North Carolina from the Southern Historical Society, Chapel Hill, North Carolina. "23rd October 1863, Frid. The Yankees shot a deserter today. The Yankees are greatly scared, had we gone to see the execution we might have broken out."

On October 23, 1863, Stout was executed by a firing squad on the east shore of the island facing the stockade. After the Hoffman Battalion (the security guard of Johnson's Island) formed a hollow square, open side toward the water, where Stout was seated upon his coffin, the orders and sentence were read. Clergymen offered prayers, one in English and one in German. The eyes of the prisoner were blindfolded, the execution squad fired, killing him. Stout was pronounced dead by the Command Surgeon and then the battalion marched off past the corpse, while the band played the dead march. Stout was buried in the Prison Cemetery and remains there today under a gravestone marked unknown.

REFERENCES:

We are most heavily indebted to Roger Long of Port Clinton, Ohio who is the authority on everything and anything about Johnson's Island P.O.W. camp.

Military Personnel Records, RG-#94

Court Martial Proceedings, RG-#153 LL 451

Diaries cited above, courtesy of Roger Long.

"Rebels on Lake Erie," by Frohman

"Yankee Rebel, the Civil War Journal of Edmund DeWitt Patterson," edited with an introduction by John C. Barrett, the University of North Carolina Press, Chapel Hill, 1966.

Sandusky Register, May 16, 1863.

Case #72
Pvt. John Roberts
Co. H, 15th Regiment, Mass. Infantry
Executed for Desertion
October 30, 1863

DESCRIPTION:
21 years of age, 5 feet 6-½ inches tall, brown hair, blue eyes, light complexion, born in St. John, New Brunswick, Canada, occupation blacksmith.

Roberts was drafted and mustered into service on July 28, 1863 and was assigned to Company H, 15th Massachusetts Infantry Regiment being forwarded from Long Island, Boston Harbor on August 8, 1863. He deserted, was captured, confined and tried by court martial.

A General Court Martial was convened at Headquarters, 2nd Division, 2nd Army Corps near Somerville Ford, Virginia and on October 9, 1863 tried Private John Roberts, Company H, 15th Massachusetts Infantry Regiment on a charge of desertion.

Testimony showed that on or about September 3, 1863, Roberts and another unnamed soldier, while on the march returning from Banks Ford, Virginia fell out of ranks near Hartwood Church without permission altho they complained of sore feet. Roberts had been with his Company and Regiment since August 14, 1863 and had heard the Articles of War read to the Company.

Roberts was arrested by the Provost Marshall of the 2nd Army Corps. on September 24, 1863 as a deserter.

"US Str. Teaser, Potomac River, September 7, 1863

Sir: I respectfully report that while cruising off Liverpool Point at 2-45 this A.M. I overhauled and captured a boat containing five (5) deserters, who gave their names as follows: *John Roberts*, Charles Davis, John Dawson, Peter Kelly and Michael Warren. I hailed the boat 3 or 4 times but received no reply, the occupants kept pulling towards the Maryland shore, I fired at them but they kept on I then manned my cutter and started in pursuit, when near the shore, one of the men jumped overboard, but I overhauled the party and brought them on board, one claims to be a paroled prisoner belonging to the 9th Massachusetts Regiment three others say they enlisted as substitutes, while the remaining one (Davis) disclaims all attachment to either Army.
I am Sir Respectfully your Obedient Servant
(sig.) Philip Sheridan, Act. Ensign Commanding."

The accused offered no witnesses but did present a statement of defense.

"Statement in Defense"
"When I was hunting for the Camp at Morrisville; (VA) I lost my road and got down to the river, I did not intend to desert. I met the men I was with and I could not walk. They said they were going to the sick camp and I could get into the boat and go to Alexandria and I could get to my regiment in that way. I was on picket when the Articles of War were read to the Regiment and they were never read to me."

The Court then deliberated, found the accused guilty, and sentenced him to be shot to death with musketry.

The execution took place on October 30, 1863 near the Camp of the 2nd Division near Morrisville, Virginia.

REFERENCES:
Military Personnel Records, RG-#94
Court Martial Proceedings, RG-#153   LL 987

Case #73
Private Mitchell Vandall
Co. K, 8th Conn. Infantry Regt.
Executed for Desertion
November 9, 1863

DESCRIPTION:

27 years of age, 5 feet 8½ inches tall, brown hair, hazel eyes, dark complexion, born in Canada, occupation laborer, illiterate.

Vandall was drafted and mustered into service on September 3, 1863 at Norwich, Connecticut into Company K, Connecticut Infantry Regiment. Vandall deserted from his Regiment September 19, 1863 near Portsmouth, Virginia in the Company of Private Francis Wales, Company D, 8th Connecticut Infantry Regiment. They both were apprehended on September 20, 1863.

A General Court Martial was convened at Portsmouth, Virginia and on September 28, 1863 tried Private Mitchell Vandall, Company K, 8th Connecticut Infantry Regiment on a charge of desertion.

Testimony disclosed that Vandall was enlisted on September 3, 1863, came to the Camp of the 8th Connecticut near Portsmouth, Virginia (in a party of conscripts) on September 9, 1863 and was assigned to Company K. On the morning of September 19, 1863 he had disappeared and on the following day was returned to the Company under guard.

The details of his case are nearly identical with those of Private Francis Wales, Company D, 8th Connecticut Infantry Regiment (case #74 Francis Wales).

Vandall called no witnesses but did present a statement to the court.

Statement of the Prisoner

"When I left my camp between 9 and 10 o'clock I started to go to the 10th Regiment to see a man to have a letter written, he was not there. I went down to the sutlers and drank some 24 bottles of ale in company with a friend. I went with my friend. I was a stranger and knew not where he was taking me. We went in the woods to drink some beer and fell asleep. Woke up and started for Camp. Lost the way. I told my friend we were going the wrong way, he said we were not and told me to keep up with him. We walked through the mud and wet until 9 and 10 o'clock in the evening when we saw a light. I told him we would go to the light, as we were very tired and might find friends and could rest. He told me to keep still and stop my noise. As we came near the light the sentinel halted us. I replied friends from the 8th Connecticut, they then took me under guard and tied me hand and foot."

The Court then deliberated, found Vandall guilty and sentenced him to be shot to death with musketry near Portsmouth, Virginia on November 9, 1863.

The original date set for execution was October 26, 1863, but was delayed until the actual day of execution, November 9, 1863.

Private Henry Marshall, a Civil War Soldier, in a letter home, mentions the impending execution of Vandall and Wales. (For the execution description see case #74 Francis Wales.)

"This day two deserters from the 8th were to be shot and the men to do the shooting were taken from our Regiment. Two from each Company. But just before the time came, up came a reprieve till Monday, tomorrow. So if nothing happens to prevent we shall see the two men shot tomorrow. They were some of the substitutes the 8th received and tried to get through our picket line and were brought in by some of our boys the day we went to South Mills."

REFERENCES:

Military Personnel Records, RG-#93
Court Martial Proceedings, RG-#153 MM 897
Manuscript Division, Civil War soldiers letters, Schoff collection, Clements Library, University of Michigan, Ann Arbor, Michigan, letters of Henry Marshall.

Case #74
Private Francis Wales
Co. D, 8th CT Infantry Regt.
Executed for Desertion
November 9, 1863

DESCRIPTION:

23 years of age, 5 feet 5½ inches tall, brown hair, blue eyes, fair complexion, born in Canada, occupation laborer, substitute.

Wales was drafted and mustered into service at Hartford, Connecticut on September 1, 1863 into the ranks of Company D, 8th Connecticut Infantry Regiment. Wales deserted military service on September 19, 1863 near Portsmouth, Virginia, and was apprehended on the 20th of September, 1863.

A General Court Martial was convened at Headquarters Portsmouth, Virginia and on September 26, 1863 tried Private Francis Wales, Company D, 8th Connecticut Infantry Regiment on a charge of desertion.

Wales was enlisted on September 1, 1863 and on the 9th of September, 1863 was one of 166 conscripts sent to the Regiment. On September 12th the accused was missing from roll call and was returned to his company under guard, with two other soldiers on September 13th. They were all punished and returned to duty on September 16th or 17th and on September 19th he deserted again. He was arrested on September 20th accompanied by another soldier (Vandall) and placed under arrest and charged.

Witnesses verified Wales transgressions, while he attempted to establish the fact that he was drunk and unwilling to escape, even asking his captors to tie his bonds tighter as he could loosen his hands.

The prisoner offered no witnesses on his behalf but did present a statement to the Court.

Statement of the Prisoner

"We started on the 19th from our Regiment in the afternoon. We went to the sutler of the 10th New Hampshire Volunteers and on arriving there we began drinking. We drank liquor we counted 24 bottles of ale and porter. Then we thought it was time for us to go to our regiment. But after going a short distance, turned and went back to the sutlers and got 2 more bottles and some segars. We went from the sutlers into the woods to finish our spree. When we got in the woods we drank one bottle. Could not tell whether we drank the 2nd one or not. We were so drunk when we started for our regiment and walked through the woods and fields until we found a track. And saw a light about a mile or two off. We went straight up to the light and were taken prisoners. If I had wanted to desert I would not have went straight up to the light but would have went through the woods."

The court deliberated, found the accused guilty and sentenced him to be shot to death with musketry.

The execution took place on November 9, 1863 at Portsmouth, Virginia.

The date of the sentence was originally set for October 26, 1863 and for some undisclosed reason, was delayed until November 9, 1863.

Private Henry Marshall, a Civil War Soldier, in a letter dated November 9, 1863 to the "home folks" describes witnessing the execution of Wales and Vandall. For the introduction to this description see Case #74 Mitchell Vandall which contains excerpts from Marshall's letter of the previous day. "And now I come to the great event of the day, and that is the shooting of the two deserters of the 8th. They were two of the substitutes and tried to get out of our lines, the day we went down to South Mills. They were sentenced to be shot last Friday but a reprieve was obtained till today and today they suffered the penalty due to their crime in presence of the whole Brigade on a plain in front of Fort Reno. The troops marched up there at 9 A.M. and formed a square with one side open. General Harland and staff sat on their horses opposite and facing this open side where the men knelt who were to be shot. The right side of the square was occupied by the

15th in line of battle. The back side by the 16th and the left side by the 8th and a company or two of Battery Boys. There we waited while spectators and outsiders began to collect and the wind blew up chilly and cold and the clouds looked like snow but none came and we shivered and waited till at last the procession came. The band playing a mournful dirge, the 20 men who were to do the shooting, the two coffins, taken by the bearers, the carriages with the prisoners and priests and last the escort of two platoons from the 8th. They marched along behind our Regiment up to the open side and then into it round the three sides up to the left of the 8th. There the prisoners were lead by the Chaplain and priests to the coffins which had been placed upon the ground and the executioners drawn up in line about a rod from them behind these stood the Commandant then the escort and then the band and then the General and staff. A little draft will show you the procedure much easier and quicker than I can tell. It was a solemn time and still enough while they descended from the carriages, walked slowly to the coffins, knelt and prayed, embraced and kissed the priests, knelt in front of their coffins and had their eyes blindfolded. The priests and officers in charge bade them good bye and retired behind the 20 men and then the commands were give, `*Ready*' - `*Aim*' - `*Fire*' and the two fell on their right side, dead, pierced by several bullets and all was over with them. Then `By Co. right wheel' `Forward March' and we all marched round and by the side of the two and so back to camp while those detailed stayed and buried them, not far from there near the edge of the woods. The priests going through their formula over the grave. Both were foreigners I believe. Thus are the rigorous edicts of Martial law fearfully executed on the guilty by their comrades in fight. One could not but think after it all that any who witnessed it would never want to desert and run the risk of meeting such a death as that. The effect cannot but be salutalory. Their names were Wales and Vanvert (sic). One man in our regiment helped them and received 10 dollars from them for showing how to get away. He has been arrested and sent to Portsmouth to await his trial and he may have to be shot for the penalty is the same. It will go hard with him. Such a sight I had curiousity to see for once and now that I have seen an execution I don't care to see another. Once is enough and my curiousity is satisfied."

REFERENCES:

Military Personnel Records, RG-#94
Court Martial Proceedings, RG-#153 MM 897
Manuscript Division, Civil War soldiers letters, Schoff Collection, Clements Library, University of Michigan, Ann Arbor, Michigan, letter of Henry Marshall.

Case #75
Pvt. Erastus C. Daley
NV: Dailey
Co. D, 88th, IL Infantry Regt.
Executed for Desertion
November 13, 1863

DESCRIPTION:

35 years of age, 5 feet 7½ inches tall, brown hair, blue eyes, fair complexion, born in New York City, occupation harness maker, literacy undetermined.

Daily enlisted at Princeton, Illinois on August 5, 1862 and was mustered into service at Chicago on September 4, 1862 in Captain Bross' Company, 88th Regiment Illinois Infantry. The unit designation was subsequently changed to Company D, 88th Illinois Infantry Regiment. The Regiment was deployed from Illinois into Kentucky and on October 13, 1862 while pursuing the enemy, Daily deserted near Harrodsburg, Kentucky.

On November 1, 1862 a letter was written to Captain Bross concerning Private Daily. It read as follows:

"Polo, Ogle Co., Ill, Nov 1, 1862

Capt John A. Bross, Dear Sir By request of E C Daily, I take pen in hand to say a few words to you concerning his whereabouts. He is at my house and pretty sick. I will state to you the circumstances of his being here he fell back from your Company on account of not being able to keep up Was picked up by the rear guard and sent to hospital The Superintendent of the Hospital told him he had better find a Private house as they were full he being a stranger and out of money stayed at a private house a few days and concluded he would try and get home and accordingly he is here. I know Sir you would confer a favour by giving him a leave of absence for a short time until he can recover and be able to return to his Regiment which I think will be before long He told me to tell you what he done with his things He left his gun Knapsack overcoat Blanket shirt socks and towel with Miller the Waggoner of your Regiment and his dress coat J.W. Densmore has got He would like to have you see to them James Welch told him to put them on Millers Wagon

I am respfy,

Jas. L. Deon

P.S. Captain Please send the boy a furlough for a short time He will soon be around.

JL Deon"

In the charge sheet filed against Private Daily for desertion there is the phrase, "arrested by the Provost Marshall of the 3rd District of the State of Illinois at Polo on or about the 6th day of August 1863."

Obviously Daily continued his absence for another eight months after his friend disclosed his whereabouts.

A General Court Martial convened on August 25, 1863 at the Headquarters of the 1st Brigade, 3rd Division, 20th Army Corps at Bridgeport, Alabama for the trial of Private Erastus C. Daley, Company D, 88th Illinois Infantry Regiment on the charge of Desertion.

Testimony revealed that Daley deserted his Regiment near Harrodsburg, Kentucky while it was pursuing the enemy on October 13, 1862 and that he was absent until arrested in Polo, Illinois on August 6, 1863. He apparently deserted and returned immediately to Polo, Illinois where he claimed to have been ill. Daley attempted to claim that he had not completed the enlistment process and was not sworn into the service nor received bounty hence was not in the service or under Army Jurisdiction. He claimed he was sick and reported for sick call, the morning he disappeared. The surgeon, after examining Daley, stated he was fit for duty and gave him medicine.

Daley was located in Polo by a letter, written to his Company Commander, on his behalf explaining he was ill.

During the trial, Daley questioned many of the witnesses but offered no defense or statement to the court.

The court deliberated and found Daley guilty and sentenced him to death by musketry. Daley was executed on November 13, 1863 at Chattanooga, Tennessee.

REFERENCES:

Military Personnel Records, RG-#94

Court Martial Proceedings, RG-#153 LL 1173

Case #76

Pvt. Valentine Benjamin

Co. C, 44th, IL Inf. Regt.

Executed for Desertion

November 13, 1863

DESCRIPTION:

39 years of age, occupation carpenter, no further description found.

Benjamin enlisted on July 1, 1861 at Wenona, Illinois and was mustered into service on September 13, 1861 at Chicago, Illinois in Captain Russell's Company, North Western Rifle Regiment U.S. Volunteers. The designation of the unit was later changed to Company C, 44th Illinois Infantry Regiment. On October 5, 1861, Benjamin was confirmed in his position as Regimental Carpenter. On May 27, 1862, Benjamin deserted the service at Hamburg Landing, Tennessee as the Regiment was advancing toward battle at Corinth, Mississippi.

A letter in Benjamin's personnel file from his Company Commander John Stoner written, apparently, to the Chicago area Provost Marshall intimates his location and eventual arrest. "Camp Schaefer, near Murphysboro, Tenn, June 11th, 1862:

Dear Sir: Having been informed that Valentine Benjamin (Private) of my Co. who deserted at Hamburg Landing, Tenn. May the 27th or 28th, 1862 is now in Chicago working at his trade (carpentering) you will arrest him immediately and send him to the Regt. If you will call on James Lacey, Marion Hospital Ward #32 Chicago he can point him out to you or tell you where he is to work but if Lacey has left the Hospital you will find him to work on a house some where in the city. I think you had better attend to the matter as soon as you receive this as I have heard it intimated that he would be apprised of my intention to have him arrested & in that case he would leave Chicago.

John B. Stoner, Capt. 44th Regt. Ill Inf Comdg. Co. C."

Private Valentine Benjamin, Company C, 44th Illinois Infantry Regiment was tried on August 17, 1863 for desertion by a General Court Martial at Camp Harrington, Alabama. Testimony stated that Benjamin deserted his Regiment at Hamburg Landing, Tennessee sometime between the 27th and 30th of May, 1862 just before the Regiment marched to Corinth, Mississippi to face the enemy. He apparently returned to Chicago and the practice of his carpentry trade as both a letter in his personnel file and trial testimony allude. He was finally located in the Chicago area by the Chicago Provost Marshall, arrested and returned to his Regiment for trial. Benjamin's only defense was a statement prepared for him by his counsel. It was not very effective, being largely devoted to a verbose exposition of Benjamin's "good character" and an appeal to the mercy of the court.

Benjamin was found guilty and sentenced to be shot to death by musketry. The sentence was carried out on November 13, 1863.

REFERENCES:

Military Personnel Records, RG-#94
Court Martial Proceedings, RG-#153

Case #77
(Sgt./Pvt.) Lawson Kemp
Co. A, 55th Regiment USC Infantry
Executed for Rape
November 19, 1863

DESCRIPTION:

19 years of age, 5 feet 9 inches tall, black eyes, black hair, black complexion, born Tuscaloosa, Alabama, occupation farmer, illiterate.

Kemp enlisted at Corinth, Mississippi on May 1, 1863 and was mustered into service May 21, 1863 in Captain Sammon's Company 1st Regiment Alabama Infantry, A.D. (African Descent). This unit changed its designation later to Company A, 55th Regiment USC Infantry. Kemp was appointed as a Sergeant but was reduced to Private on June 3, 1863 for drunkenness and neglect of duty. A comment on his service record states, "This man was a desperate villian. I sent him from Fort Flodd, Tennessee to the stockade at Corinth, Mississippi for swindling, with a request that he be kept until I could prefer charges. Captain Reeves of Company D at Corinth, got him out of prison, took him in his own Company, went foraging near Pocahantas, Tennessee when this fellow ravished a white girl for which he was shot next day, November 19, 1863." Kemp was the first member of the USCT's executed.

On his muster roll (attendance) card for November, December, 1863 under remarks, is a notation, "died of disease, November 19, 1863." The preponderance of documentary evidence however verifies the fact of execution on that date.

REFERENCES:

Military Personnel Records, RG-#94

Case #78
Pvt. Homobono Carrabajol
NV: H. Molino Carrabajol, Caravagal
Co. D, 1st New Mexico, Vol Cav Regt
Listed as Executed
November 27, 1863
But Never Executed

DESCRIPTION:

22 years of age, dark eyes, dark hair, dark complexion, born in Mexico, illiterate. The descriptive list of Carrabajol has never been found and a memorandum in his file dated November 3, 1865 states, in part, "no papers to that effect can be found at present, they have either been lost or destroyed." The memo is in response to a request for the descriptive list request as it was needed for Administrative purposes relating to his discharge from the Army and admission to the Insane Asylum in Washington, D.C.

Carrabajol enlisted and was mustered into service at Fort Craig, New Mexico on November 16, 1861, and assigned to Company D, 1st Regiment New Mexico Volunteers. In May 1862, this regiment was consolidated with the 2nd, 4th and 5th Regiments into the 1st Regiment New Mexico Cavalry, with his Company designation remaining as Company D. He served the usual cavalry tasks of escort duty, scouting, guard and patrolling until May 21, 1863. A letter from the Fort Commander describes the murder committed by Carrabajol.

"Headquarters - Fort Garland, Colo. Terr.

May 21, 1863
A. A. Genl
Dist of Colorado
Sir,

"It is my sad duty to inform you that this day one of the most diabolical murders ever perpetrated was committed at this post by a private of Capt. Eaton's Company 1st New Mexico Volunteers named Carrabajol the murdered man was named Lujan both Mexicans, at the time the murder was committed the murdered man was laying in his bunk asleep his face down Carrabajol went into the room crawled upon him holding his pistol at the back of Lujan's head and the ball went in the back of his head and came out at his forehead killing him almost instantly and strange to say no person saw him in the act. When he went in the room every person was asleep and when the pistol went off he ran out the 1st Sergeant hearing the shot ran and as he got to the door of the squad room he met Carrabajol the Sergeant asked him "who done that" and was answered "I done it" the Sergeant not yet knowing what had been done went into the room and saw the dead man he then ran after the murderer, caught him and took his pistol from him with one load out, the murderer does not deny his guilt he is in double irons hand and foot We increased the guard to keep the excited men from lynching him.

From what little I can learn of the cause, it was caused by whisky. I learned that there has been a few Mexican whisky peddlers along the creeks since payday selling whisky

at three dollars a canteen and the men go there after Tattoo and get good and drunk and it seems as though these two men while on one of the drunks had a quarrel when they came home one of them was put in the guardhouse and they had not been together since until this morning, when Lujan was released and went to his quarters to sleep this other man killed him. They were both sober at the time of the murder. I have taken all caution to find out the whisky peddlers! What shall I do with them if caught?
Please let me know soon.
I am Sir
Your Obt Servt

J. C. Davidson, Capt Comdg
Fort Garland"

A General Court Martial convened at Fort Garland, Colorado Territory on June 6th, 1863 to try Private Homobono Carrabajol, Company D, 1st New Mexico Infantry Regiment on the charge of murder, to which Carrabajol pleaded guilty. Carrabajol spoke little English and a Spanish translator/interpreter was appointed by the Court.

Testimony was offered that Carrabajol and Private Francisco Lujan of Company D, 1st New Mexico Volunteers had apparently been drinking heavily together when they became involved in some dispute over paying for or custody of the liquor. They continued their dispute at the squad room at their barracks. At the barracks Lujan struck Carrabajol several violent blows with a "stick." The accused was ejected from the barracks but later returned when all the occupants were asleep. He leapt upon Lujan who was lying face down on his bunk asleep, placed his revolver against the back of Lujan's head and fired one shot. The bullet traveled through the brain cage emerging over the left eye causing immediate death on May 21, 1863.

Carrabajol asked to present a written statement to the Court, which request was granted.

"To the honorable President and Court,
Ft. Garland, C.T., June 5, 1863

The undersigned though delinquent in the actuality for having had the misfortune to touch in an ugly manner, one of my own kind, I know sirs that this was by the great temptation of the devil, and not because my former acts or life has been such as in any way to lead me to commit such an act. Now Mr. President, finding myself before the Court, which the law gives power to try and punish the guilty and protect the innocent, I have no other right nor can I expect other favor than that of the God of Heaven, and from the compassionate hearts of my always respected Officers I may receive the compassion and pardon which an unfortunate needs. Also honorable Court I offer myself with good will and upon my solemn oath to the service of arms in the United States five additional years, and to support the widow of the deceased with my pay as a soldier until such time as she may choose to take another husband and to explain myself better honorable Court, that I will fulfill my promise. I offer nothing more, being one of the weakest and most feeble of God's creatures on Earth. And I hope from the honor that adorns you, that I may not be left without the favor that as a helpless delinquent I solicit, and at your meritorious feet I await your decision.
Signed, Homobono Carrabajol"

The Court adjourned and confirmed Carrabajol's guilty plea sentencing him "to be hanged by the neck until dead, dead, dead."

On the appointed day of execution, a report from Col Chivington, Commanding the Colorado District, stated that "the execution of Carrabajol has been indefinitely suspended on account of the prisoner being crazy, and "that the information as to the condition of prisoner Carrabajol should have been reported previous to the day upon which his execution and sentence was to be carried into effect. The General commanding the Department had no alternative in consequence of the state of the case, save to approve the action of Col. Chivington."

From this point on there were a number of medical examinations of Carrabajol. Most stated that he was in no condition to be sent to Denver City for execution as planned. One report states, "the prisoner Carrabajol is guilty of a cruel and cowardly assassination of a fellow soldier, without a single circumstance to palliate the damning enormity of the deed; yet to hang him in his present, apparent, condition of mind; would be inhuman and unjust, in the extreme." Others stated -"Carrabajol is still insane and unfit to travel." "Sir; we have the honor to report that we met and examined private Carrabajol and find him in a state of unsound mind and not in a condition to have the death penalty executed."

In 1865 a final attempt was made to carry out the sentence of the Courtmartial of Pvt. Carrabajol. "Special Order #47, dated February 16, 1865, Headquarters Dept. of Missouri, Fort Levenworth, Kansas. - Extract - Paragraph II - The sentence of death in the case of Private Homobono Carrabajol of Company D - 1st Regiment of New Mexico Volunteers, will be carried into effect as directed in General Orders *No. 104,* Dept. of the Missouri Series 1863 under the direction of the *Commanding Officer,* District of *Colorado.*

By Command of Major General Dodge - "This was followed by the execution directive." Headquarters District of Colorado, Denver, C. T., April 5, 1865 - Captain - The Colonel commanding directs that under your supervision, the sentence of death in the case of Private Homobono Carrabajol - Co. D - 1st New Mexico Volunteers will be carried into effect as directed in General Order - No. 104 - Department of the Missouri - Series 1863 - To Wit - _To hang by the neck until he is dead, dead, dead, on Friday the 14th inst. at 2 O'Clock P.M. Should there be no gallows erected at this place for executing persons sentenced to be hung, you will erect a temporary one at some suitable place in the suburbs or vicinity of Denver for this purpose. You will make all the necessary arrangements for the interment of the body, previous to the hour of execution, such as providing the coffin, digging the grave etc., the grave to be dug in the place set apart by the City Authorities for the interment of persons executed for crime; if there be no such place, then in such place as you may deem most suitable!

Very Respectfully
Your Obedient Servant
Ira D. Haber
1st Lieutenant and A.A.A. General

To - Capt. Silas S. Soule
Acting Pro. Mar. Gen'l. - Dist. of Col.
Denter - Col. Ter."

On april 13, 1865 another message was sent to Captain Soule. "Hdqrs. Dist. of the Plains, Denver, Colorado, April 13, 1865.
To - Capt. Silas Soule, Acting Pro. Mar. Gen'l.

Sir: The General Commanding directs that you postpone the execution of the death penalty upon Private Homobono Carrabajo, Do. D, 1st New Mexico Vols. as ordered to take place on the 14th inst. (as per letter of instructions directed to you from Headquarters, District of Colorado, Denver, G. T. - April 5, 1865) until further orders from these Headquarters.

Very Respectfully,
Your Obedient Servant
Geo. F. Price, A.A.A.G."

A further communication set the stage for the ultimate conclusion of the Carrabajol case.
"Headquarters District of the Plains, Denver, Colorado, April 17, 1865.
To - Major J. W. Barnes, Asst. Adjutant General, Dept. of the Missouri, St. Louis, Missouri

Sir: I have the honor to enclose herewith communication of Surgeon Hamilton - Vet.

Batt. 1st Col. Cavalry in reference to the sanity of Private Carrabajol, Co. D, 1st N. M. Vols. now in confinement and under sentence to be hung. On the representation of many respectable citizens i commanded the examination to be made and have postponed the execution until the decision of the Major General commanding on the subject is received.

I am of the opinion from personal observation and the testimony of the Provost Marshall and Guard that the prisoner is of unsound mind and therefore respectfully recommend that his sentence be commuted to imprisonment for life.

I have the Honor to Remain,

Your Obedient Servant

O. Edw. Connor - Brig. Gen'l. Comdg."

A telegram approved the request for a final mental examination.

"Julesburg, May 3rd, 1865 by Telegraph from St. Louis, May 3rd,1865.

To - Brig. Gen'l. Connor - Julesburg

Maj Gen'l. Dodge directs that you cause a thorough examination to be made by board of Surgeons of Homobono Carrabajol, sentenced to be hung, if found beyond a doubt to be crazy, send him to the Insane Asylum at Washington, D.C.

J. W. Barnes - A.A.G."

The verdict of the Board was insane and Carrabajol was sent under escort to the Government Asylum for the Insane at Washington, D.C. and was apparently admitted during late September, 1865. He was reported cured, requiring no further treatment and discharge from the Asylum was recommended by February 7, 1866. A delay of a few weeks was occasioned due to administrative documentary problems. Carrabajol was finally freed and was never heard from again.

REFERENCES:

Military Personnel Records, RG-#94

Court Martial Proceedings, RG-#153 NN 382

Case #79

Corporal) Paul Kingston

Co. M, 1st Missouri Cav. Regt. November 27, 1863

Executed for Murder & Desertion

DESCRIPTION:

24 years of age, 5 feet 11 inches tall, brown hair, gray eyes, dark complexion, born in Gillespie, Illinois, occupation farmer, married with children, literate.

Kingston enlisted on August 1, 1861 at Bunker Hill, Illinois and was mustered into service at Jefferson Barracks, Missouri on September 6, 1861 as a corporal in Company M, 1st Missouri Cavalry Regiment. On May 22, 1862, Kingston was placed on detached service with Company F, 1st Missouri Cavalry Regiment near Corinth, Mississippi. Company F was the escort for Brigadier General Gordon Granger.

Kingston deserted on February 5, 1863. A letter in his file states:

"Camp Near Nashville, Tenn., February 28, 1863

Col. J. W. Ritter

Comdg. 1st Mo. Cav.,

Sir:

I have the honor to inform you that Paul Kingston a Corpl. of Co. M, 1st Mo. Cav. has deserted from my company, on the 5th of February, 1863 at Tell City, Ind. in defiance of Maj. Genl. Halleck's order attaching him to the same. If he has rejoined his company you will please have him arrested for desertion and theft, he having taken a belt, revolver and holster with him when he left have the honor to be

Your obedient Servant
James Clifford,
Capt. Co. F, 1st Mo. Cav.
Maj Genl's G. Granger's Escort."

Another letter describes Kingston's place of hiding.

"Headquarters 1st Mo. Cavalry
Camp near Fair View, Ark.
June 5, 1863
Provost Marshall Gen. Farrar, St. Louis, Mo.
Sir:

Information has been received at these Head Quarters that said `Kingston' is at Gillespie, Macoupin Co., Ill. You will therefore be pleased to take steps for his apprehension and confinement until a proper court can be assembled.
Your Obdt Servt
F. lieut. Wm Lewis."

Kingston fled from Gillespie, Illinois southward and, on August 29, 1863, shot and killed a local resident of Cape Girardeau, Missouri. He was promptly arrested and imprisoned, awaiting custody of the military. A court martial trial for the crime of murder, charging Kingston with the "murdering of one John R. Charters, a resident of Cape Girardeau, Missouri on the 29th day of 1863 without cause or provocation."

A General Court Martial was convened at Cape Girardeau, Missouri, and on September 22, 1863 tried Corporal Paul Kingston, Company M, 1st Missouri Cavalry Regiment on a charge of murder.

Testimony revealed the following course of events, beginning about 9 P.M. on August 29, 1863 in the city of Cape Girardeau, Missouri. Mrs. Adelaide Harrison, a resident of Cape Girardeau, who witnessed a murder, gave the following account:

About 9 P.M. she was in her room in a house across the street from where John R. Charters was mortally wounded. She heard someone cry, "Guard!" She went to her window and looked out on the street and saw two men scuffling near the street curb. She saw the flash and heard the report of a pistol shot and John Charters, one of the two combatants, staggered backwards toward a house holding his chest and screaming, "Murder!" As Charters tried to open the door and enter the house his assailant fired two more shots and Charters fell without entering the house. A crowd collected and found Charters dead. He was removed to the Pest Hospital (Smallpox hospital). His assailant, a soldier, departed the scene quickly on foot, having been preceded by another soldier on horseback. The soldier walking was Kingston, and the mounted soldier was Private G. R. Sutton, Company M, 1st Missouri Cavalry Regiment, a friend of Kingston. They had been drinking together at a beer saloon and were proceeding through the city streets, Kingston on the sidewalk, Sutton riding horseback in the street. Kingston saw a man standing on the sidewalk and jostled him in trying to pass by. The citizen called him names and they scuffled. Kingston drew his revolver and as they wrestled for it, he fired striking the citizen, who endeavored to back away from Kingston. Kingston then fired twice more at him, and left the scene. Sutton, who had continued riding ahead of the dismounted Kingston, heard the shots and galloped his horse to the Union picket line, where he was arrested. Kingston continued on foot to the picket line, where he was admitted.

A First Lieutenant Fred R. Vincent, who was the Sergeant of the Provost Guard of Cape Girardeau, Missouri at the time of the murder, stated that between 9-10 P.M. on the night of August 29, 1863, he heard the sound of pistol shots. He immediately made his way, on foot, toward the area where the shots were fired, and arriving there found a group of people gathered about a body lying on the ground. The Questioning of a few bystanders revealed that a suspect had fled, on foot, toward the Union picket lines. Vincent set off after the suspect on foot, and as a horseman passed, halted him, commandered his horse, mounted, and continued his pursuit of the suspect. Arriving at the Union Picket post, he inquired of the sentinel if he had seen any man on foot enter recently. He was told there was a man who entered a few minutes earlier who complained of being robbed, and that he was running away from his assailants. Vincent rode in the direction the sentinel pointed out and quickly caught up with the suspect. Asked if he was armed, the suspect replied in the affirmative. Vincent asked to examine his revolver, and the suspect handed it over. Vincent noted that three chambers had been fired and that the weapon was still warm. Vincent arrested the suspect who was identified as Kingston.

Witnesses testified that Charters did not use a weapon and, in fact, was unarmed. That Kingston was "somewhat intoxicated" after drinking beer, to the extent that he staggered as he walked. Kingston was described as sane, altho very quarrelsome.

The accused had no witnesses to offer in his defense, but did present a confession to the court.

Confession of Paul Kingston given to Court
September 25, 1863

"On the 29th day of August I left Camp in the morning about 9-o'clock and went to a saloon near Fort `C', Cape Girardeau, Mo. and while I was there I was gaming for the beer and drank some eight or ten glasses. I had a difficulty with a soldier about a water melon and struck him. I then pulled out a small pocket revolver but did not attempt to shoot him. A man told a Lieutenant who was standing by to take the revolver away from me, but he did not attempt to do it. I went from one saloon to another drinking beer all the while until I had drunk some five or six more glasses. I then went back to camp. After I had gotten back Sutton came to me and asked me to ride out, this was about sundown. We got on our horses and came back to the saloon near Fort `C' and then turned and rode out to the pickets in the dirt road and then turned and came back to the same saloon and there remained about an hour and a half and drank two or three glasses of beer. We then went out and untied our horses and I went to get on mine but slipped and fell and the horse got loose and run in the direction of camp. Then we came on down in town. We came to a cross street where we turned and started back. I was on the side walk and Sutton was on his horse in the street. I overtook a man in front of a house a short distance from the corner, and in going to pass him I staggered against him and knocked him some two or three feet from where he was, he turned his face to me and called me a drunken rascal and I told him I was no rascal and not to call me that name and put my hand down on my revolver by my side. After I stopped I staggered against him again and he put his hand against me and pushed me back and told me to leave. As I put my hand on my revolver he took hold of me and between us we got the revolver out. We then had a scuffle which should have the revolver, he had hold of the barrel and I had the breech and when he jerked it, the hammer was pulled back and the pistol fired. He then let loose of the pistol and I staggered back and he gave back also. He was doing something with his hands and I thought, he was trying to get a weapon and I shot him again. He then hallowed `Guards' twice and then I started towards Camp and got about two or three steps when I fired at him again. I then started in a run towards Camp. I ran until I came to the corner. I crossed the street and walked about fifty yards then ran about one hundred yards, then walked again. I was overtaken by a soldier on horseback and arrested. My revolver taken away and I was put in prison. This is a true confession. In the eyes of the Law I am a murderer but not in heart. I did this deed while intoxicated. I ask your clemancy
Fred Kingston"
witness Lt and Judge Advocate L. E. Irion

The Court deliberated, found Kingston guilty and sentenced him to be hung by the neck until dead. The execution was carried out on November 27, 1863 near Cape Girardeau, Missouri.

A letter pleading for clemency for Kingston from the Commissioned Officers of the 1st Missouri Cavalry Volunteers was presented. It read as follows:
"Pilot Knob, Mo., Nov. 13, 1863
Major:

We the undersigned Commissioned Officers of the 1st Cavalry Mo. Vols. have the honor to request that such portions of the sentence against Paul Kingston Corporal Co. M, 1st Cavalry Mo. Vols. be mitigated as far as the interests and the good of the service will allow. We make the request in consideration of the previous good conduct, the fighting abilities and the faithfulness and efficiency of the prisoner.

He entered the service the 1st day of August 1861 and has given valuable service to the Government since that time, and we therefore urgently recommend him to the merciful consideration of the Major General Commanding this Department.

To: Major O. D. Greene
A. A. G. Dept. of the Mo.
St. Louis, Mo."

Appended thereto were ten signatures of Commissioned Officers of the 1st Missouri Cavalry Volunteers. The plea was not acted upon.

Kingston himself wrote a letter indicating his acceptance of death and making two specific requests.

"Cape Girardeau, Mo., Nov. the 23rd, 1863
Brig. Genl. Fisk,

On the 27th Inst. I am to be exicuted. My wife and children are here with me, who I love dearer than my own life. At the same time by the laws of the land I must be seperated from them in a few days *forever.*

I ask one favor of you before I am exicuted. That is as follows. To be removed from this post. & for you to be present at the time of my exicusion.

Your obt. servt.
Paul Kingston, 1st Cav. Mo. Vols."

There is no record of any action on his requests.

REFERENCES:
Military Personnel Records, RG-#94
Court Martial Proceedings, RG-#153 NN 420

Case #80
Pvt. Philip Raber
NV: Raver
Co. K, W. Virginia Inf Regt
Executed for Desertion
November 27, 1863

DESCRIPTION:

20 years of age, 5 feet 9 inches tall, black eyes, black hair, dark completion, born in Marion County, Virginia, occupation farmer, literacy undetermined.

Raber enlisted on March 31, 1862, in Marion County, Virginia, was mustered into service on April 30, 1862, at Camp Paxton, Guyandotte, Virginia and assigned to Captain Boggess Company, 9th Regiment Virginia Infantry. The designation of this unit was later changed to Company K, 9th West Virginia, Infantry Regiment. Raber had a series of desertions beginning on September 30, 1862 at Point Pleasant, Virginia. On December 16, 1862, he was arrested in the Moorefield/Petersburg area. One account states he was masquerading as a member of Company D, 3rd Virginia Cavalry. He was court martialed during the January/February period of 1863, for desertion and sentenced to one month hard labor and a fine of three mouth's pay ($39.00). On April 10, 1863, he was again reported on the list of deserters leaving his Company at Winchester, and was "returned from desertion on September 5, 1863.

A General Court Martial was convened at Gawley Bridge, West Virginia and on September 8, 1863 tried Private Philip Raber, Company K, 9th West Virginia Infantry

Regiment on a charge of desertion, 2nd time and Breaking Guard.

The testimony recorded was vague and at times confusing. A list of the enlisted men of Company K, 9th West Virginia Infantry Regiment indicates that Philip's father, William Raber and his brother Christopher all enlisted at the same time and place. Both Philip's father and brother were dishonorably discharged and drummed out of camp on November 4, 1863. Philip Raber deserted the 9th West Virginia Infantry Regiment and enlisted in Company D, 3rd Virginia (Union) Cavalry Regiment later designated Company D, 3rd West Virginia Cavalry Regiment. He was Court Martialed in early March 1863 for this desertion and sentenced to six months "Ball and Chain," and to have his head shaved and be "drummed out of service." General Cluseret is said to have commuted his sentence to one month "Ball and Chain," the stoppage of three month's pay and then to be returned to his Company for duty. Raber was said to have been in the custody of the Cavalry Regiment in which he falsely enlisted and deserted, in Winchester, Virginia. He escaped from the Guard House in Winchester on March 3rd, 1863 and Raber's home area neighbors wrote to his original Regiment and Company and reported seeing him at home. Raber was arrested and brought to Fayetteville, Virginia on August 2, 1863. Records show that Raber was at Charleston, West Virginia on August 24, 1863, having been brought there from Wheeling, West Virginia.

During the final Court Martial Raber offered neither witnesses nor statement in his defense. The Court then deliberated, found Raber guilty and sentenced him to be shot to death with musketry between 6 and 7 A.M. on November 27, 1863 at Fayetteville, West Virginia.

An order contained in his file stated, "Headquarters 2nd Brigade, 3rd Division, Dept. of West Virginia, Fayetteville, W. VA, November 27, 1863, 3-1/2 O'clock a.m. Col., I am directed to inform you that the order issued last evening requiring the parade this a.m. to witness the execution of Pvt. Philips Raber, 9th Regt. Va Vols has been revoked the prisoner being respited.

By order of Col. C. B. White "

A final order from "Headquarters 2nd Brigade, 3rd Division, Dept. of West Virginia, Fayetteville, W. VA, November 27, 1863, Col., The sentence in the case of Philip Raber Private 9th Regt. VA Vols. will be executed between the hours of two (2) and three (3) O'Clock this P.M. The troops will be paraded as required in General Orders No. 14 from these Headquarters, of yesterday, at two (2) O'Clock.
By order of Col. C. B. White"

REFERENCES:

Military Personnel Records, RG-#94
Court Martial Proceedings, RG-#153 NN 439
G.O. #14, Department of Virginia, October 15, 1863

Case #81
Private Cyrus H. Hunter
Company G, 3rd Maine Infantry Regiment
Executed for Desertion
December 4, 1863

DESCRIPTION:

19 years of age, 5 feet 10¼ inches tall, brown hair, blue eyes, light complexion, born in Clinton, Maine, occupation farmer, not married.

Hunter enlisted on April 30, 1861 at Waterville, Maine and was mustered into service, in Company G, on June 4, 1861 at Augusta, Maine. While the Regiment was in the Falmouth, Virginia area, Hunter deserted Camp Pitcher on or about January 20, 1863. He was finally arrested at Biddeford, Maine on September 3, 1863 by a Special Agent

James P. Hill. The expense of Hunter's capture was $22.31 which included a $10.00 reward for Agent Hill and transportation charges from Biddeford to Portland, Maine.

A General Court Martial was convened at the Headquarters of the 3rd Brigade, 1st Division, 3rd Army Corps and on November 12, 1863 tried Private Cyrus H. Hunter, Company G, 3rd Maine Infantry Regiment on a charge of desertion.

Hunter applied to the Court for permission to introduce Lieutenant Charles W. Lowe, 3rd Maine Infantry Regiment as his counsel. The application was granted by the Court and Lieutenant Lowe appeared but declined to act. Hunter then withdrew his application.

Testimony revealed that on or about January 21, 1863 near Falmouth, Virginia Hunter did desert his Company and Regiment, which was under marching orders. Hunter abandoned his gun and equipment and was absent until returned to the Regiment under arrest. Several members of his Company reported seeing Hunter amongst a miscellaneous group of convalescents, prisoners and replacements from Alexandria, Virginia, on the railroad near Bristow Station, Virginia about the end of October or first of November of 1863. One of his old comrades asked him where he was arrested and he replied in Biddeford, Maine.

The accused offered no witnesses on his behalf and declined to make a statement in his defense.

The Court deliberated, found the prisoner guilty and sentenced him to be shot to death with musketry.

Major General D. Birney, Commanding 1st Division, 3rd Corps, in approving the findings and sentence of the General Court Martial stated: "In my opinion this is an agravated case and is to be made an example of."

Hunter was executed at Brandy Station, Virginia on December 4, 1863.

REFERENCES:
Military Personnel Records, RG-#94
Court Martial Proceedings, RG-#153 NN 675

Case #82
Pvt. John Kendall
NV: (aka Thomas)
Co. G, 3rd NH Infantry Regt.
Executed for Desertion
December 17, 1863

DESCRIPTION:

21 years of age, 5 feet 7¼ inches tall, brown hair, hazel eyes, dark complexion, born in St. John's, New Brunswick, Canada, occupation sailor, substitute.

Kendall was enlisted as a substitute and mustered into service on October 8, 1863 at West Lebanon, New Hampshire and was forwarded to Morris Island, South Carolina where he was assigned to Company G, 3rd New Hampshire Infantry Regiment.

Kendall deserted the camp of his Regiment at Morris Island, South Carolina on the night of November 28, 1863. When captured on Black Island, he is said to have stated that his last name was Thomas and that he was a deserter from the enemy. Kendall was placed in confinement and tried by court martial for desertion.

A General Court Martial was convened at Morris Island, South Carolina and on December 3, 1863 tried Private John Kendall, Company G, 3rd New Hampshire Infantry Regiment on a charge of desertion.

Kendall sought permission of the court to be allowed Captain M. Topping, 100th New York Volunteers as his counsel, which request was granted.

Testimony was offered to prove that Kendall deserted his company and regiment encamped on Morris Island, South Carolina on November 28, 1863. Kendall attempted to evade capture and punishment by approaching another union force and pretend to be a rebel deserter named Thomas.

Kendall was a substitute, drafted on October the 8th, 1863 and arrived for duty with Company G, 3rd New Hampshire Infantry Regiment on the 17th of November. Eleven days later he deserted.

1st Lieutenant Josiah C. Beal of the 9th Maine Infantry Regiment stated that on Sunday, December 1, 1863, about noon while acting as Officer of the Guard he was in his tent on Black Island, South Carolina preparing to eat his dinner when he was interupted by a Corporal Harmon who came to his tent and reported a deserter, at the Cook's tent, who had come from James Island. The deserter was naked and the Corporal felt something should be done for him. The Lieutenant brought the deserter to his own tent, found some old clothes for him, as he was clad only in a black silk handkerchief about his neck and black boots, and then fed him. The Lieutenant asked the deserter if he came from James Island and he replied in the negative, saying he was from Fort Johnson. He said he swam a creek just before he came in to the Maine Regiment Camp. He nearly drowned as he developed cramps while swimming. He was taken to the Colonel's Headquarters of the 9th Maine Infantry Regiment on Black Island, South Carolina.

The object of the defense was to depict the captured deserter as a rebel, and the object of the prosecution was to show that his most intimate acquaintances in the Company, Company G, 3rd New Hampshire Infantry Regiment, such as his tent mates and one soldier that he knew prior to entering the service and with whom he had voyaged to the West Indies, all identified the deserter as John Kendall which the deserter stubbornly denied.

Kendall had no witnesses to testify in his behalf but offered a written Statement of the Defense.

"United States
vs.
John Kendall"

"May it please the court there are two questions involved in this case, both of which must be decided affirmatively before a conviction can be had. First, did John Kendall enter the service of the United States as a soldier? Second, is the prisoner at the bar that person?

In considering the first question we must look at two things, the evidence, and the quality of it, if it be satisfactory in kind, is it of such quality as the case requires? It need hardly be said that a case like this, involving the life of a fellow man must be complete in the amount of the evidence but that evidence must be of such a quality or character as stamps it the best which the case admits the existence of, or that it is possible to obtain before conviction can be had. There are two kinds of evidence to which we call attention: Viz: primary and secondary. In this case it should have been shown by the descriptive list itself or other official records that John Kendall was ever a soldier; since all the testimony assumes to be based upon it. The law excludes such evidence of facts as open the nature of the thing supposes still better evidence behind in the party's possession of power. [Benet-Mil. Law & C.M. -266]. Though not showing if the Official Records of the enlistment of John Kendall is the absence of a link in the chain which if not fatal to the prosecution, should be looked at very cautiously. The testimony of Lt. Frickey is that he learned from "the Books" and from the "descriptive List" that John was drafted, etc. Why were not "the Books and Descriptive List" presented to this court? Without them how can this court determine that the John Kendall there described is the prisoner at the bar and if there is a doubt: as there most unquestionably is, it arises from the fact that only in a general way, though with remarkable uniformity, the witnesses say he is John Kendall. For the use of this secondary evidence in this case by the prosecution, while the reasons for it are not given deserve attention. The rule of law is plain and the presumptions are in favor of the prisoner. None have described his height or the color of his eyes which in identifying a soldier are of the highest importance. Again it has been held that in order to render a person liable to the charge of desertion it must be shown that he was regularly enlisted (or drafted) or that he had received pay from the Government of the U.S. for Military Service - here is another failure of an important character. If the court find that he was not enlisted and has not received pay, which is not attempted to be shown, the prosecution fails.

The accused has from the first moment that he was found on Black Island coming from the direction of the enemy's lines asserted that his name is Thomas and that he is a deserter from the enemy, his giving himself up as such when first found, his apparent exhaustion and nakedness and the fact that so soon as he reached the picket line, announced himself as a deserter from Fort Johnson, all lead to the belief that is a true statement. It hardly seems probable that a soldier intending to desert would run the hazard of detection by coming into the camp from which he deserted and announce himself as from the enemy.

I will not detain the court by referring to cases where similarity of shape of features, color of hair and complexion, have not infrequently led to mistakes of the gravest character. Probably every member of the court has met such cases, at least so far as similarity is concerned, which will readily occur to them if the court shall think that there is a reasonable doubt as to the identity of the prisoner at the bar it will be it's duty to acquit."

"To this the Judge Advocate replies that it has been the province of the prosecution to assert the facts, upon which the accused bases objection and asks the decision of the court in his favor. He has attempted to show by clear and uncontravertible testimony that the accused is a member of Company G, 3rd New Hampshire Volunteers. The concurrent testimony of the Officer commanding the Company and the non-commissioned officers thereof is that John Kendall is an actual member of his command, that he has been held in the ranks voluntarily and liable to the performance of such duty, with no objection whatsoever or representation to the contrary. It is not possible for the prosecution to present the primary evidence of his enlistment to the court will hold the fact of his enrollment and actual duty with the company as a de facto admission of his previous enlistment all necessary (illegible) has been produced which in the opinion of the Judge Advocate is necessary to set forth that John Kendall was and is actually a member of the Company and Regiment as alleged in the charge. As to the identity of the accused with the John Kendall mentioned in the specifications, the prosecution has presented testimony which unrefuted by the defense, must have it's due rights with the court and is properly such that the Court may adjudge as to it's integrity or discredit."

The court then deliberated, found Kendall guilty and sentenced him to be shot to death by musketry.

The execution took place on Morris Island, South Carolina on December 16, 1863.Emilio in his book, mentions the execution with all details corresponding except that he states the name of the soldier executed was Joseph Lave, 3rd New Hampshire Volunteers.

E. J. Copp's memory of the Kendall case facts, as he related them in his book, do not correspond to the facts as related by witnesses at the Court Martial. Copp states Kendall was mired in marshy ground and unable to free himself until aided by his captors.

REFERENCES:

Military Personnel Records, RG-#94
Court Martial Proceedings, RG-#153 NN 781
"A Brave Black Regiment the 54th Mass," Lewis Emilio, 1894
"Reminiscences of the War of the Rebellion, 1861-65," E.J. Copp, 1911, Nashua, New Hampshire, Telegraph Publishing Company.

Case #83
Private Winslow H. Allen
Co. H, 76th NY Inf. Regt.
Executed for Desertion
December 18, 1863

DESCRIPTION:

No physical description of Allen has been found.

Allen enlisted at East Hamilton, New York on December 4, 1861 and was mustered into service on January 16, 1862 at Albany, New York in Company H, 76th New York Infantry Regiment. He deserted May 18, 1862 from Camp Doubleday near Washington City. He seemingly teamed up with Private W. H. Devoe (case #85) at some point after deserting. They were apprehended, arrested, and confined.

The Court Martial testimony at the trial of Winslow N. Allen disclosed that on May 18, 1862, while the Regiment was stationed at Fort Massachusetts near Washington, D. C., Allen and another member of Company H, obtained one day passes to visit Washington, D. C. Allen did not return to his Company but his companion did. Allen was subsequently placed on the list of deserters, and was neither seen nor heard of until September 27, 1863. On that date, Allen was in a group of 7 or 8 drafted men or substitutes delivered to Company H, 76th New York Infantry Regiment as replacements, which was Allen's original Company from which he had deserted 16 months previously. Allen, although using the assumed name of William Newton, was quickly identified by veteran members of H Company who remembered him as Winslow Allen, the deserter. Allen was arrested and charged with desertion. At his trial, Allen was positively identified by fellow members of the Company who had served with him before his desertion in 1862, thus sealing his fate.

Allen offered no defense, excuse, or explanation or final statement in his behalf. The Court found him guilty and sentenced him to be shot to death with musketry, which sentence was carried out on December 18, 1863 at Kelly's Ford, Virginia.

A Union Soldier commented on their impending death in a letter to his parents. "There is two men to be shot in our division next Friday, one in 57th and one in the 76th N. Y. for desertion. it is hard for the poor fellows. But then they ought to know their penalty is death. But I pity their Parents and sisters it will be hard for them to think of their miserable end. rather would I suffer twice the privation I have went through."

REFERENCES:

Military Personnel Records, RG-#94

Court Martial Proceedings, RG-#153 NN 794

Manuscript Division, Civil War Soldiers letters, Schoff Collection, Clements Library, University of Michigan, Ann Arbor, Michigan, Letter of Hugh Roden.

History of 76th Regiment New York Volunteers, A. P. Smith, Cortland, New York, Truair Smith and Miles Printers, 1867.

Case #84
Pvt. George E. Blowers
Co. A, 2nd, Vermont Inf. Regt.
Executed for Desertion
December 18, 1863

DESCRIPTION:

23 years of age, 5 feet 11 inches tall, brown hair, blue eyes, light complexion, born in Washington, New York, occupation farmer.

George Blowers enlisted on August 14, 1862 at Arlington, Vermont and was mustered into service at Burlington, Vermont on September 15, 1862 in Company A, 2nd Vermont Infantry Regiment. He deserted his Regiment from Camp near Manchester, Maryland on July 1, 1863, and was arrested on October 19, 1863 at Day, New York and delivered, on October 26, 1863, to the Military Post at Brattleboro, Vermont. "He is stated to have resisted the attempt to arrest him, is considered a desperate character who while confined in jail was grossly insulting to people visiting the place." His arrest cost $30.00 in charges for reward and expenses.

George E. Blowers, Company A, 2nd Vermont Infantry Regiment was the subject of a General Court Martial on November 19, 1863 at Headquarters, 2nd Division charged with desertion and Blowers pleaded guilty. Testimony revealed that the Regiment was moving from Manchester, Maryland to Gettysburg, Pennsylvania on July 1, 1863 and Blowers was gone on the morning of July 2, 1863. He was captured at Day, New York, arrested and returned to the military post at Brattleboro, Vermont as a deserter on October 26, 1863. One witness commented that Blowers' wife influenced his desertion and "guessed she is not very patriotic."

Little testimony was introduced by the prosecution in view of Blowers' guilty plea. He offered no defense other than a brief verbal statement. "I had been drinking a good deal. A man that was with me (probably his brother William) induced me to go. I told him we had better not but he persuaded me to go. I am sorry I left now. I have nothing more to say."

The court confirmed Blowers' guilty plea and sentence him to be shot to death with musketry at Brandy Station, Virginia on December 18, 1863.

George Blowers had a brother, *William Blowers*, 25 years of age who enlisted and was mustered into the military service at the same dates and place, and was assigned to the same Company and Regiment.

On September 30, 1862, William Blowers deserted from Alexandria, Virginia. He was arrested in Hadley, New York on October 19, 1863 where he and his brother were confined briefly as noted above. His arrest cost an additional $30.00 as in his brother's case. He is said to have "rejoined" his Regiment on November 29, 1863. Tried by court martial, he was found guilty and sentenced to loss of all pay and allowances that are due or may become due and further will be required to serve an additional period of time equal to the period of his desertion and shall receive a dishonorable discharge from the service.

William was wounded on June 5, 1864 and hospitalized. By September 1864, William was performing light duty at the Divisional Hospital and deserted the second time on September 19, 1864.

William Blowers following his second desertion on September 19, 1864 at Winchester, Virginia leaves no further record of his whereabouts or military disposition. His earlier sentence stated he was to serve two years and eleven months commencing the 15th day of October, 1863.

REFERENCES:
Military Personnel Records, RG-#94
Court Martial Proceedings, RG-#153 NN 794

Case #85
Pvt. William H. Devoe
Co B, 57th New York Inf Regt
Executed for Desertion
December 18, 1863

DESCRIPTION:

44 years of age, 5 feet 8 inches tall, gray hair, blue eyes, light complexion, born in Albany, New York, occupation butcher.

Devoe enlisted on September 15, 1861 and was mustered into service on September 24, 1861 at Utica, New York in Company B, 57th New York Infantry Regiment. Devoe's service record is poor. While he served at the battles of Fair Oaks, Virginia on June 1, 1862 and at "Seven Days Battle" June 25, 1862 to July 2, 1862, he was absent without leave at Antietam, Maryland September 17, 1862; present "before Fredericksburg" December 11, 1862; absent without leave at Fredericksburg Heights, Virginia December 1862; left the field at Chancellorsville, Virginia May 3, 1863; was court martialed for misconduct at the same place. In June 1863, he was reported as "straggled"; missing in action at Gettysburg, Pennsylvania July 2, 1863; arrested August 23, 1863 at Albany, New York for which a $20.00 reward was paid. He was sent as a deserter/prisoner to Fort Columbus, New York City Harbor September 5, 1863 and thence to Washington, D.C. He was delivered to his Regiment under heavy security on September 29, 1863 and charges of desertion were filed on September 30, 1863. He was court martialed and convicted, sentenced to be executed by a firing squad December 18, 1863 at Stevensburg, Virginia. He was also fined the sum of $10.00 per month to be deducted from his pay beginning November 1, 1863. (Also see Case #83, Winslow H. Allen.)

REFERENCES:
Military Personnel Records, RG-#94
Court Martial Proceedings, RG-#153 LL 883
Manuscript Division, Civil War soldiers' letters, Schoff Collection, Clements Library, University of Michigan, Ann Arbor, Michigan letter of Hugh Roden.

Case #86
Pvt. John McMann
Co.B, 11th Infantry Regt US Army Reg
Executed for Desertion
December 18, 1863

DESCRIPTION:
23 years of age, 5 feet 9 inches tall, light hair, hazel eyes, dark complexion, born in Scioto County, Ohio, occupation laborer, illiterate.

McMann enlisted at Pittsburgh, Pennsylvania for a three year period rather than the standard five year period of service on May 27, 1862 for service in Company B, 11th Infantry Regiment US Army regulars. McMann deserted his regiment which had been assigned to service with the Army of the Potomac on May 14, 1863 and was apprehended on September 24, 1863.

A General Court Martial was convened at the headquarters of the 2nd Division, 5th Army Corps in Camp near Culpeper, Virginia and on November 5, 1863 tried Private John McMann, Company B, 11th U. S. Infantry (regulars) on a charge of desertion.

The accused pleaded guilty to the charge and specification. The crime was described as taking place near Potomac Creek where his regiment was stationed. He acquired a pass for "a few hours" on May 11, 1863 and failed to return.

On September 24, 1863 he was brought to Company B, 1st Battalion, 11th U. S. Infantry Regiment (regulars) as a substitute for a conscript of the District of Columbia. This of course was the Company and Regiment from which he deserted!

The prosecution closed it's case and the accused having no witnesses to testify on his behalf offered the following statement.

Prisoners Statement

"I got a pass to go to Aquia Creek. I was under the influence of liquor or I would never have gone away. If I had not have been drugged, I never should have gone as a substitute if I had known what I was about. I was afraid to come back to any regiment. I was in New York and Philadelphia from the time I left Aquia Creek to the time that I found myself as a substitute in the City of Washington. I have nothing more to say and leave myself at the mercy of the court."

The Court deliberated, confirmed the plea of guilty of the accused and sentenced him to be shot to death with musketry.

The execution took place on December 18, 1863 at Benton's Station, Virginia.

As an informational data item, the sheet upon which McMann's military record appears contains the names of 41 men of which 19 are recorded as having deserted!

REFERENCES:
Military Personnel Records, RG-#94
Court Martial Proceedings, RG-#153 NN 794

Case #87
Pvt. John Tague
Co. A, 5th VT Infantry Regt.
Executed for Desertion
December 18, 1863

DESCRIPTION:

22 years of age, 5 feet 1½ inches tall, dark hair, blue eyes, dark complexion, born in Shelborn, Vermont, occupation farmer.

Tague enlisted August 29, 1861 at St. Albans, Vermont and was mustered into service on September 16, 1861 at St. Albans, Vermont in Company A, 5th Vermont Infantry Regiment. Tague's service record is confusing as to details and dates from this point on. One chronology is as follows:

Tague deserted his Regiment while on the march somewhere near Fredericksburg, Maryland on or about June 28, 1862. He was apprehended on October 28, 1862, tried and $10.00 per month of his pay was stopped (withheld) and returned to duty. On December 11, 1862 he again deserted from the area near Belle Plaine, Virginia. He was apprehended on September 21, 1863 in Frederick County, Maryland and transferred to his headquarters area near Brandy Station, Virginia on September 24, 1863. The cost of capture for expenses and the reward was $11.00.

A General Court Martial was convened at headquarters of the 2nd Division, 6th Army Corps and on November 19, 1863 tried Private John Tague, Company A, 5th Vermont Infantry Regiment on a charge of desertion, to which the accused pleaded guilty.

Testimony was presented to the court which showed that Tague deserted the military service on December 11, 1862 while with his regiment marching to meet the enemy from White Oak Church to Fredericksburg, Virginia. Tague is said to have fallen out of the marching column to warm himself at a fire without permission. It was emphasized that the average soldier was fully aware that the regiment was marching to engage the enemy in battle and further that the sound of cannonading was heard in the direction to which they were marching. Tague was dressed in a soldiers uniform when he deserted and in citizen's clothing when he was returned under arrest in mid-November, 1863.

The accused offered neither witnesses nor statement in his own defense. He did state, "I am 25 years old; am a laborer; have no family; have relatives at Rouse Point, New York and at Burlington and Fairfield, Vermont."

The Court deliberated, confirmed the plea of the prisoner and sentenced him to be shot to death with musketry.

The execution took place in the field on December 18, 1863.

REFERENCES:
Military Personnel Records, RG-#94
Court Martial Proceedings, RG-#153 NN 794

Case #88
Pvt. Charles Turner
Co. C, 114th NY Infantry Regt.
Executed for Desertion
December 28, 1863

DESCRIPTION:

24 years of age, 5 feet 11 inches tall, brown hair, blue eyes, light complexion, born in Courtland, New York, occupation laborer, married.

Turner enlisted at Norwich, New York on August 5, 1862 and was mustered into service on August 7, 1862 in Company C, 114th New York Infantry Regiment. On June 1, 1863, Turner deserted his Regiment while engaged against the enemy at Port Hudson,

Louisiana. He was arrested on July 26, 1863 at Baton Rouge, Louisiana.

A General Court Martial was convened at Berwick (Benwick?) City, Louisiana and on September 19, 1863 tried Private Charles Turner, Company C, 114th New York Infantry Regiment on charges of misbehavior before the enemy, disobedience to orders, conduct to the prejudice of good order, military discipline and desertion.

Testimony by witnesses stated that the accused, while on the march with his Regiment on April 13, 1863 near Fort Bisland, Louisiana, did ask permission to drop out of the ranks for a few moments, promising to shortly return to his place in the ranks. Permission was granted but Turner was not seen again until the morning of the 15th of April, 1863 when he was arrested and confined at Brashear. On or about April 31, 1863 near Brashear, Louisiana, Turner was found by his superior officer outside the regimental camp and was ordered to return. He replied, "I'll be damned if I'll go" and called the Lieutenant a "Son of a Bitch." He was, however, taken along by force. On or about June 1, 1863, the Regiment, including Turner, arrived at Port Hudson, Louisiana and marched to the front to receive ammunition. Turner was again absent. After a search, Turner was found and ordered to take his issue of ammunition and not to leave his Company again. When the Company moved out to their attack positions, Turner was gone and was not seen again until about mid-July, 1863. He was arrested garbed in citizens clothes in Baton Rouge, Louisiana and returned to his Regiment where he had been constantly under guard since.

Turner called one *defense witness* and asked him:

Q: "How long have you known the accused?"

A: "3 or 4 years."

Q: "What is his character?"

A: "Not good."

The prisoner offered a statement to the court.

Statement of the Accused

"Accused states that he was sick etc. leaving Brashear City, and on the Boat on the way to Port Hudson and marched from Springfield Landing to Port Hudson. He fell out to lay down being unwell. When he got well and went on he could not find his Regiment. He asked a man with a mule and cart. Man asked him if he didn't want to go to Baton Rouge. Accused asked if it would be all right, man said he did not know, he was going, accused went with him, On arriving at the guard at Brashear Ridge, Guard stopped him and arrested him and sent him to the Guard House for 15 days. After 15 days was up, he went to Provost Marshall for a Pass to go to Port Hudson, pass was refused and accused sent to Convalescent Camp where he remained until arrested."

The Court deliberated, found Turner guilty and sentenced him to be shot to death with musketry.

Turner was pronounced dead by Surgeon Ferguson of the 165th New York Volunteers and his burial took place on December 28, 1863 at Cypress Grove Cemetery, New Orleans, Louisiana.

REFERENCES:

Military Personnel Records, RG-#94

Court Martial Proceedings, RG-#153 NN 835

1864
"The Peak Year"

Bounty Jumpers Proliferate
Cases #89-#183
(95 Executions)

Case #89
Private James Murphy
AKA: Joseph Strobel
Co. I, 55th PA Inf. Regt.
Executed for Desertion
January 6, 1865

DESCRIPTION:

22 years of age, 5 feet 1 inch tall, brown hair, hazel eyes, light complexion, born in New York state, occupation locksmith, substitute, literacy undetermined.

Murphy was drafted and mustered into service at Reading, Pennsylvania on October 15, 1863, and was assigned to Company I, 55th Pennsylvania Infantry Regiment. His regiment was stationed in the Beaufort, South Carolina area. Murphy deserted from the guard quarters of the Rifle Pit Picket, near Beaufort, Port Royal Island, South Carolina on the night of November 27, 1863. He was arrested on November 30, 1863 on St. Helena Island, South Carolina and confined.

A General Court Martial was convened at Beaufort, South Carolina, and on December 10, 1863 tried Private James Murphy, Company I, 55th Pennsylvania Infantry Regiment on a charge of desertion.

Murphy asked permission of the court to introduce Lieutenant M. McMartin, 115th New York Infantry Regiment as his counsel, which was granted.

The charge and specifications were objected to in writing by the accused as follows:

"The accused objects to the several charges and specifications on the ground that it is not alledged that the accused is an enlisted man or that he is in any way subject to the military jurisdiction of the United States."

The courtroom was cleared and the court deliberated. The decision was that the objection was over-ruled.

Testimony was begun but was interrupted by another objection in writing by the accused.

"The 20th Article of War provides that all Soldiers who have received pay or have been duly enlisted into the Service of the United States shall be punished and so forth. The accused therefor objects to any evidence tending to establish the fact that he is an enlisted man on the ground that such fact is not alleged in the charges and specifications and secondly, on the ground that such fact if proven can only be proven by the enlistment papers or some record evidence."

The courtroom was cleared and the court deliberated. The court announced to the accused that his objections to the witness testimony was over-ruled, "and the enlistment papers of the accused will be produced at a future period."

Testimony was offered showing Murphy to be a member of I Company and performing duty therewith. He answered roll calls up until the evening of November 27, 1863. When he was on picket duty about 8 PM he walked out of the picket quarters to get water, and never returned voluntarily. He was searched for, unsuccessfully. He was in full uniform with accouterments, but without his gun when he deserted.

The accused was identified as being listed on the Company Muster Roll as James Murphy, however some men in the company knew him as Joseph Strobel. He was generally believed to be of German origin as he spoke German.

A colored man, from the area testified that he was setting "Coon traps" on the river shore at St. Helena Village when he noted two men approaching. He was not visible from their vision but he could see them, and as they approached quite close, he could hear their conversation. One man said to the other, "What will become of us two on this point?" The accused was heard to reply "If we could get a boat we could go over and not stay here." The first man said "We have got to hunt for one till we find one." The accused had no rifle, the other man had one. The colored man ran home and told his male family members that "Rebels was trying to get across the creek." The boys ran down to the two men and caught and disarmed them. The accused was found to be carrying a revolver. Both men were fully clothed in Union Army Military clothing. When interrogated by their captors as to the reason for their presence and where they had come from, they replied they were from Beaufort, South Carolina and that they had come over to go to the Main (mainland). The captors told the accused and his companion that they were taking him to the village where Union Cavalry was, as they suspected the two prisoners were rebels in Union uniforms. The accused replied "I am not a rebel, but I want to get on the Main (mainland) to walk to New York." The chief captor asked the accused if he was a "run-away" (deserter) and the reply was "Yes he was a "run-away" and wanted to get back to the North." He further stated that "he gave a black man five dollars to put him on the Main and the black man put him down there and told him that was the Main." A Lieutenant and some men from the Cavalry Unit in the village approached and took charge of the prisoners.

A witness testified that Murphy stated he was a skidaddler, and that his name is not James Murphy but Joseph Strobel, and had belonged to a New York Regiment as a Sergeant and was caught after skidaddling brought back and reduced in rank to private.

The accused at this point presented another objection in writing. "The accused objects to any evidence that he ever deserted from any other regiment as it is not legitimate evidence to prove the commission of the offence charged."

The courtroom was cleared and the court deliberated, then announced that the objection raised by the accused was sustained.Testimony continued by a witness who stated that the accused was as far as he knew in a party of conscripts in his charge, brought to the 55th Pennsylvania Regiment.

The accused objected in writing to the testimony. "The accused objects to the evidence offered by the last interrogation on the grounds that the evidence does not prove or tend to prove that he was duly drafted or enlisted in the service of the United States."

The courtroom was cleared, the court deliberated and then announced that the objection was over-ruled.

The witness continued to testify that he was provided with muster rolls (lists of names etc. of each man in the draft group being taken from Philadelphia to the 55th Pennsylvania Regiment) and that the muster rolls were presented to him personally by Brigadier General Hatch.

The accused again objected to the testimony in writing.

"The accused objects to what was said by General Hatch on the grounds that it is hearsay evidence."

The courtroom was again cleared and the court deliberated, then announced that the objection of the accused was over-ruled.

The muster roll and descriptive lists were turned over to the court as evidence (marked #B).

The accused objected in writing as follows:

"The accused objects to the paper marked B as evidence in this case upon the following grounds:

1st On the ground that the paper offered is not properly proven or authenticated.

2nd There is no law authorizing a Brigadier General Commanding a rendezvous to certify to such a roll nor is there any law making such certificate evidence in any court.

3rd The facts set forth in the certificate could not have been officially known to the person making the certificate.

4th The enrolling board consisting of the Provost Marshal, the Enrolling Office, and the Surgeon appointed for that purpose, are the only persons competent to give such certificate.

5th The signatures to the paper are not proven."

The courtroom was again cleared and the court deliberated. The court then announced that the foregoing objections are over-ruled by the court.

Testimony was given that another man was missing at roll call, in addition to the accused. He was identified as Joseph Dagenfelt of Company D, 55th Pennsylvania

Infantry Regiment and he was seen to have personal conversations with the accused. The presumption was that Dagenfelt was the man who was with Murphy in his desertion attempt.

The accused had no witnesses to offer in his behalf but did present a written address to the Court (read by his counsel).

"On General Court Martial
In the matter of the charge
against James Murphy of Desertion

The accused is charged with the crime of deserting the Service of the United States on the 27th of Nov. last, at Beaufort, South Carolina. If the accused is convicted at all it must be under and by virtue of the 20th Article of War. That Article provided that, all Officers and Soldiers who have received pay or have been *duly* enlisted in the Service of the United States and shall be convicted of having deserted the same, shall suffer death or such other punishment as by sentence of a Court Martial shall be inflicted: It will be perceived that this Article refers to two classes of persons "Namely Officers and Soldiers who have received pay or have been duly enlisted in the Service. And the Specification should have been in the language of the Statute itself." that the accused was duly enlisted in the service of the United States and that being so enlisted, he did desert the same. The allegation that he was an enlisted man or that he received pay is just as necessary to be stated as that he deserted because it is one of the facts which go to constitute the offense. Benet in his work on Court's Martial says all the ingredients of the offense, the facts and the circumstances constituting it, must be set forth with certainty and precision. And he refers for his authority to Archbolds, "Criminal Pleading." In cases of (illegible) and indictments in Civil Courts, Wharton in his treaties on American Criminal Law says that the facts should be set forth in the indictment with such certainty that the offense may judicially appear to the court and the omission of any fact or circumstance, necessary to constitute the offense, will be fatal. This is unquestionably the law in the trial of offenders in civil courts and it will be found that their charges before a court martial, and their sufficiency are determined and ascertained by the same rules as that of an indictment in a Civil Court. No valid judgement could be pronounced upon an indictment, which failed to state the substantive facts constituting an offense. Once the objection might be taken at any stage of the trial or even after verdict.

But supposing that the specifications were sufficient and that the mere description of the accused as a Private belonging to some Company and Regiment were equivalent to a distinct and positive overment that the accused had been duly enlisted in the service of the United States. How stands the case then? It is necessary to prove all the material overments set forth in the specifications. Or in other words it is necessary in order to convict the accused of the offense charged in the specification to prove that he was duly enlisted in the Service of the United States or that he received pay and that he deserted the same or left it without permission. And this must be shown by legal competent proof. And the language of the statute is guarded. The accused must not only be shown to have been enlisted but he must be shown to have been duly enlisted. The object of the statute was evidently to guard the accused against fraudulent enlistments. And there is no hardship in this. That original enlistment papers are made one is to be retained by the officer commanding the company, one to be on file at the Adjutant General's office at Washington and one at the Adjutant General's office of the State in which the enlistment is made and the procurement of either of these papers and production in court would be proper and competent to prove, the regularity and validity of the enlistment. Because in that case you would have the obligation of the accused signed by himself and his voluntary affiant in Court showing the regularity or irregularity of the enlistment.

But if only (illegible) that the accused was not enlisted within the meaning of the 20th Article of War but that he was drafted under the Conscription Bill or that he is a substitute for some person who was drafted. But what evidence is there before this court that the accused was drafted under the Conscription Act? It is respectfully submitted that there is no evidence whatsoever. The paper purporting to be a Muster Roll and descriptive list was not proven. There is no evidence to show by whom it was made or that the certificate attached to it was ever signed by any officer whatsoever.

But supposing that it had been proved that this certificate attached to this paper was signed by a Brigadier General Commanding a rendezvous by what authority is it claimed that his certificate is evidence of any fact whatever. Unless there is some Act of Congress making his certificate evidence it is not evidence in any Court whatsoever. The paper is no record, and of itself it imports no verity. Would it not be a strange act for congress to pass that a Brigadier General commanding a rendezvous should be authorized to give a certificate stating who were and who were not duly drafted when he could not be supposed to be conversant with the facts as to which he certified. The only certificate authorized by the Conscription Bill which has come under my observation is the certificate of the Enrolling Board discharging those who have shown them to be exempt. And I believe there is a general Act of Congress providing that where an official Certificate is authorized by law to be made that such certificate when properly attested may be read in evidence in any court. But I cannot conceive that a Brigadier General Commanding a Rendezvous is authorized by law to certify to facts which can be known only to the enrolling board.

It may be said that the Conscription Bill is defective in this respect but if it is that defect can not be removed by a Court Martial. Benet says that "The rules of evidence that obtain in the criminal courts of the country must be the guides for courts martial (see page 224). And it is most respectfully submitted that unless there is some statute which makes the certificate of a Brigadier General Commanding a Rendezvous evidence of the regularity of the enrollment and conscription, the paper purporting to state that the accused was duly drafted is of no more value as evidence in the case than so much waste paper. These views have been submitted hastily and without that opportunity for examination and review which the importance of the case seems to demand. The liberty and even the life of the accused may depend upon the opinions which you may severally entertain of the correctness of these views. And while I feel I have discharged my duty very imperfectly, yet I doubt not you will give the whole case your earnest and candid consideration, and that you will examine to some extent at least the views herein expressed. It would be idle to deny that the accused deserted and left the island but it will also be borne in mind that the evidence shows that he did not intend to join the enemy but to return again to his northern home. And if after mature deliberation the court shall be of the opinion that the legal defences set up were insufficient then the accused can only point to his youth, his inexperience and the weakness of our common nature in exteneration of his guilt."

The Court then deliberated, found the accused guilty and sentenced him to be shot to death with musketry. The execution took place at Beaufort, South Carolina on January 6, 1864.

REFERENCES:

Military Personnel Records, RG-#94
Court Martial Proceedings, RG-#153 NN 898

Case #90
Pvt. John Coffield
NV: Cofield - Canfield
Co. K, 1st NM Vol Cav Regt
Executed for Murder
January 19, 1864

DESCRIPTION:

25 years of age, 5 feet 6-1/2 inches tall (HV: 5 feet 5½ inches), hazel eyes, sandy hair (CV: brown), complexion florid, born Durham, England, occupation soldier, illiterate,

paid one month's pay in advance and $25.00 (1/4 of bounty due), enlisted in Company K, 1st New Mexico Volunteer Cavalry Regiment on July 1, 1862 at Fort Marcy, New Mexico. He served on detached service at Sante Fe, New Mexico, at Fort Stanton, New Mexico, and in the Navajo Campaign. Arrested and in confinement at Fort Canby, New Mexico awaiting trial, apparently for murder. A report by a Captain Carey, 13th Infantry dated October 8, 1863 from Fort Canby, New Mexico mentions the capture of Pvt. Coffield and a civilian, Luciano Valencia who had escaped from the post. He was reported to have been received at Fort Wingate, New Mexico in late September 1863, and confined until October 10, 1863.

On January 18, 1863 the Post Commander of Fort Canby, New Mexico reported the execution of Pvt. Coffield, Company K, 1st New Mexico Volunteer Cavalry Regiment at 1:30 p.m., that day.

Epilouge:

A letter in Coffield's file states:

> "In confinement at this post there is one Valencia, a citizen who was apprehended on the ____ day of ________ 1863 near this post, in company with Pvt. John Caufield (sic) Compy K, 1st Cavy NM Vols: I would respectfully enquire if there are any charges against this man? and if there is, what is the nature of said charges? and what are the orders in relation to him? from the records at this post I can find nothing against him and I dislike to hold a man in *durance vile* without some reason for doing so. any information in relation to this man will much oblige."

There is no record in the file of the disposition of Valencia's case.

No court martial record of this case has been found.

REFERENCES:

Military Personnel Records, RG-#94

"Forts of the West," Robert W. Frazer, 1988. University of Oklahoma Press, Norman, Oklahoma.

Case #91

Pvt. John Marcum

NV: Sgt, Cpl

Co. F, 5th West Virginia Vol Inf Regt

Executed for Murder

January 19, 1864

DESCRIPTION:

27 years of age, no further description available.

John Marcum had two brothers, one entering service on the same day and the other on October 1, 1861. All served in the same Company. Brother James was discharged at Washington, D.C. on November 30, 1862 for physical disability. Brother Randolph continued in service, re-enlisting as a Veteran Volunteer in February 1864. He was transferred to Company G, 1st West Virginia Veteran Infantry Regiment when the 5th and 9th Regiments were consolidated on November 9, 1864.

John Marcum enlisted and was mustered into service as a Corporal on September 2, 1861 at Camp Pierpont, Virginia in Captain Kirk's Company, 5th Regiment Virginia Foot Volunteers. The designation was changed to Company F, 5th Regiment West Virginia Infantry. He later was promoted to the rank of Sergeant.

Another version of his record states he enlisted on August 10, 1861 at Camp Anthony, Virginia. After nearly two years of service, Marcum shot Private Andrew J. Farley, same

Company and Regiment at or near Gauley Bridge, West Virginia.

A General Court Martial was convened at Charleston, West Virginia and on October 7, 1863 tried Sergeant John Marcum, Company F, 5th West Virginia Infantry Regiment on a charge of murder.

Testimony offered described the events as they occurred. It seems that the accused and a Private Andrew J. Farley also a member of Company F, 5th West Virginia Infantry Regiment while stationed near Gauley Bridge, West Virginia had entered a business proposition as partners in the purchase and sale of a barrel of cider. Farley had apparently collected the money for the sale of the cider and had "neglected" to give the accused his share.

A soldier witness stated that prior to the shooting, while on guard duty with the accused, Farley had passed their post with a pass. The accused halted Farley and broached the matter of his share of the proceeds from the sale of the cider. Farley said little in way of explanation and continued out of the camp. The accused remarked as he viewed the departing Farley that, "if he did not pay it, God damn him, he would take it out of his hide." His soldier companion somewhat later remarked that "Farley was a pretty stout fellow and may be you would not get much out of his hide" The accused, while they were in their quarters, replied, as he pointed to his revolver lying on his cot, that "he kept it for such damned rascals as Farley."

Witnesses generally regarded Farley as one of the strongest men in the company, far stronger than the accused.

On the morning of September 22, 1863 about 7:30 - 8 AM the accused rode up to Farley's quarters, dismounted, and called for Farley to come out as he wanted a settlement made concerning the division of money for the sale of the barrel of cider. Farley came out and proffered a one dollar bill to the accused as his share of the profits. The accused refused to accept it claiming at least two dollars was due him. They continued quarreling and then agreed to fight about the matter. Farley pulled off his blouse and the accused entered a tent and came out with his blouse off and his revolver in his hand which he held behind him to conceal it. Farley inquired, "What are you going to do with the revolver?" The accused said, "What revolver?" "The revolver you have behind you!" "You need not think you can scare me with a revolver. I cannot be suckered by you or any other man." The accused asked, "Farley, do you want to die?" Farley said he did not want to die, "You may shoot me but I am nothing but a man if you do." The accused told Farley to go away and leave him and Farley replied that he was not going away as he was not afraid of him nor was he going to be run by any damned man.

They continued quarrelling Farley being extremely profane and abusive to the accused and Lieutenant Eba was summoned, came and told them both to stop. He particularly told Farley to shut up and leave then turned to the accused and tried to convince him to put up his revolver. the accused did lower the hammer on the revolver and dropped the arm holding the revolver to his side, the gun muzzle pointing down. Farley then took a step or two toward the accused, who then raised the revolver cocked it and leveled it at Farley. He shouted to Lieutenant Eba either, "Stand aside Lieutenant or take care Lieutenant" and fired, the Lieutenant having jumped back out of the line of fire. Farley was struck in the abdomen and immediately bent over grasping the lower trunk area of his body. The accused maneuvered closer to him and pointed the revolver at Farley's back and pulled the trigger again. This time only the cap exploded and the ball was not discharged. Farley then fell to the ground and the accused ran away. He was seized by a group of soldiers but broke loose and was captured by Sergeant Johnson of the Regiment and taken to the Guard House. The accused was believed to be intoxicated at the time he shot Farley.

Farley was removed from the Company street and his wound and death was described at the trial by Assistant Surgeon, D. Mayer, 5th West Virginia Infantry Regiment as a wound of the abdomen which "he probed but failed to locate the ball or any fragment thereof. The wound was dressed and about six hours after he was wounded, anything that was administered to him would pass out through the wound. Mortification set in the eve after he was wounded. I did no more for him, knowing he would die." He died the next day. (about 8:30

PM) He was also shot, by the same ball, in the middle finger of the right hand.

The accused seems to have made a statement in his defense but it is almost entirely illegible and can only be minimally deciphered. What is barely visible deals with the details of the business entered into by the accused and Farley in the purchase and sale of a barrel of Cider. One statement is legible and pertinent. "I knew he was a stronger man than I and if he got hold of me would be very apt to hurt me."

The Court then deliberated, found the prisoner guilty and sentenced him to be shot to death with musketry. The execution took place on January 19, 1864 near Charleston, West Virginia.

REFERENCES:
Military Personnel Records, RG-#94
Court Martial Proceedings, RG-#153 NN 861

Case #92
Pvt. William E. Ormsby
Co. E, 2nd Mass. Cavalry Regt.
Executed for Desertion
February 7, 1864

DESCRIPTION:

23 years of age, 5 feet 3½ inches tall, brown hair, blue eyes, fair complexion, born in New York State, occupation expressman.

Ormsby had a previous enlistment with an honorable discharge from the 3rd Regiment of U.S. Artillery (regular Army) on November 7, 1862. While in San Francisco, California he subsequently enlisted in Company E, 2nd Massachusetts Cavalry Regiment on February 15, 1863. He and other enlistees were forwarded from California to Readville, Massachusetts where on April 26, 1863 they were mustered into service, in Ormsby's case in Company E, 2nd Massachusetts Cavalry Regiment. A history of the 2nd Regiment Massachusetts Volunteer Cavalry states that recruiting for the regiment was carried on in California, Company A being the first recruited and sent to Boston, Massachusetts for muster into service. Subsequently Companies E, F, L, and M were recruited in California and sent to Boston. This latter group was termed the "California Battalion." The remaining Companies of this Regiment were recruited in Boston and eastern Massachusetts. Ormsby was with his Company near Vienna, Virginia when he deserted on January 24, 1864. On February 6, 1864 a telegram was sent to Colonel Taylor, chief of staff, from Fairfax, Virginia by R. O. Tyler Brigadier General Commanding Division. "I have the honor to report all quiet. The scouting party sent out yesterday returned this afternoon from Aldie and Middleburg (Virginia). Their rear guard was attacked yesterday noon by eight (8) of Mosby's men. They were dispersed and the leader proved to be William E. Ormsby who deserted from 2nd Mass. Cavalry on the night of January 24th was captured and is now being tried by *Drum Head Court Martial*. Two men of the 2nd Mass. Cavalry and three (3) rebels were wounded. Five (5) citizens were arrested under suspicious circumstances. No evidence of any force being in the vicinity."

A Drumhead Court Martial was convened at Vienna, Virginia on February 6, 1864 and tried Private William E. Ormsby, Company E, 2nd Massachusetts Cavalry Regiment on a charge of desertion to the enemy.

The accused asked for the assistance of counsel which was granted.

Testimony was offered by witnesses which stated that on Sunday January 24, 1864 Ormsby was on mounted picket duty near Lewinsville, Virginia during the period which began at 8 PM of January 24th and ended about 1 PM on the 25th of January, 1864. He was not seen thereafter until February 5, 1864 near Aldie, Virginia. When Ormsby disappeared he took his arms, accouterments and two horses with him.

Ormsby and three other men were enlisted in San Francisco in the Massachusetts

Regiment and were sent to Readville, Massachusetts where they were mustered into service. At the time of Ormsby's enlistment it seemed that he was a few months (at most) under the enlistment age of 21 years. By the time the men in California, Ormsby being one, arrived in Massachusetts for mustering into the Regiment he had reached his 21st birthday, thus obviating the age problem.

About noon on February 5, 1864 near Aldie, Virginia the rear guard of a patrol of the 2nd Massachusetts Cavalry was attacked by nine of Mosby's guerillas. The rear guard of the Massachusetts Cavalry hastily retreated drawing the rebels into an ambush formed of the bulk of their patrol strength. Ormsby was reported to have been identified by several members of the rear guard as one of the leading assailants and he fired at them. As the charging rebels entered the trap and were greeted with a volley of shots, Ormsby swerved his horse and rode briefly cross country up to a creek which he attempted to make his horse jump over. The horse however landed in the creek and Ormsby was either thrown off or dismounted. In any case he scrambled up the bank of the shallow creek and halted upon command of a pursuing Massachusetts Cavalry Sergeant. Ormsby was brought back to the camp of his old regiment under arrest. When captured Ormsby was wearing a grey jacket with brass buttons and a light colored hat. He wore a pistol belt and by some witnesses carried 2 revolvers, others noted only one.

Ormsby presented no witnesses on his behalf but did offer the Court a statement.

"Statement of William E. Ormsby, Company E, 2nd Mass. Cavalry"

"I had no idea of leaving this place to join any rebel command at all. I deserted from here to go home and see my parents. My mother was in Boston the last time I heard from her and she wished me to get a furlough and come home to see her. They expected her in New York. I took the horses away from here. I were going to sell them to get money to go home on. When I got out at Aldie there were three of Mosby's men met me and they took my horses and arms from me. I were taken from there up above Middleburg (VA) and left with a widow lady. And yesterday morning they come to where I was and a young fellow wished me to go down with him to his house. He lives below Aldie and I was acquainted down there with some ladies. I was going down to see them and before I got to Aldie I met another man named Davis and he wanted me to go over between the two Pikes with him and get some liquor, and I went over with him and I got drunk and we followed down between the Pikes to very near where they come together at Aldie. Just before we come to Aldie we met a wagon and one of the men rode up to it and asked them if they saw any Yankees and I don't recollect the answer he gave him. And just as we passed the wagon I heard somebody coming up behind and I saw five more men. I knew two of them, they were brothers and their names were Underwood and one of them asked a nigger if he had seen any Yankees around and he said he had seen nine and Davis rode up to my side then and he pulled out his revolver and says he "there's the damn Yankees!" and fired. I drew my revolver then and cocked it and it went off. Then I turned in my saddle and fired off up the hill. I was so drunk that I couldn't see nothing at all and I turned down and tried to jump a creek but my horse couldn't and I could scarcely stand up, I was so intoxicated. When we were over at the house where we got the liquor, one of the boys asked me to come down to Aldie with him. I told him I wouldn't without arms. He told me to come over to Middleburg with him and he'd get me some. I went and he gave me a horse and two revolvers. I saw Mosby twice and he promised to give me a pass Monday to go into Texas or he'd set me across the river at Point of Rocks. I know I done wrong and I'm sorry for it and I think I was always counted a sober man when I was here and always done my duty very well until I got into a scrape about a horse-trade down here. That's what caused me to desert more than anything because I had my pay taken away from me."

The Court deliberated, found the accused guilty and sentenced him to be shot to death. The sentence was approved and Ormsby was shot to death on February 7, 1864 at the Cavalry camp near Vienna, Virginia.

A telegram dated February 7, 1864, Fairfax CG1-VA. to Colonel Taylor from R. O. Tyler, Brigadier General Commander, stated: "I have the honor to report all quiet. The deserter from the 2nd Massachusetts Cavalry captured in arms against the United States was convicted by *Drum Head Court Martial* and shot at twelve (12) O'Clock this noon."

REFERENCES:
Military Personnel Records, RG-#94
Court Martial Proceedings, RG-#153 CMSR
"Massachusetts's Soldiers, Sailors and Marines in the Civil War," 2nd Regiment Massachusetts Volunteer Cavalry.

Case #93
Private James Thompson
NV: Thomson
Co. K, 97th PA Inf. Regt.
Executed for Desertion
February 7, 1864

DESCRIPTION:
28 years of age, 5 feet 6 inches tall, hair dark, eyes blue, complexion light, born in Ireland, occupation sailor, literacy not determined.

Thompson enlisted and was mustered into service on September 23, 1863 at Pottsville, Pennsylvania. He was assigned to Company K, 97th Pennsylvania Infantry Regiment arriving at the regiment stationed in the Fernandina, Florida area on November 5, 1863. He deserted on February 14 and was recaptured on February 15, 1864.

A General Court Martial was convened at Fernandina, Florida and on January 18, 1864 tried Private James Thompson, Company K, 97th Pennsylvania Infantry Regiment on a charge of desertion.

The accused applied for permission to introduce James M. Latta, Esquire, as his counsel, which was granted.

The accused, Thompson was one of four men who deserted together. Thompson had been accidentally shot by one of his companions during the attempted desertion, was hospitalized and thus the last to be tried.

All the testimony presented in this case and in the cases of James WIlson (case #94), and Peter Goodrich (case #98) is virtually identical. To spare redundancy, the reader is referred to the above listed cases.

While the accused filed a lengthy statement as did the Judge Advocate, both are citing the same points as were given in the other three cases.

The Court then deliberated, found the accused guilty, and sentenced him to be shot to death with musketry.

His execution took place on February 7, 1864 at the Camp of the 97th Pennsylvania Infantry Regiment.

REFERENCES:
Military Personnel Records, RG-#94
Court Martial Proceedings, RG-#153 LL 1338

Case #94
Private James Wilson
Co. B, 97th PA Volunteer Inf. Regt.
Executed for Desertion
February 7, 1864

DESCRIPTION:
25 years of age, 5 feet 5 inches tall, brown hair, hazel eyes, dark complexion, born in Scotland, occupation laborer, substitute, literacy undetermined.

Wilson, a substitute, was enlisted and mustered into service on September 23, 1863 at Pottsville, Pennsylvania. He was assigned to Company B, 97th Pennsylvania Infantry Regiment, and arrived for duty on November 5, 1863. The Regiment, while stationed in the Fernandina, Florida area, offered the opportunity for Wilson to desert. He took advantage of the opportunity, deserting on the 14th of December, 1863, and was captured and confined in the guard house on December 15, 1863.

A General Court Martial was convened at Fernandina, Florida and on January 15, 1864 tried Private James Wilson, Company B, 97th Pennsylvania Infantry Regiment on the charge of desertion.

As the trial was being organized before the members of the Court were sworn in, a Captain Isaiah Price, 97th Pennsylvania Infantry Regiment, presented a petition requesting to be excused from serving on this Court Martial trial. The petition read as follows:

"Provost Marshall's Office, Fernandina, Florida, January 14, 1864.

Major G. Pennypacker, Prest. Court Martial.

Major, I have the honor to suggest the following consideration as constituting an impropriety in my sitting as a member of the Court Martial, in the cases of Privates Wilson, Goodrich, Williams and Thompson of the 97th Pennsylvania charged with *desertion*. These men have been in my charge since their arrest and daily visited by me to ascertain their condition and safety! And from my present position must necessarily be brought into constant personal supervision of them during their confinement and in the event of a conviction for the offense with which they stand charged, my position may become still more embarrasing and painful.

I should regard it as highly improper that I should, while having custody of these men, be placed in the position of a member of the Court to try them for the very serious offense with which they stand charged.

I therefore respectfully ask that I be excused from serving on these cases.

I remain your obedient Servant
Isaiah Price
Captain 97th Pennsylvania
Provost Marshall"

The Court was cleared and the members, without Captain Price, deliberated. The Court was then reopened and the Court announced that "Captain Price is not excused from serving as a member of the court."

All members of the Court, the President, and the Judge Advocate were sworn in.

Wilson requested the Court to admit a J. M. Latta Esq. to act as his counsel, which request was granted.

Wilson was charged with deserting his unit on December 14, 1863 and endeavoring to go over to the enemy on December 15, 1863.

Evidence was introduced by testimony of witnesses that Wilson was present at Tattoo Roll Call (prior to taps) on the night of December 14, 1863 but was absent at Reveille Roll Call on the morning of September 15, 1863.

Wilson was accompanied on his desertion effort by Private Peter Goodrich of Company I, Private James Thompson, Company K, and Private John Williams, Company I, all of the 97th Pennsylvania Infantry Regiment, and each was tried separately on the charge of desertion. Briefly, the four men planned to desert, build a raft from material salvaged from a deserted house on the island and float and paddle to the mainland. As they approached the beach on the morning of the 15th of December, they noted a boat containing a Mr. H. Helper and several negroes. They made an attempt to escape by seizing a row boat and managed to get off the beach without Goodrich. Goodrich ran out into the water with a loaded cocked pistol in his hand and as he caught hold of the gunwale of the boat, the pistol fired wounding Thompson. Helper meanwhile approached, and by his clothing and speech, convinced them he was a confederate and would guide them to the rebel lines. They were intercepted by a Captain Hawkins, Commander of Company I, who was searching for the deserters, arrested and confined them to await trial. Thompson recovered from his wound. All four were tried and found guilty, but Williams was not sentenced to death. He was instead awarded a dishonorable discharge, imprisonment at hard labor for the balance of his period of enlistment and forfeiture of all pay and allowances. The other three received death sentences. The statements presented by the defense and the prosecution are of interest in displaying a fair view of the legal talents available during the Civil War. They are consequently quoted in toto.

The testimony runs too many pages, and is summarized for the defense by a statement of the accused and by the prosecution in a rebuttal by the trial Judge Advocate as follows.

Defense Statement

"I would call the attention of the court to and ask their consideration of the following statement and argument on my defense.

I ask that the evidence of H. H. Helper, the man claiming to have arrested me be thrown out of court for the reason that a part of it is *inconsistent* and a part *impossible* to his `to wit.' He states that the negroes who were with him at the time were joined [by others] dresed in the Uniforms of soldiers of the United States Army. While he strangely enough insists that we supposed him to be a rebel and in face of the fact that as [Harry] Young testified of his coming directly from the Island where he had told me there were Union Troops. How entirely inconsistent it is to suppose that seeing a boat approaching from where we had been told there were Union troops, it's occupants being mostly negroes, dresed in the Uniforms of soldiers in the United States Army, we should make no attempt to secrete ourselves but on the contrary meet the boat at the beach and get in, all the while supposing him (Helper) to be a *rebel*. He states also in his testimony that he was on Tolbert Island distant between a mile and a half and two and a half from Amelia Island, where we were, the day being rainy, as shown by the testimony of Captain J.M.C. Savage, and at that distance he heard the discharge of the pistol alledged to have been fired by one of the accused, and saw three men walking on the beach, both of which are *physical impossibilities*.

Now to believe this testimony of Helper's to be true, you must ignore practical experience and observation and discard every principle of common sense and reason. For these reasons we ask that it be wholly disregarded in the consideration of any case under the [rule] of law, that where gross contradictions or palpable inconsistencies exist in any part of the testimony of a witness it casts doubt upon the whole and should in cases of Court's Martial be wholly rejected.

That if the testimony of Mr. Helper is to be accepted as evidence it be with that degree of allowance which is fair to the case of an *interested witness*: as his over-anxiety to convict me shows but too plainly that he is not forgetful of the reward he will be entitled to upon my conviction.

As an evidence of my not desiring to desert, I would call the attention of the court to the testimony of Harry Young who states that the boat was in the undisputed possession of the three men with me, and that there was nothing to hinder our going where we felt disposed: yet *I* remained standing upon the bank and did not approach the boat, nor in any other way make an effort to escape.

The court will not fail to observe that there is an entire absence of evidence of any complicity on *my* part in the effort alledged to have been made to [steal] or take possession of the boat.

As to my voluntary statement to a negro that I was a deserter, it is too absurd to fear the courts believing it. When they call to mind the fact that the admission is alledged to have been made when I was yet on the Island where the Regiment were stationed.

Mr. Helper's testimony being ignored, and I having Young's statement discredited, there remains but my absence to be disposed of. It is not attempted to be proven that I forced the guard. I am precluded from showing by the guard that I had the permission to absent myself as I might have supposed by them.

The evidence is by no means positive nor conclusive that *I* was the absent *one* at `Roll

Call' on the morning of the 15th. The morning report is silent as to the name of the absentee, and it being the best evidence, therefore the [parol] evidence of Sergeant (Laurie) could only be introduced to explain an ambiguity which was not done. The evidence admitting of a doubt as to *my* being absent at `Roll Call' on the morning of the 15th. Am I not entitled to the benefit of the doubt? And are you not to take it for granted that I absented myself after `Roll Call' in broad day light and therefore did not leave in a manner which would indicate I intended to desert and consequently was only absent at the `Roll Call' on the evening of the 15th and could not be guilty of desertion.

I would also add that the disparity of dates as to Helper's testimony affords another argument for it's rejection. All of which is respectfully and hopefully submitted. James Wilson."

The trial Judge Advocate, Henry W. Carruthers, then submitted his rebuttal of the defense.

"Gentlemen: In the trial of James Wilson, before this honorable court, upon a charge of Desertion, it is my duty as Judge Advocate to lay before you the *Law* and the *facts* of the case. Whilst I prosecute in the name of the United States, I am also bound to see that no injustice is done the accused. How that duty has been here performed this Record must show.

The hand the evidence taken in connection can alone enable you to decide justly and according to the merits of the case.

The law is simply this: (I quote from General Orders No. 53, from Hd. Qrs., Dept. of the South, dated Hilton Head, Port Royal, South Carolina, June 29, 1863.) `To *desert* means to quit or abandon the post or command of the individual and there is no authority requiring the animus with which the party left, to be established; XXXX, the Highest Military Authority declares that Officers and enlisted men, absent from their command without proper authority are, in fact, *Deserters.*'

Of course, that `individual,' must be a *soldier*, and the 20th Article of War would seem to require that, that soldier should be a soldier who has received pay *or* have been duly enlisted in the service of the United States.

Now does the *evidence* meet the requirements of the law. Let us see—

Capt. Savage swears that the accused was regularly assigned as a Recruit to his Company in November last. The original Muster Roll of men drafted and mustered into the service of the United States and assigned to the 97th Regt. Penn. Vols. bears upon it the name and description of a man named James Wilson. Captain Savage swears that it is the name and description of the man assigned to his Company, and that the accused is the same man. The accused, if this evidence is to be believed, is then a `soldier.' Is he then a soldier who has received pay *or* been duly enlisted in the service of the United States? There is no evidence that he has been paid; but the original and Official Muster Roll shows that he has received clothing from the Gov't to the amount of $28.00 which is tantamount to the same thing, and has been so decided by the War Dept. *or* taking the alternative of the requirement of the Article of War, the same Muster Roll says that he was `*Drafted*' and mustered into the service of the United States on the 23rd of September 1863.' That this is equivalent to the words `Duly Enlisted' the action of the Government establishes beyond cavil, objection or doubt.

Next, did James Wilson quit or abandon his command? Did he absent himself from his company without authority?

Captain Savage swears that on the morning of the 15th December last, he was absent, and absent without authority; that in consequence of that absence he made pursuit and search for him but without avail. 1st Sergeant Jacob G. Lowrie, who called the Roll, and who was the de facto Commander of the Company swears that he was present at Tattoo Roll call on the night of December 14th, but that at Reveille Roll Call on December 15th he was absent, he swears further that neither sleepiness, nor sickness, nor duties prevented him from being present. That he was not in his *bunk.* That James Wilson was *absent*, and absent, too, without authority. He tells you further that the standing orders are that enlisted men, not on duty, must not be absent between Tattoo and Reveille. Next pursuit is made, and it is a rainy morning. The prisoner asks you in his argument to believe that he may have had permission to pass the guard or picket. Newly made tracks are found in the sand, coming out between the Picket Posts, coming out at a place where the `Officer of the Day' tells us no one, although armed with the proper `pass' *or* with the `countersign' has a right to come out, *i.e.* between the Posts. Now there were tracks, Capt. Savage says he followed to within a mile of the lower part of the Island, when he lost them, to the lower part of the Island where the accused was found on the afternoon of the same day by Mr. Helper. Now it is for you to decide whether they were the tracks of the accused and his party. If you believe they were, then his argument that he rightly passed the Pickets falls to the ground, because the presumption of the *law* is, that the Pickets did their duty, until the contrary is proved. But Mr. Helper swears that when the party of four men answered his hail, made at gun shot distance, he was answered by them that `they were deserters and wanted to go to the other side, to the Rebels.' He swears that the accused was one of the four men, and that from his conversation he supposed him to be the `Leader of the Party.' He told Mr. Helper of his strategy in evading the pursuit. They spoke of their intention to go over to the enemy. They spoke of having cooked their breakfast at a little shanty, and that they intended to make a raft of that shanty at night `with which to cross over to the mainland.' They exhibited the rope which they said they had provided for that especial purpose. They said they had not provided themselves with everything they needed, such as nails, as they feared discovery. They said they had conceived a previous plan to desert, but said that it had been frustrated. They all offered to give anything Mr. Helper might ask, if he would but land them on the other side. Mr. Helper swears that James Wilson was one of the four men. He is very positive, and he recognized the accused also by the scar on his face. Mr. Helper took them all into his boat. They were under the impression they were going to rebeldom. But were delivered into the hands of Capt. Hawkins who had come out in his boat with an armed party with a view of intercepting them in their attempted escape.

The prisoner, in his argument, asks you to reject or discredit, the testimony of Mr. Helper on the ground of inconsistency, impossibility, and interest.

Whether Mr. Helper's testimony is inconsistent or whether it is the plain unvarnished statement of facts, I leave to you to decide. I may not make any assertions. Whether they believed Mr. Helper to be a rebel or not. You will decide, by a consideration of their assertions, and their actions.

Whether it was impossible too, that on a rainy morning, at a distance of a mile and a half from Amelia Island to Talbot Island, Mr. Helper could have heard the report of a gun or a pistol and seen three men on the beach, you must decide. Yet it is very clear, that *something* attracted Mr. Helper's attention. That something was more probably what he says it was, than anything else.

With regard to the interest of the witness, if there is any at all, that can only affect the credibility, and not the competency of the witness. You must, legally, receive it, but you may place such a degree of credit upon it as your wisdom suggests. A consideration of the high character and demeanor of the witness may aid you in placing upon his testimony it's proper degree of credit.

Henry Young, a witness called by the defense, says that he recognizes the prisoner as one of the four men who were captured. He says that they said they were deserters. That they attempted to take his boat, that one of the party ran for the boat with a cocked pistol in his hand; that in getting into the boat the pistol went off, and one of their number was shot.

The prisoner, in his argument, asks you to believe that because he did not escape in Henry Young's boat, that therefore, he was not a deserter, and did not want to escape.

If this point enters into the case at all, you will of necessity, judge of their motives at that time, by a review of the circumstances which surround them. You will remember that one of their number was not yet in `the boat,' another of the number had been accidently shot by his comrade, *which* would necessarily create a feeling of anxiety and excitement. Henry Young had also told them that there were Union Troops on the opposite shore. He gave the alarm by waving his cap and `Hooping' to the persons in `the flat' on the Talbot Island shore, who answered the signal by firing a gun. It may have been intention, or it may have been excitement and fear that kept them back at that time. You must decide.

Believing that this Honorable Court will guard the rights of the accused as carefully as it will uphold the dignity and authority of the Military service of the United States in this hour of peril to both, I submit the case to the court without further remark or comment.

Henry W. Carruthers
Judge Advocate."

The Court deliberated and found the accused guilty and sentenced him to death by musketry, the identical verdict of his three companions. The execution was to take place at Fernandina, Florida on February 7, 1864. Thompson and Goodrich were to be executed at the same time and place with Wilson. On the night of February 6, 1864, Goodrich escaped, although handcuffed and under guard, while being escorted to the latrine. Thompson and Wilson were executed on February 7th as ordered. Goodrich managed to elude capture until February 12th when he was wounded and apprehended as he attempted to evade his searchers. New orders for his execution had to be issued, as the original orders called for his execution on the 7th of February, and he was finally executed on February 27, 1864 at the same place his companions were.

REFERENCES:

Military Personnel Records, RG-#94
Court Martial Proceedings, RG-#153 LL 1335
"History of the 97th Regiment, Pennsylvania Volunteer Infantry during the War of the Rebellion, 1861-65, Isaiah Price, Philadelphia, Pennsylvania, 1875, (published by Price).

Case #95
Private John Wesley Cook
NV: Cork
Co. B, 55th MA Vol. Inf. Regt. (Colored)
Executed for Rape
February 18, 1864

DESCRIPTION:

23 years of age, 5 feet 6 inches tall, black hair, brown eyes, brown complexion, born at Wilmington, Delaware, occupation laborer, illiterate.

Cook enlisted May 21, 1863 at Readville, Massachusetts, and was mustered into service on May 31, 1863 at Readville, Massachusetts. On February 17, 1864, Cook, in company with three other soldiers, committed a rape.

A Military Commission was convened at Camp Shaw, Florida on February 17, 1864 for the trial of four soldier's of the 55th Massachusetts Infantry Regiment (colored). The first man tried was Private John Wesley Cook, Company B, 55th Massachusetts Infantry Regiment (colored) on the charge of rape. Cook requested admission of Captain Apthorp of the 2nd South Carolina Volunteer Infantry (Colored) as his counsel and the commission consented thereto.

Sarah Hammond (the rape victim) of Cedar Creek Bridge, Florida testified as follows.

"This man with three others came to my house this morning, and I left to go to their camp after some provisions that some of them said they had left, and I had not got more than 200 yards from the house before they overtook me and they asked me if they might not hug me as one did, the others did not, this was not the one, I tried then to get out of his way, he, the black one took his gun from his shoulder and I hallooed, he threatened to shoot me if I hallooed so as to be heard at the house, He then threw me down, I asking him to let me go back to my babies at the house, the prisoner was present and saw this, I struggled with the black one till he told me if I did not lie still, he would take his gun and kill me, he then violated my person, he then got up and broke and ran away in the direction of Jacksonville, the prisoner present was the next one that went to my person and threw me down, and one with shingled hair held me down by the arms till the prisoner had connexion with me, I screamed so that if the man in the house had not been hard of hearing he could have heard me or my little boy screaming, to the risk of fits. When this man laid hold of me, I cried and screamed and begged them to let me loose and they would not do it. I was afraid to scream my best for fear they would kill me, this one staid till all had got through and the last three went off together. Capt Hodges then came up and I told him about it, i.e. after I went back to the house and I told Mr. Fleming in the house, I had started for Mr. Carmichael's for help when I saw Capt Hodges approach. He followed after and caught three of the four men."

Captain Hodges verified Mrs. Hammond's testimony and stated that he followed the four rapists until he met Quarter Master Lieutenant Mussey, 55th Massachusetts Infantry Regiment (colored) and had Mussey trail the rapists while he rode to the camp and secured a detail of a Sergeant and eight men who arrested the rapists took them to camp and then to the Provost Marshall in Jacksonville, Florida.

The accused offering no defense or statement. The Commission deliberated and found the accused guilty and sentenced him to death by hanging. The body was left hanging for 24-hours as an example of the penalty for rape.

Cook was executed on February 18, 1864 at Camp Shaw, Florida.

(Also see Cases 96 and 97.)

REFERENCES:
Military Personnel Records, RG-#94
Court Martial Proceedings, RG-#153 SR

Case #96
Private Spencer Lloyd
Co. B, 55th Mass.
Executed for Rape
Vol. Inf. Regt. (colored)

DESCRIPTION:

21 years of age, 5 feet 3 inches tall, black hair, brown eyes, black complexion, born in Wilmington, Delaware, occupation porter, illiterate.

Lloyd enlisted and was mustered into service on May 31, 1863 at Readville, Massachusetts. He was assigned to Company B, 55th Massachusetts Regiment Volunteer Infantry (colored). On the 17th of February, 1864 near Jacksonville, Florida, Lloyd and other members of the 55th Massachusetts Infantry Regiment (colored) (Privates John Cook, Company B, and John Smith, Company A) raped and maltreated a white female, Mrs. Sarah Hammond, a citizen resident of Cedar Creek, Florida. He was arrested and confined.

A Military Commission was convened at Camp Shaw near Jacksonville, Florida, and on February 18, 1864 tried Private Spencer Lloyd, Company B, 55th Massachusetts Colored Volunteer Infantry on the charge of rape.

The prisoner asked to have Captain W. Lunthorp, 22nd South Carolina Volunteers, admitted as his counsel. The request was granted.

The defense had no testimony or statement to make.

The Court deliberated and found the accused guilty and sentenced him to be hung.

The execution took place at Camp Shaw, near Jacksonville, Florida on February 18,

1864.

The other rapists were similarly tried, found guilty, and executed by hanging at the same time. All three were left hanging for 24-hours as examples of the penalty for rape. (See case #'s 95 and 97)

REFERENCES:
Military Personnel Records, RG-#94
Court Martial Proceedings, RG-#153 CMSR

Case #97
Pvt. John M. Smith
Co. A, 55th Mass Vol. Inf. Regt. Colored
Executed for Rape
February 18, 1864

DESCRIPTION:

21 years of age, 5 feet 4½ inches tall, dark eyes, dark hair, light complexion, born in Old Town, Maine, occupation stove maker, literacy undetermined.

Smith enlisted on June 9, 1863 at Readville, Massachusetts and was mustered into service there on June 22, 1863. He was assigned to Company A, 55th Massachusetts Volunteer Regiment Infantry (colored). He deserted from Readville, Massachusetts on July 20, 1863, and was apprehended and returned to his Regiment on october 19, 1863. He was not Court Martialed for this offense as his Regimental Commander Lieutenant Colonel Alfred S. Hartwell recommended mercy. He was, however, required to make up the time lost during his "desertion" and forfeit all pay due up to the date (October 19, 1863) of pardon.

On February 17, 1864, near Jacksonville, Florida, Smith, in company with three other soldiers, raped and maltreated a white woman, Mrs. Sarah Hammond, a citizen of Cedar Creek, Florida.

A resume´ of the Court Martial testimony states that Smith and three other colored soldiers went to the home of Mrs. Hammond and told her that a lot of provisions had been left behind in their camp, which they had left. She left her home and took a path toward the camp, by the time she had gone more than 200 yards the four men following her, overtook her. One of the men asked her for a hug and she attempted to walk around him and return to her home. He stopped her and she "hallooed". The soldier said he would shoot her if she "hallooed" again to alarm the people at her house. The soldier then threw her to the ground and she resisted him. He told her if she did not lie still he would take his gun and kill her. Each soldier in turn raped her, while the others held her arms. One soldier told her if she would not be quiet he would kill her and her child.

When the soldiers left she returned to her home crying and shouting and unexpectedly met Captain T. O. Hodges of the 1st North Carolina Volunteers whom she told of the assault. He ran after the men and caught three of them, one Wallace Baker escaped. Mrs. Hammond emphasized in her testimony that she screamed and resisted the assaults to her physical capacity.

Captain Hodges testified that about noon on February 17th he was on horseback proceeding down a road past Mrs. Hammond's home when he saw her and rode to her side. Mrs. Hammond told him of what had just transpired. He rode after them, saw them, met another officer who he assigned to trail them, while he rode back to his Regimental Camp and secured a detail of a Sergeant and eight men. He then returned and was guided by the other officer toward the criminals. He surrounded, arrested, and had them confined.

A Military Commission was convened at Camp Shaw, near Jacksonville, Florida and on February 18, 1864 tried Private John W. Smith, Company A, 55th Massachusetts colored Infantry Regiment on a charge of rape.

The Court allowed Captain Apthorpe, 2nd South Carolina Volunteer (A.D.) to serve as counsel for the accused.

Smith offered no defense witnesses or statement to the Court.

The Court deliberated, found the accused guilty and sentenced him to be hung by the neck until he be dead. Smith, Cook and Lloyd were executed on February 18, 1864 while Baker who had escaped was executed on June 18, 1864 on Folly Island, South Carolina for the offense of Mutiny. (See Case #122.) Baker apparently was never tried for the rape offense.

The sentence was carried out on February 18, 1864 at Camp Shaw, near Jacksonville, Florida. The body was left hanging for 24-hours as an example of the penalty for rape.

REFERENCES:
Military Personnel Records, RG-#94
Court Martial Proceedings, RG-#153 CMSR

Case #98
Private Peter Goodrich
Co. I, 97th Pennsylvania Infantry Regt.
Executed for Desertion
February 27, 1864

DESCRIPTION:

23 years of age, 5 feet-3½ inches tall, hair black, eyes dark, complexion dark, born in England, occupation sailor, literacy undetermined.

Goodrich was drafted and mustered into service on September 23, 1863, at Pottsville, Pennsylvania. He was assigned to Company I, 97th Pennsylvania Infantry Regiment, arrived for duty on November 5, 1863. The Regiment, at the time was stationed in the Fernandina, Florida area. Goodrich deserted on February 14, 1864 and was apprehended December 15, 1863 and confined.

A General Court Martial was convened at Fernandina, Florida, and on January 20, 1864 proceeded to the trial of Private Peter Goodrich, Company I, 97th Pennsylvania Infantry Regiment on a charge of desertion.

The accused applied to the court for permission to introduce J. M. Latta Esq. as his counsel, which the court granted.

The prisoner, Goodrich, submitted in writing an objection to the jurisdiction of the court, "I hereby respectfully object to the jurisdiction of the court, on the ground of my not being a citizen of the United States of America."

Appendix A

"In support of my objection to the jurisdiction of your honorable court, I urge the following points.

1st That I am a lawful citizen of her Britanic Majesty never having by act or word renounced allegiance to the Queen, nor committed any act which would absolve me from service due her as my sovereign nor to England as my country.

2nd That I have never taken any oath of fealty or allegiance to the United States nor declared my intention to become a citizen thereof: and by the Act of Congress approved March 3, 1863, I am not subject to do military duty.
Can I be tried here for an offense against the military services? Clearly not!

3rd By the Muster Rolls which is the best evidence which can be produced, I am shown to be a drafted soldier. Has the United States the power to draft aliens? The Act above referred to would indicate that Congress did not intend to confer that power. By their own construction of the Extradition Laws, the United States never claimed they had more than the right to the *Voluntary Services* of Aliens. Will they now claim control over his services and invade the sacred rule of life too? I think not. The Queen of Great Britian cannot be expected to yield her right to the lives of her subjects.

4th The Articles of War were intended to apply exclusively to citizens of the United States and were not contemplated as extending to Aliens who might fall into the

Military Service of the United States.

For these reasons I claim the Court has no jurisdiction in my case.
Peter Goodrich"

Appendix B
The Trial Judge Advocate Replied

"1st The objection to the jurisdiction of the Court, even if it were a valid one, comes *too late*. The defense is estopped from contraverting it's jurisdiction now, inasmuch as he has already acknowledged it, by pleading the *General Issue - Not Guilty*. By the rules of pleading, this alone disposes of his objection.

2nd This being a *General* Court Martial, it is competent to try every offense against the Articles of War, and every description of persons known to them: Benet-page 38. By the 10th and 60th Articles of War, it has jurisdiction over any soldier, and over *all persons whatsoever* serving with the Armies of the U.S. in the field. The prisoner is serving with the Army in the field, and the law presumes jurisdiction over him. To abut that presumption, *evidence*, not argument or assertion, must be produced.

3rd Martial Law exists in the Department of the South, and in the State of Florida. His presence here, being an undeniable fact. He falls under the provisions of General Order number 100, series of 1863, from War Dept. which holds that Martial Law to the property and persons of Aliens. [Par. 7] The offices, persons, property, and businesses of even Foriegn Consuls are not exempted. They may be punished for offenses against Military rules by Courts Martial and such punishment furnishes no reasonable ground for international complaint. [Par. 8.]

4th He objects to your jurisdiction on the ground of alienage, and also upon the Act of Congress of March 3, 1863. The same Act required him to prove his exemption before the Enrolling Officers of his Congressional District. Now the law presumes that everything that is done in pursuance of Law is rightly done, until the contrary is established. The muster roll showing that he was duly drafted and mustered into the Service, is therefore conclusive against him; being *Official Record Evidence* that his claim if ever made has been disallowed, and that he is liable to Military Duty.

5th The fact of his having been drafted as shown by the Muster Roll, makes him a Soldier, and amenable to the Articles of War, from the fact of being drafted. [Gen. Orders No. 112, series of 1863, from War Dept.]

6th Having committed a crime as a Soldier, he cannot at this stage, throw off his Martial Cloak, and claim immunity from the consequences of his act. The Maxim of the Law is that `No one can take advantage of his own wrong.'

Lt. Henry W. Carruthurs, 97th Regiment
Judge Advocate"

The court deliberated on the matter, reconvened and announced "that the objection is overruled, and the court deems that it has jurisdiction of the case now before it."

The trial began with the presentation of the case for the prosecution, followed by the presentation of the case for the defense.

After both prosecution and defense had offered their testimony. At this point the defense made a motion for the introduction of Goodrich's accomplices as witnesses as follows.

"I move the Honorable Court for the introduction of James Wilson, James Thompson, and John Williams, now prisoners and charged as accomplices, as witnesses in my defense, verily believing their testimony necessary to a fair trial of my case."

Appendix C

"In support of my motion, I read from *BENET-pages 242-243*, which says, `*For the admission of an accomplice to testify, a motion should be made by the public prosecutor and the court under the circumstances of the case, will admit or disallow the evidence as may effectually answer the purposes of justice.* This clause in the law having especial reference to the introduction on the part of the prosecution, thus pointing out the manner in which it may be introduced. It is but fair to presume that a similar proceeding on the part of the prisoner would be followed by a like result, when we find on the same page the following language used. `*As an accomplice is not an incompetent witness for the prosecution, it follows that he will be also a competent witness on behalf of the prisoner* not withstanding he may himself be charged on a *seperate indictment.*'

The same author goes on to specify in what *particular* cases such testimony will *not* be admissible thereby leaving us to infer that the *latter* are the *exceptional* and the *former* the *General* rules to be observed.It would certainly be a strained construction of the law as laid down by this author in cases of this kind to suppose he intended to be understood as saying that *rights* were conceded to the *prosecution* which were *denied* the *prisoner.* While it is the well established doctrine of the law that in all *penal offenses* the *prisoner* shall have the *benefit* of *every doubt* which applies no less to the *evidence* than to the *law* and shall have the protecting arm of caution thrown around him as a shield against hasty, inconsiderate and unjust decisions. I say it would be at variance with the *tendency* of the *law* as expounded by other and no less reliable authorities should you place so *uncharitable* a construction upon it.

It may be urged by the prosecution that the introduction of such testimony would offer a *premium* to *perjury* by the *accomplice.* But that could scarcely be while we are *charged seperately.* The evidence elicited in *my* favor could with difficulty be perverted to affect *his guilt* or *innocence*; but on the contrary it would, from the very nature of the case, be quite free from personal or individual interest.

I have in my *motion* shown the Court the *necessity* of the evidence to a full and fair hearing of my case. This being my *Dernier resort*, in the only way I am permitted to do so. And I hope the court will not cut me off from the only evidence I can rely upon to show my innocence.

Peter Goodrich"

The Judge Advocate offered the motion and said "the Court will admit or disallow the evidence, as may most effectively answer the purpose of Justice. But the motion for the admission of the accomplices as witnesses must show that their testimony is *absolutely essential*, and that the persons proposed to be admitted are not more guilty than the prisoner himself."

"The defense on the contrary shows nothing, but simply makes an allegation unsustained by even the slightest evidence."

The court deliberated on the matter and later announced to the assemblage "that James Wilson, James Thompson, and John Williams cannot be called as witnesses for the defense in this case."

Prisoners Statement

"I would call the attention of your Honorable Court to and it's consideration of the following statement and argument in my defense.

I ask that the evidence of H. H. Helper, the man claiming to have arrested me be thrown out of court for the reason that a part of it is contradictory, a part contradicted by other and disinterested witnesses, a part inconsistent and the balance impossible: in his towit, he states that the negroes who were with him at the (illegible) he claims to have inveigled us into his boat under the delusion that he was a rebel, while we were dressed in the clothes of a soldier in the United States Army. He states that he took us to the shore of the Island we thought was the mainland and where we remained until two hours of the clock and yet we made no effort to escape nor to go on shore. That although we had a guard placed over us and were forbidden to go on shore, yet under all these circumstances we yet supposed him to be a rebel until we met Captain Hawkins. All of which would bear upon it's face sufficient marks of inconsistency. But to brand it as a complete falsehood we have only to examine the testimony of James Hibbard who says, `I got out of the boat at Tolbert Island

and attempted to push it off from the shore, that he told me prior to Mr. Helper's coming over that there were Union Troops upon the land we could see Mr. Helper coming from. When we took into consideration the fact that the oarsmen of Mr. Helper's boat were clothed in the uniforms of U. S. Soldiers, it renders it's inconsistency so *flagrant* that it assumes the worst form of falsehood.

Helper also states that I told him on the way to Amelia Island that I attempted to shoot one, James Hibbard. But when Harvey Young is placed upon the stand he swears he was on the same boat at the time the alleged conversation was said to have taken place but that he heard no such conversation.

Helper testifies that he hailed us at gunshot distance and asked us what we wanted and narrates a long story inflating his (*evangelical*?) powers. Yet the same Harry Young, who seems to be a truthful witness, says no such colloquey took place.

Helper says he demanded my pistol and upon my resisting to surrender it he told me that until I did surrender it I could not get into the boat. While Harry Young swears that Helper asked to see it and when I handed it to him he put it in his pocket saying I guess I will keep this too. All of which makes up quite a sum of contradictions and goes to show the general inaccuracy of his testimony. Helper also states that he was on Tolbert Island, distant two miles from Amelia Beach, where it is alleged we were, and at that distance he heard the discharge of the *pistol* alleged to have been fired by one of our party. That he also saw three men walking on the beach, not withstanding I proved by him that he is wholly blind in his right eye. This last assertion you must conclude to be false. In the first place it is impossible for a man to see at a distance of two miles with the naked eye, sufficiently distinct to make out a human being. In the second place Helper only had one eye and was not aided by any field or other glass. It is a physiological fact that the overstraining of a visual organ instead of having a tendency to strengthen, as is the case with other parts of the human organism which are called upon for physical exertion has the directly opposite effect. Now it was definitely a physical impossibility for Helper to have either seen the men or heard the report of the pistol at that distance.

For these reasons I ask that the testimony of the said Helper be wholly disregarded in the consideration of my case under the rule of Law that where gross contradictions and inconsistencies exist in any part of the testimony of a witness it casts doubt upon the whole and should be wholly rejected in cases of Courts Martial.

2nd That if the testimony of Mr. Helper is to be received as evidence, it be with that degree of allowance which is fair in the case of an interested witness, as his own over-anxiety to convict me displays his *Avaricious* eagerness for the reward he will be entitled to should he succeed in having me convicted of desertion.

3rd As an evidence of my not desiring to desert I would remind the Court that it is shown that I was in the boat and the boat was out in the stream and that there was nothing whatever to hinder me in company with those who were with me from going over to the rebels if we had desired: but of our own volition we released the boat to the negroes and came on shore. And again to the fact we were upon the beach of what we supposed was the mainland for two hours in the darkness of the night and yet made no effort to escape. All of which is shown by the evidence of James Hibbard.

4th The evidence admitting of a doubt, am I not entitled to the benefit of that doubt?

All of which is hopefully submitted to your honorable court.

Peter Goodrich"

No further testimony being offered by the Prosecution or the Defense the Court deliberated and found the Prisoner guilty and sentenced him to death by firing squad.

The execution took place on February 27, 1864.

REFERENCES:

Military Personnel Records, RG-#94
Court Martial Proceedings, RG-#153 LL 1335

Case #99
Sgt. William Walker
Co. E, 21st Regt Inf, USCT
Executed for Mutiny
March 1, 1864

DESCRIPTION:

23 years of age, 5 feet 7 inches tall, black eyes, black hair, dark complexion, born at Hilton Head Island, South Carolina (also stated born at Savannah, Georgia), occupation Ship Pilot, literate.

Walker enlisted in Company A, 3rd Regiment South Carolina Infantry on April 24, 1863 at Hilton Head, South Carolina. The Company and Regiment later changed designation to Company E, 21st Regiment Infantry, USCT. Walker was enrolled as a sergeant but was reduced to private on November 22, 1863.

Walker was a slave who was liberated by the Union Army. He had been a civilian river pilot and later stated he was the pilot for Captain Worden of the "USS Monitor Montauk" during its operations on the Big Ogeeche River against Fort McAllister and the engagement resulting in the sinking of the confederate steamer Nashville. We have been unable to secure documentation of this service. Walker has the double distinction of being the first negro soldier executed for mutiny as well as being the one most often mentioned in articles and books in connection with the early pay problems of the U.S. Colored Troops.

The U.S. Colored Troops experienced and overcame great obstacles in their campaign for acceptance as combat troops and equality with white troops in all matters relating to their military service.

Colored troops were, in the beginning, reluctantly recruited, poorly clothed, armed and equipped with obsolete weapons, used primarily as labor troops, trained in many instances by incompetent white officers, and despite original promises of equal pay and allowances, were paid at the scale of $7.00 per month, cash regardless of rank plus an allowance for clothing of $3.00.

Walker was highly incensed by the unequal pay problem particularly after the men had been promised by the government equal pay, with that received by white troops. White privates were paid $13.00 per month plus an allowance of $3.00 for clothing. A white hospital steward received $30.00 pay whereas a negro hospital steward was only paid $7.00. And in one notorious case an outstanding negro physician, commissioned as a Major in the Medical Corps originally received only $7.00 per month.

On the morning of November 19, 1864, Walker is said to have marched Company A (and it is said men of other Companies of the Regiment) to their Colonel's tent quarters and stacked arms. Walker, when asked what was going on, "Replied that they would no longer do duty for seven dollars per month." His Colonel warned him to return to duty. Walker then ordered the men to leave and return to their quarters, as he did. On that evening, Walker was placed under arrest and directed to remain in his tent quarters. The following day he was confined in the guard house after leaving his tent without prior permission. Walker was demoted as a sergeant to the grade of private on November 23, 1863. Charges were prepared against Walker and on January 9, 1864 he appeared before a General Court Martial at headquarters, Hilton Head, South Carolina. Trial began on Janury 11th, 1864 and Walker was counseled by a Lieutenant of a New York Regiment.

The charges against Walker were four in number.

#1 - Mutinous Conduct - Walker's angry oratory on August 23rd and October 31, 1863.

#2 - Conduct prejudicial to good order and discipline - Walker was alleged to have prevented the Regimental band Drum Major from arresting one of the Band Drummers.

#3 - Mutiny - for marching his Company before the Colonel's tent on November 19th, 1863 and having them refuse to perform their duties, and to have ordered his Company to release a private under arrest.

#4 - Breach of Arrest - while confined to his tent under arrest, he had left the place of confinement without permission.

Walker's defense to refute the charges included testimony that on charge #1 and #2 the NCO's were jealous and prejudiced. Charge 3, that he was not in command but rather the entire affair had been a spontaneous movement by the men. Charge 4, admission that he did leave his tent to go to the latrine after waiting vainly for over an hour for a guard escort.

The Court was in session all of the 11th of January 1864 and when testimony was concluded retired and deliberated, returned and announced the verdict of Guilty, "to be shot to death with musketry."

Walker made one significant statement which would seem to characterize one of the basic problems of Civil War Military Justice, "On military law, and the rules of the service, we are entirely ignorant. Never, since the organization of the Company, have the Articles of War been read to us nor any part of the 'Regulations' even. We have been allowed to stumble along." A complaint voiced by other convicted men.

Walker was returned to confinement at Hilton Head, South Carolina, while his regiment was preparing to embark on a military expedition to Florida using Jacksonville as its base.

While confined in the Provost Guard House at Hilton Head, South Carolina, wrote a letter appealing for clemency to the Provost Marshall.

"Provost Guard House, Hilton Head, South Carolina, February 7, 1864.

"Colonel Hall, Provost Marshall General

"Sir: I am a poor colored soldier of the 3rd South Carolina Volunteer Infantry who appeal to your generosity and justice and also hoping the following statement will cause you to forgive the intrusion on your time. Sir, I have been now some three months a prisoner in the Provost Guard House I am now awaiting sentence of Court Martial charged with crimes I am entirely guiltless of I have always done my duty as a soldier and a man and I hope to do so in future My former good character has never been doubted I am suffering very much in consequence of my close confinement and absence from my family who are suffering from want and destitution My family receives no assistance whatever from government and I have received no pay for the last six months causing them and myself to suffer much if under these considerations you would use your influence in the proper quarter you could I am confident procure my release and return to duty I assure you sir I shall never give you cause to regret your kindness I will say no more You can easily learn the circumstances connected with my case if you are not already acquainted With hoping sir you will use the influence you possess in my behalf I have the honor to sign myself sir your most humble obediant servant to command, Wm Walker Sergeant, Co A, 3rd S.C. Vol Infantry.

"P.S. Sir if you should wish any reference with regard to my former character I refer you sir to Captain Worden of the Monitor Montauk I was his Pilot for six months

I also destroyed the rebel steamer Nashville on the Big Ogeeche river near Fort McAllister by order of Admiral Dupont Sir these are facts Captain Worden can testify to.

"I am sir very respectfully
Your humble servant to command
William Walker"

Walker's court martial sentence was confirmed and he was sent from South Carolina to his Regiment in Jacksonville, Florida under escort commanded by an officer of his regiment.

Walker was executed, according to the "Official List," on March 1, 1864. Other dates given include February 28th or February 29th, 1864 from military records and newspaper reports. It is reported that the first firing squad failed to kill him, only one bullet of eleven fired struck him. The reserve firing squad completed his execution.

Walker's death stimulated action by high ranking members of the military and congress as well as state governors to correct the inequality of pay and allowances that was a manifest injustice. In the end, the pay was made the same for colored troops as for white troops. Bounties were paid where applicable under the individual state and federal law. Best of all, the difference in pay between white and colored troops was made payable retroactively to those properly entitled to same and such statements appear on colored troops record files.

REFERENCES:

"Forged in Battle," Joseph T. Glatthaar, 1990, the Free Press of MacMillan & Company, New York City, New York.

"Negro Casualties in the Civil War" by Herbert Aptheker, in the Journal of Negro History, Volume 32, 1947, January, #1.

"Reminiscences of My Life in Camp with the 33rd USCT, Late 1st South Carolina Volunteers," Susie King Taylor, Boston, 1902, (Published by author).

"Army Life in a Black Regiment," Thomas W. Higginsson, Beacon Press, Boston, Massachusetts, Reprint, 1962, (original in 1869).

"Black Union Soldiers in the Civil War," Hondon B. Hargrove, MacFarland & Company, Jefferson, North Carolina, 1988.

"The Negro's Civil War," James M. McPherson, 1967, Vintage Books of Random House, New York City, New York.

"The Sable Arm," Dudley T. Cornish, University Press of Kansas, 1987, Lawrence, Kansas.

"The Negro in the Civil War," Benjamin Quarles, 1989, De Capo Press Paperback reprint of original, New York City, New York.

"The Cause and Consequence of a Union Black Soldier's Mutiny and Execution," Howard C. Westwood, Civil War History, Volume XXXI, #3, Kent State University Press, Kent, Ohio.

"Negro Casualties in the Civil War," Herbert Aptheker, Journal of Negro History, Volume XXXII January 1947, #1, The Association for the Study of Negro Life and History, Washington, D.C.

Military Personnel Records, RG-#94

Court Martial Proceedings, RG-#153

Case #100
Pvt. Thomas Abraham
Co. G, 139th, NY Infantry Regt.
Executed for Various Charges
March 7, 1864

DESCRIPTION:

26 years of age, 5 feet 5½ inches tall, dark hair, hazel eyes, dark complexion, born in Ireland, occupation laborer, illiterate.

Abraham enlisted on August 23, 1862 and was mustered into service on September 9, 1862 at Brooklyn, New York in Company G, 139th New York Infantry Regiment. Abraham was with his Regiment stationed at Fort Magruder near Williamsburg, Virginia and on or about the 29th of January, 1864 Abraham was arrested and jailed. Private Thomas Abraham, Company G, 139th New York Infantry Regiment was tried by a General Court Martial at Fort Monroe, Virginia on February 11, 1864. He was charged as acting and lurking as a spy in that he did obtain valuable information as to a Union Army expedition to be launched against the enemy at Richmond, Virginia on or about February 1, 1864. Abraham was also accused of communicating the information concerning the Union Army proposed plan of attack to a Private William J. Boyle, Troop H, 1st New York Mounted Rifles, a prisoner convicted of murder awaiting execution confined within the guard house. The third charge placed against Abraham was that of advising and persuading another soldier to desert the service of the United States in violation of the 23rd Article of War. Abraham, well aware that Boyle would reveal this important information to the enemy, should he escape and reach their lives, did while on guard duty offer Boyle aid, advise and assist Boyle to escape from the Guardhouse and the Union Army lines. On January 29, 1864, Boyle did enter the rebel lines and relate the details of the impending Union Army attack to the enemy as directed by Abraham.

Private Thomas Abraham, Company G, 139th New York Infantry Regiment was tried by a General Court Martial at Fort Monroe, Virginia on February 11, 1864.

The trial proceedings records are lengthy and much of the record is contradictory and repetitious. The writers, therefore, wish to present only a resume of the most pertinent aspects of the case.

Private William J. Boyle, Troop H, 1st New York Mounted Rifles, a convicted murderer under sentence of death, was confined in the guard house at Fort Magruder awaiting execution. The guard house was described, in the trial testimony, as three "A" tents joined together to form one long tent. Boyle and another convicted murderer named Blake were confined at one extreme end of the tent away from other prisoners detained there. Guards consisted of two guards on the outside of the tent and two, Privates Ludwig and Abraham, on the inside assigned solely and specifically to watch the prisoners Boyle and Blake. The special orders for Ludwig and Abraham included to never allow Boyle or Blake out of their sight and to permit no unauthorized conversation with them. There was no apparent assignment of a particular guard to a single prisoner. Both guards were equally responsible for either or both prisoners who were each attached to an iron ball by a chain about their ankle. The two balls and chains were estimated to weigh about 24 lbs. each.

Boyle managed to escape from the guard house tent on the night of January 29, 1864 and was tracked by the Officer of the Guard and some of his men. First search made in the moat which surrounded Fort Magruder and it's drainage outlet was fruitless. They tracked the prisoners to the "sink" (Privy, outhouse) but found neither. A ball and chain was found and believed to have been found by the guard Ludwig and both guards were promptly placed under arrest. A search of the guardhouse turned up a knife made into a saw. Examination of the abandoned ball and chain was said to have revealed that the fastening rivets had been sawed through apparently with the knife found in the guardhouse.

Testimony disclosed that Abraham had escorted Boyle to the sink at the time he escaped.

The Sergeant of the Guard testified he had examined the ball and chain of the prisoners prior to the escape, but did not try and lift the ball by the chain.

Further testimony stated that Abraham and Boyle had had intimate conversations out of earshot of guard Ludwig. Further, that Boyle was aware of Union Army preparations for an attack on Richmond about February 1, 1864 and had communicated same to Boyle.

On the night of the escape, Abraham escorted Boyle, still with ball and chain attached, to the sink. When Abraham returned to the guardhouse alone, Ludwig asked where Boyle was and Abraham denied any knowledge of Boyle. Ludwig became highly excited and rushed to the sink in search of Boyle. The sink was empty but the ball and chain which had been attached to Boyle's leg were on the floor. Ludwig raised the alarm and an immediate and thorough search was mounted which was fruitless. Boyle had disappeared. Abraham and Ludwig were arrested and after extensive interrogation Ludwig was freed and Abraham was charged as previously noted.

At the trial, evidence was introduced by a deserter from the Confederate forces in Richmond and from a rebel newspaper, the *Sentinel* of Richmond. Both of the foregoing testified to the successful escape of Boyle to Richmond. The *Sentinel*, on it's front page under date of February 8, 1864, carried an article stating that a Yankee deserter, Boyle, described the Yankee plan for a raid on Richmond which was postponed by the revelation of the plan by him and other Yankee deserters.

Abraham made a *statement* which is reproduced here.

"The *statement* I have to make is that when I relieved this man the orders were to take care of both the prisoners. I always done my duty, and I can get that character. I never refused to do my duty. I was often over those men and had I been there that day I would have kept them. Ludwig was neglectful of his duty all day. In walking he struck against a prisoner. It's me says Boyle. They stood outside and were talking together alongside the tent. I never went to the back house (privy) with him any more than with one of you gentlemen. I saw number 8 (guard post #8 Ludwig's post). I sat there one day 3/4 of an hour and saw him speak to the prisoners. They seemed intoxicated. All the guard was ordered out. Number 8 he lay outside of me, and I was lying in the bunk all the time. He would not let me out and said what a fool I was. I would get my whiskey I said. I could buy my whiskey, and get an order (to purchase same) from my Captain if I wanted it. Ludwig sat at the door. I heard the order he got from the sentry he relieved. The Officer of the day stood at his side of the tent listening and then he said is that the way you do Guard duty? They said they were only talking a little. The officer put his head in to see if all was right. I straitened myself this way. Boyle said he wanted to go to piss. I said well why don't you go and piss and be damned. He stood up as if to go to the back house. I was going to the door. Ludwig he stood up. Boyle was in the middle of the tent and I suppose Ludwig was going out with his man. Kirby was outside. I said to him good day. He turned his back to me. I turned again and seen Ludwig sitting down. I said why don't you go out with the man? He said nothing. Then he said he would shoot me. Boyle should not make a fool of him. That is the time he capped his musket (made it ready to fire). Blake straightened himself in the tent, afraid Ludwig would shoot him. I don't know said I. I will if you come out said he. No said I stay where you are. But he said come out. Just as I went out with Blake there was a man and he says Blake heres the Ball and Chain and Boyle is gone. I thought it was no business of mine, but I thought I would halloo (call out)! and report it anyhow. That is the way things are done. One is blind and another deaf all trying to get a discharge (out of the army). This Ludwig was in the Hospital 7 days before this, and a man who always done his duty has to suffer for the likes of him."

The Court found Abraham guilty and sentenced him to death before a firing squad at Yorktown, Virginia on March 7, 1864.

Only one question remains, what ever happened to Private William J. Boyle, Troop H, 1st New York Mounted Rifles?

REFERENCES:

Military Personnel Records, RG-#94
Court Martial Proceedings, RG-#153 NN 1857

Case #101
Pvt. Francis Ely
Co A, 1st Oregon Vol Cav Regt
Executed for Desertion
March 11, 1864

DESCRIPTION:

36 years of age, 5 feet 7-3/4 inches tall, blue eyes, black hair, dark complexion, born in Canada, occupation miner, illiterate.

Ely enlisted and was mustered into service on February 7, 1862, at Camp Baker, Oregon in Company A, 1st Oregon Volunteer Cavalry Regiment. Apparently Ely furnished his own horse and equipment for which the government was to reimburse him. His duty was routine until August of 1863 when his Regiment was campaigning against the Snake Indians. His company was encamped on the Port Neuf River, at Camp #42 near Fort Hall, Idaho Territory. On the morning of August the 27th, 1863, Ely deserted the Regiment while on duty as a sentinel in charge of horses and mules of the expedition. He was pursued and on August 28th was captured by Lt. John T. Apperson, 1st Cavalry Oregon Volunteer Regiment at a point 65 miles away.

He was taken to Fort Walla Walla, Washington Territory, and confined in the guardhouse there until a court martial was convened.

A General Court Martial was convened at Fort Walla Walla, Territory of Washington and proceeded on November 27, 1863 to the trial of Private Francis Ely, Company A, 1st Oregon Cavalry Regiment on a charge of Desertion, Deserting his Post, and Stealing.

Testimony recorded at the trial stated that Ely deserted August 27, 1863 in the field, while on a campaign against the Snake Indians, encamped at Port Neuf River at Camp #42 near Fort Hall, Idaho Territory. He had been posted as a sentinel guarding horses and mules of the expedition and left his post before he was relieved.

He took with him a new Colt's revolver, the property of the United States with the evident intention of appropriating same to his own use.

He was captured on August 28th 1863, 65 miles from Camp #42. Ely pleaded guilty to the charges, offered no defense but offered the Court the following statement.

"I had been sick some days previous to my leaving. I requested the 1st Sergeant to take me over to the hospital to be placed on sick report, I had been taking Blue Mass pills and was not fit to do duty. My mouth was very sore and I was unfit to do anything. The Sergeant said I had to go on guard as I had been detailed for that duty. I went on guard according to his orders, while out I felt very sick and bad and under the influence of this feeling, I became disgusted with the service, myself and everything surrounding me, and while so left my post and deserted. In regard to the pistol, I would state that I had it hanging on my belt. I never thought of it and never for a moment intended to steal it or anything else."

A 2nd Lieutenant of the 1st Oregon Cavalry made a brief statement under oath in the accused behalf.

The Court then deliberated, confirmed the prisoners guilty plea and sentenced him to be shot to death with musketry.

On February 23, 1864, Col. R. F. Maury, commanding 1st Oregon Volunteer Cavalry Regiment, then at Fort Dalles, Oregon sent a telegram to General G. Wright, San Francisco, California. The message on the telegram form is garbled and difficult to read. We have interpreted it as follows.

I ask you to commute the sentence of Private Ely of Company A, 1st Oregon cavalry now under sentence order to be shot after almost two years service as an exemplary soldier spare him as this was his first crime of which he stands justly convicted and deserves the forfeit of his life as an example but I think the proceedings of the court in the approval of commutation of execution will have an effect equal to the execution of the sentence. In accordance with the order he will be shot on the fourth day of March if my request is not granted. Please telegraph to me at Ft. Dalles, Oregon.

Very resply, Your obdt servt,

R.F. Maury, Col. 1st O.C.

Ely was executed by a firing squad at Fort Walla Walla, Washington Territory on March 11, 1864.

Some controversy developed over the execution being carried out prior to the trial review. When it finally was submitted for review the execution had taken place.

"The Portland Daily Oregonian" of March 17, 1864 carried a brief paragraph entitled "Deserter Shot." "Francis Ely, sentenced to die for desertion, was shot at Ft. Walla Walla on the 11th inst. If the telegraph had reached the post, it is probable that his life would have been saved, as the President by Proclamation last week commuted the punishment of all deserters under sentence and ordered them to be confined at Tortugas during the war."

(President Lincoln ordered sentences of deserters to confinement at Fort Jefferson, Dry Tortugas for the balance of the war to be substituted for the death penalty on February 24-26, 1864.)

REFERENCES:

Military Personnel Records, RG-#94
Court Martial Proceedings, RG-#153 LL 1586
"Portland Daily Oregonian," March 17, 1964

Case #102
Private Robert Kerr
Co. A, 1st Calif Vol Cav Regt
Executed for Murder
March 20, 1864

DESCRIPTION:
(34/36) years of age, 5 feet 6 inches tall, blue eyes, black hair, florid complexion, born in County Tyrone, Ireland, occupation drayman, literate.

Kerr enlisted in Company A, 1st California Volunteer Cavalry Regiment at the Presidio, San Francisco, California on August 12, 1861 and was mustered into service on August 16, 1861. The regiment was placed in service in the south west, Arizona, New Mexico and Texas. Kerr was engaged in escorting prisoners, paymaster and supply trains. By March 12, 1862, however, he was in arrest for assaulting an officer, Lt. Harvey and was sentenced to hard labor for the balance of his enlistment.

On July 31, 1862, he wrote the following letter:

Fort Yuma, July 31, 1862, Col. David Ferguson, 1st Cavalry Cal Vols.

"Sir: From the confidence I have in your kind and humane disposition, I am induced to ask your favorable interposition in my behalf. At the time I committed the offence for which I am now suffering, I was totally unconscious as to my actions and was in reality no more responsible than a maniac. I have been in irons ever since I have been here and am so reduced physically that I am unfit to perform the simplest duties. Prior to the unfortunate occurance that caused my confinement, I am confident there was no soldier who performed his duties with more cheerfulness than myself as the officers I think will testify. May I not then beg you to write to Genl. Wright and have my sentence commutted. I am confident through your influence that I can be released and if you should be pleased to take an interest in my welfare you will receive the heartfelt thanks of an unfortunate man.

I have the honor to beVery Respy Yr Obt Servt
Robert Kerr"
Private Co. A, 1st Cav Cal Vols

The letter was received and forwarded with the following letter.

"Company A, 1st Cav Cal Vols
Fort Fillmore, NM
September 1, 1862

"To 1st Lieut. Ben C. Cutler
1st Infantry Cal Vols
Act Asst Adjt Genl
Column from California

"Lieut

Please find enclosed a communication from private Robert Kerr of this company. I have no official information as to this man having been tried and sentenced, though I have no doubt it is so. Lieutenant Harvey, against whom the offense was committed, is quite willing that anything that could might be done to mitigate Kerr's punishment. I have the honor respectfully to ask that this man's letter be laid before the General and beg his favorable consideration thereto."

I am Lieut very respectfully
Yr Obvt Sent
J.W. Card
Capn 1 Cav CV
Com Co. A"

On August 7th, 1862 he wrote another long desperate appeal for clemency addressed to Capt. William M. Close.

"Fort Yuma, August, 6th, 1862.

Capt. William M. Close Sir:

From the confidence I have in your kind and humane disposition, I am induced to ask your favorable interposition in my behalf as I am placed in a condition almost beyond endurance. I have been confined five months at this place in irons. the first two months solitary. Since that time I have been at work, and I am now destitute of everything in the line of clothing. I have never drawn any since last December, consequently I am in a manner naked I have to go bare footed over this hill which is a great punishment as flesh can stand and cannot get shoes or pants to cloth my nakedness. As the commanding officer will not issue prisoners anything other prisoners is better situated than me as they have all had officers to provide for them of there own company or regiment whilst I have been left here entirely alone a stranger, to every officer and soldier here and I have been treated as such for no officer has spoken to me since my stay at this place. Captain if you will take an interest in having my sentence changed or remitted, I shall be ever thankful to you. It is asking a great favor but I hope and trust you will confer it. At the time I committed the offense against Mr. Harvey I was unconscious of what I was doing and he knows and every number of the company knows that few if any had the love or the respect for the commissioned officers that I had. But I have committed a crime and I believe deserved punishment and would have never complained if I had been treated as a human or tried by a court martial of men of judgement that would have tried me impartially as I believe the cavalry officers would have done. I am sorry to have to inform you of the fate of (Forster) of our company. He died ten days ago very suddenly, he was taken sick and died in one hour after. Patrick Carr is here on the sick report awaiting his discharge. Bradley, McManus, and Martin is here doing nothing. The other boys left about one month ago for San Francisco. I have not heard from them since.

In conclusion, I will say that if I should ever be fortunate enough to be returned to duty, I will do my duty, as a man and a good soldier should serve his country in time of need, but placed as I am here I am doing my country no good nor anything else. The only hope I have for an honorable change in my present condition is through your interposition in my behalf and by so doing you will receive the heartfelt thanks of an unfortunate man.

I have the honor to be.

Respy Yr

Obt Svt.

Robert Kerr"

P.S. My sentence is the balance of my enlistment to wear a ball and chain 24 lbs. weight but in place of 24 lbs. I have a 31 lbs. with all pay and allowance stopped."

R.K.

The appeal was apparently successful as Kerr was returned to the rolls of his Company and resumed his duties.

A General Court Martial was convened at Mesilla, New Mexico and on January 3, 1864 tried Private Robert Kerr, Company A, 1st California Cavalry Regiment on a charge of murder.

The prisoner applied to the court for counsel and Judge Henry Jenkins was admitted as counsel for the prisoner.

Testimony disclosed that on the night of December 29, 1863 Kerr was on picket duty on the road between Franklin and San Elizarie, Texas and Lieutenant Samuel H. Allyne, 1st California Cavalry Regiment was in command of the picket guard.

Lieutenant Allyne was to bring the relief (replacement) to the picket post where Kerr was stationed. Lieutenant Allyne did not return from bringing the relief guard to the picket post. About 11 PM that night Private James Milne of Company A, 1st California Cavalry Regiment appeared at the quarters of Captain A. H. French, Commanding Company A, 1st California Cavalry Regiment and reported that Kerr had shot Lieutenant Allyne. The Captain immediately dressed, had his horse saddled and ordered the Company to follow him. At a point about 2 1/2 miles from camp, at the side of the road, they found the dead body of Lieutenant Allyne. The Captain issued orders to transport the body to camp and he set off, with an escort in pursuit of Kerr. A short distance from the place where the Lieutenant was found, the Captain discovered two soldiers, Privates Kennedy and Youngson, of his command lying drunk on the road. On the morning of December 30, 1863 Privates Martin and Shure located Kerr.

Kerr was arrested. Kerr's revolver which was fully loaded was confiscated. Kerr was asked where he had been and replied that "he was on the plains and was trying to find his way home." He was said to have been sober.

The body of Lieutenant Allyne was examined and it was determined that he had been shot in the back under his right shoulder, the ball traversed the chest and halted just under the skin below the left nipple. The fatal pistol ball was extracted from the body of Lieutenant Allyne by Private Clark of Company A. The pistol was later offered in evidence at the trial. Lieutenant Allyne's revolver, "a colt make Navy size old pattern" was found and turned over to Captain French.

Testimony was offered that described the events prior to and the fatal event itself.

Lieutenant Allyne relieved the pickets shortly after sundown and was returning to San Elizarie accompanied by Privates Milne, Kerr, Kennedy and Youngson. They stopped at the town of Isletta where they got something to drink remaining only thirty minutes. Lieutenant Allyne and Milne had at most one drink of liquor. Kerr, Kennedy and Youngson had up to four glasses of liquor. Kerr was so intoxicated he had to be helped on to his horse and was able to ride but very erratically.

After all the parties were mounted, the Lieutenant led them out of Isletta and continued the journey toward San Elizarie. A few minutes out of town, Kennedy fell off his horse and lay helplessly intoxicated. Lieutenant Allyne ordered Milne to remain with the man and to bring him in when he could. The Lieutenant had said to Kerr: "Kerr you are not treating me like a man to act this way. I have treated you like a gentleman." Youngson rode up to the Lieutenant and said "There is no use taking any notice of him because Captain French and Major McCleavo knew what he was when he was in liquor."

About three miles from San Elizarie, Milne rode up with Kennedy, to Lieutenant Allyne and his halted party. Youngson was lying on the ground drunk. Milne was ordered to get Youngson on to his horse. After much exertion this was done. Then Kennedy fell off his horse. Kennedy was assisted back into the saddle and then Youngson fell off his horse again. For an hour and a half these two drunks were assisted onto horseback only to have them fall off shortly thereafter. The exasperated Lieutenant then took the intoxicated cavalrymen's revolvers and ordered Milne to lead Youngson's and Kennedy's horses remarking that when the two sobered up they could walk in themselves. At a point about a mile and a half from where they left the two drunken soldiers, Kerr galloped up to the Lieutenant and said something to him. The Lieutenant then turned in his saddle and said to Milne "We'll go back and try to get those men along." The Lieutenant, Kerr and Milne returned to the place where the drunken men lay. For over a half an hour they again attempted to mount the two troopers, without success. Lieutenant Allyne said for Milne to take Youngson's horse and proceed to camp and he would follow as he would not stop any longer. Kerr again appeared and asked the Lieutenant to leave the arms and horses of the two men with him and he would be responsible for same and bring the men to camp when sober. The Lieutenant replied "he would do no such thing." Kerr drew Kennedy's carbine out of the bucket (Holster) on the horse. Allyne went over and took the carbine away from Kerr after a brief scuffle. Kennedy in relinquishing the carbine said, "take the gun I don't want it." Milne then rode off toward camp as ordered. He had proceeded only 20-25 yards away when he hear Kerr shouting "it is more than your commission is worth to leave these men in an Indian Country like this!" This was followed by a shot and Milne rode back and found the Lieutenant lying on his back, barely breathing. Youngson and Kennedy were dead drunk and Kerr was no where to be seen. Milne then took the reins of the Lieutenants and Youngson's horses and rode toward the Camp of Company A. The horses however broke loose from his grasp about 600 yards away from the place where the shooting occurred. The Lieutenant's horse bolted away and returned to the Cavalry Camp while Youngson's horse galloped off into the Mesa. Milne returned to the Camp of Company A and reported the events to Captain French.

Questioned about the weapons the mounted party carried, Milne replied that the enlisted men carried carbines in leather buckets attached to their saddles and in addition each was carrying on his waist belt a colt revolver, New Army Pattern. The Lieutenant however was armed with a colt Navy 6 shot revolver of the old pattern.

Kerr was captured by a search party in the chapparral some miles from camp mounted on Youngson's horse which had bolted into the area while Milne was trying to lead it to camp. Kerr had a Mexican also on the horse who leaped off and successfully evaded Kerr's captors. Kerr was returned to camp in irons.

Kerr had a reputation of being "all right when sober" but of being very quarrelsome when under the influence of liquor. He had a previous court martial conviction for drawing and pointing a carbine at a Sergeant. The sergeant took the carbine away from Kerr, struck him over the head with it, rendering him unconscious.

The trial having consumed ten full days was terminated as the accused had no witnesses to bring before the court but did offer a statement in his defense which extended to fifteen pages of nearly totally faded or illegible writing. The court deliberated, found Kerr guilty and sentenced him to be shot to death in Franklin, Texas on March 20, 1864.

A letter dated April 27, 1862, Headquarters, Franklin, Texas addressed to a Captain Ben C. Cutler, Asst. Adjt. Genl., Dept. of New Mexico read as follows:

"Captain:

In compliance with Department Gen'l. Orders #4, Feby 29th, 1862, Private Robert Kerr, Company A, 1st Cavly. Cal. Vols. was executed at this post on the 20th day of March last at the hour of 2 O'Clock P.M. by being shot to death by a detachment of Company E, 1st Cavly. Cal. Vols.

He made a will, leaving to his nephew, Robert Kerr some real estate, which he owned in Washington County, Illinois and appointed his brother, Thomas Kerr, the father of his nephew, executor.

The will, he desired me to forward to his brother; and also $50.00, which he left in my hands, to another brother by the name of William J. (Kerr) of Stockton, California. I had written to William J. of Stockton to ascertain if he still lived there and where Thomas is, as soon as I learn, I will send the will and money to them.

Very Respectfully
Your Obt. Servt.
C. W. Boure
Col. 3rd Infty. Cal. Vols.
Comdg.
N.B. This report has been inadvertantly neglected heretofore.
C.W.B."

REFERENCES:
Military Personnel Records, RG-#94
Court Martial Proceedings, RG-#153 LL 1689

Case #103
Private John Eagen
NV: Egin
Co. A, 2nd NH Inf. Regt.
Executed for Desertion
April 15, 1864

DESCRIPTION:

21 years of age, 5 feet 7½ inches tall, dark hair, hazel eyes, fair complexion, born in

England, occupation laborer, literate.

Eagen enlisted and was mustered into service on November 23, 1863 at Concord, New Hampshire in Company A, 2nd New Hampshire Infantry Regiment. On the 10th of April, 1864, Eagen deserted the Regiment then stationed near Yorktown, Virginia. He was arrested on the 11th of April, 1864.

A General Court Martial was convened at Headquarters of the U. S. Forces, Yorktown, Virginia and on April 12, 1864 proceeded with the trial of Private John Eagen, Company A, 2nd New Hampshire Infantry Regiment on the charge of desertion.

Testimony offered showed that Eagen deserted his Company on April 10, 1864. On the night of April 11th about 4 A.M. a negro came to the picket post of a sentry, Private Thomas Nolan, Troop C, 1st New York Mounted Rifles, and requested Nolan to come to his house as some men were trying to cross the creek (Skiffs Creek), and that they were building a raft. Nolan mounted his horse and rode to the creek, crossed it and found Eagen on the opposite bank. Nolan said that Eagen was attempting to make his escape, and Eagen said that the night before there were three comrades with him and that he got strayed from them and did not know his course. He was making for the James River when Nolan came up to him. Eagen offered no resistance in accompanying Nolan back to camp. Nolan arrested him and brought him to camp, and turned him over to Captain Cronin, Troop C, New York Mounted Rifles. This man (Eagen) admitted to Nolan that he was trying to desert. He admitted that he had been as far out as Kings Mills (10 miles from the Union lines).

The accused offered no defense nor statement. The Court deliberated, found the prisoner guilty and sentenced him to be shot to death with musketry.

The execution took place on April 15, 1864 near Yorktown, Virginia.

A rather curious communication appears in Eagen's file. A letter from the office of the "Provost Marshall, Hdqtrs of the Dept of Va and NC at Fort Monroe, Va, dated Sept 9, 1864 addressed to Brig Genl Barnes, Comdg Point Lookout, Md,

General:

By direction of Major General Butler I have the honor to request of you any information now in your possession, or which may be conveniently attained, concerning Private John Eagen, Co. H, 2nd N. H. Vol. whose sentence is promulgated in Genl. Court Martial orders #233, dated War Dept. Adjt. Genls. Office, Washington, D. C. August 8, 1864. It is not positively known here whether his sentence was, or not carried into effect before being Commuted by the President.

very respectfully

Your obt. Servt,

D. W. Shelley

Lieut and Asst. Pro. Mar."

Perhaps Eagen was executed before the arrival of a reprieve. We have been unable to identify and locate the document mentioned.

REFERENCES:

Military Personnel Records, RG-#94

Court Martial Proceedings, RG-#153 MM 1422

Case #104

Pvt. Henry Holt

Co. F, 2nd N.H. Infantry Regt.

Executed for Desertion

April 15, 1864

DESCRIPTION:

25 years of age, 5 feet 6 inches tall, black hair, gray eyes, dark complexion, born in England, occupation mechanic, illiterate.

Holt enlisted on November 17, 1863 and was mustered into service on November 19, 1863 at Concord, New Hampshire in Company F, 2nd New Hampshire Infantry Regiment. No details are known of his military service beyond the bare details here listed. He deserted, apparently on April 1, 1864 at Yorktown, Virginia and was apprehended April 13, 1864.

A General Court Martial was convened at Yorktown, Virginia and on April 13, 1864 tried Private Henry Holt, Company F, 2nd New Hampshire Infantry Regiment on a charge of desertion.

Holt applied to the court for permission to introduce as his counsel, Captain Hugh R. Richardson, 2nd New Hampshire Infantry Regiment which the Court granted.

Testimony offered disclosed that Holt deserted his company on April 10, 1864 from it's encampment near Yorktown, Virginia and was apprehended in an open row boat at or near the mouth of the James River. Holt and his two companions, on April 12th, encountered a mail steamer and were compelled to come on board where they were detained and delivered to a Provost Marshall for confinement and questioning.

One witness testified that Holt possessed excellent character, was a good soldier and had never attempted to desert previously.

The accused offered no defense witnesses but did present a statement of the defense which was read by his counsel.

"I would respectfully call the attention of the court to the following facts: First, on or about the 10th of the month I got some whiskey and gin and drank very freely and then went looking around the Fort and roads. About three o'clock in the afternoon, myself and two other fellow soldiers took a small boat and went down one of the creeks out into the bay. The next morning at day break we saw land and made for it. About that time we met the mail boat and one of the men aboard of her hailed us but could not tell what he said but we immediately made for her where we were taken aboard and brought to Yorktown in irons. I never had any idea of deserting and have always tried to do my duty in my company like a soldier and if I had not had too much Whiskey I would not have gone this time. I would like to be returned to my company and regiment and pay all expenses and I know that I never will be caught in the like manner again.

Henry "X" (his mark) Holt"

The Court deliberated, found Holt guilty and sentenced him to be shot to death by musketry. The execution took place near Yorktown, Virginia on April 15, 1864.

Apparently there was an inquiry made in October 17, 1865 as to the whereabouts of Private Henry Holt, as a letter dated October 17, 1865 from the Adjutant Generals Office, War Department Washington, D. C. to the Commanding Officer of the 2nd New Hampshire Infantry Regiment raises the question. The reply is vague, stating only that Private Henry Holt was executed in the latter part of April, 1864." A notation in the Court Martial Proceedings file states "proceedings, findings, sentence approved execution ordered immediately, Benjamin F. Butler, Major General Commanding.

In a letter to the President dated May 10, 1864 Judge Advocate General Holt (no relation to the deceased) wrote about the matter:

"General Butler approved the proceedings and ordered the execution immediately upon the receipt of the order, and forwarded the record.

A letter from General Butler on file in this office, dated January 28, 1864 says: that in consequence of directions from the President, that no persons sentenced to death in his department should be executed until further orders, he had issued an order suspending all executions, he further states, that all sentences of death are, under his orders, to be executed within forty eight hours after the sentence is read to the prisoner and that sentence is not ordered to be read to the prisoner, until the time and place are fixed for his execution; it is therefore supposed that the sentence in this case is suspended, until the orders of the President are made known."

The trial and execution were completed on April 15, 1864, two and one half months after General Butler's letter of January 28, 1864. Obviously, either some administrative procedure was overlooked in permitting the execution or some change in the directive from the President relative to the suspension of executions occurred.

REFERENCES:
Military Personnel Records, RG-#94
Court Martial Proceedings, RG-#153 MM 1427

Case #105
Pvt. Henry Miller
NV: Heinrich Muller - Hugh Muller
Co. F, 3rd NH Vol Inf Regt
Executed for Desertion
April 16, 1864

DESCRIPTION:
26 years of age, 5 feet 7 inches tall, gray eyes, brown hair, born in Germany, occupation barkeeper, literate, enlisted at West Lebanon, New Hampshire on November 18, 1863, $300.00 bounty and $2.00 premium credited to Plainfield, New Hampshire. The 3rd New Hampshire Volunteer Infantry Regiment was on duty in the Jacksonville, Florida area.

Elbridge Copp, in his book, relates that there were desertions from the Regiment and his Colonel decided to try and halt the practice. He therefore established, unknown to the majority of troops, a second picket line beyond the regular picket line. Apparently, Miller, while trying to desert on April 15, 1864, passed through the usual picket line at night in the belief it was the only one in place. Then he called over to what he thought was the rebel picket line, announcing his intention to desert to the Rebels. The secret Union second picket line soldiers made the reply however and encouraged him to come over. When he arrived, to his amazement, he was seized by members of his own Company and brought before Colonel Plimpton who ordered an immediate "Drumhead Court Martial" which quickly found Miller guilty. He was shot by a firing squad early on the morning of April 16, 1864. No record of the trial or Drumhead Court Martial has been located.

REFERENCES:
National Archives, Military Personnel Records, RG-#94
"Reminiscences of the War of the Rebellion, 1861-65," Elbridge Copp, 1911, Nashua, New Hampshire, Telegraph Publishing Company.

Case #106
Private Henry Schumacker
NV: Schumaker
Co. C, 6th Conn., Inf. Regt.
Executed for Desertion
April 17, 1864

DESCRIPTION:
24 years of age, 5 feet 8¼ inches tall, dark hair, blue eyes, light complexion, born in Germany, occupation painter, substitute.

Schumacker enlisted as a substitute for a drafted man and was mustered into Military Service on October 7, 1863 at Bridgeport, Connecticut. He was forwarded as a replacement to the 6th Connecticut Infantry Regiment on duty at Hilton Head, South Carolina and was assigned to Company C.

Together with Stark and "Hoffman" he deserted on February 9, 1864. Details of his misadventures are virtually identical with those of his two comrades.

(See the Henry Stark, case #107, for further details.)

A General Court Martial was convened at Hilton Head, South Carolina and on March 7, 1864 tried Private Henry Schumaker, Company C, 6th Connecticut Infantry Regiment for desertion.

Alexander Naumann was sworn as the interpreter of record as testimony in the German language was anticipated.

Witnesses testified as to the absence of the accused and to his subsequent capture. One witness stated that not only had the Articles of War been read to the Company but that they were explained in German.

Testimony was given that showed Schumaker to have deserted on February 9, 1864 and was not seen until returned to his Regiment in arrest after being captured and in arrest aboard the U. S. Steamer Oleander, near Ossabaw Island, Georgia on February 24, 1864 in the company of two other 6th Connecticut Regiment deserters.

Schumaker offered no testimony on his behalf but offered a brief statement to the court which simply said "I object to the whole proceedings for the reason that I have never been sworn into the Service of the United States."

The Court deliberated, found the accused guilty and sentenced him to be shot to death with musketry on Hilton Head Island, South Carolina on April 17, 1864.

Schumacker and Stark were shot to death on April 17, 1864 on Hilton Head Island.

REFERENCES:

Military Personnel Records, RG-#94
Court Martial Proceedings, RG-#153 NN 1643
"The Old 6th Regiment, It's War Record, 1861-5," Charles K. Cadwell, New Haven, Connecticut, 1875, Pages 83-86.

Case #107
Pvt. Henry Stark
Co. E, Conn. Infantry Regt.
Executed for Desertion
April 17, 1864

DESCRIPTION:

24 years of age, 5 feet 7¾ inches tall, light hair, gray eyes, light complexion, born in Germany, occupation farmer, substitute.

Stark was drafted and mustered into service as a substitute at Bridgeport, Connecticut on October 20, 1863. He was forwarded with a group of recruits to the 6th Regiment Connecticut Infantry stationed at Hilton Head, South Carolina and assigned to Company E. He became acquainted with Privates Henry Schumaker and Gustav Hoofan and deserted the service with them on February 9, 1864. Stark's record indicates he was captured on February 10, 1865 in a boat near Ossabaw Sound by a crew from the U.S. Side Wheeler, S.S. Oleander and returned to confinement. Sergeant Charles K. Cadwell, of the 6th Regiment Connecticut Infantry writing in 1875 stated that upon the return and confinement of these men, they were "chained hand and foot to a post inside of the Provost Quarters. A strong guard was stationed surrounding the area of confinement." Despite all these precautions, the three deserters again escaped on April 8, 1864. They again stole a boat and set out for the mainland but ran aground in Warsaw Sound and were captured by a crew from the U.S. Monitor, Patapsco on April 12, 1864.

The General Court Martial was convened at Hilton Head, South Carolina on March 8, 1864. Stark pleaded guilty to the specification and not guilty to the charge. A German language interpreter was provided and sworn in.

Stark offered neither testimony nor a statement in his defense, nor were any witnesses called.

The Court deliberated, confirmed the plea of guilty of the accused and sentenced him to death by musketry.

General Orders #7 was issued.

"In obedience to General Orders No. 50, Department of the South, Hilton Head, S.C., April 15, 1864, the sentence of private Henry Schumaker, of Co. "C," and private Henry Stark, Co. "E,"

Sixth regiment Connecticut Volunteers, who were tried before a court martial assembled at Hilton Head, S.C., March 4, 1864, for the crime of desertion, and were sentenced to be shot to death with musketry, will be carried into execution at this Post on Sunday the 17th day of April, 1864, at three o'clock P.M., on the field beyond the causeway and in the presence of all the troops of this command. All fatigue work within the line of the entrenchments will be suspended on that day during the afternoon, and every officer and man not upon the sick list or upon other duty, will be present. The firing party will be furnished by the Sixth Connecticut Volunteers. Capt. E. S. Babcock, 9th U.S.C.T., Provost Marshal, will make the necessary arrangements for the execution. The several regiments and detachments comprising the command will report at two o'clock P.M. to Lieut. Woodruff, A.A.D.C., who will be stationed there to direct them to their positions.
By order of Col. REDFIELD DURYEE, WALTER FITCH 1st Lieut. 6th Conn. Vols., Post Adj.

Official:
D.A. WOODRUFF,
1st Lieut. 6th Conn. Vols., A.A.D.C."

Sergeant Cadwell describes the details of the execution as follows:

"As soon as the time had been fixed for their execution they were visited by the Provost Marshal, who informed them of their fate and advised them to prepare for death. They seemed stolid and indifferent at first, but upon reflection they gave way to their feelings and desired to have a priest sent to them (they were both Roman Catholics), and Rev. Mr. Hasson, a Catholic priest who was in the department, was sent for and ministered to them. It was for a long time difficult to convince them that their case was hopeless, but Mr. Hasson's arguments finally forced conviction, and, after hearing their confession twice, he performed all the rites of the Church that were practicable. The prisoners were taken from their cells at about two o'clock, placed in army wagons and seated on the coffins in which they were to be buried. The column was formed as follows:

Capt. E. S. Babcock, Provost Marshal, mounted. Capt. J. P. King, Asst. Provost Marshal, mounted. Drum Corps in two ranks. Firing Part of 24 men detailed from 6th Conn. The Prisoners in wagon seated on their coffins. Ambulance containing Rev. Mr. Hasson, and Chaplain Woodruff, of the 6th Conn.; Rev. Mr. Taylor of the Christian Commission; the Surgeon of the Provost guard house, and the Surgeon of the 6th Connecticut.

The funeral escort, consisting of a corporal and eight men, marched to funeral music, with arms reversed. Slowly the procession proceeded to the appointed place; the square was formed on three sides, and the victims were driven around once that all might see them and avoid their fate. They maintained a calm demeanor to all, except as they passed our regiment they took off their caps several times to their old comrades. On reaching the end of the square they were assisted to alight from the wagons, the coffins were placed on the ground, the culprits sitting down upon them while the Provost Marshal read the charges, findings and sentence. After a short prayer by the priest they were blindfolded and their hands tied behind them and made to kneel upon their coffins, facing the center of the square. The firing party came up and were halted at six paces distance, when, at a signal from Capt. Babcock, they fired and the victims fell upon their coffins. Schumaker was pierced with nine bullets and Stark with eight. They lay just as they had fallen till the whole command marched past them on the way to camp, when they were put into the coffins and buried."

Gustav Hoffman convicted with Schumacker and Stark of desertion was also sentenced to death by musketry. To the dismay of the court it was discovered and acknowledged that his name had been misspelled. The correct spelling being HOOFAN which made the sentence of the court inoperative. Hoofan was released from the sentence of death and returned to duty.

Some months later, while at Staten Island, New York City, New York, he deserted and was never heard of again.

REFERENCES:

Military Personnel Records, RG-#94
Court Martial Proceedings, RG-#153 NN 1643

"The Old 6th Regiment, its War Record, 1861-65" by Charles K. Cadwell, late Sergeant Company F, New Haven, Connecticut, 1875.

Case #108
Pvt. Thomas R. Dawson
Co. I, 20th Mass Infantry Regt.
Co. A, Mass Infantry Regt.
Executed for Desertion
April 25, 1864

DESCRIPTION:
32 years of age, 5 feet 8 inches tall, dark hair, blue eyes, florid complexion, born in Ireland, occupation laborer, literacy undetermined.

Dawson originally was drafted apparently as a substitute on August 1, 1863 at Boston, Massachusetts and was assigned to Company A 19th Massachusetts Infantry Regiment. He deserted the regiment at Morrisville, Virginia on September 9, 1863 and through some unspecified and bewildering process was transferred to Company I, 20th Massachusetts Infantry Regiment on January 14, 1864. Notations in his military records file include one brief statement "in arrest since date of transfer (from) Company A, 19th Massachusetts on January 15, 1864." Thus Dawson had little more than 5 weeks of actual service time in the 19th Regiment and none in the 20th Regiment. He had somehow however managed to create the impression of the beau ideal of a soldier. Dawson claimed to have been in the British Army during the Crimean War (1854-56) and while serving in the Crimea to have been decorated with the prestigious Victoria Cross for Valor and something called the "Cross of Honor." British Military service records are unable to verify his claim of service in the British Army or Crimea. He is not listed in either the Wilkins, Smyth or Knollys books which collectively contain all accounts of the Crimean Awards of the Victoria Cross. The award termed "Cross of Honor" is unknown as an award during the Crimean period.

Dawson's crime, in brief, is that he and two unidentified and uncaptured soldier companions left camp without leave and entered homes in the area, where they found one or another alcoholic beverages from which he became drunk and nearly unconscious. A woman of about 60 years of age attracted some passing officers and accused Dawson of rape.

Thus we have a man of little service time, a little over one month actually, who then deserted that regiment and manages somehow to be transferred to a second regiment, claims to be a decorated hero of the British Army, absent without leave, drunk and accused of rape and is defended by the officers of the original regiment! The studied conclusion is that Dawson was a superb confidence man.

A General Court Martial was convened at Morrisville, Virginia on September 11, 1863 for the trial of Private Thomas R. Dawson, Company A, 19th Massachusetts Infantry Regiment charged with desertion of his post, Rape.

Testimony of witnesses disclosed that Dawson, while on guard duty at the camp of his brigade, on the night of September 9, 1863, left his post and entered the home of an elderly widow, Frances West, residing near Morrisville, Virginia. The corporal of the guard heard the screams of a woman about 10 PM and reported it to the officer of the guard. About 1 AM Mrs. West came to his guard post and reported she had been abused and raped. He sent a file of men to her house, the officer of the guard directing them to bring the perpetrator back "dead or alive." They found Dawson under the influence of liquor in back of her home with a lighted candle in his hand. He had no hat or shoes on. A search of the home revealed Mrs. West's bed linens wet and a pair of men's suspenders, which Dawson acknowledged were his. Dawson's shoes and hat were subsequently found in her home and he again admitted ownership of the items found.

At the trial, Mrs. West was unable to appear so the court and the accused were taken to her home where her testimony was recorded. Mrs. West stated she was 60 years of age, a widow and feeble as she was recovering from a recent severe illness. Dawson forcibly entered the house and threw her on her bed and attempted to rape her, but she got away from him and ran outside the house. Dawson caught and beat her then threw her on the ground as she screamed. This was the screaming heard by the sentinel about 10 PM. Dawson raped her on the ground in the yard then dragged her back into the house and threw her on her bed and raped her again. She then escaped and found a sentinel who ordered the search for Dawson. Mrs. West positively identified Dawson saying "I shall never forget his face while I live."

Dawson offered no defense but did offer a statement which the court accepted. "In regard to the first charge to which I pleaded guilty. I was relieved at 7 o'clock from post and went to camp and went to sleep and when I woke up I found my cap and slippers off. I know nothing whatever of the 2nd charge when I woke up I found myself in charge of the picket (guard), I have served 12 years in the British service one year and ten months in the 4th Maine Volunteers and was honorably discharged and I just came out as a substitute to the 19th Regiment of Massachusetts Volunteers and I had at this time been drinking and do not know anything about it."

The court deliberated, found Dawson guilty and sentenced him to death by hanging. Dawson was executed on April 20, 1864.

The officers of the 19th Massachusetts Infantry Regiment on April 17, 1864 drew up a petition addressed to the Honorable Abraham Lincoln, President of the United States asking for a complete pardon for Dawson and his return to duty!

The Reverend Father William Corby, chaplain of the Irish Brigade was persuaded to personally carry the petition to Washington and present it to the president. Father Corby carried out their request. President Lincoln declined to offer an immediate pardon but did agree to give the matter consideration. Father Corby argued rather persuasively and President Lincoln finally agreed to grant the pardon if Major General Meade would state in writing that Dawson should be pardoned. General Meade however declined to make the statement requested and Dawson's fate was sealed. The morning of the execution, Father Corby was asked if the Provost Marshall should grant Dawson's request for whiskey. Father Corby refused to sanction the request. Dawson was hung, on April 20, 1864 at Stevensburg, Virginia.

REFERENCES:

Military Personnel Records, RG-#94

Court Martial Proceedings, RG-#153 MM 792

"Memoirs of Chaplain Life, 3 years chaplain in the famous Irish Brigade," Army of the Potomac, Reverend William Corby, CSC, Schoester Pros Notre Dame, 1894-South Bend Indiana.

"The Victoria Cross in the Crimea," Major W. W. Knollys, London N. D., Dean and Son Printers.

The Victoria Cross, 1856-1964, Sir John Smyth, VC 1965, London, Frederick Huller Ltd.

"Massachusetts Soldiers, Sailors and Marines in the Civil War" 19th Regiment Massachusetts Volunteers.

"The History of the Victoria Cross," Philip A. Williams, London, 1904.

"British Orders, Decorations and Medals," Donald Hall, 1973, St. Ives, Huntingdon, England.

Case #109

Pvt. Charles Carpenter

AKA Charles McCarty

Unassigned Recruit, VT. Vol. Infantry

Executed for Desertion

April 22, 1864

DESCRIPTION:

21 years of age, 5 feet 4 inches tall, red hair, blue eyes, light complexion, born in Syracuse, New York, occupation laborer, literate, not married.

Carpenter apparently enlisted on December 4, 1863 at Sunderland, Vermont and was sent to a recruit training camp as an unassigned recruit to some Vermont Regiment. It is believed, but unable to document, that Private Carpenter was related to E. H. Carpenter, Sutler of Company E, 15th Vermont Volunteer Infantry Regiment. Private Carpenter deserted from camp, was apprehended and charged with desertion. He was tried, convicted and sentenced to be shot near Fort Warren, Massachusetts on April 22, 1864. Carpenter enlisted on the same day and place as Case #110 Private Matthew Riley (AKA John Roach). Both deserted together, were arrested, tried together, executed before a firing squad together and buried at the same cemetery near Fort Warren, Massachusetts. Both bodies were subsequently disinterred and returned to Cohoes, N.Y. for permanent burial at the request of and the expense of their relatives.

A General Court Martial was convened at Galloups Island, Boston Harbor, Massachusetts on March 31, 1864 for the trial of Private Charles Carpenter, unassigned recruit, Vermont Infantry on the charge of Desertion.

Carpenter had requested to have counsel, but the person he desired was unable to appear and he requested the court to admit Captain D. W. Hughes as his counsel, which request the court granted.

Testimony at the trial by Major S. Colburn, Vermont Recruiting Officer, documented Carpenter's lawful enlistment on December 4, 1863 at Manchester, Vermont. He had arrived with four companions, who also enlisted, and two brokers (substitute brokers). Carpenter and the others remained in Manchester, Vermont for about 24 hours until they were forwarded to Battleboro, Vermont which was a troop replacement shipping point.

On December 5, 1863, Carpenter arrived in Battleboro, Vermont with his companions and brokers. The brokers were most persistent in their effort to persuade the officials to process the men quickly, to no avail. The reason being that the State Bounty of $500.00 was paid in two installments. Two hundred dollars ($200.00) was paid when the men were actually mustered into service and the balance, three hundred dollars ($300.00), on leaving the state of Vermont. The brokers finally collected the two hundred dollars ($200.00) for each of the men and they all, two brokers and five enlisted recruits, disappeared the next morning. One of the five who fraudently enlisted was called John Roach, an alias for Matthew Riley, who was also tried for the offense of desertion and would be found guilty and be executed with Carpenter.

Maj. Colburn testified that on December 22, 1863 he was at Manchester, Vermont with a draft of twenty men to be sent to Battleboro, Vermont. While at the railroad depot, the train arrived and Carpenter got off, went into the restaurant in the depot and purchased a piece of fruit and a glass of ale. Major Colburn followed Carpenter as he reentered the railway car and had him arrested. Carpenter was dressed in civilian clothing and his normally red hair had been dyed black. His face also had been darkened by a dye or some material, all in an attempt to disguise him. Carpenter was found to have some four men with him that he was taking to enlist (he acting as a broker). Carpenter was turned over to the custody of the District Provost Marshall. Carpenter and his four companions were described in a bulletin sent to all recruiting offices in the district warning that "an organized gang of" what were termed, "Bounty Jumpers" were operating in Vermont and some should be detained when recognized.

After the above testimony was presented, Carpenter stated his witnesses were not available and he presented a written application for postponement of the trial to the court.

"Galloups Island, B.H. (Boston Harbor) March 31st, 1864, I, Charles Carpenter do solemnly swear that Charles Thompson of Albany, New York is a material witness for my defense and that said witness will testify as to the coloring of my hair some months previous to the date of time I am accused of having enlisted at Manchester, N.H. I have used due diligence to secure his attendance before this General Court Martial, I have reason to believe that I will be able to have him in attendance as a witness within a week from this date."

The court announced that the application for postponement was denied.

The accused then said he did not want to say anything to the court.

The court room was cleared and the court deliberated on the testimony. The verdict was guilty and the sentence to be shot to death by musketry.

As commented on earlier in recitation of the testimony, Carpenter's partner, Matthew Riley (alias John Roach) was also tried, similarly found guilty, and sentenced to suffer death at Fort Warren, Boston Harbor, Massachusetts on April 22, 1864 with Carpenter.

Carpenter made an appeal to President Lincoln.

"Fort Warren, Boston Harbor, April 18, 1864, To his Excelency Abrham Lincoln President of the United States of America.

Sir I take the liberty adressing my self to you hoping that you will listen to me. I am under that most aful sentance of death at this fort. I am to be executed on the 22nd day of April, 1864 witch was approved by your selfe and I think if you knew my real character it never would come to pass. I am a very young man to have sutch an aful sentance read to me and what is more to have it put in execution I am only in my 20th year and the son of Poor but Resectble parents entirely depending on m for suport and there fore have no one to intercede for me but my selfe for witch I am poorly fit, if I am to be shot why not guive me a chance to die like a man on the Field of Battle or prove my selfe something or if not send me to some place whare I will be of use to the government and to my selfe and Family if I was the most hardened Vilian in the world this would be awarning to me I should think. I know it is not my chagies that has brought this sentance to me but the charecter that was given of me by men who met or saw me before and if I had time __________ witnesses I could at least have a __________ witch goes agrate ways in a mans favor I know that you will do justice by me as I have no one to go to you and state the ____ but I trust in god that you will _____ this aful sentance.

I am your Obdt subject

Charles Carpenter."

Riley also made a similar appeal and it is included in Carpenter's file.

"Fort Warren, Boston Harbor, April 18, 1864,

To His Excellency Abraham Lincoln President of the United States of America.

Sir I take the liberty of addressing you hoping that you will listen to me. I am that most aful sentance of death now at the Fort on the charge of desertion I am to be executed on 22nd day of April 1864 as approved by your selfe but I think if you knew the circumstances that you would not approve of it. I have served two years faithfully in the field under Col. M. Murphy in the 15th N.Y. and have an honorable Discharge now with me I was discharged on the 17th of June 1863 I think it is rather hard after going 2 years on the field without being shot to come home and then be shot and I trust you will think the same. if I am to be shot why not let me go back to the field and take my chances with the rest of my felow soldiers hoping this may reach you in time to save me

I am your Obdt. Subject

Matthew Riley"

The sentence of the Court was executed as ordered.

REFERENCES:

Military Personnel Records, RG-#94
Court Martial Proceedings, RG-#153 NN 1535
Albany, NY, *Atlas & Argus,* April 25, 26, 27, 1864

Case #110
Pvt. Matthew Riley
AKA: John Roach
Unassigned Recruit, Vt. Volunteer Infantry
Executed for Desertion
April 22, 1864

DESCRIPTION:

22 years of age, 5 feet 5 inches tall, auburn hair, blue eyes, light complexion, born in Saratoga, New York (?), occupation moulder, literate.

Riley has two duplicate sets of enrollment forms, one in the name of Matthew Riley, the other in the name of John Roach. Roach is stated to be an alias that Riley assumed for which no purpose is specified.

Riley/Roach enlisted at Sunderland, Vermont on December 4, 1863 and was mustered into service at Sunderland, Vermont on December 8, 1863. He was forwarded to a recruit training center as an unassigned recruit of the Vermont Volunteer Infantry. He was apparently an acquaintance of Case #109 Carpenter having the identical service pattern from enlistment to execution as Carpenter. They were both executed for desertion at Fort Warren, Massachusetts on April 22, 1863.

A General Court Martial was convened at Gallup's Island, Boston Harbor, Massachusetts and on March 29, 1864, tried Private Matthew Riley, unassigned recruit, Vermont Infantry on a charge of Desertion.

The accused asked the Court to postpone swearing in of the court, its officers and other proceedings for one day as the counsel he wished to represent him was absent. The Court granted the request and the proceedings were postponed for one day.

On March 30, 1864, the Court reconvened and the prisoner Riley advised the Court that the original counsel he desired, not having arrived, asked permission of the Court to introduce Captain D. W. Hughes, additional A.D.C. as his counsel, which request the Court granted.

Testimony offered the Court described the events as related in Pat Carpenter's Case #109 trial.

The Court deliberated, found Riley guilty and sentenced him to be shot to death by musketry. The execution was carried out at Fort Warren, Boston Harbor, Massachusetts on April 22, 1884.

His body was claimed by his relatives and removed for final burial two days later at his home, Cohoes, New York. His funeral and burial took place on April 24, 1863, his fiancee being present.

REFERENCES:

Military Personnel Records, RG-#94
Court Martial Proceedings, RG-#153 NN 1535
Albany, NY, *Atlas & Argus,* April 25, 26, 27, 1864

Case #111
Pvt. Jacob Morgan
Co. D, 8th CONN Infantry Regt.
Executed for Desertion
April 28, 1864

DESCRIPTION:

37 years of age, 5 feet 4 inches tall, brown hair, blue eyes, fair complexion, born in England, occupation shoemaker, substitute, literate.

Morgan was drafted as a substitute and mustered into service on February 22, 1864 at Norwich, Connecticut. Morgan was forwarded to Norfolk, Virginia and assigned to Company D, 8th Connecticut Infantry Regiment. He deserted from his Regiment on March 14, 1864 near Deep Creek, Virginia and was arrested near Portsmouth, Virginia on March 26, 1864 and confined in Norfolk jail.

A General Court Martial was convened at Portsmouth, Virginia and on April 6, 1864 tried Private Jacob Morgan, Company D, 8th Connecticut Infantry Regiment on a charge of desertion.

Witnesses testified that the accused enlisted and was mustered into service on February 22, 1864 and assigned to the 8th Connecticut Regiment and Company D then on duty encamped at Deep Creek, near Portsmouth, Virginia. On or about March 14, 1864, he left his Company and Regiment without any permission or authority and remained away until arrested on March 27, 1864 in Norfolk, Virginia from where he was returned on March 30, 1864 to his Regiment and confined in the guardhouse to await trial.

Morgan's adventures in Norfolk, Virginia, where he spent most of his time as a deserter, present a picture of wartime morals and life style.

In Norfolk, the accused spent a large portion of this time drinking and discussing the war. He did frequently spend his nights lodged with admitted prostitutes whom he paid $4.00 or $5,.00 for their bed and services. The accused realized quickly that he had to get out of his uniform and into citizen's clothing to avoid drawing attention to himself by the Provost Marshall guards who would demand seeing his "pass," which he did not have. He bought citizen's clothes, and donned them, bundled up his uniform and left it in charge of one of the prostitutes he patronized. His drinking removed his inhibitions and revealed that subconsciously he favored the Southern Cause. This combination of intoxication and "secesh" talk inevitably lead to severe physical beatings by Union Army soldiers and/or Northern sympathizers.

He became so outspoken and anti-Union that he was warned, by several of the few friends he had made, to hush his mouth. Despite this warning, he continued his drunken and public tirades which led to his being reported as a deserter, in disguise. Warned of the approach of Provost Marshall guards and detectives to arrest him, he went to the prostitute who was hiding his uniform and changed into it. He hoped to lessen the gravity of his offence by claiming he had not tried to conceal his military presence.

Witnesses from all walks of life, the seamy, poor civilians and soldiers testified to his presence in Norfolk, his "secesh" talk and failure to voluntarily return to his Regiment.

The accused having no further testimony to offer asked permission to make a verbal statement to the Court, which was granted. The statement was duly recorded and entered into the trial proceedings.

Statement of the Prisoner

"When we left camp our intention was to come no further than Portsmouth. We started on drinking on the first morning. We met a soldier in a drinking saloon. He said, "are you going over to Norfolk?" I said, "we could not get over, we had no pass." He said, "he could furnish us with two passes." We went over to the city. We stopped at the Old Point tavern that night. The next morning we met the man that had given us the passes. He then took us down to the "shebang." We got drinking there rather freely. I then said to Charlie, "we can't move around here, for the Provost Marshall will be asking for our pass; we will have to change our clothes and leave our soldier clothes where we can get them when we want them." After that I became sick and laid in bed three days. I came to my senses and resolved to return home the moment I could get out of bed. I had no pass and could not get across the river. I went to a person whom I thought would send over to this side to get me a pass. She said that "her husband would not be over that night, I would have to wait until Sunday." Says I, "Rather than bother any more about it, I will go to the Provost Marshall, and give myself up." I leave my case to the mercy of the Court. I had not intention to desert."

The Court deliberated, found the prisoner guilty and sentenced him to be shot to death with musketry.

On April 9, 1864, General Benjamin Butler wrote, "The proceedings, findings and sentence approved. The prisoner was not content with deserting but spread sedition among the inhabitants of Portsmouth. There is nothing in his case, conduct or life that entitles him to clemency."

Judge Advocate General Holt, in a review and summary of the case, dated May 12, 1864, stated his views of the matter.

"To the President:

In this case, Private Jacob Morgan, Company D, 8th Regiment, Conn. Vols. was tried at Portsmouth, Va. on the 6th Day of April, 1864 for desertion, convicted and sentenced to be shot.

General Butler approves the sentence, and forwards the record. He says; "the prisoner was not content with deserting, but spread sedition among the inhabitants of Portsmouth. There is nothing in his case, conduct or life that entitles him to clemency."

A letter from General Butler on file in this Office dated January 28, 1864 says that in consequence of directions from the President that no persons sentenced to death in his Department should be executed until further orders, he had issued an order suspending all executions; and also states that all sentences of death, are under his orders to be executed within forty-eight hours after the sentence is read to the prisoner, and that sentence is not ordered to be read to the prisoner, until the time and place are fixed for his execution.

"It is therefore supposed that the sentence in this case is suspended until the orders of the President are made known.

The proof shows that the prisoner was enlisted and mustered into the service on the 22nd day of February 1864 and that he absented himself from his Regiment, then encamped near Portsmouth, Va. on the 14th day of March 1864, without leave and remained so absent until about the 26th day of some month, when he was arrested at Norfolk, Va., he had been in Norfolk during the time of his absence, dressed most of the time in citizen's clothes and represented himself as being a citizen of Philadelphia. While at Norfolk, he frequently used, in the presence of citizens of that place, such disloyal and seditious language as the following: "That he did not think the Northerners had any right to disturb the Southerners about their slaves; that the Southerners had as much right to emigrate their niggers to the territories as the Northerners had to emigrate there, that they had to fight for the territories; that the Southerners were not to blame; that Lee would give the Northerners "Hell on the Potomac." When arrested, he was dressed in soldier uniform, and claimed he was intending to deliver himself up to the Provost guard, but the evidence shows that his resumption of his soldier's dress was in consequence of having reason to believe that he was suspected of being a deserter.

He proves that he was a good soldier during the time he was with the Regiment.

There are no mitigating circumstances proven in this case, and his conduct, after deserting, aggravates the offense.

It is recommended that the sentence be carried into execution.

Holt

Judge Advocate General"

General Court Martial Orders #233

War Department Adjutant General's Office

Washington, August 8, 1864

III. The proceedings, findings and sentences of the Courts in the above cases have been approved by the proper Commanders, and the records forwarded for the action of the President of the United States, who directs that the sentence in each case be commuted to "discharge from the United States service, with forfeiture of all pay and allowances due, and imprisonment during the war, at the Dry Tortugas, Florida to which place the prisoners *Private Jacob Morgan, Company D, 8th Connecticut Volunteers* and Private John Eagen, Company H, 2nd New Hampshire Volunteers will be sent, under suitable guard, by orders from the Army or department commander.

By Order of the Secretary of War

E. O. Townsend, Assistant Adjutant General"

However, on April 27, 1864, General Orders, number 2, from Headquarters of Norfolk and Portsmouth was issued.

"In obediance to General Orders Number 48, Head Quarters Department of Virginia and North Caroline, Private Jacob Morgan, Co. D, 8th Connecticut Volunteers, now under sentence of death for desertion, will be shot to death with musketry, at the Fairgrounds, near this city between the hours of 10 AM and 12 M, Thursday, the 28th inst.

By command of Brigadier General
G. F. Shepley"
He was buried at Hampton National Cemetery, Virginia.Epilogue:
On August 8, 1864, G.C.M.O. #233, A.G.O. *commuted* the sentence of Private Jacob Morgan, Company D, 8th Connecticut Infantry Regiment to forfeiture of all pay and allowances due, discharge from the US service and imprisonment during the War at Dry Tortugas, Florida.
Unfortunately, Morgan had already been executed.

REFERENCES:
Military Personnel Records, RG-#94
Court Martial Proceedings, RG-#153 MM 1452

Case #112
Sgt.(Pvt.) John Meyers
Co. G, 7th IL Infantry Regt.
Executed for Murder
April 28, 1864

DESCRIPTION:
No description is available. The use of a descriptive record was apparently not in force in the early part of the war.

Meyers enlisted and was mustered into service at Mound City, Illinois on October 28, 1861 in Company G, 7th Illinois Infantry Regiment. The 7th Regiment was originally organized as Infantry, but was mounted by order of General Dodge on June 1863 and were dismounted and returned to duty as Infantry per S.O. #126 Headquarters 16th Army Corps, May 20, 1865. On August 31, 1862, Meyers was promoted to rank of Sergeant directly from rank of Private. He was reduced back to rank of Private on December 4, 1862. His muster roll records indicate absence in Hospital at Paducah, Kentucky at some point during the period January 1 to June 30, 1862.

On December 3, 1862 Meyers did threaten and did shoot his Company Commander, Captain Henry W. Allen, so that he died a few hours later at the camp of the 7th Illinois at Corinth, Mississippi. He was arrested, confined, reduced in rank to private and tried by Court Martial on December 4, 1862. Convicted of the charges, he was sentenced to be hung. The execution was carried out on April 28, 1864 at Pulaski, Tennessee.

Two Springfield, Illinois newspapers carried brief accounts of Captain Allen's murder. Most of the articles describe the biography of Captain Allen, who was born in New York state, arrived in Illinois in 1858 and was a teacher by profession. The statement that his body would be returned to Springfield for burial concludes one article. There was no indication of the reason for the murder.

A General Court Martial was convened at Corinth, Mississippi and on December 22, 1862 tried Sergeant John Myers, Company G, 7th Illinois Infantry Regiment on a charge of murder.

The accused asked for a delay of the trial in order to permit him more time to obtain counsel which the Court granted. No counsel seems to have been obtained and the trial commenced.

On the evening of December 2, 1862, the day previous to the murder of Captain Allen, there was great excitement in the regimental camp and especially in the street of Company B, commanded by Captain Perrin. An elderly negro man, said to have been in his 80's, was brought into the tent of his wife who cooked for Company B. Another crowd of soldiers were milling around on Company H street. Captain Perrin and several others went there and Perrin inquired who the person was who had knocked the old man down and the reason for it. A man in the group said that he was the one who did it, offering no explanation for his act. The Officer of the Day and two guards took the man, who admitted assaulting the elderly negro, to the guard house. The excitement increased as officers and men broke up in groups discussing the matter of the striking of the negro. In Lieutenant Colonel Rowell's tent, men and officers gathered to discuss the affair. The accused, Myers, was present and spoke up saying, "I want that man (the person who assaulted the negro) out of the guardhouse." The Lieutenant Colonel said, "Have that man arrested." Captain Allen, also present said, "Myers I will have you arrested and put in the guard house if you don't keep still." The Lieutenant Colonel asked Myers if he meant what he said as a threat? Myers replied "No." The Lieutenant Colonel then said, "this is a public discussion and you have as much right to speak perhaps as I have." Myers exclaimed, "Do you hear that?" and then said after he left the tent and the immediate area thereof, "Captain Allen is a son of a bitch, if he fools with me I will shoot him."

Prior to the fatal day, Myers had attempted unsuccessfully to secure a transfer from Captain Allen's Company to another in the same Regiment.

Witnesses described the events of the crime. About 6 or 7 PM in the Camp of the 7th Illinois Infantry near Corinth, Mississippi a Captain Perrin heard the accused pass his tent using "pretty strong language" in a loud tone of voice. Some witnesses testified that he was talking loudly about loading his gun and getting "the man" out of the guard house. Two men heard him loading his gun and remarked "let's go out he is loading his gun, there will be some fun." Moments later Myers entered their tent, gun in hand, saying, "Come on boys follow me, I will shoot the first son of a bitch that tries to arrest me." Perrin came to Captain Allen's tent and said, "Captain there is one of your men raising the devil." Allen replied he had summoned the Officer of the Day to arrest the accused. When Lieutenant Knowlton, the O. D. reported, Allen told him to take Myers to the guard house. Knowlton seemed hesitant about performing this task. Allen then said to Knowlton, "If you are afraid, I will go myself." Allen stood up, took his revolver and left the tent, followed by Perrin and Knowlton. The accused was at the head of the Company street and saw Captain Allen approaching and addressed him, "Captain Allen, you are the son of a bitch I mean, I will shoot you." He then brought his musket up to the "Ready," keeping an eye on Captain Allen who moved about among the groups of soldiers present to evade the prisoner's observation. The accused brought his gun to the aim and began tracking Captain Allen's movements while warning the bystanders to stand back, which they quickly did. Captain Allen held out his hand toward the accused saying, "hold on." which he repeated, then shouted in desperation "Why don't some one get hold of him and get the gun away from him?" Two or three soldiers then started toward the prisoner as he fired and mortally wounded the Captain. The accused threw down his gun and said, "I have done what I wanted to do." He was seized and delivered to the guard house.

While in the guard house, the accused kept up a stream of remarks such as, "I killed him, the Company wanted him killed." He was told to stop talking but continued saying, "I killed the son of a bitch and I was the only man in the Company that had the heart to do it." The Captain told him to quit such language or he would shoot him and ordered the prisoner to be "bucked and gagged." He ordered the guard to allow no one to talk to the accused or approach him. The Captain rode to Corinth to arrange for the Provost Marshall to hold the prisoner and upon his return to the regimental guard house heard the prisoner still talking and saying, "I have killed him, the Company wanted him killed." The Captain irked by the failure of his men to carry out his orders demanded to know "Why the prisoner had not been gagged?" The accused replied, "It is not worthwhile, he would quit talking." The Captain then issued orders for the transfer of the prisoner to the Provost Marshall's jail in Corinth, Mississippi saying, "if the prisoner tries to escape, kill him!" The accused then spoke up saying "I shall not try to get away; I am a man, every inch of me, I killed him and expect to die for it, but I am a good soldier and I want you to treat me well and have mercy."

When Captain Allen had been shot, he fell down, face forward exclaiming, "I am shot, I am shot." After a moment or so he asked, "where is my revolver? Where is my revolver?" and finally, "There is my revolver pick it up!"

Dr. James Hamilton, Assistant Surgeon of the 7th Illinois Regiment testified that he examined Captain Allen after he had been removed to his tent. He found a ball wound of entrance on the right side about two inches from the backbone, the eighth rib being fractured. Another wound, the exit site, on the left side about three inches from the back bone between the 7th and 8th ribs, the liver being pierced. It was the doctor's opinion that Captain Allen, who died about twenty minutes to eleven o'clock, bleed to death of internal hemorrhage.

The prisoner having no witnesses to offer did present a statement to the court.

Gentlemen of the Court

"In this unhappy affair, I can only appeal to you men as this is the first in my life that I have been ever accused of an offense against the laws of my country. I served faithfully through the Mexican War, and early responded to the call for troops to crush this unholy Rebellion. Rum has been the cause of any ruin. Captain Allen, on the last day of his life, gave me unlimited permission to get Whiskey from his quarters, as I was at work for him; and drank too much; so that when the excitement arose in camp I was in a fit state to commit an act, the memory of which will embitter the remainder of my days, whether few or many.

"From the details of the testimony you cannot but perceive that I had no long cherished malice against Captain Allen; that should, in the state in which I then was, have offered violence to any one who should attempt to arrest me. I cannot now recollect by any means clearly, the transactions of that dreadful night. I should not, in my sober moments, have dreamed ever of committing violence upon my Captain. If malice aforethought is necessary to constitute the crime of murder, I am not guilty. I committed the act in a moment of intense excitement, caused by whiskey and the circumstances which surrounded me on that evening.

If it is within the scope of your power, gentlemen, to spare my life, so that by years of penitence I can atone for one misdeed, I shall be ever grateful.

(signed) John Myers"

The Court deliberated, found the accused guilty and sentenced him to be hung by the neck until he be dead.

The trial records and proceedings were very delayed in forwarding through the chain of command for approval. A letter from Major General U. S. Grant, dated June 1, 1863, Headquarters of the Tennessee, in the field at Vicksburg, Mississippi. "The proceedings, findings and sentence in the foregoing case (Sgt. John Myers) are confirmed; but as the law at the time of the trial and conviction in this case was had, prohibited the carrying into execution of the sentence of death, until the same should be approved by the President, the execution of the sentence in this case is suspended in pursuance of the authority conferred by the 89th Article of War, until the pleasure of the President of the United States, to whom these proceedings are respectfully forwarded, can be known."

On October 28, 1863, the Judge Advocate General Holt wrote, "Sergeant Myers of the 7th Illinois Volunteers was sentenced to be hung for the murder of his Captain. The proof is indubitable that the shooting was wilfull and premeditated. The prisoner claimed he was under the influence of liquor at the time, but the evidence is clear that he was in full possession of his reason, and fully understood the penalty attached to the commission of the deed.

The offence having been committed prior to the enactment authorizing the execution of death sentences by Commanding Generals, the case is forwarded by General Grant for the approval of the President. The review was concluded in January (1863) but was not received in this office until the present month. It is recommended that a speedy enforcement of the sentence be ordered.

Holt, Judge Advocate General."

An endorsement to the Judge Advocate General's memorandum is dated February 10, 1864 and reads, "Sentence Approved"

A. Lincoln

The execution took place on April 28, 1864 at Pulaski, Tennessee. The 7th Illinois Infantry Regiment having been assigned there for duty from Corinth.

REFERENCES:

Military Personnel Records, RG-#94
Court Martial Proceedings, RG-#153 MM 989
Springfield, Illinois, Illinois State Journal, December 5, 1862.
Springfield, Illinois, Illinois State Register, December 5, 1862.

Case #113
Pvt. Owen McDonough
Co. K, 2nd NH Vol Inf Regt
Executed for Desertion
April 29, 1864

DESCRIPTION:

29 years of age, 5 feet 6 inches tall, blue eyes, brown hair, fair complexion, born in England, occupation mechanic, literate.

Enlisted in Company K, 2nd New Hampshire Volunteer Infantry Regiment at Concord, New Hampshire on November 17, 1863 and a bounty of $300.00 and $2.00 premium, was assigned to the City of Concord. Deserted his company at Yorktown, Virginia on the 11th of April 1864 and was arrested on the 20th of April 1864. Was court martialed and found guilty of desertion, sentenced to be shot near Fort Magruder, Virginia on April 29, 1864 together with Pvt. James Scott of Company G, 2nd New Hampshire Volunteer Infantry Regiment.

REFERENCES:

Military Personnel Records, RG-#94
No record of the trial or court martial proceedings have been found.

Case #114
Pvt. John Reily, Jr.
NV: Riley - Reilly
2nd Batty L, 2nd Mo Vol L Arty Regt
Executed for Murder
April 29, 1864

DESCRIPTION:

21 years of age, 5 feet 4 inches tall, hazel eyes, brown hair, fair complexion, born in New Orleans, Louisana, occupation boatman, received $60.00 bounty, $2.00 premium, and one month's pay in advance.

Enlisted at St. Louis, Missouri on January 4, 1864, and apparently on duty with his unit in the Warrensburg, Missouri area, about midway between Kansas City and St. Louis, when in February 1864 he committed murder, was arrested, confined in the County Prison, and court martialed. He was found guilty as charged and sentenced to be shot by a firing squad on Friday, April 29, 1864 at 3:30 p.m.

The execution order directed all troops participating to form in the street adjoining the County Prison. The procession to the place of execution was led by the Provost Marshall, followed in turn by the Brigade band, the firing party, the coffin borne by four men, the hearse containing the prisoner and Chaplain, provost guard and balance of troops all proceeding to the place of execution to the west of the town. When the ten man firing squad had completed their task, the assembled troops marched past the corpse in slow time. The military district Quartermaster provided the coffin, transportation, and supervised the interment of the body.

REFERENCES:
Military Personnel Records, RG-#94
No court martial records or proceedings were located to provide more explicit details of the crime.

Case #115
Pvt. James Scott
Co. G, 2nd NH Vol Inf Regt
Executed for Desertion
April 29, 1864

DESCRIPTION:
22 years of age, 5 feet 8¼ inches tall, blue eyes, light hair, light complexion, born in Scotland, occupation sailor, illiterate.

Enlisted Concord, New Hampshire, bounty and premium assigned to Nashua, New Hampshire. His regiment served in the Williamsburg, Virginia area and his Muster Roll record (attendance record) for January and February 1864 bear the notation, "detailed on Mortar Schooner," a logical assignment for one whose civilian occupation was that of a sailor.

Scott deserted his Regiment, was captured and tried on April 18, 1864, found guilty and shot to death on April 29, 1864 together with Pvt. Owen McDonough of Company K, 2nd New Hampshire Volunteer Infantry Regiment near Fort Magruder, Virginia.

REFERENCES:
National Archives, Military Personnel Records, RG-#94
No record of the Court Martial has been found.
"History of the 12th Regiment, New Hampshire Volunteers in the War of the Rebellion," Abe W. Bartlett, 1897, Concord, New Hampshire, Ira Evans Publishing.

Case #116
Pvt. John H. Thompson
Co. E, 1st Ohio Cavalry Regt.
Executed for Desertion
April 29, 1864

DESCRIPTION:
18 years of age, 5 feet 4½ inches tall, black hair, black eyes, dark complexion, born Licking County, Ohio, occupation farmer, literacy undetermined.

Thompson enlisted at Newark, Ohio on August 25, 1861 and was mustered into service at Camp Chase (Columbus, Ohio) on September 12, 1861. He was assigned to Company C, 1st Ohio Cavalry Volunteer Regiment. His unit was conducting military operations in the area around Drainsville, Virginia when he deserted on or about March15, 1863. He was apprehended on July 21, 1863 and according to most records, escaped from his guards on the same day. He was captured by local civilians toward the end of November, 1863 and taken to Fort Ethan Allen. A Major Young, of the U.S. Army at Fort Ethan Allen, had announced that he would arrest and imprison the civilian population of the community if they did not capture and deliver Thompson to him. Three men in the area carried out the capture to forestall the Major's threat.

A General Court Martial was convened at the court rooms on Fairfax street, Alexandria, Virginia and on January 16, 1864 tried Private John H. Thompson, Company C, 1st Ohio Cavalry Regiment on the following charges: Desertion, Desertion to the Enemy, Robbery.

Thompson pleaded guilty to all charges and specifications except, serving as a Guerilla.

The testimony presented to the court by witnesses showed that Thompson, while serving with his Regiment near Drainsville, Virginia, deserted the military service on or about March 1, 1863. The accused later escaped from his guard after apprehension on July 21, 1863. He remained in the neighborhood, however, until the end of November 1863 when he was captured and delivered as a prisoner for confinement to Fort Ethan Allen, Virginia. The accused admitted to his captors that he had engaged in horse stealing and had joined one partisan band of guerillas. The prisoner also had, on October 15, 1863, stolen $239.00 from a citizen named James Trammel and admitted it to the men who captured him. The people in the area generally considered Thompson to be a member of one of Mosby's guerilla gangs that preyed on the unwary Union Soldiers and Citizens of the area alike.

The accused offered neither witnesses nor statement to the court.

The court deliberated and confirmed his pleas of guilty as well as finding him guilty on his plea of not guilty. He was sentenced to be shot to death with musketry.

Following his Court Martial trial and conviction, Thompson wrote the following letter of appeal for clemency to President Lincoln.

"Alexandria Jail, January 16th, 1864
To His Excellency Abraham Lincoln
President of the United States
Dear Sir

I was Court Marshalled yesterday and one of the gravest of charges was brought against me Viz: that of deserting the federal army and joining a confederate guerilla band known as White's. In relation to this charge I am perfectly innocent: that is of joining any guerilla band and this I can prove by the most substantial testimony. I can also prove that the men that testified against me in respect to the above charge are disloyal men and are constantly carrying on illicit trade with the South and have been known to pilot "Whites" men to the Union Camp at Loonsville for the purpose of stealing horses. This I can prove by men who have always known the men who swore against me. Viz: the men who reside at the Big Falls, Fairfax County, Virginia. They are two-faced men assuming to be loyal when with loyal men and disloyal when with rebels. This they do to promote their own selfish ends. As the testimony of the false-hearted men who swore against me is calculated to deprive me of my liberty and perhaps my life, I solemnly appeal to you to set aside the sentence of the Court-Marshall and allow me the privilege of another trial. I will briefly stat how I happed to be absent from my regiment, when it was stationed at Drainsville I sometimes like many other soldiers visited some of the families in that vicinity inside of our lines and at the time the Regiment left, I happened to be absent and afterwards stopped at one of the families at Spring Vale, a place two miles this side of Drainsville. I can prove that I never aided, abetted or given comfort to the enemy in any way. Nor even resided within their lines. I seriously hope you will interpose and be instrumental in preserving my liberty or at least life.

Your Humble Servant
John H. Thompson"

Major General C. C. Augur, Military District Commander, confirmed the proceedings, findings and sentence of the court but suspended execution of the sentence until the pleasure of the President of the United States is made known. General Augur recommended that the sentence be mitigated to dishonorable discharge from the service and confinement at hard labor in a penitentiary for the term of five (5) years.

"Judge Advocate General's Office
January 22nd 1864

The record of the trial referred to has not been received at this office and nothing is

known in regard to the case beyond what is stated by the prisoner in the writer's letter and by Brig. Gen. Slough. It is for the Secretary to determine whether the unsupported representations of the former in his own behalf will justify a suspension of the death sentence until the record can be received and reviewed.
Holt
Judge Advo General"

"Judge Advocate General's Office
February 26th 1864
Private *John H. Thompson* of the 1st Ohio Cavalry was convicted of "Desertion," "Desertion to the enemy," and of "Robbery" and was sentenced to be shot.

Gen'l. Augur suspended the execution of the sentence and recommends commutation to dishonorable discharge from the service and confinement at hard labor for five years in the Penitentiary. The prisoner plead guilty to having deserted on the 15th of March '63 remaining absent until apprehended on the 21st of July: and to having escaped from the guard on the 21st of July and deserting again, remaining absent until apprehended, and also guilty of having robbed a citizen near Great Falls, Virginia of $239.00.

No reasons are shown or suggested by the record whey the sentence pronounced should not be rigidly and speedily enforced.
Holt
Judge Advo General"

"United States Military Telegraph
By Telegraph from Alexandria
Dated April 29, 1864
To Asst. Adjt. Gen'l. Hdq. Dist. Dept.
Sir: Private John H. Thompson, Company C, 1st Ohio Cavalry was shot to death with musketry this 29th day of April 1864 in pursuance of Gen'l. Orders No. 170 dated War Dept. Adjt. Gen'l. Office, Washington April 21st 1864.

Nothing else unusual has transpired in this command today.
John Slough
BGV
Mil. Gov."

REFERENCES:
Military Personnel Records, RG-#94
Court Martial Proceedings, RG-#153 NN 1153

Case #117
Pvt. Henry Burnham
Co. E, 5th N.H. Infantry Regt.
Executed for Desertion
May 9, 1864

DESCRIPTION:
29 years of age, 5 feet 11 inches tall, brown hair, gray eyes, florid complexion, born in New York City, New York, occupation farmer, substitute, illiterate.

Burnham was drafted, as a substitute, and mustered into service at West Lebanon, New Hampshire on October 3, 1863 and was sent in a draft of men to the 5th New Hampshire Infantry Regiment and assigned to Company E.

On November 19, 1863, Burnham deserted his Regiment near Camp Lookout, Maryland. He was arrested on January 12, 1864 and was tried by court martial.

A General Court Martial was convened at headquarters of St. Mary's district, Point Lookout, Maryland on April 28, 1864 to try Private Henry A. Burnham, Company E, 5th New Hampshire Infantry Regiment on a charge of desertion and fraudulently reenlisting in the Army.

The prisoner applied to the court for admission of Captain Young of the 2nd New Hampshire Volunteers as his counsel, which was granted.

Burnham's Military career consisted of enlisting as a substitute in New Hampshire on October 3, 1863 and was assigned to Company E, 5th New Hampshire Infantry Regiment from which he deserted on November 19, 1863. He returned to New Hampshire and reenlisted on November 25, 1863 as a substitute and was assigned to the 2nd New Hampshire Infantry Regiment stationed at Point Lookout, Maryland where he was discovered on January 12, 1864, arrested and confined in the guardhouse as a deserter. Burnham escaped from the guardhouse on February 1, 1864 and no date is found for his recapture and final confinement to the guardhouse pending his trial.

The accused pleaded guilty to all charges and his counsel requested a postponement of the sentence for 24 hours to permit the preparation of a statement of the prisoner, which was granted.

Statement of the Accused

"I, Henry A. Burnham now under charges for desertion enlisted at first under false impressions having been deceived by the parties so common in New England, substitute brokers, I received no bounty, in fact was very drunk when I enlisted, and entirely unable to understand the nature of my oath. Upon arriving at Point Lookout was placed in the 5th New Hampshire Infantry Regiment and then did my best to become a soldier but one day while I was drunk I was induced to desert, which I did and a few days after found myself in Boston when I was introduced to some gentlemen who asked me to drink. I remember little else until I found myself in Concord, New Hampshire again and enlisted as a soldier. I had been drugged, I found that I had one hundred and seventy five dollars in my pocket and I immediately resolved to go where they put me and do my duty.

I was taken to Point Lookout once more, this time to be placed in the 2nd New Hampshire Infantry Regiment where I tried to do my duty as a soldier. I think I succeeded in this, but after five weeks I was discovered by Lieutenant Hale and arrested. I had been sober all the time I had been with the 2nd and when I found myself again in the guardhouse and was told that I surely would be shot. I felt so badly that I once more got intoxicated, and then attempted to escape again, I have no other excuse to offer to the court than that I, in attempting to escape was drunk each time. I have been the dupe of designing men in Boston who drugged me, stole my bounty and placed me in this wretched condition. I ask the indulgence of the court and whatever punishment you may deem proper to inflict, I will endeavor to bear like a man and a soldier. If I am allowed to return to my regiment I promise to do my whole duty, whether in the camp or in the field, and if I am to be shot I will die like a true American Soldier.

This statement I declare to be true as I hope for peace hereafter.

"Henry A. Burnham"

The Court retired to consider the case and rendered the verdict of guilty confirming the plea of the accused and sentenced Burnham to be executed before a firing squad near Point Lookout, Virginia. The execution took place on May 9, 1864 and curiously enough there are documents in the file dated August 26, 1864 authorizing the execution!

On May 7, 1864 a memorandum request from the Provost Marshall having custody of Burnham to the Acting Assistant Adjt. General at Headquarters both located at Camp Lookout, Maryland stated: "I am requested by Private Burnham 5th N.H. Vols. now under sentence of death, to procure for him a copy of the findings and sentence of the court martial. Will you please furnish me with copy."

On May 9, 1864, a report of Burnham's execution states in part, "Private Henry A. Burnham, Co. E, 5th NH Vols. was at eight o'clock this morning shot to death with musketry."

Special Orders No. 282, War Department, Adjutant General's Office, Washington,

August 26, 1864 (extract).

2-By direction of the President of the United States, the sentence, "to be shot to death" of the General Court Martial, in the case of Private Henry A. Burnham, Company E, 5th New Hampshire Volunteers, promulgated in General Orders, No. 56, Headquarters, Department of Virginia and North Carolina, May 4, 1864, is approved, and will be executed under the orders of the Department Commander.

By order of the Secretary of War

E. D. Townsend, Assistant Adjutant General"

The above published order stimulated the sending of a telegram on August 27, 1864 to a Captain Nelson, A. A. Adjt. General, "Please ascertain and report whether Private Henry A. Burnham, Company E, 5th N.H. Vols. is now with his regt. and if not where is he confined, an order has been received directing that the sentence of death be carried into execution."

A reply to the telegram (preceding) was sent from Headquarters, 5th Regiment New Hampshire Volunteers near Petersburg, Virginia August 29, 1864 to Captain G. H. Caldwell, A. A. General, 1st Brigade,

"Sir: I have the honor to report that Private Henry A. Burnham, Co. E, 5th Regt. New Hampshire Vols. found guilty of desertion by a G.C.M. convened by virtue of S.O. no 116, Hdqrs. Dept Va and NC of April 26, 1864 and sentenced to be shot to death with musketry, was accordingly executed on the morning of May 9, 1864, the proceedings etc. having been approved by Maj. Genl Butler Comdg. Dept. Va and NC.

I am, Capt.

Very Respectfully

J. E. Larkin

Maj. 5th NH Vols Comdg. Regt.

The preceding series of communications indicate that there was an unnecessary request for approval from the President of the United States as the law as amended permitted executions for convictions of desertion permitted death sentences in such cases to be carried out with the approval of the Commanding Officer of the Major Command in the area. The approval of the sentence of execution arriving after the execution had been performed is a variant from cases where the President directed executive clemency, a pardon or a reprieve and the order arrived after the execution had taken place.

REFERENCES:

Military Personnel Records, RG-#94

Court Martial Proceedings, RG-#153 NN 1733

Case #118

Private John D. Starbird

Co. K, 19th Mass. Vol. Inf. Regt.

Executed for Desertion

May 20/21, 1864

DESCRIPTION:

20 years of age, 5 feet 8 inches tall, dark hair, gray eyes, light complexion, born in Manchester, New Hampshire, occupation clerk, literate.

Starbird enlisted September 3, 1861 at Boston, Massachusetts and was mustered into service September 16, 1861 at Boston, Massachusetts in Company K, 19th Massachusetts Volunteer Infantry Regiment. Starbird began a series of desertions and false enlistments for bounty, following an early desertion. Reports indicate him AWOL on April 18, 1862 from Yorktown, Virginia, and on June 29, 1862 was declared a deserter. In September, 1862 he enlisted in the 47th Massachusetts Volunteer Infantry Regiment as Lawrence J. Hoyt. In November, 1862 he deserted the 47th Massachusetts, and enlisted in the 2nd Rhode Island Cavalry Regiment and received a bounty of $325.00. He deserted the 2nd

Rhode Island in August, 1863 and in September 1863 enlisted in the 35th New Jersey Volunteers under the name of John D. Ford, and received a $200.00 bounty, then deserted three days later. Starbird's luck expired when he returned to Boston, Massachusetts and was arrested by Police Officer T. H. Adams who was paid $30.00 for expenses incurred in Starbird's capture. On November 10, 1863 he was in confinement at Military Headquarters, Boston, Massachusetts and by March 22, 1864 had been returned to his original regiment, the 19th Massachusetts Volunteer Infantry in the Stevensburg, Virginia area.

"A General Court Martial"(*) was convened at the headquarters of the 19th Massachusetts Infantry Regiment and on May 19, 1864 tried Private John D. Starbird, Company K, 19th Massachusetts Infantry Regiment on a charge of deserting the Colors of the Regiment in the face of the enemy.

Testimony was provided that indicated Starbird had deserted while his Regiment was engaged with the enemy in the Wilderness at or near Chancellorsville, Virginia on or about May 7, 1864. Starbird also repeated this offense on May 10, 1864 while the regiment was going into action at or near Spottsylvania Court House. Five witnesses are said to have testified, three for the prosecution, two for the defense. The accused presented no statement on his behalf. The Court deliberated, found the prisoner guilty and sentenced him to be shot to death with musketry.

The execution was by one report carried out on May 20, 1864 in the field.

This case generated a good deal of correspondence and at least two versions of the Court Martial proceedings are extant. The original was apparently written in haste by a penman with poor writing skill. The second version is prepared more conventionally and by an accomplished clerk. The proceedings were forwarded to the Judge Advocate General's office in Washington, D. C. from which the first letter of correspondence emanates.

"Judge Advocate General's Office, June 28, 1864

Respectfully returned to Major General Meade. The record in this case is incomplete. The testimony of the five witnesses, who appear to have been examined by the court, is not reported.Holt—

Judge Advocate

General Meade replied.

"Headquarters A. of P.

July 5, 1864

Respectfully returned to the Judge Advocate General. The trial of this case occurred when we were in the immediate presence of the enemy and in actual and constant engagement with them. In my judgement, an immediate example was necessary to check a growing disposition to desertion. I consider I would have been perfectly justified in ordering the instant execution of the person without trial, but it was thought better to conform to the ordinary modes of procedure so far as circumstances would permit. The case therefore was brought before a *"Drumhead Court Martial"* and no record was made of the evidence.

Geo. C. Meade

Major General Commanding"

Another letter dated May 17, 1864 from the commander of the 19th Massachusetts Infantry Regiment states "his execution took place as ordered."

A letter from a James D. Thompson of Boston, Massachusetts is referred to in a letter dated March 24, 1865 Treasury Department, Washington, D. C. from second auditor E. B. French.

"Encloses letter of James D. Thompson relative to John D. Starbird (deceased), Company K, 19th Massachusetts Volunteers asks if the statements as to *Starbird* being *pardoned* are true and requests with reply a full military history."

On March 31, 1865 a letter from the Adjutant General's Office Washington D. C. stated:

"Respectfully referred to the Bureau of military Justice for information relative to the alleged *pardon* of this man.

These papers to be returned with report.

By order of the Secretary of War,

Signed ________________

Assistant Adjutant General"

On April 13, 1865 another letter was written on the matter.

"War Department

Bureau of Military Justice

April 13, 1865

Respectfully returned to the Adjutant General and record in case of *Private John D. Starbird, Company K, 19th Massachusetts Volunteers* exhibited. It is probable that he died May 20th as stated in the within letter, but that it was by execution for desertion, which, it will be seen, was ordered to take place on that day.

A. A. Hasmer, Major and Judge Advocate

In the absence of the Judge Advocate General"

And finally on May 17, 1865 a letter from the Headquarters, 19th Massachusetts Volunteers.

Respectfully returned.

This man was executed by shooting, May 20, 1864 pursuant to sentence of General Court Martial.

Signed ______________

Lt./Col. 19th Massachusetts Commanding Regt."

General Meade commented in writing at the conclusion of the original Court Martial.

"The Major General Commanding is determined to exercise the utmost, rigor of the law in punishing those cowards who disgrace their colors by basely deserting them in presence of the enemy."

(*) See statement of Meade as to the trial being a drumhead Court Martial.

REFERENCES:

Military Personnel Records, RG-#94

Court Martial Proceedings, RG-#153 NN 1943

Case #119

Pvt. John Callahan

Co. H, 2nd NJ Cavalry Regt

Executed for Rape & Theft

June 10, 1864

DESCRIPTION:

18 years of age, no further description was located.

Callahan enlisted at Hudson City, New Jersey on August 6, 1863 and was mustered into service at Trenton, New Jersey on August 12, 1863 in Company H, 2nd New Jersey Cavalry Regiment. A notation on his military record states, "September 25,-October 31, 1863 deserted and captured, $10.00 paid for his apprehension." No other details of this incident appear in his records. He was involved with Case #121 Snover and Case #120 Johnson of the same Regiment in the crime of Rape and Theft for which he also suffered their fate. See the above listed cases for more details.

A Military Commission convened at Memphis, Tennessee on March 21, 1864, charged Private John Callahan, Company H, and Private Jacob Snover, Company M, both of the 2nd New Jersey Cavalry Regiment on the 12th of March, 1864 with offenses of Rape and Robbery. Both pleaded not guilty and requested admission of Captain Van Rensalaer as their legal counsel. A third man, Private Thomas Johnson of Company D, 2nd New Jersey Cavalry Regiment had been included in the original draft of the charges, but was not brought to trial with Snover and Callahan.

Testimony at the trial indicated that Callahan and Snover were sent out from their unit Headquarters about 4PM on March 12, 1864, to investigate a report of a robbery. They were said to have returned about 8PM or so, well after dark. A George Washington Bradshaw, an employee of a Mr. Brooks was driving a two mule wagon from Memphis toward the Brooks residence, accompanied by Mrs. Margaret Brooks and a Mr. Moore in a buggy. At the Nonconah River, while trying to ford the stream, the wagon became mired at the bank of the stream. Bradshaw unhitched the team, tied one mule to a tree and mounted the other to secure aid in pulling the mired wagon free. On the Pidgeon Roost Road he encountered three Union soldiers about 300 yards from the stream at dusk. Mrs. Brooks had remained with the bogged down wagon. Bradshaw went to the Brooks' residence and returned toward the site of the stalled wagon when about 9:30 PM he saw Mrs. Brooks about 1/2 mile from the bank of the stream. She said something had happened and that some soldiers had treated her most cruelly. Questioned about Mr. Moore, Bradshaw stated he had been left at the wagon but had not been seen thereafter. Mr. A. T. Forbes, a citizen residing on the Pidgeon Roost Road near the Nonconah Creek testified that three Union soldiers appeared at his home on March 12, 1864 before dark and demanded supper. The supper was prepared by Mrs. Forbes, the men ate and left.

He identified Callahan and Snover as two of the three men. Mrs. Margaret I. Brooks testified she was married and had two children. She recounted the events of the day, leaving Memphis for home, Bradshaw's wagon being stalled at the stream, unhitching the Mules and Bradshaw riding one mule to her house for aid. She and Moore remained at the stream. Three mounted soldiers came riding up, "hooting and hollering," one untied the remaining mule while the other two soldiers rode into the creek to see what the wagon contained. Mrs. Brooks got into her buggy and the soldiers shouted "stop there God damn you, or I'll shoot you." Mrs. Brooks ignored them and began to turn the horse and buggy around but the three soldiers rode up and ordered her "not to move a peg or they would blow my brains into hell!" They questioned her as to the details of the stalling and whether anyone was with her. She replied, "Moore," her buggy driver was there, but he had disappeared and was not found to testify at the subsequent trial. Snover and Johnson rode out looking for Moore and Callahan remained with Mrs. Brooks.

Callahan then demanded "Green Backs" and Mrs. Brooks replied she had none. Finally Callahan said if you don't have money we will take something else. She said she didn't know what he was talking about. He said they wanted a little "FUCKING" and we intend to have it right here and the stiller you are the better it will be for you. Mrs. Brooks replied, "I will die right here before I will submit to any such thing." Callahan said, "We will shoot you dead" and drew up his gun and aimed it at her head, then pulled the hammer back and said, "do you submit," she replied, "No, I would rather die right here first!" Callahan then said, "We won't ask you anymore, we will do it anyhow." He jumped into the buggy where Mrs. Brooks was seated and she began screaming and calling for Moore. Callahan placed one of his hands over her nose and mouth and with the other began choking her until she was semi conscious. Then he and his two companions arranged her in the buggy overcoming her feeble resistance. Callahan continued to choke and punch Mrs. Brooks saying, "God damn you, you had just as well come to it, for we will do it or kill you right here." Callahan raped her while the other two held her helpless. Then Snover and Johnson raped her. Callahan then declared she had not permitted him to penetrate her person and raped her again. The three rapists then examined the mule Wagon contents and returned to the buggy and one asked, "is that gal dead?" another answered, "No, but damn near it!" They then searched Mrs. Brooks clothing and person and found two hundred and fifty ($250.00) "in her bosom" and had one hundred dollars ($100.00) in her "companion" (purse or brief case).

A Dr. T. F. Payne testified to examining Mrs. Brooks at the home of Dr. F. J. Malone. He found her condition to indicate that she had been "roughly handled."

An enlisted man of the Regiment testified to being told by Callahan that he and two others got some "screwing" and that it occurred while they were drunk.

No other testimony or statements were made and the court adjourned to deliberate. The prisoners, Callahan and Snover, were found guilty and sentenced to death before a firing squad on June 10, 1864. Strangely enough, Private Thomas Johnson, Company D, New Jersey Cavalry Regiment who was not charged at this trial, was also executed at the same time and manner as Callahan and Snover.

REFERENCES:
Military Personnel Records, RG-#94
Court Martial Proceedings, RG-#153 NN 1740
State of New Jersey Military Records

Case #120
Pvt. Thomas Johnson
Co. D, 2nd, NJ Cavalry Regt.
Executed for Rape & Theft
June 10, 1864

DESCRIPTION:

18 years of age, no further description located.

Johnson enlisted on August 21, 1863 at Jersey City, New Jersey and was mustered into service at Trenton, New Jersey on August 26, 1863 in Company D, 2nd New Jersey Cavalry Regiment. Johnson was appointed to rank of Corporal on August 26, 1863 and reduced to rank of Private on October 23, 1863. He was involved with Case #121 Snover and Case #119 Callahan (same Regiment) in the crime of Rape and Theft. See the above individual cases for more details.

A Military Commission was convened at Memphis, Tennessee on March 31, 1864 tried Private Thomas Johnson, Company D, 2nd New Jersey Cavalry Regiment on charges of Rape and Robbery.

Johnson stated he did not desire counsel. Johnson was one of a trio of 2nd New Jersey cavalrymen involved in the rape and robbery of a Mrs. Mary J. Brooks on Pigeon Roost Road at Nonconah Creek Ford about 7 or 8 miles from Memphis, Tennessee. Two of the three, Jacob Snover and John Callahan, had been previously tried and convicted on the same charges and sentenced to death. The testimony presented in this case differed very little from that presented in the two prior cases. To reduce repetition, only previously unstated evidence will be referred to or quoted.

Witnesses testified that they were reasonably sure that Johnson was one of the trio of perpetrators of this horrendous crime, but the appearance of Johnson had materially changed. Where he had been obese, he now was thin, where his skin color had been red or flushed it now was sallow or colorless.

The difficulty was resolved by the testimony of Corporal Lemuel Shook, Company E, 103rd Illinois Infantry Regiment on detached service at the Irving Military Prison where Johnson was confined since the middle of March. Corporal Shook stated that on arrival at the prison, "Johnson was healthy, robust, of good color. He has however been quite sick and is much reduced" (in body bulk) "and his color not so good." When asked what the nature of his illness was, Shook replied, "I can't tell what his disease was."

The accused offered no testimony in his behalf but presented a statement to the court.

"Statement of Accused"

"All I have to state is that I know nothing about the case I never heard of the robbery until I came to the Provost Marshall's Office, I never received any of the money and know nothing about it."

The commission then deliberated, found Johnson guilty and sentenced him to be shot to death with musketry. The execution took place on June 10, 1864 near Memphis, Tennessee.

Captain Channing Richards, 22nd Ohio Infantry Regiment who was Judge Advocate at Johnson's trial wrote a letter on April 10, 1864:

"I certify that I have made every effort in my power to obtain the testimony of the man Moore, but the detectives to which I applied report that he is keeping out of their way and they cannot find him. This statement is made mainly because I do not wish to appear in the record unexplained that any witness who could probably throw considerable light upon the affair was not summoned."

These three men were buried in Memphis National Cemetery.

REFERENCES:
Military Personnel Records, RG-#94
Court Martial Proceedings, RG-#153 NN 1740
State of New Jersey Military Records

Case #121
Pvt. Jacob F. Snover
Co. M, 2nd NJ Cavalry Regt.
Executed for Rape and Theft
June 10, 1864

DESCRIPTION:

40 years of age, 5 feet 10 inches tall, dark hair, gray eyes, dark complexion, born in Sussex County, New Jersey, occupation farmer.

Snover was enlisted on August 29, 1863 at Stillwater, New Jersey and mustered into service on September 2, 1863 at Trenton, New Jersey in Company M, 2nd New Jersey Cavalry Regiment. Snover was promoted to Corporal on September 3, 1863 and reduced again to rank of Private on November 1, 1863.

Snover was involved in a crime on March 15, 1864 of rape and theft, was arrested, confined and tried by court martial, found guilty and sentenced to be executed by a firing squad on June 10, 1864 at Memphis, Tennessee.

For more details see cases #120 and #119.

REFERENCES:
Military Personnel Records, RG-#94
Court Martial Proceedings, RG-#153 NN 1740
New Jersey State Military Records

Case #122
Pvt. Wallace Baker
Co. I, 55th Mass
Volunteer Infantry (colored)
Executed for Mutiny
June 18, 1864

DESCRIPTION:

19 years of age, 5 feet 4½ inches tall, brown eyes, black hair, brown complexion, born in Hopkinsville, Kentucky, occupation farmer.

Baker enlisted and was mustered into service on June 22, 1863 at Readville, Massachusetts. He was assigned to Company I, 55th Massachusetts Infantry Regiment (colored). By 1864 the regiment was encamped at Folly Island, South Carolina when Baker was involved in "mutinous conduct" on May 1, 1864. Charges filed were four in number, Mutiny, disobedience of orders, contempt and disrespect to his superior officer, and conduct prejudicial to good order and military discipline. Baker, ordered to go to his quarters by Lieutenant T. F. Ellsworth, refused to obey, saying "I shan't do it; I'll be damned if I'll go; I'll go to the guardhouse first!" He then struck Lieutenant Ellsworth two violent blows in the face, and attempted to take Lieutenant Ellsworth's sword, striking him again several times. He shouted "You damned white officer, do you think you can strike me, and I not strike you back again? I will do it, I'm damned if I don't." All the preceding in the full presence of Company I, 55th Massachusetts Volunteers Infantry (colored).

On May 1, 1864 at the camp of the 55th Massachusetts Infantry Regiment (colored) on Folly Island, South Carolina, Company I was lined up for an inspection with Second Lieutenant T. F. Ellsworth of Company I in charge of the formation. Private Wallace Baker of Company I arrived late for the formation and did not have his jacket or his equipment belt on his person, he was holding them in his hand together with his musket. Lieutenant Ellsworth asked Baker to hurry up and get his jacket and equipment on his person. Baker replied he would not hurry and that he hadn't had time to prepare for the formation. Baker continued to argue loudly with the Lieutenant in the presence of the men in the company formation. The Lieutenant told him to "shut his mouth" and come to attention but Baker continued to talk loudly in a rambling fashion. Finally the Lieutenant ordered him to shoulder arms and return to his tent, pack his knapsack and report back after the formation was dismissed. Baker left the formation, went to his tent, removed his equipment belt and leaving his musket in the tent, returned to the company formation taking a position on the extreme left of the company and three or four paces in front of the 1st Rank.

The men of the Company in the assembled formation, noting Bakers complete disobedience to the Lieutenant's order, began to laugh. The Lieutenant dismissed the company and went over to Baker and ordered him to go to his tent and pack his knapsack and return. Baker said "I won't go." "You are going to make me stand at attention." "I won't do it." "I'll be damned if I will." The Lieutenant again ordered him to obey the original instructions. Baker replied, "Lieutenant I won't stand to attention for you or any other damned white officer." The Lieutenant then seized Baker by the collar of his uniform jacket and shoved him in the direction of his tent. Baker then struck the Lieutenant several times in the face with his fist. The Lieutenant drew his sword and attempted to strike Baker who grasped the sword blade as it struck him on the arm and shoulder area. As they wrestled for possession of the sword, Baker struck the Lieutenant several more times. Baker managed to maneuver the sword so that it was pressing on the Lieutenants neck, but the Lieutenant prevented injury by holding on to the sword blade. The Lieutenant shouted for the Orderly Sergeant and another Sergeant to assist him but they apparently were out of earshot. The Lieutenant finally wrestled the sword away from Baker and sheathed it, while being struck by Baker's fists. The Lieutenant then seized Baker by the throat and held him until the Captain came up and helped the Lieutenant take Baker to the guardhouse.

During the altercation the Lieutenant was severely bitten on the thumb by Baker.

Baker was charged with Mutiny, disobedience of orders, contempt and disrespect for his superior officer, conduct prejudicial to good order and military discipline.

During the Court martial trial Baker was afforded every opportunity to question witnesses, which he took ample advantage of.

The Company Commander, Captain Gordon, was asked if the Articles of War had been read to the Company and he replied it was done frequently.

Company members testified that Baker seemed mentally retarded, and was described as simple-minded, having difficulty in speaking clearly and an inability to understand even simple instructions. Testimony also was presented that Baker tended to be physically aggressive as he thought "he should not be ruled by any other man."

Baker was found guilty by the court and sentenced to be executed before a firing squad at Folly Island, South Carolina on June 18, 1864. (Baker was previously in serious trouble. See Case #97.)

REFERENCES:
Military Personnel Records, RG-#94
Court Martial Proceedings, RG-#153 LL 2112

Case #123
Pvt. John Flood
AKA/NV: J. Schmidt, Smith
Executed for Desertion
Co. D, 41st, NY Infantry Regt.
June 19, 1864

DESCRIPTION:
22 years of age, 5 feet 7 inches tall, brown hair, gray eyes, dark complexion, born in Ireland, occupation laborer, substitute, literacy undetermined.

Flood enlisted November 6, 1863 at Albany, New York as a substitute. He was assigned to Company D, 41st New York Infantry Regiment. By order of June 10, 1864, he was transferred to Company E, 41st New York Infantry Regiment due to consolidation of Companies. While stationed on Kiawah Island, South Carolina, he attempted to desert to the enemy on April 26, 1864 and was apprehended on the same day. He was arrested, and held for trial by Court Martial.

A General Court Martial was convened at South End, Folly Island, South Carolina and proceeded on May 4, 1864 to the trial of Private John Flood, alias John Smith, 41st New York Infantry Regiment on the charge of desertion.

Trial testimony, as recorded, has badly faded, to the extent of illegibility in over 50% of the text. What remains, and is minimally legible, provides only a shadow of the original testimony. What testimony is cipherable, states that Flood (although his Company muster rolls name him as Smith/alias Flood) was a regularly enlisted member of the 41st New York Infantry Regiment and had received pay for his military service. Further that the Regiment was stationed on Folly Island, South Carolina and provided sentries for guard posts on the Island. That adjacent Kiawah Island was said to contain Rebel Troops and some Union Army picket posts were established there.

Flood was posted on guard duty on the night of April 26, 1864 and when the Corporal of the guard was called by a sentry, who then reported several unidentified men near his post, the Corporal noted the absence of Flood from his sentry post. A squad of ten men was immediately assembled to search for the unidentified men and Flood. Footprints were found on the beach which seemed to indicate a group of six men. Nearby Flood was found alone, lying face down and either asleep or feigning sleep. When questioned about his leaving his post and weapon, Flood only at first would reply "what do you want with me?" He finally admitted that he and one other man had tried to desert, although four other men left earlier, he insisted he was unaware of their identity. Flood was arrested and with his arms pinioned was marched with the search party who had orders to shoot him down if he tried to escape. Flood asked his guards, as they trudged along, what punishment he would receive. They said that he would not get any "hard punishment." He finally admitted that the other deserters had left him behind, because he could not swim. He was waiting for low tide to wade across a narrow section of the water to the adjacent rebel held island when he was found.

Flood had been in trouble previously having left camp without written permission (a pass) from his Commanding Officer. Upon his return, he was very excited and was placed under arrest. He was using "very bad language" and was intoxicated. His officer "punished him severely" and tied him up to a tree, despite the restraints he tore his clothing off until he was nearly naked.

The accused offered no defense but made a brief statement in his behalf in which the trial proceeding reproduction is very faded.

Statement

"All I have to say is that (the man I was out with that night -?) He was at me day and night to go with him, to get out (of Killing rebels?) On the next I (?) went to picket he said (illegible) gun. He was a sailor and said there was a ship in Charleston Harbor and he would get me on board."

The Court deliberated, found Flood (alias Smith) guilty and sentenced him to be shot to death with musketry. He was executed on Hilton Head Island, South Carolina on June 19, 1864.

REFERENCES:

Military Personnel Records, RG-#94
Court Martial Proceedings, RG-#153 LL 2112

Case #124
Pvt. Cornelius Thompson
Co. A, 48th Inf Regt, USCT
Executed for Murder
June 24, 1864

DESCRIPTION:

35 years of age, 5 feet 5½ inches tall, black eyes, black hair, black complexion, born in Claybourne County, Mississippi, occupation farmer, illiterate.

Thompson enlisted and was mustered into service at Lake Providence, Louisiana on May 1, 1863 and was assigned to Company A, 10th Regiment Louisiana Infantry (A.D., African Descent). The unit designation was later changed to Company A, 48th Infantry Regiment USCT.

A General Court Martial was convened at Vicksburg, Mississippi, and on June 15, 1864 tried Private Cornelius Thompson, Company A, 48th Infantry Regiment, USCT. on a charge of murder.

The accused was permitted to introduce counsel but had none. Testimony by witnesses disclosed the following events.

At about seven or seven and a half o'clock on the morning of June 10, 1864, Thompson shot a colored woman, Martha Richardson, a civilian laundress employed by Company A. An examination by Surgeon H. C. Davis, M.D. of the 48th USCT, who happened to witness the shooting revealed that the ball had entered at the right hip, passed through the uterus and bowel, then exited from the left side of the abdomen. The wound was fatal and Richardson died about 10 A.M. that same day.

Thompson was arrested promptly and confined.

Colonel F. M. Crandall, commander of the 48th USCT stated that Thompson had come to him on several occasions asking for advice or requesting changes in regard to himself or Richardson. Thompson and Richardson had been "living together" in an apparently mutually satisfactory arrangement up until a few weeks prior to her death. Thompson had requested the Colonel to bar Richardson from the Camp or to transfer him to another regiment. Neither request was possible. Thompson was upset primarily because he believed Richardson was also living with another man, although he did not identify the suspected "other man". The Colonel had also interviewed Richardson on the matter and she swore that Thompson was insanely jealous and that there was no "other man", that it was entirely imaginary on his part.

Thompson had on several occasions told members of his company that he would shoot Richardson if she were not sent away.

On the morning of June 10, 1864, Thompson took up his musket, loaded it and when asked what he was going to do, replied, "he was going to kill somebody or somebody would kill him." He left his tent went toward the Cooking Quarters, where the laundresses labored. He was seen to survey the area, apparently looking for Richardson.

Finally he raised his gun to his shoulder, moved the barrel from side to side as he tracked his victim in the gun sights. He fired, Richardson fell mortally wounded and Thompson remained rooted to the spot. He and his musket were quickly seized, and he said, "he did not give a damn what they done with him now, he had done all he wanted to" and he was marched off to the Guardhouse.

The accused having no witnesses to bring before the Court on his behalf did make a final statement.

"Statement of the Accused"

"I never threatened to shoot Martha Richardson. I told the Lieutenant of my company that if she was not sent away from the Company, it would be the cause of trouble! But I did not want to injure myself or anybody else. Martha Richardson threatened my life three different times: I told her that I would like to live peaceably with her, not that I wanted her to be my wife, again, but that I wanted to live on friendly terms with her, as I did with everyone. I asked her if she was willing to let every difficulty that had occurred before drop? She said she was not satisfied with me and would not be this side her grave. I then said to her, the Lord be with and take care of you as long as you may live: this was the last word I ever said to her."

The Court then deliberated, found the prisoner guilty and sentenced him to be shot to death with musketry.

The execution took place in near Vicksburg, Mississippi on June 24, 1864.

Some notations on the copy of the trial proceedings forwarded to the Judge Advocate General's Office reads "The execution of the sentence in this case *was* illegal but the record was not received in this office in time to correct the error."

Brigadier General John P. Hawkins, commanding the 1st Division of USCt at Vicksburg, Mississippi commented on the case as follows.

"The proceedings, findings and sentence in the foregoing case are approved, and I earnestly request that the District Commander will see the propriety of ordering the immediate execution of the sentence. This is the third murder committed by men in this regiment, and other regiments have had killing cases. The negroes have the same notion of chivalry and ideas of avenging private wrongs, real or imaginary, that their masters had. They must be made to respect law and human life. The guilty of such crimes, they have seen go unpunished all their lives. It is now time that they should have learned better. Talking has had no effect to reform the matter. Nothing remains but immediate and severe punishment. To wait for the approval of Generals Sherman or McPherson would cause a delay of several months."

The story of his crime and execution (which took place on June 24, 1864) is also related in the "Vicksburg Daily Herald" of June 25, 1864. "A Military Execution — Yesterday we witnessed the sentence of a General Court Martial in the case of Pvt Cornelius Thompson, A Company, 48th Regiment U.S. Colored Troops, convicted of murder of a colored Trull that followed that regiment carried into execution near this city. The prisoner was taken from the jail to the camp of the 48th, and thence seated on his coffin in an ambulance, accompanied by the Chaplain of the Regiment, Reverend Thomas Calahan, he rode to the place of execution, which was at the southeast angle of the fortifications near the Washington street road leading south.

"The First Division of colored troops was formed on three sides of a square around which the prisoner was conveyed, the bands playing the "Dead March." The fourth side of the square was next to the works and was left open. Here the coffin was placed, the prisoner being seated upon it, the finding and sentence of the court were read. The Chaplain led in prayer, after which the prisoner asked leave to speak, which being granted he said: "It is right that I should die. I believe I am willing to die, but I am sorry to see you (meaning the firing squad) standing before me. Never do as I have done, but always look to God for Grace. I have nothing more to say."

"The Chaplain having withdrawn, the prisoner was blindfolded and the firing squad was directed to fire. The condemned fell backward upon his coffin and died without a struggle, having been pierced by six balls, five taking effect in the breast and one in the neck. The criminal never manifested the least repentence for his deed and met his death without a tremor."

REFERENCES:
Military Personnel Records, RG-#94
Court Martial Proceedings, RG-#153 NN 2171
Vicksburg Daily Herald, cited above

Case #125
Pvt. Pedro Garcia
Co. E, 1st Texas Vol Cav Regt
Executed for Desertion
June 27, 1864

DESCRIPTION:

25 years of age, 5 feet 10 inches tall, blue eyes, dark hair, fair complexion, born in Mexico, occupation farmer, illiterate.

Garcia enlisted and was mustered into service in Company E, 1st Texas Volunteer Cavalry Regiment on December 1, 1863 at Brownsville, Texas. He was assigned to a variety of duties such as a scout, attending sick and unserviceable horses and general escort duty. He was apparently on detached service with the Independent Company of Partisan Rangers, Texas Cavalry, when on May 26, 1864 near Edinburgh, Texas he deserted. He was apprehended and jailed at Brownsville, Texas.

A General Court Martial was convened at Brownsville, Texas, and on June 6, 1864 proceeded with the trial of Pvt. Pedro Garcia, Company E, 1st Texas Cavalry Regiment on charges of Desertion, leaving his post before being regularly relieved, and conduct to the prejudice of good order and military discipline.

Since Garcia spoke little English, the court appointed Joseph Henana, a citizen of Brownsville, Texas as his interpreter.

Testimony given showed that Garcia on May 10, 1864, was stationed at a picket post at Punta Del Monte. This post was about one mile from a ranch named Punta Del Monte and about 22 miles from Santa Rosa where the Company Commander had his headquarters.

At Punta Del Norte, seven men and a corporal were stationed while at the picket post beyond Punta Del Norte there were three men who stood sentry duty of from 2-4 hour periods. On the night of Garcia's defection, May 10th, 1864, one guard, not on duty saw Garcia on duty about 1 a.m. and another man together at the Sentinel post. Garcia and another soldier were found missing about an hour before daybreak. The Corporal was notified and a search of the post was conducted which disclosed that Garcia and another soldier (unnamed), their horses, firearms, plus one carbine of another guard and equipment all missing. The Corporal and two soldiers saddled up their horses and took up the pursuit of the deserters. The search party located Garcia and his companion about 15 miles from Punta Del Monte and hailed them, demanding they halt. The two deserters spurred their horses to a full gallop, the pursuers following managed to get within one hundred yards of them and fired at them unsuccessfully. The deserters rode into a wooded area and dismounted abandoning horses, saddle, equipment, even Garcia's saber. The pursuers searched the area to no avail, rounded up the two abandoned horses and returned to their post.

On or about May 12, 1864, Captain A. B. Slaughter, Company B, 1st Texas Cavalry Volunteers was on duty at Santa Rosa when one of his sergeant's brought into camp Garcia and his companion. Garcia, under questioning (indicated that he could speak a little English) said he had been out turkey hunting, with permission of his Commander. The two men had a couple of small bundles of clothing which they said they received from a wash woman as they were returning from hunting. They had gotten lost and strayed into a picket post at Como de Llamo. The picket post there had been ordered to come into Santa Rosa that evening and the Captain said if the members of the Picket Post would verify Garcia's and his companion's statements they would be free to go. Garcia replied, "Bueno".

Garcia was unable to have his story verified and the Captain asked why he deserted his post. Garcia admitted he deserted and, at that time, offered no excuse. He did beg to be let off and said he should be hanged or have his throat cut if he ever did such a thing again. Garcia did not say where they were going when they deserted.

Garcia offered no defense at his trial but made a verbal statement to the court, "that he left the guard post for the purpose of coming to Brownsville, Texas to see his wife; that he intended after seeing her to report to camp; that he may be ignorant of orders forbidding him to do this, and that he begs to be excused this time and he will never do the like again."

The Court deliberated, found Garcia guilty and sentenced him to be executed before a firing squad at or near Brownsville, Texas on June 23, 1864.

An excerpt from the letter of approval of the court martial proceedings states, "the great number of desertions from the Texas Cavalry Volunteers, and the large amount of government property thereby lost, demands an immediate example. It is therefor ordered that the accused Pvt. Pedro Garcia, Co. #, 1st Texas Cavalry Volunteers be shot to death with musketry as provided by the sentence of the court, at 6 O'Clock in the afternoon on Wednesday, June 23, 1864, in the presence of the Second Brigade."

(The "Official List" cites June 27, 1864 as the actual date of execution.)

No other mention has been located of Garcia's companion.

REFERENCES:
NA, Military Personnel Records, RG-#94
Court Martial Proceedings, RG-#153 LL 2228

Case #126
Pvt. Francis Gillespie
Co B, 15th New York Cavalry Regiment
Executed for Murder
July 11, 1864

DESCRIPTION:

23 years of age, 5 feet 9¾ inches tall, brown hair, blue eyes, dark complexion, born in Rochester, New York, occupation farmer, literacy undetermined.

Gillespie enlisted and was mustered into service on July 4, 1863 at Syracuse, New York in Company B, 15th New York Cavalry Regiment. He was sick in a hospital during the period October 1-20, 1863. Gillespie was discharged and immediately re-enlisted in the same Regiment as a Veteran Volunteer in September 1863. On July 8, 1864, Gillespie murdered 1st Lieutenant William B. Shearer, 15th New York Cavalry Regiment at a point on the railroad between Parkersburg and Grafton, West Virginia. Gillespie, for whatever reason, drew his revolver and shot Lieutenant Shearer in the head, causing his death. Gillespie was arrested.

A Military Commission was convened at Cumberland, Maryland, and on July 9, 1864 proceeded to the trial of Pvt. Francis Gillispie, Company B, 15th New York Cavalry Regiment on a charge of Murder.

Testimony revealed that the regiment boarded a railroad train at Parkersburg, West Virginia, between midnight and daybreak on July 8, 1864. Gillispie was observed to have been drinking and reluctant to board the train with the rest of his unit. His company commander, 1st Lt. William B. Shearer, ordered him to board several times but Gillispie's only response was abusive language. Shearer, unable to contain his exasperation, finally struck Gillispie and seizing him by the throat, choked him, saying "damn you - get drunk again will you!" The Lieutenant summoned other soldiers who pulled Gillispie onto the railway car and the train soon began its' journey. In the railroad car, Gillispie remarked that he was going to shoot Lt. Shearer, that he would strike no more soldiers, etc.

When the train made its first stop Gillispie, with a loaded revolver in his possession, went to a railroad car containing the officers and asked for Shearer. Upon being told he was not there, Gillispie continued his search. He finally located the Lieutenant asleep in a berth, in the last car of the train. He placed the muzzle of the gun close to the Lieutenant's head and pulled the trigger, the bullet entering at the junction of the left eye and nose, causing death immediately. Gillispie ran back through the train to his own railroad car where he whispered to one of fellow soldiers a confession that he had shot Lt. Shearer. He further was reported to have said that Shearer was dead enough and that he would not command the Company again as he had put an end to the son of a bitch.

The accused offered no defense but did make a statement to the court.

"All I recollect is I came up from the Grocery pretty drunk, he caught me by the throat and struck me. I asked him what he did that for. He said, shut up you son of a bitch or I will kill you. They then put me into the cars and I took another drink and laid down and fell asleep and that is all I know about it, I was arrested while I was asleep. I did not know what for until afterwards. That is all sir."

The commission then deliberated, found Gillispie guilty and sentenced him to death by hanging. The sentence of the commission was carried out in Cumberland, Maryland on July 11, 1864.

REFERENCES:
Military Personnel Records, RG-#94
Court Martial Proceedings, RG-#153 NN 2086

Case #127
Private Daniel Geary
NV: Garry - Gerry
Co. G, 72nd NY Vol Inf Regt
Executed for Rape
July 15, 1864

DESCRIPTION:
18 years of age.

Geary originally enlisted on July 17, 1861 at Westfield, New York in Company G, 3rd Regiment Excelsior New York Infantry Brigade, whose designation was changed to Company G, 72nd New York Volunteer Infantry Regiment. He entered service at Camp Scott, Staten Island, New York, on July 23, 1861.

Geary has an extremely erratic military history filled with disciplinary problems which is difficult to sort and arrange chronographically. Some of the milestones recorded include: December 11, 1862 deserted near Fredericksburg, Maryland; Reported wounded at Fredericksburg, Maryland; December 13, 1862 reported at Westfield, New York (his home); January 20, 1863 discharged from hospital, Pt. Lookout, Maryland; March 11, 1863 reported at Buffalo, New York as a deserter under President Lincoln's Amnesty Proclamation; May 2, 1863 sent from Buffalo, New York to Washington, D.C.; May 10, 1863 deserted from Washington, D.C.; September/October, 1863 reported wounded at Gettysburg, Pennsylvania; at home in Westfield, New York; October 20, 1863 sent to New York City; November 13, 1863 imprisoned at Ft. Colombus, New York Harbor; arrested November 16/17, 1863, reward of $30.00 paid; November 16, 1863 forwarded to Washington, D.C.; November 21, admitted to Stone Hospital, Washington, D.C. for treatment of Syphilis; labeled deserter/prisoner; November 22, 1863 deserted from Stone Hospital; January, 1864 returned from desertion awaiting Court Martial decision; May/June 1864 sick in Corps Hospital. June 18, 1864 committed crime of rape, arrested, tried for rape, found guilty. Executed for Rape, July 15, 1864.

General Court Martial convened at the Headquarters Camp of the Provost Marshall General (in the field) on June 27, 1864.

Objection by Judge Advocate to introduction of Gordon as defense witness for Geary - as Gordon had been tried for the same offense and was mentioned as the companion to Geary in the specifications to the charge. Court pondered the objection and sustained it, barring Gordon as witness on behalf of Geary.

Geary made a verbal statement to the court - (long)

President Abraham Lincoln's return and disapproval of case. July 4, 1864, *same place,* case reopened per Abraham Lincoln.

Geary declined to call Gordon, or any other witness.

For full details, see Gordon Case #128.

REFERENCES:

Military Personnel Records, RG-#94
Court Martial Proceedings, RG-#153 MM 1481

Case #128
Pvt. Ransom S. Gordon
Co. E, 72nd New York Vol Inf Regt
Executed for Rape
July 15, 1864

DESCRIPTION:

23 years of age.

Gordon enlisted in Company E, 3rd Regiment Excelsior Brigade on May 16, 1861 at Demkirk, New York. This unit was later designated Company E, 72nd New York Volunteer Infantry Regiment. He entered into service at Camp Scott, Staten Island, New York, June 20, 1861. He was variously listed as a Wagoner, Musician, Teamster, Private and Ambulance Driver. He had no recorded desertions, arrests, court martials, or other service disciplinary problems.

The crime of rape, for which Geary and Gordon were executed, is related in the diary of Brig. General Marsena Rudolph Patrick, Provost Marshall of the Army of the Potomac.

In the trials of Ransom S. Gordon and Daniel Geary charged with rape, an example of legal procedure safeguarding the rights of one of the accused was invoked by President A. Lincoln.

Gordon was tried first and during the course of the trial Geary was called as a witness for the defense. Gordon was found guilty of the charge of rape.

Geary was then tried and during the course of his trial, Gordon was called as a witness for the defense. The Judge Advocate objected to Gordon Testifying on behalf of Geary, claiming that Gordon was already convicted of the crime of rape and further that Gordon and Geary were accomplices in the rape of the same woman at the same time and place. The objection of the Judge Advocate was sustained.

During President Lincoln's review of the Court Martial trial proceedings, he wrote: "July 1st, 1864, Upon examining this record submitted to me for my action, it appears that the court erred in refusing to hear the evidence of Private Gordon, the alleged accomplice of the prisoner. Said Gordon, was a competent witness, his conviction and sentence of the infamous crime referred to not having been approved by the President, and being therefore at the time inoperative, wherefore the case is remanded to the Court for its reconsideration, and with a view to the correction of the error committed to the prisoner's prejudice.

A. Lincoln"

The Court was reassembled on July 4, 1864 to reconsider the case of Geary, but lacking a quorum adjourned until the morning of July 5th when the Court called Geary and informed him that he could call Gordon as a witness in his behalf. Geary replied he did not wish to call Gordon as a witness, that he had no other witnesses to offer on his behalf and that he had no further statement to make to the Court.

The Court then deliberated and found Geary guilty of the charge of rape and sentenced him to be hung until he is dead.

General Patrick recorded the following in his diary — "25 June, 64 - I have had a Mrs. Stiles here, who identified a man named Gordon of the 72nd N.Y. as the man who had committed the outrage upon her person last Saturday. He will be tried tomorrow." "26th June. Today has been terrible hot and no let up. A court martial has been in session all day, trying the rape case on the person of Mrs. Stiles. Tonight we have caught the other culprit and he will be tried tomorrow." "27th June - Have been busy since ever I got up this morning. The court martial has finished the trial of the Rapers this evening, I believe."

"28th June - We had on Sunday and yesterday a court martial in session at my Office Tent for the trial of two men who had committed a crime upon the person of Mrs. Stiles living near Prince George's Courthouse. There seemed to be no clue to the perpetrators, at first, but the leader could not keep away from the spot, after the crime, and was the first to speak of it as an outrage, before any person knew of it. He was arrested and to make his own story good, he had to tell of his comrade. They were identified by the woman and her cousin and both have been tried; with what results is not known. The woman feels terrible and has come to see me."

Photo copies of the original handwritten record of the court martial proceedings in the case of Geary and Gordon run to 35 pages. The court martial detail consisted of a Judge Advocate and five officers and the prisoners were assigned counsel. The court martial trial revealed the details of the crime.

Herewith in brief, a Mrs. Mary E. Stiles, a married woman, residing in a isolated farm house, a quarter of a mile from the nearest neighbor, in the vicinity of Prince George's Courthouse, Virginia was the victim. With her in the small two-story farm house at the time of the events were her 48-year-old unmarried cousin, Lucy E. Williams, and her (Mrs. Stiles') two children, a daughter eight years and a son aged three years. Her husband, stated to be a Union sympathizer, had been away from home for about 10 days.

The entire area had been occupied by Union soldiers and the usual theft of food from gardens and fields including livestock made life difficult for the local inhabitants. At about 4 p.m. on June 18, 1864, Pvt. Gordon and two other Union soldiers appeared at the Stiles farm and demanded meat and vegetables, to which Mrs. Stiles replied she hadn't tasted meat in a long time and needed, for her own family, what few vegetables remained in the ground. The three soldiers remained in the farmyard for a while then rode off.

About 7 p.m. on the night of June 18 Gordon returned accompanied by Geary, bearing coffee and sugar which they insisted Mrs. Stiles and her cousin prepare for them. After drinking the coffee the women prepared, Gordon inquired if they would like him and Geary to remain as guards through the night. The woman replied they would appreciate guards but that they could not ask for such aid. Gordon and Geary stated that they would stay in the house and that it was time for all to turn in.

Mrs. Stiles asked if they would sleep in the upstairs bedroom, to which they replied no. The women therefore finally dragged the mattress from the upstairs bedroom down into the passageway outside their first floor bedroom door where Geary and Gordon insisted they would sleep. Mrs. Stiles stated that she had not undressed for many nights, as Union soldiers roamed the area and pounded on the cabin door at all hours of the night. This necessitated her answering their summons promptly in order to prevent damage such as broken doors and windows.

About an hour after retiring behind the locked door of their bedroom, the women were awakened by Gordon knocking on their door and demanding some drinking water. Mrs. Stiles' cousin took a pitcher of water off the mantel and went to the door, but was unable to get the door unlatched, Mrs. Stiles came to the aid of her cousin and unlatched the door and returned to her bed while her cousin handed the pitcher of water to Gordon.

Gordon set the pitcher of water on the passageway stairs and quickly entered the room, seizing Mrs. Stiles by the arm while Geary entered and seized her other arm. Between them they dragged Mrs. Stiles quickly out of the bedroom into the passageway, slamming the door shut behind them and deposited her upon the mattress on the passageway floor. Geary firmly held her upper torso upon the mattress while Gordon disarranged her clothing and raped her. Then they changed places. Gordon constricting her movement while Geary raped her. Following the second rape and her release, she groped her way back to the room where she was admitted by her cousin.

Geary and Gordon returned to the Union Army camp about 11 p.m. Mrs. Stiles, her cousin and two children waited until well after the departure of Gordon and Geary before fleeing into the nearby woods, with a few bundled-up possessions where they remained, frightened, until daybreak. They then slowly made their way to the home of Mrs. Stiles' mother and Mrs. Stiles reported the crime to the Union Army authorities.

On June 25, Mrs. Stiles identified Gordon as one of her assailants. On June 26, Geary was caught following Gordon's statement of implication. The court martial began on Sunday, June 26, in General Patrick's headquarter tent and continued through Monday. Under questioning by the court and defense lawyer, Mrs. Stiles stated that she had resisted the efforts of the rapists to the full extent of her physical ability and that screaming and crying out would have attracted no one in such an isolated area except other Union soldiers who might have joined the rapists.

Her cousin verified all Mrs. Stiles' statements and stated that she personally was so terrified that she could neither move nor speak during the attack. Gordon and Geary claimed that Mrs. Stiles willingly consented to the rape because of the food already given and promise of more to be provided. The court believed Mrs. Stiles and her cousin and both men were found guilty and sentenced to death by hanging.

General George Gordon Meade, commanding general, Army of the Potomac, in his endorsement to the court martial transcript says in part "I think it is unfortunate for the discipline of this Army and the dignity of Arms that I am not empowered by law to order an immediate execution of the sentences of these cases. Prompt punishment adds very much to the efficacy of the example, and I request that you will take special opportunity to present their cases to the President at as early a period as possible that the Army not be embarrassed by the custody of these prisoners." As noted in General Meade's endorsement, all sentences of death had required review and approval by the President.

President Lincoln read the court martial transcript carefully and noted that the trial Judge Advocate had ruled against Gordon appearing as a witness for Geary stating that he was already under sentence of death as an accomplice in the crime and hence not competent to testify. Mr. Lincoln in his review summary stated; "July 1, 1864 — Upon examining this record submitted to me for my action, it appears that the court erred in refusing to hear evidence of Pvt. Gordon, the alleged accomplice of the prisoner. Said Gordon was a competent witness, his conviction and sentence of the infamous crime referred to not having been approved by the President and being therefore at the time inoperative, wherefore the case is remanded to the court for its reconsideration and with a view to the correction of the error committed to the prisoner's prejudice." "A. Lincoln."

On July 5 at 9 a.m., the court martial reconvened in accordance with President Lincoln's directive. Pvt. Geary was called and advised of his right to reopen his case and to call Pvt. Gordon as a witness in his behalf. Upon being asked if he desired to pursue this course of action Pvt. Geary replied that he did not wish to call Pvt. Gordon or any other witness and had no further statement to make to the court. The court then deliberated and again found Pvt. Geary guilty as charged and sentenced him to be hung. The time and date of the execution was set for 9 a.m. on July 15, 1864.

General Patrick notes in his diary: "14 July, '64 — Slept well and rose up in tolerably good season — breakfast late — That over and morning matters disposed of, I took Chaplain Rammell with me and started off over to see Mrs. Stiles and the Robertson family. I read the Order to her and Rammell had quite a long conversation with her. At their request we had prayers and I then left. The Chaplain came back, perfectly satisfied of the truth of her statement. He and a Catholic Priest, Father William Corby, have both been very anxious and diligent in behalf of their two patients. Arrangements have been made for the execution near the Wagon Camp, as a public place and also near the Teamsters, who, to a large extent, are the persons committing these outrages." "15 July, '64 — Up in good season and found work enough to be done until it was time to move to the place of execution. Was there by 9 o'clock and the Cavalry holding the ground — the 68th NY and 114th Penn. regts. soon came into position and then the guard, with the condemned in a wagon, with the ministers.

"They mounted the scaffold and there I read the Order of the Court and sentence. The clergy talked with them a few minutes and at their request, Rammell said for them, that they died hoping for mercy through Jesus Christ and acknowledged the justice of the sentence about to be executed.

"Rammell made a short prayer and both clergymen took leave of the condemned and left the scaffold. The hands and feet were tied, the eyes bandaged, the ropes adjusted, the tap upon the drum and the drop fell! Scarcely a convulsion, both being killed instantly. They hung, perhaps, five minutes, when I remounted the scaffold and said such words of warning and reproof and of correction as seemed proper in the presence of such a mass of life as stood before and around me, with the dead hanging beneath my feet. My words will not soon be forgotten by those who stood before me. Leaving the scaffold I turned over the whole to Col. Collins who afterwards had them cut down, put in their boxes and sent down to me, to City Point (Va.), where I had ridden from the place of execution, with Col. Gates. Arrangements were made, by me, to have them embalmed tonight and sent off with the brother of Geary (as escort) by the morning boat."

(The charges were $15 for embalming and $25 for the coffin for each man. They were transported at government expense to their former homes in western New York state.)

In the embalming case book of William J. Bunnell, in consecutive order, were the records of two Union Soldiers embalmed, coffined, and shipped back home for burial on July 15, 1864, "by order of Brig. Genl. Marsena Rudolph Patrick, provost marshall of the Army of the Potomac." Written across the two entries was the phrase:

"These two men was hung at City Point for committing a rape on a lady."

Father Corby, the Very Reverend William Corby, C.S.C. relates his participation as a religious counselor to Geary and Gordon in his book, "Memoirs of Chaplain Life: Three years Chaplain in the Famous Irish Brigade; Army of the Potomac."

It began with a letter from General Meade received on July 12, 1864.

"Headquarters Army of the Potomac
July 12, 1864
Rev. W. Corby, Irish Brigade, Second Corps, Rev'd Sir: There are two men to be executed on the 15th inst., one of whom, especially, is very anxious to secure the services of a priest. If you will be pleased to attend him, the Provost Marshall at Headquarters will be instructed to furnish you all facilities to discharge the functions of your sacred office.
By order of Major General Meade
Commanding Army of the Potomac"

Father Corby became both famous and beloved by the Irish regiments of the Union Army as he performed many religious services as well as non-religious acts for the troops, non-Catholic as well as Catholic. There is a statue erected at Gettysburg to his memory.

Father Corby describes Geary as a young, healthy, strong person with a good mind, not depraved. The military service record however overwhelmingly contradicts Father Corby's first impression. Father Corby describes his ministrations to Geary, the execution, and the presence of Geary's brother at same in his book. He also publishes the full text of a letter he received from Geary's mother dated December 22, 1864. In her long somewhat rambling letter, filled with religious overtones, she states that the coffined body of the executed Geary escorted by his brother, arrived at Westfield, New York, his home, two hours before official notification of Geary's death. In the letter she states she had not seen him in three years, yet his military records at least twice report that he was at Westfield, NY. Geary would seem to be a rather disturbed individual.

Epilogue:

Burke Davis' writing in his "The Civil War — Strange and Fascinating Facts," states, "The Southern woman (Mrs. Stiles) who had accused these men of rape (they were soldiers of the 72nd New York) confessed on her death bed, years after the war that she swore the lives of these men away in order to contribute her mite toward the extermination of the Yankee Army." Communications with author Davis concerning documentation of this matter were disappointing as his manuscript and research documents were donated to the College of William and Mary, Williamsburg, Virginia. No copies of the newspaper account of Mrs. Stiles death bed declaration have been relocated.

REFERENCES:

Military Personnel Records, RG-#94
Court Martial Proceedings, RG-153 MM 1481
Embalming Case Record Book, Embalming Surgeon William J. Bunnell, City Point, 1864
Diary of Major General Marsena Rudolph Patrick, Library of Congress
"The Civil War — Strange and Fascinating Facts" by Burk Davis, 1982, Fairfax Press
"Memoirs of Chaplain Life: Three Years Chaplain in the Famous Irish Brigade; Army of the Potomac," Notre Dame, South Bend, Indiana, Scholastic Press, Very Reverend William Corby, C.S.C., 1894

Case #129
Pvt. Isaac B. Whitlow
AKA: John Hall
Co. D, 23rd Ohio Infantry Regt.
Executed for Desertion
August 5, 1864
(two enlistments)

DESCRIPTION:

17 years of age, 5 feet 6 inches tall, dark hair, blue eyes, fair complexion, born in Franklin County, Virginia, occupation farmer, substitute.

Whitlow may be the youngest soldier executed during the Civil War. His records state 17 years as his official age, most often, however there is no consent form for a minor to enlist amongst his file documents. He enlisted and was mustered into service on September 21, 1863 at Camp White, Charleston, Virginia (West Virginia) in Company D, 23rd Ohio Infantry Regiment. He deserted from Camp White on October 2, 1863.

Whitlow again entered service as a substitute under the alias of John Hall at Cincinnati, Ohio on July 23, 1864. He was assigned to Company D, 23rd Ohio Infantry Regiment at Monocacy, Maryland where he was recognized by some of his former Company comrades.

A Drumhead Court Martial was convened at Monocacy Junction, Maryland and on August 5, 1864 tried Private Isaac B. Whitlow (alias John Hall), Company D, 23rd Ohio Infantry Regiment on charge of deserting to the enemy.

Whitlow had enlisted on or about September 20, 1863 in the 23rd Ohio Infantry Regiment from the Military Prison at Charleston, West Virginia where he was confined as a Confederate deserter from a Virginia Infantry Regiment.

Whitlow deserted the service in early October 1863, some witnesses citing the second or third, others the fifth day, and remained absent until he was captured, as a member of the rebel force at the Battle of Cloyd's Mountain, West Virginia on or about May 9, 1864*. Whitlow was among the Confederate prisoners held in confinement at Blacksburgh, West Virginia.

Whitlow was identified at the Blacksburgh Prison Camp by several members of the 23rd Ohio Infantry Regiment as a former member of their Regiment. Whitlow was said to have admitted his guilt to witnesses who testified that he had been a member of a Virginia Infantry Regiment (Confederate) and had deserted their service.

Whitlow questioned witnesses at his trial but offered no defense other than a statement to the court.

"I deserted the Confederate Service (Co. B, 24th Va. Infty) about Sept. 1, 1862. I enlisted in the United States Service in Sept. 1863 and deserted about Oct. 1, 1863 with the intention of going after my mother in Franklin County, South Eastern, Virginia. I found my mother and she started before me to go North. I also started North and fell in with Gen'l. Averill's Cavalry (CSA) near Rocky Gap, West Va. about the 15 of May, 1864. General Averill sent me with other prisoners to Pepper's Ferry on New River and turned me over to General Crook's Command. I was then sent to Meadow Bluffs, West Va. and from there was sent with other deserters to Gallipolis, Ohio and released after taking the oath of Allegiance. I have never borne arms against the Government of the United States since I deserted the Rebel Service. I enlisted again as a substitute in the United States Service in the month of July, 1864* (using the name John Hall) and received five hundred dollars bounty."

The court deliberated, found the accused guilty and sentenced him to death by musketry. The sentence was carried out near Monocacy Junction, Maryland on August 5, 1864.

The final notation on the muster and descriptive roll, etc., for "John Hall" states "Kiled with Isaac Whitlow."

* (These dates do not coincide, but are listed as cited in the original documents.)

REFERENCES:
Military Personnel Records, RG-#94
Court Martial Proceedings, RG-#153 NN 4023

Case #130
Private Frank McElheny
NV: McElhenney, McElheney
Co. F, 24 Mass. Inf. Regt.
Executed for Desertion
August 8, 1864

DESCRIPTION:

18 years of age, born in Boston, Massachusetts, a teamster by occupation, his mother a widow, no other description available.

McElheny enlisted on November 25, 1861 at Readville, Massachusetts and was mustered into service on November 26, 1861 at Readville, Massachusetts in Company F, 24th Massachusetts Infantry Regiment. Described as a troublesome, insubordinate soldier, who was fined a half months pay on May 20, 1862 and finally tried for an unstated offense by a court martial trial at Newberne, North Carolina, August 7, 1862. The sentence was confinement in Fort Macon Prison near Beaufort, North Carolina for the remainder of his enlistment period. Despite the geography of the prison, situated at one end of a long narrow island, McElheny managed to escape by swimming from the island to the mainland. Once on the mainland he made his way to Raleigh, North Carolina where he secured employment, briefly, at a shoemaker's shop. He left Raleigh for Richmond and enlisted in the Confederate Army under an assumed name in a company of Heavy Artillery, 19th Virginia Battalion. He was, he said, for a time a guard at Libby Prison over seeing Union Army prisoners. After a while military life again paled and he planned to desert, having been told that the U. S. Federal government (Union) was offering to send any rebel deserter to any place in the north which he wished to go.

His Confederate Regiment was ordered to frontline duty facing the Union Army at Deep Bottom, Virginia. On July 27, 1864, McElheny made his decision to desert the confederates and carry out his plan to be sent North as a Rebel deserter.

McElheny, during a lull in the gunfire, leapt from the Confederate line and raced to the Union line. By extraordinary bad luck, against all possible odds, McElheny chose to enter the Union lines at a point manned by his old Company (F) and regiment (24th

Massachusetts Infantry). Contemporary reports indicate that the regiments "on the line" rotated day to day and actually were in frontline position only one day out of three. Further his old regiment, 24th Massachusetts Infantry was within ten minutes of completing it's tour of duty and would not again be on the line until the third day hence. As he entered the Union front lines, manned at this particular point by Company F, 24th Massachusetts Infantry Regiment from whom he had originally deserted, he was recognized and called by name. "Hello Frank", "I'm not Frank" he replied. The company drummer boy in particular, as well as other veterans recognized McElheny and he was arrested and removed to the headquarters for interrogation. Under questioning, he broke down and admitted his true identity and the fact of his escape from prison.

A General Court Martial was convened at Fort Monroe, Virginia, and on August 5, 1864 tried Private Frank McElheny, Company F, 24th Massachusetts Infantry Regiment on a charge of desertion. (He appeared in court in Rebel Uniform.)

Testimony was given that showed the accused had a long history of military violations of Army rules and regulations as well as of the Articles of War.

In August, 1862, the accused was a member of the 24th Massachusetts Infantry Regiment. In July, 1862 the prisoner returned to camp very drunk, and used abusive language to his Company Commander, Captain Clarke, saying "he could lick Captain Clarke or any other son of a bitch." and further that "he was just the boy that could do it." "That rather than serve in the U. S. Army he would desert to the Rebels and he was just the boy that could do it." The prisoner was court martialed on August 6, 1862 on the following charges:

1. Violation of the 21st Article of War (going outside the Union lines without permission).

2. Disrespect to a sentinel (ran away from a guard taking him to the river to bathe) and failure to obey order to return to camp.

3. Insubordination (refusal to go to guard tent, said he didn't care if he served the rest of his enlistment in confinement at Fortress Monroe).

4. Using insulting and abusive language to a superior officer (called his Captain a son of a bitch and didn't care a God damn for any Officer in the 24th and he could lick them all).

5. Violation of the 9th Article of War (tried to kick and bite his Captain and attempted to strike his Sergeant whilst being put in the guard tent).

6. Treasonable Language ("I ain't going to do a days duty in the 24th Regiment, I'll desert to the Rebels first. I'm just the boy that will do it too).

7. Fraud (he purchased some pies from a colored woman and paid her with a *facsimile* of a ten dollar Confederate note and received his change in good money).

He was sentenced to receive a dishonorable discharge, loss of all pay and allowances then due or which might become due, and confinement in the Penitentiary in the District of Columbia for five years.

On June 3, 1863 his sentence was commuted to confinement for the balance of his term of enlistment at Fort Macon, North Carolina.

The accused wrote a statement for the Court which reveals the balance of his activities.

"Headquarters Department of Virginia and North Carolina,

July 31, 1864

My name is Frank McElheny, I belong to the 19th Virginia Battalion, Colonel Eckerson. I have been in the Regiment for two months, I enlisted in Richmond.

I was born in Salmon Falls, New Hampshire. When two years old my parents moved to Boston. When 15 years old I went back to Salmon Falls lived there four years and then returned to Boston where I have lived until the war broke out, driving team for a living. I first enlisted in the 24th Massachusetts regiment and went with them to North Carolina. While there I got into a drunken scrape and abused a sentry. For that I was court martialed and sentenced to Fort Macon. I left Fort Macon in November last (1863). I was not confined in the Fort but had the run of the island. One Sunday another man and myself walked to the lower part of the island opposite Swampton, a deserter said rebels were picking up all within the reach. When the Cavalry pickets of the Rebels station who have swam their horses across the river, and captured us, they had to remain (*illegible*) half a mile (*illegible*) horseman came over in a boat and took us across, a major of the 3rd Virginia Cavalry was in command of the Fort at the time.

From there, we were taken to Richmond where I enlisted in the 19th Virginia Battalion, I came within your lines July 27th having escaped from the enemy.

Frank "X" (his mark) McElheny

witness, Lieutenant Manning

By leave of the Court the accused made the following *Statement*.

"If I deserted in the first place, from this side, I should not come back, I think. So it looks reasonable I was captured. I was about twenty miles from Fort Macon when I was captured. All the prisoners used to go all around there, fishing."

The prisoner having no other witnesses or statements to present to the Court and the prosecution ended the court deliberated. The accused was found guilty and the court sentenced him to be shot to death with musketry.

The firing squad was composed of 24 men (two squads of 12 men each) from his former company, Company F, 24th Massachusetts Infantry Regiment. 24 rifles were loaded, 22 with ball ammunition, two with blanks. The procession to the execution site was lead by the regimental band playing a dirge, with drums muffled. Following them was an army wagon containing the prisoner, seated upon a rough pine coffin, and beside him a Catholic Priest. The firing squad, with rifles reversed, followed the wagon. At the site of the execution was an open grave. The procession halted, the wagon, near the grave, the priest and prisoner alighted and the coffin was removed and placed near the open grave. The prisoner was blindfolded, his arms previously shackled and led to the coffin where he knelt upon it. The first firing squad took their position, the commands being given, they fired. McElheny fell onto the coffin, said to have received at least five bullets in the chest. The Regimental Surgeon, Dr. Samuel Green, upon examination of the prisoner found life still present which occasioned the employment of the second firing squad to ensure death. The surgeon then declared life extinct. The assembled troops who had witnessed the execution then marched past the corpse led by the band playing a lively tune. When the troops had departed the corpse was placed in the coffin "face downward" (this is the only reference to such a practice we have noted) and buried. The grave was filled in level and no headboard or marker indicated McElheny's grave.

The execution took place on August 8, 1864 in his divisional area near Deep Bottom, Virginia.

The 24th Massachusetts Infantry Regimental Surgeon Samuel Green stated that on the forenoon of the day of McElheny's execution he rode seven miles to the headquarters of General Benjamin Butler at point of Rocks, Virginia to beg for a commutation of the sentence of McElheny, to no avail.

REFERENCES:

Military Personnel Records, RG-#94

Court Martial Proceedings, RG-#153 LL 1342

"The 24th Regiment Massachusetts Volunteers, 1861-1866, New England Guard Regiment." Worchester, Massachusetts 1907 Alfred S. Roe. (incorporating accounts by Regiment Surgeon Samuel A. Green, 24th, Captain John N. Partridge Company F, 24th).

Chaplain H. C. Trumbull, 10th Connecticut) "War Memories of an Army Chaplain" New York City, 1898.

Case #131

Pvt. Barney Gibbons

Co. A, 7th Regiment U.S. Infantry

Shot for Desertion

August 17, 1864

DESCRIPTION:

No Military Personnel Records were located for Barney Gibbons. All the information recorded here was contained in the records of Gibbons' Court Martial.

Gibbons enlisted in the U. S. Army during 1859 at Newport, Kentucky and was sent as a replacement to Camp Floyd, Utah Territory where he was assigned to Company A, 7th

Regiment U. S. Infantry. At some point in his service, the 7th Regiment was transferred for duty to Ft. Fillmore, New Mexico. Ft. Fillmore was evacuated on July 27th, 1861 because of the approach of Confederate forces from Texas. The 7th Regiment set out across a desert toward San Augustine and ran short of water resulting in large numbers of the regiment unable to continue the withdrawal at the normal march pace. One Lieutenant, a Sergeant and eleven men finally reached San Antonio where they were surrendered to a Confederate force that marched them to Las Cruces, New Mexico and there paroled.

Gibbons deserted the Parole Camp and was observed to be serving with a Confederate unit operating against the Union Troops in the Las Cruces area.

By sheer chance, Gibbons was seen and recognized by a former Sergeant of the 7th Infantry Regiment, Richard C. Day, on the street in St. Louis in 1864. Gibbons was arrested and confined pending a General Court Martial on charges of Desertion and deserting to the enemy and joining with them in arms against the government of the United States, to which he pleaded not guilty.

The Ex-Sergeant of the 7th Infantry who recognized Gibbons was the principal witness for the prosecution.

Gibbons presented a statement in his defense to the court. "All I have got to say is the charge against me is false. I never belonged to the U. S. Infantry, but there was a man, my brother, who went by the name of Barney Gibbons that did and he belonged to that Company. I was in Texas at the time and was in a light battery. My brother pretended to say he was not treated well and left them and joined us. He resembled me very much and I suppose this man arrested me under that name for this reason. My name is Benjamin Gray. I never assumed the name of Barney Gibbons, my brother did, he joined under that name, he got into trouble and assumed that name to get out of it. I have a cut on my lip* and so has he. I was born in Pennsylvania. I came up to Fillmore in Colonel John Baylor's command. I never was in the service of the United States. The Company, the Rebel Company that I belonged to was broken up and I was assigned to a gunboat, The Sachem, but I was dissatisfied and the first opportunity I left them. I never saw this man before that I know of. I might have seen him at the time stated, but I don't recollect it. I was in the Rebel since at the time this Company of the 7th U. S. Infantry surrendered. I was in a battery when the Regiment was taken."

The court, desiring to insure the truth of ex-sergeant Richard C. Day's testimony, recalled him for further questioning.

Day stated emphatically that Gibbons possessed unmistakable physical characteristics, that were collectively impossible to duplicate. Gibbons had a harelip and a posture which thrust his head forward and hips and buttocks backward somewhat bent forward from he waist. He marched with his hands open and fingers spread apart, even with gloves on.

Day also assured the court he had no personal enmity toward the prisoner.

The court then deliberated and found the prisoner guilty as charged and sentenced him to death by musketry. The sentence to be carried out in St. Louis, Missouri on the 12th day of August 1864.

*Harelip

REFERENCE:
Court Martial Proceeding, RG #153 LL 2210

Case #132
Private William H. Howe
Co. A., 116th PA Vol. Inf. Regt.
Executed for Desertion & Murder
August 26, 1864

DESCRIPTION:

22 years of age, Married, 2 children, a farmer and cigar maker of Frederick Township, Montgomery County, Pennsylvania. No further physical description located.

Howe enlisted on August 8, 1862 at Philadelphia, Pennsylvania and was originally listed as a Wagoner in Company H, 116th Pennsylvania Volunteer Infantry Regiment. The unit designation was changed to Company A, Battalion A, 116th Pennsylvania Volunteer Infantry by transfer of men from Companies A, D, F and G (same Regiment) by order dated January 26, 1863.

The Regiment was formed and taken by train to Washington, D.C. and thence into Maryland, finally to the Harper's Ferry area, then to Warrenton and Falmouth, Virginia. On December 11, 1862 the attack on the Confederate positions at Fredricksburg, Virginia began and the 116th Pennsylvania Volunteer Regiment participated. Prior to the battle, and continuing on well after, Howe had, in common with countless other soldiers, developed severe and debilitating diarrhea. Howe apparently walked from the 116th Regiment to Falmouth, seeking medical attention but was given "short schrift" as the Army Hospitals were filled to over flowing with badly wounded men. Howe decided, it seems, to simply walk home to Pennsylvania and secure rest and such medical treatment for his ailment as was there locally available. The date was officially December 27, 1862 and Howe had committed the act of desertion. At his home, Howe recovered his health and strength and was present on February 6, 1863 for the birth of his third child.

Howe's return home did not remain unnoticed and on or about June 21, 1863 two members of a provost's staff attempted unsuccessfully to arrest Howe at his home. On the evening of the day following, another attempt was made to arrest Howe at his home. It is stated that the provost arresting party consisted of David Y. Eisenberry, Abraham R. Bertolet, Michael Wagner and an unnamed negro servant of Bertolet. They approached the house late at night in total darkness and demanded Howe surrender himself. Being refused, they attempted to force their way in. Shots were said to have been fired from the house and one struck Bertolet in the chest, eventually causing his death. Howe left his home after the shooting but returned after the provost men left with Bertolet's corpse. Howe later fled his home area. He was arrested in Allentown, Pennsylvania on July 13, 1863 and was transferred to Philadelphia. His Court Martial, on December 26, 1863, resulted in a guilty verdict on the charge of desertion and murder. The sentence was death by hanging.

Howe wrote a letter to President Lincoln on August 23, 1863.

"Philadelphia Provost Marshals Headquarters, August 23, 1863

Mr: President: Sir. I will inform you a few lines this is that I William H. Howe from Frederick Township Montgomery County PA. have enlisted in the 116th P.V. Reg. as private i enlisted on the eight of August 1862 and left the Regiment one day before crismas and Received home the 21 of January the reason that i left the Regiment was this i was not well the hole time that i have been in serves and i could not get in no Hospital i hat to do my duty like the rest that was well and so i thought i would live the Regiment and go home till i was well again and when i was at home about three months i was nere over it then i was going to go out againe and then my Nabors found it out and they came to my house and told me that you hat let Printed in the news papers that every deserter that would not be in his Regiment till the first day of April would get shot or hung they make me afraid because i was to late then and further they told me that i should stay at home they would fite for me before they would lieve me go and so i did not no what to do i was afraid to go out and I was afrait to stay at home and then i thought i would stay two three weeks yet then i would, i would go and in that time they commenced to enrole the Peoples for the Draft and so one Sunday Nite three men came at my house to catch me one was the Enrolen Officer from Newhanover Township and the others was two citicence from the same Township and one on Sunday nite at Eleven O'Clock somebody came nocking at the dore and my wife heret it and she went down to see what was the matter then she ask what was the matter and then somebody outside set she should open the dore and she ask what for then she got no anser rite away then he set if she would not open the doore he would push her in and then he tried to push her in and my wife came running upstairfs then i seen two men out side so soon i looked out they shot at me two times and then i went back again and got my gun and then i hert them at the doore again and i seen one outside to but i could not tell who he was and then i shot at him and then i went upstairs againe opened at window and looked out but everything was all quiet and then i jumped out and hollart Murder Murder Murder and runt to my next nabor and told him and to a *candle* more and whent there came back again then i hat shot the Enrolen Officer from New Hanover township he was going to cetch me and then they caut me and tucked me to Philadelphia and put me in a sell about eight feet long and about four feet wite an almost smaterring in here i been in now six weeks it is no air coming in atall and dark to if he would come there like a man he could cetch me but not like a murder and this I can prove by a dossen of witnesses

Wm. H. Howe.The Army Judge Advocate General, Joseph Holt, stated in a memorandum his comment on Howe's letter which was addressed to the President.

"Office of the Judge Advocate General

31 August '63

Howe addresses the President from Provost Marshall's Headquarters, Philadelphia. He acknowledges that he deserted on the day before Christmas, because, he says, he was in ill health, and could not get into hospital, but was made to perform duty as if well. He states he went home to get well, and intended to return. in July, he states on a Sunday night three men came to his house to catch him at about 11 O'clock and attempted to enter it by violence. That his wife informing him of it, he looked out of the chamber window and was immediately shot at twice: He got his gun, and hearing them at the door again looked out and seeing one man outside of the others fired and shot dead a man he did not then know, who proved to be the enrolling Officer of New Hanover Township. He was arrested, taken to Philadelphia and confined in a cell from which he writes. He declares that he is sorry he shot the man, and should not have done so if he had come for him like a man, instead of like a murderer.

This statement by Howe is not accompanied with any petition or complaint, and does not present a case on which this office can take any action.

Holt

Judge Advocate General"

A review of the proceedings of the trial by the Judge Advocate's office in Washington, D.C. resulted in the overturning of the verdict of the trial and sentence because of "the informality" of the entire proceedings.

An additional unaddressed or dated letter to President Lincoln is in Howe's Military file.

"i enlistet to fite for the Union and left two little Children's and a Wife behind me and when i did come out i was treated like a dog not like a soldier and i am willing to fite for the union anytime yet and further that man be the name of Barttolette what i have shot he was trafted last year then he went Harristown and tucked an oath that he hat his rite since and then he got free but he hat allways sence enufh to cheet somebuddy Mr: President i am sorry that I cant talk English better so that i could explane it write But i hope you will do for me what is write i am willing to suffer for what is write and no more i have a wife and childrens and I cant see how they can get thru the world this way and I am sorry that i shot that man but i could not help it he did not come like a man he came like a murderer if a sholder would come there i would went along with him.

My address is William H. Howe,

Perkiomenville Post Office, Montgomery County, Pennsylvania and further is wish you would not forget me

Yours truly William H. Howe"

The records of the trial of Private Howe which had resulted in his conviction and sentence of death were forwarded for review and confirmation. The reviewing authority overturned the verdict on the basis of the "informality" with which the trial had been conducted.

The second General Court Martial was convened at Philadelphia, Pennsylvania and on February 15, 1864 tried Private William H. Howe, Company A. 116th Pennsylvania Infantry Regiment. The accused was asked if he objected to any member of the Court named, to which the accused challenged Lieutenant Colonel H. A. Frink, 11th Pennsylvania Volunteer Infantry upon the ground that Colonel Frink had prepared the charges against the accused.

(In a sworn statement to aid a plea for clemency on the 24th of June, 1864 at Washington D. C. attorney for Howe, Edmund Randall stated in reference to Colonel Frink, "Having tried the Prisoner Howe *some two months before for the same offence*, which trial however *was set aside for informality. This last mentioned fact does not appear on the Record, for the reason stated*, but it is nevertheless *true*, as can be fully verified by an examination of the two orders from General Couch Headquarters detailing the various officers to constitute the two Courts." No copy of the first Court Martial record has been found.)

Colonel Frink responded to the challenge by stating that he had no knowledge of the facts of the case and further that his name was appended to the charges against the accused by order of Colonel Frink's superior Officer.

The Court room was cleared and the Court deliberated. Reaching a decision, the Court summoned the accused and announced the Challenge/Objection to Colonel Frink's presence on the Court was not sustained.

The accused requested to be allowed counsel, Edmund Randall of Philadelphia, former Adjutant of the 116th Pennsylvania Volunteer Infantry, which the Court granted.

Howe was charged with Desertion and Murder.

The Prisoner pleaded Not Guilty to the charge of Desertion but refused to enter a plea on the Charge of Murder on the grounds that The Court now convened "has no jurisdiction in this case, in as much as the offense is laid as having been committed in the murder of one Abraham R. Bertolet, Enrolling Officer of New Hanover Township, who was in nowise an Officer or Soldier in the Military Service of the United States and that the Defendant is amenable, therefore, only to the laws of the State of Pennsylvania and the Court of Ozer and Terminer for Montgomery County in the State of Pennsylvania."

The Courtroom was again cleared and the Court deliberated. The Court returned to session, the accused appeared and the Court announced that it had decided not to admit the plea of the accused for the following reasons to wit:

"Section 30 of the Act of Congress of the United States approved March 3, 1863 entitled `An Act for Enrolling and calling out the National forces and for other purposes,' reads as follows: And be it further indited that in time of War, Insurrection or Rebellion, Murder, assault and Battery, with intent to kill, manslaughter, Mayhem, wounding by shooting or stabbing with an intent to commit murder, robbery, arson, burglary, rape, assault and battery with an attempt to commit rape, and larceny shall be punishable by the sentence of a General Court Martial or Military Commission when committed by persons who are in the Military service of the United States and subject to the Articles of War; and punishments of said offenses shall never be less than those inflicted by the laws of the State, Territory or District in which they may have been committed."

One of Howe's defenses was that he claimed not to be the person named as the accused since his name was William H. Howe and the Company roster carried the name William Howe. This was not accepted after an intermission of the trial to permit substantiation of the claim. After much maneuvering to attempt to rebut damaging testimony to the accused the second trial was concluded. The verdict, guilty as charged and the sentence, death by hanging on June 24, 1864 at Fort Mifflin, Philadelphia, Pennsylvania.

The murdered Bertolet's brother wrote to President Lincoln on June 24, 1864 concerning the Howe case.

"Philadelphia, June 27, 1864

To the President of the U.S.

Respected Sir I communicate

These few lines in behalf of the family of my Brother Abraham R. Bertolet who was murdered by William H. Howe about one year since the time for his execution having passed his sentence having been commuted to an indefinite period. We fear some bad influence has been used in representing his case before you if any petitions or anything of the kind have come before you perporting as coming from his wife or friends that he should not be executed we have only to say that it is false and a forgery we have waited patiently and long for Justice to be meted out to him and when upon the eve of realizing those expectations we are unhappily informed that execution has been stayed The enemies of our glorious union are already rejoicing hoping and expecting that their friend Howe who has not only murdered my brother but also deserted the flag of his country will be again released and amongst his friends. however we hope and pray that those hopes of theirs may be blasted.

There have quite a number of Union men been murdered through the state that it seems but proper that an example should be made of this man Howe. For if all are pardoned it only licenses traitors to murder our citizens I would earnestly solicit an early reply to this letter.

Henry Bertolet"

Several continuances were granted on the basis of petitions such as one from the officers of his regiment. These however were eventually declined, the execution taking place at Fort Miflin, Philadelphia, Pennsylvania on August 26, 1864.

A very thorough study of the Private Howe case has been made by Robert I. Alotta in a book entitled"Stop the Evil", Presidio press, San Rafael, California, 1978.

Unfortunately Alotta interprets the events and facts which occurred in the Civil War (1861-1865) by the laws, legal standards, military justice and court room procedure as exists today. One can only fairly judge events in history in light of the contemperary mores.

REFERENCES:
Military Personnel Records, RG-#94
Court Martial Proceedings, RG-#153 NN 1528

Case #133
Pvt. Emanuel Davis
NV: Drummer, Manuel Davis
Co. A, 48th Infantry USCT
Executed for Murder
August 31, 1864

DESCRIPTION:
18 (also 17) years of age, 5 feet tall, black eyes, black hair, black complexion, born in Madison Parish, Louisiana, occupation farmer, illiterate.

Davis enlisted and was mustered into service in Company A, 10th Regiment Louisiana Infantry (A.D., African Descent) at Goodrich Landing, Louisiana on September 2, 1863. His unit changed its designation to Company A, 48th Infantry Regiment, USCT. In March of 1864, while the Regiment was on duty near Haines Bluff, Mississippi, Davis murdered a soldier of his own Company. He was arrested, confined and court martialed.

A General Court Martial was convened at Haines Bluff, Mississippi and on March 19, 1864 tried Private Emanuel Davis, Company A, 48th Infantry Regiment USCT for murder.

The testimony provided by the witnesses stated that at the regimental dress parade, at the Brigade Parade ground at Haines Bluff, Mississippi on the morning of March 18, 1864, Ephraim Woodward (the victim) and Huston Gray, both privates in the 48th Regiment band were standing next to each other in formation. Emanuel Davis, given a drum by the Drum Major, stepped into the interval between Gray and Woodward. Woodward told Davis that was not his place and Davis said he would stay there. Woodward shoved him out of the formation, whereupon Davis drew out his pocket knife, opened it and told Woodward "he would kill him." Gray advised Davis "not to make any fuss on the parade ground." Woodward told Davis to wait until they were dismissed and they could go away from the area and settle the matter. After dismissal of the Regiment, Davis pulled off his coat and drew and opened his pocket knife when Woodward told him if he would give his knife to one of the spectators, he would whip him. Davis replied, "No, he was going to keep his knife and kill him with it." Woodward then went off and secured a "switch" (described as "big as my two fingers at the big end and all sprangen out at the other end") and Davis found a club. Woodward then advanced toward Davis and struck him a blow across the shoulders with the switch. Davis ran up to Woodward and stabbed him in the chest area with his knife. Woodward turned around, took four or five steps, said "I'm going to die" and fell face foremost on the ground. He was dead within twenty minutes.

Surgeon A. C. Davis of the 48th Regiment testified that Woodward had been "killed by some sharp instrument. He was struck about the lower portion of the breast bone and the instrument glanced about 3/4 of an inch and then entered the cavity between the 5th and 6th ribs on the left side, making an orifice about 1 inch in length. I probed the wound and found that the instrument had entered the heart producing necessarily almost instantaneous death. I have no doubt whatever that the death was caused by the wound and the blow that produced the wound must have been struck with full force." The knife was described as a four inch single bladed pocket knife with a stag horn handle.

Davis questioned some of the witnesses, but offered no defense or statement.

The Court deliberated and found Davis guilty and sentenced him to be executed by hanging.

The execution took place on August 31, 1864 at the Camp of the Brigade.

The Vicksburg Daily Herald of September 1, 1864 carried an account of his execution at Vicksburg on August 31, 1864. "A large crowd of spectators, in addition to the Military, viewed the execution. Davis, nearly overcome with fear of his pending fate, prayed aloud for mercy on his soul. He begged to be freed under promise of never committing another wrong deed. While weeping, he begged his comrades, in a tremulous voice, not to do as he had. The noose was placed about his neck, the hood covered his head, the trap door sprung and Davis was dropped into eternity."

REFERENCES:

Military Personnel Records, RG-#94
Court Martial Proceedings, RG-#153 NN 1707
Vicksburg Daily Herald (as above quoted)

Case #134
Pvt. Roger Johnson
NV: aka Johnson Roger
Co. H, 6th Heavy Arty Regt, USCT
Executed for Murder
September 1, 1864

DESCRIPTION:

29 years of age, 5 feet 5 inches tall, black hair, brown eyes, black complexion, born in Wilkson County, Mississippi, occupation farmer, illiterate.

Johnson enlisted and was mustered into service at Natchez, Mississippi on November 1, 1863 and was assigned to Company H, 2nd Regiment Mississippi Artillery A.D., (African Descent). The unit was redesignated Company H, 5th Regiment U.S. Colored Heavy Artillery and finally as Company H, 6th Heavy Artillery Regiment, USCT. Within a month after enlistment, Johnson became ill of Smallpox. He was reported variously as sick in Post Hospital and in Variola Hospital at Natchez, Mississippi.

The Regiment seems to have been on duty in the Natchez area throughout its existence. Johnson committed murder, was arrested and tried.

A General Court Martial was convened at Natchez, Mississippi and on June 9, 1864 tried Private Roger Johnson, Company H, 6th Heavy Artillery Regiment, USCT on charges of murder, assault with intent to kill and Conduct Prejudicial to Good Order and Military Discipline.

Witnesses testified that on February 11, 1864, Johnson who was a nurse in the "Pest Hospital" (smallpox) near Natchez, Mississippi, came into the Cook's kitchen of the hospital, which was presided over by Private Andrew Belleville, Company F, 4th Illinois Cavalry Regiment. Present also at the time were Sergeant Bedford Symes, Company K, 6th Heavy Artillery Regiment USCT and Clementine McKellup who had been both a patient and more recently cook and nurse at the Pest Hospital. Johnson demanded his supper, but Belleville told him to wait outside until another man who was eating finished. When Johnson did not leave, Belleville seized Johnson and pushed him out of the kitchen. Johnson then disappeared. Johnson returned and Belleville said, "Have you come back again?" The accused replied, "yes". Sergeant Symes spoke to Belleville saying, "Keep cool and let him (Johnson) have his supper." Belleville replied, "Well, I want him to go out until I fix the Colored Peoples Supper." Belleville then again told Johnson to leave the kitchen. When Johnson did not move, Belleville seized hold of him and put him out of the kitchen again and threw two or three plates after him. Belleville returned to his duties in the kitchen and as he raised his hand to take down some provisions from a shelf, Johnson came into the doorway of the kitchen and Mrs. McKellup screamed when she saw him with a pistol in his hand. Belleville turned around, saw Johnson and threw up his hand, as though to ward off a bullet. Johnson fired and the shot struck no one, and he fired a second time and the shot struck Belleville in the left breast. Johnson pulled the trigger a third time, but the pistol did not fire. Belleville ran out of the kitchen toward the Surgeon's office holding his hand over his left breast, but fell before he reached the Surgeon's office. Belleville was taken into the hospital where he lived until the 13th of March, 1864.

The pistol Johnson used was described as an Allen's patent six shot revolver, a pepper box. The ball projectile was described as the size of a turkey or buck shot.

A postmortem examination of the body of Belleville was performed by a Dr. Walker, Surgeon, and Hospital Steward, F. C. Steinel. "The bullet entered the left chest wall 2 ½ inches from the nipple of the mammary gland between the second and third ribs. The bullet penetrated the left lung and we thought the ball lodged in the spine, but the bullet was not found. The left lung was entirely mortified and broken down, the right lung partially mortified. Five and one half pints of pus were taken out of the chest. Although we did not find the ball, we were satisfied that the wound caused by a bullet produced the death of Andrew Belleville.

Johnson was arrested by Private Thomas McRevy, Company I, 29th Illinois Infantry Regiment assigned to the Pest Hospital. McRevy brought Johnson to Dr. Walker's office where he was interrogated. Dr. Walker asked the accused why he shot Belleville and Johnson replied, *"I shot him for throwing or shoving me out of the kitchen."*

The accused offered neither witnesses nor a statement for his defense.

The Court deliberated, found the accused guilty and sentenced him to be shot to death with musketry.

The execution took place on September 1, 1864 at Natchez, Mississippi.

REFERENCES:

Military Personnel Records, RG-#94
Court Martial Proceedings, RG-#153 LL 2577

Case #135
Pvt. (Cpl.) James Williams
Co. G, 5th Heavy Artillery, USCT
Executed for Murder
September 1, 1864

DESCRIPTION:
29 (25) years of age, 5 feet 11½ inches tall, dark hari, dark eyes, yellow complexion, born in the York District, South Carolina, occupation carpenter, illiterate.

Williams enlisted and was mustered into service at Natchez, Mississippi on October 10, 1863 in Company G, 2nd Regiment Mississippi Artillery, USCT. He was promoted to Corporal on the 20th day of October, 1863 and was reduced back to rank of Private on March 25, 1864 as a result of his arrest on a charge of murder.

A General Court Martial was convened at Natchez, Mississippi and on June 15, 1864 tried Private James Williams, Company G, 6th Regiment Heavy Artillery, USCT on the charge of murder.

Private James Williams stabbed Private Harry Williams also of Company G, 6th Regiment Heavy Artillery on March 15, 1864 at Camp McPherson thereby causing his death. (Harry and James Williams are not related.)

Witnesses testified that Harry Williams was at the cook stoves, within the Fort McPherson Fortification at Natchez, Mississippi. He had secured a cup of coffee and was waiting for the coffee grounds to settle when James Williams arrived and demanded Harry's cup of coffee. Harry refused to surrender it, and James grasped the cup and attempted to wrest it from him. James then kicked Harry and Harry, in turn, struck James and knocked him down. James got up and walked away from the scene amidst the laughter of bystanders. james whirled about and strode toward Harry saying, "If I can't whip you one way I can another" while drawing a knife. James made two "rakes" (slashing motions) at Harry, the first penetrated his lower left rib area, the second only cut through his shirt. Harry walked about 100 yards to the entrance to his Captain's tent, where he collapsed in the Company street. He was taken to the regimental hospital and lived for nine days. The Hospital Assistant Surgeon, F. W. Ferris, testified that the wound was in the region of the spleen and that if no untoward symptoms occurred, the patient might recover and that the wound was not necessarily fatal but was of such a character which might produce death.

No further testimony was given and James Williams offered no statement, the court then deliberated. The court found Private James Williams guilty and sentenced him to death by musketry.

The sentence was carried out at Fort McPherson, Natchez, Mississippi on September 1, 1864.

REFERENCES:
Military Personnel Records, RG-#94
Court Martial Proceedings, RG-#153 LL 2577

Case #136
Pvt. Seldon S. Chandler
Co. K, 4th, Artillery, US Army, Regular
Executed for Desertion
September 2, 1864

DESCRIPTION:
39 years of age, 5 feet 8½ inches tall, dark hair, gray eyes, dark complexion, born in Enfield, Connecticut, occupation soldier, literate, married to Lovina Chandler of Claremont, New Hampshire.

Chandler enlisted on May 27, 1861 and was mustered into service on June 5, 1861 at

Portsmouth, New Hampshire as a corporal in Company H, 2nd New Hampshire Infantry Regiment. He was discharged for disability at Fairfax Seminary, Virginia on November 1, 1862 to enlist in Battery K, 4th US Artillery, Regulars for the term of the balance of his original enlistment, 1 year six months 27 days. He had been reported absent without leave on October 29, 1862 but apparently encountered no difficulty in having the record expunged. Chandler deserted from the regulars (Battery K 4th US Army Artillery Regulars) on July 15, 1863. He next appears on February 1, 1864 as a patient at the Stone General Hospital Washington, D.C. where the record states he was admitted from the Forrest Hall Prison and listed his military unit as Company H, 2nd New Hampshire Infantry Volunteers. He was discharged from the hospital or deserted same, no record remains available to consult. He was finally apprehended on July 16, 1864 by the 2nd New Hampshire Infantry Volunteers and delivered to the Provost Marshall as a deserter from Battery K, 4th US Artillery Regulars.

A General Court Martial was convened at the headquarters of the Artillery Brigade, 2nd Corps. on July 26, 1864 for the trial of Private Seldon S. Chandler, Battery K, 4th U. S. Artillery on the charge of desertion.

Testimony of witnesses revealed that Chandler left the Battery on July 10, 1863 near Gettysburg and was apparently brought back to the Battery by the Provost guard. On July 17, 1863 he deserted near Middletown, Maryland. He was arrested on July 21, 1863 as a deserter, and returned to his unit. Other testimony did not mention the second act of desertion on July 17, 1863 as described above and set the date of his apprehension as January 29, 1864.

A statement was read into the record.

"Headquarters Department of Washington, office of Chief Quartermaster, Washington, D.C. February 25, 1864"

"Sir: I have the honor to inform you that Private S.S. Chandler, Company K, 4th Regiment U. S. Artillery has been apprehended as a deserter from the military service of the United States and has been delivered to Captain Henry A. Schutz, Provost Marshall-District of Columbia and that the reward and expenses amounting to thirty dollars have been paid at this office."

"Very respectfully, your obediant servant
Horatio C. King, Captain A. Q. M."

The defense offered no testimony but Chandler supplied the following written statement concerning the matter.

Statement

"At the time I left the Battery I was sick, or, in fact, the battery left me, for I was unable to go with it. I was on the sick report and the doctor had given me medicine that morning. At the time that the Battery went away from me, they were on the double-quick and I went with them until I fell and asked some of the boy's to tell Lieutenant Seeley. They said they would, but he was wounded and they did not see him. I got to the Battery as quick as I could find it and reported to Lieutenant James. He would not listen to me; put me under guard with handcuffs on and told me he would court martial me for leaving the Battery on the field of battle. I then went with it as far as I could and it again left me. When I went to Captain Schutz, I was sick and told him who I was and all about it. The surgeon sent me to the hospital, where I remained from February 1, 1864, till the latter part of April. I was sent from the hospital to Fortress Monroe. After more than two months I was sent here."

The Court was closed while the Court deliberated and then announced the verdict of guilty and sentenced Chandler to be executed before a firing squad.

Chandler, still awaiting execution, was the subject of official correspondence in August, 1864.

On August 6, 1864 a message was sent certifying that Chandler was indeed forty one years of age. No explanation is found for the communication.

On August 24, 1864 a telegram was sent from Major General George C. Meade to the

Judge Advocate General Joseph Holt in Washington, D. C. The message read, "General Meade requests that the records in the cases of Private W. Alimetter, Battery A, 1st New Jersey Artillery and *S. S. Chandler*, Battery K, 4th U. S. Artillery be returned to him immediately by mail. It is said that G. C. M. Order #30 of August 12th from these Headquarters confirming death sentences in these cases contains a misstatement of fact in the case of Chandler. Viz: that he twice deserted and reenlisted under an assumed name. If this is the case General Meade desires to correct the order before execution. Execution in both cases have been postponed one (1) week in order to reexamine. it is for this purpose that he desires to have the records temporarily returned to him. if the records cannot be sent please inform him whether the recital of facts in cases of these men in the last paragraph of the order are correct.

George G. Hastings - Major and Acting J. A."

Since no further correspondence relative to the matter has been located, it must be assumed the matter was satisfactorily resolved as Chandler was executed on September 2, 1864.

REFERENCES:
Military Personnel Records, RG-#94
Court Martial Proceedings, RG-#153 LL 2292

Case #137
Pvt. John Rowley
Co. D, 7th CONN Infantry Regt.
Executed for Murder and Treason
September 3, 1864

DESCRIPTION:

22 years of age, 5 feet 6 inches tall, black hair, black eyes, dark complexion, born in England, occupation sailor, substitute, literacy undetermined.

Rowley was drafted as a substitute and mustered into service on November 2, 1863 at Bridgeport, Connecticut. He was forwarded for assignment to Company D, 7th Connecticut Infantry Regiment. On February 20, 1864 while the Regiment was engaged in the battle of Olustee, Florida, Rowley shot and killed Pvt. Jerome Dupay, Company D, 7th Connecticut Infantry Regiment on the firing line. Rowley was arrested, tried by court martial on April 25, 1864 at Gloucester Point, Virginia charged with Murder and Treason. The treason charge was based upon the assumption that the murder of one union soldier by another during battle gave "aid and comfort to the enemy."

A General Court Martial was convened at Gloucester Point, Virginia and on April 26, 1864 tried Private John Rowley, Company D, 7th Connecticut Infantry Regiment on charges of murder and treason.

The accused asked permission of the court to have Captain Jeremiah Townsend, 7th Connecticut Volunteer Infantry act as his counsel. The Court granted the request.

The accused asked for a postponement of the trial to enable his counsel to make preparations for the trial, which the court granted, postponing the trial for 24 hours.

Witnesses described the events which had occurred. On February 20, 1864 at the battle of Olustee, Florida. Rowley was a member of a "composite Company" composed of remaining members of Companies D, F and I of the 7th Connecticut Infantry. His position was in the second line of battle. Immediately in front of him a distance of only 10-15 feet in the first rank, was Private Jerome Dupay, Company D, 7th Connecticut Infantry Regiment. The men were equipped with the Spencer Repeating Carbine, capable of firing 15 shots per minute.

Dupay was described as kneeling near a tree firing at the enemy beside Private Eleazer Nodine of Company F, 7th Connecticut Infantry Regiment also kneeling and firing at the enemy, about 18 inches to the left of Dupay. A shot was fired from the line of men behind them and Dupay fell forward on his face. The powder blast burned Nodine's face and he quickly turned his head toward the rear rank and shouted "What in the hell did you do that for?." A man, in the second rank, later identified as Rowley then fell prone without replying.

Dupay's wound was described as a small hole in the rear center of the head, surrounded by powder burned hair. The exit wound in the forehead was much larger, and a witness said, "his brains was slopping out."

In the confusion of battle, Rowley was not immediately identified as the killer of Dupay.

Analysis of the military formations and positions of the opposing forces at the time Dupay was killed indicated that the fatal wound could not have been inflicted by the enemy.

When the rumors of Rowley's involvement in Dupay's death began, it was found that Rowley had indeed uttered threats against Dupay. It seems that when the regiment had been encamped on Saint Helena Island, Dupay was observed running out of Rowley's tent and Rowley followed screaming that Dupay had stabbed him. Examination of Rowley's body bore out his claim as a shallow knife wound was found on his back. Rowley publically stated Dupay would "pay him for it." Before the battle of Olustee, Florida as the troops were forming battle lines, Rowley was heard to say, Dupay is the only man he wanted to see hurt, and he would like to see him killed.

First Lieutenant T. C. Wildman, Company D, 7th Connecticut Infantry Regiment stated that on April 1, 1864, he had occasion to punish Rowley. The punishment consisted of having Rowley stand on the rim of a topless wooden barrel for two hours with a full haversack. When punishment was concluded Rowley asked permission to speak to Lieutenant Wildman. As the company orderly conducted Rowley into the Lieutenant's tent, he remarked that, "Rowley says he shot Dupay." Rowley then confirmed his statement to the orderly and told the Lieutenant. "By God I did shoot him, and I acknowledge it." When asked why he did it, he replied that Dupay had tried to kill him twice, the last time was when he shot him. Dupay, Rowley contended, had his carbine pointed at him. Rowley further stated that the cause of his being in the Army was that he had killed a man in New York.

Rowley commented that "Dupay's ghost appeared to him every night and he could not sleep and he hollered in the night time." The accused called no witnesses on his behalf but did offer a written statement to the Court in his defense.

"May it please the Court, in submitting my case to it's decision, I bring forth no witnesses in my defense, for I see the need of none, the plain facts as they have appeared from the evidence of the prosecution are seemingly enough to secure an innocent man from an ignominious death. In summoning up the evidence against me, I find it of two fold character, direct evidence which is contained in the testimony of Private Eleazer Nodine, Company I, and Private Charles Vibberts, Company B, and indirect and presumptive evidence which is contained in the testimony of the rest of the witnesses of the prosecution. I would by leave to call the attention of the Court, first to the direct evidence, in examining the testimony of Private Nodine you find that it is not evidence against me, but rather for me. He, Nodine, was acquainted with the deceased as well as with myself, he was within a few feet of the deceased when he was shot and *he* testifies that to the best of his knowledge that the deceased was shot by a party other than myself. The testimony of Private Vibberts is very incomplete he did not know the deceased and had never seen me to know me until the day of the battle, he says he saw me aim and fire my rifle and thinks that it hit a man who he saw fall at that time, he acknowledges that it is possible that my shot did not hit the man he saw fall and that shots were flying in all directions at the time, his description of the manner and locality as regards the man he saw shot differs materially from the manner and locality of the death of Dupay as described by Nodine. Such is the summing up of the direct evidence against me and it is so contradictory and incomplete that there cannot be a shadow of *proof* embodied in it. Now let us look at the presumptive evidence. We find that the two chief points in this consists first in a quarrel the deceased had with me, second in confessions made by me, the quarrel was one that occurred several months previous to Dupay's death, one thing must have already presented itself to the mind of the court, if I had such a deadly purpose against the deceased, why did not it develope itself in the many opportunities I had in the long marches, frequent scouts isolated, picket duties and so forth in which we were thrown into close relationship during the march from Jacksonville, (Fla) to Olustee if there had been any evidence to the fact that I was of a vindictive disposition this point might have some weight but such is not the case and the mere fact of my having had quarrels with the deceased ought not to condemn me. And now lastly let us look at the grand point and on which the decision of the court must pend that is the confession made by myself. I find in referring to Benet that confessions are reduceable to three classes, First - a confession made in open Court by the prisoner himself which is conclusive and no other proof necessary, Second -a confession made before a magistrate, Third - a confession made to any other person, this last says Benet, is the weakest and lowest of all and such is the sort of confession made by myself, a sailor by occupation, full of love for the marvellous and having a strong desire for telling extravagant stories partly to intimidate my officers who were punishing me partly from my love of relating the horrible and startling story once told with the stubborness characteristic of the English nation to which I belong and stuck to it, but the changes I made in telling the story as must have been seen by the court from the evidence of the prosecution was enough of itself to show the untruth of it. But the question may be asked by some can it be possible that a man would jeopardize his life in such a manner without being guilty. Benet says in reference to such cases, although it can hardly be conceived that any one would make a free and voluntary confession of guilt so diametrically opposed to the feelings and principles that govern our actions, if the facts confessed were untrue, yet instances have occurred in which innocent persons have confessed themselves guilty of crimes of the gravest character.

It *should be considered* that the confessions as generally made in want of advisors, under circumstances of desertion by the world, in chains and degradation, with spirits sunk, fear predominant, hope fluttering around, purposes and views momentarily changing, a thousand plans alternating, a soul tortured with anguish and difficulties gathering into a multitude. How easy it is for the hearer to take one word for another, or take a word in a sense intended by the speaker! And for want of an exact representation of tone of voice. Emphasis, countenance, eye manner, and action of the one who made the confession how impossible is it to make a third person understand the exact state of his mind and meaning. For these reasons, such evidence is received with great distrust, and under apprehensions for the wrong it may do. Such was the state according to the facts brought up to *this* court of any mind at the time I made the first confession, low spirited, suffering from punishment, reckless to a degree beyond thinking or caring for the future and from utter desperation, I let fall those words for which I am now being tried for my life. Such are the mainpoints in my case and I submit it to you Gentlemen, to your decision well knowing that I can rely upon your justice and humanity.

John Rowley."

The Court then deliberated, found the accused guilty and sentenced him to be hanged by the neck until dead.

The execution took place on September 3, 1864 near the camp of the 7th Connecticut Infantry Regiment.

The second paragraph (II) of General Orders No. 97 August 23, 1864 H.Q. Dept. of Virginia and North Carolina reads as follows:

"Private Rowley has been convicted of the most heinous offence known to the annals of crime. It cannot be said to be criminal law, for the law has never presupposed a crime of so great malignity, and is silent upon the subject, as the Roman law was said to be silent against parricide."

A soldier in the army of the United States, he had a comrade, Jerome Dupay, in the same Company with him, with whom he had had some weeks previously a foolish quarrel. Because of this he had threatened revenge, and this revenge he took when Dupay, deployed in the skirmish line of his regiment, was bravely fighting the enemies of his country at Olustee, Florida, by deliberately shooting him from behind through the brain, causing his instant death, from so close proximity that the powder burned the hair of the deceased, and scorched the faces of his comrades skirmishing with him; thus committing murder and treason at the same time, by giving aid and comfort to the enemies of the United States in the same act that killed his comrade.

Is it not wonderful that, in the language of Rowley's confession, he "cannot sleep, because Dupay's ghost appears to him." Rowley has had an impartial trial, was defended by counsel of his own selection, and has been convicted in due form upon what appears to be sufficient evidence; which conviction, after careful review, has been approved. The Commanding General, Therefore, is constrained to order this sentence to be carried out."

REFERENCES:
Military Personnel Records, RG-#94
Court Martial Proceedings, RG-#153 LL 2366

Case #138
Pvt. William C. Dowdy
Co. E, 1st Regiment of U.S. Vols
Executed for Desertion
September 9, 1864

DESCRIPTION:
22 years of age, 5 feet 9¾ inches tall, blue eyes, red hair, fair complexion, born in Bedford, Tennessee, occupation Blacksmith, illiterate.

Dowdy originally served in Company E, 66th North Carolina Infantry and was captured at Parkville, North Carolina on October 12, 1863, transferred to Fort Norfolk, Virginia on November 6, 1863. He was subsequently transferred to Prisoner of War Camp Lookout, Maryland where he remained until February 1, 1864 when he took the oath of allegiance to the U.S.A. and enlisted in the 1st Regiment of U.S. Volunteers (Galvanized Yankees) and was mustered into service at Norfolk, Virginia on May 1, 1864. The 1st U.S. Volunteer Infantry trained diligently and marched to Elizabeth City, North Carolina as a training exercise.

The U.S. Volunteers (Galvanized Yankees) were not to fight the Confederates but were solely to be employed against the Indians of the west. Dowdy's Regiment was ordered to the western plaines.

On August 15, 1864, the regiment sailed on a transport from Norfolk to New York City where it was loaded on railway cars for the journey. New orders sent four companies, A, F, G and I to Milwaukee while the remainder, including Company E and Dowdy traveled to St. Louis, Missouri. The regiment, shrunken in numbers by transfer of four companies was ordered to board a river boat, the Effie Deans and sail up the Missouri River to Fort Rice, Dakota Territory. The diminished regiment on the river boat was under the direct command of its Colonel, Charles A. R. Dimon. Col. Dimon was appointed as a Sergeant in the 30th Massachusetts Volunteer Infantry from civilian life in Lowell, Massachusetts at 20 years of age. He was a protege of Major General Benjamin Butler also of Massachusetts and was rapidly promoted to Major in the 2nd Louisiana Volunteer Infantry and finally Colonel of the 1st U.S. Volunteers Infantry. As the Effie Deans churned north on the Missouri River, a number of desertions began to occur as it was customary for river boats to anchor along the shore at night and travel only in the daylight. Col. Dimon, 23 years old at the time, with no real command experience became apprehensive of a large scale general desertion and ordered his officers and NCO's to be more watchful.

On September 5, 1864 the Company Commander of E Company was advised that Dowdy had threatened to desert. On September 7, 1864, Dowdy was tried by Court Martial convened aboard the Effie Densis and was charged with violation of the 7th Article of War, which broadly refers to mutiny and the 21st Article of War, Absent Without Leave.

Dowdy was specifically charged with cursing his superior officers and making seditious statements such as "that he'd be damned if he wouldn't take the first opportunity to desert the regiment." The second charge stipulated that Dowdy had absented himself from his Company without leave from his Commanding Officer, and did remain absent until apprehended. Dowdy had counsel appointed who advised him to plead not guilty to violation of the 7th Article of War and guilty to the 21st Article of War. Testimony disclosed that Dowdy complained of illegal training expeditions in the Norfolk area as well as being critical of some of his officers which is a common soldier trait from ancient times to the present. His Company Commander testified that he personally watched Dowdy all during a heavy rain filled night, but never stated that Dowdy had ever left the boat.

The Court then deliberated, found Dowdy guilty as charged and sentenced him "considering the best interests of the Service and the Regiment, he be shot to death by musketry in the presence of his Regiment at such time as the Commanding Officer may direct."

Records state Dowdy was executed two miles north of Florence, Nebraska territory on the Iowa side of the river on September 9, 1864.

Dowdy thus became the first "Galvanized Yankee" executed during the Civil War. (See Case #173, Private William M. Smith, 2nd U.S. Volunteer Infantry.)

REFERENCES:

Military Personnel Records, RG-#94
War Department Collection of Confederate Records, RG-#109
Court Martial Proceedings, RG-#153 LL 2566
"Galvanized Yankees," Dee Brown, 1963, University of Illinois Press, Urbana, Illinois

---

Case #139
Pvt. John Mitchell
NV: Mitchel, Micheal
Co. B, 53rd Inf Regt, USCT
Executed for Desertion
September 15, 1864

DESCRIPTION:

20 years of age, no further data found.

Mitchell apparently enlisted at Nanenton, Mississippi on June 19, 1863 and was mustered into service at Milliken's Bend, Mississippi on October 28, 1863 and assigned to Company B, 3rd Regiment Mississippi Infantry A.D., (African Descent). The unit designation was changed to Company B, 53rd Infantry Regiment, USCT. Mitchell deserted on November 22nd, 1863, with his rifle and accouterments and did not return until August 3rd, 1864 when he was arrested. A General Court Martial was convened at Vicksburg, Mississippi and on June 15, 1864 tried Private John Mitchell - Company B - 53rd Infantry Regiment - USCT on a charge of desertion.

Testimony was given by witnesses that the accused deserted the military service when his Regiment and company was at Millikens Bend, Mississippi, on November 22, 1863. He was not seen again until he was arrested on board the Steamer "SHENANGO" on April 15, 1864 at Vicksburg, Mississippi. He had been seen by members of his Regiment after they arrived in Vicksburg. The accused had been employed aboard the steamer as a cabin boy. He offered no resistance to the arresting party. When brought back to camp he was given labor duty with a ball attached to his leg with a chain.

"Statement of the Prisoner"

"I told the Captain previous to going away that I should leave his company and go to some others if he continued to kick and cuff me about as he had been doing. I told him that I was willing to go into any other company in the Regiment."

The Court then deliberated, found the accused guilty and sentenced him to forfeit all pay and allowances now due on which may become due for the next four (4) months and be at hard labor under charge of a regimental guard with a ball weighing twelve (12) pounds attached to his right leg by a four (4) foot long chain. On June 20th, 1864, General John P. Hankins, Commander of the 1st Division of United States Colored Troops Vicksburg, Mississippi addressed a letter to accompany the copy of the Court Martial Proceedings in the trial of Private John Mitchell, which he was returning to the Court. It read as follows: "The Proceedings in the foregoing case are respectfully returned to the Court for reconsideration of it's sentence. The Prisoner was absent five months and until arrested, and by his own admission - he shows his desertion was premeditated. There is nothing in the evidence to palliate the guilt and by comparity there should be no letting up on the extreme punishment prescribed by the Articles of War. Desertions have been too common in this command and they will become more frequent unless soldiers are made to understand the severe punishment they must suffer for not being faithful to their Oath of Allegiance to the Government. They know very well they should not desert. It is time they learned as well the just punishment due a deserter."

The Court deliberated and revised the sentence to be shot to death with musketry.

On June 28, 1864, Major General Slocum, District Commander at Vicksburg, Mississippi commented "The proceedings, findings and sentence in the foregoing case are approved and respectfully forwarded for action of Department Commander - with a recommendation that the sentence be commuted to loss of pay and to hard labor four months with ball and chain attached to his leg."

The sentence had already been reconsidered once and was not reconsidered a second time. The execution took place near Vicksburg, Mississippi, on September 15, 1864.

REFERENCES:

Military Personnel Records, RG-#94

Court Martial Proceedings, RG-153 LL 2350

Case #140

Pvt. Samuel W. Downing

AKA: John W. Ball

Co. H, 4th MD Inf. Regt.

Executed for Bounty Jumping

September 16, 1864

DESCRIPTION:

30 years of age, no other description available. It is believed he was literate and was of course a substitute many times. Although there are others who lay claim to being the all time champion bounty jumper of the Civil War, Downing is the *only one* with a self confessed accurate listing and description of his 18 enlistments as a substitute for which he received $7,750 in a relatively short span of time. His ability to outsmart jailers and detectives was of a very high order, regrettably he did not direct his obvious talents to a business or professional career where he would have in all likelihood achieved a very real success.

Downing's own statement covers completely the details of his career as a bounty jumper from about August 15, 1861 to his execution on the morning of September 16, 1864 in the open field northwest of the Sickles Barracks Hospital.

Statement of Samuel W. Downing. Alias John W. Ball Co "H" 4th Md Infy.

"I enlisted in Co "H" 4th Md. Infy at Baltimore Md about the middle of August 1861 and went with my Reg to Williamport Md. About the last of July 1863 I left the camp without permission, and went to Greencastle Pa, where I put on Citizens Clothes, and went as a Substitute. about the 16th of August 1863 receiving therefor ($500.) Five Hundred Dolls, and a Pass, to go about the Village. I then went to New York City, where I went as a Substitute. at the Cor of Broome, and Mercer St. N.Y. receiving therefor ($375.) Three Hundred & Seventy five Dolls, and was sent to Rikers Island, where I paid an Arty Sergt ($50.) Fifty Dolls, to let me go, which he did. I putting on Citizens Clothes. I then paid a Boatman ($5.00) Five Dolls, to take me to New York City. I then went into another Office, and went as a Substitute, again, under the name of John W. Ball, and received ($375.) Three Hundred and seventy five Dolls, this about the 19th of August 1863 and was again sent to Rikers Island. I again paid the same Sergeant ($50.) Fifty Dolls, and the same Boatman ($5.00) Five Dolls, to take me to New York City. having previously put on Citizens Clothes, while on the Island. I then went to Harrisburg Pa, where I went as a Substitute under the name of Samuel W. Downing, about the last of August 1863, receiving therefor ($1500.00) Fifteen Hundred Dolls, and was sent to Camp Curtin, when I bought of a Sergt a Pass, paying ($10.00) Ten Dolls for it, and put on Citizens Clothes. and went to Philadelphia the same day. About the 7th of September 1863, I went as a Substitute at 11th and Girand Street receiving ($250.00) Two Hundred & Fifty Dollars and was sent to Barracks Cor Buttonwood & 22nd Street where I paid the Serg. of the Guard ($30.00) Thirty Dolls to let me out. I then put on Citizen's Clothes, and to Frankford, Pa. where about the 10th of September 1863 I went as a Substitute, receiving ($450.) Four Hundred & Fifty Dolls, and was sent to the same Barracks Cor of Buttonwood & 22nd St. where I paid the same Sergeant another ($30.00) Thirty Dolls to let me go. I again put on Citizens Clothes and went to New York City, where about the 15th of Sept. 1863. I went as a Substitute in the upper part of the City receiving therefor ($375.00) Three Hundred & Seventy-five Dolls and was sent to Alexandria, Va. and landed at the Coal Warf Sept. 24, 1863 when I put on an Officers Coat, which I had prepared, on board the Transport, for the purpose, and passed myself by the Guards, to Alexandria as an Officer, where I bought Citizens Clothes, and put them on also. A Pass, paying ($40.) Forty Dolls for the Pass. I then went to New York City, where I again went as a Substitute, about the 1st of October 1863, receiving ($375.) Three Hundred & Seventy Five Dolls and was sent to Alexandria, Va., and landed again at the Warf, about the 8th of October 1863, when I again put on the Coat, and passed myself to Alexandria, Va. as an Officer, and bought Citizens Clothes, and a Pass, of the same parties as the first time. I then went to Jersey City, N.J. about the 15th of Oct. 1863, when I again went as a Substitute, receiving therefor ($350.) Three Hundred & Fifty Dolls. and was sent to Brandy Station, Va. About the last of October 1863 I purchased an Officers Uniform, and put it on, and went to Washington D.C. where I purchased Citizens Clothes, and put them on and went to New York City again. About the 10th of Nov. 1863 I again went as a Substitute, receiving therefor ($375.) Three Hundred & Seventy-five Dolls, and was sent to Alexandria, Va. and landed at the Coal Warf about Nov. 16, 1863, when I again put on an Officers Uniform, and passed myself to Alexandria, Va., as an Officer, where I put on Citizens Clothes, and bought a Pass for ($20.) Twenty Dolls. and went to Phila, where about the 20th of November 1863 I again went as a Substitute in 3rd St. receiving therefor ($250.) Two Hundred & Fifty Dolls, and was sent to Ruttonwood Barracks, and the next day I paid the Sergeant of the Guard ($30.) Thirty Dolls to let me go out. I then put on Citizens Clothes, and went to New York City where about the 12th of December 1863. I again went as a Substitute in the Bowery, receiving therefor ($375.) Three Hundred & Seventy five Dolls. and was sent to Alexandria, Va. and landed at the Coal Warf about the 15th of December 1863 when I put on a Naval Officers Uniform and passed the Guard to Alexandria, Va. as a Naval Officer, and again purchased Citizens Clothes, and put them on, and bought a Pass for ($40.) Forty Dolls, and went to Baltimore, Md. and then to Cincinnati, Ohio where I about the last of December 1863 went as a Substitute and receiving ($300.) Three Hundred Dolls therefor, and was allowed to go where I pleased, but to report every day. About the 15th of January 1864, I went to Louisville, Ky. where I remained until the 15th of Feby 1864 and went to Cincinnati, Ohio, where I again went as a Substitute receiving ($450.) Four Hundred & Fifty Dolls therefor, and was sent to some place beyond Fortress Monroe. Upon arriving at Fortress Monroe, I paid the Chief Engineer ($100.) One Hundred Dolls to hide me on the Boat. He hid me, and Fed me, until the Boat returned to Washington D.C., the same party furnishing me with Citizens Clothes, which I put on about the 1st of March 1864. I then went to Columbus, Md. about the 15th of March 1864. I went as a Substitute, receiving ($250.) Two Hundred & Fifty dolls therefor and was sent to Camp near Columbus, Md. about the 18th of March. I paid the Sergeant of the Guard ($20.) Twenty Dolls to let me pass, which he did. I then put on Citizens Clothes, which i had with me and went to Columbus, Ohio April 1, 1864 where I went as a Substitute receiving ($700.) Seven Hundred Dolls, and was sent to Alexandria, Va. and stopped at the Soldiers Rest. About the 12th of April 1864, I paid the Sergeant of the Guard ($50.00) Fifty Dolls to let me pass out of the Rest. which he did. I then purchased Citizens Clothes, and bought a Pass of the same parties, who had furnished me with them before paying ($40.) Forty Dolls for it and went to Cincinnati, Ohio, where I was arrested about the middle of April 1864 by a Soldier, and taken to the Provost Marshal who confined me and sent me to Baltimore, Md. where I was confined in the Slave Pen. About the last of June 1864 I passed myself out of the Slave Pen as the Doctor attending the Pen. I then stopped about the City until about the last of June 1864 when I went as a Substitute, receiving therefor ($500.) Five Hundred Dolls, and was allowed to go to the Express Office, under Guard, from whom I escaped, and stopped around Baltimore, Md. until about the 7th of July 1864 when I went to the Provost Marshal and offered myself as a Substitute, but, was arrested by a Detective who recognized me and was confined by Prov. Marshal in Fort McHenry. I was then sent to Camp Distribution, Va., and then to Prince St. Milt Prison, Alexandria, Va. where I now am, confined as a Deserter."

Signed, Samuel W. Downing

"August 13, 1864
Witnesses
R. D. Pettit
Capt. 12th Reg. V. Re. C. in charge of
Prince St. Milt Prison
R.F.W. Roberts
1st Lt. 12th Reg. V. Re.C.

I was assisted in all of the transactions above named, that occurred in New York City, Jersey City, Baltimore, and Philadelphia by a man names William Jones, who has a Brokers Office for Substitutes in the Bowery, New York City, just above Canal St. on the right hand side. He met me at the different Provost Marshals Offices and "put me through" taking for his pay, about half the proceeds. He also gave me instructions how to proceed. I was assisted at Columbus, Ohio, Columbus, Md., and Cincinnati, Ohio by a Doctor named Brown in the same manner. He is known at Provast Marshal Jones Office Cincinnati, Ohio.

Signed
Samuel W. Downing"

Witnesses
R. D. Pettit
Capt. 12th Reg. U.R.le.
In charge of Prince St. Milt Prison
R.f W. Roberts
1st Lt. 12th Reg. VRC

Enlistee Co. "H", 4th Mae Rigt. Aug 61
1st Desertion last - July 1863, Williamsport Map

1st Reenlistment	Aug 16/63 at Green Castle, Pa.	$500.00
2nd Reenlistment	Aug 16x19 at New York	$375.00
3rd Reenlistment	Aug 19,63 at New York	$375.00
4th Reenlistment	Aug 31,63 at Harrisburg	$1500.00
5th Reenlistment	Sep 7.63 at Philadelphia	$250.00
6th Reenlistment	Sep 10.63 at Frankford, Pa.	$450.00
7th Reenlistment	Sep 15.63 at New York City	$375.00
8th Reenlistment	Oct 1.63 at New York City	$375.00
9th Reenlistment	Oct 15.63 at Jersey City, N.J.	$350.00
10th Reenlistment	Nov 10.63 at New York City	$375.00
11th Reenlistment	Nov 20.63 at Philadelphia	$250.00
12th Reenlistment	Dec 12.63 at New York City	$375.00
13th Reenlistment	Dec 31.63 at Cincinnati, Ohio	$300.00
14th Reenlistment	Feby 16.64 at Cincinnati, Ohio	$450.00
15th Reenlistment	Mar 15.64 at Columbus, Indy	$250.00
16th Reenlistment	Apr 1st.64 at Columbus, Ohio	$700.00
17th Reenlistment	June 31.64 at Baltimore, Md.	*$500.00*
		$7550.00

Arrested July 7th 1864 in Baltimore, Md.

Samuel Downing

His conviction by courtmartial on Sept. 14, 1864 was predictable. Downing was executed by a firing party on the morning of Sept. 16, 1864 in the open field northwest of the Sickles barracks hospital, Washington, D.C.

REFERENCES
Military Peronnel Recrords, RG #94
Court Martial Proceedings, RG #153   NN 2518

Case #141
Pvt./John Sweeney
NV: Corporal, Sweeny
Co. C, 1st Maryland Vol Inf Regt
Executed for Desertion
September 20, 1864

DESCRIPTION:
22 years of age, gray eyes, brown hair, 5 feet 7 inches tall, complexion fair, born in Maryland, occupation blacksmith, literacy not determined.

Sweeney was a substitute credited to the 2nd District of Maryland and enrolled on January 4, 1864 and was sent to the Draft Rendezvous on Masons Island, D.C. on January 28, 1864 and forwarded to his unit, Company C, 1st Maryland Volunteer Infantry Regiment. He apparently remained in service until May 5, 1864 when he deserted near the Rapidan River. He was apprehended and court martialed on July 15, 1864 on the charges of desertion and deserting to the enemy. He was found guilty of the first charge and not guilty of the second charge and was sentenced to execution by firing squad.

A curious memorandum is included in his Military Record file. Dated the 29th of August, 1864, on the printed stationary of the Headquarters, Army of the Potomac, Judge Advocate Office appears the following addressed to Brig. General Ayres, Commanding 2nd Division, 5th Corps: "The Major General Commanding directs that you obtain from Comdg. Oficer of Co. C, 1st Md Vet. Vol Infty, a certified statement of the age of Private

John Sweeny of that Company and Regt. tried for desertion and forward the same to this office (balance illegible)."

It would appear as though Sweeney was appealing his conviction by pleading under age for enlistment. There has been no reply to this request found.

Sweeney was said to have been executed but the listed dates of execution vary. The court martial order states execution to have taken place at 9 a.m. on Friday, September 16, 1864. "The Official List" records the date of execution as September 20, 1864 as do some of his military file records. Another document lists September 27, 1864 as the date.

REFERENCES:

Military Personnel Records, RG-#94

Case #142
Pvt. Sgt. George W. McDonald
NV: M.M. Dunning
Co. F, 3rd MD Cavalry Regt.
Executed for Desertion
September 21, 1864

DESCRIPTION:

31 years of age, 6 feet 1¾ inches tall, dark hair, dark eyes, dark complexion, born in White County, Illinois, occupation boatman, illiterate.

McDonald enlisted on September 18, 1863 and was mustered into service on September 23, 1863 at Baltimore, Maryland in Company F, 3rd Maryland Cavalry Regiment as a Sergeant. A notation on his service record states that McDonald was "sick in camp" at some time during the period 18 September-31 October, 1863 at Fort Delaware Maryland. On or about January 1, 1864 he deserted from the vicinity of Baltimore, Maryland. He was not heard from until March 15, 1864 when at Clarksburg, Maryland he assaulted, without provocation, one Ezekial Moxley by firing a pistol at him and wounding him. On March 30, 1864 McDonald's hideout in Montgomery County, Maryland was discovered and a Sergeant Haugh and detail of soldiers attempted to arrest him which he violently resisted, firing a revolver and using other weapons to prevent capture. Fortunately, his efforts produced no wounds and he was finally arrested and confined at Baltimore, Maryland.

A General Court Martial was convened at Baltimore, Maryland and on September 5, 1864 tried Sergeant George McDonald, Company F, 3rd Maryland Cavalry Regiment on charges of desertion and assault with intent to kill.

Several witnesses did not appear as the trial began and the Judge Advocate was very disturbed by their absence, and he requested that they be arrested and brought to the trial under guard. He received a letter from the Provost Marshall on the matter which read as follows: "I sent Detective Taft up to Monocacy, Maryland on Saturday with a letter to General Tyler to furnish a squad of mounted men to arrest the witnesses. I have not heard from them yet, although I expect them here this morning. I will notify you as soon as they arrive."

The trial was urged to begin as the prisoner had been held in close confinement for four months. The trial was therefore begun.

Witnesses present, testified that McDonald had deserted his Company and Regiment on January 1, 1864 and remained absent until captured on March 30, 1864. McDonald was hiding in Montgomery County, Maryland, southwest of Baltimore, during his absence. At his capture on March 30, 1864, McDonald admitted he was a deserter.

Ezekiel Moxley, aged 26 years, a horse dealer employed by the government to purchase horses for the Artillery, Cavalry and wagon trains and similar uses. rode, in company with a U.S. Postal carrier, from Washington to Clarksburg, Maryland. Upon arrival at Clarksburg, he was greeted by friends and while engaged in conversation with them was interrupted by a man who inquired, "Do you belong to the Government Service?" "No" replied Moxley. The stranger then asked "Does that horse belong to the Government Service?" Moxley asked in way of a reply, "Are you a detective?" The stranger angrily shouted, "You dirty son of a bitch, I will give you detective!" and drew a revolver which he pointed at Moxley's breast. Moxley, trying to keep calm said, "You are not going to shoot me. I have never done anything for you to shoot me." The stranger ordered Moxley to, "Draw your hand off that horse, you damned dirty son of a bitch." "It is very hard for a man to have to take his hand off his own horse." The stranger than fired his revolver at Moxley striking him in the calf of the leg. (The witness displayed the wound to the Court.) The stranger previously referred to was then positively identified as McDonald.

Moxley continued to relate the event. He took the reins and made ready to ride off, still pointing his revolver at Moxley who exclaimed, "You shot me!" "You son of a bitch, that is not half as much as I intended to do!" McDonald mounted the stolen horse and rode away. Moxley commented that he was fortunate that the revolver failed to fire when McDonald aimed at this breast, which would have killed him and also pointed out that some thirty people were present when he was shot, including two constables and two magistrates, but all seemed to be afraid of him.

Moxley's horse was found, apparently having been turned loose, and was returned to him by the finder.

Sergeant Jesse Waugh, Company G, 3rd Maryland Cavalry Regiment testified concerning the capture of McDonald.

On March 30, 1864, Sergeant Waugh and five men plus a local citizen, William F. Talbott as guide, located McDonald's hide out at a farm owned by a Joseph Thompson 16-18 miles from Mt. Arey on the Baltimore and Ohio Railroad near Laytonville, Montgomery County, Maryland. Arriving about 8PM, the Sergeant had his men surround the farm house and ascertained that McDonald was in the house on the second floor. The Sergeant entered the house, which was in total darkness except for the light cast from a burning fireplace. He secured a lamp, after McDonald threatened to shoot them, and began ascending the stairs to the second floor, the accused cocked his revolvere and called out, "Come on upstairs, I am ready for you, you damned son of a bitch!" The Sergeant demanded that McDonald come down and surrender, but McDonald said, "if he wanted to take him or did take him, that he would only have his body, for he would not be taken alive!" The Sergeant shouted, "I will smoke you out as I had smoked crows out before tonight and will smoke you out!" The Sergeant went out of the house and secured several matches from his soldiers, returned inside and set fire to bed clothing. McDonald fired at the Sergeant but the cap only exploded without setting off the ball powder. With that, the Sergeant set the entire lower floor afire. The Sergeant ordered his men to fire into the second floor and McDonald replied with a number of shots. The fire began to gain headway and the second floor began collapsing. McDonald came to a window and begged for his life, but the Sergeant remained adamant in his demand for McDonald to throw down his weapons. McDonald finally threw down his revolver (which was presented to the Court as evidence), a double barreled shot gun, another revolver and a bowie knife. McDonald was then permitted to surrender and escape the portent of hellfire. He was seized, tied up very securely and returned to the camp of the 3rd Maryland Cavalry Regiment where he was turned over to the Provost Marshall.

No further testimony by either the prosecution or the accused and no statement of defense was offered by the accused, the Court then deliberated. The prisoner was found guilty and sentenced to be shot to death with musketry.

The execution was carried out at Fort McHenry, Baltimore, Maryland on September 21, 1864.

REFERENCES:

Military Personnel Records, RG-#94
Court Martial Proceedings, RG-#153 LL 2430

Case #143
Pvt. Giles Simms
NV: Sgt, Sims
Co. F, 49th Inf Regt, USCT
Executed for Mutiny
September 25, 1864

DESCRIPTION:
31 years of age, 5 feet 11 inches tall, black eyes, black hair, black complexion, born in Grand Gulf, Mississippi, occupation field hand, illiterate, married.

Simms enlisted at Grand Gulf, Mississippi on May 21, 1863 and was mustered into service at Milliken's Bend, Louisiana on June 4, 1863 and assigned to Company F, 11th Regiment Louisiana Infantry, A.D., (African Descent). The unit designation was changed to Company F, 49th Infantry Regiment, USCT. On June 7th, 1863, he was wounded in the battle of Milliken's Bend, Louisiana. On April 3rd, 1864, Simms was promoted to the rank of Sergeant, the Regiment then being stationed in Vicksburg, Mississippi. On June 13, 1864, however, he is said to have led a mutiny, ordering his men to "stack arms." He was arrested.

A General Court Martial was convened at Vicksburg, Mississippi and on June 20, 1864 tried Sergeant Giles Simms, Company F, 49th Infantry Regiment USCT on a charge of mutiny. In all, there were 21 members of Company F, including Simms so charged.

Testimony revealed that on June 13, 1864, sixteen men of Company F marched up before the tent of the Company Commander, Captain James P. Hall, and stacked their arms and remained in formation awaiting the arrival of Captain Hall. When the Captain arrived, one soldier, Washington Fontaine (see case *#144*) stepped out of ranks, approached the Captain, saluted and said, "Captain, we have stacked our arms and are not going to do any more duty until we can have the promise of better treatment from you." The Captain left and went to the Colonel commanding the Regiment and reported the mutiny. The Colonel returned with Captain Hall to the Company street and ordered the Captain to take their arms and accouterments. This done, the Colonel marched the men to the guardhouse. Six more were arrested in the afternoon of the 13th including Simms who vigorously attempted to persuade all remaining Company members to join the mutiny. Simms, strangely enough, did not march all the way up to Captain Hall's tent, dropping out enroute and returning to his own tent.

The mutineers claimed that on Saturday, Captain Hall had broken open their boxes (Civil War prototype of the present day army foot locker), had treated them (the mutineers) as though they were thieves, had burned the boxes and taken their candles.

The Captain explained his actions as the result of an inspection of the Company F quarters by the Regimental Surgeon on the day previous to the breaking open of the boxes and complained that the boxes contained some foul smelling objects. The surgeon further pointed out that a soldier had no business with any box or extra luggage which would not fit into his knapsack. When the Captain broke into the boxes, he found mutilated candles, spoiled meat, rotten bread, green apples, and gloves and stockings previously reported as stolen from the soldiers. All boxes were in a very filthy condition.

At roll call at noon on June 13, 1864, the Captain stated he informed the men of his inspection findings and actions regarding the boxes. He stated that boxes were not permitted and if any more were found in their quarters he would not only destroy the boxes but also punish the owners.

Of the prisoners confined in the guardhouse, Simms was the loudest and most frequent speaker. Simms was reported to have said he would "not allow any white man to put him in the Guardhouse."

No witnesses or statement being offered by the accused the Court deliberated, found the accused guilty and sentenced him to be shot to death with musketry.

The balance of the 20 men arrested for mutiny received the following varied sentences: Washington Fountain was sentenced to death and was executed at the same time and place with Simms. Seventeen men were sentenced "to forfeit all pay and allowances that are or may become due to them; and to be imprisoned at hard labor for life at such place as the Commanding General may direct." One prisoner was sentenced to forfeit all pay and allowances that are or may become due to him; to be imprisoned at hard labor during the remainder of his term of enlistment, with a ball and chain attached to his leg, in such place as the Commanding General may direct." One man was "released from confinement and returned to duty."

No record has been located as to a later reduction in the punishment of those awarded life imprisonment sentences.

The Vicksburg Herald of September 27, 1864 carried a story concerning the execution.

"Military executions" — "On Sunday morning last (September 25, 1864), two soldiers, Sergt. Giles Sims and Private Washington Fountain of Company F, 49th Regiment USC Infantry, were shot to death with musketry, without the inner fortifications of this post, pursuant to sentence of court martial, for the crime of mutiny. They were both stout, fine-looking soldiers, one apparently a man of fifty years of age.

"The different colored regiments of the post were all present at the scene of execution, besides a great many spectators of the white troops and citizens. The condemned men were seated upon their coffins in front of the firing squad, when the proceedings of the Court Martial were read to them and to the troops — After the reading of the finding and sentence of the Court Martial, a brief prayer was made by the chaplain, at the conclusion of which the bandages were placed upon the eyes of the condemned men, and the order to fire given to the squad. One of the men was instantly killed; the other, however, had to be dispatched by a pistol, immediate death not resulting from the wounds by the muskets." (See also, Case #144 Private Washington Fountain.) Simms' widow, Hetty, received his effects, one pair trousers and two woolen blankets.

REFERENCES:
Military Personnel Records, RG-#94
Court Martial Proceedings, RG-#153 LL 2350
Vicksburg Herald, as previously quoted

Case #144
Pvt. Tontine Washington
NV: Fountaine, Fontine
Co. F, 49th Inf Regt, USCT
Executed for Mutiny
September 25, 1864

DESCRIPTION:

35 years of age, 6 feet tall, black hair, dark eyes, black complexion, born at Grand Gulf, Mississippi, occupation field hand, illiterate.

Washington enlisted at Grand Gulf, Mississippi on May 21, 1863 and mustered into service at Milliken's Bend, Louisiana on June 4, 1863. He was assigned to Company F, 11th Regiment, Louisiana Infantry (A.D., African Descent). Participated (June 7, 1863) in the battle of Milliken's Bend, Louisiana. He participated in a mutiny at the camp near Vicksburg, Mississippi, was arrested, tried and convicted. Sentenced to execution on September 25, 1864 before a firing squad. (See Case #143 as Sergeant Giles Simms was similarly involved in the mutiny.) Washington's sentence included the stipulation that he "forfeits all pay and allowances now due." His mother, Jennie Washington, receive his effects, one woolen shirt, one pair of trousers and one woolen blanket.

REFERENCES:
Military Personnel Records, RG-#94
Court Martial Proceedings, RG-#153 LL 2350
Vicksburg Herald, 27 September 1864

Case #145
Private William J. Lynch
AKA: "Polly" Lynch
Co. B and K, 63rd, NY Infantry Regt.
Executed for Desertion
September 30, 1864

DESCRIPTION:

22 years of age, 5 feet 8 inches tall, brown hair, gray eyes, fair complexion, born in Albany, New York, occupation bricklayer.

Lynch enlisted and was mustered into service on September 25, 1861 at Albany, New York in Company K, 63rd New York Infantry Regiment. While enroute to Virginia, in March 1862, Lynch deserted. Returned to his Regiment, he again was reported missing as of April 2, 1862 from Alexandria, Virginia and as the records seem to indicate again was returned to the ranks of his Company which by December 1863 was Company B, 63rd New York Infantry Regiment. Comments about Lynch contained in his Military Personnel file include, "Is an old offender having deserted 12 or 15 times, the last time from Fort Columbus within a week" and "Is a dangerous man, this is his fourth offense." His military career seems to have consisted of deserting and escaping from military prisons with little if any actual "Soldiering." Why he was permitted to re-enlist as a Veteran Volunteer is inexplicable.

A General Court Martial was convened at the headquarters, 1st Division, 20th Army Corps and on September 2, 1864 tried Private William I. Lynch, Company B, 63rd New York Infantry Regiment on a charge of desertion.

Testimony showed that Lynch reenlisted for a third period on December 21, 1863 and received a furlough which expired on February 5, 1864. Lynch did not report and his Regiment left New York City for the field. Lynch was returned, in citizen's clothes, to the Provost Marshall on August 1, 1864.

Lynch's personnel record disclosed the following prior offenses:

"Lynch was arrested by members of his own company and afterwards escaped from the Albany Barracks at least three times before the Regiment went into the field. He escaped from David's Island, New York Harbor, July 1, 1862 and September 25, 1862 was arrested by Officer Bart and a reward of $5.00 and $12.50 expenses was paid by Major Sprague Mustering and Disbursement Officer at Albany, New York. He was then conveyed to Ft. McHenry, Baltimore, Md. whence he escaped and reached Albany, NY even before the return of the Officer who took him there. He was again arrested by Officer Muliman on the 19th of Dec., 1862 and $5.00 was paid by Major Sprague. He was then taken to Wash. D.C. whence he soon made his escape. On the 14th day of Aug., 1863, he was brought to these hdqtrs., (Albany, N.Y.) and on the 20th of the same month was transferred to Fort Columbus, New York Harbor. A reward of $10.00 was paid for his arrest. Lynch succeeded in making his escape from Fort Columbus, in a few days and on the 25th of August, 1863 was arrested and on the 27th of August was again sent to Fort Columbus. A reward of $10.00 was paid for the arrest. He again escaped and on the 22nd of October, 1863 was again arrested and a reward of $30.00 paid for his arrest. The matter in detail was referred to the Provost Marshall General and an order returned that Lynch be sent direct to his Regiment for trial. He was accordingly forwarded to his Regiment on the 6th of November 1863. He was then tried by General Court Martial and sentenced to be shot, the sentence being approved by the President. The President was then petitioned and Lynch was pardoned and restored to duty. He re-enlisted and was given a furlough of thirty days, came home (Albany, NY), was paid his local bounty of $300.00 in this City (Albany) and again deserted. He was again arrested, on or about the 10th of July 1864 in Buffalo, NY by order and a reward of $30.00 paid for his arrest. He was forwarded to his Regiment, in accordance with instructions from Major General Dix, commanding the Dept. of the East."

A summary of the expenses incurred in arresting Lynch was attached to the report. Rewards totaled the sum of $92.50 and a notation states, "Other expenses probably have been incurred in the several arrests attended to, but this is all that can be found on record at Albany."

The Court deliberated, as no further testimony of either the prosecution or defence was offered. The Court found Lynch guilty and sentenced him to be shot to death with musketry.

On September 19, 1864, Lynch addressed a letter to President Lincoln.

"Your Excellency Abraham Lincoln, President of the United States, by the will of God and the vote and voice of the American People.

I beg your Excellency to allow a few lines from the humblest of your subjects to find favor in your sight.

I, Wm. Lynch, Co. B, 63rd NY Volunteer am sentanced to be shot for desertion on the 30th inst. I will not undertake to excuse myself Since I have been tried, found guilty and Sentanced by Court-Marshal. This, to say the least of it would be unsoldierly. But for my life I now plead and I trust, in your clemency, You will commute the sentance. I am a young man and in the full vigor of manhood and I do not wish to die now if it please God and the Chief ruler of these U. States to let me live. Any sentance for me but death.

If my life be saved it shall be devoted to whatever Your excellency may direct.

Your most humble and obediant Servant

Wm. Lynch, Co. B,

63rd NY Vet. Vols."

The sentence was carried out in Washington D. C. on September 30, 1864. On October 12, 1864, the Judge Advocate General Holt writing from the War Department, Bureau of Military Justice:

"Resply returned to Maj. G. G. Hastings, Judge Advocate A.P.

Attention invited to omission from the record of the prisoner's plea, by which the entire proceedings are invalidated, unless, the sentence not being yet executed, the Court can be reconvened and the error, if merely clerical, be corrected."

The reply on October 17, 1864 from Major Hastings, Army of the Potomac read:

"Respectfully reforwarded to the Judge Advocate General. The within named prisoner was duly executed, pursuant to the sentence, on the 30th of September, and it is too late to remedy the defect in the record. The Certificate of the Judge Advocate of the Court (appended to this record) shows that the omission referred to was a *clerical* error, and that the accused was duly arraigned and pleaded Not Guilty.

George G. Hastings,

Major, acting Judge Advocate,

A. of P."

REFERENCES:

Military Personnel Records, RG-#94

Court Martial Proceedings, RG-#153 NN 2533

"Albany Atlas and Argus" September 24 - October 27, 1864

Case #146

Pvt. Peter Keiffe

NV: Keaf, Keith, Keefe, Kieffe

Co. B, 2nd Arkansas Volunteer Cavalry

Executed for Murder

October 7, 1864

DESCRIPTION:

27 years of age, 5 feet 7¾ inches tall, blue eyes, brown hair, fair complexion, born in County Kerry Ireland, occupation laborer, literate.

Keiffe was enlisted on June 26, 1863 at the Benton Barracks, Mo in the 2nd Arkansas Volunteer Cavalry Regiment and was mustered into Company B of the Regiment on July 1, 1863. Much of his military service was spent on escort duty at Fort Smith, Arkansas and in Missouri. Arrest and confinement orders in Keiffe's personnel file tend to indicate he had previous violations of Military Laws as early as August of 1863 and again in July, 1864.

On the 3rd of August, 1864, Keiffe stabbed a local citizen in the vicinity of Springfield, Missouri and subsequently related the crime to members of his company. Two men of his company, learning of the matter, and of his plan to desert, informed the Company Commander of the entire affair. Later testimony divulged that Keiffe was quite drunk when he returned to camp and stated he was going to desert. On August 7, 1864 Keiffe was arrested.

A General Court Martial was convened at Springfield, Missouri and on August 10, 1864 tried Private Peter Keiffe, Company B, 2nd Arkansas Cavalry Regiment on a charge of murder.

Keiffe was granted permission for D. C. Dade, Esq. to appear as his counsel.

Witnesses revealed the following events. On August 5, 1864 Keiffe left his encampment, on foot, and walked via the Capville Road toward Springfield, Missouri, a distance of one and one half miles. Enroute he encountered Calvin Newman a resident of Green County, Missouri but a stranger to him. They exchanged words. Newman asked Keiffe who he was and Keiffe replied, "an Arkansas soldier." Keiffe then asked Newman who he was and Newman replied, "A Missourian," and then added, "Yes, you are a damned Arkansas whipped Rebel." They then scuffled and according to what Keiffe reportedly related to a tent mate, Keiffe drew out a pocket knife and stabbed Newman twice in the right breast near the nipple the knife blade measuring 1/4 inch wide and three (3) inches long. Newman's body fell on the side of the road and was not discovered until the following day. A coffin was brought out from Springfield, Missouri and the body placed therein and later moved to the courthouse in Springfield Missouri. The coroners jury having previously assembled at the place of death and examined the body, concluding death was due to knife wounds in the chest.

One of the witnesses, George Harrington testified that Newman resided with him for eight or nine months and that he had been called during the inquest to view the body for the purposes of positive identification. He, under questioning, stated that Newman had a prominent scar on his head which had been caused by being kicked by a horse. He further testified that Newman became "ill and fractious" if he consumed even a dram of liquor. He did not consider Newman crazy. He further stated Newman had not consumed any liquor before leaving the house and meeting Keiffe unexpectedly.

Keiffe related the entire details of his encounter with Newman to his tent mate and even had him examine the fatal weapon, which had dried blood on one blade. The only reason he advanced for his actions was that he considered Newman's remarks a slur, not only on him but on the entire regiment and he was willing to defend them.

A fellow soldier witness appearing on behalf of Keiffe described the accused as, "a good soldier, as quiet a man as is in the company."

Keiffe offered no more witnesses nor a statement in his behalf.

The Court deliberated, found Keiffe guilty and sentenced him to be shot to death by musketry.

Keiffe guilty of murder was shot for the murder on October 7, 1864 at the regimental camp near Springfield, Missouri.

REFERENCES:

Military Personnel Records, NA, RG-#94
Court Martial Proceedings, RG-153 NN 2958

Case #147
Pvt. Charles H. Merling
NV: Merlin
Co. H, 2nd MD Infantry Regt.
Executed for Desertion
October 14, 1864

DESCRIPTION:

25 years of age, 5 feet 5 inches tall, brown hair, hazel eyes, dark complexion, born in

Wales, occupation sailor, substitute, literacy undetermined.

Merling enlisted as a substitute on August 22, 1864 at Baltimore Maryland and was mustered into service at Lafayette Barracks, Baltimore, Maryland on August 30, 1864. Merling "attempted to desert to the enemy" shortly after arriving at the front lines in September 1864. He was seized and confined, tried by court martial on charges of desertion and attempting to desert to the enemy.

A General Court Martial was convened at headquarters 2nd Division, 9th Army Corps at the New Weldon Railroad, Virginia and on September 15, 1864 tried Private Charles H. Merling, Company H, 2nd Maryland Veteran Volunteers on charges of desertion and attempting to desert to the enemy.

Testimony of witnesses disclosed that the accused deserted his Company and Regiment on the night of September 5, 1864 from a fatigue duty detail taking with him his personal effects. The prisoner had only joined the regiment on September 1, 1864.

On September 7, 1864 after daybreak, the accused, alone and in Federal U. S. Uniform was challenged by a picket guard to halt. He, however, ignored the challenge and continued on his way toward the enemy lines. The guard was joined by a mounted sergeant in pursuit of the interloper and despite their quarry efforts to hide he was finally halted and captured in a wooded area and marched out to the road. When questioned by his captor as to what he was doing out there, he replied "viewing the country." He stated he was a member of the 5th Massachusetts Battery and wanted to know what was to be done with him. The guard said he would be taken to guard headquarters. The prisoner put his hand in his pocket and drew out a wad of currency (later found to be $264.00) saying "here is plenty of money, let me pass" and offered it to the guard if he would let him through. The guard refused the bribe and escorted the prisoner to a Lieutenant Clark who then sent him. to guard headquarters. The prisoner was alone, dressed in the federal uniform with no knapsack, haversack or bundle but did carry a revolver. He then admitted he was a member of the 2nd Maryland regiment and was drunk the night previous and had only been in the regiment three days. He gave no explanation as to why he attempted to bribe the guard.

The accused had no witnesses but did present a statement.

Statement of the Accused

"I was drunk and did not know what I was about when I left. I have been in the Navy a long time. I was told I could get transferred to the Navy if I wanted to. I did not know whether I was going to the front or the rear. The enemy would be the last place I would want to go."

The Court deliberated, found the accused guilty and sentenced him to be shot to death by musketry.

The execution took place on October 14, 1864 near Peebles House, Hancock Station, Virginia.

REFERENCES:

Military Personnel Records, RG-#94
Court Martial Proceedings, RG-#153 NN 2570

Case #148
Private Jefferson Jackson
Co. B, 9th MO State Militia
Executed for Murder
October 28, 1864

DESCRIPTION:

22 years of age, 6 feet tall, black hair, hazel eyes, dark complexion, born in Boone County, Missouri, occupation farmer, unmarried, literacy undetermined.

Jackson enlisted and apparently was mustered into service at Sturgeon, Missouri on

January 20, 1862 in Company B, Guitar's Mounted Rifles, Missouri Militia. The unit designation was changed twice, first by simply omitting "Mounted" from the preceding title, and finally was titled Company B, 9th Regiment Missouri State Militia. Jackson provided his own horse and saddlery, a not uncommon practice, for which he was to receive a monthly allowance. As of January 1, 1863, Jackson was appointed Company B Wagoner.

On August 27, 1864, Jackson committed the murder of Private John Greene, Company K, 1st Iowa Cavalry for which he was arrested and court martialed.

A General Court Martial was convened at St. Joseph, Missouri, and on September 5, 1864 tried Private Jefferson Jackson, Company B, 9th Cavalry, Missouri State Militia on a charge of murder.

Jackson applied to the Court for permission to introduce Henry Tues as his counsel, which application the Court granted.

Testimony was given that Jackson, on August 27, 1864, did murder a Private John Greene, Company K, 1st Iowa Cavalry Regiment. Greene came into the Depot Saloon and ordered a drink. He was followed shortly thereafter by the arrival of Jackson, who complained about being called a bushwacker apparently by Greene, and Greene spoke to Jackson. Jackson threw a glass at him and Greene ran out of the saloon taking his beer glass with him, heading towards the Waverly House, a boarding house and restaurant. In a few minutes, however, he returned his beer glass to the Depot Saloon, Jackson having left the premises. The deceased then left the saloon, and was walking toward the Waverly House when Jackson was observed to strike him two or three times and discard the fatal weapon, a club. The weapon described as formed of hickory wood, originally intended to be used as a cross bar for a sawbuck, was on a woodpile near the place of the fatal attack prior to it's use.

The body of Greene was removed, from the sidewalk where he fell after being struck, to the Cottage Home where it was placed upon a counter. A physician, J. F. Brunner, was called by the police to examine the body, and he described the wounds as, "the right half of the occipital bone (rear of skull) had been mashed into fragments. The skin itself was broken through, and the blood still flowed copiously showing there had been a rupture of internal blood vessels and from the feeling, the brain had been mashed into a jelly, a pulpy mass...the wound in the occipital region was about two and a half inches wide and between three and four inches in length..."

Witnesses testified to Greene's poor character. He was said to have come into a saloon, drew his pistol, and ordered beer, but declined to pay for it saying, "charge it to Uncle Sam." The saloon keeper reported the incident to an officer of the 1st Iowa Cavalry (Greene's Regiment) and was told Greene was a desperate man, and to avoid fooling with him. Other members of the 1st Iowa told the saloon keeper that Greene had hardly served a single day on duty, having instead been under confinement almost constantly. Others characterized Greene as worthless, good for nothing, and insulting to everybody. In fact, he was advised it was a great wonder that Greene did not draw his revolver and shoot the saloon keeper when he ordered Greene out of his saloon. Greene was also reported to have drawn his pistol on the saloon keeper's little boy. Jackson was described in an affidavit as having performed his duties as a soldier in a highly satisfactory manner and at all times conducted himself as a quiet ordinary soldier.

The accused made no statement in his defense. The Court deliberated, found the prisoner guilty, and sentenced him to be shot to death with ball and musketry.on October 21, 1864.

On October 20, 1864, the following telegram was sent:

"Jackson, Jefferson, a soldier of my command at St. Joseph is sentenced to be shot tomorrow. I have the honor to request that his execution be postponed four a week. He had always been one of the best of soldiers but in a fit of intoxication committed the deed for which he is to die. He is of good family and his mother earnestly desires that he have more time to prepare for death."

Signed, C. B. Fisk, Brig Genl

Comdg. Dist. Nor. Mo.

The Herald and Tribune Newspaper, St. Joseph, Missouri of October 22, 1864, carried the following story relating to Jackson:

"A Murderer Reprieved," Execution of Jackson, Jefferson postponed for one week.

This individual, a member of the 9th Cavalry, who was sentenced to be shot yesterday, was reprieved for one week. Efforts had been made for a reprieve, and the execution was accordingly delayed as long as possible, which delay gives the prisoner another week's lease of life. At three o'clock P.M. the companies of the 43rd now here, all the militia, and a large number of citizens, comprising Men, Women and Children, repaired to the ground selected for the execution, which was directly South of the Patee House, near the Bluffs. The four companies of the 43rd formed a square open on the east facing the bluff, and the militia formed in two ranks in the rear of the 43rd. Citizens were formed on the outside, many standing in wagons and carriages so as to be able to see. When the guard arrived at the jail to take him out for execution, his cell door was found barricaded, and the prisoner threatened to kill anyone who should attempt to enter. After some time an entrance was effected, when he peaceably submitted, and was placed in an ambulance with his coffin, and the procession moved away. At half past four the prisoner arrived on the grounds, accompanied by his spiritual adviser, Rev. Mr. Hagerty, some friends, a guard, and the detail made for the execution. The prisoner and guards moved at once to the center of the square, where the coffin was placed. It was here that all eyes were riveted upon him, and he met the gaze with a steady and firm countenance, evincing but little agitation, not even shedding a tear. Some friends came forward and shook him by the hand, and bid him, as they supposed, a last farewell. Preparations were completed for the execution, when Lt. Harding rode up, and dismounting, read the following dispatch:

"Lamine Bridge, October 21, 1864

To Lt. Harding, A.D.C.: Postpone the execution of Jefferson Jackson one week.

Signed Clinton B. Fisk, Brigadier General"

The reading of this order brought tears to the eyes of the prisoner, and he received the congratulations of his friends with much emotion.

The prisoner is a fine large man, dark hair and eyes and has a powerful and well built frame. The circumstances of his condemnation will be remembered by all. In addition to the crime for which he was sentenced, it is generally believed he has committed many others of nearly as serious a character, but of this there is no proof. His friends even pronounced him "a hard case," but the fact of his being a soldier is sufficient to excuse him from many a crime in the eyes of many. We suppose the execution will take place next Friday."

The news article elicited a letter of response.

"We notice in the Tribune and Herald of the 22nd an article in relation to the postponement of the execution of Jefferson Jackson, Company B, 9th Cav. M.S.M." Also a paragraph where he states the murderer was reprieved and should have his career in St. Joseph be investigated, that the murder in question is not the only one, that the above named soldier has been implicated in—

This from a public Journal will do the prisoner great injustice, and it is thought that the error should be corrected, or sufficient reasons given to substantiate the fact. We would be glad to see the correction made through the papers who have published so great a falsehood. It is also currently reported in St. Joseph that Jefferson Jackson, has been in the Rebel Army this I will say for the benefit of loyal citizens of St. Joseph is false, Mr. J., ever has been a loyal, honest, sober man until his arrival in St. Joseph, Missouri where he has met with men (citizens) who have lead him from the paths of morality and have made him a drunkard as well as a murderer. We hope to hear no more of such language from loyal men of St. Joseph, Missouri.

Signed, Soldiers of Co. B, 9th M.S.M.
W.O. Blanchard, Sgt. Co. B, 9th Cav., M.S.M."

On October 29, 1864 the St. Joseph, Missouri Herald and Tribune contained the following account:

EXECUTION OF JACKSON JEFFERSON

The march from the jail-Affectionate farewell-Reading of the sentence-Dying speech-The execution.

At two o'clock yesterday afternoon, the doomed man, Jackson Jefferson, was taken out of his cell in the military prison, and placed in an ambulance, preparatory to moving to the place of execution. He was accompanied by his spiritual adviser, Reverend Mr. Hagerty, and an old acquaintance, Lieutenant Ray, and by Captain Wright with a guard of six or eight men. It was not generally known that the execution would take place, but as the solemn cortege moved along, quite a number of personel followed, and by the time the procession arrived at the place of execution, a large crowd of men, women and children was assembled. The prisoner was taken to the Provost Marshal's office at the Patee House, and there bid an affectionate adieu to many of his friends, who were visibly affected at the parting; the prisoner, however, remained calm throughout, speaking cheerfully to all. This mood be maintained throughout the solemn march, and with a Testament in his hands, conversed freely with Mr. Hagerty upon religious topics. At the Provost office he entrusted to Mr. Blanchard, an old acquaintance, some letters, one of which was for his mother, and one for Mr. B., giving him directions how to dispose of his body, which he was very anxious should be sent to his mother. He also gave directions for the purchase of a metalic coffin, and for the disposition of some money which he had.

While this affecting scene was being enacted, the four companies of the 43d Missouri marched by on their way to the bottom below the Patee House. The prisoner soon followed in the ambulance, and after all came Lieutenant Harding, Provost Marshal, with twelve men detailed as executioners. The ground selected for the solemn tragedy, was well chosen, and gave all a fair opportunity to see. The soldiers were formed in a hollow square, with an opening to the east, and the citizens were not permitted to pass this line. The prisoner was allowed some time to converse with his friends before alighting from the ambulance, and calmly spoke to those around him, and lifting the cover of the ambulance, coolly surveyed the solemn preparations. He was as calm as man could be, and frequently said he was prepared to die. We failed to notice any of that nervousness which affected him a week ago, but his every act and move showed the brave man who had nerved himself for the scene, and who was left with only the certainty of a speedy death. His handcuffs were removed and he was permitted again to shake his friends by the hand. On alighting from the ambulance, some difficulty was experienced in adjusting the handcuffs, and the prisoner himself helped to fasten them. Attended by Mr. Hagerty and Surgeon Bruner, the prisoner was marched around the hollow square, following the guard detailed to do the firing. The coffin, a rude, rough affair, had previously been placed in the center of the square, and as the procession came to the opening, the guard was marched to the western side of the square, the prisoner being conducted to his coffin. Lieutenant Harding, Provost Marshal, then read the findings and sentence under which the execution was to take place, and manifested considerable emotion as he did so. The entire crowd was much affected by the solemnity of the scene, and we saw many who were shedding tears. The prisoner was then asked if he had anything to say, and after an interval of thought, spoke as follows:

Friends, I love you all. I have grieved much over this affair. I put my trust in God, and hope this will be a warning to every soldier. I hope to meet you all in a better world. I am prepared to die. I am not afraid to die. I am not afraid to lose my breath. I have been a soldier for a long time, and no soldier ever did his duty better than I. This is a solemn affair, and I committed the act in the heat of passion, and as I think in self defense; and

I did just as anybody else would do. I guess I had justice done me, but I am not guilty of many things with which I am charged. I shall soon be better off. I love you all. Goodbye to you all.

Calling to Lieutenant Harding and Mr. Blanchard, he reiterated his instructions to them about his body, and then kneeled beside his coffin with Mr. Hagerty, who offered an *affecting* prayer, the prisoner continued praying audibly. The prayer ended, he bid farewell to those around him, and kneeling again by his coffin, was blindfolded, he himself assisting to adjust the blind. Not a single tear did he shed, but stern resignation marked his countenance. Being blindfolded, he first crossed his arms, but quickly threw them to his side, and straightened himself on his knees. The guard of twelve, detailed from the 43d regiment, were divided into two squads of six each, each commanded by a sergeant. The word was given, "Ready! aim! fire!" and with one report the missiles of Death were sent to do their work, and Jackson Jefferson fell back, dead! having thus expiated with his life his crimes. Without a struggle, or the moving of a single muscle, he died.

The shots were well aimed, two striking on the chin and almost cutting off the neck, while another entered the center of the breast, and another striking the left shoulder. The scene was solemn, and we hope never again to witness another such.

REFERENCES:

Military Personnel Records, RG-#94
Court Martial Proceedings, RG-#153 LL 2610
St. Joseph, Herald & Tribune as above cited. October 22, and October 29, 1864.

Case #149
Pvt. John Velon
Co. G, 5th NH Infantry Regt.
Executed for Desertion
October 28, 1864

DESCRIPTION:

20 years of age, 5 feet 2¾ inches tall, sandy hair, blue eyes, light complexion, born in Prussia (Germany), occupation peddler, substitute.

Velon was drafted as a substitute and mustered into service August 16, 1864 and sent to the Petersburg, Virginia area where he was assigned to Company G, 5th NH Infantry Regiment. On September 27, 1864, while on picket duty near Petersburg, Virginia, Velon deserted his duty post with the intention of going over to the enemy. He remained absent until found, arrested and returned under a guard. He was confined, tried and by court martial

A General Court Martial was convened at Headquarters of the 1st Division 2nd Army Corps and on September 29, 1864 tried Private John Velon, Company G, 5th New Hampshire Infantry Regiment on a charge of desertion.

Testimony of witnesses stated that on September 27, 1864 Velon and two other soldiers were on picket duty before Petersburg. Velon was on alert and the other two went to sleep at 9 AM and Velon was to awaken them at 11 AM. One soldier awoke, noted Velon absent, awakened his companion and both searched unsuccessfully for Velon. They then noticed their rations were gone and their gun barrels contained a stick of wood driven well down into them. A further search disclosed tracks in the mud along a nearby creek.

Velon was found outside the Union Picket lines hiding under the exposed roots of a large tree along the bank of the Appomatox River, by another picket guard on the forenoon of the 27th of September. The guard and an armed Corporal took Velon back to the Union Picket Support Line. When Velon emerged from his hiding place, his clothing was covered with drying, caked mud from shoe sole to waist, indicating an attempt had been made to ford the river and reach the enemy lines. Velon had left his musket and accouterments on the picket line when he deserted. A witness stated that Velon had been present when the Articles of War were read.

The accused called no witnesses on his behalf but did offer a statement to the Court.

Statement of Prisoner

"It was a quarter past nine, my comrades went to sleep, the lieutenant came and found the men asleep. After the lieutenant had gone there was two men came out from hiding behind a bush on the front. I asked them where are you going. they said they belonged there. they came up near me, I let them come up. I had my gun at order arms; one of them said, let go your gun and at the same time put his hand in his pocket and drew a pistol and said to me if you want to live leave your gun. One man stood by me and the other took the gun of my comrade and put a stick in the tube. they then told me to go with them and I told them I would wake up my comrades. I cannot go from my place. they told me you don't want to wake up these men. I wanted to go for my things and thought if I could go. I could wake up the men as they were very near where the men were laying. but they put the pistol to my head and made me go with them. I went with them towards the River and jumped into a mud hole. I thought as I went in up to my waist they would leave me but they pulled me out. I went a little farther and told them I could not walk. I laid down and went to sleep. that is all I have to say."

The Court deliberated, found the accused guilty and sentenced him to be shot to death with musketry.

The execution was carried out on October 28, 1864 near Petersburg, Virginia.

REFERENCES:

Military Personnel Records, RG-#94
Court Martial Proceedings, RG-#153 LL 2605

Case #150
Pvt. Henry Hamilton
Co. I, 2nd Inf. Regt., USCT
Executed for Mutiny
November 4, 1864

DESCRIPTION:

23 years of age, 5 feet 3½ inches tall, black hair, hazel eyes, black complexion, born in Easton, Maryland, occupation farmer, illiterate.

Hamilton enlisted at Baltimore, Maryland on September 10, 1863 and was mustered into service at Arlington, Virginia on October 10, 1863 in Company I, 2nd Infantry Regiment, USCT. By 1864, the Regiment was on duty in southern Florida and Hamilton became involved in a mutiny which resulted in his arrest and confinement at Key West, Florida in February, 1864.

A General Court Martial was convened at Key West, Florida, and on April 15, 1864 tried Private Henry Hamilton, Company D, 2nd Infantry Regiment USCT on charges of Joining in a Mutiny, Offering Violence against his Superior Officer, and Disobedience of Orders.

Hamilton applied to the court for the introduction of Lt. O. A. Carpenter, 2nd Regiment, USCT as his counsel, which request was granted.

Witnesses testified that on December 27, 1863 the Regiment was encamped at Ship's Island, Mississippi and on the morning of the 27th a riot occurred. The officer of the day, Lt. Edward Pease, was attempting to arrest Private Henry Cornish but was prevented by the action of Hamilton and some 30 other soldiers most of whom were armed. It was stated that as many as 200 to 300 men of the Regiment crowded about the scene of the attempted arrest. Hamilton stood, some three yards in front of Cornish, who had his bayonet affixed rifle in his hands. Lt. Pease ordered Hamilton to go to his quarters and he refused saying, "no man should be sent to the guardhouse." The Lieutenant stepped forward and Hamilton assumed the "charge bayonet" position, his bayoneted rifle lowered and pointing at the body of the Lieutenant and declared, "he would run his bayonet through the first who touched him (Cornish)." The Lieutenant stepped forward and grasped hold of the bayonet near it's mid point and attempted to wrest the rifle away from Hamilton at the same time he shouted to the Sergeant and guards who accompanied him to arrest Cornish and take him to the guardhouse. The rioters threw showers of stones at the Lieutenant and his men and frightened the guards to the extent that they were unable to arrest Cornish. Finally, the Regimental Commander, Colonel Fellows accompanied by resolute guards succeeded in arresting Cornish and taking him to the Guardhouse. Lieutenant Pease and Colonel Fellows then ordered the rioters to disperse and return to their quarters which order was not immediately obeyed.

An enlisted man witness of Company I, when asked by the defense if the Articles of War had been read to the Regiment, as required by Army regulations, the reply was affirmative.

The defense offered one novel piece of evidence in explanation of the bayoneted rifle used by Hamilton. Hamilton was illiterate, hence unable to read the serial number of his issued rifle and in order to identify it quickly and positively when in the rifle rack with other identical appearing rifles, left his bayonet attached to his piece.

The defense counsel prepared a statement by the accused to be presented to the court in his behalf.

"I was out in my company street, cleaning my gun when the guard came after Cornish, and the way I happened to have my bayonet fixed, there were four or five together in the tent, and the way I could tell mine was by fixing it. I did not intend to hurt any one, I went to my quarters when the Officer of the Day ordered me to. I can't read or write, and I beg the mercies of the Court on account of my ignorance."

The court then deliberated and found Hamilton guilty, and sentenced him to be shot to death with musketry.

A petition for executive clemency was filed by members of the General Court Martial who tried Hamilton.

"We the undersigned members of a General Court Martial convened by virtue of Special Orders #39 Head Quarters District of Key West and Tortugas, Fla., April 4, 1864, would respectfully recommend to Executive Clemency Henry Hamilton, Private Co. I, 2nd U.S. Col. Troops, a prisoner tried by said court.

We do this on account of his manifest ignorance and in consideration that while his criminality was far from being the highest in degree of it's kind, the extreme measure of punishment was affixed thereto by the sentence of the court.

The proposition made at the Session of the Court held on the 20th day of April to reconsider the sentence of Private Henry Hamilton, Company I, 2nd Infantry Regiment, USCT, failed to receive the votes of a majority of the court.

The execution took place at Key West, Florida, on November 4, 1864.

REFERENCES:

Military Personnel Records, RG-#94
Court Martial Proceedings, RG-#153 LL 2628

Case #151
Pvt. Charles Lockman
NV: Lachman, Lockmann
Co F, 2nd Volunteer Cavalry
& Co H, 2nd Colorado Volunteer Infantry
Executed for Murder
Official List cites date as November 10, 1864
However, Lt. Wise states
Execution took place on November 12, 1864

DESCRIPTION:

31 years old, 5 foot 2 inches tall, blue eyes, light (colored) hair, complexion is fair,

occupation miller, born in Saxony (Germany), literate. Enlisted September 15, 1861 at Central City, Colorado Territory, original muster into Company H, 2nd Colorado Volunteer Infantry Regiment on November 26, 1863. That unit became Company F, 2nd Colorado Volunteer Cavalry Regiment.

Pvt. Lockman had the usual assignments and experiences of all enlisted men in war time. In 1862 he was ill in hospital at Denver and in 1863 sick at Fort Larned, Kansas. In 1864 was on extra or daily duty as a cook and in October, 1864, was reported on detached service with a Quartermaster Train. No details have been discovered as yet as to the reason why Private Lockman murdered Private John Grace (Groce), aged 27 years, also of Company F, 2nd Colorado Volunteer Cavalry on November 12, 1864.

Two newspaper accounts of the incident have been found. "The Leavenworth Daily Conservative," for November 13, 1864 states, "as a Company of the Second Colorado was going to Lawrence, yesterday, a difficulty took place at Elhart's Five Mile House, between a couple of soldiers. In the affray one of them shot the other, inflicting a mortal wound. Report says the offender was hung." "The Conservative," Leavenworth, Kansas, November 15, 1864, published a letter from Lt. Wm. Wise, giving a full account of the murder. The Editorial Comment of the newspaper highly criticized Lt. Wise as a person who violated not only military law procedure but also of encouraging mob action.

Lt. Wise's letter follows:

"Camp Detachment Co's, D&F, 2nd Colo. Cav.
Big Stranger, Kansas, November 12, 1864

Editor Conservative - In order to inform the 2nd Colorado Cavalry and the public, in regard to the shooting of a member of our regiment, and the hanging of the offender, I herewith make the following statement as reported to the Adjutant General's Office:

"This morning, while in Command of detachments of Company D and F, 2nd Colorado Calvary, marching to Lawrence, about six miles from your city, two men in the rear of the command had a few words of dispute, after which one Charles Lockman, Co. F, fell back and in a few minutes, riding up on a gallop, deliberately shot John Gross, of the same Company, through the region of the heart, killing him instantly. After ascertaining he was dead, I called together the command, and getting all the information we could, I proposed to leave the case with the members of the company to which the parties belonged. Company F, without a dissenting voice, voted to hang him (Chas. Lockman) to which the whole command assented.

"At 1 O'Clock p.m., he was hung by a Sargeant and three men of his own company, who volunteered their service. All was done in a quiet and orderly manner. No excitement manifested, all expressing their entire approbation.

After he was dead, he was buried on the spot. The body of Gross* I sent in charge of a Sargeant to Ft. Leavenworth. I respectfully state that they were justifiable in hanging the said Lockman, for the security of the members of their company and the good of military discipline.

Very respectfully your obedient servant,
Wm. Wise, 1st Lieutenant, 2nd Col. Cav.
Commanding Detachment"

(*Note - The name of the murdered man is herein given as GROSS, but the official military records indicate the name as either GRACE or GROCE.)

REFERENCES:

Colorado State Military Records
Military Personnel RecordsRG - #94
Newspaper accounts cited above.
"History of the Military Organizations of the State of Colorado 60-1935," by Nankivell

Case #152
Pvt. Joseph Prevost
NV: Provost
Co. A, 1st (NY) Lincoln Cav. Regt.
Executed for Murder
November 10, 1864

DESCRIPTION:

25 years of age, 5 feet 5¾ inches tall, dark hair, blue eyes, dark complexion, born in Montreal, Quebec, Canada, occupation seaman, literate.

Prevost enlisted and was mustered into service on August 16, 1861 at New York City, New York in Company A, 1st New York (Lincoln) Cavalry Regiment. He was discharged on December 31, 1863 and immediately reenlisted in the same Company and Regiment as a Veteran Volunteer on January 1, 1864 at Charlestown, Virginia.

A Military Commission was convened at Cumberland, Maryland and on May 5, 1864 tried Private Joseph Prevost, Company A, 1st New York Cavalry Regiment on a charge of Murder.

Witnesses testified that early on April 19, 1864, four Union soldiers, Private Joseph Prevost, Company A, 1st New York Cavalry Regiment, Private William Bruce, 2nd Maryland Volunteers, Sergeant James T. Cross, Company F, 2nd Maryland Volunteers, and a stranger only identified as a member of 1st New York Cavalry, were seen in the early morning riding up a rural road, in Morgan County, West Virginia toward a still house. Later, about an hour before sundown, they rode into the front yard of the Christian Miller farm. They dismounted, walked into the house and announced that they were ordered to search the house for firearms and immediately began opening drawers and dumping out their contents, knocking over furniture and generally tearing up the premises. The head of the household, Christian Miller was cutting wood in the wood yard, his wife, was out of the house but on the farm somewhere. Confronting the soldiers were Miller's two daughters, Lavina, aged 17 years and Martha Jane aged 15 years. Also in the household was a younger brother variously described as aged six to eight/nine years of age. An older married brother, William, occupied an adjoining farm but was not present. The search apparently turned up a child's four inch revolver, not further described as to whether it was a toy or a working derringer, belonging to the Miller boy. The soldiers threatened to shoot the entire family. At about that point, Christian Miller, the head of the family entered and was threatened in a like manner. At some point, it is unclear from the trial record, the soldiers threw newspapers on the floor together with broken wooden furniture and set it on fire. Prevost, either just before or just after the fire was ignited, took Christian Miller upstairs. Prevost, for whatever purpose, had previously taken a handful of flour from a flour barrel and carried it upstairs with him. Shortly thereafter a shot was heard and Prevost came down the stairs alone. At that point, Prevost announced that there was a dead man lying on the upstairs floor. Mrs. Miller arrived about this time and as the soldiers went out of the house, told her if any of them reported this to the authorities, they would kill every damned one of them. They then mounted their horses and prepared to ride away. The three women were in the doorway observing the departing soldiers and Prevost turned his horse, while drawing his revolver and fired a shot at the group clustered in the doorway which lodged harmlessly in the door frame. The youngest boy had, in the meantime, been sent to his brother's farm to fetch him to help to fight the fire and remove possessions. Mrs. Miller, being told of Prevost tale of the dead body upstairs, ran up the staircase and came immediately back down exclaiming, your father has been killed by the soldiers. Lavina then went upstairs and saw her father lying on the floor on his side, with two bullet wounds in his temple, blood flooding his face and pooling on the floor. He was still alive, barely breathing, unable to speak. A grotesque touch was that his eyes and face were covered with flour. He died within five minutes.

William (eldest son of Christian Miller) later stated the two wounds entered, about 1 inch apart, the right temple and exited behind and below the left ear.

When William arrived, in response to his sister's message for help, he found the fire smouldering, the house quite smoky but not in danger of being destroyed.

When the four renegade Union soldiers left the Miller farm, they stopped at the farm of a Mr. Fleece on their way to Bath, West Virginia. At the Fleece farm, they demanded eggs and Mr. Fleece reminded Prevost, ever the spokesman/leader, that he had taken all the eggs on the day before and at the moment there were no more eggs. Prevost asked who lived at the farm house down the road a ways and Fleece told him Christian Miller. He then went out, followed by the other three, and mounted his horse saying, "I have done good business today, I have killed a rebel." Fleece asked, "how many?" He replied, "but one." And they rode away. Fleece remarked that he was left with the impression that there was some mischief at the Miller's.

Fleece also stated that he viewed the dead body of Christian Miller at Miller's home and paid his respects to the grieving family. As the corpse was laid out, the wounds were visible.

Prevost's companions testified, as might be expected, mainly in his favor.

Prevost attempted to depict Christian Miller as a Confederate sympathizer, recruiter for the rebel army and/or a member of a rebel guerilla band.

Sergeant Cross, one of the four marauders, admitted he was under arrest and confinement for his part in the affair.

Prevost had a poor military record having been arrested recently in Winchester, Berryville, and Martinsburg, Virginia for various offenses previous to his final arrest on the Murder charge.

Prevost called two of his companions, William Bruce and Frank Cross, as witnesses in his defense. He offered no statement to the Court.

The Court deliberated, found the accused guilty, and sentenced him to be hung by the neck until dead.

Prevost was transferred for confinement to the military prison at Wheeling, West Virginia on June 11, 1864 to await execution.

On September 19, 1864, Prevost wrote an appeal to President Lincoln from prison in Wheeling, West Virginia.

"To his Excellency, President Lincoln, Sir. I now take this present opportunity of writing you a few lines to ask you to reprieve me from this act. I am a Veteran in the 1st N.Y. Cav. Regt. and now sentenced to be hung for Murder. I have served 3 years in the army faithfully. Can you do anything for me in this case. The case is this: This man has been trying to capture Union men in that County to put in the Rebel ranks before our Army got them, I myself and 3 others was among where this man lived & two of these men that were along with me had been drove from there homes by the same man. Afraid to be put in the Rebel ranks and swore to have revenge on him, while in his house the man was shot and I was the only stranger in the house the men that had the spite against him made away and I was the victim and I was taken to Cumberland, Md. and tried by a Court Martial (sic) this was in the month of May 1864. I was sent to Wheeling, W. Va. and never heard anything about my sentence until today and the execution will take place on the 25th inst. You see that I have very little time to myself. The execution will take place in Cumberland, Md.

I am yours Very Respectfully,

Joseph Prevost, 1st N.Y. Lincoln Cavalry

Co. A"

The President granted Prevost a reprieve on the grounds that his appeal could not be evaluated without the written copy of his trial record. Same being, at the time unavailable, President Lincoln ordered a postponement of the execution until October 25, 1864.

Upon receiving word of his execution postponment, Prevost again wrote the President from the Cumberland, Maryland jail where he had been transferred on September 22, 1864.

"Cumberland Jail, Md. Sept 25, 1864
His Excellency President Lincoln
Sir.

I thank you from the bottom of my hart, by the favor you bestowed on me, by posponing my exacution another week (actually another month) not that I was not prepared, although a man never could be to well prepared to face Death even if it is a shameful one. But if anything to avoid this terrible blow from my old parents knowledge, for indeed it would kill them for they don't know nothing of this, and I hope, they never will, for I was in the navy service under Capt. Bankhead previous to my enlisting in the arme that account for not seeing them since so long. As to my conduct as soldieer I refer you to Capt. Jones, Capt. of Co. A, under wich I served during the whole thre years. I have a young brother of mine, that came away from Canada, to list in your arme, he is now in the fourth Michigan Cavalry, so that we are nearly all away from home and if nothing as reprieve could be effected on my behalf, no matter what it would be you would have the prayers of grateful harts both form my old parents and myself. But otherwise if the execution have to take place god's will be done, and god bless you, at least I will dye with the full conviction that I am innocent of this crime, for as god almighty is our Juge, Christian Miller never dye through means of mine, although the evidence are against me. I will not trouble you witht the Details of the occurence all I know that it was Donne for revenge by the one that done it. but I never saw nor know the man until that day.

I am with respect your humble servant.
Joseph Prevost, 1st N.Y. Lincoln
Cavalry, Co. A"

After the trial records were forwarded to Washington, D.C. and reviewed by the Judge Advocate General Holt, who made his recommendations to President Lincoln, who in turn declined to interfere further in the case.

Prevost was hanged, by the Civil Authorities, at Cumberland, Maryland on November 10, 1864.

REFERENCES:

Military Personnel Records, RG-#94
Court Martial Proceedings, RG-#153 LL 2497

Case #153
Pvt. John Carrol
NV: Carroll
Co. D, 20th Wis Vol Inf Regt
Executed for Desertion (Official Record)
November 11, 1864

DESCRIPTION:

38 years of age, no further data available.

Carrol enlisted in Company D, 20th Wisconsin Volunteer Infantry Regiment at Madison, Wisconsin on August 18th, 1862. He served in the Regiment's battles at Prairie Grove, Arkansas and the siege of Vicksburg. He is recorded as having deserted April 4, 1863. Noted in arrest at New Orleans Police Jail, September 29, 1863, and released on October 24, 1863 to some other authority.

A General Court Martial was convened at Brownsville, Texas on November 30, 1863 for the trial of Private John Carroll, Company D, 20th Wisconsin Infantry Regiment on charges of Conduct Prejudicial to Good Order and Military Discipline, Assault with Intent to Commit Rape, Assault with Intent to Kill.

Testimony disclosed that Carroll was a member of the Divisional Provost Guard, a unit whose purpose is to maintain law and order. As some of the witnesses who were to testify spoke no English, a Spanish interpreter was provided by the Court.

The events of the evening of the 19th of November, 1863 were recounted as follows. A fellow member of the Provost Guard, Private John L. Thiry, 20th Wisconsin Infantry Regiment, stated that he and Carroll were out together early in the evening and were drinking in a saloon in Brownsville, Texas. They both separately returned to their quarters in camp where they were confronted by a Lieutenant Clawson of the Provost Guard who noted that they were intoxicated. He ordered them both to bed and ordered them not to go out any more that night. When the Lieutenant left they both got up and went back to town and to the same saloon but were refused service. They then wandered to the plaza where a Mexican brass band was playing and listened to the music for a half hour or so and Thiry went back to camp leaving Carroll in town. About Midnight, while quite dark, a negro citizen, Elisha Gidon, of Brownsville noticed Carroll standing in the yard of his home. He shouted at Carroll but was ignored. He then picked up a hoe handle and as he slowly approached, Carroll drew his bayonet from it's scabbard. Carroll announced he was a guard and demanded Gidon give him a light for his pipe, which Gidon provided. Carroll then verbally abused Gidon stating, "all you damned Niggers" and that he had a mind to run his bayonet through him. Gidon tried to pacify him, beg him to excuse the approach with the hoe handle and that he was unaware of who he was. Carroll ignored Gidon's apology and pulling a piece of paper out of his pocket and asked for his name saying he might bring him up before the Provost Marshall General on charges in the morning. He also inquired if Gidon was a "secesh" (a confederate sympathizer) and Gidon replied no. Carroll then inquired if Gidon had any women in his house and Gidon replied only his wife and six children. Carroll then left, pacified as he smiled and shook hands. Carroll then apparently returned to camp, secured his rifle and ammunition and returned to the Gidon house within an hour of his departure. He demanded that the door be opened and light be provided or he would shoot Gidon. The door was opened and a candle lit, Carroll entered with his rifle, bayonet affixed, pointed straight before him. Gidon retreated out the opposite end of the house and into a ditch where he hid. He was followed closely by a small white dog. Carroll fired at Gidon or the dog and killed the dog. Carroll returned to the house and approached Mary Gidon, wife of Elisha, put his hand on her shoulder and told her to put down the child she held in her arms. She replied that she wanted to put the child in it's bed first. Carroll angrily retorted that he wanted her to lie down on the bed quick, as he was in a hurry, and if she didn't make haste he would shoot her. She seemed to agree to his demand and said she would shut the door first, but instead she ran out of the house, still carrying the child in her arms, across the street to a "shanty" occupied by a Mexican family named Flores. She remained there for about thirty minutes when, concerned about her three other children in the house with Carroll, she ventured out to see to their safety. About 20 paces from her house, she saw Carroll coming towards her with his bayoneted rifle and she turned and ran back to the Mexican's house with Carroll in pursuit. As he approached the Mexican's home, the owner Reyes Flores, met Carroll and seized hold of the rifle. They then wrestled for possession of the weapon, Flores being cut on the chest in the melee. Carroll cursed him and told him to let go of the gun under threat of death and to order all the women in the house to come out. Finally, Flores released his grip on the weapon and fled while all the women remained in the house. Carroll then proceeded to try and pry the board siding off the house while threatening to set the house on fire. Carroll fired his gun twice into the house. The first shot passing harmlessly through the battered structure, however, the second shot struck Mrs. Flores, passing through her right arm, then through the chest wall, emerging from her back. She screamed in agony and rolled on the floor. Carroll, hearing the screams, left the scene and returned to the camp.

Elisha Gidon, saw Carroll and asked soldiers what his name was. Upon being told, John Carroll, 20th Wisconsin Infantry, Gidon then went to the guard headquarters and asked for John Carroll. Carroll being absent, Gidon was asked what he wanted with Carroll. He replied Carroll had attempted to kill him as well as other offenses. The guard officer accompanied Gidon through the guard barracks and assembly area and eventually Gidon saw Carroll and made a positive identification whereupon Carroll was promptly arrested and charged.

Carroll offered little in the way of a defense except for a statement.

"All that I know that I did that night was to bring out my coffee and go down to the river and get some water. I brought the coffee to the cook fires back of the building, put the water on the fire and set down on a log and fell asleep. when I waked up the water had all boiled away. I went to my quarters and went to bed. This all I know as to what I did that night."

The court considered the testimony and found the defendant guilty and sentenced him to death by musketry.

The trial proceedings, however, were returned for corrections and revisions as the recorder had omitted a series of required legal phrases. The court reconvened and corrected and revised the testimony to the satisfaction of the reviewing authority.

Carroll was executed on November 11, 1864.

REFERENCES:
Military Personnel Records, RG-#94
Court Martial Proceedings, RG-#153 MM 1372

Case #154
Pvt. Edward Eastman
Batty. B, 2nd MO Lt. Arty.
Executed for Pillaging & Plundering
November 25, 1864

DESCRIPTION:

19 years of age, 6 feet 1 inch tall, dark hair, black eyes, light complexion, born in Bolivar County, Mississippi, occupation farmer, literate.

Eastman enlisted on May 31, 1864 and was mustered into service on June 1, 1864 at Springfield, Missouri in Company B, 2nd Regiment of Missouri Light Artillery.

A General Court Martial was convened at Rolla, Missouri on September 16, 1864 and proceeded to the trial of Private Edward Eastman, Battery B, 2nd Missouri Light Artillery Regiment charged with deserting the colors to pillage and plunder, a violation of the 52nd Article of War.

Testimony revealed that on the night of September 12, 1864, Eastman and another soldier of his company named Frank Jones, put on civilian clothing and left their camp without any permission to do so. They went to the farm of Thomas Cole and pounded on the front door of his house, demanding admission. Cole was suspicious but after some conversation through the latched door, he opened the door and asked what they wanted. One of the two men wanted water. Cole brought it to him. The other declined. They then asked Cole questions as to whether he was a soldier or a teamster and if he had any firearms. Cole said he had firearms. Eastman and Jones demanded them and Cole declined to surrender any. One of the men then drew and cocked his revolver, Cole moved aside and shot him. Eastman and Jones then ran off. About three hours later the wounded man returned to Cole's house followed by an Army scout. The wounded man admitted his name was Jones and he was a Union Soldier. A William A. Strachan, Special Agent of the United States Secret Police, questioned the accused and elicited the following information. Eastman confessed he was with Jones on at least two previous robbery expeditions. Eastman's companion, Frank Jones, died of his wound in the Military hospital on the 13th of September 1864 about 10AM. He made a death bed confession corroborating the testimony of Cole.

Eastman was described as a wild and reckless character, having only been in service since June 1864, a period of about 3-1/2 months.

Other crimes committed by Eastman and Jones included a robbery on September 2,

1864 at Diebel's farm where they robbed Philip Sommerlot of one pocket book, and various articles of clothing and jewelry to the value of $60.00. They also robbed Mrs. Nancy Davis, of Diebel's Farm, on the same occasion, of a revolver valued at $30.00.

Eastman declined to offer a defense or written statement although he orally stated, "that he was coaxed into it, and never done anything of that sort until this time, this being my first freak. I hope the court will be as easy with me as possible, and I will try to be a good soldier."

The court then deliberated, found the accused guilty and sentenced him to be shot to death with musketry, which was carried out on November 25, 1864 at Rolla, Missouri.

On October 5, 1864, S.O. 276, Headquarters, Department of the Missouri, Paragraph 2, states, "The execution of the sentence of death in the case of *Edward Eastman*, Co. B, 2nd Arty MO Vols as promulgated in Gen'l. Orders #174 current series from these Head Quarters is suspended until further orders.

By Order of Maj. Genl. Rosecrans
(Signed) Frank Eno
Asst. Adjt. General."

That order was countermanded by S.O. #296, Paragraph 2, "Head Quarters department of the Missouri, St. Louis, Mo. October 25, 1864:

The sentence of death in the case of *Edward Eastman* promulgated in General Orders #174, (c.s.) from these Head Quarters will be carried into effect on the 25th day of Nov. 1864 as directed in said orders.

By Command of Major General Rosecrans
(signed) Frank Eno
Asst. Adjt. Genl."

The execution took place at Rolla, Missouri as ordered.

REFERENCES:

Military Personnel Records, RG-#94
Court Martial Proceedings,RG-#153 LL 2601

Case #155
Pvt. James Quinn
Co. A, 11th Heavy Artillery, USCT
Executed for Murder
November 25, 1864

DESCRIPTION:

21 years of age, 5 feet 6 inches tall, black hair, hazel eyes, mulatto complexion, born in Baltimore, Maryland, occupation Seaman, literacy undetermined.

Quinn enlisted and was mustered into service at Camp Smith near Providence, Rhode Island on August 28, 1863 in Company A, 14th Regiment, Rhode Island Colored Artillery. The designation of this unit was later changed to Company A, 11th Heavy Artillery, USCT. His Regiment was stationed at Camp Parapet, Louisiana, near New Orleans where he committed murder.

A General Court Martial was convened at Fort Jackson, Louisiana and on August 23, 1864 tried Private James Quinn, Company A, 8th Heavy Artillery Regiment, USCT on a charge of Murder.

Witnesses described the events of the crime as occurring on the 27th day of July, 1864 at the camp of the 8th Heavy Artillery, USCT at Fort Jackson, Louisiana about supper time. The Company was procuring their coffee at the various Company messes and as Quinn was approaching his mess line he accidentally bumped into Private Charles Cisco of his Company. Cisco, enraged, turned to face Quinn, saying, "didn't want any God damned (some said he used the term Black) son of a bitch running into him" and struck Quinn in the face (or head as some testified) with his coffee cup. Quinn staggering back asked what he done it for. Cisco replied, "I will rip your damned heart (other witnesses said guts) out of you" and reached into his pocket as though searching for a knife. Quinn retorted that, "he wasn't going to be struck for nothing, that the man who struck him should suffer for it." At that moment, Cisco began pulling off his coat and Quinn said he'd shoot him. Quinn turned about and entered the barracks. Cisco remained there, jawing and threatening what he would do to him. Quinn shortly returned, went up to Cisco and dared him to strike him again, other witnesses reported he urged Cisco to cut his guts out. Cisco, at this point, ran toward the barracks and Quinn lifted up his revolver and fired at him, striking Cisco in the neck. Cisco fell, and lay, his body part in and part out of the barracks entrance. Quinn was promptly placed in arrest and confined in the guardhouse.

Surgeon Rowland R. Hazzard was called and found Cisco still alive, barely breathing, unable to speak and clearly terminal. Cisco expired in fifteen minutes. Examination of the wound disclosed that the pistol ball entered the left side of the neck at a point about one half way between the top of ear and the point of the shoulder. There was no exit wound, however, the pistol ball was located just below the skin on the right side of the neck about an inch and a half below the mastoid process of the temporal bone. The surgeon dissected the pistol ball out of its place of lodgement and presented it to the Court as evidence.

Cisco was depicted as quarrelsome, having several such encounters previously and this occasion was the second on that day. When reproached by a Sergeant about his conduct, Cisco is reported to have said, "he wouldn't stop, but would do as he pleased, would fight as much as he liked."

Quinn was called to make his final defense and was cautioned by the Court to make no statement which might incriminate him. He then offered the following oral defense.

"The way it fully commenced, I came out of the barracks to get my supper and met Charles Cisco and a kind of pitched up against him. He hauls off with his cup, and then he says, 'You black son of a bitch are intruding upon me.' I asked him, wanted to know what he struck me for, he wouldn't say. Said he 'would cut my damned black heart out' and then I carried my coffee in the barracks and then I came out and asked him, what did he hit me for? He couldn't give no account. Then he made the expression again, he 'would cut my damned heart out.' Then he ran his hand in his pocket. At the time, I jumped off from the barracks, I sung out, Look out and then I fired. That is all."

The Court deliberated, found Quinn quilty and sentenced him to be shot to death with musketry. The execution took place on November 25, 1864 at Fort Jackson.

REFERENCES:
Military Personnel Records, RG-#94
Court Martial Proceedings, RG-#153 LL 2714

Case #156
Charles Williams
Unassigned Recruit, USCT
Hung for Murder
November 25, 1864

DESCRIPTION:

No military personnel records of Williams were located at the National Archives. All that is known is that he was an unassigned recruit at Camp Casey, Virginia when he was arrested and confined, charged with the murder of a colored woman on September 14, 1864.

A General Court Martial having been convened in Washington, D.C. did on September 30, 1864 proceed to the trial of Charles Williams, unassigned Recruit of the U.S. Colored Troops on a charge of murder. Specifying that Charles Williams, unassigned recruit,

USCT, did willfully and with malice aforethought deliberately shoot and kill a colored woman (name unknown), all this near Camp Casey, Virginia on or about the 14th Day of September 1864. To which charge and specification the prisoner plead - not guilty.

Witnesses for the prosecution presented the following version of the murder. Williams was seen walking toward the Camp Casey Sutler's with a negro woman on his left with their arms virtually touching. They were not quarrelling. At a short distance from the Sutler's establishment, Williams was seen to draw a pistol from his right hand jacket pocket and point it at the woman and fire one shot. She screamed and fell to the ground while Williams ran about 15 feet toward the Sutler's store then slowed to a walk and continued on to the Sutler's store. An Army ambulance took the wounded victim to her house.

Several soldiers testified to seeing Williams with the pistol some hours before the shooting. One witness stated that Williams on the forenoon before the incident said he was going to shoot a woman. Another witness testified that Williams brandished the pistol prior to the shooting and when cautioned by his companions not to shoot anyone, declared he didn't "care a damn if he did," and further that in reference to the woman that "if he did not shoot her he hoped hell would be his heaven."

An acting assistant surgeon stationed at the Abbott Hospital near the Freedman's Village, Virginia stated he was called to visit the wounded woman at her residence in the Village. He saw a wound in the lower abdomen typical of a pistol wound and that the victim was moribund. Thomas Williams, the father of the victim, testified that he came home and that his daughter Sallie Williams (the victim) was lying on the bed with a bullet wound in "the flank." She died at 6 AM the following morning.

The prisoner presented a statement on his behalf which read: "I was drawing my handkerchief from my pocket and the pistol went off accidentally. I did not know the woman and had nothing against her."

With no further witnesses to testify, the court deliberated and found the prisoner guilty, and sentenced him to be hung by the neck until he is dead.

The execution was carried out on November 25, 1864.

REFERENCE

Court Martial Proceedings, RG #153 LL 2979

Case #157
Pvt. William Loge
NV: Aka, French Bill
Executed for Desertion/Murder
December 2, 1864

DESCRIPTION:

Not located.

Loge's military unit is unknown but has been variously reported as the 61st New York Volunteer Infantry Regiment, the 28th New York Volunteer Infantry Regiment, and the 15th New York Volunteer Cavalry Regiment. The records of these units to this date fail to verify his membership in any of them. "The Official List" does not indicate his service in a specific military unit, only states he was hanged for desertion and murder on December 2, 1864 per S.O. #107, Military District of Harper's Ferry. The full text of the order is, "William Loge, known as "French Bill" being a deserter from the services of the United States, a noted bushwacker, murderer and assassin, as a just punishment for his crimes, should at once be hanged. It is ordered that Captain A. D. Pratt, Provost Marshall do hang him by the neck at 2 o'clock p.m., Friday, December 2nd, 1864 until he be dead." OR, I, 43, Part 2, Correspondence, contains all the remaining pertinent correspondence that has been found concerning William Loge (aka "French Bill").

Item One:

General Stevenson to General Sheridan, Harper's Ferry, December 1, 1864. "Merritt burned down to the river yesterday and is now on his return. I have not heard what he did beyond destruction of property. My command in Gaps report no attempt of enemy to pass through. I caught French Bill, a notorious murderer and bushwacker belonging to White's Battalion, who was with the party that murdered the Surgeon of the Sixth Pennsylvania Cavalry. He is a deserter from the Sixty-First New York Infantry."

Item Two:

General Sheridan to General Stevenson, December 1, 1864, 1:45 p.m. "As soon as you can have fully ascertained that you have French Bill as your prisoner, take him out and hang him. This will be your authority."

Item Three:

General Stevenson to General Sheridan, December 1, 1864. "I have undoubtedly French Bill. He will be hanged at 2 p.m. tomorrow."

Item Four:

Captain D. Henry Burnette to General Stevenson, Point of Rocks, December 1, 1864. "Mosby was encamped near Waterford last night, watching the burning of property. He had about 300 men. Our forces were in the vicinity of Lovettsville, seven miles from Waterford. I fear his command will escape. Yesterday seized 10 horses escaping to this side from our conscription; some of them I know belong to Union men. Shall I send them to Harper's Ferry without distinction? The officer commanding squadron of Ninth New York Cavalry at Lovettsville says General Sheridan's order is to take all horses. French Bill, of Mobberly's Freebooters, was yesterday taken by Keye's men, I understand; if so, he is an important capture, as he is a deserter from Twenty-Eighth New York Volunteer Infantry. The destruction of property in this vicinity is now complete. Colonel Root, of Fifteenth New York Cavalry, now at Pleasant Valley, will furnish you evidence against French Bill; also a clerk in employ of Mr. Bush, who was sutler for Twenty-Eighth Regiment. I will bring him to Harper's Ferry."

REFERENCES:

OR as cited above Official List Military Correspondence

Case #158
Pvt. William Henderson
Co. B, 66th Inf Regt, USCT
Executed for Murder
December 1, 1864

DESCRIPTION:

25 years of age, 5 feet 6 inches tall, black eyes, black hair, dark complexion, born in Louisburg County, Virginia, occupation hunter, illiterate.

Henderson enlisted December 12, 1863 and was mustered into service on Island 76, Mississippi on December 17, 1863 and was assigned to Captain Bullock's Company, 4th Regiment of Mississippi Infantry, A.D., (African Descent). This designation was subsequently changed to Company B, 66th Infantry Regiment, USCT. A notation in his personnel file states that on February 12, 1864 he was absent, in Smallpox Hospital. Harrison committed a murder, was arrested and tried by Court Martial.

A General Court Martial was convened at Little Rock, Arkansas and on November 28, 1864 tried Private William Henderson, Company B, 11th Infantry Regiment USCT on a charge of murder.

The accused applied to the Court for permission to introduce Lieutenant William

Getchell, 66th Infantry USCT as his counsel. The request was granted.

Testimony was offered that stated Henderson inquired of negroes at the Rosson Plantation located about one mile from Union Picket lines if Mrs. Rosson had any gold, silver or greenbacks and if Mrs. Rosson was not afraid to stay there alone.

On the night of November 17, 1864, a negro, Armistead Rosson, heard a shot fired and Mrs. Virginia Rosson screamed and asked Armistead to come out. But he refused as he heard someone say, "If he pokes his head out I'll blow his brains out." She ran into Mosely's house crying out that Mrs. Fannie Tombe had been killed. Mr. Mosely got out of bed and opened the door to the room and Mrs. Rosson ran in and jumped into bed next to Armistead's wife. Moments later Henderson came to the door and ordered her to come out. When she did not obey, he shouted he would put her to death if she did not come out. When she did not emerge he opened the door, searched for her, found her in bed and struck Mrs. Rosson over the head several times with his rifle butt, then shot her and left the house.

Henderson returned to his camp. The murders were reported the following day by wagon teams carrying farm products from the countryside to the camp. It is unclear from the testimony as to how suspicion of the commission of the murders was fastened on Henderson. Various items stolen during the murders, clothing, a silver knife and other unnamed items were found on the night after the murders were committed, buried in the ground under Henderson's bed. They were identified as possessions of either Mrs. Tombe or Mrs. Rosson, the murdered women.

The defense offered only one witness who testified to Henderson's being regarded as "a first rate soldier but a wicked man."

Henderson's counsel prepared a written defense which he submitted to the Court.

"Headquarters General Court Martial
St. Charles, Ark, Nov 28, 1864
Captain William T. Sullivan, Judge Advocate.

I have the honor to submit the following as a defense in the case of Private William Henderson, B, Company, 66th USC Infty. You are well aware of the necessity of punishing the guilty man whoever he might be, and that speedily. In such a case as the one under consideration, it should be viewed impartially. I have no doubt but such will be the case, but charged as I am with the defense of a man whose life is at stake I pray he may be strictly looked upon as innocent until he is fairly beyond a doubt proven to the contrary. The crime is well calculated to rouse any ones passions, and such will cast dishonor on the service unless the guilty ones shall be punished. The charge is Murder. The specification asserts that the accused is guilty of murdering two women, on or about the 17th day of Nov. 1864, with malice aforethought, that he did shoot Mrs. Virginia Rosson and Mrs. Fannie Toombe, residents of Arkansas Co., Ark., thereby causing their deaths. From the testimony adduced, is there anything, to establish the guilt upon the accused, sufficiently to justify a sentence of death? There is no evidence that he shot Mrs. Fannie Toombe. Armistead Rosson (col'd) the first witness called on behalf of the prosecution, is one of the poorest class of nigros, and judging from the fright he was in, it is altogether probable he took no notice of the murderer, but ran and hid himself. I would judge him to be of the class, whether swearing to the truth or an untruth, swears positively. This is too much the case with many of them. They would soon, if it would shield them from punishment, swear falsely. So far as my observation has gone, I have found this to be the case generally. No wonder it is so. They have been held in bondage all the days of their lives. From childhood such an espionage has been excused over them, and in many cases even forced to steal their daily bread, and lying deceit had to be practiced to shield themselves that it has become to them a second nature almost. Having not been trusted in Slavery and in ignorance, they do not value their oaths as sacred as a white man does. So they can escape the earthly punishment, they care not for the Heavenly. Their idea of prayer is no matter what crime they commit, if they only have time to pray before death, God will grant them a remission of their sins. This witness being of that class his testimony should be taken with the greatest degree of allowance. The one and only positive witness for the prosecution was Armistead Mosely, a good looking and athletic colored man. (writing here illegible) He (writing faded) or in other words they agreed here. Did his actions correspond with his oath? He swears he saw no other young man present. (faded) Rosson never outside the door against the murderer, but hid himself in bed, covering themselves snugly in bed and Armistead Mosely never as much as said to a man of his own color, stop don't kill the woman. Why was he not begging for help and (faded). Another remarkable coincidence, although so terrified, he took particular notice of the murderer even that he noticed the pimples on his face. He swore positively to all that was done, although he hid in bed. When asked if he was certain beyond a doubt that the accused was the guilty one, answered, "I am pretty certain" but immediately afterwards said, "I am certain." The reason for being certain was that the accused had pimples on his face. The accused like hundreds and thousands of his colored comrades in arms has had the variola. In identifying a colored man and especially one who has had this disease, it is to all white men at least very difficult and I have no knowledge of a difference between the vision of a white and black man. The opinion often expressed is that they favor each other.

Some ladies dresses were found buried in the house where the accused lives. No one saw him with them. No one saw him put them there and although it was diligently tried to be proven that he placed them there, signally failed.

Lt. Buchan Adjt. of 63rd US Col'd Infantry was called as a witness for the prosecution to identify the Articles of clothing found in the accused house. That also failed. The witness swore he had seen Mrs. Toombe wear similar dresses; but was not positive the dresses alluded to were hers.

Lt. Col. Geo. G. Simpson, 66th U S Col'd Infy. swore these were dresses taken from the accused house but they were not presented to him consequently his testimony was neither pro nor con. The only witness called on part of the defense was a Corporal from the accused's own company who swore he was a good soldier but a wicked man. I presume his meaning of a wicked man is the same as held by his people generally viz: one who swears and never prays to God. It is a principle of law that all men are to be held innocent until proven to the contrary. "By the mouth of law *(illegible)*." This being done in this case. Is there a person who would not shudder at the thought of having his life placed in the hands of such witnesses as Armistead Wesley and Armistead Rosson who are the only material witnesses in the case. Can any officer who holds bravery as a merit believe these poltroons? Can such errant cowards be truthful men? They hid themselves and let a man of their own race murder an innocent woman. This is too absurd for belief. Sooner would I think them guilty of the crimes. They make no sense but remained at home until morning before telling the crime to be known. (*very faded*) as to the nature of an oath. No one knows as they properly knew (*faded*).

I have the honor to appeal as
Your Obt. Svt.
Wm.Gitchell
1st Lt. 66th USCT
Counsel for the accused.

The Court deliberated, found the accused guilty only of the murder of Mrs. Rosson and sentenced him to be shot to death with musketry.

The execution was carried out at St. Charles, Arkansas on December 7, 1864.

REFERENCES:

Military Personnel Records, RG-#94
Court Martial Proceedings, RG-#153 NN 3192

Case #159
Private Edward Rowe
Co. C, 179th NY Inf. Regt.
Executed for Desertion
December 11, 1864

DESCRIPTION:

21 years of age, 5 feet 10 inches tall, brown hair, light eyes, fair complexion, born in Berkshire County, Massachusetts, occupation clerk, literate.

Rowe enlisted and was mustered into service at Elmira, New York on April 12, 1864. Rowe and Smith (case #160), were in the same Company, deserted together, were tried, convicted, and executed together. For more details see (Case #160 Smith).

A General Court Martial was convened at City Point, Virginia and on December 1, 1864 tried Private Edward Rowe, Company C, 179th New York Infantry Regiment on a charge of deserting to the enemy.

Testimony offered the Court showed that the accused was put on Picket Duty at Peebles Farm about October 15, 1864 near Petersburg, Virginia. Rowe deserted his post at about 4 A.M. on October 16, 1864. He was described as a volunteer, enlisting at Elmira, New York and receiving $300.00 bounty.

Three other men deserted about the same time, abandoning their guns and blankets. It was a very foggy night and the presence of Rebel picket posts only 30-40 rods away made desertion easy. Rowe was taken by the Rebels and sent to Castle Lightning (P.O.W. camp) in Richmond, Virginia. When he arrived at the camp, he was dressed in civilian clothing and declared he was a Yankee deserter. On October 20th, the prisoners left Richmond and Rowe carried a "paper" which he stated entitled him and others to the benefits of Order #65 War Department, C. S. A. which referred to treatment of Yankee deserters which the prisoners said was given them by General Heth. The prisoners traveled in a group through the Rebel lines to the Union lines near the mouth of the Big Sandy River (Kentucky). The prisoner was on a boat, and was arrested at Covington, Kentucky and taken to Lexington, Kentucky where the Provost Marshall separated the prisoners into groups, Rebel soldiers, Citizens, Union Soldiers. The accused was left in the group of Rebels. Several other witnesses testified that they were in a group of prisoners with the accused and that he represented himself constantly as a Yankee deserter.

The accused had no witnesses to bring before the Court, but did present a statement on his behalf.

Statement of the Prisoner

"I left my regiment about the middle of October, it was then near Petersburg. I was captured with Daub Smith while my Co. was on picket, about the 15th of October and taken to Gen'l. Heth (C. S. A.) and sent to Petersburg and from there to Richmond. I told Gen'l. Heth I had intended to desert anyhow, I took no oath of any kind, from Richmond they took me to Abingdon (Virginia) and from there to Pound Gap, and thence to Greenwichburg. I reported to the Provost Marshall there and told him I was captured on the lines and passed through as a Union deserter. I was sent from Greenwichburg to Portsmouth (Ohio) on the Ohio River, nobody was with me but Smith. I hired myself on the boat at Portsmouth to go to Cinncinnatti, but when I got to Covington, I was arrested by the Officer who had the rest of the prisoners in charge. I was taken to Lexington, and from there to Washington via Cincinnatti. Smith and I were captured together, nobody else was with us.

(signed) Edward Rowe."

The Court then deliberated, found the accused guilty, and sentenced him to be hung by the neck until dead. The execution took place on December 10, 1864 at or near City Point, Virginia.

REFERENCES:

Military Personnel Records, RG-#94
Court Martial Proceedings, RG-#153 LL 2812
Manuscript Division, Civil War Soldiers letters, Schoff Collection, Clements Library, University of Michigan, Ann Arbor, Michigan, letter of Nathaniel W. Bunker.
(See text Of Pvt. Daniel C. Smith, Co. C, 179th NY Inf. Regt., Case #160, page .

Case #160
Private Daniel C. Smith
Co. C, 179th NY Infantry Regiment
Executed for Desertion
December 11, 1864

DESCRIPTION:

21 years of age, 5 feet 9½ inches tall, light hair, blue eyes, light complexion,born in Saratoga, New York, occupation boatman, literacy undetermined.

Smith enlisted and was mustered into service on April 12, 1864 at Elmira, New York in Company C, 179th New York Infantry Regiment. Smith and Private Rowe, also of Company C, deserted the Regiment to serve with the confederates and were captured in the Shenandoah Valley, recognized, arrested, and confined.

A General Court Martial was convened at City Point, Virginia, and on December 2, 1864 tried Private Daniel C. Smith, Company C, 179th New york Infantry Regiment on a charge of deserting to the enemy.

Testimony given the Court showed that Smith was on picket duty, before Petersburg, Virginia, on the night of October 15, 1864 and deserted from his post on the morning of October 16, 1864. Smith was with the Company from the end of June 1864, having received $300.00 enlistment bounty. Smith and other Company members were apparently aware of the oft mentioned Rebel War Department General Order #65 of August 15th 1864. The order was "said" to have outlined a procedure along the following lines. A Union soldier was to desert to the Rebel forces and then take an oath of allegiance to the Confederate Government and enlist in the Rebel Army. He then would be "escorted" north toward Louisa, Kentucky where he would enter, unescorted, and report to the Union Army Provost Marshal as a Confederate deserter. *If* he were accepted as such, he would take the oath of allegiance to the United States and he would be issued a certificate permitting him to travel freely in the North and to be exempt from military service. No copy of this G.O. #65 has been located at the time of this writing.

Smith was discovered missing between three and four o'clock on the morning of October 16, 1864 as were the two other members of the Post. They left their guns and blankets behind.

Smith was accompanied by Rowe (case #159) and the account of Rowe's case duplicates the facts in Smith's case. Rowe, already convicted and sentenced for desertion to the enemy, was a witness for Smith at the trial.

Smith offered no other witnesses but did present a statement on his behalf to the Court.

Statement of Prisoner

"At the time I was captured (October 16, 1864) Rowe and I went to the creek outside of the videttes for the purpose of getting water from the creek. After filling our canteens we attempted to return when the enemy's videttes (2 of them) halted us and told us to come over to them, said if we did not they would blow our brains out—we went over, and were taken before General Heth, I told him I intended to come over, my intentions in telling him so were that I might get through the lines. We were taken to Castle Thunder, Richmond, were kept there 3 days, then passed thro the lines into Ky. as deserters from the Union Army. We traveled on to Portsmith, a town on the Ohio River, in the State of Ohio, hired on a boat there, to go to Cincinnatti, when boat stopped at Covington, Ky. an officer came to me and told me I was a deserter. They took me to Lexington, Ky. and when first asked what I was, said I was a citizen, I afterwards acknowledged my command.

(signed) Daniel C. Smith"

The Court deliberated, found the accused guilty and sentenced Smith to be hanged by the neck until dead.

He was executed at the same time and place as Rowe at City Point, Virginia on

December 10, 1864.

The Journal of a Civil War soldier mentioned the execution.

"On the 11th of Dec. 1864 I was compelled to attend, with the regiment to witness the hanging of two men. They deserted from the 179th N.Y. Vols. to the rebels and were taken prisoners while fighting on the side of the enemy, in the Shenandoah Valley and recognized by men in Genl. Sheridan's Army. One was named Edward Rowe, the other Daniel C. Smith. Such was the doom of deserters."

(Also see case #159)

REFERENCES:
Military Personnel Records, RG-#94
Court Martial Proceedings, RG-#153 LL 2812
Manuscript Division, Civil War Soldier's letters
Schoff Collection, Clements Library, University of Michigan
Ann Arbor, Michigan, from The Bunker Journal

Case #161
Private Charles Hummel
NV: Carl, Hommel, Himmel
Co. E, 7th NY Volunteer Infantry Regt. (New)
Executed for Desertion
December 7, 1864

DESCRIPTION:

21 years of age, 5 feet 8 inches tall, brown hair, brown eyes, fair complexion, born in Germany, occupation merchant, substitute, literate.

Hummel enlisted as a substitute and was mustered into service on July 19, 1864 at New York City, New York, and was assigned to Company E, 7th New York Volunteer Infantry Regiment (new). The Regiment was stationed near Petersburg, Virginia. Hummel deserted while on Picket Duty on October 18, 1864, and on November 9, 1864 was "captured" and confined.

A General Court Martial was convened at City Point, Virginia, and on December 7, 1864 tried Private Charles Hummel, Company E, 7th New York Infantry Regiment on a charge of Deserting to the Enemy.

The accused pleaded guilty.

Evidence was introduced which showed that Hummel absented himself without authority while on picket duty in front of Petersburg, Virginia on or about October 16, 1864. Hummel was described as a very good soldier, only six months in the U.S.A. from his birthplace, Germany, well educated, but unacquainted with American customs, and he had the Articles of War and Army Regulations read to him.

Hummel and a Sergeant Rose were absent from roll call on the night of October 16, 1864. Sergeant Rose was said to have a canteen, and a bottle full of liquor and Hummel liberally partook of it. Hummel was arrested in Louisa, Kentucky as a deserter and sent to Lexington, Kentucky. From there he was sent to Washington, D.C. and finally back to the Provost Marshall in City Point, Virginia.

The accused having no witnesses to call upon submitted a "Statement of the Prisoner" to the court.

"Statement of Prisoner"

I am about 22 years of age, have been in this country six months. Sgt. Rose gave me liquor and afterwards persuaded me to go over with him. I reported at Louisa, Kentucky. Sgt. Rose staid at Abingdon, Va. He asked me to go with him to a post to recover some guns and then said we would go out further after we got down to the creek between our line and the rebel line the Sgt. said we had better go on over as our men would shoot at us if we went back, we went over to the rebels and were taken before their General.

(signed) Charles Hummel"

A Volunteer Descriptive list, etc., accompanied Hummel when he was returned under arrest. It contained various statements in addition to the Descriptive Listings. One notation reads, "The above states that he deserted his command in front of Richmond on October 16th and surrendered himself to guards who brought him to Louisa." A second notation states, "Surrendered at Louisa, Received at Lexington, November 9, 1864." A third statement says, "The man surrendered himself as a rebel deserter at Louisa, Ky. and after being brought to take the Prisoner's Amnesty Oath, confessed himself a deserter from the Army of the Potomac."

The court deliberated, found the accused guilty and sentenced him to be hung by the neck until dead. The execution took place at the encampment of the 1st Division, 2nd Army Corps on December 16, 1864 near Ft. Wheaton, Petersburg, Virginia.

(Also see Privates Christopher Suhr Case #165, Company E, 7th New York Volunteer Infantry Regiment (new), and Private John Thompson Case #166 Company H, 5th New Hampshire Volunteer Infantry Regiment.

REFERENCES:
Military Personnel Records, RG-#94
Court Martial Proceedings, RG-#153 NN 3085

Case #162
Private William Kane
AKA: William Carter, NV: Cain
Company A, 8th MD Volunteer Infantry Regt.
Executed for Desertion
December 16, 1864

DESCRIPTION:
25 years of age, 5 feet 7 inches tall, auburn hair, gray eyes, fair complexion, born in Montreal, Quebec, Canada, occupation sailor, substitute, literacy undetermined.

Kane, a substitute, enlisted and was mustered into service at Baltimore, Maryland on June 1, 1864. On duty with his Regiment in the Petersburg, Virginia area, he deserted seemingly while on duty on June 28, 1864, and was apprehended and confined.

A General Court Martial was convened at City Point, Virginia, and on December 6, 1864 tried Private William Kane, Company A, 8th Maryland Infantry Regiment (alias William Carter, Company A, 8th Maryland Infantry Regiment) on a charge of deserting to the enemy.

Testimony presented showed that Kane enlisted as a substitute about June 17, 1864, and arrived for service with the 8th Maryland Infantry Regiment, then stationed before Petersburg, Virginia on June 26, 1864. Kane deserted the service on June 28, 1864, five other men deserting from Company A at about the same time. Kane appeared in Court in a rebel uniform and was described as having been wearing a Union Army Uniform when he deserted. Kane was arrested in Lexington, Kentucky and returned to City Point, Virginia on November 20, 1864.

A most interesting question to a witness was whether Kane knew of the Confederate War Department, General Order #65, dated August 15, 1864. The order purported to relate to a procedure wherein Union Soldiers deserted to Rebel forces, took an oath of allegiance to the Confederacy, then were conveyed north by Rebels to Union lines near Louisa, Kentucky and released. When entering the Union lines, they were arrested as Confederate deserters. They then took the Oath of Allegiance to the United States of America and were released, permitted to go anywhere in the North and remain free of the draft and further military service. This Confederate War Department order is frequently referred to in Court Martial testimony, but we have not been able to document it nor have any individuals with knowledge of Confederate Military history verified it.

The reply by the witness to this query was that Kane had deserted before the order had been issued.

A Captain Harry Rulon, 114th Pennsylvania Infantry Regiment, who examined prisoners returned from desertion under arrest stated that Kane represented himself as a British subject who arrived in the country aboard a blockade runner and had never been in the Union Army. At Lexington, Kentucky, Kane was said to have insisted he was a British subject named Carter and had been in neither the Union or Rebel armies, but was a private citizen of the south.

The accused offered no witnesses in his behalf, but did present a statement of defense.

Statement of Prisoner

"When I first enlisted in Baltimore I was sent to camp, when I got there what little Bounty I got was taken from me, also a silver watch, when I was sent to the Regiment the Col. or Maj. at Baltimore, said he intended sending my money on, some $200.00, when I got to my regiment and inquired for it, I found that none of it had come along with me, and the watch did not come either, I thought it was too hard to lose my money and stay in the service, I only received about $50.00 of my bounty, I am a Scotch man, was known in the Regiment by the name of Wm Kane, I was trying to escape North and was picked up by 6 rebel scouts, I did not intend going to the enemy at all, They took my uniform off and gave me these clothes, I never said I was a Rebel deserter, I gave myself up as having come in a blockade runner.

signed William `X' (his mark) Carter"

The Court then deliberated, found the prisoner guilty, and sentenced him to be hung by the neck until dead.

The execution took place on December 16, 1864 in the City Point, Virginia area. *Epilogue*: A letter in Kane's file concerns his will.

"Adjutant Generals Office, Wash. D. C., May 3, 1865.

General, I have the honor to acknowledge the receipt of a communication forwarded by you to this office on the 25th day of March last from Chaplain Wm. O'Neill, 118th Penn Vols enclosing copy of the last will and Testament of William Kane 8th Md Vols executed for desertion on December 16, 1864, and requesting that Lt Col W. H. Comegys 1st Eastern Shore Md Vols be called upon to account for the money and watch belonging to the deceased if in his possession.

In reply I have the honor to inform you that from an affidavit of Col Comegys on file in this office it appears that he received from Private Kane two hundred and forty dollars ($240.00) and but no watch; that he paid to him before leaving camp, one hundred and forty seven dollars ($147.00) and that the balance due him, ninety three dollars ($93.00) was, after he was assigned to a regiment, turned over at Alexandria, Va to be forwarded with the man to the Army of the Potomac.

I have the honor to be,
Very respectfully
Your Obediant Servant
Asst. Adjt. Genl."

REFERENCES:

Military Personnel Records, RG-#94
Court Martial Proceedings, RG-#153 MM 650

Case #163

Sgt./Pvt. George R. Prince
NV: George W. Prince
Co. B, 22nd Ohio Vol Inf Regt
Executed for Desertion
December 16, 1864

DESCRIPTION:

31 (AV: 30) years of age, 5 feet 7 inches tall (HV: 6 feet 1 inch), eyes gray, hair brown,

complexion fair, born in Portland (CV: Larence), Ohio, occupation furnaceman, literate (if he wrote the letter of appeal for clemency quoted here).

Prince is recorded as enlisting in Company B, 13th Missouri Volunteer Infantry Regiment at Portsmouth, Ohio on September 2, 1861 and was mustered into service at Benton Barracks near St. Louis, Missouri on November 1, 1861. He was appointed a Sergeant and assigned to detached duty by orders of January 3 and 5, 1862 as a member of a permanent recruiting party on south 4th Street, St. Louis, Missouri. By March 1862, Prince is listed as a private (reduced from Sergeant). By July 1862, the unit designation was changed to Company B, 22nd Ohio Volunteer Infantry Regiment and Prince deserted on August 18, 1862. The regiment was engaged in the vicinity of Corinth, MIssouri in August 1862 and a record notation states that he was captured and paroled August 24, 1862 at Corinth, Missouri and in another record he was noted as a deserter on August 18, 1862 at Corinth, Missouri. From this point on his records are confusing and conflicting. The most clear statements seem to indicate that Prince was caught about the end of October or early November 1863 in the vicinity of Covington, Kentucky and was temporarily lodged in the Greenup County (Kentucky) jail at Cattlettsburg, Kentucky, situated at the junction of the Ohio and Big Sandy rivers in North Eastern Kentucky, from which Prince promptly escaped. He was recaptured at Cincinnati, Ohio and returned to the Cattlettsburg jail in late July 1864. He was finally taken in November 1864 to his Regiment's new station at Little Rock, Arkansas where he was confined in the Military Prison, tried for desertion, found guilty and sentenced to be executed. Several vouchers and paid bills in his file indicate that subsistance for the prisoner cost an average of $0.75 per day plus railway transportation cost. A reward of $30.00 was paid and another bill for $6.51 for cost of delivery paid. While awaiting execution, Prince wrote a long eloquent letter begging for clemency. The letter is reproduced verbatim.

"Military Prison, Little Rock, Ark. Nov. 22, 1864 Major Genl. F. Steele, Commanding Department of the Arks.

Sir I seat myself today to make one last effort if possible to avert the awful sentence that hangs over my now friendless and forsaken head. And in attempting to make a plea to you in order if possible to save my life — I hardly know how to proceed, for conscious am I that I have been guilty of the grosest military crime But yet I cannot willingly and contentedly pass my few remaining days away upon this earth without at least making one feeble effort to prolong my life which is as dear to me as the life of any other of God's creation — however bad I may have spent this portion of it which is past and gone and can never be recalled.

"And while I do not here pretend to plead innocence, nor would I have you, Genl. to supose that I now wish to escape punishment for the offense that I have been guilty of, yet I must say that in accordance with other cases simular to mine if not of a more agravated nature, that have come under my observation during my imprisonment — and were only punished by confinement — some of them but for a short time. that my sentance when compared to theirs seems to be a very hard one. But in this conexion I will say that I do not wish you to believe that I consure you with the hard sentance that I have been so unfortunate to receive. Not atal Genl. for well I know that you was in no way conected with my trial — But that sentance has your approval. And without it, it would be of no effect. Hence it seems to me that if you have the power to sentance one to death you at the same time must have the power to mitigate or change that sentance according to your own option.

"Hence it is Genl that I presume to beg your attention to this my feeble petition to you to spare to me my life. There is other modes of punishment that seems to me would be severe anough in their caracter to sufficiently punish me. And at the same time make my case one of example. Any of which I would cheerfully receive if you will only spare my life that I may yet have an oppotunity of atoneing for the past by thorough and true repentance. Remember Genl. that I have an aged Father and Mother with kind Sisters and Brothers whom I fondly and devotedly love and would like to greet them again when this cruel and unwholly rebellion is at it's finale. Around the family circle and be enabled to relate to them that I had been so unfortuante as to have been condemned to death on the 19th day of Decem 1864. And through the goodness of you Genl. my life had been spared, — You will have the great pleasure of knowing then that instead of attaching any additional burthen upon the now afflicted minds of my grey haired Parents, having a tendency to make thier paths to thier graves more thorny, and rugged. That instead of this the receipt of the to them joyful intelligence of my pardon thier hearts would be made glad with joy. And you would have thier united prayers for your future welfare and prosperity.

"That God may help you to consider my case and incline your heart to Mittigate my punishment is my prayers, believing this I have the honor Genl. to be your most Obedient servant

George W. Prince, Co. B, 22nd Ohio Inft. Vols.

Passed by Supt. of Mil Prison, Nov 24, 1864"

Prince was executed by a firing squad on December 16, 1864 at Little Rock, Arkansas.

REFERENCES:

Military Personnel Records, RG-#94

There is no remaining copy of the transcript of his trial by court martial according to both National Archives and "The Official List."

Case #164
Pvt. Darius Stokes
NV: 1st Sgt.
Co. I, 2nd Inf Regt, USCT
Executed for Murder
December 16, 1864

DESCRIPTION:

23 years of age, 5 feet 2 inches tall, black hair, black eyes, black complexion, born in Baltimore, Maryland, occupation seaman, not married.

Stokes enlisted at Baltimore, Maryland on September 10, 1863 and was mustered into service on October 10, 1863 at Arlington, Virginia. He was assigned to Company I, 2nd Infantry Regiment, USCT, was appointed 1st Sergeant on November 1, 1863 and reduced back to rank of Private on December 1, 1863. His Regiment was stationed on Ship Island, Mississippi and on January 29, 1864, he shot Sergeant John Waugh, Company I, 2nd Infantry Regiment, USCT.

The 2nd Regiment USCT was stationed on Ship Island, Mississippi at the time of the shooting but was under orders to move to Key West, Florida. This resulted in a delay of the order for the convening of the Court Martial, as the entire Regiment including the accused was transferred to Key West.

A General Court Martial was convened at Key West, Florida and on April 20, 1864 tried Private Darius Stokes, Company I, 2nd Infantry Regiment, USCT on a charge of Murder.

Stokes applied to the Court for permission to introduce Chaplain James H. Schneider of the 2nd Regt. USCT as his counsel, which request was granted.

Testimony presented to the court stated that on January 29, 1864 while the Regiment was stationed at Ship Island, Mississippi, Stokes shot Sergeant John Waugh, Company I, 2nd Regiment, USCT. This occurred while the company was in formation on dress parade. Stokes had his musket loaded and capped and as Sergeant Waugh called "Company Attention", Stokes raised his weapon, cocked it and fired. The ball struck Waugh on the left side and he fell immediately on his back. He never moved or spoke, dying in about 4 or 5 minutes. Stokes was immediately seized, arrested and confined in the Guardhouse.

Assistant Surgeon Jacob M. Wurtz, M. D., 2nd Regiment, USCT examined the body and described the wound to have been caused by a musket ball which entered his body between the 5th and 6th ribs on the left side passing under the heart and exited between the 4th and 5th ribs on the right side, having penetrated both lungs.

Stokes, when interviewed by the Colonel of his Regiment, stated that he was quartered in the same tent with Sergeant Waugh Sergeant Freeman and Corporal Brown, all of whom abused him. Sergeant Waugh had struck him several times and at the time of the shooting he (Stokes) bore evidence of a blow on his forehead. Stokes was advised by a comrade that he couldn't fight the big men. Stokes testified that he and the Sergeant had engaged in a mock bayonet fencing duel and it concluded with the Sergeant seizing him and holding him up in the air.

Stokes counsel became suddenly ill and he requested a delay in the trial proceedings to allow his Counsel to recover. The court deliberated on the matter and declined the request on the grounds of the improbability of speedy recovery of his counsel.

The accused had no witnesses to bring before the Court in his behalf, but did make an oral statement to the Court which was read by the Judge Advocate who reduced the oral statement to writing.

Statement of the Prisoner

"I was cleaning my gun for inspection. After I had cleaned it, I laid it in my tent on the bed. I went from the tent down to the Cook house, when I came back to the tent I took one side of the tent (curtain like) and threw it back and got my gun out. After I got my gun out, there was a lot of sand in the nipple and in the barrel. I said `what damned rascal done that mean trick?' I said `whoever done it was a damned rascal!' Some one in the tent replied to me and said `a rascal had one stone' then he said `I have two, I'm no rascal.' Moses Brown, he draw'd back with the brush and was going to hit me with it. I jumped back from him and laid my musket side of the tent. In the meantime (sgt.) John Waugh run out past Corporal Brown and grabbed me by the collar and struck me and then I showed him fight. He picked me up and tried to throw me on the ground and I ketch him by the whiskers and held him there and he a hold of me. Then he says let me go and I let him go then he ran to the corner of the tent and picks my musket up and run to me and was agoing to strike me with it. I picked up a piece of rock and struck him on the shoulder. Then I ran to get another. By that time I got the rock he went into the tent and got his musket and put a bayonet on it and said he was agoing to stick me with it. Then I run and grab up my musket and told him if he come out there and tried to stick me with his bayonet, I would try and knock him down with the butt end of my musket. Then he taken the bayonet out of the scabbard and the hilt of it struck me in the stomack. He threw it at me. I then walks up to the Captain and i says Captain, Moses Brown, Sergeant Waugh and 1st Sergeant Freeman, they are always after me and I told him that Corporal Brown was agoing to strike me for asking about my musket and I said Sergeant Waugh and Sergeant Freeman had struck me already. Then the Captain says, `Stokes if you can't get along in the tent, I'll move you down to Sergeant Cambash's tent. Sergeant Freeman after I went away from there told me the Captain's order was to move into Sergeant Cambash's tent. Then I came there and took my equipments out and all that belonged to me and carried them down to Sergeant Cambash's tent except my musket and equipments. Before I came back to the orderly Sergt's. tent, I put on my dress coat. Then I take my equipments behind the 1st Sergt's. tent, and hung them on a tree. Then I went to work cleaning my musket again. About ten or twenty minutes before the first call for dress parade, Sergt. John Waugh come to where I was behind the tent, and says to me in a low voice, 'You son of a bitch you reported me didn't you?' and says ' the first time I catches across the lines, outside the camp, he meant, 'I mean to kill you' I replied to him, 'You are only funning.' Then he went away from there and I did not see him again until the first call for dress parade. I put on my equipments from off the tree and hurried up as quick as I could. After I got fixed I taken my musket up, carrying it at a trail Army. I went between the first and second tent. Sergt. Waugh says to me, 'Mind or you'll catch it before you come off from dress parade.' I did not make him no reply.

So I fell into ranks, the rear rank of the extreme left of them what had fallen in. I was standing there at Order Arms, I seen Sergt. Waugh carry his hand round to his cartridge box and take his cartridge and hold it up front and one side of him. Then I take and loaded my musket. I saw him bit the paper. I stepped backwards and right face and fired to shoot him in the arm. That's all I done then sir.

The Captain he come to me and told me to give my musket up and I gave it up. Then the Captain sent me to the guard house. The Colonel came to me and asked me what I do that deed for. I told him I shot not intend to kill. I said it was not the first time I was challenged for my life in the company. Then I told him it was done once at Camp Casey and the Captain never done much about it and I told him that the man had his gun loaded and turned it on me and I run'd away from him and told the Captain of it at Camp Casey. Then I stopped then sir. That's all I said to the Colonel sir. I told the Colonel I was angry at the time I done it and I was feared of the man and thought maybe he would kill me. The Colonel never said anything to me at all. After that Captain Bartholf said in the street that he had a notion to shoot me down in the street."

The Court then deliberated, found Stokes guilty and sentenced him to be hung by the neck until he is dead. The execution took place on Decembeer 16, 1864 at Key West, Florida.

The Special Order concerning the execution stipulated that the Provost Marshall was responsible for the erection of a scaffold from lumber, material and labor to be furnished by the Acting Assistant Quartermaster. Included in the personnel file for Stokes is a document infrequently encountered, a description of his place of burial. It states Private Stokes was to be buried on the southwest point, Island of Key West, Florida. The surgeon filing the report requested that burial should be accompanied by the usual military honors. The latter, military honors for a criminal interment, was seldom carried out. It would seem that this was a routine form request.

REFERENCES:

Military Personnel Records, RG-#94
Court Martial Proceedings, RG-#153 NN 2905

Case #165
Pvt. Christopher Suhr
Co. E, 7th NY Infantry Regt. (New)
Executed for Desertion
December 16, 1864

DESCRIPTION:

24 years of age, 5 feet 8 inches tall, brown hair, hazel eyes, fair complexion, born in Germany, occupation laborer, substitute, literate.

Suhr was enlisted and mustered in as a substitute at Hart's Island, New York City on July 13, 1864 and assigned to Company E, 7th New York Infantry Regiment (new). Records indicate that Suhr deserted from picket duty between October 16 - 18, 1864. He was returned to the regimental rolls on December 12, 1864, and court martialed, convicted and sentenced to death by hanging on December 16, 1864 at Fort Wheaton, Virginia. Executed at the same place and date were Privates Charles Hummel, Company E, 7th New York Infantry Regiment (New) Case #161 and John Thompson, 5th New Hampshire Infantry Regiment Case #166.

A General Court Martial was convened at City Point, Virginia and on December 7, 1864 tried Private Christopher Suhr, Company E, 7th New york Infantry Regiment on a charge of deserting to the enemy.

Testimony was presented that showed Suhr to have been on picket duty before Petersburg, Virginia on the night of October 15, 1864 and that he deserted his post between 10 and 11:00PM without permission or authority. Examination of the Picket Post revealed it unmanned and Suhr's gun and knapsack abandoned there. It was believed that two other men of the Regiment deserted on the same night.

Suhr was alleged to be a deserter from the Danish Army who spoke German. One of his officers testified that the Articles of War were read and explained carefully to Suhr in *both* English and German. He also was strongly impressed with the importance of the constant manning of all picket posts.

During the trial a copy of Rebel Order #65 August 15, 1864 was shown to a witness. (This would seem to be proof that such order did exist!)

Suhr was arrested at Louisa, Kentucky on November 9, 1864 pretending to be a Confederate deserter. He was sent to Lexington, Kentucky where he admitted he was a Union Army deserter and tried to take advantage of the Presidential Amnesty Offer. He was returned to City Point, Virginia via Washington, D.C. on November 20, 1864 where he was tried.

Suhr had no witnesses nor statement to present to the court.

The court then deliberated, found Suhr guilty and sentenced him to be hung by the neck until he be dead. The execution took place at City Point, Virginia on December 16, 1864.

REFERENCES:
Military Personnel Records, RG-#94
Court Martial Proceedings, RG-#153 NN 3058

Case #166
Private John Thompson
Co. H, 5th NH Vol. Inf. Regt.
Executed for Desertion
December 16, 1864

DESCRIPTION:
31 (AV-19) years of age, 5 feet 7½ inches tall, hair black, blue eyes, light complexion, born in Yorkshire England, occupation boatman, substitute, literacy undetermined.

Thompson, a substitute, was drafted and mustered into service at West Lebanon, New Hampshire on October 3, 1863, and assigned to Company H, 5th New Hampshire Infantry Regiment. The Regiment was on duty in the Petersburg, Virginia area. On October 15, 1864, while on picket duty, Thompson deserted to the enemy. He was arrested and confined.

A General Court Martial was convened at City Point, Virginia and on December 5, 1864 tried Private John Thompson, Company H, 5th New Hampshire Infantry Regiment on a charge of deserting to the enemy.

Thompson pleaded guilty to the charge except for the words "to the enemy."

Testimony offered the Court stated that Thompson, a substitute who had enlisted on September 9, 1864, had attempted to desert from the recruit depot shortly after arriving there. He and 15 other recruits were delivered to the 5th New Hampshire Infantry Regiment in irons. Their valuables, which had been taken in charge by the escourt officer were then delivered to them.

The regiment had heavy demands placed upon it to provide Picket line guards. About 100 of the new recruits were armed and quickly assigned to such duty. Some *sixty six of them deserted*, the prisoner among them, *in the first three days and nights of such assignment*.

The Court inquired whether the recruits had ever received instruction on their duties as picket guards. The reply was that they received training, literally on the job. A question was also asked as to whether instruction had been received by the recruits on loading and firing their musket or on attaching and unfixing the bayonet. The reply was negative. Some of the recruits loaded their guns with the ball first, then the powder, others inserted the minie ball into the muzzle point first. Questioned as to having been read the Army regulations and the Articles of War, the reply was that this was invariably done at the Recruit

Depot.

Thompson deserted from the Picket Post, before Petersburg, Virginia, on October 1, 1864 and was next seen as a prisoner in Castle Lightning, Richmond, Virginia. He was then escorted by Confederates to Pound Gap, Virginia and given directions to proceed, unescorted to Union held Louisa, Kentucky where he reported to the Union Army Provost Marshall. He was then sent to Lexington, Kentucky and failed, initially to identify himself as a Union Army deserter. He later, on November 9, 1864, admitted he was a deserter from the Army of the Potomac. He was sent to City Point, Virginia via Washington, D. C. arriving there on November 20, 1864.

The prisoner offered no defense Witnesses but did present a statement to the Court.

Statement of the Prisoner

"I have been 4 months in this country, I am an Englishman, born in London, am 21 years of age, I was persuaded to enlist by a substitute broker in Canada who promised he would get me into the Navy, I was put in as a substitute and assigned to the 5th Regiment New Hampshire Volunteers, when I left the Regiment I came on the cars to City Point, Virginia and crossed the James river in a boat with 2 others, we were making our way North when we were picked up by Rebel Scouts near White House, Virginia, they took us all to Richmond, I told them I was a Yankee Deserter and was sent through the lines and arrested at Louisa, Kentucky. I was asked what regiment I belonged to, I told them the 5th New Hampshire, they sent us to Lexington, Kentucky and thence to City Point, Virginia via Washington.

signed John Thompson"

The Court deliberated, found the defendant guilty and sentenced him to be hung by the neck until he be dead.

The execution took place at City Point, Virginia on December 16, 1864.

He was to be executed at the same time with Privates Christopher Suhr, and Charles Hummel, both of Company E, 7th New York Volunteer Infantry Regiment. (See case #165 and Case #161)

REFERENCES:

Military Personnel Records, RG-#94
Court Martial Proceedings, RG-#153 NN 3058

Case #167

Pvt. Alexander Vess
NV: Ness - Vass - Voss - Viss
Co. E, 3rd Heavy Artillery, USCT
Hanged for Murder
December 16, 1864

DESCRIPTION:

21 years of age, 5 feet 4 inches tall, black eyes, black hair, brown complexion, born in Virginia, occupation farmer, illiterate.

Vess enlisted in Company A, 2nd Battalion, 1st Regiment Tennessee Colored Heavy Artillery and was transferred to Company E of the same regiment which later was redesignated as Company E, 3rd Regiment U.S. Colored Heavy Artillery. His term of service seems to be almost entirely spent in the Fort Pickering area of Tennessee. He committed murder some time prior to January 20, 1864 as a notation indicates he was confined in Military Prison, Fort Pickering, Tennessee since January 20, 1864. He was hanged for murder on December 16, 1864 at Fort Pickering. No record of the trial or court martial has been located so the details of the crime remain unknown.

REFERENCES:

Military Personnel Records, RG-94

Case #168
Private Thomas Dix
Co. G, 1st CONN Hvy. Artillery Regt.
Executed for Desertion
December 21, 1864

DESCRIPTION:

22 years of age, 5 feet 5-1/2 inches tall, brown hair, blue eyes, fair complexion, born in Ireland, occupation umbrella maker, literate.

Dix enlisted and was mustered into service on November 28, 1864 at New Haven, Connecticut into Company G, 1st Connecticut Heavy Artillery Regiment. The Regiment was stationed in the area of Petersburg, Virginia and Dix deserted from Redoubt Dutton, Virginia. He was apprehended and confined.

A General Court Martial was convened at the Headquarters of the Army of the James in the field on December 19, 1864, and proceeded to try Private Thomas Dix, Company G, 1st Connecticut Heavy Artillery Regiment on the charge of desertion.

Dix pleaded guilty and the prosecution did not offer it's case. The accused declined to offer any defense but did make the following statement to the Court.

"When these other men in the guardhouse started out to go, all of them were in the guardhouse and they asked me if I wanted to go home. They said they were going to go down the river to get to City Point and there were gun boats on the river so we couldn't get down, and so we went down to the shore along the river and lit a fire and staid there and warmed ourselves. Then we were going along down the river and we met five or six cavalrymen, we told them we had lost our way and wanted to get back to camp and they told us to go around the woods and go down to the river, there we found a fort and sentry and went down to him. I was only about five or six days in camp before this and did not intend to desert to the enemy."

The Court then deliberated and confirmed the accused plea of guilty and sentenced him to be executed by musketry. The execution took place on December 21, 1864.

See also Case #169 John Hall, Case #170 Henry McCurdy, Case #172 James Thompson, and Case #171 John Smith.

REFERENCES:
Military Personnel Records, RG-#94
Court Martial Proceeding, RG-#153 NN 3254

Case #169
Private John Hall
Company G, 1st Conn. Heavy Artillery Regt.
Executed for Desertion
December 21, 1864

DESCRIPTION:

31 (AV-37) years of age, 5 feet 11¼ inches tall, brown hair, gray eyes, sallow complexion, born in New York, occupation Joiner, unmarried.

Hall enlisted and was mustered into service at Hartford, Connecticut on November 25, 1864 into Company G, 1st Connecticut Heavy Artillery Regiment which was stationed in the Petersburg, Virginia area. He deserted from his Regiment at Redoubt Dutton, Virginia November 27, 1864. Was captured and returned to his regimental camp.

A General Court Martial was convened at Headquarters of the Army of the James and on December 19, 1864 tried Private John Hall, Company G, 1st Connecticut Heavy Artillery Regiment on a charge of Desertion.

Hall pleaded guilty to the charge and offered the following statement.

Statement

"I started with five others with the intention of going home and went down to the James River where we built a little log raft to cross on, I crossed over on that with two others. One of them left as soon as we were across and two of us staid together; then I told the man who was with me that we had better go back to our company again. We called across the river to a couple of colored men to bring us acroos the river to the Bermuda Hundred side; the guard stood on the shore as we crossed and we went with him from the riverbank over to the Provost Marshall at Bermuda Hundred. We knew that the guard was on the river bank before we crossed."

No further testimony was offered and the court deliberated and confirmed Private Hall's plea of guilty. He was sentenced to be shot to death with musketry.

The execution took place on December 21, 1864.

(There are variants noted as to dates including date of execution.)

In his file is a letter:

"Dec 23rd, 1864, Lieut. I am the Chaplain of the 8th Conn Vol. last evening, who took the pocket book of private John Hall, Company G, 1st Conn. H. Arty. at his request. At the time Hall told him there was a receipt in it for two hundred (200) Dollars from a Provost Marshall. The receipt was given at your Head Quarters and is dated Dec. 17th, 1864 and reads as follows. `Received of Private John Hall, Co. G, 1st Connecticut Heavy Artillery, One Hundred and ten (110) dollars for safe keeping.

signed D. W. Mertan Clerk"

This man gave the Chaplain his true name and his father's address and desired him to forward the money to his father. None of the others claimed to have left money with the Provost Marshall.

This is the same subject I mentioned to you yesterday.

Respectfully your
obt Servant
A. B. Sharpe
Capt AAG and Provost Marshall"

A notation in reply states: "The money referred to belonging to Hall, one hundred and ten Dollars ($110.00) is here. Please notify the Chaplain of the 8th Conn Vols that he can receive the money by calling at this office."

Also see:
Case #170 *Henry McCurdy*
Case #171 *John Smith*
Case #172 *James Thompson*
Case #168 *Thomas Dix*

REFERENCES:

Military Personnel Records, RG-#94
Court Martial Proceedings, RG-#153 NN 3254

Case #170
Private Henry McCurdy
Co. G, 1st Conn Hvy. Artillery Regt.
Executed for Desertion
December 21, 1864

DESCRIPTION:

21 years of age, 5 feet 10 inches tall, brown hair, hazel eyes, sallow complexion, born in New york, occupation cooper, unmarried, literate.

McCurdy enlisted and was mustered into service at Hartford, Connecticut on November 25, 1864 in Company G, 1st Connecticut Heavy Artillery Regiment which was stationed in the

Petersburg, Virginia area. He deserted from Redoubt Dutton, Virginia on December 17, 1864, was captured on December 20, 1864.

A General Court Martial was convened at headquarters of Army of the James, and on December 19, 1864 tried Private Henry McCurdy, Company G, 1st Connecticut Heavy Artillery Regiment on a charge of desertion.

The accused pleaded guilty to the charge. The accused left his station without permission, deserting the Military Service at Redoubt Dutton, Virginia on December 14, 1864.

The accused offered the Court a verbal statement which was recorded.

Statement of the Accused

"There were five besides myself who wanted to go home. We did not intend to go to the enemy we came to the James River, I was informed that it was near Jones landing, it was not far from the Citizens that lives near Bermuda Hundred, and three of us crossed the river on a raft. After we crossed we seperated, myself and Hall (case #169) started off together and I did not see the third person until I saw him in the guard house here.

We gave it up, and went down the river a little ways and then it was proposed by the man who was with me to go back to camp and so we called to some niggers that were across the river to come over in a boat and bring us across; We knew there was a sentry over there before we did so.

The sentry asked us where we were going, we told him, to camp, He told us that we would have to go down to Bermuda Hundred and satisfy the Major as he was ordered to bring all men that he found straggling round and so we went with him there."

The Court then deliberated, confirmed the accused guilty plea and sentenced him to be shot to death with musketry.

The execution took place on December 21, 1864 in the division area.

See also Case #169 John Hall, Case #171 John Smith, Case #172 James Thompson, Case #168 Thomas Dix.

REFERENCES:

Military Personnel Records, RG-#94

Court Martial Proceedings, RG-#153 NN 3254

Case #171

Private John Smith

Co. G, 1st Conn. Hvy. Artillery Regt.

Executed for Desertion

December 21, 1864

DESCRIPTION:

23 years of age, 5 feet 7¼ inches tall, brown hair, blue eyes, florid complexion, born in Canada, occupation boatman, illiterate, unmarried.

Smith enlisted and was mustered into service at Hartford, Connecticut on November 20, (November 25th by another set of records) 1864 into Company G, 1st Connecticut Heavy Artillery Regiment. The Regiment was stationed in the Petersburg, Virginia area. Smith deserted the Regiment from Redoubt Dutton, Virginia on December 14, 1864 and was arrested and confined.

A general Court Martial was convened at Headquarters, Army of the James, in the field, Virginia and on December 19, 1864 tried Private John Smith, Company G, 1st Connecticut Heavy Artillery Regiment on a charge of desertion.

Smith pleaded guilty to the charge of desertion admitting he deserted from Redoubt Dutton, Virginia on December 14, 1864 without permission.

Smith offered the only testimony in the case in a verbal statement to the Court.

"I am guilty of desertion, that is so far as to get home. I did not intend to desert to the enemy and never thought of such a thing. I know that I did not do right, I intended to stay, but some of them wanted to go and I went too."

Questioned by the Court, Smith stated that he had received $410.00 bounty and had enlisted the day after Thanksgiving. (November 25, 1864) The Articles of War he said had never been read to him.

The accused having no witnesses and nothing further to tell the Court, the trial was closed.

The Court then deliberated, confirmed the accused's plea of guilty and sentenced him to be shot to death with musketry.

The execution took place at the headquarters of the 24th Army Corps in Virginia on December 21, 1864.

Also see Case #172 James Thompson, Case #168 Thomas Dix, Case #170 Henry McCurdy, and Case #169 John Hall.

REFERENCES:
Military Personnel Records, RG-#94
Court Martial Proceedings, RG-#153 NN 3254

Case #172
Private James Thompson
Co. G, 1st Conn. Hvy. Artillery Regt.
Executed for Desertion
December 21, 1864

DESCRIPTION:
21 years of age, 5 feet 3 inches tall, black hair, gray eyes, dark complexion, born in Ireland, occupation laborer, unmarried, literate.

Thompson enlisted and was mustered into service at Hartford, Connecticut on November 16, 1864 in Company G, 1st Connecticut Heavy Artillery Regiment. He was forwarded to his regiment which was stationed in the Petersburg, Virginia area. He deserted from Redoubt Dutton, Virginia on November 17, 1864. He was apprehended and confined.

A General Court Martial was convened at the headquarters of the Army of the James in the field, and on December 19, 1864 tried Private James Thompson, Company G, 1st Connecticut Heavy Artillery Regiment on a charge of desertion.

Testimony revealed that Thompson deserted the Military Service on or about December 14, 1864 at Redoubt Dutton, Virginia.

Thompson pleaded guilty and offered a brief verbal statement to the Court.

"I had no intention of deserting to the enemy, I was trying to go North. I enlisted on the Tuesday after election and have never been in the service before." In answer to the amount of bounties he received, Thompson replied "Four Hundred and ten dollars."

The Court deliberated, confirmed Thompson's plea of guilty and sentenced him to be shot to death with musketry.

The execution took place on December 21, 1864 in the regimental area.

Also see Case #168 Thomas Dix, Case #171 John Smith, Case #170 Henry McCurdy, and Case #169 John Hall.

REFERENCES:
Military Personnel Records, RG-#94
Court Martial Proceedings, RG-#153 NN 3254

Case #173
Pvt. William M. Smith
Co. C, 2nd US Vol Inf
Executed for Desertion
December 22, 1864

DESCRIPTION:
23 years of age, 6 feet 2 inches tall, blue eyes, light hair, light complexion, born in Roanoke,

Virginia, occupation farmer, illiterate.

Smith originally enlisted in Company F, 27th Battalion, Virginia Mounted Rifles, Confederate Forces on September 1, 1862 and the designation was changed to Company F, 25th Regiment of Virginia Cavalry and he attained the rank of Sergeant. Apparently Smith stated his military unit as Company F, 27th Virginia Cavalry and same was recorded as the 27th Virginia Cavalry Regiment when he was taken a prisoner at Strasbourg, Virginia on September 23, 1864. Confederate records indicate he deserted June 1, 1864 en route to the Shenandoah Valley. Smith was confined at Point Lookout, Maryland Prisoner of War camp.

During the Civil War, the Union Army beginning in 1864 offered confederate prisoners of war their release from P.O.W. camps if they would sign an oath of allegiance to the USA and enlist in one of the US Volunteer Regiments. Some 6,000 Confederates eventually accepted this offer and served in the six US Volunteer Regiments (numbered 1-6). The US promised that no Volunteer Regiment would be employed against the Confederacy and that all such military service would be in the western USA against the Indians, which promise was fulfilled.

These troops were often referred to as "Galvanized Yankees" or "Repentant Rebels." Their organization followed loosely that employed for the USCT. Union army officers and some Union army NCO's in command with the balance of the units composed of ex-rebels.

One other "Repentant Rebel" is on "The Official List," see Case #138, Private William C. Dowdy, 1st Regiment, US Volunteers.

The Confederates also sought to swell their depleted regiments with "Galvanized Confederates" recruited from rebel prisoner of war camps. Recruits, however, were few in number and were used against the Union army. Large numbers of these men deserted back to the Union forces at the first opportunity and proved of little, if any, value to the rebel cause.

For the most complete study of the Volunteer Regiments, based upon massive research, see Dee Brown's "Galvanized Yankees," 1963, University of Illinois Press, Urbana, Illinois.

Smith took early advantage of the opportunity to enter a US Volunteer Regiment and enlisted in the 2nd US Volunteer Regiment at Fort Monroe, Virginia on October 17, 1864, designation later changed to 4th US Volunteer Regiment. The Regiment was being organized in the Portsmouth, Virginia area and on or about November 9, 1864, Smith decided to desert the US Military service.

A number of communications in Smith's file delineate his escape attempt.

November 10th, 1864, telegram, from Fort Monroe, Virginia. Provost Marshall Major John Cassell's to Baltimore, Maryland Lt. Col. Woolley, Provost Marshall. "Please arrest John Alexander, alias Wm Smith deserter from 2nd US Vols he left here this evening on boat for Baltimore is twenty three (23) years old, blue eyes, light hair, light complexion, height six (6) feet two (2) inches, telegraph me result."

Lt. Col. Woolley, Provost Marshall, Baltimore, Maryland issued a memorandum, "Attend to this. Have a man at boat at 5 o'clock. No excuse for not catching this man as he is on Norfolk boat and can't get off till he gets here."

November 11th, 1864, Baltimore to Col. John Woolley, Provost Marshall, "I have the honor to report the arrest of John Alexander alias Wm Smith a deserter from the 2nd US Vols as per telegram enclosed."

Very respectfully, Lt. H. Babcock, USA"

Smith was returned to Norfolk and confined in the city jail on November 13, 1864. Smith was tried by court martial on November 15, 1864 at Norfolk, Virginia and in the usual trial procedure, Smith was asked if he had any objections to the presence of any member of the court. He stated he had none. The court was then, in his presence, sworn by the Judge Advocate and the Judge Advocate sworn by the President of the Court.

Smith was charged with desertion and pleaded guilty as charged and offered no testimony in his defense. Asked if he had a statement to make to the court he replied he had, as follows:

"My only reason for deserting was that there was talk of our getting $300.00 bounty and I saw nothing of it, and I wanted to go North as a citizen. I did not want to go to the Confederacy, I have no more to say gentlemen."

Smith was sentenced to be executed by a firing squad in the presence of his Volunteer Unit on December 22, 1864 at half past 11 o'clock at Norfolk, Virginia.

REFERENCES:

US Court Martial Record, Civil War, RG - #153 NN 3174
"Galvanized Yankees," Dee Brown, 1963, University of Illinois Press, Urbana, Illinois.
U.S. Federal Army Personnel Records RG #94
Confederate Army Personnel Records

Case #174
Pvt. Charles Billingsley
AKA: Cooper & Robinson
7th Battery, IND Vol. Artillery
Executed for Desertion
December 23, 1864

DESCRIPTION:

18 years of age, 5 feet 6 inches tall, light hair, gray eyes, light complexion, born in Putnam County, Indiana, occupation farmer, illiterate, substitute.

Billingsley enlisted on March 21, 1864 at Greencastle, Indiana and was mustered into service on March 23, 1864 at Indianapolis, Indiana in the 7th Battery of Indiana Light Artillery. Billingsley deserted from the Battery on June 20, 1864 near Kenesaw Mountain, Georgia. By September 8, 1864, Billingsley was under arrest in Indianapolis, Indiana and was using aliases to conceal his true name. On September 8, 1864, the Provost Marshall's office in Indianapolis, Indiana received one Charles Froman, 7th Indiana Battery, for confinement. An inquiry by the Provost Marshall of the Adjutant General of Indiana on September 9, 1864 inquires, "Does the name of Charles Donahue (alias Froman) appear on your muster-in-roll for the 7th Ind. Battery, I think he was recruited in March or April 1864. D. Braden, Pro. Mar" Another letter sent on September 9, 1864 to Captain Stansifer, Provost Marshall, 4th District, Indiana, asks, "A man calling himself Charles Froman whose real name is *Charles Billingsley* has been arrested as a deserter from the 7th Battery Ind. He says he was enlisted by you some time in August as a substitute for some man in your district. Does your book show such enlistment? D. Braden, Pro. Mar." Captain Stansifer replied, "Yours of date is just received, the records in this office show, that Charles Froman, aged 18, blue eyes, dark hair, dark complexion, 5 feet 7 inches high, was enlisted at this office as a substitute for William C. Newcomb of Sand Creek Township, Bartholomew County, Ind. for one year. The date of his enlistment was August 12, 1864. He was enlisted for the 5th Ind. Cavalry, Co. B. He was mustered into service at Indianapolis August 13, 1864 by Lieut. Fletcher, Mustering Officer and credited to Sand Creek Township."

On the 15th of September 1864, D. Braden wrote, "Respectfully referred to Colonel J. Jones A.A.P.M. Gen'l. Ind. with the information that the within mentioned Charles Frohman, *Sub*, was arrested as a deserter in this city (Indianapolis) on the 9th Inst. Upon investigation it was ascertained that his real name is *Charles Billingsley*, and that he deserted from the 7th Ind. Battery on June 20, 1864. These facts he subsequently admitted and I have sent him to the 7th Ind. Batty. as a deserter."

Colonel J. Jones A.A.P.M. General, Indiana indicated in his letter of September 15, 1864 to Captain S. Stansifer, Provost Marshall, 3rd District, Indiana, another difficulty arising from the bounty jumping/false enlistment/substitute activity, the penalty paid by the person who hired the substitute.

"Prima facie Frohman (alias Billingsley) was in the service already and could not be a substitute. You will therefore correct your record of enlistments and notify Wm. C. Newcomb that he is subject to the draft. Capt. Braden Prov Mar 6 Dist will *not* give him a certificate of Exemption or if he has done so he will reinstate his name on the enrollment."

Billingsley was tried by court martial on November 22, 1864 together with Thomas Doyle, Case #179 John Murray, and Case #180 Thomas Ryan. All were found guilty and sentenced to be executed by firing squad on December 23, 1864 at Burnside Barracks, Indianapolis, Indiana.

An account in an Indianapolis newspaper stated that Billingsley's wife visited him in jail but that he was utterly indifferent to her presence.

The details of Billingsley's biography and execution details for all the condemned men will be related here, in detail. For biographical details of the other three prisoners see their respective Case #174, 179, and 180 as previously recorded.

A letter written to Colonel A. J. Warner, dated December 17, 1864, Terre Haute, Indiana stated, "Colonel, I notice in yesterdays Commercial that Chas. Billingsley, 7th Battery has been tried by your court and sentenced to death for 'Bounty jumping.' As he is a deserter from my battery or rather from the Div. Prov. Marshall, while awaiting the publication of the action of a court martial in his case, I have concluded to advise of it: his case was an aggravated one, 'committing rape on a defenseless woman'; while our army was near Dallas, Geo. last summer and I hoped he would receive his reward ere this: he deserted the day his trial closed and rumor has it that he went over to the enemy but of that I cannot speak definitely.

Signed, O.H. Morgan,

Late-Capt. of 7th Ind Battery"

Private Charles Billingsley (AKA Charles Cooper or Charles Roberts), of an unstated unit of the 7th Indiana Battery, was tried for rape by a General Court Martial at the Camp near Burnt Hickory, Georgia on May 30, 1864.

Testimony during the trial disclosed that Billingsley and a Private William Cutsinger, also of the 7th Indiana Battery, left the camp on the night of May 28, 1864 and went to the home of a citizen named James Smith, near their camp, and did arrest and remove Smith from his home under the pretext of a military order. Billingsley later returned to the Smith residence and compelled Louisa Smith, wife of James Smith, to accompany him to headquarters where her husband was being detained. She dressed and accompanied Billingsley through wooded areas and Billingsley began calling for "Charles." Finally he halted, seized Mrs. Smith and threw her to the ground while she begged him to go away and leave her alone. She stated that he intended "to frig me right there or kill me," and she attempted to push him away, to no avail. Having consummated his passion, Billingsley dragged Mrs. Smith onto a road and continued along it until they met the man called "Charles." Billingsley and "Charles" then threw Mrs. Smith down on the ground and "Charles" raped her and Billingsley followed him again raping Mrs. Smith. Mrs. Smith had attempted to scream but one covered her mouth with his hand while the other seized her by the throat, choking her. They then took her back to her home and she went upstairs to her bedroom followed somewhat later by Billingsley and "Charles." They each raped Mrs. Smith again. Asked if she resisted their advances, she replied she had outside the house, but in the house she "just gave up." She stated, "I was afraid they would kill me."

Newspaper accounts describe Billingsley as a hardened criminal who used a number of aliases and admitted to fellow prisoners that he enlisted and deserted on numerous occasions and worse that he had killed a woman and child.

On December 23, 1864, the day of execution for the four deserters, a Special Order No. 202, Headquarters, State of Indiana (extract), "The execution of John Doyle, Lemon alias Thomas Doyle, will be postponed for 10 days in accordance with the directions of His Excellency, Abraham Lincoln, President of the United States," By order of Brevet Major General Alvin P. Hovey, Colonel Ambrose A. Stevens, Colonel commanding the Camp.

The three men to be executed, Billingsley, Murray and Ryan were marched to the execution site at Camp Burnside where they had been preceeded by about two thousand soldiers and about 100 bounty jumpers. The latter were tied together and to a rope running the length of the center of their column. Some were draped with placards proclaiming their crime. Heavily guarded, they were marched through Indianapolis to the execution grounds, led by a large negro who incessantly clanged a large brass bell to attract the local citizens attention. Their attendance at this solemn affair was designed to deter any further similar criminal activity.

The prisoners were accompanied by a Catholic Priest, Father August Bessonies, who provided the religious support for those about to die. The usual arrangement of the procession included the bearers of the three coffins, the firing squad and escort. The coffins were placed on the ground at the selected place for the execution. The prisoners were stripped of their outer jackets, seated on their respective coffins, had their feet tied and eyes blindfolded. Spectators remarked at the chill of the day and of how cold the men to be executed must have been. Finally, all the prescribed orders and requirements having been completed the three firing squads were drawn to attention, then the commands: ready, aim, fire! Murray and Ryan fell back on their coffins quite dead. Billingsley fell off his coffin and lay on the ground, panting hoarsely, still alive. One member of the firing party was ordered forward to complete the execution. He fired into Billingsley's chest and ended his life.

After the assembled troops marched past the dead, the bodies were placed in their coffins, and the coffins loaded into a covered wagon and driven away.

For the other individuals see Case #180 Thomas Ryan, Case #179 John Murray, and Thomas Doyle.

REFERENCES:

Military Personnel Records, RG-#94
Court Martial Proceedings, RG-#153 NN 2165
Indiana Military History Journal, Volume 5, #2, "Military Execution of 3 Bounty Jumpers near Camp Morton, 1864" by F.M. Wiley, submitted by Howard Lord.
"Daily Sentinel" Indianapolis, December 23, 1864.
"Daily Evening Gazette" Indianapolis, December 23, 1864.
"Indianapolis Daily Journal" December 24, 1864.
"Daily Evening Gazette" Indianapolis December 27, 1864.
"Indianapolis Star" December 12, 1971.
"Frank Leslies Illus. Newspaper" December 24, 1864. (Includes Illustration)
Indianapolis News" February 11, 1909.
Indiana Commission on Public Records, Civil War Military Records.

Case #175
Pvt. George W. Bradley
AKA George Bates
Co. H, 5th NH Infantry Regt.
Executed for Desertion
December 23, 1864

DESCRIPTION:

24 years of age, 5 feet 8 inches tall, brunette hair, hazel eyes, dark complexion, born in Canada, occupation farmer, married substitute.

Bradley was drafted and mustered in as a substitute on August 19, 1864 at Concord, New Hampshire and assigned to the 5th New Hampshire Infantry Regiment, Company H. On October 15, 1864, while on picket duty before Petersburg, Virginia, Bradley deserted his assigned duty post and deserted to the enemy. Bradley was subsequently arrested, confined and tried by court martial.

Private George Bradley, Company H, 5th New Hampshire Infantry Regiment was charged with deserting to the enemy at a General Court Martial which took place at City Point, Virginia on December 14, 1864.

Bradley was assigned to Picket Duty on the night of October 15, 1864 in front of the Union Army lines near Petersburg, Virginia. Another soldier of the same regiment on similar duty, was assigned to a position some 20 feet away. About 10PM on October 15th, Bradley was seen running bent over, his head covered by a blanket, towards the Rebel lines. The witness, upon noting his intent, fired at him as did another soldier on picket duty. Bradley was unscathed and entered the rebel lines. He was re-captured and delivered to the Union Army authorities at City Point, Virginia on November 29, 1864. Testimony mentioned a "Rebel War Department" order-G.O. #65, which apparently urged Union Army Soldiers to desert to and enlist in the Confederate Army. They then could desert as Rebel soldiers back to the Union and after swearing allegiance to the U.S.A. be free to go anywhere in the U.S and be exempt from military draft.

The prisoner offered no defense witnesses, although he directed questions at the prosecution's witnesses. He did prepare a written statement which was read in court.

Statement of Prisoner

"The way I was enlisted was this. I was living in Canada, and a substitute broker came and got me drunk, and brought me to Concord, New Hampshire and had me enlisted. I knew nothing about it until I found myself in Camp at Concord, they gave my name as George Bradley, instead of George W. Bates, which is my right name. When I got to the Regiment the Lieutenant was pretty hard on me. Sometime after, I was almost destitute of shoes and stockings, besides being unwell with a severe cold, chills and fever, and was still compelled to do duty. I am a married man and have my wife, mother and sister depending on me for support."

The Court found Bradley guilty and sentenced him to be hung by the neck until dead. Sentence was carried out at City Point, Virginia on December 23, 1864.

REFERENCES:

Military Personnel Records, RG-#94
Court Martial Proceedings, RG-#153 NN 3098

Case #176
Pvt. John C. Dixon
Co. H, 1st Mass. Hvy. Artillery Regt.
Executed for Desertion
December 23, 1864

DESCRIPTION:

21 years of age, 5 feet 9½ inches tall, brown hair, blue eyes, light complexion, born in Montreal, Canada, occupation boot crimper.

Dixon enlisted August 18, 1864 at Concord, Massachusetts and was mustered into service at Boston Harbor on September 3, 1864 and was forwarded to Company H, 1st Massachusetts Heavy Artillery Regiment. Dixon attempted to desert to the enemy on November 21, 1864 near Petersburg, Virginia. He was seized, confined, and tried by court martial.

A General Court Martial was convened in the field near Petersburg, Virginia and on November 28, 1864 and proceeded to the trial of Private John C. Dixon, Company H, 1st Massachusetts Heavy Artillery Regiment on charges of desertion and deserting his post.

Testimony presented during the trial disclosed that on November 21, 1864, Dixon had been posted as a sentry on the picket line in front of Fort Alexander Hays, Petersburg, Virginia. One witness stated "the prisoner was in a pit with me and under my charge on or about that date. I posted him about 3 o'clock P.M. as a vidette to stand for one hour, and he could not be found later. His gun was found about three rods in front of his post, leaning against a tree. I took the gun and gave it to the sergeant. A short time afterwards word came that he had been taken and sent to headquarters under guard." Dixon had wandered along the picket line of the Union Army when he was halted by a Union Army Picket of another regiment. Another witness testified, "I went out and saw the prisoner (Dixon) there. I asked him where he came from and he replied that `he had left the Yanks and come over'. The sentry who first detained Dixon stated that Dixon told him "he wanted to desert the Yanks they used him so bad, that he had received a good bounty but that it had been stolen in the Post Office and that he had been used hard generally." I asked him what Regiment and Brigade he belonged to and he told me. I then took him to the Reserve post and he was asked the same questions there. Some of the men remarked, `We are the Yanks', when he seemed greatly surprised and much confused. Another witness testified Dixon was bewildered and confused. He was then sent to Brigade Headquarters under guard.

Dixon questioned some of the witnesses but declined to present a formal defense but offered as statement to the court as follows.

"I did not intend to desert. I was discharged from the British Service for disability. I sometimes get light in the head."

The court deliberated, found Dixon guilty and sentenced him to be executed by musketry.

A letter addressed to Secretary of War, Stanton from Lieutenant Colonel L. I. Lyman, Brigade of Montreal Garrison, Artillery-Montreal, Canada was dated December 22, 1864.

Sir: I have the honor to address you with reference to a soldier in Company H, Massachusetts Heavy Artillery who is under sentence as a deserter. I have already forwarded to his Commanding Officer certificates of character from his employers, Mssrs. Scholes and Ames, testimony from the Commanding Officer of the Volunteer Company to which he belonged here, also certificates of character from several respectable citizens. All of these testify to his excellent character. This young man, John Cochlan Dixon was enlisted by a bounty broker who defrauded him of his money, yet determined to serve the time and was led in an evil hour to desert but did not pass out of the Federal lines. I can offer no palliation or excuse for the crime of desertion. I beg however in this case you will exercize all the clemency in your power consistent with discipline of the Army. The young man is a British subject and has resided in this city (Montreal) for a number of years. Your consideration of this case will, I am sure be highly appreciated by many in the community and be the means of sparing a life which from the character of the young man will be yet useful to the Army of the United States

I have the honor to be sir
your obedient servant
Lyman-Lt. Colonel"

The reply from the Adjutant Generals Office, Washington D. C. dated January 13, 1865 stated:

"Sir: I have the honor to acknowledge the receipt of your communication of the 22nd Ultimo, requesting a pardon for Private John C. Dixon, Company H., 1st Regiment Massachusetts Heavy Artillery under sentence for desertion.

In reply I have the honor to inform you that it appears upon investigation that this soldier was tried by Court Martial for desertion, and deserting his post, found guilty and sentenced to be shot to death by musketry December 23, 1864 at noon, which sentence has been executed."

I am sir, very respectfully your obediant servant
(signed) Samuel Preck Asst. Adjutant General

REFERENCES:

Military Personnel Records, RG-#94
Court Martial Proceedings, RG-#153 NN 3098

Case #177
Pvt. John Lynch
NV: John Wood
Co. F, 5th NH Infantry Regt.
Executed for Desertion
December 23, 1864

DESCRIPTION:

21 years of age, 5 feet 7-3/4 inches tall, brown hair, blue eyes, fair complexion, born in St. John's New Brunswick, Canada, occupation machinist, substitute.

Lynch was drafted and mustered in as a substitute on August 29, 1864 at Portsmouth, New Hampshire and forwarded to Virginia where he was assigned to Company F, 5th New Hampshire Infantry Regiment. On October 10, 1864, Lynch deserted while on picket duty near Petersburg, Virginia. Lynch was apprehended and placed in confinement.

A General Court Martial was convened at City Point, Virginia and on December 8, 1864 tried Private John Lynch, Company F, 5th New Hampshire Infantry Regiment on a charge of deserting to the enemy.

The accused pleaded guilty except for the words "to the enemy."

Testimony was provided showing that the accused was a duly enlisted and assigned member of Company F, 5th New Hampshire Infantry Regiment and that the Articles of War had been read to him. He was assigned to picket duty on the lines before Petersburg, Virginia from which he left his post without permission or authority thus deserting the service of the U. S. Government between midnite and half past four o'clock in the morning on or about October 11, 1864, abandoning his gun, knapsack and haversack.

Corporal Heaton, a witness, testified that the accused, with whom he had been imprisoned, gave the name Lynch in Richmond, Virginia but in Lexington, Kentucky used the name John Wood. Heaton and the accused were imprisoned at Castle Lightning, in Richmond, Virginia and on October 14, 1864, 278 federal soldiers, held prisoner by the rebels, were sent north under armed escort. They were sent to Abingdon, Virginia thence to Pound Gap, Virginia and then to the head waters of the Big Sandy River where the rebel escort left them to make their way to Louisa, Kentucky. The accused separated himself from the main body of federal prisoners and took a different route directly to Lexington, Kentucky. Apparently the accused assumed the name of John Wood of the 24th North Carolina Infantry Regiment C. S. A. and took the Oath of Allegiance to the U. S. A. Lynch at some point confessed that he was a Union Army deserter and was sent to City Point, Virginia under guard to be tried by court martial.

The prisoner having no witnesses to offer did present a statement to the court.

Statement of Prisoner

"I was picked up by the enemy's scouts between Petersburg and Richmond, I claimed to be a Yankee Deserter after I found that I was caught. I arrived in Kentucky with another man and was advised by several persons to go and give myself up as a rebel deserter and was advised the same after I arrived in Lexington, to take the oath in order to get released from prison. I gave my name as Wood in Richmond, that is my right name. I was told to give the name of Lynch by those who enlisted me. When I enlisted, I was drugged in Boston and from there was taken to Portsmouth, New Hampshire I did not know what was going on until I reached the latter place. I had no idea of enlisting. On arriving there, I was threatened if I did not enlist I would suffer before I left Portsmouth. I thought it safer to enlist and escape from their hands. Those who enlisted me were men styling themselves "brokers." They induced me to believe that I would get $1,000.00 or $1,300.00, but I never received more than $100.00, which was taken away from me in the Camp at Concord, New Hampshire. I was acting sergeant of the barracks there for some time.

(signed) John Wood."

The Court deliberated, confirmed the plea of guilty by the accused and sentenced him to be hung by the neck until he be dead.

Tried at the same court session were Privates George Bradley alias George W. Baker Company H, 5th New Hampshire Infantry Regiment and William Miller alias James Craig Company F, 5th New Hampshire Infantry Regiment both charged with deserting to the enemy and also found guilty. All three were sentenced to be executed by hanging on December 23, 1864 near Fort Wheaton near Petersburg, Virginia.

Also see Case #175 George Bradley and Case #178 William Miller.

REFERENCES:
Military Personnel Records, RG-#94
Court Martial Proceedings, RG-#153 NN 3098

Case #178
Pvt. William Miller
AKA: James Craig
Co. F, 5th New Hampshire Vol. Inf.
Hung for Desertion
December 23, 1864

DESCRIPTION:

Born in Canada, 20 years of age, blue eyes, brown hair, complexion florid, 5 feet, 1¾ inches tall, literacy undetermined, occupation Seaman, Dyer.

William Miller was a substitute for Romanzo Cressey of Chesterfield, New Hampshire and was paid $200.00, although he stated other substitutes were paid as much as $1,100.00.

He was drafted and mustered in at West Lebanon, New Hampshire on September 3, 1864 and was sent with a replacement draft to City Point, Virginia where on September 10, 1864 was assigned to Company F, 5th New Hampshire Voluntary Infantry Regiment which was on duty in the trenches before Petersburg, Virginia.

On October 10, 1864, he absented himself without authority from his company and was dropped from the Company rolls as a deserter on October 15, 1864. He was arrested in Louisa, Kentucky and returned to City Point, Virginia on November 20th, under arrest for deserting to the enemy.

A General Court Martial was convened at City Point, Virginia and on December 16, 1864 tried Private William Miller, Company F, 5th New Hampshire Infantry Regiment on a charge of deserting to the enemy.

Testimony by witnesses showed that the accused enlisted as a substitute on September 3, 1864 and he joined the Regiment on September 10, 1864 near Petersburg, Virginia. The accused absented himself without authority on October 10, 1864 and was declared a deserter.

Witnesses declared the Articles of War had been read to the prisoner for certain at least once and possibly twice. One witness, when asked if the Rebel War Department G.O. #65 was generally known in the Regiment, replied that some men surely knew of it, but the witness had no way of knowing if the accused was aware of it.

Another witness, who was captured by the rebels testified that he saw the accused at Abingdon, Virginia about the 16/17 of October or November 1864 on their way to Pound Gap, the entrance into Kentucky. The accused went directly to Lexington while the majority of men went first to Louisa, Kentucky where they were then transferred to Lexington, Kentucky for interviews and processing. At Lexington, the accused was seen to take the Oath of Allegiance to the U.S. having successfully convinced the Army authorities that he was a Confederate Army deserter. The certificate, made out in the alias the accused had adopted, James Craig, was produced in Court and the signatures identified.

The accused having no other defense to offer presented a statement to the Court.

Statement of the Prisoner

"I was boarding with a man in Quebec, Canada who brought me to this country, for the purpose of joining the Navy, at least that was the promise. I am a sea faring man. At West Lebanon, N.H. I was told to ask two hundred dollars for bounty, and I found out later that some others got eleven hundred dollars ($1,100.00). I enlisted with the expectation of joining the Navy and I spoke about it after enlisting and was told I could get transferred into the Navy, instead of which I was sent to the Army near Petersburg. After leaving Camp, I was picked up by two Rebel Scouts. It was useless to try and get away from them. I never was in the Army before, I have only been about four months in the country. The man who enlisted me gave my name as William Miller, which is my right name. I never gave the name of Craig until after I left the Regiment.

(signed) William Miller"

The Court then deliberated, found the accused guilty and sentenced him to be hanged by the neck until he be dead.

The sentence was executed on December 24, 1864 near Fort Wheaton, Virginia.

REFERENCES:

Military Personnel Records, RG-#94

Military Court Martial Proceedings, RG-#153 NN 3098

Case #179

Pvt. John Murray

Unassigned 11th IND Cavalry Regt.

Executed for Desertion

December 23, 1864

DESCRIPTION:

27 years of age, 5 feet 5¾ inches tall, black hair, black eyes, fair complexion, born in Dublin, Ireland, occupation laborer, illiterate.

Murray enlisted and was mustered into service on November 22, 1864 at Lafayette, Indiana as an unassigned recruit for the 11th Indiana Cavalry Regiment. He and another soldier named Doyle deserted together after one night at the Cavalry Camp, leaving camp on a train from Lafayette to Indianapolis. Both men were arrested on the train and taken to Indianapolis where they were charged with desertion and incarcerated.

Murray and Doyle had been shipmates on Doyles brother's Canadian registered ship (he being the Captain) which plied the Great Lakes. The pair left ship in Chicago, went to Indianapolis and enlisted in the 11th Indiana Cavalry. Murray, at first, denied that Murray was not his true name, but under questioning finally admitted his name was Maloney, but had used the name Murray after his widowed mother had remarried a man named Murray. Murray is said to have been an old practitioner of bounty jumping and a generally hard and reckless person.

(For the details of the execution see Case #174 Billingsley.

A General Court Martial was convened at Indianapolis, Indiana and on December 6, 1864 tried Private John Murray, unassigned, 11th Indiana Cavalry Regiment on a charge of desertion.

Testimony given the Court showed that the accused, Thomas Doyle (another defendant) and a George Thompson were drinking together in Lafayette, Indiana on November 22, 1864 at a saloon called the "9 Bramble House." The Bar Keeper asked them if they would enlist in the Army. All three finally consented to enlist and were taken by the bar keeper's partner and the person who paid them their bounty ($400.00) to a hotel where they instructed the three candidates on what to do and what to say at the mustering office. They went to the mustering office, were examined by the surgeon and passed, and were not further questioned but mustered into the military service with seven or eight other men. On the following day, November 23, 1864, they were sent to Camp Carrington near Indianapolis, Indiana and issued a complete Army uniform except an overcoat. They were allowed to retain their citizens overcoats. They had arrived in Camp Carrington about 10 AM and left (deserted) at 8 or 9 o'clock that same evening. In their recruit detachment at the camp were two gamblers from New York who had citizen's clothing on under their uniforms. One of the gamblers gave one of the deserters a citizen's coat and he removed his uniform and left it on his bunk.

The two New Yorkers and the three others deserted together. The night was cold and dark the guards more interested in clustering about a roaring campfire than stopping deserters. All five simply walked out of camp and eventually boarded a railroad train where Murray and Doyle were arrested.

The accused had no witnesses to bring before the Court but did offer a statement to the Court.

Gentlemen of the Court Martial

"I came from the city of Chicago with another man; we were going down to the river to get work on a Steam boat during the winter. We got as far as Lafayette, Ind. and all my money was spent and I could not go on. The man who was with me went on and I remained at Lafayette where I met with Thompson and Doyle and another man. We all went into the saloon at the Bramble House to get something to drink and then we went down and enlisted. After I had got my bounty there was a man there who wanted me to gamble with him which I did and he won from me two hundred and forty dollars. I was drunk at the time and it was he that coaxed me out of the camp that night. He said he would give me back half the money he had won from me if I would go out with him. We got some whisky and he got me drunk and I did not know where I was going to and the first thing I knew I was arrested, I never had any intention of deserting at all, This is all I have to say in the case."

John Murray - Private

11th Regt. Ind. Cav."

The Court deliberated, found the accused guilty and sentenced him to be shot to death with musketry.

The execution took place on December 23, 1864 on the Parade Ground at Burnside Barracks near Camp Morton, Indianapolis, Indiana.

REFERENCES:

Military Personnel Records, RG-#94

Court Martial Proceedings, RG-#153 II 523

See other references in Case #174 Billingsley.

Case #180

Pvt. Thomas Ryan

AKA: Thomas Reagan, John Hanrahan

Unassigned 51st, Ind. Infantry Regt.

Executed for Desertion

December 23, 1864

DESCRIPTION:

No military Personnel Records are available from either National Archives or State of Indiana Archives. Meager descriptions are available, most from newspaper sources.

Ryan enlisted in the 51st Indiana Infantry Regiment under the name of Reagan, stated he received $433.50 as bounty for enlisting. He deserted the evening of his arrival at camp by bribing a camp guard with $10.00 to allow him to leave to get his supper. He was arrested at the railway station with a railroad ticket for Chicago in his pocket. He, at first, denied ever enlisting or deserting but finally admitted the crime. He later boasted of enlisting and deserting for the bounty on over 30 occasions. Ryan, using aliases of Reagan and Hanrahan, said he was from Roundout, New York and since the age of nine had been employed on the Canal. Ryan and two other men and a man named Burns, described as an agent for deserters, came from Roundout, New York where Burns had first made his acquaintanceship. Burns is said to have told Ryan that he had worked hard enough and long enough and could make eight or nine hundred dollars bounty by enlisting in the army and that I could get away easily and he told him to use the name Thomas Reagan. The detective who arrested Ryan asked Burns if he had brought them there and also told Burns if he did not do the square thing he would arrest them. Burns told him to go ahead and arrest him, which he did. The detective who arrested them allowed Burns to remain free but upon delivering Ryan and his companions to jail, was ordered to bring Burns in for questioning. The detective obliged by sharing a supper of oysters with Burns and then escorted him to the 4:00 AM train to leave town. Burns was reported to have paid the detective $80.00-$100.00 to let him escape.

Ryan eventually admitted bounty-jumping many times. It was the opinion of those who observed Ryan that he was both a hardened criminal and gang member.

A General Court Martial was convened at Indianapolis, Indiana and on December 3rd, 1864 tried Private Thomas Ryan, unassigned, 51st Indiana Regiment on a charge of Desertion.

Testimony stated Ryan deserted from the 51st Indiana Infantry Regiment on or about October 22, 1864 at or near Indianapolis, Indiana and went to Cincinnati, Ohio and enlisted as a substitute in October (day unknown) 1864. He was arrested and returned to Indiana where he was tried together with Private Charles Billingsley, 7th Indiana Battery, Private Thomas Doyle, unassigned, 11th Indiana Cavalry Regiment, and Private John Murray, unassigned, 11th Indiana Cavalry Regiment.

Ryan was found guilty and sentenced to be shot to death with musketry on December 23, 1864 on the parade grounds of the Burnside Barracks near Camp Morton, Indianapolis, Indiana.

For description of the execution and other subsequent events, see Case #174 Billingsley.

REFERENCES:

See references under Case #174 Billingsley, as there are no Military Personnel Records at National Archives nor in the State of Indiana Military records on Thomas Ryan.

Case #181
Private Larkin W. Rhea
NV: Ray
Co. D, 7th KY Inf. Regt.
Executed for Murder
December 24, 1864
However probably 12/30/64
correct date

DESCRIPTION:

19 years of age, 5 feet 8 inches tall, light hair, light eyes, light complexion, born in Hawkin's County, Tennessee, occupation farmer, illiterate.

Rhea enlisted on August 19, 1861 at London, Kentucky, and was mustered into service at Camp Dick Robinson, Kentucky on September 22, 1861 in Captain McNeill's Company, 3rd Regiment Kentucky Volunteers. The unit designation was later changed to Company C, 3rd Regiment Kentucky Volunteers and again to Company C, 7th Regiment Kentucky Infantry. On March 17, 1864, several Companies and the 19th

Regiment Kentucky Infantry were consolidated with Company C, becoming (New) Company D, 7th Regiment Kentucky Infantry.

Rhea deserted near Raymond, Mississippi on May 11, 1863 and was captured by the Confederates at Jackson, Mississippi on May 12, 1863 and sent to Richmond, Virginia for confinement on May 16, 1863. He was paroled at City Point, Virginia on May 23, 1863 and was received at Camp Parole, Maryland on May 25, 1863. He was then placed in Company F, 2nd Battalion Paroled Prisoners, U. S. Army at Camp Chase, Ohio. This organization was formed from Paroled Prisoners of War for duty compatible with their parole and were returned to their original commands as soon as practicable. By the period November/December, 1863, he was returned to Company C, 7th Regiment Kentucky Infantry stationed at Baton Rouge, Louisiana, and was Court Martialed for desertion. The verdict acquitted Rhea of the charge, with reinstatement in his Company with full pay.

On October 5, 1864, he completed his period of Military service and re-enlisted as a Veteran Volunteer. On December 2, 1864, while with his Regiment at Baton Rouge, Louisiana, Rhea murdered the 19th Kentucky Regimental Surgeon, Dr. William K. Sadler, aged 28 years, of Oxford, Ohio. Rhea was arrested and charged with murder.

A General Court Martial was convened at Baton Rouge, Louisiana and on December 5, 1864 tried Private Larkin Rhea, Company C, 7th Kentucky Infantry Regiment on charges of murder, assault and battery with intent to kill, conspiring, aiding and abetting, and attempting to commit murder.

Rhea asked for and received permission to introduce Captains Hogg and Stephens of the 7th Kentucky Infantry as his counsels.

Witnesses testified that on or about 8 PM on December 2, 1864 in the Sun Billiard Room in Baton Rouge, Louisiana a group of five officers were conversing when a young man, later identified as Roarch, in an enlisted soldiers uniform, came up to them and said, "he did not care a God Damn for any citizen, officer or soldier." He and another enlisted man had been interfering with the billiard players by seizing the billiard balls and rolling and throwing them about the tables. Surgeon Sadler came up to them and told them to desist disturbing those playing. No one had spoken to him at the time he made the unsolicited remark. Another soldier, also later identified as Rhea, then stepped up and said, "he did not wish to see anyone imposed upon, that he would not stand it." He was advised that if he took his friend to his quarters there would be no imposition. Rhea seemed to be sober and Roarch quite drunk. They were both further advised that if they remained and continued quarreling they would be in trouble. Roarch then said to a Lieutenant Roberts, "I am an officer and a 1st Lieutenant by God, I don't think you are an Officer." To which Roberts replied, "You say I am not an Officer." Roarch replied, "That's what I think." Lieutenant Roberts grabbed Roarch by the coat collar and dragged him out of the Billiard room. As Roberts ejected Roarch, Rhea threw a half brick, which he had concealed on his person, at the Lieutenant. Rhea then approached the Lieutenant and said the man ejected was a friend of his and no one could abuse his friend while he was around. Roberts reply was that if he insulted him (Roberts) he'd be treated in the same way. Rhea replied he didn't think he could. Whereupon Roberts grabbed Rhea, and marched him out of the billiard room. One of the two loudly remarked that they would "get square" with Roberts for what had occurred. The five Officers left the premises about 5-10 minutes later, and as they sauntered along the sidewalk, noted two men across the street who were observing them. It was believed that the two men were Rhea and Roarch.

About 10-15 minutes after the five Officers left, Rhea and Roarch returned to the billiard room armed with bayoneted rifles. And as the door had been locked by the proprietor, pounded on the door, with their rifle butts, for entrance. Fearing damage, the proprietor unbolted the door. A Dr. W. K. Sadler, Surgeon in Chief of the Military District of Baton Rouge and Port Hudson, was present together with Mr. P. Billiard, owner of the Sun Billiard Saloon, and Mr. W. W. Edwards, a citizen of Baton Rouge. One soldier stood inside the entrance to the billiard room while the other approached Dr. Sadler who was seated at a table. Dr. Sadler asked, "What's the matter, what do you want?" "We are Provost Guard" was the answer. W. W. Edward started to leave but was halted when both men leveled their guns at him. Dr. Sadler spoke up, "You don't know who you are speaking to." The two soldiers, later identified as Rhea and Roarch, then ordered Dr. Sadler to leave the room as they were going to shoot him, he refused to go. Dr. Sadler continued to question the soldier. "Was he drunk? Was he a guard? What was his military unit? What did he mean by pointing his gun at him (Sadler)?" To all of his queries he answered, "none of your business." At about this point Rhea shot him. Both men fled the premises, as did Mr. Edwards. Dr. Sadler wrapped his arms about the trunk of his body groaning and staggering half bent over. Sadler was assisted to seat himself in a chair. A surgeon Charles Dean, 2nd Louisiana Infantry, was passing the premises and heard the shot fired, he went in to investigate, ran to the billiard parlor, saw Dr. Sadler who died about five minutes after Surgeon Dean arrived. The wound was described as entering the left side, passing through the hip bone and the abdomen, exiting at the right front of the abdomen. Sadler was wrapped in blankets and carried to his boarding house.

The defense declined to present any evidence or statements. The Court then deliberated, found Rhea guilty and sentenced him to be hung by the neck until dead.

The execution took place on the Commons, one mile east of the City of Baton Rouge, Louisiana on December 24, 1864.

The records are not concise nor do they agree on the date of execution. The Official List states December 24, 1864 while the majority of other report sources indicate the 30th as the date. This is most logical as documents indicate a change of overall command in a number of telegrams exchanged and dated December 28, 1864. General Benton was personally charged with the overall responsibility of Rhea's execution. When he was relieved of command and replaced by Brigadier General George L. Andrews, the original order became inoperative. A telegram from Major General Hurlbut's Assistant Adjutant General on the 28th of December, 1864 stated that General Andrews was charged with the execution of Private Rhea. No mention of the 29th of December, 1864 appears anywhere in the documents on this case and it would be logical to assume that the 30th of December, 1864 would be correct as it would provide enough time for the newly arrived General to issue necessary orders for the execution.

REFERENCES:

Military Personnel Records, RG-#94
Court Martial Proceedings, RG-#153
Also see Case #190, Private Lewis Roarch.

Case #182
Pvt. James F. Brown
Co. G, 3rd NH Infantry Regt.
Executed for Desertion
December 26, 1864

DESCRIPTION:

23 years of age, 5 feet 5¼ inches tall, brown hair, blue eyes, light complexion, born in Lancaster, New Hampshire, occupation teamster.

James F. Brown was enlisted and mustered into service at Concord, New Hampshire on December 2, 1863 and assigned to the 3rd New Hampshire Infantry Regiment, Company G. A difficulty exists in accurately recording his service record as there was in Company G, 3rd New Hampshire Infantry Regiment, another enlisted man, *John F. Brown* and over the years there had occurred some intermingling of their service records. On June 24-25, 1864, *James F. Brown* deserted his Regiment near Wilson's Landing, Virginia and was subsequently apprehended in the ranks of the 47th New York Infantry Regiment. *James*

F. Brown was arrested, confined and tried by court martial for desertion.

On December 20, 1864, a General Court Martial was assembled at the Headquarters of the 1st Division, 24th Army Corps in the field at which Private James F. Brown, Company G, 3rd New Hampshire Infantry Regiment was tried for desertion.

Testimony disclosed that Brown had entered the service of the 3rd New Hampshire Infantry Regiment in July or August, 1861 and been discharged for disability in April or May of 1862. He subsequently volunteered to re-enter the Regiment in December, 1863 at Morris Island, South Carolina. On duty with the 3rd New Hampshire Regiment on June 25, 1864, he and another soldier were sent to secure water while the Regiment was at Wilcox Landing, Virginia. Brown was not seen again until December 18, 1864 when he was arrested at Laurel Hill, Virginia as a member of the 47th New York Infantry Regiment under the assumed name of James Barrett. Brown had enlisted in New York City and been sent (along with 87 others) as a substitute recruit under the assumed name of James Barrett to the 47th New York Infantry Regiment. His 47th New York Inf. Regt. records indicate the name James Barrett, drafted into service December 2, 1864 and ordered assigned to the 47th on December 8, 1864, arriving about December 15, 1864 at their camp near Laurel Hill, Virginia. Brown was recognized by one of the men of the 3rd New Hampshire, who had served with him. The 47th New York and the 3rd New Hampshire were encamped in the same area.

Brown was arrested and the testimony of members of the 3rd New Hampshire, who had known him before his desertion, confirmed his identity. Brown offered no defense but he did file a statement with the court.

Statement

"In the first place I knew nothing about enlisting in the N.Y. Regt. Another young man besides me was told how we were drugged and our bounty (enlistment money bonus) taken from us by brokers (substitute recruiters) of the city must have done it. So far as the desertion is concerned I had no intention whatsoever of leaving the regiment. We had leave to go after water. In search of it we lost our way back. there were a good many more rambling around through the woods at the same time and enquiring of some of them that were after water where the Regiment was they said they didn't know, anymore than we did, we traveled around until it got to be about dark and I told this fellow we had better lie down and not try to find it until morning. I think it was about 9-10 o'clock in the night we heard some horses coming. he said get up or they will run over us. so we roused up and they rode up and told us they wanted us, they wanted to know if we were yankees and we told them. They said they wanted us to go with them. We started and we walked about 3 miles. As we were going along I dodged out into a bush. I staid there about 15 minutes. Three (3) of them came back and went right by me and when they went by I kept in the bushes and I came to a small stream of water. I crossed it on a log. The next stream I came to was the Chickahominy River. I got to that river about dark the next night and went to a negro shanty and a boy rowed me across. The next river I came to was the York. There was a Schooner laying in the river. I went on board of the Schooner and asked them where they were going He said he was going to Boston. I asked him if I could get a passage with him. He asked me if I had any money. I told him I had not much only $2.17. He said I could go if I had a mind to work my passage. I went with him. I went with him to Boston."

The Court deliberated and found Brown guilty. He was sentenced to be executed by a firing squad on December 26, 1864 near his division encampment.

REFERENCES:

Military Personnel Records, RG-#94

Court Martial Proceedings, RG-#153 NN 3171

Personal letter from M.E. Pilgrim, National Archives, Re: John F. Brown and James F. Brown records.

Case #183
Pvt. Michael Genan
NV: Genow, Jenos, John Martin
Co B, 5th New Hampshire Inf Regt
Executed for Desertion
December 30, 1864

DESCRIPTION:

21 years of age, 5 feet 3¾ inches tall, brown hair, gray eyes, florid complexion, born in St. Paul, Canada, occupation farmer, substitute, illiterate.

Genan enlisted and was mustered in as a substitute on September 7, 1864 at Concord, New Hampshire and assigned to Company B, 5th New Hampshire Infantry Regiment stationed in the Petersburg/ Virginia area. While on picket duty, near Petersburg, Virginia on October 15, 1864, Genan deserted his duty post and entered the enemy lines. He remained absent until arrested at Lexington, Kentucky on November 20, 1864. Genan was returned, under guards, to City Point, Virginia where he was confined.

A General Court Martial was convened at City Point, Virginia and on December 20, 1864 proceeded to the trial of Pvt. Michael Genan, Company B, 5th New Hampshire Infantry Regiment on the charge of "Deserting to the Enemy."

The court appointed an interpreter for Genan (language not specified) as he spoke little English.

Testimony presented portrayed the following chain of events.

Genan, a substitute, arrived at Petersburg, Virginia during September, 1864 in company with some 400 other replacements, for the most part substitutes. On or about October 15, 1864 Genan deserted from his post as a sentinel on the picket line. It was mentioned that 16 other Union soldiers deserted at the same time. The distance between the Union and Rebel picket outposts was only on an average about 200 yards. Genan was said to have stated that he left his gun at the guard post and ran over to the Confederate lines and surrendered. He was taken to Petersburg, Virginia and then to Richmond, Virginia, at each place stating he was a Yankee deserter. At Richmond, he was confined at Castle Lightning (a Confederate prisoner of war place of confinement) for four days and then taken, under guard, to Pound Gap, Virginia, where he was released. He made his way to Louisa, Kentucky and reported to the Provost Marshall, whom he told he was a southern citizen. He was sent to the local prison in Louisa for eleven days and then taken to Lexington, Kentucky. From the latter place he was sent to City Point, Virginia via Washington, D.C. arriving there on November 20, 1864. Genan used the alias of John Martin in some of his interrogation sessions.

At one point in Genan's questioning by the examining Officer of Prisoners while confined at the Provost Marshall's in Lexington, Kentucky, Genan stated that he was from Abingdon, Virginia, and had enlisted in Col. Prentice's Command (a Confederate cavalry unit) and served about three weeks when he deserted. Genan related a sorry tale as he was unfamiliar with the Abingdon, Virginia, area or the Rebel cavalry.

Genan offered no defense during his trial nor any statement although he did question some of the prosecution witnesses.

The court deliberated, found Genan guilty and sentenced him to be hung at City Point, Virginia. The execution was carried out on December 30, 1864.

REFERENCES:

Military Personnel Records, RG-#94
Court Martial Proceedings, RG-#153 LL 2888

1865
"Capital Offenses Decline as the Army Demobilizes"

Cases #184 - #263
(80 Executions)

Case #184
Private John Foster
Unassigned, 58th Penn Vol Inf Regt
Executed for Desertion
January 3, 1865

DESCRIPTION:

19 years of age, 5 feet 9⅞ inches tall, blue eyes, brown hair, dark complexion, born in Hamilton, Ontario, Canada, occupation horseman, substitute, literacy undetermined.

Foster was a substitute for a William E. McCall of Plula, Pennsylvania and was enlisted at Philadelphia, Pennsylvania on November 18, 1864. He was sent to the 58th Pennsylvania Regiment of Infantry. Little is discovered about him safe that he was not assigned to a specific Company within the regiment prior to his desertion and capture.

A General Court Martial was convened at Fort Monroe, Virginia, and on December 8, 1864 proceeded to the trial of Pvt. John Foster, 58th Pennsylvania Volunteers unassigned, charged with desertion.

(The testimony at the trial was interwoven with that of the case of Sergeant William Johnson, 21st V.R.C. as they were involved with one another in their respective offenses.)

Foster was mustered into the service of the United States at Philadelphia, Pennsylvania on November 19, 1864 as a substitute and received a bounty of $300.00. Foster arrived at Bermuda Hundred on or about the 21st of November, 1864 and promptly made an attempt to desert. He left the recruit reception depot, Camp Distribution and went aboard the Steamer Thomas Collyer where he spent the night. He bribed Sgt. Johnson, giving the money ($100.00) to one of his associates, to get him aboard the Collyer for its return to Philadelphia. The scheme involved Sgt. Johnson placing Foster among his guard unit members and getting them aboard ship., Unfortunately for Foster, Johnson was not sincere in his effort to provide the service for which he was paid. Johnson's intent was to collect the money and then to denounce Foster as a deserter just before the ship reached City Point, Virginia, have him arrested and taken off. The scheme back fired as both Johnson and Foster were arrested and tried. Foster testified at Johnson's trial and was instrumental in securing Johnson's conviction. Foster offered no defense or final statement.

The Court deliberated, found Foster guilty and sentenced him to be executed by a firing squad.

He and Johnson were executed together at Bermuda Hundred on January 8, 1865.

For additional details, see Sergeant William G. Johnson, 21st V.R.C. Case # *185.*

REFERENCES:

Military Record File, RG-#94
Court Martial Proceedings, RG-#153 NN 3426

Case #185
Cpl./Pvt./Sgt. William G. Johnson
NV: Johnston
Co. F, 21st Veteran Reserve Corps
Executed for Desertion
January 3, 1865

DESCRIPTION:

22 years of age, 5 feet 8 inches tall, eyes blue, hair light, complexion light, born Londonderry, Ireland, occupation bookkeeper (he signed his name as Johnston not Johnson), literate.

Johnson re-enlisted in the Veteran Reserve Corps on March 31, 1864 at Washington, D.C. where his infirmity was stated as "ORCHITIS" (an infection of the testicles most frequently caused by the gonococcus, cause of gonorrhea) sarcocele and varicocele are also genital afflictions. He had been originally mustered into service on October 31, 1861 at Philadelphia, Pennsylvania in Company D, 2nd Pennsylvania Heavy Artillery Regiment. Upon expiration of service he enlisted in Company F, 21st Regiment Invalid Corps which designation was changed to Company F, 21st Regiment Veteran Reserve Corps.

His principal duty in his last period of service was to take charge of escort details which delivered recruits to various commands, usually by railroad.

A General Court Martial was convened at Fort Monroe, Virginia and on December 8, 1864, proceeded to the trial of Sergeant William G. Johnson, 21st Veteran Reserve Corps on the charge of "persuading and advising another soldier to desert the service of the United States."

Testimony offered at the trial traced the relationship of a new soldier, Pvt. John Foster, a substitute assigned to the 58th Pennsylvania Regiment and Johnson.

Johnson was on duty as the Sergeant in charge of a party of recruits being brought to Bermuda Hundred, Virginia on board government transport.

The detachment of recruits were delivered to Camp Distribution, Virginia (a replacement assignment camp) and Johnson returned to the wharf at Bermuda Hundred. The testimony from this point on is long, repetitious and convoluted. The case against Johnson was well stated in the charge, as follows: "Sergeant William G. Johnson, 21st Veterans Reserve Corps, did willfully advise and persuade Pvt. John Foster 58th Penn. Vols. a soldier lately enlisted as a substitute in the service of the United States, to desert the service, and did receive a bribe of one hundred dollars therefor and did, in pursuance of this object, willfully permit the said Pvt. Foster, 58th Penn. Vols. to come aboard the transport Thomas Collyer, starting from Bermuda Hundred, for the purpose of unlawfully transporting him to Philadelphia, Pennsylvania, on or about the 22nd day of November, 1864."

Johnson and several associates, conspired to extract bribes of $100 each from two soldiers, Foster and Frederick Bouden an unassigned recruit. Foster left camp distribution after being reported in, as he said the tent (to which he was assigned) was filled with mud and water. He went back to the wharf and boarded the Thomas Collyer and persuaded the boat Sergeant to permit him to sleep in one of the state rooms for a dollar or two. In the morning the boat was cleared of all non-operating persons and Johnson brought a guard detail on board which contained Foster and Bouden among its members. The guard was being returned to Philadelphia.

Johnson's statement rather well describes his crime and his betrayal of the naive bribers.

"Statement in Defense"

I left Philadelphia with a detachment of Substitutes under charge of Capt. Riley & Lieut. Johnson of the 187th Pa. Vols. We arrived at Baltimore by the train and came from there to Bermuda Hundred on the Transport Gen. Meigs. We started Friday afternoon and arrived at Bermuda Hundred on the afternoon of the 21st, with 89 substitutes all together. We turned them over to the proper officer there and got a receipt for them. We started back to the boat and stayed there all night. In the boat I applied to the Captain for a berth. I got a state room and Hermon (one of his associates) and I slept there all night. The next morning I saw Foster and Cherry (another of his associates) talking together and I suspected Foster wanted to get back on the boat. I asked Cherry about it, and at first, refused to tell me. Afterwards he told me that Foster did want to get back. I told Cherry we will manage this affair so as to get his money and then we will deliver him to the Provost at City Point. Cherry took me to his state room. And there he told me he would give fifty dollars. I told him, I would not do it for fifty, but if he would make it a hundred, I would try and do it.

Afterwards he met me and told me he would give the hundred dollars. Afterwards I saw the Sergeant of the boat, as I would not do it on my own risk, I told him I would give fifty dollars if he would pass him with these men as a part of my guard, and then have them arrested at City Point and confined. He told me he would do it, under those circumstances. I stood at the gangway and they were passed on, and the Sergt. knew they were passed on.

A little while after the Lieut. came to me and told me he believed some of his men (recruits) were aboard the boat. I said there are two men who have offered me one hundred dollars to put them aboard the boat. I said we have got them aboard the boat, said I, we have got them there and the Sergt. of the boat is to deliver them to be confined at City Point. I don't know whether the Lieut. made any remark or not, he told me to call the roll. I got my sword on one side and then I pointed out the two men and gave them in charge of the Lieut. But a little before, I had received one hundred dollars from Cherry. I went to one of my comrades and asked if he could change a hundred dollar bill. He said he could not. I asked if he could lend me fifty dollars till I got to Philadelphia. He said yes, and gave me a new fifty dollar bill which I determined to give to the Sergt. of the boat. The other hundred dollars was left to be divided between Hermon and Cherry. I could not find Cherry when we started, to give it to him, but I saw the Lieut. and went to Cherry and got the other hundred dollars from him and went with him to the Provost Marshall's office.

Before I got off the boat I said to the Lieut. I thought I would not get off that day and asked leave to get my blanket. Said he, you need not mind, we will send you down to City Point in a tug, the boat stops there an hour. I went up to the Provost Marshall's and told the tale just as I tell it here. He would not believe it, and we were put in the guard house. My honest thoughts and actions would have been, they may not have been honest towards the men, but would have been towards the government, would have been to hand them over at City Point. Because I believe it is right to take the money of a man who will offer to desert, and turn him over.

My commanding officer, the Adjt. Gen. has instructed us in Camp, if men offer money, to take the money and immediately report them. It has been done in several instances. We had one man shot for the same thing. The kind of duty we are on is a duty that requires men to be wide awake and know what they are about.

If this is a bribe, it is the first time. I didn't look at it in that light; because I didn't intend to let the men go.

That is about the sum and substance of all I have to say."

The court deliberated, found the accused guilty and sentenced him to death by musketry.

One interesting observation is the consistent advice by the Judge Advocate to the witnesses that it was his privilege to decline answering any questions which might incriminate him. In the file of the Court Martial Proceedings are several letters attesting to the character of Sgt. Johnson.

Camp Cadwalader, Pennsylvania
December 7, 1864
"Dear Johnson,

Enclosed please find a document, which may be of use to you, if you are court martialed, and need further testimony, call on me for a witness, I am sorry you are in the scrape and my being so far from you, prevents me from doing much for you, but keep up your spirits - for all will be well yet—"

"Yours
Harry Rockafeller,
Captain—"

Camp Cadwalader, Pennslyvania
December 7, 1864

"To whom it may concern,

I beg leave to bear witness as to the good character, of Sergt. Wm. Johnson and Privates Cherry and Hermann, of Co. F, 21st Regt. V.R.C., since they have been under my command, I have always found them to be, good, honest, faithful soldiers, ready and willing to obey and execute any order given them. I have never had occasion to reprimand them for a single fault, and can only regret to find them in their present position. Pvt. Cherry's time of service expired on Nov. 23, 1864." I am sir

"Very respectfully
your obt. servant
Harry Rockafellar
Capt. Com'd., Co. F, 21st V.R.C."

Foster's trial followed the same general line of testimony.

Both Johnson and Foster were executed together on January 8, 1865 at Bermuda Hundred, Virginia before a firing squad.

Some correspondence between Judge Advocate General Holt and Headquarters Department of Virginia is of interest. On December 21, 1864 General Benjamin Butler stated, "Sentence approved and will be executed at Bermuda Hundred in view of all the employees and troops there within 48 hours after this order is received."

A letter from Judge Advocate General Holt on January 30, 1865 read as follows:

"Respectfully returned to the Commander of the Dept. of VA. The sentence in this case, death, cannot legally be executed until approved by the President. It would seem from the endorsement of Major Genl. Butler that it has been already carried out. Information upon this point is desired.
J. Holt, Judge Advocate General"

On February 8, 1865 a reply was sent to General Holt,

"Respectfully returned to the Judge Advocate General. It appears from the report of Bvt. Major Gen'l Ferrero, Comdg. defenses of Bermuda Hundred, on file at these Headquarters that the sentence in case of these men was executed January 8, 1865."
Ord - Maj Genl Comdg

A soldier of the 2nd Pennsylvania Heavy Artillery Regiment in writing to his mother comments about Johnston's execution. "I was to the execution of two deserters this morning at the hour of Ten O'clock before they was shot. One was a Sargent in Company D of our Regiment. he was captured at Fort Eathen Allen and then he went into the Invalid Corps and then he was discharged when his time was up and enlisted in some other Pennsylvania Regiment and then he deserted over to the enemy and then got a rebel suit and come back to our lines again. Then he was tooken up he let several deserters go while he was on guard. They marched arround the hollow square which the division formed. They did not seem to take it hard a tall. They had no remarks to make as I herd of. They set on their coffins at the foot and the cofins laid side their graves. They both were shot by 12 men. 1 half blanck cartriges. Then after they was shot the chaplin of our regiment give a sermon but I did not hear it. We was marched back to camp about a mile and a half."

A letter in his Military record file from his Commanding Officer, Captain Harry Rockafeller, Company F, 21st Regiment Veterans Reserve Corps to General Ferrero, Army of the James, Bermuda Hundreds, Virginia inquired: "General, I understand, unofficially, that Sergt. Wm Johnson of my company, was executed by sentence of Genl. court martial, in your Department January 3, 1865, will you please officially inform me of the facts in his case, and what dispositon was made of his effects, as I have been called on by his mother for the facts, and have so far been unable to obtain them. I am sir, very respectfully,

Your obedient servant,
Harry Rockafellar
Capt. Comd. Co. F, 21st Regt. VRC"

His inventory of effects showed, as with almost all executed soldiers, none. A few contain a statement that the only effects were the clothing he was executed in or buried in.

REFERENCES:
Military Personnel Records, RG-#94
Court Martial Proceedings, RG-#153 NN 3426
Manuscript Division, Civil War soldiers' letters, Schoff Collection. Clements Library, University of Michigan, Ann Arbor, Michigan, Letter of Henry Pippitt.

Case #186
Pvt. John Benson
5th NH Infantry Regt.
Unassigned Recruit
Executed for Desertion
January 6, 1865

DESCRIPTION:
25 years of age, 5 feet 9 inches tall, brown hair, gray eyes, light complexion, born in Canada, occupation laborer, substitute.

Benson's records indicate he enlisted as a substitute and was mustered in on August 6, 1864 at West Lebanon, New Hampshire. About August 20, 1864, he and other replacements were forwarded to City Point, Virginia. Bradley's statement, following his apprehension for desertion takes up his military career at that point.

"John Benson, 5th N.H. Vols, I enlisted at White River Junction, near Concord, N.H.in the latter part of Sept. 1864. I rec'd $250.00 Bounty. We staid about a week in Concord and was then sent to City Point to join my Regt. but while the men were getting on the cars to go to the front, I and another got permission to go get some water, and while we were gone the cars left us, we were afraid of being put in the Bullpen, so we went out in the woods and staid all night. Next morning we started for Norfolk, Virginia, and when about 15 miles down we met 3 Rebel scouts, we started to run, and they killed a man named Williams who was with me: they then took me prisoner and robbed me of my boots and money, they then took me to Gen Fitz Hugh Lee, whom I told I was a Yankee deserter. He sent me to Petersburg and from there to Richmond. I was confined in both Castles Thunder and Lightening. I told them I was a Yankee deserter, I was taken from Richmond to Abbington and then I was taken with a squad to about 15 miles from Pound Gap and released. I then went to Louisa, Ky. I reported to the Pro. Mars. and told him to what Regt. I belonged, he sent me to Lexington (Ky.) and was sent from there to Washington."

Benson was arrested, confined and tried by court martial.

Private John Benson, unassigned recruit, 5th New Hampshire Infantry Regiment, was tried by a General Court Martial convened at City Point, Virginia on November 15, 1864 on the charge of desertion to the enemy.

Trial testimony revealed that Benson was among a large group of drafted men and substitutes sent as replacements to be assigned to various Regiments from City Point, Virginia. The replacements traveled by sea from New Hampshire (probably Portsmouth) to Fortress Monroe and City Point, Virginia where they debarked and were placed on railroad trains to reach their assigned regiments. The testimony reveals the magnitude of the desertion problem when a Lieutenant Colonel Crafts, witness for the prosecution stated that when the replacements arrived at the 5th New Hampshire Infantry Regiment, 130 of the men who were sent from Concord, New Hampshire had disappeared. At City Point, as the replacements were being loaded on the trains for their respective destinations, there were few guards to prevent their escape. The replacements took advantage of the situation by hiding behind or between buildings and railway cars. At their destination, Hancock's Station, Virginia the men left the railway cars, were placed in formations and the roll call was made, revealing a further absence, or loss of replacements, Benson amongst them.

Benson was arrested in Lexington, Kentucky in early November, 1864 and was wearing grey trousers and a light colored frock coat, not the U.S. Army blue uniform worn when he deserted. Benson was with a group of Union Army deserters who are claimed to be rebel deserters seeking sanctuary in the north.

One of the court's questions to a regimental enlisted man testifying for the prosecution, was whether the articles of War were read to replacements at the Camp in Concord, New Hampshire. The reply was that he had not known of this being done in New Hampshire but it was done after the men joined the regiment in the field.

Benson made a statement marked Exhibit A:

"Statement of the Prisoner"

I cannot tell my age exactly, but I think I am more than 22 or 23 years of age. I do not remember as giving my age as 25 years. I was taken from Canada to New Hampshire by a broker (substitute broker) and understood I was to be enlisted as a volunteer, and I found out when I came to Concord I was a substitute. I was under the influence of liquor when I enlisted and hardly knew what I was doing. I am a native of Wales and have been in Canada six years.

(signed) John "X" (his mark) Benson"

The court found Benson guilty of desertion (not deserting to the enemy) and sentenced him to be executed by musketry which took place on January 6, 1865 at City Point, Virginia.

REFERENCES:
Military Personnel Records, RG-#94
Court Martial Proceedings, RG-#153 LL 2924

Case #187
Pvt. (Sgt., Cpl.) Peter M. Cox
Co. A, 4th NJ Inf. Regt.
Executed for Desertion
January 6, 1865

DESCRIPTION:

38 years of age, no further physical description located.

Cox enlisted and was mustered into service on August 9, 1861 at Trenton, New Jersey as a Corporal in Company A, 4th New Jersey Infantry Regiment. During the period November/December, 1862, Cox was promoted to the rank of Sergeant and in December, 1862 was on Provost Guard duty in Philadelphia, Pennsylvania. He had the usual soldier experiences such as an illness requiring hospitalization at Washington, D. C. in the fall of 1862 following his capture and imprisonment in Richmond, Virginia for 40 days. Cox deserted the service after he had apparently been discharged to re-enlist as a Veteran Volunteer. When he was arrested for desertion he made a full statement which reads as follows.

"Peter M. Cox, 4th N. J. Vols. Co. A. I left my regiment on the last of March, it was then at Hazel River, near Brandy Station, Va. I left it to go home having received a Furlough for 30 days I live at Glouster, Camden Co. N. J. after my furlough had expired I was persuaded by a Canadian to go with him to Canada, I staid there about two months, and then hired on a vessel to go to St. Thomas, W.I. but instead of going there, the vessel run into Wilmington, N. C. I was in that place near 3 weeks. I gave myself to the Confederate Authorities, and told them I was a deserter from the Union Army but that I had no intention of coming in their lines. They then told me they would send me to Saulsbury and through again into our lines, I was sent from Wilmington to Saulsbury, where I met the other prisoners whom I am now with, we were all sent to Abbington, and from thence to Pound Gap, where the Confederate Guard Post is, we went to Louisa and reported to the Pro Mar, whom I told I was a citizen of Saulsbury I was sent with the rest on to Lexington and thence to City Point, via Washington.

Certified by Captain Shaw, Commanding Co. A,
4th NJ Vols
Col Ewing"

A General Court Martial convened at City Point, Virginia and on December 27, 1864 for the trial of Private Peter M. Cox, Company A, 4th New Jersey Infantry Regiment on the charge of deserting to the enemy.

Testimony of witnesses revealed that Cox had enlisted originally on September 1, 1861, had re-enlisted as a Veteran Volunteer on March 19, 1864 and left on the re-enlistment furlough of 30 days to which he was entitled. He left camp and went to Washington, D. C. where he was in the company of several members of his Regiment among whom was a man referred to only as Herbert. Cox left Washington, D. C. and went to his home in Gloucester, New Jersey to remain during his furlough. Unfortunately, he remained beyond the lawfully granted period of time and he was listed on his Company rolls as a deserter. Herbert, a Canadian, showed up and persuaded him to go to Canada with him, which he did remaining there about 2 months. He then hired on a ship as a crew member, the vessel destined for St. Thomas, Virgin Islands. The ship unexpectedly put in to Wilmington, Delaware and Cox left the ship and hid out in the city for three weeks until he surrendered to Rebel authorities. Cox was sent to Salisbury, North Carolina then to Abingdon, Virginia to Pound Gap where he was left free. He was picked up by Union Authorities taken to Louisa, Kentucky where he declared unsuccessfully under questioning that he was a citizen of Salisbury, North Carolina as he was dressed in civilian clothing. He was placed under arrest and sent to the Union Army Provost at Lexington, Kentucky then to Washington, D. C. and to City Point, Virginia where he arrived toward the end of November. Cox questioned some of the witnesses, as was his privilege, but offered no defense testimony of his own, except a written statement which the court accepted.

"Statement of Prisoner"

"I have a wife and family, and an aged mother, living in Gloucester, N. J. for whose support I have always worked, and endeavored to keep from want, I hope the court will extend mercy in, my case, as I had no intention of going to the enemy, but was deceived by those with me. I never heard of General Order, No. 65, Rebel War Dept. and was not aware, when at Wilmington, that there was such an order in existence. While going to Pound Gap I was robbed of my clothing, and had to wear what I could get. When the vessel put into Wilmington I expressed no desire of remaining there, nor of having wished to go there, and wished to be put back into our lines as soon as possible. When near Louisa, Kentucky, we met several different guards and could not be certain whether they were Union or Rebel soldiers. They would present their revolvers and demand who we were. Some of the guards gave us no satisfaction as to what they were. If I had had a chance to speak to the Provost Marshall at Louisa, Kentucky I intended to state my true character to him but could not get no opportunity, I gave my statement to Lieutenant Vance, at Lexington, Ky. as soon as I got there, giving my name, rank, company, and regiment and how I got to Lexington. Signed Peter M. Cox"

The Court deliberated and found Cox guilty and sentenced him to be shot to death with musketry. At City Point, Virginia on January 6, 1864, Cox was executed.

The execution was witnessed and commented on by a soldier writing to his parents.

"Friday, the 6th, the Whole division were called together to witness the execution of a private Soldier belonging to the 4th New Jersey of the 1st Brigade of our Division. He was sentenced to be shot at 12 AM he was brought in an ambulance in front of the Division and made to sit on his coffin near the grave. At a distance of about 10 paces were 12 men with loaded muskets only part of them having a ball in. After tying a handkerchief over his eyes, tying his hands & feet, the orders were read to all. Peter M. Cox was to be shot for desertion. After which the orders were to the guard to aim. Fire and he fell backward lifeless without a struggle the balls all entering the breast. the Surgeon pronounced life extinct. then the whole Division marched by to look at the corpse. I don't care to see another such a scene."

REFERENCES:
Military Personnel Records, RG-#94
Court Martial Proceedings, RG-#153 LL 2924
Manuscript Division, Civil War soldiers letters, Schoff Collection, Clements Library, University of Michigan, Ann Arbor, Michigan, letter of George H. Bates.

Case #188
Pvt. Charles King
Co. L, 3rd NJ Cavalry Regt.
Executed for Desertion
January 6, 1865

DESCRIPTION:

26 years of age, 5 feet 2 inches tall, light hair, hazel eyes, fair complexion, born in Wurtemburg, Germany, occupation machinist, literate.

King enlisted at Trenton, New Jersey on December 23, 1863 and was mustered into service at Trenton, New Jersey on March 24, 1864 in Company L, 3rd New Jersey Cavalry Regiment.

King's record file for March/April, 1864 states present but also contains a notation, "$30.00 for apprehension as a deserter to be stopped (withheld from his pay) and also (for) a pistol and belt." No other explanation of the desertion appears. In May/June, 1864 he is reported absent, dismounted. In July/August, 1864 he is reported absent sick and for September/October, 1864 absent, wounded. King, accompanied by Regley (same Company and Regiment) deserted on January 4, 1865. For details see Case #189 Regley.

They were both shot by order of Major General Philip Sheridan near Winchester, Virginia on January 6, 1865.

Private Charles King, Company L, 3rd New Jersey Cavalry Regiment was arrested on January 5, 1865 while attempting to desert and having given information to one of Major General Phillip H. Sheridan's Staff Officers concerning the location of General Sheridan's troops and all changes of troops with great accuracy, supposing the staff officer to be a rebel. Afterwards he replaced his union uniform with a rebel uniform.

General Sheridan ordered King to be shot to death at noon on Friday, January 6, 1865.

REFERENCES:
Military Personnel Records, RG-#94
Court Martial Proceedings, RG-#153 5453 A(eb) 1876

Case #189
Pvt. Henry Regley
NV: Regly, Rigle
Co. L, 3rd NJ Cavalry Regt.
Executed for Desertion, Treason, Spying
January 6, 1865

DESCRIPTION:

27 years of age, 5 feet 6 inches tall, brown hair, brown eyes, dark complexion, born in Switzerland, occupation clerk.

Regley apparently enlisted at Trenton, New Jersey and was mustered into service on

September 30, 1864 and assigned to Company L, 3rd New Jersey Cavalry Regiment and arrived for duty on October 1, 1864 at Bridgewater, Virginia.

On January 4, 1865, Regley and King (same Company and Regiment) did desert the Regiment near Winchester, Virginia and approached a small group of soldiers whom they presumed were rebels. They told one, whom they thought to be a rebel officer, the position of all Union troops in the area and indicated fully the changes in troop units. They further changed their Union Army uniforms for rebel uniforms. To their utter surprise, the "rebel officer" revealed that he was an officer on General Sheridan's staff and that they (Regley and King) were under arrest for desertion, treason and spying! Regley and King were shot near Winchester, Virginia by order of Major General Philip Sheridan on January 6, 1865 as spies.

See also case #188 King.

REFERENCES:
Military Personnel Records, RG-#94
Court Martial Proceedings, RG-#153 5453 A(EB) 1876

Case #190
Private Lewis Roarch
NV: Roark
Co. D, 7th KY Inf. Regt.
Executed for Murder
January 6, 1865

DESCRIPTION:

19 years of age, 5 foot 9 inches tall, black hair, black eyes, fair complexion, born in Clay County, Kentucky, occupation laborer, illiterate.

Roarch enlisted on August 19, 1861 at Booneville, Kentucky and was mustered into service on September 22, 1861 at Camp Dick Robinson in Captain Treadway's Company, 3rd Regiment, Kentucky Volunteers. The unit designation was changed several times, first to Company A, 3rd Regiment Kentucky Volunteers, then to Company A, 7th Regiment Kentucky Infantry. On December 24, 1864, a consolidation of several other Companies of the 7th Kentucky and the 19th Regiment Kentucky Infantry changed the unit designation to (New), Company D, 7th Kentucky Infantry Regiment. Roarch served with no recorded offenses for three years and reenlisted at Baton Rouge, Louisiana on the 17th day of March, 1864 as a Veteran Volunteer. The Regiment continued to be stationed in the Baton Rouge area. Late in 1864, Roarch deserted the Army, was arrested and tried by Court Martial.

A General Court Martial was convened at Baton Rouge, Louisiana and on December 8, 1864 tried Private Lewis Roarch, Company C, 7th Kentucky Infantry Regiment on charges of murder, conspiring, attempting and assisting to commit murder.

Roarch also requested Captains Hogg and Stephens to be admitted as his counsels (as Ray had) and the Court acquiesced.

The only difference between the cases of Rhea and Roarch was that Rhea fired the fatal shot and Roarch aided and abetted. The defense contended that Roarch was unaware of what Rhea intended to do and that he was not present when the shot was fired. The contention was that he was *outside* the room, not inside the room where the murder was committed.

The defense called witnesses who testified that Roarch was a good soldier, not a drunkard and had not been previously in trouble.

Counsels for Roarch offered a statement to the Court on the accused's behalf.

"May it please the court,

I desire to arrange and compare some of the evidence offered in this case, and to refer to some points of law having a bearing upon them. The evidence has in all material points agreed as to the identity of the accused, there is and has been no question. All the witnesses concur and swear positively that he is the man who accompanied Rhea on the fatal night, and who was his comrade and friend. It is also in evidence that his subsequent actions at the time of being arrested were those of a confederate. He refused to betray the real perpetrator and deliver him over to justice. Rhea speaks of the prisoner as his friend and takes his part in the quarrel with Lt. Roberts. Indeed there is every reason to suppose that both were actuated by the same feelings of revenge and that the accused was well aware of all that was intended.

It is impossible that two men could have acted as these men did, without the most complete and thorough understanding. Smarting under the punishment inflicted by Lt. Roberts, they went from the Saloon under the common influence of one bad poison, Revenge. True no one saw them steal into quarters and take their guns, but can there be any doubt but that they did so? Follow them back to the Saloon and listen? It is arranged that the prisoner shall stand at the door and guard against surprise: while Rhea, the bolder criminal, wreaks the revenge which is to satisfy the hatred of both. The accused stands at the door. He carries out the part assigned him by preventing Mr. Edwards from going out and causing alarm or procuring assistance. Mr. Edwards stated that he halted him and told him not to come there. There is no contradiction in the testimony here both witnesses agree, but the accused could plainly see both Doctor Sadler, and Rhea, that he could not but have heard the angry threats of Rhea, when he ordered the Doctor out of the Saloon.

One witness is nearly, if not quite certain that the accused must have seen the shot fired. But the evidence on this point conflicts. Mr. Billiard testifies that the accused stepped back into the hall a moment before the deed was done. The latter is the most reasonable supposition. He however remained in the hall while the fatal shot was fired, there the accused and his twice guilty friend ran out, and made good their escape. No regrets had they, they returned to their quarters and slept as soundly as though not the perpetrators of the cruel deed. In fact they exhibited no remorse whatsoever.

And here I wish to call the attention of the Court to the actions of the accused next day. He goes out a member of the detail sent to find the murderers. Fancy him pretending to look with hypocritical eyes for some indication which should lead to a discovery of the murderers, and carrying in his own bosom at the same time all the secrets of the horrible deed. And yet he betrays no feelings, does not even shudder or turn pale at the thought of his crime. Does not this evince a degree of stolid indifference almost unequalled? Even Judas after betraying his master and frantic at the thought of the crime he had committed, endeavored to made amends by hanging himself, but not so here. The accused betrayed no feeling and manifested no remorse. The gratification of his revenge was accomplished and though the wrong man had been killed and the whole community mourned the victim, only he and his guilty associate expressed no sorrow, shed no tears.

And during his trial before this Court he has shown himself a fit associate of his friend Rhea, who since his trial boasts of having committed three murders before the atrocious murder of Surgeon Sadler. And now permit me to call the attention of the Court to the degree of guilt which attaches to the accused as the proven associate and confederate of the actual murderer, Larkin W. Rhea, the law seems to be most clear in this regard. Greenleaf on page forty two, Vol. III says "Persons participating in a crime are other principals or accessories: If the crime is a felony they are alike felons. Principals are such in the first or second degree. Principals in the first degree are those who are the immediate perpetrators of the act. Principals in the second degree are those who did not with their own hands commit the act, but who were present aiding and abetting it." Greenleaf further says that "It is not necessary even that this presence be strict, actual and immediate, so as to make the person an eye or ear witness of what passes. It may be a constructive presence. Thus if several persons set out in concert, whether together or apart upon a common design which is unlawful, each taking the part assigned him, some to commit the fault and others to watch at proper distances to prevent a surprise or to favor the escape of the immediate actors." See also O'Brien, on American Military Law, page two hundred and sixty six. If then the Court believe the accused to have been in company with Rhea, for an evil purpose which is evinced by the fact that both were concerned in the original quarrel with Lt. Roberts and that both went for their arms and returned to the Saloon for the purpose of revenge. It matters little whether he actually saw the fatal deed done. It is enough that he performed faithfully the part assigned him and as to the specification alleges, by his presence and support aided and assisted in the crime. It cannot even be said that the accused is an accessory to the murder. The law applied to the evidence makes him a principal. For he who would otherwise be an accessory, being present when the crime is committed becomes a principal and deserves the same punishment as he who commits the deed. But it is not necessary or proper for me to suppose any member of the Court uninformed upon this, one of the clearest rules of criminal law. I feel certain that they will, well and truly try and determine the case according to the law and the evidence as each has sworn to do. We have only this week followed the dead body of our friend on the way to it's final resting place. We scarcely yet miss him from among us and can hardly realize that he is gone from us forever. But so it is and no one who knew him can fail to mourn deeply his loss. He was so courteous, and affable, a gentleman, a thorough officer, and a warm friend. He performed in the fullest degree his public duties and won the respect of all his associates, and though his young life was cut short in a moment, before he had reached the meridian of life, he has left a record of kind words and noble human deeds which will make his memory immortal. There remains to the Court however the stern duty of administrating justice upon the man who by his presence and active assistance contributed so largely in the commisssion of the cruel wrong.

Gentlemen: I leave the case in your hands."

The Court deliberated, found Roarch guilty and sentenced him to be hung by the neck until dead.

The execution was carried out on January 6, 1865, on the Commons east of Baton Rouge, Louisiana.

(For other details of the crime consult, Larkin Rhea, Case #181.)

The Court Martial proceedings were submitted for review and approval to the Judge Advocate of the Headquarters Department of the Gulf. The Judge Advocate studied the records of the proceedings and then wrote the following reply.

"Headquarters, Department of the Gulf, New Orleans,

December 20, 1864

W.P. Benton

Brigr Genl etc

General:

By direction of the Commanding General I herewith return to you the proceedings of General Court Martial in the case of Private Lewis Roarch, Co. C, 7th Kentucky Vol. Infantry for revision.

The record does not show accused present at a session of the court Dec. 10th, 1864 when the address of the Judge Advocate was read. It is the duty of the court to have the accused present during the *entire* proceedings (the deliberations of the court excepted) and the record should show that fact.

If accused was present during the part of the proceedings above mentioned, the Court can on coming together revise it's records; accordingly i.e.: add a statement of the fact. If not present then the prisoner will be brought before the reconvened court and the address read in his hearing, and such proceedings be added to this record.

By the form of the sentence to wit: '*All* the members of the Court concurring therein,' the oath that each took at the commencement of the trial' not to disclose or discover the vote or opinion of any particular member etc was violated. Yet as the rights of the prisoner are not prejudiced. It is not in this instance a fatal error, the sentence should be in the language of the statute, to wit: '*two-thirds* etc.'

I am very respectfully,

Your Obediant Servant,
E. D. Benedict
Major and Acting Judge Advocate

The foregoing is an example of Judicial review which was available and increasingly monitored the legal aspects of the Court Martial trial records.

Roarch was executed by a firing squad at Baton Rouge, Louisiana on January 6, 1865.

REFERENCES
Military Personnel Records, RG - 94
Court Martial Proceedings, RG - 153 NN 3251
Also see Case #181 Prive Lewis Roarch

Case #191
Pvt. Waterman Thornton
Co. E, 179th NY Infantry Regt.
Executed for Desertion
January 6, 1865

DESCRIPTION:

40 years of age, 5 feet 7 inches tall, dark hair, dark eyes, dark complexion, born in Canada, occupation laborer, drafted, literate.

Thornton was drafted and mustered into service at Syracuse, New York on August 22, 1864 and assigned to Company E, 7th New York Infantry Regiment (New). On October 15, 1864, his records disclose his transfer to the 52nd New York Infantry Regiment. But no further mention is found of his service with this unit in the available records. Thornton was reported to have deserted to the enemy on or about September 30, 1864.

A General Court Martial was convened at City Point, Virginia and on December 21, 1864 tried Private Waterman Thornton, Company E, 179th New York Infantry Regiment on a charge of deserting to the enemy.

Testimony disclosed that Thornton, while a member of the 179th New York Regiment on duty since September 1, 1864 in front of Petersburg, Virginia did without permission leave his Company and Regiment on or about the 30th day of September 1864 while on the march toward the South Side Railroad. Thornton asked to fall out as he was limping, but permission was denied twice. At a rest point, he claimed he was unable to get up and march. The Regiment marched and was preparing to engage the enemy about two miles from where Thornton refused to continue. Thornton was not seen again until his return under guard to City Point, Virginia on November 20, 1864.

A witness testified that he saw Thornton at Rebel General Young's Headquarters near Petersburg, Virginia on October 2, 1864. Thornton had brought his gun and accouterments except his bayonet, which he lamented. He stated he was a Yankee deserter, a drafted man from Brooklyn, New York and further that he had written to his friends at home that he had intended to desert. The witness, a prisoner of War, was sent to Louisa, Kentucky by the rebels arriving there prior to Thornton's arrival on October 26, 1864. Thornton was heard to say he was a farmer from Union County, Virginia. Thornton, in conversation with the witness at Louisa, Kentucky, stated he was well aware of Rebel War Department Order #65, August 15, 1864 concerning the treatment of Union Army Deserters. Thornton betrayed himself when the group of men he was with at Louisa, Kentucky were ordered to have all Union Army soldiers take one step forward. Thornton stepped forward. He was then arrested and returned to the charge of the Provost Marshall at City Point, Virginia arriving there on November 20, 1864.

Another witness stated that when he saw Thornton at General Young's Headquarters near Petersburg, Virginia he was wearing a Union Army uniform with the exception that he wore boots rather than shoes. The witness described how Thornton traded off various items of his uniform until he was clad in grey pants, gray cap, dark pants and a loose frock of reddish colored material like those worn by farmers. He exchanged the grey cap for a black slouch hat.

Surgeon Joseph W. Robinson, M.D., 179th New york Regiment stated that he and an assistant surgeon had examined Thornton's hip at sick call prior to his desertion and could not find any serious ailment located in the hip area. He was excused from duty for a day or two but was not "off duty" on the day of his desertion. The prisoner had no witnesses on his behalf but did present a statement to the Court.

Statement of the Prisoner

"We started from Camp, I should judge about 11 o'clock in the morning. After crossing the Weldon Railroad, we went towards the left, the main direction was westward. We proceeded about 3 miles and halted in the woods to load our pieces; there was firing in advance of us at that time. We went about three quarters of a mile where there were some dead men lying. I passed the first line of works taken from the enemy and the fort also, to the right and beyond the White House. I was with the column at the time; after passing the fort we marched to the left. I there told the Sergt: I was not able to go on. He told me to sit down when I got the chance. I kept up with the column about a half mile, when I told the Sergt. again I was unable to march, and he told me to stop when the column halted for rest. I did so. The Regiment then went ahead into the woods out of sight. I remained behind. I afterwards went into the woods and did not find them there. I enquired where they had gone and was told they had gone to the right, I followed up and the fighting commenced. I did not get up with the Regt. The enemy seemed to be driving our line on the left and men came running back where I was. I did not know them but I went back with them to a little beyond the White House on the Pamunkey River. I supposed our Regt. would come back, but as I did not see them, I turned back towards the front again. Beyond and at the left of the White House I was captured. This was about dark, the fighting lasted until about sunset. I was taken into the woods about a mile from there, where there were some of 7 or 8 Rebel soldiers by a fire. I was captured by 2 rebels and was taken to the fire by one of them. Remained there until about 11 o'clock the next morning. One other man started to take me to another place and before starting asked of the others whether I was a Prisoner of War or a deserter. They hesitated about answering and I told them I had come in. They took me to another place where there was also a fire, where Cpl. Heaton and about fifteen others among whom were some Germans from the same Regt. as myself. There we staid all night. Next day they took us to Gen'l. Youngs Hd. Qrs. I told the rebel guard various stories and did not think it made much difference what I told them. I wanted to get through if I could. At General Young's headquarters I did not say anything to anyone about having intended to desert, or that I had written to that effect. They kept me at Petersburg two or three days and from there I was taken to Richmond, where I remained about two weeks; after that I was sent to Lynchburg and stayed there two days, from there I was taken to Abingdon. We then started from there, under guard, to go to Kentucky. The guard remained with us until some ten or fifteen miles of Pound Gap where we were released. From there I went alone to Louisa, Kentucky some two hundred miles. When I arrived there I went direct to the Provost Marshall's office, who was not in at the time, I saw Heaton at the door. He heard what I told the Provost Marshall. I said I was a farmer from Virginia; there were so many afloat with regard to us which was the reason I made that statement I was sent to prison and the same evening asked the Sergt.: of the Guard to see the Provost Marshall. I intended to state to him just how it was, but I did not get to see him for two or three days after that. When I did see him I said I belonged to the 179th New York Volunteers and was captured as before stated. I have a wife and one child at home and when I entered the army

I closed my shop and gave up business for the purpose of enlisting. On the day I was last with the Regt. I wrote the address of the family on an envelope and gave it to a member of the Co. so that he could communicate to them if I was killed. I entered the service with good intentions. If I had intended to desert I would have enlisted for three years and taken a larger bounty."

(Signed) Waterman Thornton"

Thornton, in a letter appealing for clemency, relates his version of the events which lead to his arrest, trial, conviction and sentence of death.

"Headquarters, 2nd Div 9th A.C., January 4th, 1865, Maj. Genl. J. G. Parks, Comdg. Army of the Potomac,

General:

It is appointed unto all men once to die, but by some inevitable fatality it seems that a premature death awaits me by sentence of a Court Martial, unless that rare virtue clemency, which you possess in so eminent a degree, be exercized toward me.

The grounds upon which I base this appeal will appear in the sequel.

In the first place I was captured in action Sept. 30, 1864 at the Peebles House, VA, after some days retention as a prisoner of war, & changing hands different times, it happened through omission of vigilance on the part of my enemies, that an opportunity of escaping presented itself to me by misrepresenting myself to be a refugee, which I much preferred, rather than linger in the loathsome Prisons of the South. Then followed two weeks of confinement after which a number of us were transported through the rebel lines, making our way thence, we encountered two hundred (200) miles toilsome and dangerous traveling which brought us to the interior of Kentucky, after which I reported myself to the Provost Marshall of the Post at Louisa, Ky. preparatory to being forwarded to my command, but to my astonishment found myself confronted and falsely accused before the Provost Marshall aforesaid by an escaped prisoner who was captured the same day I was made prisoner, and further the aforesaid prisoner at my trial jeopardized his immortal soul by swearing three (3) unmitigated lies, for which I am sentenced to be hanged.

In face of these facts and to the end that justice may be shown me, I would most respectfully urge upon you the propriety of at least postponing the execution until I can bring conclusive evidence of my good conduct upon the unfortunate day of my capture, and also if time were given to show how inflexible my loyalty and zeal for my country have been and in my private character how irreproachable.

In conclusion I will thank you, for your patience and indulging this encroachment upon your valuable time, and I assure you a numerous and respectable family will be made happy, and a large circle of friends will sing praises to the humanity of a great General for the interposition of an act of clemency.

Waterman Thornton,

Private, 179th NY Vols."

Thornton's version of the facts of the incident was disputed by the military authorities. Their version states, "This man (Thornton) surrendered himself as a rebel deserter at Louisa, Ky. after being brought to the place to take the President's Amnesty Oath. Was made to confess himself a deserter from the Army of the Potomac. Above man captured 11th September by 2 of Hamilton's men east of Petersburg, Va."

The Court deliberated, found the accused quilty and sentenced him to be hung by the neck until dead.

The execution took place near City Point, Virginia on January 6, 1865.

REFERENCES:

Military Personnel Records, RG-#94

Court Martial Proceedings, RG-#153 LL 2924

Case #192
Private Michael Wert
NY-Wort
Co. G, 184th PA Inf. Regt.
Executed for Desertion
January 6, 1865

DESCRIPTION:

38 years of age, 5 feet 5 inches tall, brown hair, blue eyes, fair complexion, born in Northumberland, Pennsylvania, occupation laborer, illiterate.

Wert enlisted on March 31, 1864, and was mustered into service on May 17, 1864 at Harrisburg, Pennsylvania into Company G, 184th Pennsylvania Infantry Regiment. Wert, while serving with his Regiment near Fort Connalley in the Petersburg, Virginia area, deserted on December 7, 1864. He was caught and confined.

A General Court Martial was convened at Headquarters, 2nd Division, 2nd Army Corps, and on December 11, 1864 tried Private Michael Wert (Wort), Company G, 184th Pennsylvania Infantry Regiment on charge of deserting his post.

Wert requested admission of Lieutenant W. R. Bell, of the 184th Pennsylvania Infantry Regiment, as his counsel, which was granted.

Wert deserted his post as a picket guard in front of Fort Conalley, near Petersburg, Virginia on December 7, 1864.

On December 7, 1864, about an hour before daylight, Wert was captured off of his post, wandering idly about without weapon or equipment. When questioned by a Union Officer, at the time of his capture, Wert replied, "the Yankees were going to make a charge in the morning. They were going to make a charge on the left and the 5th Corps was to do it." (Wert *believed* he had left his post and crossed the lines to a Rebel post.) Wert added, "There were three Corps, the 5th 6th, and 2nd were in mass and would charge on us (the rebels) either there or to the left" he did not know which. Wert, in reply to a query as to the whereabouts of his rifle and equipment, said, "I thought you (Rebels) wouldn't let me in if I fetched them along."

Wert had testimony offered on his behalf which indicated mental deficiencies. His Company Commander testified, "I am almost certain that he (Wert) is very weak minded. He is easily controlled and would believe almost anything a man, who got his confidence, would tell him. He has scarcely judgement enough to know right from wrong." "He believes all sorts of rumors, if told him; any simple thing told him he will believe, no matter how unlikely."

The accused offered neither any further defense or a statement. The Court recessed to deliberate and found the defendant guilty and sentenced him to death before a firing squad.

Case of Private William Wert
Memo - Headquarters, Army of the Potomac
Office of Judge Advocate
December 24, 1864

Respectfully returned for compliance with Par. 3, current series, of General Orders Number 3, from these Headquarters which says, "In all cases of trial of soldiers for capital offenses, the *age* of the accused will be ascertained and noted on the record of the trial."
J.P. Brinton,
Bvt. Colonel Acting Judge Advocate

The execution took place on January 6, 1865.

REFERENCES:

Military Personnel Records, RG-#94
Court Martial Proceedings, RG-#153 LL 2924

Case #193
Pvt. James Collins
Co. D, 8th Conn. Vet. Vol. Infantry
Executed for Desertion
January 7, 1865

DESCRIPTION:

21 years of age, 5 feet 7 inches tall, brown hair, blue eyes, florid complexion, born in Ireland, occupation boatman, substitute.

Collins was drafted as a substitute and mustered into service on November 17, 1864 in Hartford, Connecticut and was assigned to Company D, 8th Connecticut Infantry Regiment. He deserted his Regiment encamped at Chapins Farm, Virginia on December 12, 1864 in company of William Dix, Company E, 8th Connecticut Infantry Regiment. Both men were arrested on December 19, 1864 confined, tried by court martial.

A General Court Martial was convened on December 27, 1864 at the Headquarters of the 24th Army Corps in the field for the trial of Private James Collins, Company D, 8th Connecticut Infantry Regiment on the charge of desertion.

Trial testimony provided by the witnesses summoned, stated that Collins disappeared from the camp on December 17, 1864 and was on report as "absent without leave" until December 21, 1864 and thereafter reported as a deserter. He was returned to his regiment on the night of December 21, 1864 by guards of Company B, 158th New York Infantry Regiment stationed at Deep Bottom, Virginia. An Acting Corporal of the Provost Guard testified that he saw Collins, at Deep Bottom on December 16, 1864 and questioned him concerning the reason for his presence in the area. Collins said he was looking for whiskey but was vague about other matters. The guard escorted him out of the area. On December 18th the same guard recognized Collins in the area again. Collins told him that he had been hiding in the woods since he was escorted out of the Deep Bottom lines on the 16th and did not intend to return to his regiment. Collins said he wanted to cross the river and make his way to City Point, Virginia and that he would give the Acting Corporal of the guard ten dollars for information permitting him to escape the sentinels and provost guards in the area. The Acting Corporal stated he was not acquainted with City Point but would make inquiry concerning the other information requested. Collins then asked if he could obtain a meal, for which he offered to pay. The Acting Corporal obtained a meal from a negroes house. While Collins was eating, the Acting Corporal left him, saying he was going to get some cigars. Instead, he went to the Lieutenant Commanding the Guard and informed him of the entire procedure. The Lieutenant assigned him a guard to post across the river and he returned to Collins and gave him information which would lead him to believe that he could successfully desert however the directions would lead Collins to the place where the sentinel had been posted. Collins paid the Acting Corporal and left while the Acting Corporal joined the sentinel at his post. Collins crossed the river by boat furnished by the negro who provided his meal. The Acting Corporal and his men continued the search for Collins all night and finally at 8AM found him at Jones Landing and brought him before a Lieutenant Parsons, Commander at Deep Bottom. Collins was turned over to the custody of the Provost Marshall who returned him, in arrest, to his regiment.

The accused offered no defense but filed a statement with the court which was accepted. Regretably the statement is almost illegible in many sections and the exact text is not possible to be presented. The thrust of Collin's statement seems to dwell on the belief that he was persuaded to desert and entrapped by the guards at Deep Bottom.

The court deliberated over the testimony presented and found Collins guilty and sentenced him to death before a firing squad. The execution took place on January 7, 1865 near the Camp of his Regiment in Virginia. (Also see Case #194 William Dix.)

REFERENCES:

Military Personnel Records, RG-#94
Court Martial Proceedings, RG-#153 NN 3301

Case #194
Pvt. William Dix
Co. E, 8th, Conn. Infantry Regt.
Executed for Desertion
January 7, 1865

DESCRIPTION:

19 years of age, 5 feet 9¼ inches tall, brown hair, gray eyes, dark complexion, born in Canada, occupation moulder, substitute.

Dix was drafted and mustered into service as a substitute on November 17, 1864 at Bridgeport Connecticut and assigned to Company E, 8th Connecticut Infantry Regiment. Dix is reported absent sick immediately upon his arrival at Chapin's Farm, Virginia in his assigned unit. In the company of James Collins, Company D, 8th Connecticut Infantry Regiment Dix deserted the Regiment on December 12, 1864 and they were apprehended on December 19, 1864. Among the documents in the Dix Military Record File are receipts given by officers for $5.00 in Greenbacks taken from William Dix at the time of his arrest as a deserter.

A General Court Martial was convened at the headquarters of the twenty fourth army corps, Army of the James, and on December 27, 1864 proceeded with the trial of Private William Dix, Company E, 8th Connecticut Infantry Regiment, charged with desertion.

Dix was the companion of Private James Collins (Case #193), Company D, 8th Connecticut Infantry Regiment and was tried by the same court on the same day. Testimony offered was essentially the same.

Dix presented a statement to the court.

"Head Quarters 8th Conn. Vol.

"24th Army Corps.

"Statement of Private William Dix of Company E, 8th Regiment Connecticut Volunteer Infantry 24th Army Corps.

"I William Dix of Company E, 8th Conn. Vol. did on the 17th of (December, 1864) leave my company to go to Deep Bottom to get some liquor and while I was there an unknown man came to me and told to me that he had orders to arrest all suspicious characters seen about there I then asked him if he thought I looked like one he told me that the guard mite I then asked him if he could get me some liquor He then said that I am the man to get it if anyone can he then said that he was Acting Corporal of the Guard around there he then said that he had more authority than the Sergeant he then asked me to come to his tent and had already sent for the liquor by an unknown man to me and that he would be in a few minutes when it was growing dark when he proposed that we take a short walk with him he then asked me if I did not wish to cross over I then asked him what he meant by crossing over across the river of course he then said that he was an Irishman and could be trusted and depend on what he said He told me that he could get me a boat on either side of the Potomac He then said that he could not depend on none of the men around there except him he then left us to get the liquor and to get the boat and told us to go to a certain place to stay at which place I stayed about ten or fifteen minutes when I got up to go to camp and was too late and too dark to reach camp so I remained in the woods all night between the two pontoons (boats supporting a pontoon bridge) I didn't see the corporal until between 11 and 12 o'clock the next day when he was in company with four others 2 of them whom he had sent to the sutlers at the pontoons when they came back they seemed intoxicated they then handed me a canteen of spirits I took some of the liquor the corporal again proposed to get us across the river the corporal said that he would get dinner for us and when it got dark he introduced us as his friends to the colored man who fed us when we had finished dinner he proposed to get a boat he stayed about 2 hours with us it was then settled that we would cross the river after dark in a boat procured by the corporal he then appeared after dusk with his waist belt on a horseman happened then to be riding by and the corporal told us to hide our selves until he had passed he then told us where we could get the boat he then left us and we crossed the river between the two pontoons when we were arrested by the corporal and his guards.

William Dix

True Statement of William Dix

Company E, 8th Conn. Vol.

(The preceding statement, like a similar one by his companion, James Collins, is considerably faded to the extent that some words are totally faded. The statement, therefore, cannot be said to be an exact duplication but rather a close replication.)

The Court deliberated, found Dix guilty and sentenced him to be executed by musketry.

Both Dix and Collins were tried together by court martial, convicted and sentenced to be executed before a firing squad together on January 7, 1865 near Fort Harrison, Virginia at the place of previous executions near the New market road.

See also Case #193 James Collins.

REFERENCES:

Military Personnel Records, RG-#94

Court Martial Proceedings, RG-#153 NN 3301

Case #195

Private Abraham Purvis

Co. C, 21st MO Inf. Regt.

Executed for Murder

January 13, 1865

DESCRIPTION:

18 years of age, 5 feet 7 inches tall, black hair, hazel eyes, dark complexion, born in Scotland County, Missouri, occupation farmer, literacy not determined.

Purvis enlisted at Hannibal, Missouri on February 12, 1864 and was mustered into service near St. Louis, Missouri on February 20, 1864. He was assigned to Company C, 21st Missouri Infantry Regiment. In March and April, he was on detached service. In early November, Purvis, along with Ephram Richardson (Case #196), committed a murder and was confined in arrest at St. Louis, Missouri.

A General Court Martial was convened at St. Louis, Missouri, and on December 6, 1864 tried Privates Abraham Purvis and Ephraim Richardson, both of Company C, 21st Missouri Infantry Regiment on a charge of murder.

Witnesses testified that on November 18, 1864, about five miles from St. Louis, Missouri on the St. Charles Rock Road about sundown, Privates Abraham Purvis and Ephraim Richardson, both of Company C, 21st Missouri Infantry Regiment, and armed with rifles, were engaged in stopping wagons and demanding fifty cents from each driver to pass on. Most wagon drivers paid. One colored man had no money and was allowed to proceed. A hearse was halted but the driver whipped up his horses and fled the scene. One soldier took up his rifle, aimed and fired at the fleeing hearse unsuccessfully as the cap failed to ignite the powder charge. Another wagon pulled up and the demands were made for tribute. Some further conversation took place between the soldiers and the wagon driver which resulted in one of the soldiers shooting the wagon driver. As the victim fell over into the wagon, the horse reins being wrapped about his hands conveyed to the horses the impression to gallop and the horses ran off, pulling the wagon behind them. Purvis and Richardson ran toward St. Louis.

A citizen of the neighborhood, Josephine Haberstock, a witness to the entire affair and the mother of Joseph Haberstock, could not speak English. Lieutenant Frank Blucher was appointed and sworn in to act as the interpreter of the German language in which Mrs. Haberstock related the events. She said she ran out after the soldiers but her son took over the chase and captured them. Her son, Joseph, had been observing the actions of Purvis and Richardson, he ran into his house, took up a revolver and a saber, then mounted his horse to pursue the fleeing soldiers.

Haberstock caught up to them, disarmed them, and with the assistance of another citizen, Casper Hinury, compelled them to go with him aboard railway cars to town where he turned them over to the Provost Marshall.

Examination of their weapons showed that Richardson's was discharged (fired) and Purvis' weapon had a burst cap but the charge had not been fired. This indicated that Purvis was the one who fired at the hearse driver, and Richardson had fired the fatal shot at the wagon driver.

The runaway wagon was found halted by Clark Hooper, a citizen, near Six Mile House on the St. Charles Rock Road. The reins were lying down on the ground, near the horses. Hooper halted his carriage, got out and went to the halted wagon. Hooper saw the wounded driver, Dominick Patton, lying in the wagon, groaning. Hooper picked up the reins and put them in Patton's hands, got the team onto the road and started them toward the Six Mile House telling Patton to come on that he would lead the way. At Six Mile House, Hooper told the proprietor, a Mr. George Krinkle, about the affair, and just then the wagon with the wounded driver pulled up and stopped. Hooper and Krinkle lifted Patton from the wagon and took him into Krinkle's establishment where they examined his wounds. He had a bullet wound which pierced the right arm then entered the right chest.

Benjamin Tyler, a physician, was summoned to examine Patton, the wounded man, and found him dying. Patton died about one half hour after Dr. Tyler arrived. The wound was described by Dr. Tyler, ignoring the wound through the right arm, as entering the right chest about one inch back of the nipple on the right side, passing directly through the lungs and liver and apparently lodged in the spinal vertebrae. The ball did not exit the body. The cause of death was given as hemorrhage.

No defense witnesses or statement was presented by either of the accused.

The Court then deliberated, found Purvis and Richardson guilty, and sentenced them to be hung by the neck until dead.

The execution took place on January 13, 1865 in a St. Louis, Missouri Jail.

The Missouri Republican, St. Louis, Missouri, January 13, 1865 carried the story of the execution of Purvis and Richardson under local news.

"The Military Executions today—At noon today Abraham Purvis and Ephram Richardson, both privates in the 21st Missouri Infantry, will be executed in the St. Louis Jail Yard for the murder of a farmer en route to the city near the Six Mile House on the Bellefontaine Road on the 17th of October last. Purvis and Richardson are both natives of Scotland County, Missouri, and both fine specimens of boys, sixteen to eighteen years of age, and both are one year in government service. They state that on the march of the regiment from St. Charles to this city, they had permission from their Captain to 'fall out,' being much fatigued, and were left behind. At the Six Mile House they drank. Richardson states that what he did he does not know, further than that Purvis proposed that they should kill the farmer. Purvis says that he himself was sober, and that he repeatedly removed the caps from Richardson's gun to prevent him doing injury. Both the boys are remarkedly open faced, free-spoken, and prepossessing, and it is difficult to conceive them guilty of the dastardly crime of which they have been convicted, but the jury of a military commission would hardly convict them of the offence without very pointed testimony. The many murderous outrages committed during the past year have rendered it necessary that examples of the perpetrators should be made, and if they are guilty, let them suffer."

One small lingering question about the Purvis case remains. He is most often listed as being 18 years of age, but on one "Company Muster Out Roll" he is listed as 17 years of age. This is, possibly, a copyist error, as there are no consent forms in his file, as required, for underage enlistment. The newspaper account also refers to "boys 16-18 years of age."

(Also see case #196 Richardson.)

REFERENCES:
Military Personnel Records, RG-#94
Court Martial Proceedings, RG-#153
Missouri Republican, St. Louis, Missouri, January 13, 1865

Case #196
Pvt. Ephraim Richardson
Co. C, 21st MO Vol. Infantry Regt.
Executed for Murder
January 13, 1865

DESCRIPTION:
16 or 17 years of age; notation on muster in roll states, "Produced Guardian's Consent." His age is not well established by documentation. No other descriptive data available.

Richardson enlisted on October 24, 1862 and was mustered into service on November 1, 1862 at Memphis, Tennessee in Company C, 21st Missouri Infantry Regiment at one point on his records there is a notation that his "name cancelled on the roll." It may be that he was dropped from the service or that the enrollment data was changed.

He must, at some point, have managed to enlist and be mustered into service as he was in confinement at St. Louis, Missouri as of November 19, 1864 on a charge of murder. He was referred to at the time as a recruit.

A General Court Martial was convened at St. Louis, Missouri, and on December 6, 1864 tried Private Ephraim Richardson, Company C, 21st Missouri Infantry Regiment on a charge of murder.

Richardson was tried at the same time as Private Abraham Purvis, Company C, 21st Missouri Infantry Regiment. All the testimony presented there applies equally to Richardson, including the finding, sentence and execution.

See Case #195 Purvis for full details.

Richardson is surely a candidate for the title of the youngest Union Soldier executed by the Union Army during the Civil War.

REFERENCES:
Military Personnel Records, RG-#94
Court Martial Proceedings, RG-#153 LL 3012

Case #197
Private Newell W. Root
AKA: George W. Harris
Co. H, 1st CT Hvy. Arty. Regt.
Executed for Desertion
January 27, 1865

DESCRIPTION:
18 years of age, 5 feet 9 inches tall, sandy hair, blue eyes, sandy complexion, born in East Hampton, Connecticut, occupation farmer, unmarried, literate.

Root made the following statement after his arrest and confinement from desertion.

"Henry W. Root, 1st Conn Heavy Artillery. I enlisted the 2nd of December, 1863 at Hartford, Conn. I am a volunteer and rec'd $350.00 bounty. I was last with my battery the 16th of last September it was at Dutch Gap. I left it in the morning about 8 o'clock there was 2 of us we crossed the River to get some grapes, we saw 10 or a dozen Rebels, who stopped us, and we told them we were deserters, we did not intend to desert when we started across the River. I was taken before General Pickett's Adjt Genl whom we told we were Yankee deserters, we were then sent to Richmond and confined in Castle Lightning, on the 18th of Oct. we left Richmond, and was taken to Abbington, and thence to Pound Gap, where we was released, I went to Louisa (Kentucky) and reported to the Pro. Mar. I told him I was a rebel deserter, I wanted to get out of the Service, I was sent to Lexington (Kentucky), from thence to Cincinnatti and finally to Washington. When I came here I gave the name of Geo. H. Harris."

The statement is verified by Captain Hubbard, Comdg. Co. H, 1st Conn, H. A."

A General Court Martial was convened at City Point, Virginia, and on December 19, 1864 tried Private Newell W. Root, Company H, 1st Connecticut Heavy Artillery Regiment on a charge of Deserting to the Enemy.

Testimony offered disclosed that Root was assigned to a "Water Battery" (mortars mounted on Barges), designated Battery Spofford on the James River about seven miles above Bermuda Hundred. On or about September 16, 1864, Root and another soldier of the same Company and Regiment named Finch, left the battery without permission and crossed the river to the North Bank, near the Rebel lines. A witness stated he saw Root and Finch on September 16, 1864 standing on the bank of the James River as he was entering a boat to cross the river back to the Battery Spofford. He called to Finch and asked if they wanted to cross over in the boat with him. Finch replied, "We are not going back," or words to that effect. The boat with the witness aboard sailed for Battery Spofford and Root was not seen again until November 29, 1864 under arrest. Finch had not been seen since.

The officer in charge of the Provost Prisoner's Barracks at City Point, Virginia testified that he interrogated Root who told him that he and Finch were captured by rebel scouts after they were last seen on the river bank. Root told his captors they were deserters, but had not intended to desert when they left the Battery that day. Their original purpose was to search for wild grapes. They were taken before General Pickett's Adjutant whom they told they were deserters, and were taken to Richmond, then to Pound Gap and released to make their way to Louisa, Kentucky where he went to the Union Provost Marshall and stated he was a Rebel Army deserter. His object in doing this was to get out of the Service (military). (This was in accordance with the reputed general gist of the often alluded to Order #65, Confederate War Department.) Root was sent to Lexington, Kentucky then to Washington, D. C. and finally to confinement at City Point, Virginia where he used the alias of George H. Harris.

The defense had no witnesses to call before the Court but did offer a statement of defense.

"Statement of the Prisoner"

"I and Finch left the Company that morning and went to the Canal. We went to see the "Mud Digger." After we got down there, some of our Pickets (Colored Troops) had just been relieved and were coming in with Grapes in their hands. We inquired where the Grapes were obtained, they told us on the bank of the river. We went very near the upper end of the Peninsula some three quarters of a mile from the canal, we passed along up the Picket line to a point which seemed to be the end of the line; beyond that there no pickets. We continued in that direction for about 500 yards in the Woods; we obtained some grapes. I had my blouse off and the sleeves of it tied and filled with grapes. We were about to return and were captured by armed Scouts of the enemy. It was no use to make resistance as there were some ten or twelve of the Rebel Scouts. I left Finch, who was captured with me, at Pound Gap; sick. In going through in to Kentucky from Pound Gap the men who were with me were all sure of getting through by representing themselves as Rebel deserters, and advised me to do the same. I am in my nineteenth year. I was in the service about seven months before joining the 1st Conn. H. Artillery and was honorably discharged for disability.

(signed) Newell W. Root"

The Court then deliberated, found the accused guilty and sentenced him to be hung by the neck until dead.

The execution took place in or near City Point, Virginia on January 27, 1865.

As the result of an appeal to President Lincoln for clemency, from an unidentified source, the President telegraphed to General Grant. "Wash, Jan 24, 1864, to General Grant:

If Newell W. Root of first Conn. Heavy Artillery is under sentence of death please telegraph me briefly the circumstances. A. Lincoln"

General Grant replied on January 25, 1864 by telegraph, which included the following report from Captain P. T. Whitehead: Judge Advocate to Brigadier General Marsena R. Patrick, Provost Marshall General, Army of the Potomac. "I have the honor to report in regard to Private Newell W. Root alias George H. Harris, Co. H, 1st Conn. Heavy Artillery; that he was tried by this court on December 19, 1864 and convicted of `Deserting to the enemy' and sentenced to be hung. His sentence is approved by General Meade and ordered to be carried into effect at City Point on Friday 27th inst. under the direction of the Provost Marshall General. The facts in the case show that Root deserted to the enemy near Dutch Gap and gave himself up to the rebels as a Union deserter; was released under Rebel Order #65 and on making his way through to Louisa, Ky. represented himself as a rebel deserter for the purpose of getting out of the service, he gave the name of Harris and came to City Point in arrest under that name. Capt. Dimock, Co. H, 1st Conn Artillery proves that Root left camp on James River without authority and never returned. Private Potts, same company proves that he saw Root near the canal on that day and asked him if he was going back to camp. Root answered that, he was not going back so much as he was! Potts never saw him after that until on trial. The fact of Roots giving himself up as a deserter is proven by his own statement made voluntarily to the examining Officer. In his statement he claims to have been captured and that he then represented to his captors that he was a deserter and also that when he was sent from Richmond and released near Pound Gap he was advised by others with him to pass for a rebel deserter when he entered our lines in Ky." Upon receipt of this information President Lincoln telegraphed General Grant on January 25, 1864, as follows, "Lt. General Grant, having received the report in case of Newell Root I do not interfere further in the case.

A. Lincoln"

REFERENCES:

Military Personnel Records, RG-#94
Court Martial Proceedings, RG-#153 NN 3456
ALS (telegram sent) DNA, RG-#107
Telegrams Collected (bound), Lincoln, Works, VIII, 237
"The Papers of Ulysses S. Grant," Volume XIII, page 521, Edited by Dr. John Y. Simon.

Case #198
Pvt. James Devlin
AKA: Patrick Diamond, Frank Tully
Co.'s E & D, 43rd, NY Infantry Regt.
Executed for Desertion
February 3, 1865

DESCRIPTION:

28 years of age, 5 feet 8¾ inches tall. Brown hair, blue eyes, light complexion, born in Ireland, occupation butcher, literate, substitute.

Devlin made a statement on January 21, 1865 after his arrest which, to a large measure, describes his bounty jumping career.

"James Devlin states: I am a native of Ireland, am 29 years of age, am a butcher. Enlisted as a Substitute at the Provost Marshalls office, Tarreytown, on the 31st of May 1864, under the name of Pat Diamond. From there was sent on the 1st of June 1864 to

Hart's Island (NY Harbor) from there was sent to City Point (Va.), about the 5th of June 1864, to the 43rd Reg NY Inftry. which was then in the 6th Army Corps in front of Petersburg. Was with my regiment nine days. Was then sent, in consequence of an attack of Chronic Diarrhea, to the Hospital at City Point, was in Hospital one day, was then sent to Camp Distribution, Alexandria (Va.) to be forwarded to my regiment, which had gone to the Valley. (Shenandoah) On my way to my regiment, passing through Washington, I disrobed, changed my clothes in Washington at a clothing store in 7th Street near the Postoffice. I do not know the number, nor the name of the man who keeps the store. Remained in Washington five days. Then came north was arrested in Baltimore at the depot. Remained in arrest two days. Represented myself as in the employ of Brown & Hunter Sutlers in Baltimore. Was then released. Came to New York. Remained in New York one month. Returned to Washington and worked as assistant wagon master to wagon master Norris at Washington for three months, at $43 per month. Then came to New York, went to New Haven (Conn) in September of 1864. Enlisted there under the name Frank Tulley, received $600.00 bounty, was sent from New Haven to City Point. On arrival there was forwarded to Camp Stevenson, Washington D.C. to be sent to the 1st Connecticut Cavalry.

"On my way through Washington to join my regiment I saw the wagon master at the Rail Road Park just above the Depot. I had leave for two hours to go around the City before the train left. Norris told me, in reply to my question, where I could get citizens clothing, that I could get it at a rum shop near the Depot called the Swamp Poodle. I went there bought the citizens clothes, for $15.00 leaving my uniform with the man who kept the rum shop and who sold me the citizens clothes. Norris knew that I was an enlisted man and intended to desert and that I wanted the clothes to enable one to desert,, I did desert. Came to New York, enlisted in the Navy on the 18th Jany 1865, and was arrested on the 20th Jany 1865 by Officer Murphy on the Receiving Ship North Carolina, Brooklyn Navy Yard. Norris wanted me to stay in Washington and work for him at the time. He informed me where I could get citizens clothing near the R.R. Depot.

(signed) James Devlin

Sworn before me the 21st of Jany 1865" (signature and title undecipherable)

A General Court Martial was convened at New York City and proceeded to the trial of James Devlin alias Pat Diamond alias Frank Tully on charges of desertion on January 30, 1865.

Devlin was charged with desertion, as he was a substitute duly enlisted on May 31, 1864 into the United States service and assigned to the 43rd New York Regiment, Company E, at City Point, Virginia. He became ill and eventually was sent to Camp Distribution near Alexandria, Virginia and he deserted in Washington, D. C. Devlin then enlisted in the 1st Connecticut Cavalry Regiment and subsequently deserted in September 1864. He then enlisted in the U. S. Navy at New York City on January 18, 1865 and was assigned to the receiving ship North Carolina where he was arrested on January 20, 1865 and held in confinement for trial.

Devlin pleaded guilty to all charges and the prosecution did not present it's case. Devlin offered a statement in full of his activities.

The Court deliberated and confirmed Devlin's plea of guilty, sentencing him to be executed by musketry. The execution took place on February 3, 1865 at Fort Columbus, New York Harbor.

An account of the execution appeared in the New York Times.

"Military Execution at Governor's Island.

TRAGIC END OF A BOUNTY-JUMPER

Yesterday afternoon, Governor's Island was the scene of a solemn and imposing tragedy, JAMES DEVLIN, a deserter from the army, was executed, in the presence of a thousand persons, in accordance with the findings of a court-martial. The sentence was approved by Gen. Dix, Commander of the Department of the East, for the purpose of checking the rapidly increasing crime of desertion. A perfect system of bounty-jumping has been adopted by recruits, until it has become a serious evil, which the authorities have resolved to stop. The accused, JAMES DEVLIN, was about thirty years of age, of compact, well-built form, and five feet nine inches high. His features were full, and his complexion dark, with a sensual face. He first entered the army under his right name, and deserted. He then entered the army under the name of Patrick Diamond, and having deserted a second time, entered the army under the name of Patrick Sully.

Devlin was married to a woman about ten years his senior by whom he had three children. In June last he deserted his wife, and cohabited with a woman at No. 111 Mott-street. His wife becoming incensed at his conduct, recently gave information to the policeman stationed at Gen. Dix's office, which led to his arrest on board the recruiting ship **North Carolina**, on the 20th of January. He was subsequently tried by a court-martial, and convicted of desertion from the First Connecticut Cavalry and the Forty-third New York Volunteers. The sentence having been approved, the time of execution was fixed between the hours of twelve and two o'clock yesterday.

As soon as DEVLIN'S wife heard of his sentence, her affection for the prisoner appears to have returned, and she became almost frantic. On Thursday night she visited the office of Gen. Dix for the purpose of obtaining a reprieve. The General was in Washington, and those at the office could give her no encouragement. Yesterday she went to the island, and obtained permission from the Provost-Martial to see her husband, who was in the guard-room, on the right of the sallyport of Fort Columbus. The lamentations of the wretched woman were painful to witness. They appeared, however, to have but little effect upon DEVLIN, who maintained his composure throughout the trying interview.

At noon the troops were ordered out on the parade-ground by Capt. Ryer, of the Twentieth Battery, Officer of the Day. The coffin of the condemned man was placed on the plateau in the presence of the soldiery, and all minds were fixed upon the dread tragedy which was soon to take place. Visitors gathered in small groups and talked of the execution, while the soldiers moved about in a quiet and subdued manner which showed that their thoughts were all bent upon the one subject. As the hour for the execution approached, however, they became more animated, and each one seemed anxious to secure a commanding view of the closing scenes.

After remaining beside her husband a short time, Mrs. DEVLIN procured the attendance of Father Healey, of St. Peter's Church, in Barclay-street, who remained with and comforted the prisoner until the last moment.

At 1 o'clock the firing party, consisting of twelve men belonging to the Twentieth New-York Volunteer Artillery, entered the sallyport of Fort Columbus, preceded by a drum. On hearing the music the prisoner's wife, who stood near the entrance, fell upon her knees in a paroxysm of agony, calling upon God to look upon her orphan children. Her violence subsided, however, before DEVLIN left his cell. He came forth at the Command of Capt. Ryan, attended by the priest, who held a prayer-book and golden crucifix in his hands, and took his place between the soldiers, who were drawn up in single file. The order was given, and the solemn procession marched to the parade-ground, where the troops were drawn up, and waiting for the prisoner. DEVLIN was taken close to his coffin, when the officer in command directed him to bid farewell to his wife. Before leaving the cell his hands had been tied securely behind him so that he could only kiss the poor woman. Mrs. DEVLIN threw her arms around his neck, and gave him an earnest embrace, when she was taken away from the painful scene by a detail of soldiers. Again she gave vent to her agony by crying to God to look upon her poor orphans, her shriek resounding over the island, so as to be heard to the water's edge. Even this scene, trying as it was to those who witnessed it, did not seem to affect DEVLIN.

The order "Forward!" was then given, and to the solemn music of the "Dead March," the procession moved to the place of execution. Immediately in front of the condemned, four soldiers carried his coffin on a bier. Father HEALEY walked at his side, reading from the prayer-book, the prisoner paying respectful attention, but showing no emotion.

The place selected for the execution was on the beach, just below Castle William, and directly in front of the uppermost poplar tree. The entire garrison of the island, together with the recruits, numbering in all about four hundred men, were drawn up in double lines, forming three sides of a hollow square, the fourth, facing the bay, remaining open. The columns faced each other, and the procession slowly marched between the open ranks, giving all the men an opportunity to see the accused. He was then taken to the place of execution.

All of the inhabitants of the island, both male and female, including many children, appeared to have assembled to witness the execution. Boys and girls, from ten years of age upward, were to be seen passing through the crowd, to obtain a good view of the tragedy. The excellent arrangements of the military, however, prevented too near an approach, but the eagerness of the women to witness the shooting was most disgusting.

After entering the square, the priest prayed with the prisoner about a quarter of an hour, when the sentence of the court-martial was read, and the order for execution was given. At three minutes to two o'clock the white handkerchief was placed over his eyes, and he knelt in front of his coffin. The firing party was drawn up in front of him, and ten men were chosen to fire, two having been reserved, to see that, if he were not killed at the first discharge, they could finish the work. By accident, the unloaded musket was reserved, so that each of the guns discharged was loaded.

For three minutes the wretched man knelt motionless, awaiting the order to send him to eternity. To the spectators it seemed an age, so dreadful was the suspense. At precisely two o'clock Capt. Ryan gave the order, in a loud, firm voice, "Ready," when the muskets were pointed with steady arms, at the breast of the doomed man. The command "aim," was given, and at a flourish of his sword, ten balls sped upon their deadly errand, passed through his body, and sank into the bay. The body stood poised in the air a moment, and then fell forward with a heavy thud upon the coffin. An examination of the remains showed that ten balls had passed through, although there were but eight holes. Four of the bullets had passed through two holes. One of the balls cut the spine in two, and another passed through the right lung. His death must have been instantaneous.

The body remained in the position where it fell until the troops marched by to the music of a quickstep. Many of the men avoided looking at the corpse, marching forward with firm-set features, as though they dreaded the sight; but the majority cast a curious glance at the body, some of them turning to look at it after they had passed. The remains were placed in a coffin and removed, to be given to Mrs. DEVLIN.

Among those present were Col. Ludlow, Inspector-General of the Department of the East, to whom DEVLIN confessed his crime, and Maj. Gen'l. Dix and Capt. Blake of Gen. Dix's Staff. The execution took place under the direction of Col. Bumford, Commandant of the Island, whose arrangements were excellently planned. The utmost courtesy was shown to the members of the press by both those in command of the island and the members of Gen. Dix's Staff."

The last paragraph of General Order No. 9, Headquarters Department of the East, New York City, February 1, 1865 contains an eloquent statement concerning bounty jumping by Major General Dix.

"The Major General Commanding is thus prompt in the execution of the sentence pronounced upon the accused, on account of the aggravated circumstances of the case. Within the period of eight months he enlisted twice in the Army and once in the Navy, having twice during the same period, deserted the flag of his country. His case is one of those in which bad men, tempted by enormous bounties, enlist into the service for the sake of making money, with the deliberate purpose of deserting, and in which the profit is proportioned to the number of successful repetitions of the crime. By common consent, these infamous men are designated by the expressive appellation of Bounty Jumpers. They might, more properly be termed traitors and public plunderers, and the Major General Commanding, in approving the sentence of death pronounced by the Court, deems it his duty to the Army and the Country to announce, that, in all like cases, he will cause the punishment awarded, to be executed with the utmost inflexibility and promptness.

By Command of Major-General Dix"

Most records state the execution took place on February 3, 1865, however a few indicate the date as February 5, 1865.

REFERENCES:

Military Personnel Records, RG-#94
Court Martial Proceedings, RG-#153 NN 3654
New York Times, February 4th, February 5th, 1865

Case #199

Pvt. Joseph H. Sharp
NV: Samuel Trangler
Co. A, 12th NH Infantry Regt.
Executed for Desertion
February 9, 1865

DESCRIPTION:

30 years of age, 5 feet 9 inches tall, brown hair, blue eyes, light complexion, born in Burlington Co., New Jersey, occupation brick maker, literate.

Sharp enlisted and was mustered into service on December 7, 1863 at Concord, New Hampshire in Company A, 12th NH Infantry Regiment which was stationed in Virginia. On May 24, 1864 near Bermuda Hundred, Virginia, Sharp was tried by regimental court martial on the charge of forgery. Sharp was accused of forging an order to permit him to obtain a container of whiskey and further that he personally delivered the forged order to the brigade commander. During the trial, Sharp's handwriting from the clothing receipt book was compared with the forged order and the court agreed that they were dissimilar in every way. Sharp admitted he had carried the forged order as specified in the charges against him but explained his involvement in the matter. "The forged order was given to me by a soldier who belonged to the 2nd NH Volunteers who gave me some whisky out of his canteen and told me I could get another canteen full with an order which he said he would go and get for me. He went up into the 2nd NH Regiment while I was standing in the street or road and soon returned with the order. I had no thoughts of it's being fraudulent, else I should not have taken or presented it. Sharp thought he would recognize the soldier who presented him with the forged permit if he saw him again. The Court believing the prisoner at trial to be "non Compis Mentis" decided to adjourn for an hour and permit Pvt. Sharp to search for the soldier who gave him the forged order. Upon reconvening the trial an hour later, the prisoner having been unable to locate the object of his search, the soldier who provided the forged permit, the court found the prisoner Sharp acquitted of the charge and specifications "and returned to duty with his company."

On or about May 30/June 1, 1864, Sharp deserted his Regiment near White House on the Pamunky, Virginia. He was apprehended on January 12, 1865 while in the 5th Indiana Infantry Regiment. A reward of $30.00 was paid for his apprehension. Sharp was tried by court martial.

A General Court Martial was convened at the headquarters of the 3rd Division, 24th Army Corps and on January 23, 1865 tried Private Joseph H. Sharp, Company A, 12th New Hampshire Infantry Regiment on a charge of desertion.

The accused stated he did not wish to introduce counsel.

Testimony presented showed that Sharp enlisted and was mustered into service on December 7, 1863 at Concord, New Hampshire in Company A, 12th New Hampshire Infantry Regiment and deserted his Company and Regiment on May 31st, 1864 from camp near White House Landing, Virginia.

Witnesses from Company A of the 12th New Hampshire Infantry Regiment positively identified the accused as the Joseph Sharp of their Company who had served with them and deserted.

Sergeant Joseph F. Mills, Company H, 5th Maryland Infantry Regiment stated that Joseph Sharp, the accused, had enlisted as a substitute and was assigned to Company H, 5th Maryland Infantry Regiment under the name of Samuel Trangler, on or about December 6, 1864 and was arrested on or about January 10, 1865 at the Camp of the 5th Maryland Infantry Regiment.

Sharp did not offer any defense witnesses nor present a statement to the Court in his behalf.

The Court deliberated, found the accused guilty, and sentenced him to be shot to death with musketry.

The execution took place on February 9, 1865, presumably in or near the Camp of the 12th New Hampshire Infantry Regiment.

REFERENCES:
Military Personnel Records, RG-#94
Court Martial Proceedings, RG-#153 NN 3594

Case #200
Private John Hoefler
NV: Hofler, Hoffler
Co. E, 124th, NY Infantry Regt.
Executed for Desertion
February 17, 1865

DESCRIPTION:
20 years of age, 5 feet 4½ inches tall, brown hair, gray eyes, light complexion, born in Germany, occupation Cigar Maker, literacy undetermined.

Hoefler enlisted and was mustered into service at Schenectady, New York on September 8, 1864 (for one years service) and sent to Hart's Island Camp (New York City) of the 124th New York Infantry Regiment where he was assigned to Company E. The Regiment was deployed in the Petersburg, Virginia area and on November 8, 1864, near Fort Sedgewick, Hoefler deserted. He was apprehended on or about January 1, 1865 near the town of Petersburg, Virginia, arrested and confined.

A General Court Martial was convened in the field near Petersburg, Virginia at the Headquarters of the 3rd Division, 2nd Brigade and on January 30, 1865 tried Private John Hoefler, Company E, 124th New York Infantry Regiment on a charge of desertion.

Testimony revealed that Hoefler was mustered into service of the 124th New York Infantry Regiment on September 8, 1864 and received a bounty of $750.00. He was forwarded to the Regiment and assigned to Company E which was stationed behind Fort Hell, near Petersburg, Virginia. On November 9, 1864, Hoefler left his Company without permission and was not seen again until sometime in December 1864. He had been arrested by Cavalry Provost Marshalls about November 15, 1864. He had documents in his possession relating to his deposit of money from the bounty in a German bank in New York City. Hoefler, at the time of his apprehension claimed to be a deserter from the 5th Alabama, CSA. Hoefler finally confessed to the Provost Marshall that he was a deserter from the 124th New York Infantry Regiment having left their ranks on November 9, 1864.

Hoefler offered no defense but presented a statement in his defense:

"I did not try to desert at all. Guerillas caught me outside of the lines and took my clothes away and I ran away from them again and came into our lines. I was ashamed to say I belonged to the Union Army with those old lousy clothes on. When I left the Regiment I started to go on to the 7th N.Y. to see some friends who had just come out here in some new companies, and went to a Sutler who got me some whiskey and got drunk on it, and that is the way I got outside of the lines. I did not intend to desert at all."

The Court deliberated, found him guilty and sentenced him to be shot to death with musketry.

The execution took place near Petersburg, Virginia on February 17, 1865.

A brief description of the execution was noted in Bardeen's Diary, although his date is in error by about two weeks. Bardeen wrote "Went over to the First Division and saw a man shot for desertion. He belonged to Company B, 124th N.Y.S.V. He dropped dead as a nail the first pop."

REFERENCES:

Military Personnel Records, RG-#94
Court Martial Proceedings, RG-#153 OO 184
"A Little Fifers War Diary," C. W. Bardeen, Syracuse, New York, 1910.

Case #201
Pvt. Michael Landy
Co. A, 10th Conn. Infantry Regt.
Executed for Desertion
February 17, 1865

DESCRIPTION:

21 years of age, 5 feet 4 inches tall, brown hair, hazel eyes, ruddy complexion, born in Ireland, occupation farmer, substitute.

Landy enlisted and was mustered into service as a substitute on November 3, 1864 at New Haven Connecticut. He was forwarded to the Richmond, Virginia area and assigned to Company A, 10th Connecticut Infantry Regiment. Landy deserted while on picket duty on February 14, 1865 and remained outside the vidette line until discovered and arrested. Landy was confined and tried by court martial on the charge of desertion.

A General Court Martial was convened at the headquarters of the 24th Army Corps and on February 16, 1865 tried Private Michael Landy, Company A, 111 Connecticut Infantry Regiment on a charge of Desertion.

Testimony revealed that Landy was assigned to Picket line duty for the period of February 14-15, 1865 and that he was reported missing from his post without permission between 11 and 12PM on February 14, 1865.

Landy was found lying down by a soldier searching for the missing picket, just before daylight on February 15, 1865. He was approximately 15 rods outside the Union Army Picket line. He was ordered to get up and come into the Union Army Picket line several times but his only compliance was to stand up. A Lieutenant and the Commander of that section of the picket line arrived and advanced a few paces toward the accused when the Commander took a gun from a soldier aimed it at Landy and informed him to immediately come forward or he would blow his brains out.

Landy was described as dressed in overcoat, underclothes, a belt, no gun, cartridge box, haversack or canteen. He was taken to the command Post of that section of the picket line where it was established that he was Landy, the picket guard who was missing from his post. He was subsequently arrested and charged with desertion.

The accused had no witnesses for his defense but did submit a statement in his defense, as follows:

"On the morning of the 14th of February 1865 I went on picket duty with William Ryan. We got out on the picket line and he asked me to desert with him. That when we got out to the rebs. they would send us to Petersburg and then we would go to Albany (GA) where his father lived. And he said he would take me from there to New York and get another bounty and we could desert again. He told me when I was to go out, he was to be on Vidette post and he would go and talk to the next vidette until I got out then he was to come after me. I went out in the woods and did not find him coming and sat down behind a tree and stopped there until daylight. At daylight I went back to our own lines again. The first man I saw was the man that was on vidette post. He said come in Johnny. I stood awhile thinking whether I would go in or not. He called a second time, and I did not go. He called a third time. I went in the third time to within five or six paces of the vidette. I got behind a tree there. I thought when he saw me with these clothes on he would shoot me. He called for the corporal. The officer of the day came up with the lieutenant. The Officer of the Day took the gun from one of the men, cocked the gun at me and then I came in. That is all."

The court then deliberated and found the accused guilty and sentenced him to forfeit all pay and allowances that were then due or may thereafter become due and that he be shot to death with musketry.

Landy was executed behind the Union Lines before Richmond, Virginia on February 17, 1865.

On February 17, 1865 a telegram to General John Turner from Brigadier General Foster stated: "Private Landy, 10th Connecticut Volunteers who is to be executed at two o'clock this afternoon desires to see a catholic priest if there is one to be had. Will you please send him to my headquarters. Answer -"

REFERENCES:

Military Personnel Records, RG-#94
Court Martial Proceedings, RG-#153   MM 1539

Case #202
Pvt. John Brown(2)
Co. H, 10th, Conn. Infy Regt
Executed for Desertion
February 18, 1865

DESCRIPTION:

22 years of age, 5 feet 5 inches tall, dark hair, hazel eyes, dark complexion, born in Scotland, occupation cabinet maker, substitute.

One of the vexing problems of researching Civil War records is the presence of men with the same names in the same company as is illustrated by this case.

The records of John Brown(2) are complicated and confused because of the presence in Company H of "two John Brown's." The matter was settled by designating one as John Brown(1) and the other as John Brown(2). The subject of this brief study is John Brown(2) a substitute, drafted and mustered into service at Bridgeport, Connecticut on November 22, 1864 and assigned to Company H, 10th Connecticut Infantry Regiment.

On January 19, 1865, a General Court Martial was convened at Headquarters of 1st Division, 24th Army Corps in the field in Virginia for the trial of Private John Brown(2) of Company H, 10th Connecticut Infantry Regiment. Brown was charged with Desertion, Attempt to Murder, Attempt to Rob, Violation of the 23rd Article of War (persuading or advising a member of the Army to desert the service).

Testimony given at the trial disclosed that Private Peter Frantz of Company H, 10th Connecticut Infantry Regiment reported to Sgt. Sackett of Company H, 3rd New Hampshire that he had overheard a plot to desert discussed by Private John Brown(2) and Private Thomas Jones. Sergeant Sackett, in turn, reported the plot to Captain D. W. Boardman, Company H, 3rd Connecticut Infantry Regiment. Later Frantz went to Captain Boardman and advised him of the enlargement of the plan. Brown and Jones now wanted Frantz to lure a Frenchman in their company named Forbeare, who was said to possess a large sum of money, outside the encampment where they would rob him. Frantz was promised $200.00 for participating. The money would permit all of the participants to desert.

Captain Boardman, with the knowledge and consent of the Regimental Commander, directed Frantz to cooperate with Brown and Jones but to thoroughly advise Forbeare of the plot and urge him to cooperate with the authorities in their plan to catch the two criminal in the commission of the act. Accordingly, Sergeant Sackett, a Corporal, and 12 men were advised that they were to follow the conspirators and their victim, to prevent the crime taking place and to capture the perpetrators. On the night of January 4, 1865, about 11 PM, Frantz and Forbeare accompanied Brown and Jones out of the encampment into the wooded countryside followed cautiously by Sergeant Sackett and his detail. The four men halted and the group trailing them heard loud talk and scuffling and finally a pistol shot. The provost detail under Sergeant Sackett rushed in and seized Brown and Jones, and to their relief found Frantz and Forbeare uninjured. Brown had fired a bullet from his pistol which missed Forbeare during the attempted robbery. The prisoners were arrested, confined and charges were filed against them. The trial confirmed most of the charges. Brown asked questions of the witnesses against him but offered no defense of his own except a final statement.

"Prisoner Statement"

"That day I am accused of trying to desert, I was on guard that night I was coming down to my tent, where Thomas Jones and Peter Frantz were standing talking. Jones had been into our tent; they asked if I knew where to get whiskey, I told them I did not - they asked me would I come out with them and try and get some whiskey. I told them I had not time as I had to get up at half past twelve. So then I went down to my tent and Thomas Jones followed me, soon after Peter Frantz came down and called out Jones and told him he could get whiskey. I told them they could not get past the guards, four of us went down to the guard and this Peter Frantz goes up and tells the guard we are going for whiskey. One of the guards cries out to me `where are you going soldier?' I told them we were going with this man to get whiskey. The guard told me we could not get past him. So I went back to my tent and took off my belts and made up the bunk, took off my clothing and went into it. Soon after the first relief came in and then Peter Frantz came to me and told us that he knew there was a Frenchman that would let us pass. I told him I could not go to night as I had to get up at half past twelve. He came two or three times, and asked me the same thing. One of the boys told me to get up and go out for some whiskey that I should not be long. So I got up and went out with them. When we got out we were standing talking about whiskey when Peter Frantz fired one shot and the Corporal took hold of me. This is all that passed between us."

The statement was accepted and the court conferred on the testimony and found Brown guilty on all counts and sentenced him to be executed.

February 18, 1865 the sentence was sent for review and approval.

Brigadier General Joseph R. Hawley, 1st Division Commander commented on the trial and sentence of the General Court Martial tribunal as follows:

"HD. QRS, 1st Div. 24th A.C.

Before Richmond, Va., Jan 30th, 1865"

"In the foregoing case, the specifications under the fourth charge is defective in that the allegation is made in the alternative, 'did advise *or* persuade,' It should have charged that the prisoner 'did advise,' or that he 'did persuade' or that he 'did advise and persuade.' The proceedings and findings under the first, second and third charges are approved and they justify the sentence. The sentence is also approved. But as it appears that before the prisoner had committed any overt act the plot became known to a commissioned officer of the regiment, and as that officer, instead of promptly checking the plot, encouraged it's development, even to the extent of instructing the guard to let the deserters go out of camp at night, and a witness Peter Frantz, under instruction, evidently encouraged the prisoner to go on with his crime. I do earnestly recommend that the sentence of death be commuted. I make no question of the good motives of Capt. Boardman. His regiment had suffered from the desertion of substitutes and examples were needed, but I am not prepared to approve the death sentence in a case where the criminal intention was well known in advance and the overt act might have been prevented.

Respectfully Forwarded,
Jos. A. Hawley
Brig. Genl Comdg Div."

The trial proceedings were transmitted through channels for review and were approved at all levels of authority in their original form. The sentence of death by hanging was carried out on February 18, 1865 near the encampment of the Division.

One additional punishment was noted in the sentence, infrequently employed, the forfeiture of all pay and allowances that were due or thereafter become due.

REFERENCES:
Military Personnel Records, RG-#94
Court Martial Procedures, RG-#153 OO 270
See Case #203 Private Thomas Jones

Case #203
Pvt. Thomas Jones
Co. H, 10th Conn. Infantry Regt.
Executed for Desertion
February 18, 1865

DESCRIPTION:

21 years of age, 5 feet 9¾ inches tall, brown hair, gray eyes, florid complexion, born in Ireland, occupation laborer, substitute.

Jones was drafted as a substitute and mustered into service on November 22, 1864 at Bridgeport, Connecticut and assigned to Company H, 10th Connecticut Infantry Regiment. Jones deserted his Regiment on January 4, 1865 and was apprehended.

A General Court Martial was convened at the Headquarters of the 1st Division, 24th Army Corps in the field in Virginia and on January 18, 1865 tried Private Thomas Jones, Company H, 10th Connecticut Infantry Regiment on charges of desertion, attempt to rob and violation of the 23rd Article of War.

Testimony disclosed that the accused was regularly enlisted and serving in Company H, Connecticut Infantry Regiment and that on the night of January 4, 1865, he did leave the Company and Regimental area without permission. Private Peter Frantz, Company H, 10th Connecticut Infantry Regiment was of German descent, unable to speak English and the Court ordered Captain Daniel Boardman, of the 10th Connecticut Regiment to act as the interpreter for Frantz. (Frantz later said, "I can understand English but I cannot speak it much.") Likewise, Private Joseph Forbeare, a Frenchman and a witness at the trial could not understand or speak English and a Colonel George D. Doudy, New York Volunteer Infantry acted as his interpreter. Frantz then stated that about the night of the 5th or 6th of January 1865, the accused, Jones, and another soldier named Brown came to him and asked him to persuade a Frenchman named Joseph Forbeare, Company A (and a tent mate of Frantz) to go out of the Union lines to buy whiskey. They (Jones and Brown) would then rob him and give Frantz $200. After the robbery, Jones and Brown planned to desert and they urged Frantz to desert with them. Finally, Frantz told Jones and Brown that he and Forbeare would go with them, however, Frantz had warned Forbeare and his Company Commander that the pair planned to rob him. If they failed to get him outside the camp, they planned to rob him in his tent, which he shared with Frantz. All four tried to leave camp but were turned back by sentries. An attempt later that evening, however, was successful and they went about one half mile outside the guard lines. Unbeknown to Jones and Brown, the Lt. Colonel commanding the

Regiment, having been informed of both the attempted desertion and robbery plan, assigned a Sergeant Sackett and several men to maintain surveillance of the prospective deserters/robbers. Following the party of four, James, Brown, Frantz and Forbeare, they were seen to enter a wooded area. A shot was fired and Jones was observed to flee the scene, but was captured by a Private Lamphere. Jones said, "I give up, shoot the Dutchman." When the party of four entered the woods, Forbeare was asked for his money, said he had none. While Brown pointed a loaded pistol at him, exclaiming, "Your money or your life." Brown fired at him and missed and the Sergeant's men apprehended all.

The accused had no other witnesses to present to the Court nor any statement in his behalf.

The Court deliberated, found Jones quilty and sentenced him to forfeit to the United States all pay and allowances now due or thereafter may become due and to be hanged by the neck until dead.

"On January 31, 1865, In the foregoing case the specification under the third charge is improperly drawn, in the alternative the proceedings and findings under that charge are disapproved.

"The proceedings and findings under the first and second charges are approved and as they justify the sentences that also is approved, but as the intention to commit the crime was known to others and to the Officer of the Regiment and the overt acts might have been prevented, I do earnestly recommend that the sentence be commuted. Reference is made to the case of Private John Brown, Company H, 10th Connecticut Infantry Regiment involving the same occurances, the record in which case goes forward with this.

Respectfully forwarded,
Jos. Hawley,
Brig. Genl. Comdg."

Major General Cord, on February 17, 1865 (the exact date is unclear) from the headquarters, Department of Virginia, Army of the James before Richmond wrote, "The proceedings and findings upon the first and second charges and their specifications in the foregoing case of Private Thomas Jones, Company H, 10th Conecticut Volunteers are approved. The sentence is approved and confirmed. The execution will take place under the Division Commander on February eighteenth 1865 between the hours of 12M and 3PM, or should the execution be unavoidably delayed beyond that time, it will take place as soon thereafter as practical."

Jones was convicted and sentenced to be executed by hanging at the lines before Richmond, Virginia on February 18, 1865.

REFERENCES:
Military Personnel Records, RG-#94
Court Martial Proceedings, RG-#153 OO 270

Case #204
Pvt. John Parker
Co. G, 10th Conn Infantry Regt.
Executed for Desertion
February 24, 1865

DESCRIPTION:
19 years of age, 5 feet 6 inches tall, light hair, blue eyes, light complexion, born in Ireland, occupation farmer, substitute.

Parker was drafted as a substitute and mustered into service on November 14, 1864 at Bridgeport, Connecticut. He was forwarded and assigned to Company G, 10th

Connecticut Infantry Regiment near Richmond Virginia. Parker attempted to desert the Regiment on December 27, 1864 and was arrested and placed in confinement. While in confinement for desertion, he was placed on a work detail from which he did elude his guard and desert on December 29, 1864. He was arrested at Bermuda Hundred, Virginia on the 31st of December 1864 and tried by court martial.

A General Court Martial was convened at Headquarters of the 1st Division, 24th Army Corps. in the field, Virginia and on January 20, 1865 tried Private John Parker, Company G, 10th Connecticut Infantry Regiment on a charge of desertion.

Parker pleaded not guilty but admitted being regularly enlisted as a soldier in the United States.

Testimony was offered to the court showing that Parker was absent without authority from his company and regiment on the afternoon of December 27, 1864 and was returned to the regiment under guard on December 29, 1864 and placed in the regimental guard house. He remained there only two hours as an order was received to transfer Parker to the 1st Division Provost marshall Guard House. Parker was confined there until the 29th of December, 1864 when he was set at work. Parker and 14 other prisoners with guards were taken on a work detail into a wooded area 1/2 mile from the guard house. Parker deserted, while at work, from the guard placed over him and remained absent until December 31, 1864 when he was returned to custody by the Corps Provost Marshall. Parker was observed by a sentry near Bermuda Hundred who thought he recognized Parker as he walked past the sentry post. The sentry halted Parker and had him come to the post where he observed he had been mistaken and did not know Parker. He did ask for his pass and Parker had none. Just then the Sergeant of the Guard came up and he asked Parker if he had a pass. Parker replied, he did not. The Sergeant ordered Parker taken to the Guard House from where he was taken to the Provost Marshall and finally returned to his Regiment for confinement, preferment of Charges and trial.

Parker offered no witnesses but did present a statement to the court.

Statement of Prisoner

"I was enlisted for the 1st Connecticut Cavalry Regiment and was put in the 10th Connecticut Infantry Regiment. Having enlisted for that Regiment I thought I ought to get in it and I was trying to find it. I was told it was down at City Point and I was trying to get to it. When I first enlisted they told me that I could go in any Regiment I liked, and I gave my name at Bermuda Hundred as John Parker. I also gave my name at Butler's Headquarters as John Parker."

The Court deliberated, found Parker guilty and sentenced him to forfeit to the United States all pay and allowances that are now or may become due hereafter and to be shot to death by musketry.

The execution was carried out near Richmond, Virginia on February 24, 1865.

REFERENCES:

Military Personnel Records, RG-#94
Court Martial Proceedings, RG-#153   OO 292
See Case #209 Private John Brown

Case #205

Pvt. Newell Jangrow
NV: Newal, Newel, Jangro
Co. H, 64th, NY Infantry Regt.
Executed for Desertion
March 3, 1865

DESCRIPTION:

27 years of age, 5 feet 7-3/4 inches tall, dark hair, gray eyes, dark complexion, born in

Canada, occupation shoemaker, substitute, literacy undetermined.

Jangrow enlisted and was mustered in on August 12, 1864 at Plattsburg, New York and on August 24, 1864 joined Company H, 64th New York Infantry Regiment. On February 5, 1865, while on picket line duty near Petersburg, Virginia, he attempted to desert to the enemy and was arrested and confined.

A General Court Martial was convened at the Headquarters of the 1st Division, 2nd Army Corps and on February 4, 1865 tried Private Newell Jangrow, Company H, 64th New York Infantry Regiment on a charge of desertion to the enemy.

Testimony showed that Jangrow was on picket line duty on the night of February 3, 1865 and that he left his post without authority. About 10:45 PM on the night of February 3, 1865, Jangrow, accompanied by another soldier, appeared, approaching from outside the Union Army Picket line. As Jangrow approached the picket post, he was challenged and then told to come in to the Union picket line. Jangrow left his gun at the point where he was challenged and it was found in the morning. As he entered the Union lines he said, "Good evening, are you not the rebels?" He and his accomplice were then physically seized. The accomplice said to Jangrow, "New, we are wrong!" The two prisoners were taken eventually to the Provost Marshall. Jangrow stated at various interrogations that he was a member of 120th Pennsylvania Volunteers, the 121st Pennsylvania Volunteers, the 140th Pennsylvania Volunteers. Several witnesses were closely questioned as to Jangrow's sobriety and all testified that he appeared sober and spoke rationally. One witness declared he had never heard Jangrow speak of deserting or running away. When Jangrow went on picket duty, from which he deserted, he was observed to be packing all his clothing to take with him on picket duty. When questioned about this by a comrade, he replied, "So if orders come to move, no one can steal it." Jangrow had also stated that he had obtained a furlough and would leave just as soon as he could get some money.

Jangrow offered a statement in his defense.

Statement of the Prisoner

"The reason I went over there was that I had been drinking for two days before and that same morning I went on picket. I never had any intention of deserting, as I expected to go on furlough."

The Court then deliberated, found the prisoner guilty and sentenced him to be shot to death by musketry.

The execution took place on March 3, 1865.

Jangrow and Private Anthony Raymond, Company B, 64th New York Infantry Regiment, were tried during the same session of the Court Martial and were executed at the same time and place.

REFERENCES:

Military Personnel Records, RG-#94
Court Martial Proceedings, RG-#153 LL 3190
See Case #207 Private Anthony Raymond

Case #206

Pvt. Frederick Murphy
N.V.: Francis AKA: James Powers
Co. F, 6th US Cavalry (Regulars)
Executed for Desertion
March 3, 1865

DESCRIPTION:

21 years of age, 5 feet 11½ inches tall, gray eyes, brown hair, ruddy complexion, born in Liverpool, England, occupation Boatman, illiterate, substitute.

Murphy enlisted as a substitute at Harrisburg, Pennsylvania on November 22, 1864 and was assigned to Company F, 6th U.S. Cavalry (Regulars) where he reported for duty on January 20, 1863. The Regiment was operating in the Winchester, Virginia area when Murphy deserted the service on January 24, 1865 from Camp Russel, Virginia.

Murphy, alias Powers, was arrested on the night of January 24, 1865 at the Union House (a hotel formerly called the Virginia House) in Winchester, Virginia.

He was charged with Desertion and conduct to the prejudice of good order and military discipline.

During the Court Martial trial, which began on February 4, 1865 at Winchester, Virginia, it was brought out that Murphy admitted to being a bounty jumper and that his given name was Frederick not Francis as was stated on the Court Martial charge sheet later corrected by amendment.

Apparently, Murphy planned to desert and approached Private Edgar Allan, Company M, 7th Michigan Cavalry Regiment, to secure forged discharge and final statement documents. Unbeknownst to Murphy, Allan was an undercover agent for the Provost Marshall of the Area Command and later testified at his Court Martial trial. Murphy and three others secured false documents, Murphy's made out in the name of James Powers, for which it seems they each paid one hundred dollars. Allan then led the four men successfully past sentries and into Winchester, Virginia where the deserters planned to stay overnight. Murphy, according to the trial testimony, was apprehended in bed at the Union House with the forged papers in his possession.

Murphy offered no defense on his own behalf and was found guilty and sentenced to be executed before a firing squad. No mention is made of the fate of Murphy's companions. Murphy was executed on March 3, 1865.

REFERENCES:

U.S. Army Service Records, National Archives
Enlistment Records, National Archives
Court Martial Proceedings, RG #153

Case #207
Private Anthony Raymond
NV: Ramond
Co. B, 64th, NY Infantry Regt.
Executed for Desertion
March 3, 1865

DESCRIPTION:

21 years old, 5 feet 8½ inches tall, brown hair, gray eyes, dark complexion, born in Canada, occupation lumberman, substitute, literacy undetermined.

Raymond, a substitute, was enlisted and mustered into service on August 16, 1864 at Remson, New York and assigned to Company B, 64th New York Infantry Regiment. On February 4, 1865 Raymond "attempted to desert to the enemy" and was apprehended, arrested and confined. (He and Private Newell Jangrow, (case #205) Company H, 64th New York Infantry Regiment were tried at the same Court Martial session).

A General Court Martial was convened at the Headquarters of the 1st Division, 2nd Army Corps and on February 4, 1865, tried Private Anthony Raymond, Company B, 64th New York Infantry Regiment on a charge of desertion to the enemy.

Witnesses testified that the accused was on picket duty on Vidette Post on the evening of February 3, 1865 and he left his post after 9 PM without authority. Raymond told his fellow soldier on guard that he was going out to get some tobacco, but he never returned. At half past 11 O'clock, Raymond was observed by sentries on picket duty about 20 or 25 paces in front of the Union lines. Raymond approached the Union picket line saying, "Good evening boys" and then started to leave to pick up his musket and accouterments but was seized by a sentry and taken to the rear. Another man was with Raymond and when asked if they came from the Rebel side remained silent. The man was then asked his unit designation and he said the 121st Pennsylvania. The man was then taken to the rear.

The accused had no witnesses to present to the Court, but offered a statement in his behalf.

Statement

"All I have to say is the man that went with me coaxed me into going, saying he would help to support me by dividing what money he had with me. We had an understanding when we left camp to go on picket to go in the same relief, so we would have a chance to get away together."

The Court then deliberated, found Raymond guilty and sentenced him to be shot to death with musketry on March 3, 1865 in the Division area. His companion Private Newell Jangrow was executed at the same time and place.

REFERENCES:

Military Personnel Records, RG-#94
Court Martial Proceedings, RG-#153 LL 3190
See Case #105 Private Newell Jangrow

Case #208
Pvt. (Sgt) (Cpl) Charles Sperry
NV: Spery
Co. E, 13th NY Cavalry Regt.
Executed for a series of capital crimes
March 3, 1865

DESCRIPTION:

29 years of age, 5 feet 10 inches tall, brown hair, gray eyes, dark complexion, born in Ireland, occupation printer, literate.

Sperry enlisted at New York City on March 28, 1863 and was mustered into service on Staten Island, New York on April 15, 1863 in Company E, 13th New York Cavalry Regiment. On May 17, 1863, Sperry apparently was absent without leave when the Regiment left New York City for duty and was arrested in New York City on Governor's Island, New York Harbor on May 20, 1863. He was returned to duty with his Regiment and promoted to Corporal on September 20, 1863. While on picket line duty on October 17, 1863, he was taken prisoner but managed to escape with the loss of his horse, arms and equipment. He was promoted to Sergeant on May 12, 1864. On the 18th of June, 1864 while on duty, in charge of a picket post near Langley, Fairfax County, Virginia. Smith committed a series of capital crimes which were to lead to his death. He began this bizarre series of crimes by quitting his guard post without urgent necessity or leave from his superior officer for several hours. He also was drunk while on duty prior to his leaving the post. Sperry then did, while absent from his post, assault, beat, strike and bruise Annie L. Nelson, 15 years of age, with intent to commit rape. Sperry was quickly arrested and incarcerated at the Provost Marshall Jail at Alexandria, Virginia on June 19, 1864.

A General Court Martial was convened at Washington, D. C. and on August 15, 1864 tried Sergeant Charles Sperry, Company E, 13th New York Cavalry Regiment on charges of quitting his guard without urgent necessity of leave, drunkenness on duty, assault and battery with intent to commit rape, rape.

Testimony of Annie L. Nelson, aged fourteen years, provided the description of the events of the night of June 18, 1863. A group of cavalry soldiers, led by Sergeant Sperry, arrived at the Nelson home, two miles above Langley, Virginia about one half hour past midnite. (Sperry had been drinking, left his duty as Sergeant of the Guard and, with several men, stopped at the Nelson home) Sperry pounded on the front door of the Nelson home which was opened by James A. Nelson, father of Annie. Sperry informed Mr. Nelson that he and his men were going to search the house for guerillas they believed were hiding there. Nelson was placed under an armed guard on the porch, while Sperry and another soldier searched the premises. Annie had gone into her mother's room when the soldiers entered the house. Sperry entered her mother's room with a pistol in one hand and a coal oil lamp in the other. He viewed the two women, Annie and her mother, then left after another soldier called him and they continued searching the house. Annie stated that Sperry and his men tried to kill their barking dogs, but were apparently unsuccessful. Sperry returned to Mrs. Nelson's room, grabbed Annie and her mother started screaming. Sperry struck Mrs. Nelson on the head with his pistol as she attempted to leave the house through a door leading into the yard. He dragged Mrs. Nelson back into the room and pushed her onto a chair. He warned Mrs. Nelson if she again tried to leave he would shoot her. He seized Annie and dragged her into an adjoining room, her mother then got up out of the chair and commenced screaming. Sperry released Annie and aimed his pistol at Mrs. Nelson and Annie ran to escape the room but Sperry caught her and knocked her up against the wall, then punched her twice in the face with his fist. She again tried to evade him but he struck her twice on the head with his pistol knocking her down but she continued screaming. Sperry attempted to disrobe Annie and managed to pull her clothing up above her waist exposing her body. Sperry's efforts to rape Annie were aborted by the warning delivered by one of his accomplices that other soldiers were coming.

In the meantime, Annie's mother had slipped out of the room and found her husband sitting on the porch under armed guard. She berated him for doing nothing to help Annie, then ran away from the house toward a neighbor's house where she aroused the household. The neighbor, Jones, sent some of his men over to the Union Army stockade to report the crime. The soldiers came to the Nelson home and arrested Sperry and the others.

When her mother returned to the house she saw Annie with blood soaking her hair and her face, arms and hands swollen and black from the beating. She told her mother he had not been successful in his intent that she had fought him off with all her strength.

Sperry had refused to permit Mr. Nelson to put clothes on (it is unclear whether he was nude or in a night shirt) while he waited in the cool evening on the porch under guard. Sperry had also struck Mr. Nelson on the head with his pistol. Mr. Nelson was so chilled he began shivering and he begged his guard to allow him to put some clothes on. The guard shouted to Sperry to allow Mr. Nelson to put something about his shoulders. Sperry, being drunk, apparently thinking the guard shouted here come the soldiers, dropped his pistol and bolted from the house. Nelson's guard then told him to go inside and put on his clothes. The soldiers from the stockade arrived under command of a Captain Brown and had captured and arrested Sperry. They picked up the pistol he had dropped and abandoned in his flight and then took Sperry to a place of confinement.

The accused called no witnesses on his behalf but did offer a statement to the court.

Statement of the Prisoner

"At the time mentioned I got onto that Post I dismounted from the horses and left two men in charge of the Post, and took one man with me and went beyond Langley to an Infantry Camp to deliver the countersign. We came back, dismounted, put up our horses, this was about eight o'clock. A little while after I thought I heard two shots fired back of the Post. I took one of the men with me and proceeded in that direction and scouted around about an hour, then we came back again and got another man from the Post and started off and went as far as the town of Langley, outside of the town we got some tracks of horses and we proceeded on as far as this man Nelson's place and could see nothing. We thought as we went that far we would stop and search the house, as our opinion was very bad of him, as to harboring guerillas in that neighborhood, we got to the house. I knocked at the front door and he got up and opened the door, we went in and I asked for a light he got me a light that was burning dimly. I told him we were agoing to search the house. I stepped into the front room, the lower floor, and then I got out in the hall again and he seemed to be very uneasy. I told him not to be uneasy we would not trouble him, me and the other man went upstairs into a room where there was four men in bed asleep. I searched under the beds and satisfied myself of the place. I pulled the door shut and told the man to keep an eye on it and not let them out and that I would search the lower part of the house myself and I went down stairs and went through into the sleeping rooms. his wife and daughter was in the room. I looked around the room and was in the act of turning back into the room again and his wife made a rush for the back door to get out. I told her she should not go out and no person in the house should leave it and the daughter made a rush to get out between me and the jam of the door. I shoved my hand before her and headed her off. I did not want any of them out because there might be persons in the barn and it would not do for us to let them out. The daughter tried to go out the 2nd time. I shoved her back into the sleeping room and told her she should not go out. I came out into the sitting room the daughter set on a chair. I looked around in the closet and under the sofa and when I looked under the sofa the revolver dropped out. At the time I left the sitting room and went back again into the bed room and went out into the back yard, came around the house and told the men I was satisfied and told them to come out during the time I was in the room I do not recollect taking any improper freedom with the girl."

The Court then deliberated, found the accused guilty except of the charge of rape and sentenced him to be shot to death with musketry.

The execution of the sentence was postponed pending the decision of the President of the United States.

President Lincoln asked Judge Advocate General Holt to review the case and make recommendations thereupon. General Holt "recommended that the law be allowed to take it's course." On January 25, 1865, President Lincoln wrote "sentence approved" on the proceedings of the General Court Martial of Sergeant Sperry.

He was subsequently moved to the Central Guard House of Washington, D. C., Sperry was reduced to the rank of Private after the commission of the crimes. On February 12, 1865, while in the Central Guard House, Washington, D. C., he was listed as a patient in Stone General Hospital, Washington. No cause for his illness is given, nor is there any indication of an illness of more than a temporary indisposition.

He was sentenced to be executed by a firing squad at the Old Capitol Prison (where he was transferred on February 25, 1865) on Friday, March 3, 1865 between the hours of 10AM and 12PM.

REFERENCES:

Military Personnel Records, RG-#94
Court Martial Proceedings, RG-#153 NN 2427

Case #209
Pvt. David Geer
Co. D, 28th Regt, IL Infantry
Executed for Murder
March 4, 1865

DESCRIPTION:

27 years of age, 5 feet 11 inches tall, red hair, blue eyes, fair complexion, born in Franklin County, Virginia, occupation farmer, literate.

Geer enlisted at Chicago, Illinois on February 29, 1864 and was mustered into service at Camp Douglas (Chicago, Illinois) on April 21, 1864 in Company I, 28th Illinois

Infantry Regiment. He was forwarded to the Regiment which was stationed in the Natchez, Mississippi area arriving on April 29th for duty.

Associated with Geer in this most inhuman and despicable crime were Private Amsel Harmen, 4th Illinois Cavalry Regiment, Private Alexander McBride, Company I, 28th Illinois Infantry Regiment, and Private William Thomas. There are reports of a fifth participant in the atrocity but no positive identification of the soldier has been located.

Not on Official List
Pvt. Alexander McBride
Co. I, 28th Regt., IL Infantry
Sentenced to death but
commuted to Dishonorable Discharge

DESCRIPTION:

18 years of age, 5 feet 7 inches tall, dark hair, hazel eyes, dark complexion, born in Grafton, Calhoun County, Illinois, occupation farmer, not married.

McBride enlisted at Barry, Illinois on August 27, 1861 and was mustered into service at Camp Butler (Springfield, Illinois) on August 27, 1861 in Captain Hurt's Company, 28th Regiment Illinois Infantry. The unit was redesignated Company I, 28th Illinois Infantry Regiment.

McBride served with his regiment and at the Battle of Metamore (Hatchie River) on October 5, 1862 was severely wounded in the head. He was taken from the battlefield and transported to the U.S. Army General Hospital in Jackson, Tennessee where he was treated until June 25, 1863 when he was transferred to the U.S. Army (Adams) General Hospital at Memphis, Tennessee where he convalesced acting as a nurse. On march 9, 1864 he was discharged from the Hospital and returned to duty with his regiment at the Beef Yard in Natchez, Mississippi.

Not on "Official List"
Pvt. Asmiel Harmenn
NV: Armiel Harmon
Co. A, 4th Regt, IL Cavalry
Never sentenced or executed

DESCRIPTION:

20 years of age, 5 feet 9 inches tall, brown hair, gray eyes, dark complexion, born in France, occupation farmer.

Harmenn enlisted September 8, 1861 at Ottawa, Illinois and was mustered into service on September 26, 1861 at Ottawa, Illinois in Company A, 4th Illinois Cavalry Regiment. Not on "Official List" Private William Thomas, not further identified.

The victim of this senseless and despicable crime was a descendant of a famous New England family, the Sargent's. His father, Winthrop Sargent, born 1753 in Gloucester, Massachusetts had a distinguished public service career. He was an officer in the American Army during the Revolutionary War and was one of the founders in 1783 of the Cincinnatus Society, composed of Officers of the Army and Navy of the American Military Forces serving during the Revolutionary War and their male descendants. Following his service in the Revolutionary War, Winthrop Sargent became Surveyor General and Secretary of the Ohio Company, a land company that aided in the settlement of Ohio. In 1798 he was appointed the first Territorial Governor of Mississippi and served until 1801. The Capitol was established in Natchez and Winthrop Sargent built a brick mansion, named Gloucester (Gloster), in memory of his birthplace, on his plantation near Natchez. Winthrop's only child to live to adulthood, George Washington Sargent was born at Natchez on July 2, 1802. Winthrop Sargent had many interests in the natural sciences where he observed, recorded and reported on the weather and natural phenomena such as earthquakes. He died in 1820, survived by his wife who died in 1845 at Philadelphia, Pennsylvania. George Washington Sargent, as sole survivor and executor of the estate moved to Philadelphia where he remained until 1849 when he returned to Natchez and took up his residence at Gloucester.

In 1864, Natchez had been occupied by Union Forces and G. W. Sargent was at Gloucester recovering from a severe illness. On the night of May 10, 1864 he was alone in the mansion except for a single negro servant. His wife had crossed the river to Louisiana to transact some business as his poor health would not permit him to travel. About 10 PM he decided to retire and as he made his way through the house he detected some unusual noise in another room. Upon opening the door, he was immediately attacked by three men. Still not fully recovered from his illness, Sargent nevertheless grappled with one of the attackers and had nearly wrested the man's pistol from him, when one of the other intruders fired a bullet piercing he chest and lung. When he fell, they fled apparently to Natchez, avoiding the guards on the roads and outskirts of the City.

Geer and McBride were captured on June 1, 1864 and placed in confinement, while Harmenn and Thomas were never found, as they immediately deserted their regiments. The fifth man, said to be a member of a colored Regiment, was never positively identified nor apprehended.

Sargent lingered alive and fully conscious until the early morning of May 13, 1864, dying without the presence of his beloved wife, who had been prevented from returning by Union Army regulations.

McBride and Geer were charged with murder and at the trial their motive for the attempted robbery was revealed. They had planned to seize Sargent, tie him up and smother him until he disclosed the hiding place of his valuables or to arrest him on the pretense that they were sent by the local Provost Marshall and then to take him into a wooded area and torture him until he gave them the information about the location of his money, jewelry and so forth.

McBride and Geer were found guilty of murder and sentenced to be executed. For some undisclosed reason the carrying out of the sentence of the court encountered protracted delays. Finally on March 4, 1865, Geer was executed by a firing squad at Natchez. McBride however, was not executed and lingered in "durance Vile".

On September 4, 1865 Special Order #476, War Department, Adjutant General's Office, Washington was issued.

"1- The sentences of the General Court Martial, `To be shot to death with musketry, at such time and place as the General Commanding may direct' - in the cases of Privates David Geer and Alexander McBride, Company I, 28th Illinois Volunteers, as promulgated in General Orders #38, Headquarters Department and Army of the Tennessee, of October 31, 1864, is commuted to dishonorable discharge from the service of the United States, without pay, allowance or bounty. The Quartermaster's Department will furnish them transportation to their homes."

In reply the following memorandum was sent. "Private David Geer, Company D, 28th Illinois Volunteers whose sentence of death was commuted to dishonorable discharge from the service by S.O. 476, A.G.O., September 4, 1865, was shot to death with musketry at Post of Natchez, Mississippi March 4, 65." McBride, in accordance with the order, was released.

It is related that the Union Army was not active in prosecuting the perpetrators of the vicious crime and justice was only achieved because of the persistent efforts of Sargent's eldest daughter, Mary.

REFERENCES:

Military Personnel Records, RG-#94

Court Martial Proceedings, RG-#153 LL 2874

"The early Sargents of New England, Winthrop Sargent, 1853" 1922 Xerox copy, no place of publication.

Report of the Adjutant General of the State of Illinois, Volume II 1861-66, revised 1900,

Springfield, Illinois Philips Bros, State Printers.
State of Illinois Military Archives, records.
History of the 28th Illinois Volunteer.
Guide to the microfilm edition of the Winthrop Sargent Papers, Massachusetts History Sve., Boston, 1865, F.S. Allis Jr., Editor, R. Bartolomei, Assoc. Editor.
The Edith Wyatt Moore Collection, at the Judge George W. Armstrong Library, Natchez, Mississippi.

Case #210
Pvt. James Kelley
NV: Kelly
Co. D, 67th Penn. Inf. Regt.
Executed for Desertion
March 11, 1865

DESCRIPTION:

21 years of age, 5 feet 3 inches tall, brown hair, gray eyes, florid complexion, born in Ireland, occupation sailmaker, substitute, illiterate.

Kelley enlisted as a substitute and was mustered into service at Reading, Pennsylvania on December 6, 1864 and assigned to Company D, 67th Pennsylvania Infantry Regiment as a recruit arriving on December 22, 1864. Kelley deserted the Camp of the 67th Pennsylvania Infantry Regiment in the field near Petersburg, Virginia on December 23, 1864. He was arrested on January 9, 1865, confined, tried by court martial on January 31, 1865 convicted and sentenced to death by firing squad on March 10, 1865.

A General Court Martial was convened at the headquarters of the 1st Brigadier, 3rd Division, 6th Army Corps and on February 11, 1865 tried Private James Kelley (Kelly) unassigned, 67th Pennsylvania Infantry Regiment on a charge of Desertion.

Testimony offered showed that Kelley was mustered into the service of United States as a substitute (for which he received $500.00) on December 6, 1864 and arrived as an unassigned replacement for the 67th Pennsylvania Infantry Regiment on December 22, 1864 and did desert the Regiment on December 23, 1864. He was arrested in City Point, Virginia and returned to his Regiment under guard on January 8, 1865.

Witnesses swore Kelley was in a group of 86 replacements received by the Regiment on December 22, 1864 and did answer present at the Roll Call. He was absent on the following day, without permission. Other witnesses testified positively that the man returned under arrest was the Kelley (Kelly) they recognized under the same name as far back as his enlistment in Philadelphia.

Kelley (Kelly) originally told the Provost Marshall, while being questioned at City Point, Virginia, that he had gone there to send his money home by Express. Inquiring at the Express Office disclosed that no such transaction had been made by the prisoner. Kelley (Kelly) then changed his story, saying he had sent the money to Philadelphia in charge of a friend of his.

A prisoner confined in the guardhouse prior to and during the incarceration of Kelley (Kelly) said Kelley (Kelly) told him that he intended to go north and that he was arrested on the docks at City Point while waiting for his uncle, employed on a boat tied up at a City Point Dock.

The accused having no witnesses to present in his behalf did offer a statement to the court.

"Statement of the Prisoner"

"I went to City Point for the purpose of sending my money home. After I had sent it home I went to the Restaurant and got my dinner and walked around City Point and was arrested on New Year's day, between two & three O'clock. I was brought before the

Provost Marshall. He asked what Regt. I belonged to & I told him the 67th Penn. Vols. I was sent back to the Regt. on the 9th of January 1865. From there I was sent to the Div. Guard House. I was there about a week when Henry Alfords came in there. He & I and Hicks were mixing mortar together. He asked me where I was arrested? I told him at City Point. I told him that I had gone down without a pass, that I did not think that there was any harm in it. He asked me why I did not stow myself away in a boat while there and go home? I told him I did not go there to go home, but to send money home. He asked me why, when I was in the Bull ring (Bull pen, a common holding area for recently arrested persons), I did not say I belonged to some Regt. in the Valley so that I could have gone home? I told him I did not intend to desert, did not go for that purpose."

The court then deliberated, found the accused guilty and sentenced him to be dishonorably discharged the service of the United States, with loss of all pay and allowances now due or to become due and to be confined at hard labor for the balance of his enlistment on such public works as the Commanding General of the Army may direct.

"On Feb 18, 1865, the Brig. Genl. Comdg. in returning the three cases of Privates Kelley, Bates & Vawhen for the reconsideration of the court respectfully calls it's attention to the following facts that Hicks by the preceding G.C.M. a member of the same party of substitutes & deserters was sentenced to *death*. That is the usual penalty affixed by courts for the desertion of substitutes. It is the Custom of War. The sentence in the Hicks case was approved by the Maj. Genl. Comdg. the Army & the propriety of such a sentence has long since passed beyond dispute. No lesser punishment suffices for a class of men who not only betray the cause, but also the Army, by their hellish rascality.

The fact of desertion once proven is full evidence of *intention* to desert, the motive is then thrown upon the prisoner who can (if possible) show that there is no intention to desert. But the great experience of this Army with substitutes and a full knowledge of their practices should (with numerous precedents well known to the Court) have induced a leaning rather to *severe justice* than to such toleration as the Court has practiced.

The object of the Brig. Gen'l. Comdg. is simply that the Court may have another opportunity of enforcing the usages of war in these cases, trusting that it will not fail in doing it's whole duty. He cannot permit the records of the Court to go on to a Superior Authority with out the Evidence that it has been duly advised of it's duty.

Respectfully,
your most obedt. Servt.
I. Seymour,
Brig. Genl, USA"

The court then proceeded to reconsider the case of Private James Kelley (Kelly), 67th Pennsylvania Volunteer Regiment and after mature deliberation substituted the following sentence for the original sentence:

That the court sentence the accused, James Kelley, Private 67th Regiment Pennsylvania Volunteers to be shot to death with musketry.

The execution took place on March 9, 1865 near City Point, Virginia.

On March 2, 1865, Kelley had a brief note written for him. "Miss Susan Kelly, 617 Bacon St., Philadelphia, Penn. I am sentenced by a court martial to be shot to death by musketry, on Friday the 10th of March, you and John Smith go to Washington and do all you can with President Lincoln to have me reprieved, answer,

Private James Kelly,
67th Penn. Vols."

No reply is found with Kelley's military documents.

A Special Order #41 (extract), dated March 10, 1865, Headquarters, 3rd Division, 1, On account of the inclemency of the weather the Execution of Private James Kelly 67th Penn. Vols. is hereby postponed until 12M the 11th inst. - By command of Brig. Genl

Seymour"
The execution took place on March 11, 1865.

REFERENCES:
Military Personnel Records, RG-#94
Court Martial Proceedings, RG-#153 OO 285

Case #211
Pvt. William T. Griffin
NV: Griffith, George Bolter
Co. C, 8th Del. Vol. Infantry Regt.
Executed for Desertion
March 10, 1865

DESCRIPTION:
21 years of age, 5 feet 8½ inches tall, hazel eyes, dark hair, light complexion, born in Sussex County, Delaware, occupation brakeman, literate.

Griffin enlisted for one year on August 22, 1864 at Wilmington Delaware and was assigned to Company C, 8th Delaware Volunteer Infantry Regiment at Camp Smithers, near Wilmington, Delaware. He deserted the service on September 1, 1864 and was not seen or heard from until February 14, 1865, when he was recognized amongst a group of substitute replacements at City Point, Virginia by members of his old Company. He was arrested, confined and court martialed.

A General Court Martial was convened at City Point, Virginia and on February 24, 1865 tried Private William T. Griffin (alias George Bolter), Company C, 8th Delaware Infantry Regiment on a charge of desertion.

The General Court Martial proceedings at City Point, Virginia on February 24, 1865 reveal a rather creative alibi for Griffin.

Griffin states in his testimony that he left Wilmington, Delaware on September 1, 1864 and went to Philadelphia where he remained three weeks. He further stated that he was a Sergeant in the 7th Delaware Volunteer Infantry Regiment and was nominated for election to a Second Lieutenancy but lost the election by 3 votes. He was then urged, by the enlisted men, to organize and recruit a new company and to assume the Captaincy of same. He further states he recruited men for the 8th Delaware Volunteer Infantry Regiment. Wearing his Sergeants blouse he went to Philadelphia and was promptly arrested and confined in the guardhouse. While in the guardhouse a man approached him and asked if he was a member of the 7th Delaware Regiment. He replied he was discharged from the regiment. The man told him he would arrange for his release from the guard house and left. A few moments later the officer of the day came to him and asked if he had a pass. Griffin says he showed the officer his pass from Camp Smithers to go to Wilmington, Delaware and a second pass to go from Wilmington to Philadelphia. He was then released and went to the railroad station to return to Wilmington. At the depot he was arrested by a man who took him to New York City, lodged him in a hotel, got him drunk and took all his money before departing. Being without funds, he went to work to earn enough money to return to Wilmington.

Court martial testimony by Lieutenant Frank Myers, Company C, 8th Delaware Infantry Regiment, stated that Griffin had received state and local enlistment bounties and military clothing. Further he had attempted unsuccessfully to desert a day or two prior to his successful attempt on September 1, 1864. On February 145, 1865 Lieutenant Myers recognized Griffin and confronted him in a squad of substitutes at City Point, Virginia. At that time Griffin again created an alibi, stating he was drugged and was enlisted as a substitute under the name of George Bolter. He further stated he did not know he was enlisted, never received any bounty and found all this had occurred at Buffalo, New York. He was then forwarded to City Point, Virginia where he was recognized and arrested.

The verdict of the trial was guilty of desertion, penalty of death before a firing squad. The sentence was carried out on March 10, 1865 at City Point, Virginia.

REFERENCES:

Military Personnel Records, RG-#94
Court Martial Proceedings, RG-#153 OO 285

Case #212
Pvt. William Jackson
Co. A, 10th Conn. Vol. Inf.
Executed for Desertion
March 10, 1865

DESCRIPTION:

24 years of age, 5 feet 6 inches tall, light brown hair, hazel eyes, dark complexion, born in England, occupation seaman, substitute.

Jackson was accepted as a substitute and mustered into the Army on November 5,1864 at New Haven, Connecticut. He was forwarded to the 10th Connecticut Infantry Regiment which was on duty in Virginia. On November 23, 1864, he was assigned for duty to Company A and was Absent Without Leave on November 24, 1864. Jackson and several other who deserted were captured together on November 24, 1864, arrested and confined in the Provost Marshall's stockade pending investigation and the filing of charges.

A General Court Martial was convened at the Headquarters of the 1st Division, 24th Army Corps and on January 17, 1865 tried Private William Jackson, Company A, 10th Connecticut Infantry Regiment on a charge of desertion.

Testimony was given that stated Jackson was assigned to Company A about November 23, 1864 and was absent without leave on November 24, 1864. Jackson was arrested on November 24, 1864 by a Corporal Grattin of the 11th Pennsylvania who received a reward of $30.00 for the capture. Same was paid by a Quartermaster Officer. Grattin testified that he was on duty on the morning of November 24, 1864 along Four Mile Creek near Deep Bottom and in an inspection tour of his area of jurisdiction he heard suspicious noises in the brush. Upon investigation of that area, he found six soldiers hiding, whom he promptly arrested and brought to a Colonel Spear who ordered them taken to the Provost Marshall. Grattin testified that he had received a reward for eight men captured, at thirty dollars each. Grattin produced a voucher for the payment of the reward money which listed the name of Jackson and described him as a deserter. The voucher was authenticated by Colonel Spear, 11th Pennsylvania Cavalry as correct.

Jackson had no defense witnesses to call, but did offer a statement in his defense.

Statement of the Prisoner

"I was in with three others chaps on the 24th day of November last. We went to find some provisions for dinner. We went rambling about and missed our road. We came across a black man doing picket duty, when we went up and asked where the 10th Connecticut Regiment was. He showed us across to a house where the sentry was. We got a stones throw from where we were when we were arrested; we were sitting *down* smoking a pipe, in the path under a little hill."

The Court then deliberated, found the prisoner guilty and sentenced him to forfeit all pay and allowances to the United States, that were now or may become due hereafter and to be sent to death with musketry. The execution took place on March 10, 1865.

REFERENCES:

Military Personnel Records, RG-#94
Military Court Martial Proceedings, RG-#153 MM 1613

Case #213
Pvt. John Mahoney
Co. K, 10th Conn. Infantry Regt.
Executed for Desertion
March 10, 1865

DESCRIPTION:
21 years of age, 5 feet 4-1/2 inches tall, brown hair, blue eyes, ruddy complexion, born in Ireland, occupation laborer, substitute.

Mahoney enlisted and was mustered into service as a substitute on November 5, 1864 at New Haven, Connecticut. He joined his Regiment in the Richmond, Virginia area and on November 24, 1864 he deserted in Henrico County, Virginia. Mahoney was apprehended, for which a reward of $30.00 was paid, and tried by court martial.

A General Court Martial was convened at Headquarters of the 1st Division, 24th Army Corps in the field, Virginia, and on February 14, 1865 tried Private John Mahoney, Company K, 10th Connecticut Infantry Regiment on a charge of desertion.

Testimony disclosed that on November 24, 1864 he was absent from the noon roll call and remained absent until he was returned, under guard, to his Company and Regiment on November 27, 1864 at their camp near the New Market Road in Henrico County, Virginia. He was arrested by a Corporal Grattin of the 11th Pennsylvania Cavalry. Grattin testified that he had arrested six men on November 24th and two men on November 25th. The men arrested on the 24th were attempting to go outside the federal picket lines at a point about three miles from the camp of the 10th Connecticut Infantry Regiment.

The prisoner offered the Court neither witnesses nor statement for his defense.

The Court then deliberated, found the accused guilty and sentenced him to forfeit to the United States all pay and allowances that are now or may become due hereafter and to be shot to death by musketry.

The execution took place on March 10th, 1865 in the Divisional Area.

William Jackson, Company A, 10th Connecticut Infantry Regiment (case #212) was executed on the same day and place.

REFERENCES:
Military Personnel Records, RG-#94
Court Martial Proceedings, RG-#153 MM 1613

Case #214
Pvt. William Cooper
Co. E, 10th Conn. Infantry Regt.
Executed for Desertion
March 11, 1865

DESCRIPTION:
21 (26) years of age, 5 feet 5½ inches tall, dark hair, grey eyes, dark complexion, born in England, occupation seaman, substitute, literate.

Cooper was drafted and mustered into service as a substitute October 28, 1864 and was assigned to Company E, 10th Connecticut Infantry regiment. Cooper deserted his regiment at Henrico County, Virginia on November 24, 1864. He was captured on November 27, 1864, for which a reward and expenses totaling $30.00 was paid.

A General Court Martial was convened on January 14th, 1865 at the Headquarters of the 1st Division, 24th Army Corps, in the field for the trial of Private William Cooper, Company E, 10th Connecticut Infantry Regiment on the charge of desertion.

Testimony was offered to show that Cooper deserted his Regiment on November 24, 1864 where it was stationed in the rear of the main lines of the Army, within Henrico

County, Virginia. He was with the Company for only a day or two when he was arrested in the company of another man, never identified by name during the trial. Both were wandering along the picket lines outside the main Union lines when arrested. The testimony identified Cooper as an assigned member of Company E, 10th Connecticut Infantry Regiment and described his geographical position when arrested. One unusual bit of information was the statement of witness for the prosecution, Sergeant R. M. Ross, Company F, 11th Pennsylvania Cavalry Regiment to the question, "Have you or Corporal Gratten received bounty, ($30) dollars for arresting the prisoner or an order therefore?" Answer, "Corporal Gratten received a check for two hundred and forty ($240) dollars for arresting eight deserters and this man Cooper is one of them."

Cooper asked some questions of witnesses but offered no defense. He did furnish a long rambling written statement to the Court.

Statement of the Prisoner

"I slepped one night in the 10th Conn. Vols. They put me in Camp with "E" to get my rations. I answered at roll call that night and in the morning I walked around until three o'clock in the day, the man that was with me inquired about the 8th Pennsylvania Cavalry. He was told it lay out a little distance from there. He was pointed in the direction. This man that was with me knew a man that was in the 8th Pennsylvania Cavalry. They told us we could travel anyplace around. We went off to look for the 8th Penn. Cavalry. After we got out side of the Camp we inquired of a man if he knew where the 8th Penn. Cavalry was. He said there was a Cavalry Regt. down there, and we went and got a drink at the Sutlers of his beer and turned around to come back and we fell in with a man in the woods, and he sold me some whiskey. We walked along until we drank it all and became intoxicated. It came on dark and we lay down, about 3 or 4 o'clock in the morning we woke up. We tried to find our way out of the woods but could not. At day light we seen some smoke in the woods and we went for it, when we went there it was a nigger camp. We warmed ourselves by the fire and inquired of the negroes where our regiment was, they conducted us over to a cavalry camp on the hill and we asked them what Cavalry it was. They told us they believed it was the 8th Pennsy. We went right over to them. A negro corporal told us that was the 8th Pennsylvania and they would tell us where our Regiment was, we seen smoke up there and was going towards it, We had only got about forty or fifty yards from the Negro camp, two Cavalry men asked us where we were going. We asked him if he knew where the 10th Regiment of Connecticut Volunteers was. They told us to come along with them. We asked them if they were the 8th Penn. Cavalry, they said no. We told them that we were told they (the 8th Penn. Cavalry) lay over here. They told us no. They told us they were pickets and arrested us and brought us in. They asked us how we came there and we told them the negroes had told us where our regiment was, We asked the Cavalry to come and see where we came across but they would not do it."

The statement was accepted by the Court and the Court then deliberated. The accused was found guilty and sentenced to death before a firing squad. On the 16th of January 1865, the Court being convened, reconsidered Private Cooper's sentence and added "to forfeit to the United States all pay and allowances that are now due or may become due here after." Cooper was executed on March 11, 1865 near the camp of his Regiment.

The last clause concerning forfeiture of pay and allowances was increasingly used as the war entered the years of 1863 and onwards. There was an awareness of and fear that in years to come next of kin would besiege the War Department with requests for bounty or wage payments as well as possible future pension rights and payments.

REFERENCES:

Military Personnel Records, RG-#94
Court Martial Proceedings, RG-#153 MM 1613

Case #215
Pvt. John Nichols
NV: James Nicholson, Nicholus, Nicholas
Co. A, 69th NY Infantry Regt.
Executed for Desertion
March 14, 1865

DESCRIPTION:

36 years of age, 5 feet 4 inches tall, brown hair, hazel eyes, fair complexion, born in Canada, occupation farmer, substitute, literate.

Nichols was drafted and mustered in as a substitute at Lewiston, New York on September 22, 1864 and assigned to Company A, 69th New York Infantry Regiment. The Regiment was stationed near Petersburg, Virginia. Nichols deserted his regimental picket line and attempted to enter enemy lines and was arrested on October 26, 1864.

A General Court Martial was convened at Headquarters, 1st Division, 2nd Army Corps, and on January 18, 1865 tried Private John Nichols, Company A, 69th New york Infantry Regiment on a charge of desertion.

The accused did not wish to introduce counsel. Witnesses testified that the accused deserted his post on the night of October 27, 1864 while on assigned picket duty near Petersburg, Virginia without leave or permission and attempted to reach the Rebel lives. He apparently lost his way in the darkness and he traveled from one portion of the Union Army picket line to another portion of the Union Army picket line believing that he had reached the Rebel picket line opposite his starting point. He was interviewed by a federal officer, who quickly ascertained Nichols' true intention, to desert to the Rebels, and pretended he was a Rebel Officer. He skillfully questioned the accused who offered detailed information about the position, strength and so forth of the Federal positions.

Nichols had been with the Regiment only 5 or 6 weeks when he deserted and had thrown his gun away when he left his assigned post. Nichols claimed to be a Canadian citizen who went to Buffalo and then to New York City to enlist. The officer who interviewed the accused was puzzled by various aspects of Nichols story. He went to the headquarters of the adjoining picket line and finally found that they had a man missing. An officer from that sector accompanied him back to his headquarters where the accused was being "held" and instantly recognized him as one of his own men.

The accused having no testimony to offer presented the following statement to the Court.

Statement in Defense

"About 12 o'clock in the night a man came and ordered us to pack up. I got up about half awake and went down to the post where the man was standing, and told him there was a man came and ordered us to pack up and be ready for a move. I asked him to go up and see, and I would stay in his place while he was gone. He went up and that is the last I recollect of myself, until I found myself way out in the lot. I was down on my knees digging a hole, I suppose I was after water. When I got so I knew where I was I went up to where the Lieutenant was. I had no thought of going over to the other side. I was entirely lost. I did not know where I was."

The Court deliberated, found the prisoner guilty and sentenced him to be hanged by the neck until he be dead.

The prisoner was sentenced to be executed on March 10, 1865.

There are a number of errors or contradiction of dates and facts among his records. His name, for example, is confused with other individuals with different name spelling. The date of execution is recorded in several places as March 10th and in others as March 14, 1865. The original date set was listed as March 10th as were published orders concerning the execution ceremonies. Several notations seem to be at variance with the majority of the records in regard to his death. One in such regard is ambiguous in that it lists March 14, 1865 as the date and "died of disease, executed by sentence of G.C.M. (General Court Martial)." Another terse statement on a Muster-Out-Roll states, "Died March 10, 1865 at Petersburg, Virginia." One Death Disability Record specifies the method of execution, by hanging, and the Company descriptive book (Register of Deaths) states, died, March 10, 1865 at Petersburg executed (hanged)."

As stated in the introduction to the individual case histories of the men on the Official List of Soldiers Executed, during the Late War, there were clerical errors committed which while they tend at times to confuse one studying them, are understandable for what they are, simple human errors, not by and large errors of fact, or intent.

In the case of Nichols, the sentence of execution in his case specified March 10, 1865, or as soon thereafter as practicable. Another note from Headquarters, 2nd Army Corps, Assistant Adjutant General's office, dated March 10, 1865 addressed to Brevet Major General Miles Commanding 1st Division, "General: Please send by bearer the report of the execution of Pvt. John Nicholas (sic) 60 NY Vols ordered to take place today. No tri-monthly report of casualties from your Div has been seen.

Whittly, AAG"

No reply had been found to this message. The possibility of postponement of the execution from March 10, to March 14, 1865 is not an unusual respite.

REFERENCES:

Military Personnel Records, RG-#94
Court Martial Proceedings, RG-#153 OO 285

Case #216

Pvt. J. J. McNealy
1st Maryland Infantry, Unknown Company
Executed for Desertion

DESCRIPTION:

A General Court Martial was convened at City Point, Virginia and on February 28, 1865 tried Private J. J. McNealy, of the 1st Maryland Infantry Regiment on a charge of desertion.

The testimony in this case is identical to that offered in the trial of Private James Weaver, see case #219 for details of the trial.

The Court deliberated, found the accused guilty and sentenced him to be shot to death with musketry.

The execution took place at City Point, Virginia on March 18, 1865.

REFERENCES

Military Personnel Records, RG-#94
Court Martial Proceedings, RG-153 OO 316
See Case #219 - Private James Weaver

Case #217

Pvt. John Smith
(new) Co. H, 8th, NJ Infantry Regt.
Executed for Desertion
March 18, 1865

DESCRIPTION:

34 years of age, 5 feet 4¼ inches tall, light hair, gray eyes, dark complexion, born in Germany, occupation laborer, substitute.

Smith enlisted as a substitute and was mustered into service at Morristown, New

Jersey on September 8, 1864 and was sent to Petersburg, Virginia in (new) Company H, 8th New Jersey Infantry Regiment.

A General Court Martial was convened in the field near Petersburg, Virginia and on February 25th, 1865 tried Private John Smith, Company H, 8th Battalion, New Jersey Infantry on a charge of Desertion to the Enemy.

Testimony offered to the Court disclosed that Smith was a substitute, who had received $675.00 as a bounty for enlistment. He entered the service on September 18, 1864 and deserted his unit near Fort Stevens/Fort Morton, Virginia on or about October 23, 1864. He was arrested in City Point, Virginia on January 24, 1865 and returned to his military unit for trial.

Witnesses positively identified Smith as a member of their military unit, duly enrolled and further that he had left his Company without permission and did not return voluntarily.

Smith offered no witnesses to the Court but did prepare a statement for the Court.

"Statement to the Court"

"I went with two other men to City Point, Virginia to get some Whiskey. We got on to the Norfolk Railroad and went down the road, and I objected to going any further. I laid down and got asleep and the next morning six rebels arrested us and took us away. I paid one of the Rebels fifty dollars to let me go. I was three weeks in getting to our lines in Kentucky. I did not pretend to be a rebel deserter."

The Court then deliberated, found Smith guilty, and sentenced him to be shot to death with musketry.

The execution took place on March 17, 1865 at City Point, Virginia.

REFERENCES:
Military Personnel Records, RG-#94
Court Martial Proceedings, RG-#153 OO 316

Case #218
Pvt. Frederick H. Brandt
Co. E, 81st, NY Infantry Regt.
Executed for Desertion
March 26, 1865

DESCRIPTION:

26 years of age, 5 feet 9 inches tall, light hair, blue eyes, light complexion, born in Denmark, occupation Miller.

Brandt enlisted on March 11, 1864 at Oswego, New York and was mustered into service on March 14, 1864 at Oswego, New York in Company E, 81st New York Infantry. The Regiment went into service in Virginia and on May 31, 1864 Brandt was ill and hospitalized at White House Landing, Virginia where he remained until returned to duty on September 22, 1864. On October 27, 1864, he was reported as Absent Without Leave (AWOL) and was returned to his Company on October 30, 1864. On January 1, 1865, he again was reported sick but returned to duty on January 21, 1865. He attempted to desert to the enemy, was apprehended and arrested on March 24, 1865.

Private Frederick W. Brandt, Company E, 81st New York Infantry Regiment was tried by a General Court Martial at the camp of the Independent Division, 24th Army Corps on March 23, 1865 for attempting to desert to the enemy.

Brandt applied to the Court to permit the Reverend I. G. Duryee, Chaplain of the 81st New York Infantry Regiment as his counsel. The request was granted by the Court.

Testimony of witnesses disclosed that on the night of March 22, 1865, members of the picket in front of the lines of the Independent Division, 24th Army Corps between the estimated hours of 11 PM and 2 AM, two men on horseback rode up to the picket line.

One rider, dismounted and briefly addressed the members of the picket, giving the impression he was a staff Colonel or General. The other horseman was believed to be his orderly and did not dismount. After a few moments, the "Officer" remounted and the two horsemen galloped away, riding toward the rebel lines. The "Officer" and the "orderly" became separated in the darkness and the "Officer" called to the "orderly" to join him. As they both then resumed the gallop toward the rebel lines, one of the Union sentinels on the picket line fired at the "Officer." The "orderly," hearing the shot halted and was confronted by a union soldier who inquired who he was and what he was doing. The "orderly" replied that he was an "orderly" to an officer and that they had lost their way in the dark and further that the "officer" was drunk. An Officer present ordered two of his men to take the "orderly" and horse to the Provost Marshall for questioning, which they did. In the meantime, the "Officer" had escaped, presumably into the rebel lines. Witnesses testified that Brandt, who pretended to be the orderly had been drinking on the night of the 22nd and was in the Company of a private Charles Forrest of the 81st Regiment. Forrest was described as a "bad character given to thieving, drinking and fighting who was considered a crafty and dangerous man." Forrest was named as the man who pretended to be the "Officer" in the episode described.

The accused had no testimony to offer in his defense but his counsel, Chaplain Duryee, presented a final statement which was admitted by the Court.

Statement in Defense

"The undersigned, in defense of Frederick H. Brandt, would state that he believes fully in the innocence of the accused that he did *not intend to desert*. He has borne in the Regt. the character of a good and faithful soldier so far as known to me. On the night of the 22nd of March he got into a drinking carousel with one Charley Forrest, who late at night, and against his wishes accepted the proposal to take a ride. Said Forrest procured the horses and induced the accused then under the influence of liquors to go with him, first to the Sharp-Shooters back of the 96th New York Volunteers. There Forrest stole another horse and after drinking freely both started on another side, where they took the direction toward the picket line. On reaching the reserve post, Forrest rode in the direction of the Videttes and called to Brandt, as his *Orderly*, to come that way. One witness swore that he saw the accused following the Colonel and pointed down the line - On being halted, he stopped immediately and when he was arrested he was near the reserve post and made no attempt to escape whatsoever but seemed desirous of returning. Surely this was no attempt to desert. In regard to the proof that he acted as orderly for one who claimed to be Officer of the day, it may be said, that these men were in a drunken frolic. Brandt did not know that he was regarded by Forrest that he was acting in any such capacity till they reached the reserve picket post, when to cover his deception Forrest says, This Way Orderly!", Brandt was not dressed like an orderly and says he did not know that he was acting in any such capacity, but only was with Forrest for a ride. If he said he was an orderly he was too much intoxicated to know what he said or if he did say it, may it not have been understood by him, as is often the case, in a playful way, `I'll be your orderly', or Forrest who intended to desert may have told him to say that he, Brandt, was his orderly.

Brandt's character has been shown to have been previously good, getting intoxicated was not a habit with him but there is evidence that Forrest did all he could to get Brandt intoxicated for the purpose of aiding him to desert and he did desert - it was his intention to do so not so of Brandt. If I thought him guilty I would not lift a hand or say a word to shield him from the desertion punishment. But from my very soul I believe him innocent of the crime. He may deserve punishment for leaving camp, and getting drunk and allowing himself to be mislead; *but not as a deserter*. But I much prefer to leave his case in the hands of the court who will be as anxious to acquit the innocent as to punish the guilty. We are all liable to err and in view of our own frailities we should be able to say

`That Mercy I to others show

That Mercy show to me'
I. G. Duryee, Chaplain 81st New York Volunteers
In behalf of the prisoner"

The Court accepted the statement and conferred on the evidence in the case. The verdict was guilty and the sentence was execution by a firing squad which took place on March 26, 1865 behind the Union lines near Richmond, Virginia.

Five members of the Court Martial signed the following recommendation which was forwarded to the reviewing authority.

"The undersigned members of the General Court Martial in consideration of the former good character and faithful services as a soldier respectfully recommend him, Private Frederick H. Brandt, Company E, 81st Regiment New York Volunteer Infantry to the mercy of the reviewing authority."

REFERENCES:
Military Personnel Records, RG-#94
Court Martial Proceedings, RG-#153 MM 1658

Case #219
Pvt. James Weaver
NV: N.E. Baker
Co. D, 1st MD Infantry Regt.
Executed for Desertion
March 26, 1865

DESCRIPTION:

25 years of age, 5 feet 8 inches tall, brown hair, brown eyes, dark complexion, born in Virginia, occupation farmer, substitute.

Weaver enlisted and mustered in as a substitute on February 1, 1865 at Baltimore Maryland and assigned to Company D, 1st Maryland Infantry Regiment. Weaver deserted his Regiment during the siege of Petersburg, Virginia was apprehended and tried by court martial.

A General Court Martial was convened at City Point, Virginia and on February 27, 1865 tried Private N.E. Baker, alias James Weaver, 1st Maryland Infantry Regiment on a charge of desertion.

Baker alias Weaver, a substitute, duly enlisted into the Military service of the United States was sent to City Point, Virginia for forwarding to his assigned regiment, the 1st Maryland Infantry. In the recruit barracks at City Point, Virginia where he was awaiting forwarding to his regiment, Baker bribed a guard by the "gift" of ($140.00) one hundred and forty dollars on February 11, 1865 to permit him to leave the premises. Baker then purchased civilian clothing and obtained a pass under false pretenses from the office of the Provost Marshall at City Point.

The false pretenses were that Baker stated he was a deserter from the Confederate Army and had voluntarily come into the Union Army lines and surrendered in November, 1864. He then stated he took an oath of Allegiance to the United States and was permitted to leave City Point, Virginia and go to Baltimore, Maryland where he remained until the 11th or 12th of January, 1865. At that time he asserted he secured a pass from the Provost Marshall of Baltimore to return to City Point in order to secure a duplicate of his original oath of allegiance certificate which he claimed to have lost. Another deserter named McNeilly accompanied Baker to substantiate his tale.

The pass issued at City Point permitted him to proceed to Fortress Monroe and on to Baltimore. Baker was apprehended and arrested on board the mail boat James Brady on February 14, 1865.

Witnesses testified that Baker, and two companions, McNeilly being one, were seen together in City Point.

Baker was observed to have left the recruit barracks, going to City Point Oyster Saloon where he dined, went next to a barber shop for a shave and haircut, then on to a Daguerreotype shop to have a picture taken, finally stayed the night in a hotel. He spent the following day at a jewelry shop where he and his two companions persuaded a negro employee to purchase trousers for them. The Army trousers were the last vestiges of Army clothing to require replacement with citizens attire. They also purchased one pistol and later returned to unsuccessfully buy cartridges for it. All three secured passes and boarded the mail boat where they were arrested before it left the wharf.

Baker questioned witnesses but offered no formal defense but did offer a statement to the Court.

"Wishing to make a statement of a few facts concerning the charges that are preferred against me, I will now take this opportunity of doing so. First I am a native of Westmoreland in the State of Virginia. I left there, (that is Westmoreland) and came over to the federal lines and was sent to Washington and there I took the Oath of Allegiance. Second, I came over into these lines so as not to be conscripted into the Rebel services. Third, after I took the oath, I went to Baltimore where I got work as a brakeman on the Baltimore and Ohio Railroad. I was employed on the road until on or about the 30th of January, 1865, when I fell in company with a young man who said he was from the south. When I was in his company I thought myself perfectly safe, we got to drinking together, when I became in a state of intoxication after I was with him for several hours, he induced me to enlist as a substitute, I was so intoxicated that I did not know what I was doing at that time, I became so intoxicated and went so far, that he got me to enlist. But how I came into the service I was not aware until I arrived at Camp Bradford, Baltimore. I made inquiries about how I came there, nobody could tell me, only that I came in there with a squad of other recruits, and as I am a refugee from the south, and according to an order issued by Lieutenant General Grant, to the affect that no citizen or soldier, as a refugee coming within these lines should be under no liability to be drafted into the Army or Armies of the United States. Any such person enlisting should not be sent to the front of the Confederate lines. Sir, I hope you will look into my case and do all you can for me and as I have no more defence to make, I leave my case to the mercy of the court.

(signed) N. E. Baker"

The Court then deliberated, found the accused guilty and sentenced him to be shot to death with musketry.

The execution took place on March 26, 1865 at or near City Point, Virginia.

REFERENCES:

Military Personnel Records, RG-#94
Court Martial Proceedings, RG-#153 OO 316

Case #220
Pvt. Jeremiah Richards
Co. D, 55th Vol Inf Regt
(Incorrectly identified as
Pvt. Jeremiah Roberts)
Executed for Desertion
March 27, 1865

While "The Official List" carries the name of Pvt. Jeremiah Roberts of Company D, 55th Pennsylvania Volunteer Infantry Regiment, same is in error. Our research eventually discovered that Pvt. Jeremiah *Roberts* was in reality Pvt. Jeremiah *Richards*, Company D, 55th Pennsylvania Volunteer Infantry Regiment. The veracity of our discovery was attested to by Michael E. Pilgrim, National Archives and Records Service, Military Service Branch, Textual Reference Division who in a letter dated 3 May 1988, in part stated, "with the information provided by you, I was able to locate Jeremiah Richards' Court Martial Case File and his compiled service record. ... Thank you for sharing your research; we can now add this file to our microfilm publication."

DESCRIPTION:

21 years of age, 5 feet 6 inches tall, brown eyes, dark hair, dark complexion, born in England, occupation tailor, literate, substitute.

Richards was a substitute from Philadelphia who was drafted on October 3, 1863 and forwarded to the 55th Pennsylvania Infantry Regiment on October 23, 1863, and assigned to Company K, 55th Pennsylvania Infantry Regiment where he was sick much of the time. On April 1, 1864 he was transferred to Company D, 55th Pennsylvania V. V. Infantry Regiment. On the night of the 28th of April, 1864 he deserted at Gloucester Point, Virginia in the company of another soldier. Recognized and arrested at City Point, Virginia, Richards was returned to his regiment under guard on February 10, 1865. He was tried by General Court Martial in the field on Monday, February 27, 1865 and pleaded guilty to desertion. He was found guilty and sentenced to be executed by a firing squad on Monday, March 27, 1865.

While confined in prison awaiting trial, Richards wrote to President Abraham Lincoln requesting a reprieve. The letter is as follows:

"Headqurs 24th Army Corps, February 25, 1865, Abraham Lincoln President, U.S. Army.
Your Excellency,

Sir I implore your most gracious excellency in my behalf. I, your humble servant, do hereby acknowledge that I have done wrong and suffice it to say if your most gracious excellency extends your most (illegible) and most bountiful hands towards this poor wretch whom nobody seems to care anything about. I pledge your excellency my word and all thats most dear to me your leniency shall not be abused. I am waiting for court marshall which is expected for to get soon I do not know my charges and specifications at present but i have reason to believe as far as i can understand the charges are deserting to the enemy which i assure you i am not guilty of Therefore have i availed myself of this opportunity of writing to you about a reprieve the reason i have written to you beforehand is because I would not get time for to write to you after being court marshalled Whatever my sentence is it will be soon put into effect after court marshall the court will sit on the first Inst of March and my doom will be decreed before ten day's hence.

No more but I remain your obediant Servant
Jeremiah Richards, 55th Pa Vols
1st Div. Headqurs 24th Army Corps
Provost guard House"

REFERENCES:

Military Personnel Records, RG-$94
Court Martial Proceedings, RG-#153

Case #221A
Pvt. James Preble
NV: Prebble
Co. E, 49th NY Infantry Regt.
(First Military Service Period)

DESCRIPTION:

21 years of age, 5 feet 10½ inches tall, black hair, black eyes, dark complexion, born in Batavia, New York, occupation railroad man.

Preble enlisted on August 16, 1861 and was mustered into service on August 31, 1861 at Buffalo, New York in Company E, 49th New York Infantry Regiment. Records state he deserted from Harrison's Landing, Virginia shortly after enlistment but returned to his Regiment in September 1862 and in the same month was reported absent sick. Preble was returned to duty in the September/October 1862 record period. Preble was given a discharge for disability, listing the cause as "Chronic Diarrhea of long standing and Inguinal Hernia of the right side" dated January 5, 1863 at camp near Belle Plain, Virginia.

Case #221B
Pvt. James Preble
Co. K, 12th NY Cavalry Regt.
(Second Military Service Period)
Executed for Rape
March 31, 1865

DESCRIPTION:

22 years of age (sic), 5 feet 9 inches tall, brown hair, gray eyes, dark complexion, born in Batavia, New York, occupation brakeman (R.R.) (note variances between the two official descriptions, age, height, hair and eyes).

Preble's second enlistment was on September 8, 1863 at Buffalo, New York in Company K, 12th New York Cavalry Regiment. He was detailed to recruiting service in Buffalo, New York on September 10, 1863 and was relieved and sent to his Regiment, arriving for duty at Fort Anderson, North Carolina in November, 1864. He was on detached service near New Berne, North Carolina in November/December, 1864.

A General Court Martial was convened at Kinston, North Carolina and on March 17, 1865 tried Private James Preble, Company K, 12th New York Cavalry Regiment on a charge of Rape.

Preble did not wish to have special counsel.

Witnesses testified that on or about the 16th of March, 1865 a Sergeant Wood and Private Hogan of the 12th New York Cavalry Regiment wree sent to a house about 1/4 of a mile from the Snow Hill Road, about a mile from the Regimental Camp, to investigate a report that a man of their Regiment was at the house drunk. When they arrived at the house, they found the horse of the accused hitched outside. The Sergeant went to the front door and knocked, but received no reply although he heard screaming inside. He then ran to the back door, found it open and entered the house. The first person he saw was a woman emerging from a bedroom crying, and he inquired what the matter was. He received no reply but saw she was covered with blood and as she walked blood dripped from her onto the floor. The Sergeant asked if she were shot. She said, "No, raped." When asked who did it, she remained silent but pointed to the bedroom. When the Sergeant entered, he found Preble lying on the bed, his revolver in his hand, his pants unbuttoned in front and covered with blood as was his shirt. When Preble was asked what he was doing there, he made no reply except to look up and laugh. The Sergeant took Preble's revolver from his hand and ordered him out of the house, but Preble did not want to leave and the Sergeant dragged him to the door and threw him outside. The woman who had been assaulted was described as being slender and delicate, admitted to being 58 years of age, but had the appearance of a woman over 65 years of age.

Preble was estimated to have been half drunk and his canteen was half full of whiskey.

Private Hogan, who accompanied the Sergeant, remained outside the house to tend the horses. The first thing he saw was Preble being forcibly thrown out of the house by the Sergeant, his pants unbuttoned, with his privates hanging out, the front of his trousers and shirt covered with blood. Preble was laughing as he came to the place where the horses were held. As Preble mounted his horse, Hogan looking at the house, saw through the partially open door an old woman weeping bitterly. Preble remarked to Hogan that he had done more work than the whole Battalion had that day.

Rebecca Drake, aged 23, a resident of the home where the rape took place, stated that there were three women who resided there. She herself, her Aunt Letitia Craft, aged 58, and her cousin, Louisa Jane Bedard were in the home when Preble arrived. Preble used profane and vulgar language, bragged that he would have criminal connection with all the women. Walked about the premises, revolver in hand, pants unbuttoned and privates exposed. His first attempt at rape was upon Rebecca Drake who eluded him and escaped from the house and hid behind fodder stacks near the barn. He searched unsuccessfully for her and vented his ire by shooting and killing their cow. He, apparently, then also attempted to rape Louisa Jane Bedard, aged 17 years, forcing her down upon a small chest of drawers, his pants open and his penis all exposed (as the witness stated) but she too escaped his intent and fled the house. He pursued and failed to find her. He then threatened her Aunt by stating he would kill her if she didn't find the girls for him. Finally, he dragged the older woman into the house. Louisa Jane Bedard ran to a neighbor, a Mr. Maloney, and told what was happening. He apparently notified the Regiment.

Letitia Craft was dragged into the house and thrown on the bed and she screamed and Preble said, "You damned old Secesh bitch, if you do not hush hallowing I will kill you" and put his arm across my mouth to keep me from hallowing. "He stayed on top of me some twenty minutes or so." Then he rolled off her and she got out of the bed and just then a man came in (Sergeant) and asked her what happened and took Preble away.

Letitia Craft stated she had never been married and had no children. She stated the experience was painful and that she had not stopped bleeding for five minutes since the attack.

The accused offered no defense.

The Court deliberated, found Preble guilty and sentenced him to be shot to death with musketry at Goldsboro, North Carolina on March 31, 1865.

Preble was shot at 3:00 PM on the designated day at a spot one mile from Goldsboro, North Carolina. Three of the fired balls taking effect and causing death within one minute. The body was coffined and buried at the place of execution.

REFERENCES:
Military Personnel Records, RG-#94
Court Martial Proceedings, RG-#153 MM 1774

Case #222
Pvt. Samuel Mapp
Co. D (C), 10th Inf Regt, USCT
Reported Executed
April 20, 1865

DESCRIPTION:

24 years of age, 5 feet 8 inches tall, hazel eyes, black hair, black complexion, born in Pungteague, Virginia, occupation farmer, illiterate.

Mapp has discrepancies in his records both civil and military. His age is given variously (at time of enlistment as 18, 21, 24 years while his death certificate issued in 1934 (cause of death, burned to death in house fire) states he was 68 years of age. The latter would indicate his birth in 1866! The "Official List" states he was a member of Company D, 10th Infantry Regiment, USCT but most of his Muster Rolls report him as a member of Company C, 10th Infantry Regiment, USCT. Most of the physical data, from all sources coincide. Mapp is reported as enlisting on October 29, 1863 at Johnstown, Virginia and was mustered into Company C, 10th Infantry Regiment USCT on Cranny Island, Virginia on November 18, 1863. The report for September and October 1865 notes he was in the Regimental Guardhouse awaiting sentence for an unnamed offense, the only reference to any crime in all his records. The above date is nearly six months after his stated execution. From August to December 1865 he is reported as assigned to the Post Bakery and was hospitalized for mumps with an abscess of the lower right jaw from March 9 to March 16, 1866 and then returned to duty. Mapp applied repeatedly for a military pension and finally received a $10.00 per month award. The records state that he was mustered out of military service on May 17, 1866.

There is serious doubt as to the identity of the man above described with the one said to have been executed.

A General Court Martial was convened at Headquarters of the 1st Division, 25th Army Corps in the field, Virginia and on March 28, 1865 tried Private Samuel Mapp, Company D, 10th Infantry Regiment, USCT on the charges of Mutiny, Disobedience of orders, and threatening the life of his superior Officer.

Testimony revealed that on March 28, 1865 the 10th Regiment was ordered to prepare to march to a new position. While in the ranks of company formation Mapp said to his Company Commander, "Where are we going? I ain't going anywhere. I ain't going to leave this camp an inch, if I die first." "We ain't been treated right, we have not been paid." His Captain ordered him to step forward, out of the ranks, wanting to place him in arrest, but Mapp refused to come forward, instead he broke ranks and hid behind the Company formation. The Captain moved around the right flank of the formation seeking the accused. Mapp called out "Don't come here Captain, you'll be hurt!" Mapp then called for the company to load their weapons and stand by him. The Captain approached Mapp within 5 or 6 feet and pointed his revolver at him, telling him not to lift a hand. The Captain again ordered Mapp to step out of the ranks and he refused to obey. The Captain repeated the order several times and Mapp refused to obey and the men of the Company, breaking ranks, gathered about him. The Captain fired his revolver at Mapp and again ordered him to come out and the order was still not obeyed. The Captain fired a second shot and then noticed that Mapp had a revolver in his right hand and he advanced on him and took the revolver from him. (The revolver was presented to the court as evidence.) The Captain ordered Mapp to surrender his musket to a Captain Sturdevant, of the 10th Regiment. Mapp refused to obey this order. The Captain fired a third shot. Captain Sturdevant seized hold of the musket and wrested it away from Mapp, then arrested him and took him to the guardhouse for confinement.

The accused had no witnesses to offer the Court but did present a written statement in his behalf.

Statement of Samuel Mapp, Private
Company D, 10th Regiment of United States Colored Troops

"I was picked up by Colonel Nelson and a squad of Colored soldiers, on the eastern shore of Virginia and forced into the service and put into the 10th Regiment. I did not want to go but I have always been ready to do my duty.

About threatening the Captain, I never did it. I don't blame him, but I hadn't been paid in over six months and I didn't know it was right to force men into the Army and make them do everything without paying them."

X (his mark) Samuel Mapp

Witness to mark, H. V. Martin, Captain 43rd USCT, Judge Advocate.

The Court deliberated, found the accused guilty and sentenced him to be shot to death by musketry.

The execution is "recorded" as taking place in his Brigade area on April 20, 1865. (There are very serious doubts that the execution ever actually took place.)

REFERENCES:

Military Personnel Records, RG-#94
Court Martial Proceedings, RG-#153 MM 1847
Pension Record, RG-#15
Virginia State Death Certificate

Case #223
Pvt. Alexander D. McBroom
Co. B, 1st Ark Vol Inf Regt
Executed for Desertion
April 21, 1865

DESCRIPTION:

34 (also as 25) years of age, 5 feet 8 inches tall, blue eyes, dark hair, fair complexion, born in Canon, Tennessee, occupation farmer, literacy undetermined.

McBroom enlisted in Company B, 1st Arkansas Volunteer Infantry Regiment on February 4, 1863 and was mustered into service on February 23, 1863 at Fayetteville, Arkansas. records indicate McBroom deserted February 25, 1863 having been AWOL on February 23, 1863. He was returned to service on april 17, 1864 and was in confinement on May 30, 1864 at the Post Guardhouse, Fort Smith, Arkansas.

A General Court Martial was convened at Fort Smith, Arkansas and on October 12, 1864 tried Private Alexander D. McBroom, Company B, 1st Arkansas Infantry Regiment on charges of Desertion and Larceny.

Witnesses testified that the accused enlisted in February 1863 and deserted his company and Regiment on or about March 1, 1863 and was reported as being seen in Madison County, Arkansas (his home area) as a member of a Rebel gang of Bushwackers (guerrillas). The prisoner admitted that he was also in Texas for a brief period of time having some intention of going to Mexico. The accused was known to have stolen at least two horses, one in September 1863 and another in March of 1864, one being worth at least $100.00. The prisoner is alleged to have stolen the horses for his wife, who he claimed was not permitted to own a horse by the federal troops or the "Hogskin Militia" (Arkansas Militia)

A "deal" for the return of the accused is alluded to by one witness at the trial who overheard a conversation between the Regimental Commander of the 1st Arkansas, Colonel Searle and the brother of the accused who was a Sergeant Major in the Regiment. The Colonel is said to have promised the brother that if he would persuade Alex McBroom to return to the Regiment he would do all he could to keep him from being punished. The accused was in the Convalescent Camp, but it is not stated whether he returned voluntarily or was arrested and returned.

Another witness stated he was told that the accused became ill at home while on furlough in February 1863. He expressed fear of bushwackers and letters from his brother (the Sergeant Major) advised him he was listed as a deserter and to avoid Federal Troops.

The accused stated he had neither defense witnesses nor statement to present to the Court on his behalf.

The Court then deliberated, found the accused guilty and sentenced him to be shot to death with musketry.

The execution took place on April 21, 1865 at Fort Smith, Arkansas.

REFERENCES:
NA, Military Personnel Records, RG-#94
Court Martial Proceedings, RG-#153 OO 582

Case #224
Cpl./Pvt. Alfred Catlett
NV: Catlette
Co. E, 1st Hvy Regt, USCT
Executed for Rape
May 6, 1865

DESCRIPTION:

20 years of age, 5 feet 9½ inches tall, black hair, black eyes, black complexion, born

Richmond, Virginia, occupation farmer, illiterate.

Catlett enlisted in Company E, 1st Heavy Artillery Regiment, USCT at Knoxville, Tennessee on April 7, 1864. His service record indicates he was at one point the Company Cook and he was promoted to corporal. There was some dispute of his entrance date into service, apparently for pay purposes. The date was quoted as the 19th and the 30th of April. In March of 1865, his records indicate duty in the Pioneer Corps, the army's construction/labor troops.

Catlett, like other USCT privates, was paid at a reduced rate, a rate $6.00 per month less than white privates until April 30, 1864. At that time, the pay of a USCT private was made equal to the white privates at $13.00 per month and the difference between their earlier pay rates of $6.00 per month was paid retroactively to equalize the pay rates for service prior to 30 April, 1864. A statement was required which stipulated, "________ was free on or before April 19, 1861."

Catlett and two other members of Company E, 1st Regiment Heavy Artillery, USCT were tried for rape by a drumhead court martial on May 4th, 1865. The others were Alexander Colwell and Charles Turney while Washington Jackson, of Company K, same regiment, was also involved. All four were executed on May 6, 1865 at Asheville, North Carolina.

REFERENCES:
Military Personnel Records, RG-#94
No Court Martial Records have been found.

Case #225
Pvt. Alexander Colwell
Co. E, 1st Regt Hvy Arty, USCT
Executed for Rape
May 6, 1865

DESCRIPTION:

26 years of age, 5 feet 9 inches tall, eyes black, hair black, complexion black, born Maclinburg, North Carolina, occupation farmer, illiterate.

Colwell enlisted on January 16, 1865 at Knoxville, Tennessee and mustered into service on February 1, 1865. Apparently his service time was normal routine without any detached assignments.

He was tried for rape by a drumhead court martial on May 4, 1865 with three other men. For more details, see Case #224, Alfred Catlett. He was found guilty and executed on May 6, 1865 at Asheville, North Carolina.

REFERENCES:
Military Personnel Files, RG-#94

Case #226
Pvt. Washington Jackson
Co. E, 1st Heavy Artillery, USCT
Executed for Rape
May 6, 1865

DESCRIPTION:

22 years of age, 5 feet 5½ inches tall, black hair, black eyes, black complexion, born at Donaldson, South Carolina, occupation farmer, illiterate.

Jackson was enlisted and mustered into service on April 15, 1864 at Knoxville, Tennessee. He was assigned to Company E, 1st Regiment Heavy Artillery, USCT. While on duty in the Asheville, North Carolina area in 1865, Jackson committed rape, was tried by a Drum Head

Court Martial, convicted and sentenced to be executed before a firing squad by Special Order #43, dated May 4, 1865. The execution was carried out on May 6th, 1865.

REFERENCES:
Military Personnel Records, RG-#94
Court Martial Proceedings, RG-#153

Case #227
Pvt. Charles Turner, Musician
Co. E, 1st Heavy Artillery Regt USCT
Executed for Rape
May 6, 1865

DESCRIPTION:
18 years of age, 5 feet 9 inches tall, black eyes, black hair, black complexion, born Charleston, South Carolina, occupation farmer, illiterate.

Turner enlisted and was mustered into service on April 12, 1864 at Knoxville, Tennessee in Company E, 1st US Colored Heavy Artillery Regiment. He is variously described as a musician or fifer. He was to receive the difference between colored troops pay of $7.00 per month and white troops pay of $13.00 per month for privates up until April 30, 1864 when the colored troops received pay parity with the white troops. By late April, early May 1865, Turner's regiment was operating in the Asheville, North Carolina area when Turner, from the meager records available, seems to have committed rape. He was tried by Drumhead court martial on May 4, 1865 and executed by a firing squad on May 6, 1865. (See also Case #224, Private Alfred Catlett.

No records of the trial have been found so the details of the crime remain obscure.

REFERENCES:
Military Personnel Records, RG-#94

Case #228
Pvt. Cpl. William H. Harrison
Co. A, 69th Inf Regt, USCT
Executed for Murder
May 12, 1865

DESCRIPTION:
17 years of age, 5 feet 3¾ inches tall, black eyes, black hair, yellow complexion, born in Prairie County, Arkansas, occupation farmer, illiterate. (No permit for a minor's enlistment is found in Harrison's Military Personnel Records File.)

Harrison enlisted and was mustered into service on August 13, 1864 at Little Rock, Arkansas and assigned to Company A, 69th Infantry Regiment, USCT. Harrison committed a murder, was arrested and confined in the Military Prison at Little Rock, Arkansas by January 18, 1865.

A General Court Martial was convened at Little Rock, Arkansas and on March 25, 1865 tried Corporal William H. Harrison, Company A, 69th Infantry Regiment USCT on a charge of murder.

Testimony recorded states that Harrison left the regimental camp, near Little Rock, Arkansas without permission on the night of Monday January 16, 1865 taking with him his firearms and went to the home of Wyatt Temple, a citizen who resided near Little Rock, accompanied by five other members of his Regiment. Their ostensible purpose was to secure sweet potatoes. As they arrived in the yard of the Temple residence, a dog ran out barking at them and Harrison shot the dog, then reloaded his rifle. Temple came to a window, facing the yard, raised the window and asked, "What do you want? What are you here for?" Harrison replied by shooting Temple, who died on the following Friday evening. The entire group including Harrison then returned to their camp.

Major White, Provost Marshall of Little Rock, testified that when he was informed of the shooting, that suspicion was directed at members of Company A, 69th Infantry Regiment USCT. He investigated and the suspicions were confirmed by his arrest of Harrison and five others of the Regiment who had accompanied him. Harrison was held in the Little Rock Police Jail awaiting trial.

Temple's wound was described by his physician as caused by a minie ball which entered his right shoulder just above the clavicle and ranged obliquely across the scapula and exited between the spine and scapula on the left side. The nature of the wound was due to Temple's posture, stooped over to peer out through the open window.

While under arrest and in custody of Civil authority, the Police Chief of Little Rock, Harrison stated his reason for shooting Temple was that he was afraid Temple would shoot him.

The accused offered no defense testimony but did offer a statement in his behalf.

"How I came to own up to shooting this man. Jones told me that I was under age and the Court could not hurt me, but if they found that it was *him*, they would kill him, that was after we were in prison, in the cells." (The "Jones" referred to in Harrison's statement is one of the other prisoners under arrest and on trial with Harrison.)

The Court then deliberated, found the accused guilty and sentenced him to be hung until he were dead.

The execution took place on May 12, 1865 in the Military Prison at Little Rock, Arkansas.

REFERENCES:

Military Personnel Records, RG-#94
Court Martial Proceedings, RG-#153 OO 911

Case #229

Pvt. Henry Anderson
Co. D, 9th Mich, Vol. Cav. Regt.
Executed for Murder
May 13, 1865

DESCRIPTION:

21 years of age, 5 feet 7 inches tall, hazel eyes, brown hair, fair complexion, born in Ireland, occupation sailor (soldier), illiterate.

Anderson enlisted at St. Clair, Michigan and was mustered into service on May 20, 1864 at Detroit, Michigan and assigned to Company D, 9th Michigan Volunteer Cavalry Regiment. Anderson was in trouble as early as September 24, 1864 when he was sentenced by a General Court Martial trial to lose six month's pay. No details to the offense have been located to date. By 1865, his Regiment was part of Major General J. Kilpatrick's command operating in North Carolina.

A series of telegrams between General Kilpatrick and General Schofield concerning Anderson's murder of an elderly male civilian are in Anderson's record file. Greensboro, North Carolina, "May 9th, 1865, To Genl Schofield, General, A soldier of my command killed an old man today = a citizen = because he would not give up his money. A large portion of my command is here: an example is necessary. Evidence is perfect. Will I be justified in shooting him? J. Kilpatrick (Maj Genl)"

"Hdqs, Dept NC, army of Ohio, May 9, 1865 To. Pvt. Maj. Gen'l. Kilpatrick, Greensboro, The commanding General directs that you have the man refd. to in your dispatch of this date tried by Mil. Commission and forward the proceedings to him by telegraph for his action, and he will approve by telegraph.

Bvt. Col. & AAG."

"May 12, 1865, To Pvt Maj Genl Kilpatrick
Commdg Cav. Div.
Lexington, NC
The findings and sentence in the case of Henry Anderson, Co D, 9th Mich. Cav. are approved and confirmed. The sentence will be executed at Lexington, NC on Saturday the 13th of May, 1865 between the hours of 12 M and 6 PM under the direction of the Division Commander.
Maj Genl Commdg."

He was executed by a firing squad on May 13, 1865.

REFERENCES:
Military Personnel Records, RG-#94
Court Martial Proceedings, RG-#153 NN 3173

Case #230
Pvt. Willis Cowell
Co. F, 1st Cav Regt, USCT
Executed for Murder
May 26, 1865

DESCRIPTION:
20 years of age, 5 feet 6 inches tall, black eyes, wooly hair, black complexion, born in Camden County, North Carolina, occupation servant or laborer, illiterate.

Cowell enlisted at Norfolk, Virginia on February 2, 1864 and was mustered into service at Camp Hamilton, Virginia on February 26, 1864. He was assigned for duty to Company F, 1st Cavalry Regiment, USCT. During May and June of 1864 he was on detached service at Battlefield Hospital, near Petersburg, Virginia. Cowell committed murder in early March, 1865 and was in confinement on March 12, 1865 and was interned in Norfolk City Jail by May 1, 1865. He was court martialed at Norfolk, Virginia on May 24, 1865, found guilty and sentenced to be executed by hanging. The execution took place at Camp Lincoln, near City Point, Virginia. The date of execution is given variously as May 26/May 27, 1865 with the majority of reports stating the 26th as the correct date.

REFERENCES:
Military Personnel Records, RG-#94
Court Martial Proceedings, RG-#153

THE MINERVA H. AND MAJOR JARRED REESE COOK CASE

Vicksburg, Mississippi, following its surrender on July 4, 1863, became an occupied city. Union troops were encamped for miles about the city with many such camp sites on plantations. Active recruiting for the newly authorized U.S. Colored Troops took place and the 52nd Infantry Regiment, USCT, for example, was formed in the area. Many ex-slaves, having left their former owners, enlisted in the forming USCT units. Relationships between whites and newly freed negroes were uneasy as neither group were comfortable with or sure of their position in the new order of the interracial relationship.

In 1864, serious incidents began to occur involving U.S. Colored Troops and Vicksburg area white residents.

A letter to the Editor complains of part of the problem.

Vicksburg Daily Herald—July 27, 1864

(Communication)
"Vicksburg, July 26, 1864

Editor Herald: Will you be kind enough to give publicity through the columns of your valuable paper, to the many depredations committed by soldiers garrisoning this Post? It is sad to see how they are losing their reputation by marauding around and plundering the neighboring plantations. There are daily instances, where they go in squads of one to ten and steal corn and otherwise aggravate the planters. There is but little use of trying to raise crops, unless we are secured from these marauders. Will not the Commanding General please see to it and stop it, either by giving us guards or issuing stringent orders, punishing such acts according to their merits?"

On May 18, 1864, John H. Bobb and his nephew, Austin D. Mattingly, were approaching "McRaven," Bobb's home, for lunch. As the two men entered the yard of "McRaven," They noticed a number of colored troopers picking flowers from the garden. Bobb, infuriated by their presence on his property, ordered them out and received angry and profane retorts. Bobb responded by picking up a stray brick, which had been blown loose during the siege of Vicksburg and struck one of the colored soldiers, a Sergeant. The soldiers left, promising to return and burn down "McRaven." Bobb, accompanied by his nephew, immediately proceeded two squares to Major General William Slocum's U.S. Army Headquarters and filed a complaint. General Slocum is said to have promised to restrain his soldiers and end such harassments. The Sergeant, whom Bobb had previously struck with the brick, accompanied by several squads of soldiers, intercepted Bobb and his nephew Mattingly, before they had returned to "McRaven" and placed them both under arrest. Bobb reportedly asked where their officers were and received a reply to the effect that —officers be damned— we'll fix you without any Officers.

Bobb and Mattingly were marched toward the Railroad machine Shop followed by the colored soldiers. At some point on the march, one of the soldiers fired at Bobb's back. The bullet entered near his spine and exited at the exterior abdomen. Bobb fell to the ground, mortally wounded, and while dying, a second shot was fired at his head, entering the area of his cheek. Mattingly, temporarily immobilized by the vicious assault, was stimulated to run for his life as he realized he might become the second victim. As he fled, another soldier fired at him but missed the target, the bullet said to have pierced Mattingly's coat as he continued his successful escape. It is related that Mrs. Bobb had followed her husband to the Army Headquarters and upon hearing the three shots, rushed to the area of the shooting and found her husband dead. A Major Gwinden, who came from the guard station to investigate the reason for the shots fired, arrived at the death scene and is said to have found colored soldiers surrounding the corpse chanting, "We've got them." Major Gwinden ordered the arrest of all colored soldiers at the scene of the crime. Vague reports indicate only a Sergeant was arrested, but no one was ever charged or tried for the crime, nor have charges or records of investigation of the crime ever been located. An account of this tragedy appeared in the Vicksburg Daily Herald, June 14, 1864.

Major General Slocum acknowledged the occurrence of this crime when he had General Order #7, May 18, 1864, published. It was also printed in the Vicksburg Daily herald of June 7, 1864 and read as follows:

Headquarters, District of Vicksburg,
Vicksburg, Miss., May 18, 1864.
General Orders
No. 7

The attention of the officers of the command is called to the importance of maintaining discipline, and preventing all marauding and pillaging on the part of the soldiers. While every effort should be made to punish citizens who aid the enemy, or who in any manner violate military law or orders, the punishment in every case should be inflicted by the proper authority, and in a proper and lawful manner. Every act of pillage, and every unjustifiable encroachment upon the rights of citizens, serves only to bring disgrace upon our arms, and encourages a spirit which should be unknown among brave men engaged in a noble cause.

The recent murder of a citizen, by colored soldiers, in open daylight in the streets of this city, should arouse the attention of every officer serving with these troops to the absolute necessity of preventing their soldiers from attempting a redress of their own grievances. If the spirit which led to this act of violence is not at once repressed, consequences of the most terrible nature must follow.

The responsibility resting upon officers in immediate command of colored troops can not be overestimated. The policy of arming colored men, although at first strongly opposed, has finally been very generally approved by loyal men throughout the country. If this experiment is successful—if these troops prove powerful and efficient in enforcing obedience to law, all good officers connected with the organization will receive the credit which will be due them as pioneers in the great work. But if in teaching the colored man that he is free and that in becoming a soldier he has become the equal of his former master, we forget to teach him the first duty of the soldier, that of obedience of law and the order of those appointed over him—if we encourage him in rushing for his arms, and cooly murdering citizens for every fancied insult, nothing but disgrace and his honor can befall all connected with the organization.

Every wrong done to the colored soldier can and shall be punished, but he must not be permitted to take the law into his own hands; and hereafter the officers of any regiment guilty of such crimes as that which has today brought disgrace upon the colored troops, will be held to a strict accountability.

By Command of Maj. Gen. H. W. Slocum.
H. O. Rodgers
Assistance Adjutant General

On March 17, 1865, a Mr. A. B. Cook living in Warren County (Vicksburg area) was shot by negro soldiers. A letter dated April 9, 1865, Vicksburg, Mississippi to Emmee Krutcher from her brother, Marmaduke Shannon states: "A short time since A. B. Cook living in this country was shot and killed by negro soldiers, they say they ordered him to halt and he would not halt, he said before he died they did not tell him to halt." A handwritten notation concerning A. B. Cook, by a Blaine Russell was forwarded to us by Charles L. Sullivan of the Mississippi Gulfcoast Community College, Perkinston, Mississippi. It states: 'On Match 17, 1865, A. B. Cook was shot by negro soldiers of the 66th U.S. Colored Infantry. He later died of the wounds which were received on his plantation some miles from Vicksburg. No arrest or punishment followed." We have been unable to find official military records of this incident.

On April 3, 1865, a crime of such a vicious nature was committed that the military was aroused to a massive and successful effort to apprehend the perpetrators.

The scene of the crime was the Cook Plantation located less than ten miles northeast of Vicksburg, Mississippi. The plantation, known as the "Burne" at the time of the Civil War, comprised some 2,400 acres of land and employed some 85 slaves. The owner, Major Jarred Reese Cook (not related to A. B. Cook), age 50, and his wife, Minerva Hyner Cook, managed the plantation. Major Cook had served in the Army during the war with Mexico and is believed to have been acquainted with General Grant and other Civil War Army ranking officers as a result of meeting them during the Mexican War.

During the siege of Vicksburg and after its surrender, the fields of the Cook Plantation were in part occupied as camp grounds by the Union forces. In the early stages of the occupation, many male ex-slaves volunteered to serve in newly organized U.S. Colored Regiments and some of Cook's ex-slaves joined. One such recruit, Henry Johnson, was a former house servant, one who was in the main house and familiar with all family matters. He enlisted in Company D, 52nd Infantry Regiment, USCT, the Company being encamped not four miles from the Cook Plantation. It is said that the white officers of Company D, 52nd were rather lax in both their presence with the men and their enforcement of discipline. It was not unusual for the soldiers to take advantage of their unique position in a society turned upside down, where the ex-slave was now the law enforcer and the white man the governed, by occasional thefts, robbery, or home invasion.

A descendant of Major and Minerva Cook reconstructs the events of that tragic night in April, 1865, after long years of study, in an unpublished manuscript entitled "The Red Taffeta Dress" by Randolph Rives (a nom de Plume). The book is classified as historical/fiction estimated by the author to be about 90% factual history and 10% pure fiction.

In the text, he describes the meeting of some fifteen to twenty men of Company D, 52nd USCT in their camp. Apparently, no white officers were present in camp as the group of enlisted men sat around and talked endlessly about how to augment their meager pay. They all agreed they should locate a business or family which was prosperous and "persuade" them to part with whatever was valuable, portable and, last but not least important, easily converted to cash or tradeable. At some point in the discussion, the ex-slave house servant from the Cook Plantation spoke up and assured his comrades that he knew a place nearby where there were large sums of money, jewelry, watches, clothing, and guns ripe for the taking. The more he described his former plantation home, the more interested the other soldiers became. At some point in the period of time between 7:00 and 9:00 p.m., about fifteen soldiers decided to accompany the ex-slave servant to the Cook Plantation for plunder. They then drew up a plan of action, setting out the duties of each man accompanying the group such as who should enter the house to search for valuables, who should remain outside as sentinels and their plan to escape if attacked. They arrived at the plantation sometime between 9:00 and 11:00 p.m. being guided by the former servant and after setting out sentinels, the remainder of the men entered the mansion simultaneously through front and back entrances. The mansion, which was completely destroyed by fire about 1890, was described as a one story building with ceilings 12 foot high and contained a Roman Catholic Chapel.

As the soldiers entered the house, which was devoid of artificial light, some were said to have taken candles and inserted them in the muzzles of their rifles. When the candles were lighted, the rifles served as candlesticks to illuminate their areas of search. The noise of their search aroused Mrs. Cook who confronted them and demanded they leave the premises. For her words she received a blow on the forehead from a rifle butt swung by Private Morrison. Gradually other family members, three children William, Edward, and Vincent Cook, and Major Cook appeared on the scene. In the midst of denials of possession of large sums of money ,the soldiers began breaking open chests of drawers, boxes, desks and similar places of concealment. While they found female clothing, shoes, some U.S. greenbacks, a watch, some pistols and food, they still yearned for the big cache of money they had been informed of. McDowell finally threatened Mrs. Cook with death if she did not divulge the hiding place. Confused by the events taking place and by the physical abuse, she stood mute and Private McDowell shot her through the body and she fell to the floor. The Major was then shot in the shoulder by Private Four and despite his wound he managed to escape the house and make his way to his brother Alex's house. He was preceded in his escape by the children some of whom had been beaten with fists or bayonets. Mrs. Cook did not die until the following morning after relatives came to the mansion and carried her to her bed. During her ordeal she heard the conversation of the criminal though she did not recognize her ex-house servant as it is said he was too ashamed to enter the house he betrayed and remained outside during the entire outrage. After some five hours of searching, the looters, taking their meager plunder, returned to camp.

Reports of this diabolical crime quickly spread through the area and the Union Army Commander was bombarded with demands for some strong action in the matter. Major General N. J. T. Dana issued Special Order #123, Headquarters, Department of Mississippi, Vicksburg, Mississippi, April 5, 1865. It read as follows:

HEADQUARTERS
DEPARTMENT OF MISSISSIPPI
VICKSBURG, MISSISSIPPI, April 15, 1865
SPECIAL ORDERS #123

Par. 3 A reward of $500 will be paid to any person, or persons, (not in the military service of the United States), who will furnish to the Major General commanding, any information which shall lead to the detection, arrest and conviction of the party, or parties, who murdered Mrs. Cook and attempted to murder Mr. Cook, on the night of the 3rd Inst., at their house on the Jackson Railway.

A proportionate reward will be paid for the apprehension and conviction of either one of the parties, if there should prove to have been more than one person implicated.

4. A Special Commission is hereby appointed to meet in Vicksburg, at 9 o'clock a.m., on Thursday, April 6, 1865, to investigate and report all the facts connected with the murder of Mrs. Cook and the wounding of Mr. Reese Cook, on the night of the 3d inst., and the recent murder of Mr. A. B. Cook.

The commission will also inquire into, and report upon, the state of discipline of the company of the 52d United States Colored Infantry, recently encamped at the Four-Mile Bridge, near Vicksburg, and will ascertain, and report upon, such other matters as may have a bearing upon the recent irregularities and outrages in that neighborhood.

The commission will express an opinion.

DETAIL FOR THE COMMISSION
Colonel Van E. Young, 48th United States Colored Infantry, Provost Marshal General.
Lieutenant Colonel E. N. Owen, 5th United States Colored Heavy Artillery.
Major Thomas S. Free, 49th Untied States Colored Infantry.
The junior member will record the proceedings. by Order of Major General N. J. RT. Dana: FREDERIC SPEED, Assistant Adjutant General Official: Assistant Adjutant General

Within a few days, arrests of all the participants in the crime were made and they were charged with conspiracy, robbery, murder, wounding. The trial, which included Lt. Colonel Eli Lilly of the 9th Indiana Cavalry as a member of the Court, occupied seven days from May 1st to 3rd at the Vicksburg Court House and on May 4th, at the Cook Plantation to view the scene of the crime. On May 5th, the Court reconvened in the Court House at Vicksburg and continued on May 6th and concluded on May 8th,. 1865. The prisoners declined counsel and each made a statement on his own behalf. Witnesses included officers of the 52nd Infantry USCT and the 5th Heavy Artillery, USCT, Major Cook and two of his sons and Privates Thomas Richardson and Richard Simmons of Company D, 52nd Infantry Regiment, USCT..

Twelve soldiers were found guilty and sentenced to be hung on May 26, 1865 at Vicksburg. Upon recommendation of the Court and mitigating circumstances in this case, Private Cox had his sentence remitted and was returned to duty with his Regiment. He seems to have completed his term of service without further incident. On the morning of the 26th of May, 1865, an order suspending the sentence of Privates

Wilder, Washington and Carr was issued. G.C.M.O. #19, Headquarters, Department of Mississippi, May 26, 1865. Their cases were forwarded to the President of the United States for review and decision. On June 22, 1865 an order was issued remitting the sentence of death and substituting for it imprisonment for five years in the Penitentiary at Jefferson City, Missouri beginning on July 1, 1865, S.O. #346, War Department, Adjutant General Office, dated July 1, 1865. All three were released on November 8, 1866 with dishonorable discharges per letter from War Department dated November 1, 1866.

The remaining convicted men, Wallace, Willis, Rawlings, Morrison, Moore, McDowell, Johnson (the ex-house servant), Four and Pierce were hung on May 26, 1865 at a place named "O'Neal's Bottom"—a valley shut in by hills. The scaffold accommodated nine nooses and was the largest Union Army multiple execution during the Civil War. A description of the execution scene by an eye witness relates: "In a cleared space great guns are planted, for their are whispers of an effort at rescue, and if such should be the case the military orders are to mow the multitude down. The crowd gathers: the hills are covered with spectators; the drums roll, and there comes the measured sound of many, many feet. . . . . Soldiers surround the gallows;l silent sentry, fuse in hand, stands by the deep-mouthed cannon; suppressed groans smite the air; the criminals are standing in a strange house, all beams and no walls. . . . . . . a wild, moaning cry of "Farewell, brothers" from a thousand throats and nine convulsed and trembling shapes are dangling in the air. They sway, jerk and quiver and then hang motionless, black blots on a soft page of sunny space. . . . ."

Major Cook placed a claim against the government for crops furnished the Army in the amount of $57,000.00 after the War, but there is no indication of the claim being settled. He also married again and seems to have lost much of his land. Great grandchildren of the Major and Minerva Cook were able to provide some additional information about the case. One Cook descendent states there is (or was) a photograph taken after the execution disclosing the nine men hanging on the scaffold. Another descendent is in possession of a beautiful life size, well executed oil painting of Minerva Cook.

REFERENCES:

Military Personnel Records, RG-#94

Court Martial Proceedings, RG-#153 MM 2079

Personal relation of events courtesy of descendant Ted Cook

Copy of portrait and other details by descendant William C. Maute of New Orleans, La.

"In and About Vicksburg," (no author listed) 1890, Gibraltar Publishing Company, vicksburg, MIssissippi

Vicksburg Daily Herald, April 6, 1865 and May 11, 1865

"Vicksburg, 1863-1870, The Promise and the Reality of Reconstruction on the Mississippi," J.T. Currie, as a candidate's dissertation to the graduate faculty for the Degree of Ph.D., University of Virginia Corcoran Department of History, University of Virginia, May, 1975.

Letter to Emma Krutscher dated April 9, 1865 from Marmaduke Shannon Krutscher, Shannon papers (Mississippi History Department Archives).

{Vicksburg, A People at War, 1860-1865" by Peter F. Walker, Chapel Hill, North Carolina, University of North Carolina Press.

"Vicksburg, 1863-1870, The Promise and Reality of Reconstruction on the Mississippi." James T. Currie, Jackson, Mississippi. A dissertation presented to the graduate faculty, University of Virginia as a candidate for degree of Ph.D., May, 1975, Corcoran Department of History, University of Virginia.

Vicksburg Daily Herald, June 7, 1864 and June 14, 1864 "In memory of McRaven, the Haunting" by Charles W. Sullivan, 1989, Abbey Community Printers, Gulfport, Mississippi

"Diary of Minerva Hynes R. Cook, 1856-1860" courtesy of Ted Cook, Jackson, Miss.

COOK CASE—MEN NOT EXECUTED
Not On List
Pvt. Samuel Carr
Co. D, 52nd Inf. Regt. USCT
Not Executed

DESCRIPTION:

18 years of age, 5 feet 5½ inches tall, black hair, black eyes, black complexion, born in Jackson County, Georgia, occupation farmer, illiterate.

Carr enlisted and was mustered into service at Vicksburg, Mississippi on march 3, 1864 in Company D, 52nd Infantry Regiment, USCT. He was involved in the events at the Cook Plantation on April 3, 1865 which resulted in the murder of Mrs. Cook, wounding of Major Cook and plundering of the house. Carr offered the following statement in his defense during the trial.

Statement of Prisoner

"I am not to blame for anything being taken away from the house the time that the shooting was done I was not at the house I was about three hundred yards from the house. I didn't know that it was neutral ground out there. We went out for the rebels I supposed."

He was tried, convicted and sentenced to death by hanging, but in the review of the trial proceedings, he was granted a commutation of the death sentence. The sentence wwas reduced to a five year term in the Missouri State Prison.

He entered prison on July 1, 1865 and was released on November 8, 1866 after only 16 months of imprisonment. He was given a dishonorable discharge from the Army.

REFERENCES:
Military Personnel Records, RG-#94
Court Martial Proceedings, RG-#153

Not on List
Pvt. Henry Cox
Co. D, 52nd Inf. Regt. USCT
Not executed

DESCRIPTION:

22 years of age, 5 feet 6 inches tall, black hair, black eyes, colored complexion, born in Mississippi, occupation farmer, married, illiterate.

Cox enlisted on January 10, 1865 and was mustered into service on January 19, 1865 at Vicksburg, Mississippi in Company D, 52md Infantry Regiment, USCT. Cox was involved in the events at the Cook Plantation on April 3, 1865 and was tried, convicted, and sentenced to be executed.

At his trial, Cox stated: "The witnesses didn't make anything plain against me at all. I have only been in the Army since Christmas and when they said they were going on a scout I thought I would go along. I thought twasn't right to go in the house and didn't go in and when some of them offered to shoot I tried to stop them. I don't think I am to blame for what was done. I was along with them its true but I didn't do any harm, and tried to hinder the rest."

However, Cox had the sentence of death remitted upon recommendation of the Court and he was freed of all charges and returned to duty with his Regiment due to his efforts to prevent the shootings.

REFERENCES:
Military Personnel Records, RG-#94
Court Martial Proceedings, RG-#153

Not on List
Cpl/Pvt Bannister Washington
Co. D, 52nd Inf. Regt. USCT
Not Executed

DESCRIPTION:

19 years of age, 5 feet 3 inches tall, black hair, black eyes, black complexion, born in Platt Countrry, Mississippi, occupation laborer, illiterate.

Washington enlisted and was mustered into service as a Corporal on July 1, 1863 at Four-Mile Bridge, Mississippi in Captain James' Company, 2nd Regiment, Mississippi Infantry A.D. (AFrican Descent). The unit designation was later changed to Company D, 52nd Infantry Regiment, USCT. Washington was reduced to the rank of Private on December 12, 1863 for disobedience of orders.

Washington was involved in the events at the Cook Plantation on April 3, 1865 and made the following statement in his defense during the trial.

Statement of Prisoner

"I went out with the intention to catch rebels. I thought the whole party went out for that purpose. I always like to be in that kind of a crowd that goes after rebels. I stood at first with intention of catching rebels. When I found out that something else was going on I went away."

He was tried, convicted and sentenced to death by hanging, but in the review of the trial proceedings. he was granted a commutation of the death sentence. The sentence was reduced to a five year term in the Missouri State Prison.

He was sentenced to serve five years in the Missouri State Penitentiary, entering the prison on July 1, 1865 and was released on November 8, 1866 after only 16 months of imprisonment. He received a dishonorable discharge from the Army.

REFERENCES:
Military Personnel Records, RG-#94
Court Martial Proceedings, RG-#153

Not on list
Pvt. Jackson Wilder
Co. D, 52nd Inf. Regt. USCT
Not Executed

DESCRIPTION:

21 years of age, 5 feet 6 inches tall, black hair, black eyes, colored complexion, born in Carroll County, Mississippi, occupation farmer, illiterate, not married.

Wilder enlisted and was mustered into service on January 10, 1865 at Vicksburg, Mississippi in Company D, 52nd Infantry Regiment, USCT. He was involved in the events at the Cook Plantation on April 3, 1865. Wilder presented the following statement to the Court in his defense.

Statement of the Prisoner

"I went with the boys out to the place but didn't know what they were going for. I stayed outside the house and when some of them talked about shooting I told them I was going to leave for that wasn't right. I was one of the first to go away. I only come in the service last January. I didn't fetch away anything. I thought the other men know whether they ought to go or not far better than I did for they had been in the service longer."

He was tried, convicted and sentenced to death by hanging, but in the review of the trial proceedings, he was granted a commutation of the death sentence. The sentence was reduced to a five year term in the Missouri State Prison.

He was sentenced to serve five years in the Missouri State Penitentiary, entering the prison on July 1, 1865 and was released on November 8, 1866 after only 16 months of imprisonment. He received a dishonorable discharge from the Army.

REFERENCES:
Military Personnel Records, RG-#94
Court Martial Proceedings, RG-#153

Capt. Fred D. James
Commanding Officer of Co. D.
52nd Inf. Regt. USCT

Capt. Fred D. James was 27 years of age, had served in the 30th Ohio Volunteer Infantry from June 14, 1861, and reached the rank of Sgt. He applied for an appointment as an officer in the USCT and was commissioned a Capt. in the USCT on June 22, 1863 and was mustered into service July 27, 1863.

He served with his company until February 24, 1865 when, by S.O. #40, as Chief of the Fire Dept. A further notation in his military record file indicates that he was again placed on Detached Service on August 6, 1865, S.O. #8, Hdq., Post of Clinton, Mississippi. There is no statement of his assigned duties.

Capt. James was absent from his company on detached service when the crimes were committed on April 3, 1865.

There is reason to believe that Capt. James was swindling the Sutler of his Company/Regiment as well as the enlisted men. An investigation into the matter was begun as early as April 6, 1865. What he had done was to make an agreement with the Sutler to have all the items charged by his men billed to him (Capt. James) personally and he would, in turn, collect from the men who secured the goods and pay the Sutler. The men were presented due bills by Capt. James which had little or no relationship to the actual transactions. For example, he presented due bills to some of the enlisted men which exceeded their entire monthly pay. Army Regulations stated "no sutler shall sell on credit to any enlisted men more than ⅓ of his monthly pay within 1 month, without the Commanding Officer's permission and not exceeding ½ of a month's pay with permission." Capt. James violated this regulation for the 8 members of Co. D, who are convicted of the Cook crime and executed and thus was able to secure their entire pay by presenting the due bills to the paymaster, who paid Capt. James claim in full. He then requested and received a credit from the Sutler as these men had been hung.

Capt. James had quite a number of such frauds listed in the court martial proceedings. In one case he presented two accounts against the same man, one bill for $105.00 and the other for $55.00, stating that one man was at the Vicksburg General Hospital and, using the same name, stated the other was in the hospital. He received credit on his account for both sums.

On July 10, 1865, James began to realize that he had to resign from the Army before he was cashiered. He requested the Asst. Post Surgeon to certify him a physically unable to carry out his duties. He was so certified as afflicted with Chronic Diarrhea, making him unfit for duty and that his ailment was contracted on duty and rendered him ½ disabled.

On August 5, 1865, S.O. #421, Adjutant General's Office, Washington, D.C. (extract #30) accepted Capt. James resignation.

However, un undated telegram from the adjutant General's Office seems to have been sent shortly thereafter stating the discharge was revoked and such discharge order was to be withheld from Capt. James.

Capt. James was formally charged and held for a General court martial at Columbus, Mississippi. The charges were I, conduct unbecoming an Officer and a Gentleman, as reported in General Orders #81, HQs, Northern District of Mississippi, Jackson,

Mississippi, November 6, 1865. Capt. James pleaded not guilty of but was found guilty of several specifications and not guilty of others. He was sentenced to be reprimanded by the Commanding Officer of the 52nd Inf. Regt. USCT in the presence of the entire regiment and to forfeit his pay and emoluments for two months. In the review of the case the sentence was not approved on legal grounds of informality as the court found the charges and specifications were not incorporated into the record but were attached to it. The trial proceedings could only be amended by the original court numbers who heard the testimony and passed the sentence. It was impossible to amend the record as all but two of the members of the court had been discharged from the army and left the service. Consequently, Capt. James was released from arrest and returned to duty.

On November 23, 1865, Capt. James wrote to President Johnson again begging for a discharge from the army. In December, 1865, E. D. Townsend, Acting adjutant General, A.G.O., Washington, D.C., recommended his discharge "as Capt. James is not a valuable officer." S.O. #661, dated December 30, 1865, Capt. Frederic D. James, 52nd U.S. Colored Troops, having tendered his resignation, is upon the recommendation of his superior officers, hereby honorably discharged the service of the United States, with condition that he shall receive no final payments, until he has satisfied the Pay Department that he is not indebted to the Government. Adjutant General's Office, /Washington, D.C., again announced Capt. James discharge from the army. Apparently he was unable to satisfy some regulation as he again tendered his resignation on January 20, 1866 and was finally discharged on February 26, 1866.

The case of Capt. James illustrated two things. First the type of injustice inflicted on some of the USCT and the difficulty of administering military trials without the aid of trained legal officers.

It is little wonder that some of the men of Co. D., 52nd USCT found it necessary to engage in looting to replace their meager pay stolen by their Company Commander.

Case #231
Pvt. Thomas Four
NV: Fore
Co. D, 52nd Inf. Regt. USCT
Executed for Conspiracy, Robbery
May 26, 1865

DESCRIPTION:

29 years of age, 5 feet 8 inches tall, black hair, black eyes, black complexion, born in Green County, Georgia, occupation farmer, illiterate.

Four enlisted and was mustered into service on March 8, 1964 at Vicksburg, Mississippi in Company D, 52nd Infantry Regiment, USCT. Four was a member of the group who committed criminal acts at the Cook Plantation on April 3, 1865. Four shot Major Cook.

At his trial, Four presented the following brief Statement.

Statement of Prisoner

"While we were at the bridge (the Four Mile Bridge) somebody told us there were some rebels out on the Rail Road and advised us to go out and catch them, thats how I come to go. I had an old carbine that wouldn't shoot but no ammunition or anything. The witnesses try to make out that I shot but it is not so."

Four was convicted and sentenced to death. He was hung with his eight codefendants on May 26, 1865.

REFERENCES

Court Martial Proceedings, RG-#153 MM 2079

Case #232
Pvy. Henry Johnson
Co. D, 52nd Inf. Regt. USCT
Executed for Murder, Wounding, Conspiracy, Robbery
May 26, 1865

DESCRIPTION:

25 years of age, 5 feet 7½ inches tall, black hair, black eyes, black complexion, born in District of Columbia, Maryland, occupation house servant, literacy undetermined, ex-slave on the Cook Plantation.

Johnson enlisted on July 1, 1863 at Four-Mile Bridge, Mississippi and was mustered into service on July 27, 1863 at Vicksburg, Mississippi in Captain James' Company, 2nd Regiment, Mississippi Infantry A.D. (African Descent). The unit designation was later changed to Company D, 52nd Infantry Regiment, USCT.

Johnson was in the group who committed criminal acts on April 3,1865 at the Cook Plantation and was the original instigator of the plot.

Johnson made the following statement at his trial.

Statement of the Prisoner

"I didn't know where the boys was going. When I got to the house I says boys I know this place. I wouldn't have you do any harm here for the world. I wouldn't go in. I stood at the gate sometime and then went away. I told the rest to come away. I had nothing to do with the shooting. You know gentlemen there always some men in the company who lead the others astray. You know that Colored Soldiers used to be badly treated by the rebels and that makes them hate the rebels more than the white soldiers. Its natural that they should feel so. However I had nothing personal against Mr. Cook or his family, I have been away from there 2 years and one half. I didn't go with any other intention than to catch rebels."

Johnson was convicted, sentenced to death, and hung with his eight codefendants on May 26, 1865.

REFERENCES:
Military Personnel Records, RG-‹94
Court Martial Proceedings, RG-#153 MM 2079

Case #233
Pvt. Ephraim McDowell
Co. D, 52nd Inf,. Regt. USCT
Executed for Conspiracy, Robbery, Murder, Wounding
May 26, 1865

DESCRIPTION:

21 years of age, 5 feet 10 inches tall, black hair, black eyes, black complexion, born in DeKalb County, Georgia, occupation laborer, illiterate.

McDowell enlisted and was mustered into service on November 1, 1863 at Vicksburg, MIssissippi in Captain Johnson's Company, 2nd Regiment, Mississippi Infantry A.D. (African Descent), which unit designation was changed to Company K, 52nd Infantry Regiment, USCT. During the period December 22-31, 1863, McDowell was transferred to Company D, 52nd Infantry Regiment, USCT. He was one of the group involved in the criminal events on April 3, 1865 at the Cook Plantation. McDowell murdered Mrs. Cook.

McDowell made the following statement to the court during his trial.

Statement of the Prisoner

"I went out there with the intention of catching rebels. I am very sorry for what happened out there. I don't think I am to blame any farther than that I was along."

REFERENCES:
Military Personnel Records, RG-#94
Court Martial Proceedings, RG-#153

Case #234
Pvt. Peter Moore
Co. D, 52nd Inf. Regt. USCT
Executed for Conspiracy, Robbery, Murder, Wounding
May 26, 1865

DESCRIPTION:
19 years of age, 5 feet 8 inches tall, black hair, black eyes, black complexion, born in Haywood Country, Tennessee, occupation laborer, illiterate.

Moore enlisted on July 1, 1863 at Four-Mile Bridge, Mississippi and was mustered into service on July 27, 1863 at Vicksburg, Mississippi in Captain James' Company, 2nd Regiment, Mississippi Infantry A.D. (African Decent). The unit designation was changed to Company D, 52nd Infantry Regiment, USCT, Moore was among the criminals involved in the events of April 3, 1865 at the Cook Plantation.

The statement made by Moore to the Court at his trial and recorded in the proceedings is brief and enigmatic. "Peter Moore came forward but didn't seem to say anything."

Moore was convicted and sentenced to death. He was hung on May 26, 1865 with his eight codefendants.

REFERENCES:
Military Personnel Records, RG-#94
Court Martial Proceedings, RG-#153 MM 2079

Case #235
Pvty/Cpl James Morrison
Co. D, 52nd Inf. Regt. USCT
Executed for Murder, Robbery, Conspiracy, Wounding
May 26, 1865

DESCRIPTION:
25 years of age, 5 feet 7½ inches tall, black hair, black eyes, black complexion, born in Claiborne County, MIssissippi, occupation laborer, illiterate.

Morrison enlisted on July 1, 1863 at Four-Mile Bridge, Mississippi and was mustered into serve at Vicksburg, MIssissippi on July 27, 1863 in Captain James' Company, 2nd Regiment, Mississippi Infantry A.D. (African Descent). The unit designation was changed to Company D, 52nd Infantry Regiment, USCT. Morrison was promoted to rank of Corporal on November 18, 1864 and was one of the group involved in the crimes at the Cook Plantation on April 3, 1865. Morrison struck Mrs. Cook on the head with his gun butt.

Morrison made the following statement to the Court during his trial.

Statement of the Prisoner
"Well I was along with the crowd a great many things was done against my will, What I done didn't harm anybody. I wasn't at the house when the shooting was done. The rest tried to throw it on me. I didn't have any control over the party at all. I think I am not to blame for the shooting, it was a mistake about me striking Mrs. Cook."

Morrison was convicted, sentenced to death, and hung with his eight codefendants on May 26, 1865.

REFERENCES:
Military Personnel Records, RG-#94
Court Martial Proceedings, RG-#153 MM 2079

Case #236
Pvt. Otto Pierce
Co. L, 5th Hvy Arty, USCT
Executed for Conspiracy, Robbery, Shooting, Murder
May 26, 1865

DESCRIPTION:
26 years of age, 5 feet 2 inches tall, black hair, brown eyes, light complexion, born in Simpson Country, Mississippii, occupation field hand, illiterate.

Pierce enlisted and was mustered into service March 1, 1864 at Vicksburg, Mississippi in Company L, 4th Heavy Artillery Regiment, USCT. The unit designation was subsequently changed to the 5th Heavy Artillery Regiment, USCT. A notation in his military records states, "sent to Pest House April 16-64." Apparently, Pierce had contracted smallpox or some other contagious disease as the term "Pest House" was used to designate a hospital only for patients with a contagious disease. On April 30, 1864, he appeared before a regimental Court Martial, for an unspecified offense, and was fined $14.00 and five days time in solitary confinement on bread and water.

On November 17, 1864, Pierce was formally charged with absence without leave and disobedience of orders. Pierce and his Company had been ordered to be prepared for Company inspection and Pierce absented himself without permission and refused to obey the lawful order for such formation. Results of the trial are unavailable. There may be grounds for assuming the $30.00 fine mentioned (next) is his penalty for this offense.

In early 1865, Pierce again seems to have run afoul of Army regulations as another notation indicates he had $30.00 withheld from his pay as a result of another Regimental Court Martial. Examination of his military records indicates a steady list of charges against his pay for loss or destruction of issued government property.

Pierce's Regiment was encamped adjoining the 52nd USCT and he was acquainted with members of Company D. Pierce was present on the night of April 3, 1865, from the time of the planning of the plundering of the Cook Plantation to the shooting of the Cooks and the return to camp from the bloody senseless crime.

At his trial, Pierce stated: "The boys said they were going on a scout and I went just be with the crowd. If I had known they were going toward anybody I wouldn't have went. I was outside the gate when the firing took place."

Pierce was convicted and executed at the same time and place, by hanging with the eight other condemned criminals who murdered Mrs. Cook and wounded Major cook, while plundering the Cook home.

REFERENCES:
Military Personnel Records, RG-#94
Court Martial Proceedings, RG-#153   MM 2079

Case #237
Pvt. Mose Rawlings
NV: Rollins, Rawlins
Co. D, 52nd Infantry Regt, USCT
Executed for Murder, Robbery, Conspiracy, Wounding
May 26, 1865

DESCRIPTION:
20 years of age, 6 feet 1½ inches tall, black hair, black eyes, black complexion, born in Jefferson Country, Mississippi, occupation laborer, illiterate.

Rawlings enlisted on July 1, 1863 and was mustered into service on July 27, 1863 at Four-Mile Bridge, Mississippi in Captain James' Company, 2nd Regiment, Mississippi Infantry A.d. (African Descent). The unit designation was ultimately changed to

Company D,. 52nd Infantry Regiment, USCT. On November 6, 1864, Rawlings was confined in the Pest Hospital ill of an unspecified contagious disease such as smallpox, from which he recovered and was returned to duty. Rawlins was one of a group of enlisted men of the 52nd Regiment which were involved in a crime of murder, attempted murder, and robbery.

Rawlings offered the following statement during the trail.

Statement of the Prisoner

"My understanding was that I was going out after rebels. I know I was to blame for going out without orders, but that's all. When the shooting was going on I was down in the land about 300 yards from the house."

Rawlings was convicted and sentenced to death. He was hung on May 26, 1865 with his eight codefendants.

REFERENCES:
Military Personnel Records, RG-#94
Court Martial Proceedings, RG-#153 MM 2079

Case #238
Cpl/Pvt William Wallace
NV: Wallis
Co. D 52nd Inf. Regt. USCT
Executed for Conspiracy, Wounding, Robbery, Murder
May 26, 1865

DESCRIPTION:

20 years of age, 6 feet 2 inches tall, black hair, black eyes, black complexion, born in Hinds County, Mississippi, occupation servant, literacy not determined.

Wallace enlisted and was mustered into service at Four-Mile Bridge, Mississippi on July 1, 1863 in Captain James' Company, 2nd Regiment, Mississippi Infantry A.D. (African Descent). The unit designation was later changed to Company D, 52nd Infancy Regiment, USCT. On December 12, 1863, Wallace was recommended for promotion to Corporal which was granted. In the July/August, 1864 period, he was reported sick.

Wallace was one of the men who participated in the crimes committed at the Cook Plantation on April 3, 1865. During the Trial, Wallace made the following statement to the Court on his behalf.

Statement of the Prisoner

"I see them starting out of çamp. I asked them where they were going. They said they was going out to hunt some rebels, then I asked them where was they going to hunt rebels at. They said they had no particular place to go to. I fell back in the hind squad. When we got to the gate I said if you go in the house I won't go in, so if you do any devilment I won't be to blame. I didn't go in the house. I was not there when the shooting was done. I think I was not to blame for what was done because I did not know anything about it before hand nor didn't do anything myself."

Wallace was convicted, sentenced to death, and hung with his eight codefendants on May 26, 1865.

REFERENCES:
Military Personnel Records, RG-#94
Court Martial Proceedings, RG-#153 MM 2079

Case #239
Sgt/Pvt John Willis
Co. D, 52nd Inf. Regt. USCT
Executed for Robbery, Conspiracy, Murder, Wounding
May 26, 1865

DESCRIPTION:

23 years of age, 6 feet 1 inch tall, black hair, black eyes, black complexion, born in Abbeville District of Georgia, occupation laborer, illiterate.

Willis enlisted on July 1, 1863 and was mustered into service as a Sergeant on July 27, 1863 at Four-Mile Bridge (camp of colored troops near Vicksburg) in Captain James' Company, 2nd Regiment, Mississippi Infantry A.D. (African Descent). The unit designation was changed to Company D, 52nd Infantry Regiment, USCT. Willis was reported to be absent on recruiting duty on October 21, 1863 and was demoted from the rank of Sergeant during the period of July/August 1864. He, too, was involved in the criminal events which took place at the Cook Plantation on April 3, 1865.

At the trial, Willis made the following statement for his defense.

Statement of the Prisoner

"I didn"t intend to go out there to rob or do anything of that description if I had known anything of that, if I had I shouldn't have gone. I went in there to see if there wasn't rebs in there. The witnesses were mistaken about me taking things away."

Willis was convicted, sentenced to death, and hung with his eight codefendants on May 26, 1865.

REFERENCES:
Military Personnel Records, RG-#94
Court Martial Proceedings, RG-#153 MM 2079

Case #240
Pvt. John Lewis
Co. E, 13th Heavy Artillery USCT
Hung for Murder
June 13, 1865

DESCRIPTION:

Pvt. John Lewis was born in Loudon County, Virginia and was 25 years of age at his enlistment on March 27, 1865 at Louisville, Kentucky.. He was 5 feet 3½ inches tall, had black hair, eyes and complexion and was a teamster by occupation.

He was assigned to Company E, 13th Heavy Artillery Regiment, USCT and was on duty with his unit at Shelbyville, Kentucky at the time of his arrest.

About 5 A.M. on May 19, 1865 at Shelbyville, Kentucky, a small group of negro soldiers tried to break into a storage warehouse filled with agricultural implements. A white citizen, John McGrath, warned them to stay away from the warehouse, as he observed their efforts from his store adjoining the warehouse. He then went to his stable in the rear area of his store to feed and care for his horse. When he returned to the street side of his store he noted negro soldiers inside the warehouse and he went to his living quarters which he shared with his brother to notify him about the break in, as he was the custodian of the warehouse.

His brother, Thomas C. McGrath, dressed and went to the warehouse after being warned that one of the negro soldiers carried a loaded rifle. He entered the warehouse, noted several negro troopers inside the premises and ordered them out. He then turned and walked toward the door. A shot was fired which struck him in the back as he reached the door and he fell forward onto the street. His brother John and another citizen, a Mr. Hasting, carried him home where he died about five minutes later.

The person who shot Thomas McGrath, Pvt. John Lewis, readily admitted firing the fatal shot and was arrested and confined.

A General Court Martial was convened at Louisville, Kentucky and the trial began on May 25th, 1865.

Lewis claimed that Thomas McGrath drew a pistol from his pocket and pointed it at him and verbally denounced his Captain.

John McGrath, brother of the murdered Thomas McGrath, and several other witnesses denied that his brother was armed and was not carrying a pistol at the time of his confrontation with the colored troopers.

Several members of the Negro Military Company E testified that they either saw, thought they saw or were told that McGrath did have a pistol and threatened Lewis.

When the prosecution concluded its case presentation, the accused asked for a postponement to enable him to locate additional witnesses and to prepare a written statement. The request was granted by the court.

When the trial resumed, the events recounted told of Lewis seeking the key to the warehouse on his Captain's orders so that he, Lewis a cook, could prepare breakfast inside the warehouse as it was raining. McGrath refused him the key and Lewis threatened to break the door open. McGrath later went into the warehouse, found Lewis and several other negro soldiers inside the warehouse and ordered them out. McGrath turned and walked out, but as he reached the threshold of the door, Lewis shot him in the back and McGrath fell forward into the street.

Questions were raised as to the McGrath's loyalty to the Union, however, their loyalty was convincingly attested to by a Union Army Brig. General and Colonel who possessed longtime acquaintanceship with the deceased and his brother.

The court deliberated and found the defendant guilty and sentenced him to be hanged by the neck until he be dead on Tuesday the 13th Day of June 1865 in Louisville, Kentucky.

REFERENCE:S

Court Martial Proceedings, RG-#53
Army Personnel Records, RG OO 933

Case #241
Pvt./Cpl. Frank Hudson
Co I, 2nd Calif Vol Cav Regt
Executed for Murder
June 16, 1865

DESCRIPTION:

28 years of age, 5 feet 11 inches tall, gray eyes, dark hair, dark complexion, born in Ireland, occupation miner, literate.

Hudson enlisted in I Company 2nd California Volunteer Cavalry Regiment at Camp Babbitt, California on February 14, 1863 and was mustered into service at the Benicia Barracks, Benicia, California. He was reported sick in hospital shortly after his entering military service. The unit he was assigned to seems to have served almost constantly in the California area and on November 24, 1864, he was appointed Corporal. On or about April 14, 1865, Hudson deserted from Camp Bidwell, California and was later accused of murdering Lt. Levergood, Company I, 2nd California Cavalry Regiment, which deed prompted him to desert. Hudson was captured on April 18, 1865 and confined at Camp Union, California.

A General Court Martial was convened at Camp Bidwell, Chico, California and on May 4th 1865 tried Corporal Frank Hudson, Company I, 2nd California Cavalry Regiment on the charges of murder and desertion.

Testimony described the chain of events which led to the murder of 1st Lieutenant Levergood by Hudson. Hudson was mustered into service on February 14, 1864. Levergood was mustered into service on September 25, 1861 as a Private and rose through the ranks to a 1st Sergeant in the 2nd California Cavalry Regiment. He was subsequently commissioned as a 2nd Lieutenant and on or about late March or early April, 1865 was promoted to 1st Lieutenant of Company I, 2nd California Cavalry Regiment.

On April 14, 1865, Lieutenant Levergood administered punishment to Corporal Hudson by having him "double quick-time" around the Parade Ground. After the punishment was concluded, Corporal Hudson was heard by several witnesses to have remarked that, "the God damned son of a bitch has made me take my last double quick. I'll fix him before I go to sleep."

About 8pm on the night of April 14, 1865, Hudson went to the house of Private Milton Copple, Company I, 2nd California Cavalry Regiment and his wife Sarah, a laundress at Camp Bidwell, and asked to borrow a pistol as he wanted to protect himself when he went into town. During the trial it was stated that government issued revolvers were not permitted to be carried except on duty. The Copples loaned the pistol, described as a five shot revolver of an unnamed make which used the Navy ball (cal. 36). The weapon was loaded and primed by Copple before it was handed over to Hudson. Private Copple was ordered to bring in duplicates of the cartridge ball for comparison with the ball recovered by the surgeon from the Lieutenant's body.

Witnesses placed Hudson near his tent in possession of a pistol about 30 minutes before Levergood was shot. As well as in the vicinity of the place where Levergood was shot 10 to 15 minutes prior to the fatal incident.

Levergood was shot at close range in the trunk of the body, so close that his shirt was scorched and blackened. The ball entered the front of his chest and lodged under the skin of his back a little to the left of his spinal column below the sixth rib where it was recovered by the surgeon before Levergood died. The ball was presented to the court to compare with those furnished by Private Copple.

The Lieutenant was quite rational during the 50 some hours that he lived after being wounded. Lieutenant Levergood was taken after the shooting to his quarters, which he shared with his wife, and remained there until he died. He told the surgeon and others who attended him that it was Corporal Hudson who had shot him. Hudson had spoken to him before firing, saying, "is that you Lieutenant Levergood?" Levergood replied, "Yes" and Hudson fired the pistol.

The Lieutenant died on the night of April 16th or early morning of the 17th, 1865.

Hudson deserted his Company and Regiment after the shooting on the night of April 14, 1865 and was apprehended six miles from Tehama, California on or about the 18th of April, 1865. One soldier testified that he spoke with Hudson after his capture. He said that he asked Hudson if he knew the result of his shot. Hudson replied, "What was it?" The soldier replied, "We buried Lieutenant Levergood yesterday evening. I suppose you done what you intended to, you intended to kill him." Hudson made no reply. Hudson, while confined, is reported to have said that he would have shot other members of the Company if he knew then what he knew now, or words to that effect.

Hudson offered no defense witnesses but did offer a statement in his defense.

"Viz."

"Mr. President and members of the Court, I wish to make the following statement, I never had any difficulty of any nature with Lieutenant Levergood nor any ill feelings toward him. I always obeyed his orders willingly and with respect. I never had any occasion to disobey, he always used me well and I respected him as an officer and a gentleman, and as for my making threats as to killing him; such things are common in a camp: you will hear them everyday in the week. The fact that he merely ran me on a double quick, would be a very poor reason for killing a man. As to my deserting I did so as I had for some time thought I was ill treated in the Company. I went to the Captain to get reduced to the ranks and gave as a reason that I thought I could get along better as a private soldier I always have done my duty: but the Captain refused to reduce me.

Very respectfully,
Your Obt. Sevt.
Frank Hudson, Corp. Company I, 2nd Calif. Cavalry Regt."

The Court then deliberated, found Hudson guilty and sentenced him to be hung by the neck until he be dead.

The execution took place on June 16, 1865 at Camp Bidwell, California.

Hudson wrote a letter appealing for clemency.

"Camp Union, June 13, 1865.
Maj Genl McDowell, Dear Sir,

I would most respectfully make the following statement. I am under sentence of death to be executed on Friday. I have served as a soldier for two years and four months, the cause of my desertion was from continued ill usage by the 1st Sergeant of Company I, 2nd California Cavalry I was a non-commissioned in the company and repeatedly applied to my Captain to be reduced to the ranks, stating to him that I thought I could do my duty and get along better as a private soldier. I never was an enemy of Lieut Levergood's he had enemies in the company and they or some of them took advantage of my desertion to accuse me of the crime of killing him I did not kill him nor attempt to injure him in any way. I have always respected Lieut Levergood as an officer and a soldier. It is the first time I have ever been tried by any court civil or Military. I humbly beg that you will carefully look over the evidence against me, and pray that you commute my sentence to imprisonment. I am an innocent man and time will prove it.

Respectfully,
Your Obdt Sevt
Frank Hudson
Corpl. Co. I - 2nd Cal Cav"

Major General McDowell replied promptly by telegram, "California State Telegraph Company

San Francisco, June 15th, 1865
To, Brigadier Gen. G. Wright, 6:45 PM
= Commanding Dist of California =

Say to Corporal Hudson of Company I, second (2) cavalry at Camp Union that I have received his letter, that I have again carefully considered the evidence of the court in his case and have gone over it with Judge Hoffman of the U.S. District Court and Judge Field of the United States Supreme Court - They concur that the evidence fully warrants the sentence of death - Tell him that I do not modify my orders and that the execution must take place. It will be a mercy to let him know that this must be so - that he may make his last preparations in the short time that remains to him on Earth.

Irwin McDowell
Maj Genl
Comd Dept"

On June 16, 1865 at Camp Union, California, Hudson was executed. The report of his execution stated, "The drop fell at 12:20 PM and at 12:35 Surgeon C. S. Wood US Vols pronounced life extinct."

REFERENCES:

Military Personnel Records, RG-#94
Court Martial Proceedings, RG-#153 OO 1206
State of California, Archives, Records, Company I - 2nd California Cavalry Regiment 1863 - 1865

Case #242
Pvt. Henry Jay
Co. I, 57th USC Infantry
Executed for Rape
June 21, 1865

DESCRIPTION:

20 years of age, 5 feet 10½ inches tall, black eyes, black hair, brown complexion, born in Salem, Mississippi, occupation laborer, illiterate.

Jay enlisted in Company I, 4th Regiment Arkansas Infantry AD (African Descent) on November 20, 1863 and was mustered into service at Little Rock, Arkansas on December 22, 1863. The regiment changed its designation to Company I, 57th USC Infantry and Jay served in Arkansas until he committed a rape on a white woman at Dardanelle, Arkansas. He was tried by drumhead court martial, found guilty and executed on June 21, 1865. Apparently some relatives requested a Certificate of Military Service (for pension or other monetary benefits) but on October 26, 1889 same was denied on the basis of his execution for a crime.

REFERENCE:
Military Personal Records, RG-#94
U. S. Army Pension Records

Case #243
Pvt. Simon Grant
Co. H, 21st Inf Regt, USCT
Executed for Murder
June 23, 1865

DESCRIPTION:

22 years of age, 5 feet 3½ inches tall, black hair, black eyes, black complexion, born in South Carolina, occupation laborer, illiterate.

Grant enlisted on August 29, 1864 at Beaufort, South Carolina and was mustered into service August 31, 1864 at Hilton Head, South Carolina. He was assigned to Company H, 21st Infantry Regiment USCT. On or about April 10, 1865, at the camp of the 21st Regiment at Mount Pleasant, South Carolina, Grant without provocation shot and killed Private Cuffy Wright also of Company H of the 21st Regiment. Grant was arrested and court martialed.

A General Court Martial was convened at Charleston, South Carolina and on April 26, 1865 tried Private Simon Grant, Company H, 21st Infantry Regiment USCT on a charge of murder.

Witnesses stated that on April 10, 1865, in the Camp of the 21st Regiment USCT at Mt. Pleasant, South Carolina at about 12:30 PM a shot was fired which struck Private Cuffy Wright of Company H, 21st Infantry Regiment USCT in the head killing him. The body lay in the Company H tent area. Private Grant was believed to be the murderer and was arrested and confined in the guard house. Further investigation discovered the pistol that fired the fatal shot concealed in Grant's tent, where Grant was found after the shooting and from which place the shot was fired. The pistol was described as a single shot non-military flint lock of large caliber apparently obtained from some southern family. Grant voluntarily confessed that he shot Wright and that the large bruise in the center of his forehead was caused by the recoil of the pistol when it was fired. The Regimental Surgeon, Hankes, testified that the fatal wound was very large, entering behind the right ear, passing threw the brain and exiting a little forward of the left ear. The fatal bullet was made from a military leaden ball cut in half and hand shaped to fit the smaller barrel of the flint lock pistol.

Witnesses testified that Grant and Wright had quarrelled during two expeditions by the Regiment. Grant had been overheard telling Wright he would shoot him.

Grant offered no defense nor statement to the Court.

The Court deliberated and found the accused guilty and sentenced him to be executed by hanging.

He was to be confined in irons until the execution. The execution took place at Castle Pinckney, a military prison, within Charleston, South Carolina on June 23, 1865. (One casualty sheet ascribes his death to disease, a copyist error no doubt.)

REFERENCES:
Military Personnel Records, RG-#94
Court Martial Proceedings, RG-#153 MM 2139

Case #244
Pvt. Patrick McNamara
NV: McNamari
Co. K, 132nd NY Infantry Regt
Executed for Murder
June 30, 1865

DESCRIPTION:

30 years of age, 5 feet 7½ inches tall, light hair, blue eyes, light complexion, born in Ireland, occupation laborer.

McNamara enlisted and was mustered into service on July 28, 1862 at New York City in Company K, 132nd New York Infantry Regiment. McNamara seems to have a record devoid of incident until December 25, 1864 when, for an unspecified reason, McNamara engaged in an altercation at about 7 PM with Private James Shaw, Company K, 132nd New York Infantry Regiment, during the course of which McNamara stabbed Shaw twice with a pocket knife. McNamara was seized and arrested and desperate efforts were undertaken to save Shaw's life proved unavailing, when he died at 3AM on the 27th of December, 1864. A truly sad Christmas. Murder charges were filed against McNamara.

A General Court Martial was convened at New Berne, North Carolina and on February 3, 1865 tried Private Patrick McNamara, Company K, 132 New York Infantry Regiment on a charge of murder.

Testimony revealed that on December 25, 1864 in the regimental camp near Bachelor's Creek, North Carolina the accused about 7 PM entered the tent of Private James Shaw of the same Company and Regiment of the accused. When McNamara entered the tent, Shaw jumped up and pushed him out of the tent onto the Company street. Moments later the accused reentered the tent and Shaw again jumped up and ejected McNamara from the tent and followed him into the Company street. Shortly thereafter, those in Shaw's tent heard him cry out, "I am stabbed" and moments later reentered the tent with one arm folded over his breast, saying only that he had been stabbed and then laid himself down carefully on a bench. Other soldiers in the Company quickly filed into the tent.

McNamara, in the meantime, remained standing in the Company street surrounded by soldiers before being taken to the guard house.

McNamara was stated by a witness to have said to Shaw after he stabbed him, "God damn you keep away from me or I will give it to you again!"

Shaw was overheard later saying to Lt. Simpson that he was going to die and that he wanted the Doctor to write to his wife and children.

Another witness testified that he took a pocket knife from the accused at the guard house when he arrived. Assistant surgeon L. C. Grenninger, 132nd New York Infantry described Shaw's wound as an incised wound, three inches in length on the left abdominal wall about three inches from the navel. About three feet of intestines were hanging out. Shaw was taken to the regimental hospital where he died about three o'clock on the morning of December 27, 1864.

McNamara called as a defense witness one of the officers of his company who was asked as to McNamara's character as a soldier while with the Company. The reply, "At times he has been troublesome."

The accused had no other witnesses to call on his behalf but did present a statement to the Court.

"*Officers and members of the cort.* As I have a small statement to make to the Cort and as I am not capable of standing up Before you to Explain myself I will give it to you in writeing as Follows.

I must say that it is now nearly 3 years since I entered the service which I never Received aney Bounty when I did join and I defy any man in the Regt. to come Forward and say that I have not done My Duty as well as aney in the Regt. Ever since I entered and I must also say that I have always Got along Verry Well with all the Men in the Regt. Except a few in my own Company For some reason I dont no. What they have Been Very dark with me Ever since last June When we was out on A Raid When these verry men was the ons to Flinch when I spoke to them of their Cowardise and Ever since that they seem to Be taking Every advantage they Possibly can against me Not only that But my Captain has encouraged them in it as Hee told them one Day that if I said aneything to them to take up the first thing they could get hold of and Hit mee over the Head with it.

And ever since that time the Best Word I could get out of aney of them Was a sun of Bitch or Worse than that I am now a man of 35 years of age and I am all alone in this World Except one Poor old mother and sister in the old country whish I am the only support they have and I have been saveing all I could to Bring them out to this country I will also say that I have always Been Ready to aid our Government Every since I have been out Hear and My Last Words is to you all is Hopeing to Be shown Justice."

The Court deliberated, found the accused guilty and sentenced him to be hanged by the neck until he be dead.

McNamara was transferred from Fort Macon to the Provost Marshall at New Berne, North Carolina on June 25, 1865. He was considered dangerous and the order for the transfer specified that he "be properly ironed and under an officer with a sufficient guard."

The execution took place at New Berne, North Carolina on June 30, 1865.

REFERENCES:

Military Personnel Records, RG #94
Court Martial Proceedings, RG #153 OO 915

Case #245
Pvt. George Dixon
Co. D, 79th Inf, USCT
Executed for Murder
July 21, 1865

DESCRIPTION:

18 years of age.

Dixon enlisted on April 1, 1863 at Wyandotte, Kansas and was mustered into service May 2, 1863 at Fort Scott, Kansas in the 1st Regiment Kansas Colored Infantry. In 1864, the designation of the unit was changed to Company K, 79th Regiment of Infantry, USCT. A notation in his record file states he deserted from the ranks while on the march from Fort Smith, Arkansas to Roseville on December 12, 1863. He is reported as having "returned" to his unit on February 14, 1864. There is no record of any disciplinary action being taken. On November 28, 1864, he was again arrested and confined in the guardhouse. And as on the previous occasion, no punishment seems to have been administered, nor is the act for which he was confined stated. On June 22, 1865, he was arrested and confined at Little Rock, Arkansas and charged with murder.

A General Court Martial was convened at Little Rock, Arkansas, and proceeded on June 24, 1865 to the trial of Private George Dixon, Company K, 79th Infantry Regiment, USCT, charged with murder.

On the 24th of June, 1865, a memorandum from a member of the court was addressed to the Provost Marshall at Little Rock, Arkansas advising him trial witnesses failed to report and requested they be summoned at once.

Testimony disclosed the following facts.

About noon an June 21, 1865, Dixon was seen in the camp of the 79th Regiment in Company with a white man and white boy. The boy was later that day observed at the Military Headquarters with his head heavily bandaged.

According to the testimony of Louis Freinfried, son of the murdered Henry Freinfried, Dixon came to his father's store and told his father that he wanted to sell him some silver he had hidden in the woods. His father and Louis went with Dixon to the camp of the 79th Regiment. At the camp, Dixon left them with the excuse that he had a message for his Colonel and he designated a place outside of camp where they were to go, where he would meet them. Louis and his father went to the designated place and after a five minute wait were joined by Dixon and another never identified person. All four proceeded into the woods when Dixon halted them and said to wait until he and his companion returned, which they did in a few minutes. Dixon walked up to Henry, drew out a large revolver, pointed it at his chest, demanded Freinfried's money and fired the revolver. At that moment Dixon's companion seized the son, Louis, by the throat and threw him to the ground. Dixon then struck Louis a half dozen times over the head with his revolver while his companion held Louis helpless. Louis feigned death as one of the men searched his pockets while the other searched his dead father's pockets. One of them also struck his father on the head several times and then they left. Louis expressed the opinion that his father "did not live a minute." Louis got up after the murderers left the scene and made his way to his father's mill. Workers there took him to General William's Headquarters where he had his wounds dressed and he recounted the tragic events. His father, had in his possession that day about ($140.00) one hundred and forty dollars in Greenback currency consisting of a one hundred dollar ($100.00) bill and four ten dollar ($10.00) bills.

Louis described Dixon's appearance and clothing worn during the murder for identification purposes. A Lieutenant Chase of a Regiment of USCT described finding the body of Henry Freinfried after being guided to the spot by workers from the mill. The deceased was lying on his right side and close examination disclosed a pistol shot entered in the center of the breast, exiting a little to the right of the back bone (spine). The orifice of the wound was about the size of an army pistol ball. There was also a bruise on the forehead over the right eye apparently made with a club or stone. He examined the body about half past one o'clock on June 21st, 1865. One witness, a soldier of the 79th USCT testified that Dixon came to his quarters he estimated sometime between noon and 2:00 PM on June 21st, 1865 and borrowed his loaded and charged large Remington Revolver. The revolver was found in the owners bunk about two hours after Dixon borrowed it. It had two shots fired. When questioned about the two shots fired, Dixon said he had shot at a fox.

Dixon, and about five or six other members of the 79th, USCT were taken to the house of Louis Freinfried for identification purposes. Louis positively identified Dixon.

Dixon while under arrest, stated that he loaned his revolver to a soldier in another USCT Regiment and that this man murdered Freinfried and gave him (Dixon) $35.00 of the money. A search of Dixon's possessions located ($130.00) one hundred and thirty dollars in U.S. greenbacks, one hundred dollar bill and three, ten dollar bills hidden in Dixon's cap.

Dixon declined to offer testimony or a statement of the events of which he was accused.

The Court deliberated, found Dixon guilty, and sentenced him to death by hanging.

The execution took place in the courtyard of the Military Prison at Little Rock, Arkansas on July 21, 1865.

(The records in Dixon's file are somewhat contradictory. At one point he is stated to have been enlisted on August 10, 1862 at Leavenworth, Kansas. At another point his original Company of enlistment is listed as Company G, same Regiment. At another point, some information is stated to have been obtained from the "Roll of Honor" of Arkansas, page 38. Ordinarily an executed soldier's name is not placed on the Honor Roll. This is possibly a clerical error or oversight.)

REFERENCES:
Military Personnel Records, RG-#94
State of Kansas Records
Court Martial Proceedings, RG-#153 MM 2483

Case #246
Pvt. (Cpl.) William A. Wilson
Co. G, 12th Illinois Vol Cav
Executed for Desertion/Theft
July 28, 1865

DESCRIPTION:

Aged 18 years, height 5 foot 11½ inches, gray eyes, auburn hair, complexion light, occupation farmer, born in Belfast, New Jersey. (Literacy undetermined.)

Enlisted from Polo, Illinois in Company F, 4th Illinois Cavalry Regiment on 14 December 1863 and entered service on 31 January 1864. Later transferred to Company A, 4th Illinois Cavalry and on June 14, 1865 his Company was transferred to the 12th Illinois Cavalry Regiment and redesignated Company G.

Little is known of Wilson's military career prior to his execution except that he had virtually duplicated his final fatal crime at Natchez, Mississippi in 1864. In the General Court Martial trial of Wilson which took place at Natchez, Mississippi on December 20, 1864, Wilson was charged with theft of a Colt revolver, the property of the U.S. government, attempt to sell same, leaving camp without permission or knowledge of military authorities and performing a treasonable act by his conduct in this crime. Found guilty on a majority of the charges and specifications against him, Wilson was sentenced "to forfeit all pay and allowances that are now due or may become due him and to be confined at hard labor for the remainder of the time for which he enlisted, at such place as the Commanding General shall designate, and then be dishonorably discharged from the service of the United States."

The sentence was approved and the Military Prison at Natchez designated as the place of confinement. No record has, to date, been located to indicate how, why or when Wilson was released from this court martial sentence. He did, in fact, at some point in time, rejoin his Company and Regiment.

Major General Philip Sheridan was assigned to the command of the Military Division of the Gulf in 1865 and he requested Major General George A. Custer for the command of a division of Cavalry composed of the 1st Iowa, 2nd Wisconsin, 5th and 12th Illinois and the 7th Indiana Regiments which were assembled at Alexandria, Louisiana in June of 1866. The Division was to deploy into Texas to restore and maintain civilian order as well as to provide a veteran division in position to enter Mexico if the situation there required U.S. intervention.

The regiments assembled in Alexandria, Louisiana were an unhappy lot as the Civil War was ended, the troopers felt (as all soldiers from time immemorial have felt) that they had earned an honorable discharge and their return home to take up, once again, their interrupted civilian lives and careers. A further fear building in their minds was that having thus far escaped death or crippling injury, they might succumb to such during occupation duty in

Texas where guerilla type action was likely to be encountered. Even thoughts of the possibility of further military campaigning in Mexico was an ever present and foreboding prospect.

Desertions from Custer's Cavalry Division were common and Wilson was one of the deserters. On July 8, 1865, he deserted his Company taking with him his government issued mount, bridle, saddle and other accouterments including his government issued Colt revolver and ammunition. Wilson was apprehended, charged with desertion and theft, tried by a General Court Martial, found guilty and ordered to be shot on July 28, 1865. Wilson was executed by a firing squad on the appointed day. (See Sgt. Lancaster case for additional details.)

More bizarre than Wilson's career and execution, however, was that of 1st Sgt./2nd Lt. Leonard Lee Lancaster of Company L. 2nd Wisconsin Cavalry Regiment who was condemned to be shot to death with Wilson.

REFERENCES:
Military Personnel Records, RG-#94

Case #247
Pvt. (Cpl.) Dandridge Brooks
Co. E, 38th Inf Regt, USCT
Executed for Rape
July 30, 1865

DESCRIPTION:

22 years of age, 5 feet 7 inches tall, brown eyes, brown hair, light complexion, born in Essex County, Virginia, occupation teamster, illiterate.

Brooks enlisted and was mustered into service at Point Lookout, Maryland on June 21, 1864 in Company G, 38th Infantry Regiment, USCT. He was reported as a Corporal in July/August 1864 records and Sergeant in March /April 1865 records. He was arrested for rape and confined.

Sergeant Dandridge Brooks, Company G, 38th Infantry Regiment USCT was tried by a General Court Martial on April 19, 1865 at the headquarters of the 1st Division, 25th Army Corps in the field in Virginia.

Brooks was charged with the crimes of rape and plundering and pillaging.

Testimony provided the following evidence. On the night of April 11, 1865, between 10-11 PM, Sergeant Brooks accompanied by a Sergeant Jackson, Privates Anthony Branch, Sewell Knowlen, Albert Homes, Flag Corporal Sheppard, Edward Berry and another unnamed man of Company F, same Regiment, went outside of their camp and found a house with two women present. Brooks pounded on the door and demanded entrance. The older woman within the house apparently fled to the second floor screaming after Brooks broke open the door by slamming his body against it. As the woman fled, Brooks shouted, "Kill her, kill her" and Sheppard fired his revolver. Berry, Branch, Holmes and Knowlen then left the scene for their camp while Brooks, Jackson, Sheppard and the unidentified soldier entered the house. Upon entering the house, Brooks discovered Eliza H. Woodson, aged 14 years and her brother Clayton Woodson, niece and Nephew of Mrs. Fanny Crawford, wife of the owner of the premises who had fled to the upper floor.

Brooks forced Eliza Woodson into the bedroom where she had been sleeping and raped her, despite her screams and efforts to prevent him. He finally halted her screams and protests by covering her mouth and threatened to kill her. Her young brother cowered in a corner of the same room under threat of being shot if he called out or tried to interfere. After Brooks completed his sexual attack, one of the other men entered and also raped her. In the meantime, Mrs. Crawford was raped on the floor of a passageway by two of the invaders and the house was ransacked and many articles were taken away including eight pounds of butter, a tin pan, a pair of white kid gloves, a silver thimble, a silver finger shield, a white shirt, one satin vest, a towel, a dark blue overcoat, and spools of thread. Brooks and his companions boasted openly of raping the two woman and displayed the stolen goods to their regimental companions.

The Provost Marshall tracked them through the foot prints left in the muddy soil and by the peculiar heel pattern of Sheppard's boot. The men of his Company had to submit to a search of their knapsacks and the stolen articles were found in possession of Sheppard.

Brooks offered no defense and his only statement was "I was not in the house."

Brooks was found guilty and sentenced to be executed by hanging. His Regiment was ordered to duty in Brownsville, Texas and he accompanied the Regiment in irons and under guard. He was hung in Brownsville, Texas on July 30, 1865.

REFERENCES:
Military Personnel Records, RG-#94
Court Martial Proceedings, RG-#153

Case #248
Pvt. (Sgt.) William Jackson
Co. G, 38th Inf Regt USCT
Executed for Rape
July 30, 1865

DESCRIPTION:

24 years of age, 5 feet 7 inches tall, black eyes, black hair, dark complexion, born in Middlesex County, Virginia, occupation laborer, illiterate.

Jackson was enlisted on August 19, 1864 and mustered into service on August 20, 1864 at Newport News, Virginia in Company G, 38th Infantry Regiment USCT. At some point in his service, he was promoted to Sergeant and was reduced to ranks on May 1st, 1865. He was arrested for rape and court martialed.

A General Court Martial was convened at the Headquarters of the 1st Division, 25th Army Corps in the field and on April 20, 1865 tried Sergeant William Jackson, Company G, 38th Infantry Regiment USCT on charges of rape and plundering and pillaging.

Testimony revealed that on the night of April 11, 1865, Sergeant Jackson, accompanied by seven other soldiers, went to the residence of Mrs. Fannie Crawford which was located about three miles from Richmond, Virginia on the Deep Run Road. One of the group, a Sergeant Brooks, went up on the porch and knocked on the door. When his knocking was unanswered, he shouted that they had better open the door. Sergeant Jackson went up on the porch and slammed against the door which burst the door open. Mrs. Crawford, who had been standing in the hall, ran upstairs into a room, opened a window, and began screaming. Sergeant Brooks ordered someone to shoot her and the Flag Corporal fired at her, but missed. At this juncture, Privates Albert Holmes, Edward Berry, Sewall Noel, and Anthony Branch left the premises and returned to camp without ever having entered the house. Sergeants Jackson and Brooks, the Flag Corporal, and another soldier remained and entered the house.

Sergeant Jackson and his three companions entered the house and raped Mrs. Fannie Crawford and her young niece, Eliza Harriet Woodson, while threatening them with death by pistols held at their head. Then they ransacked the house taking away numerous articles including two vests, several men's shirts, a thread case, silver shield and thimble, a pair of shears, a small pocket knife, a towel, about 8-10 pounds of butter, two pairs of ladies hose, shoemakers knives, candles, handkerchief, a ladies hat, a pair of woman's kid gloves and an overcoat.

Mrs. Crawford's brother, William S. Woodson, testified that he was in his home across the road from the Crawford residence and heard the disturbance but was afraid to intervene as he too feared for his life. He did, however, run to the camp of a Union Artillery Battery and he reported the affair to General Draper that night.

The four perpetrators of the crimes returned to their Company and proceeded to brag about ravishing the white women and the articles they had stolen.

General Draper testified that on the morning of the 12th he was advised by Mr. Woodson that he had found a trail of boot prints. General Draper followed the trail of bootprints from the Crawford home to the Woodson's house and on back to near where Companies F, and G of the 38th USCT were encamped. The prisoner questioned the validity of the bootprint testimony but General Draper stated that the prisoners boot had a readily identifiable square toe, peculiar curvature on the outside edge of the sole and a broken or missing heel-iron.

Articles stolen were recovered from some of the four involved in the crime and other witnesses related what the four criminals had said they commited the crime. Sergeant Jackson was heavily implicated in the entire affair and was identified by Mrs. Crawford.

The accused offered no witnesses in his defense but did present a statement in his defense.

Statement"I did not go in the house at all. I staid in the rear of the house. When the shot was fired I was in the rear of the house behind the palings of the garden. There I staid till they come out of the house; and we all come away together then.

They had I believe two bundles. The Corporal had something hanging across his arm, looked like a coat, could not tell what color it was it was dark. I never saw no more of that."

The Court then deliberated, found the accused guilty and sentenced him to be hung by the neck until he is dead.

In a review of the Jackson Case, the Acting Judge Advocate General on May 15, 1865 wrote to the President of the United States the conclusion that "No circumstances of mitigation appear in the case."

The execution took place on July 30, 1865 at Brownsville, Texas. His Regiment having been transferred there for duty.

(Also see Case #247, Dandridge Brooks, Company G, 38th Infantry USCT.)

REFERENCES:
Military Personnel Records, RG-#94
Court Martial Proceedings, RG-#153 MM 1984

Case #249
Pvt. William Kease
NV: 1st Sgt
Co. I, 116th Inf Regt, USCT
Executed for Mutiny
August 11, 1865

DESCRIPTION:
23 years of age, 5 feet 5 inches tall, black eyes, black hair, black complexion, born in Woodford County, Kentucky, occupation farmer, illiterate. (A memorandum in is Personnel file lists the name Timothy Hughes, and the notation, "Probably name of owner.")

Kease enlisted on July 6, 1864 at Camp Nelson, Kentucky and was mustered into service on July 13th at Camp Nelson, Kentucky. Assigned to Company I, 116th Infantry Regiment, USCT, Kease was appointed a Sergeant within a week of his entrance into service and promoted to 1st Sergeant of his Company on April 26, 1865. He was executed for participating in a mutiny while in service in Texas and the record coincides with that of Sergeant Moore, Case #250.

A General Court Martial was convened at Camp Lincoln, Virginia and on May 18, 1865 tried 1st Sergeant William Kease, Company I, 116th Infantry USCT on the following charges: mutiny, disobedience of orders, violation of the 7th and 8th Articles of War. The accused asked for no counsel.

Testimony offered showed that on May 11, 1865 one Private George Seignoir, Company I, 116th Infantry USCT was confined in the guardhouse, and apparently "tied up", (hung by his thumbs or bucked and gagged, it is never quite clear) under confinement by order of Captain Warren, commanding I Company, 116th Infantry USCT. Kease marched Company I, in formation, under arms with bayonets affixed to their rifles to Captain Warren's tent where he halted them, in formation. Kease, saluted and respectfully demanded the release ("cut down") of Seignoir. Captain Warren's reply to the demand was to order Kease to march the company back to their quarters, which Kease refused to do, despite being so ordered several times. Kease told Captain Warren that the Company refused to continue to drill under his command. Finally, Kease ordered the assembled company to right face, file right, march. They marched a few yards and halted. At this point, a Captain Kirker and Lieutenant Gould arrived. Captain Kirker spoke to Kease and Lieutenant Gould seized a Corporal John Johnson and Sergeant Doctor Moore, the file leaders, and ordered them to march to the Company street. They did so and the company followed. Captain Warren followed and ordered Kease to have the company stack arms, which he did. Captain Warren then had Sergeant Kease arrested and confined to the guardhouse. Following the disturbance in Company I, a general riot and mutiny broke out in the Regiment and apparently Kease was the instigator of it. It became so serious that other nearby regiments were brought in to suppress the riots and restore order. Captain Kirker testified that he spoke privately with Kease trying to point out the serious position he placed himself in by his actions and further that the penalty for such could be death. Kease only replied that Captain Warren treated the men so harshly that they did not wish to serve under his command any longer. Kease, apparently, at no time used his position and influence as 1st Sergeant to suppress the disturbances.

Kease offered no testimony or statement in his behalf.

The Court deliberated, found Kease guilty and sentenced him to be shot to death with musketry. Kease was one of a very few high ranking non-commissioned officers executed.

The execution took place near Camp Lincoln (which was near City Point, Virginia) on July 21, 1865.

REFERENCES:
Military Personnel Records, RG-#94
Court Martial Proceedings, RG-#153   MM 2394

Case #250
Pvt/Cpl/Sgt Doctor Moore
NV: More
Co. I, 116th Inf Regt, USCT
Executed for Mutiny
August 11, 1865

DESCRIPTION:

29 years of age, 5 feet 10 inches tall, black eyes, black hair, black complexion, born in Owen County, Kentucky, occupation engineer, literacy undetermined. (The name of Wilus Roberts appears on his Personnel Record with the notation, "probably name of owner").

Moore enlisted on July 12, 1864 at Camp Nelson, Kentucky and was mustered into service on July 13, 1864 at Camp Nelson, Kentucky. He was assigned to Company I, 116th Infantry Regiment, USCT and appointed corporal within days of his muster in, and was promoted to Sergeant on November 20, 1864.

A General Court Martial was convened at Camp Lincoln, Virginia and on May 19, 1865 tried Sergeant Doctor Moore, Company I, 116th Infantry USCT on charges of Mutiny, disobedience of Orders, violation of the 7th Article of War, violation of the 8th Article of War.

Testimony of witnesses disclosed that on May 11, 1865 at the Camp of the 116th USCT at Camp Lincoln, near City Point, Virginia a mutiny occurred involving Company I, the company of the accused.

Private George Seignoir, a member of Company I, 116th USCT, was confined in the Guard House, apparently strung up by his thumbs as punishment for an undisclosed offense. The enlisted men of Company I were disturbed about his confinement and punishment. About 6 PM a portion of the Company assembled on the Company street with arms and equipment. 1st Sergeant Kease addressed the enlisted men of Company I, "All that are going to the Captain come on and I will go with you." "Sergeant Moore went with the Company." Under command of the Company 1st Sergeant William Kease, they formed up and marched to the Company Commander's quarters where they halted. Captain Warren came out of his quarters and Sergeant Kease said, "Captain the company refuses to drill under you until you cut George Seignoir down." Captain Warren replied, "March the company back to their quarters." Sergeant Kease did not obey nor did Sergeant Moore who was with the group and within hearing of the command. At no time did Sergeant Moore attempt to persuade or order the company to return to their quarters. Nor did he attempt to suppress the grumbling and complaining occurring constantly in the formed ranks. Sergeant Moore's conduct, after finally returning to the Company street was described as unbecoming a non-commissioned officer. Sergeant Moore was ordered under arrest by Lieutenant Simon Gould, 116th USCT. He refused to be taken to the Guard House. He finally was forcibly incarcerated.

The accused had no witnesses or defense statement to present before the Court.

Accordingly, the Court deliberated, found the accused guilty and sentenced him to be shot to death with musketry.

The sentence was to be carried out near City Point, Virginia on July 21, 1865. The regiment, however was transferred for duty to Ringgold Barracks, on the Rio Grande River somewhat west of present day Brownsville, Texas prior to the date of the scheduled execution.

The Ringgold Barracks had been abandoned in 1861 and were reactivated and reoccupied in June 1865. Part of the garrison consisted of the 116th Regiment USCI. The condemned prisoners accompanied the Regiment to Texas and new orders for their execution were drawn up. The new date set for execution was August 11, 1865 at the Ringgold Barracks, Texas.

Also see case #249, 1st Sergeant William Kease, Company I, 116th USCT.

REFERENCES:

Military Personnel Records, RG-#94
Court Martial Proceedings, RG-#153 MM 2394

Case #251
Pvt. Aaron Collins
Co. H, 6th Cavalry Regiment USCT
Executed for Murder
August 18, 1865

DESCRIPTION:

19 years of age, 5 feet 6½ inches tall, dark eyes, brown hair, yellow complexion, born in Kentucky, occupation farm hand, illiterate, served as a substitute.

Collins reported and was mustered into service on February 18, 1865 at Louisville, Kentucky. He was assigned to Company H, 6th Cavalry Regiment USCT. On or about the 19th of April, 1865, Collins shot and killed a Matthew Currant, with no apparent justification, at or near Paris, Bourbon County, Kentucky. Collins was arrested, confined in jail at Lexington, Kentucky.

A General Court Martial was convened at Lexington, Kentucky on July 14, 1865 for the trial of Private Aaron Collins, Company H, 6th Cavalry, USCT.

Testimony provided at the trial revealed that on April 19, 1865, Collins, accompanied by a Private Joshua King also of Company H, 6th Cavalry USCT left their camp, with the verbal permission of the Sergeant in charge of the Company (the Acting Company Commander, a Lieutenant being absent). Food rations for their unit had been short and the accused, and other members of his Company had been in the habit of leaving camp to beg for food from nearby citizens. Both Collins and King were armed with rifles as a protection against guerrillas who still roamed the uninhabited areas.

Their wandering took them down a road upon which they saw a large two story brick residence, set well back from the property frontage on the road. They conferred briefly, then decided to solicit the occupants of the house for food. They walked up the long road leading to the home and when about 75 to 100 yards from the building were challenged by an older man seated in a grape vine chair near the home but they continued up the driveway until they reached a fence which surrounded the house. They halted near a stile (a set of steps arranged on each side of a fence or wall to permit crossing) and the older man, later identified as Mathew Currant owner of the property, aged 65 years, and partially paralyzed (his right arm being virtually useless) told them that was far enough. Currant approached the fence to one side of the stile and Collins, with King behind him, also moved close to the fence and toward Currant. Currant asked them what they were doing on his property and what did they want. Currant was carrying a walking stick, which he routinely carried to assist himself in overcoming his semi-paralyzed condition. Suddenly, Currant approached the fence and wielding his stick in his left hand struck at Collins while shouting "You damned son's of bitches." Collins leapt backward, avoiding the blow, and brought his gun up, pointing it at Currant. Currant, dropped the stick, put his left hand in his jacket pocket and drew out an Allens Company "pepper box revolver" (a hand gun having five or six barrels arranged like the revolving chamber of the early multi-shot hand guns) and raised it pointing it straight up in the air. Currant then slowly brought the revolver forward and downward pointing the revolver toward Collins. Collins, believing he was to be shot, fired his rifle, the bullet striking Currant near the center of his breast. He died in a few minutes, in the presence of his son, Edward, who was quickly joined by other members of the family and entourage. Collins and King ran away immediately after Collins fired the shot that killed Currant, and returned to their Camp.

The body of Mathew Currant was not moved from the place where he fell dead until after a coroner's jury arrived and examined the body, the pocket contents of the clothing and the ground area where the shooting occurred.

The coroner summoned a physician, Dr. A. W. Davidson of Bourbon County, Kentucky, to examine the body of the deceased. The fatal wound was described as passing through the body, having entered the chest at the junction of the first rib and sternum (breast bone) continuing obliquely toward the right shoulder, severed the subclavian artery and exited through the scapula (shoulder blade), which it fractured. The coroner and members of the coroner's jury were present as Dr. Davidson examined the body. Then the clothing of the murdered man was searched and the following items were removed therefrom: One pocket knife, one handkerchief, a comb, some keys and a small piece of orange peel. All members of the coroner's jury were questioned, as well as several family members and household servants, as to the finding of any firearm such as described by Collins and King. All swore no firearm of any such description was found.

Testimony from Lieutenant Powell, Commander of Company H, 6th Cavalry USCT revealed that Currant's son, Edward, the first to reach the body after he was shot, discovered the pepper box and apparently concealed and removed it from the scene. It was also established, despite denials, that the deceased did own a pepper box revolver.

The accused made a statement describing the events and admitting he fired the fatal bullet.

Testimony being concluded, the Court deliberated, found the accused guilty and sentenced him to death by hanging. The sentence was carried out on August 18, 1865 at Lexington, Kentucky.

REFERENCES:

Military Personnel Records, RG-#94
Court Martial Proceedings, RG-#153 MM 2571

Case #253
Private Hiram Oliver
Co. A, 43rd Ohio Inf. Regt.
and in unknown PA Regt.
Executed for Murder
September 6, 1865

Military records for Hiram Oliver are virtually non existent. A Muster Roll of Company A, 43rd Ohio Volunteer Infantry Regiment was introduced at his trial for Murder. It showed that Oliver, aged 18 years, enlisted in Company A on October 21, 1861 at Steubenville, Ohio for a three year period. The same form discloses that John W. Hartup, his co-defendant in the murder trial, enlisted at 18 years of age in Company A, 43rd Ohio Volunteer Infantry Regiment on October 24, 1861 for a three year period. Oliver deserted at Clear Creek, Mississippi on or about June 23, 1862. he was accompanied by John W. Hartup and James Hartup (John's brother, aged 21 years also a Private in Company A, 43rd Ohio Volunteer Infantry Regiment).

Oliver, during his trial, claimed that he was injured or sick and received a medical discharge from the Army in July, 1862. The discharge was listed as an item among the exhibits filed during the trial, but does not appear to be included in the collection. Oliver seemingly was successful in his claim to have a discharge from service in the 43rd Ohio as his military unit designation was changed in the verdict to indicate enlistment in an Unidentified Pennsylvania Regiment. Oliver had admitted he had been a "bounty jumper" and that he had enlisted in an unidentified Pennsylvania Regiment.

The case of Hiram oliver and John Wesley Hartup is a most unusual one, perhaps a "Bench Mark Case". The trial was described by Captain J. D. Taylor, 88th Ohio Volunteer Infantry Regiment, the trial Judge Advocate, as the longest military trial of the War Period. It consumed 85 days, accumulating a ten inch tall pile of some 5000 pages of testimony, summoned some 200 witnesses, over 100 of them for the prosecution and presented nearly 100 exhibits to the Court as evidence. The accused prisoners had, at various times, as many as four civilian counsel's for their defense.

The case was long, drawn out, and had many conflicting under currents which add to the complexity of it's analysis.

One the more interesting features of this trial was the introduction of a number of expert witnesses, prototypes of present day experts. These included a Gun Smith who testified to the unique Ball Ammunition employed in Oliver's pistol with which J. B. Cook was shot to death. Handwriting "experts" were introduced to examine the handwriting of a diary and to determine whether the diary was written on a daily basis or whether the entire book was filled with entries written at a single sitting. Witnesses testified to the examination, measurements and peculiarities of the boot impressions left in the mud by the fleeing assassins. The boot prints revealed two separate sets of boots were involved. One set of prints displayed impressions of metal toe and heel plates of unusual design. The other set of boot prints displayed the application of a half sole to one boot. The boots taken from the prisoners at the time of their arrest appeared to have made the boot prints in the mud.

The most revealing single change or improvement observed was in the legal procedure employed at the trial. The accused were represented by as many as four counsels at a single time who did the actual challenging, objecting, pleading and questioning of witnesses which was a far cry from the prevailing Civil War Court procedure where the counsel for the accused could do no more than advise the accused as to what to say or ask or answer. The counsel remained mute in the Courtroom. But in this trial the counsels were unfettered and battled the Prosecution and harassed the witnesses and the Court in a flamboyant manner approaching present day Court Room trial tactics.

It would be impossible, within the scope of this work, to describe all of the hundred little separate scenarios presented and explored in this lengthy and ponderous case.

Therefore, the case will be described only in it's bare essential features, a modified resume of the critical points involved.

Oliver and Hartup were brother's-in-law as Oliver had married Hartup's sister with whom he had two small children living in Steubenville, Ohio.

In June of 1864, Oliver was hiding from authorities and met a young woman named Willama Huffard who resided with her mother and stepfather, William Hall in Fairview, Ohio. Oliver lived with the Hall's for several weeks and then proposed marriage to Willama, to which she consented. On June 16, 1864 at Cambridge, Ohio, Oliver and Huffard were married by a bogus Clergyman in what amounted to a mock ceremony.

Huffard believed the marriage genuine until she realized that there was not a marriage certificate or license ever issued. Naive and embarrassed, she continued to "act" as a wife to Oliver for several months.

In June of 1864 Deputy Provost Marshall, John B. Cook, encountered Oliver near Gibson's Station, Ohio. Remembering lists of wanted deserters and recognizing Oliver as being so listed, he attempted to arrest him. Oliver, younger and fleeter of foot, managed to escape amid a hail of bullets fired at him by Cook. Oliver, both incensed and unnerved by his brush with death vowed repeatedly, to all who would listen, that he would kill Cook at his first opportunity.

Oliver and Hartup, believing that their freedom was endangered by remaining in the area, traveled to Southern Illinois and took up residence in the vicinity of Casey and Ashmore, Illinois. Huffard and Oliver's real wife, Hartup, Oliver and his two small children made the journey. While money was very scarce, Oliver and Hartup, apparently, made a living by horse stealing, robbery and counterfeiting money. Oliver located an Ohio Doctor, then practicing in the Illinois area, and sought treatment for his gonorrhea and for one of his sick children. The child died.

Neither Oliver or Hartup were well received in the Illinois community. The house they lived in was destroyed by arson and by the end of 1864 or early 1865 they returned to the eastern Ohio area.

Both Oliver and Hartup were involved in a variety of criminal activities in Ohio which included, but were not limited to wool stealing, robbery and horse stealing. Oliver continued to tell all who would listen that he intended to kill Cook as soon as the opportunity presented itself.

Apparently this obsession with the assassination of Cook came to the point where Oliver no longer awaited a chance opportunity to murder him but made plans to carry out the project.

Accordingly, on Friday, March 3, 1865 Oliver and Hartup came to Cambridge, Ohio, Cook's home town, and stopped various Cambridge citizens asking directions to Cook's residence. Arriving at Cook's home, Oliver knocked on the door which was opened by Amarilla Cook (John B. Cook's wife). Oliver was on the doorstep, she just inside the house, as they conversed. Oliver asked for Mr. Cook and was told he was out of town and in turn was asked what he wanted to see him about. He told a tale of wanting to report a man as a deserter. Mrs. Cook said she would tell Mr. Cook when he returned on Sunday and Oliver said he would return.

At this point note that Oliver and Hartup were observed, as strangers in a small town, asking about Mr. Cook. Further that Mrs. Cook conversed with Oliver at close range. Thus a number of people were already able to identify Oliver, as well as Hartup and place them in Cambridge.

On Sunday, March 5, 1865, Oliver and Hartup returned to Cambridge arriving sometime between 6 and 8 P.M. and went to the Union Hotel where they lingered outside the establishment. Finally, they gave a negro a counterfeit dollar bill and a blue ridged glass flask, with a corn cob as a cork, and asked him to have the flask filled with liquor at the bar. The bar man readily identified the bill as counterfeit and had one of the hotel owner's sons take both the fake bill and filled flask out to Oliver and Hartup. Hartup said he would get some money and took the bill which he managed to have converted into $0.60 legal currency. The owner's son accepted the money and Oliver and Hartup went down the street, under observation, to Cook's house. Oliver was seen to enter the gate and Hartup entered an Alley which turned and extended behind the Cook home.

Oliver went to the door, knocked and the door was again opened by Mrs. Cook who remembered him from his Friday visit.

He was invited in, after being told Mr. Cook was out in the backyard, and ushered into one of the front rooms to wait for the arrival of Mr. Cook. Mrs. Cook went to the rear door and called to her husband who replied he would be in shortly. Mrs. Cook, coming back into the house found Oliver standing in the hall and after making an excuse about tending to his non-existent horse, he left the house.

Just as Oliver reached the sidewalk, he was met by William Carter, an employee of the Park's Boarding House which was next door to Cook's home. Carter followed a few steps behind Oliver to the alley which led from the street and then turned extending behind Cook's and other houses of the block.

William Carter, the witness referred to, stated that as Oliver turned into the alley he slipped in mud and cursed "God damn the Mud". He watched Oliver walk up the alley and disappear as he turned into the branch of the alley behind Cook's home. Oliver was heard to ask Cook "Are you Cook?" The reply was "yes". Moments later he heard a shot and someone saying "What did you do that for?"

Carter and several neighbors, hearing Mrs. Cook screaming, ran to the Cook yard and jumped the fence, then they ran to where Cook lay in the yard and carried him into the house where he died 3-4 minutes after being shot.

An examination of Cook's body (not an autopsy) was made for the Coroner's Jury by Dr. J. P. Tingle an M. D. having 27 years of practice. Cook was described as 49-50 years of age, 5 feet 10 inches tall, 175/180 pounds and in good health. The fatal gun shot wound entered the chest on the left side between the 5th and 6th ribs, passed through the heart and lodged under the skin below the right scapula (shoulder blade). Dr. Tingle received permission to surgically remove the revolver ball which he presented to the Court as evidence. The ball, later examined by a gunsmith, was of unique construction and matched similar balls extracted from Oliver's loaded revolver.

Several witnesses, alarmed by the pistol shot ran out of their homes, some moving toward the area of the pistol shot origin.

Oliver and Hartup were observed together and identified by many witnesses, as they ran or walked hurriedly away from the area of the pistol shot. In answer to one witness inquiring about the screaming, they replied, "Some woman making a fuss." The pair finally left the town streets, and were observed climbing a fence, into a muddy field and began their escape from the area on foot.

The following day, a search of the field previously mentioned disclosed a blue glass ridged flask, with a corn cob as a cork, frozen to the muddy ground. Warm water was poured over it, to free it from the frozen soil. It was positively identified as the flask belonging to Oliver and Hartup, filled on the 5th of March, the night of the murder.

An examination of footprints, in the vicinity of the flask, revealed two distinct separate sets of footprints, clearly recognizable in the muddy partly thawing soil. One set of boot prints were smaller than the other. One set of boot prints showed that one boot had been half soled, the other set of boot prints had unique, custom made toe and heel caps.

A posse was formed and the boot prints were followed with great difficulty for several days until they lost the tracks near Antrim, Ohio. On the morning of Thursday May 9, 1865 at Squire Carpenter's farm, near Antrim, Ohio, the posse spread out to relocate the fugitives tracks, but were unsuccessful. When the members returned to Carpenter's farm someone had a brilliant idea. The tracks ended at or near Carpenter's farm and were not found to continue beyond the farm area, yet the posse had not searched any of the farm buildings. The first building the posse approached was the main barn, which was locked or barred. The posse pounded on the doors calling for the fugitives to come out and surrender, without response. They then managed to pry open the barn doors and repeated their demands for surrender. Entering the barn, which was devoid of anything but an eight foot straw stack, they began cautiously searching and calling for the two men to surrender or they would fire into the straw stack. Finally Oliver and Hartup emerged from the straw stack and surrendered.

Oliver and Hartup were taken by the posse to Cambridge and surrendered to the custody of the Sheriff of Guernsey County, Ohio who lodged them in the County jail there.

On an unrecorded day in March, 1865 they appeared before the Grand Jury of Guernsey County, Ohio and were remanded to the Court of Common Pleas of Guernsey County where they were indicted and arraigned on a charge of murdering John B. Cook and held for trial at the next scheduled session of Court on June 12, 1865.

Subsequently Major General Hooker, commander of the Military District, ordered the military to assume custody of the Prisoners (which actually occurred on May 31, 1865) and appointed a Military Commission to conduct their trial convening at Cambridge, Ohio on May 22, 1865.

On May 25, 1865 the Commission met but several officers assigned were recalled to their regiments. The commission adjourned while substitutes were sought for.

The Commission met and adjourned several times for the same reasons as above stated until May 31, 1865 when the actual trial began. Neither Oliver nor Hartup objected to the members of the Commission and they then applied for admission of the following to act as counsels for the accused, Hiram Skinner, John W. Bushfield, Robert Savage, and Francis Creighton. Skinner would voluntarily withdraw as counsel during the trial and on August 5, 1865, the accused petitioned the commission to readmit him as counsel which was granted.

The Judge Advocate objected to the admission of Robert Savage as counsel for the accused on the grounds that he had stated that "he wished this Commission and all other Military Courts sunk so low in Hell that they would never be resurrected." Mr. Savage denied making the statement but admitted he had said that "he wished all the military spirit in the United States was sunk so deep in Hell that it would never be resurrected, for then there would have been no war, no Court Martials nor Commissions nor anything of that kind, but all would have been peace."

The commission then deliberated and reopened and announced that while they admitted three counsels without further question, Robert Savage, by disapproving the action of the government in the past four years, would be admitted as counsel for the accused only if he took the oath required of attorney's practicing in Federal Courts. Mr. Savage agreed and the oath was administered.

The accused then appealed for an adjournment to seek an explanation of the transfer of jurisdiction of their case from the Court of Common Pleas of Guernsey County to the Military and a delay in the trial by the Commission.

The Judge Advocate replied citing various objections. The Commission deliberated and granted the adjournment as requested by the accused.

The Commission resumed trial on June 2, 1865 and the Counsel for the accused pleaded lack of jurisdiction of the Military Commission to try Oliver and Hartup on the grounds that they were not in the Military service on March 5, 1865 and requested their return to the jurisdiction of the Civil Court.

The Judge Advocate replied that he had ample proof of the facts to prove Military jurisdiction.

The Court deliberated and overruled the plea of the accused.

The counsel for the accused then applied for separate trials for each defendant. The Judge Advocate objected on the grounds of duplication of the trials and thus lengthening the trial and the costs unconscionably, without any benefit to the accused.

The Court deliberated and denied the plea of severance.

At this point, the accused having pleaded not guilty to charges of Murder, Murder of a Deputy Provost Marshall, Conspiring to Murder a Deputy Provost Marshall and Robbery, the trial began.

It would be difficult indeed to list the individual testimony of each of the hundreds of witnesses called in this lengthy trial. We therefore will merely broadly outline the principal thrust of the defense and the prosecution.

The prosecution had large numbers of witnesses who saw Oliver and Hartup in Cambridge on either March 3rd or March 5th, 1865 or on both dates. Some dozen witnesses saw them just prior to or afterward in the immediate vicinity of the scene of the crime. Other witnesses testified to murder threats against Cook repeatedly made by Oliver. The material evidence such as boot prints and revolver ball were adequately presented.

The defense employed the time honored technique of not being anywhere near Cambridge, Ohio on the 3rd or 5th of March, 1865 and second, all witnesses who identified the accused were mistaken. A woman witness for the defense offered a diary she said she maintained *daily* which purported to list the item of seeing Oliver and Hartup in Florence, Pennsylvania about 70-80 miles from Cambridge, Ohio during the period March 3-5, 1865. Her testimony was unable to verify the entries in the diary and it was believed by several handwriting "experts" that the diary was not written up each day but was produced entirely at one single writing session.

The charge of robbery placed against Oliver and Hartup was based upon the invasion of the Cambridge home of Thomas Burson on Saturday, March 4th at night by two men.

The only light in the house was provided by the fireplaces and bright moonlight streaming in through window panes.

Burson and his wife were in bed when the invaders, armed with revolvers, appeared in the bedroom. They demanded money which was grudgingly surrendered after repeated threats of bodily harm including an attempt to hang Mr. Burson in his bedroom. A rope was thrown over a staple or hook in the bedroom ceiling in preparation for suspending him until he be dead. Burson eventually stated he surrendered about $1,600.00 to the robbers, who withdrew warning the Burson's not to pursue them or raise an alarm, on pain of death. Neither of the Burson's clearly saw the faces of the two robbers but the voice of Oliver was most distinctive and Hartup's voice was described as shrill or high pitched. Further, Thomas Burson was familiar with the accused prisoners and was certain that they were the men who robbed him. Little money was found on the persons of the two prisoners at the time they were arrested.

The testimony tended to cast some light on what was a life of crime and duplicity for Oliver and Hartup. Both men used assumed names and frequently hid out away from their homes. At one point they both donned women's clothing as a disguise while at other times they allowed the hair of both face and head to grow. On another occasion they even shaved their heads which were described as white and shiney. Both men were known to carry revolvers. After their capture Hartup was most anxious and voluble in his attempts to persuade members of the posse that while he was present with Oliver at the murder, he did not shoot Cook. He also stated he was Oliver's accomplice in the perpetration of many crimes.

A witness stated that Hartup told him he had shot several men but had not lingered to note whether they died or not.

The summation of the Counsel for the accused was long and as well presented as the circumstances permitted. The Judge Advocate's summation of the charges of the prosecution was even longer, more eloquent and rational. He drew a parallel between the assassination of President Lincoln and Mr. Cook, pointing out they both were in government service and both sets of murderers were tried by Military Commissions. Another major point made by the Judge Advocate was the seeming support for the alleged murders by local subversive organizations such as the Order of the Golden Circle and various Copperhead groups. A question asked by him, but left unanswered was important. Neither Oliver or Hartup possessed any large sums of money or assets which could be converted to cash. How then were they able to defray the large expenses involved in an extraordinarily long trial including costs of witnesses and the fees of four top lawyers? The intimation was that the expenses were born by contributions of members of the subversive organizations. The question of the disposition of the alleged proceeds of the robbery was not addressed.

The trial was ended and the Commission deliberated. The Commission opened the

Court and announced that the defendants, Oliver and Hartup were Guilty of Murder and were sentenced to be hung by the neck until dead.

The condemned men were transported to Camp Chase, outside of Columbus, Ohio. Some last minute misunderstandings arose as to the exact site for the execution. Camp Chase being deemed by some as unsuitable to prevent a rescue attempt. Negotiations were completed with Ohio State officials to have the execution site moved to the Ohio State Penitentiary near Columbus, Ohio. A visit to Camp Chase revealed that the premises were virtually vacant, the few inhabitants being soldiers processing for final pay and discharge. The Camp Prison was found unoccupied and the condemned Prisoners were transferred there where they were kept under surveillance around the clock with a commissioned Officer constantly in the presence of each prisoner.

The execution took place on September 6, 1865 in the Prison Yard.

The bodies were delivered to Oliver's wife and Hartup's relatives and friends and were taken home for burial.

REFERENCES:

National Archives, Personnel Records, RG-#94
National Archives, Court Martial Proceedings, RG-#153 MM 2761
Ohio Historical Society, Cincinnati, Ohio
Official Roster of the Soldiers of the State of Ohio in the War of the Rebellion, Vol IV, 37th-53rd Regts. Inf., Published by General Assembly, Akron, Ohio, 1887
"The Army lawyer, A History of the Judge Advocates General Corps, 1775 - 1975" US Government Printing Officer, 1975.

Case #254
Pvt. Juan Madrid
NV: Juan de Dios Madrid
Co. C, 1st New Mexico Vol Cav Regt
Executed for Murder
September 8, 1865

DESCRIPTION:

25 (32) years of age, 5 feet 5 inches tall, dark eyes, dark hair, dark complexion, born in Taos, New Mexico, occupation laborer, illiterate.

Madrid has a tenuous and confusing military history. He seems to have enlisted and been mustered into service at Fort Union, New Mexico on July 2, 1861 and assigned to Company B, 1st (old) Regiment New Mexico Infantry. On May 31, 1862, he was transferred to Company F, 1st New Mexico Volunteers. Records, however, show Madrid to have been a member of Company C, 1st Regiment New Mexico Volunteers which regiment was formed of men transferred from the 1, 2, 4 and 5 Regiments New Mexico Infantry. The designation was later changed to Company C, 1st Regiment New Mexico Cavalry. Madrid served at various posts such as Fort Union, Fort Craig, Fort Lyon, Fort Fauntleroy, Fort Canby and was sick in a hospital at sometime during the period January/February 1863.

Madrid was discharged and re-enlisted as a Veteran Volunteer on March 1st, 1864. He was arrested and confined at Fort Union, New Mexico on July 27, 1865 for the murder of Corporal Cruz Torres, same Company and Regiment.

A General Court Martial was convened at Fort Union, New Mexico and on August 24, 1865 tried Private Juan Madrid, Company I, 1st New Mexico Cavalry Regiment on a charge of Murder.

Since some of the witnesses testified in Spanish the Court appointed Captain Louis Felsenthal as it's official interpreter sworn under oath.

Witnesses testified that on the night of July 13, 1865 the accused murdered Corporal Cruz Torres within a hundred yards of the home of a toll gate keeper named Wooltens.

Wooltens identified the accused, Bacu and Gomes as the three men he saw the night of the murder, from the ranks of the assembled company.

The body of Torres was found with the cranium crushed by blows from a stone. The stone, covered with blood and brains was found near the body.

On the late afternoon of July 13, 1865, the accused, Baca and Gomes left their company station and rode to the toll gate where they purchased Whiskey and consumed it at one of the toll gate houses. Also present were one American and Corporal Torres. As the three left the Bar Room, Madrid asked the other two if they had any ill feeling toward Torres. They replied in the negative and the accused stated they should kill Torres. The two companions of the accused refused to even assist. When Torres came out of the bar, the accused put his arm around Torres' shoulder and they walked toward the creek where the accused killed Torres.

Neither Baca nor Gomes ever seemed to know or divulge the motive for Madrid's murder of Torres.

The three then returned to their camp and went to their separate tents.

There being no further testimony to be offered by either the prosecution or defense. A brief statement on his behalf was offered by the accused. It was written in Spanish and translated by the sworn trial interpreter.

Statement of the Prisoner

"I have nothing else to say in my defense but that these men have given false testimony against me in order to free themselves and having no knowledge of Court business, I leave my case to the consideration of the Court as it now stands."

X (his mark) Juan de Dios Madrid

The Court deliberated, found Madrid guilty and sentenced him to be hung by the neck until he be dead.

The execution took place at Fort union, New Mexico on September 8, 1865.

REFERENCES:

Military Personnel Records, RG-#94
Court Martial Proceedings, RG-#153 MM 2928

Case #255

Pvt. (Cpl.) John Shepard
Co. I, 38th Infantry Regiment, USCT
Executed for Rape/Plundering/Pillaging
October 13, 1865

DESCRIPTION:

20 years of age, 5 feet 6 inches tall, black hair, brown eyes, copper complexion, born in Virginia, occupation laborer, illiterate, a substitute.

Shepard was drafted and mustered into service January 31, 1865 at Washington D.C. He was appointed Corporal on March 15, 1865 and reduced to the ranks on August 8, 1865. By early June 1865 Shepard was under arrest, in close confinement for rape, plundering and pillaging. Found guilty by General Court Martial trial, Shepard was sentenced to death by hanging and placed in the Military Prison at Camp Hamilton, Virginia. The execution was scheduled to take place at Fort Monroe, Virginia. While there are two dates of his execution recorded, September 30 and October 13, 1865, the preponderance of evidence indicates October 13th, 1865 as the correct date. He accompanied his Regiment to Brownsville, Texas in irons where they were reassigned for duty.

A General Court Martial was convened at the headquarters of the 1st Division, 25th Army Corps in the field in Virginia and on April 22, 1865 tried Corporal John Sheppard, Company A, 38th Infantry Regiment USCT, on charges of rape, assault with intent to kill and plundering and pillaging.

Testimony was offered to the Court substantiating the charges that on or about the night of April 11, 1865 the accused raped a Mrs. Fanny Crawford in her home near Richmond, Virginia as well as her young niece, Eliza Woodson, aged thirteen. Several witnesses from the accused's own company testified to his bragging that he "fucked the old one and the young one too."

Sheppard was said, by those fellow members of the troop at the Crawford House, to have fired a shot at Mrs. Crawford as she leaned out of an open second story window and called for help.

Many of the articles stolen from the Crawford home were found in the possession of the accused.

For a more detailed description of the events of the night of April 11, 1865 at the Crawford home near Richmond, Virginia, see case #247 and #248, D. Brooks and William Jackson.

Sheppard offered no defense witnesses but made a short statement which he presented to the court.

"I was not at the house on that night."

The Court deliberated, found the prisoner guilty, and sentenced him to be hung by the neck until he be dead.

The execution took place on October 13, 1865 at Brownsville, Texas where the Regiment had been transferred for duty.

REFERENCES:
Military Personnel Records, RG-#94
Court Martial Proceedings, RG-#153 MM 2006

Case #256
Pvt. James Gripen
Co. F, 104th Inf Regt, USCT
Executed for Rape
November 20, 1865

DESCRIPTION:

20 years of age, 5 feet 5 inches tall, eyes light, light complexion, born in Charleston, South Carolina, occupation butler, illiterate.

Gripen was enlisted at Charleston, South Carolina on April 18, 1865 and mustered into service at Beaufort, South Carolina on June 25, 1865. An early duty assignment was as a Headquarters Guard at Pocotaligo, South Carolina. Gripen committed a rape in August 1865, was apprehended and court martialed, found guilty and sentenced to be hung.

A General Court Martial was convened at Hilton Head Island, South Carolina and on November 8, 1865 tried Private James Gripen, Company L, 104th Infantry USCT on the following charges: Conduct to the Prejudice of Good Order and Military Discipline, Rape, and Larceny.

Gripen obtained permission to have Major M. R. Delaney as his counsel.

Witnesses testified that on August 20, 1865, about 8 PM at or near McPhersonville, South Carolina, Gripen and a group of armed colored soldiers came to the home of a Mrs. Emily Mews, threatened the people present with violence or death, and tied up both men present and then Gripen pursued Emily Mews' young daughter Florence about the yard and into the house where he caught her and dragged her into a bedroom of the house and raped her. Two other soldiers then raped her and raped Mrs. Mary E. McTier as well. Gripen threatened to shoot all the whites present and set fire to the house if there was any resistance to their demands.

Gripen also stole a silver watch and various items of clothing from the Mews home.

Gripen offered no defense but his counsel made a brief statement:

On behalf of the Prisoner

"The prisoner was not concerned in the raping of these ladies. He was not in that part of the house at all during the night, he was in another part of the house getting flour and meat. He submits the case trusting to the favorable consideration of the court."

The Court then deliberated and found the accused guilty and sentenced him to be hung until he be dead.

Sentence carried out at Hilton Head, South Carolina, November 20, 1865 (also recorded as November 21, 1865). (Also see Private Benjamin Redding, Case #257.)

REFERENCES:

Military Personnel Records, RG-#94
Court Martial Proceedings, RG-#153 MM 3184

Case #257
Pvt. Ben Redding
NV: aka Benjamin Rudding
Co. D, 104th Inf Regt, USCT
Executed for Rape
November 20, 1865

DESCRIPTION:

20 years of age, 5 feet 9 inches tall, black eyes, black hair, dark complexion, born in St. John's, South Carolina, occupation farmer, illiterate.

Redding enlisted on April 18, 1865 at Beaufort, South Carolina and was mustered into service there on June 25, 1865. He was assigned to duty in Company D, 104th Infantry Regiment USCT. On August 26, 1865 he was arrested and confined in the Beaufort City Jail on charges of rape committed at Pocatiligo, South Carolina. (Also see Case #256, Private James Gripen, Company F, 104th USCT.)

A General Court Martial was convened at Hilton Head Island and on November 9, 1865 tried Private Benjamin Redding, Company D, 104th Infantry Regiment USCT on charges of Conduct to the Prejudice of Good Order and Military Discipline, assault and battery with intent to kill, rape and larceny.

The accused received permission to introduce Major Martin R. Delaney, 104th USCT as his counsel.

Testimony offered by witnesses stated that the crimes committed were in the town of McPhersonville, South Carolina on or about the period of the 17th to the 20th day of August, 1865. A Mrs. Emily Mew stated a party of colored soldiers attacked her house, about 1 AM on or about August 17, beginning by firing their rifles into her house, then entered and searched for her son whom they said they wanted to kill for reporting their attack on another woman's home to their superior officer. On the night of August 19th they returned to Mrs. Mew's home and again entered it. Two white men, Dr. Hazle and Mr. Morgan, who were present, were seized and tied up and placed under a colored soldier guard. The soldiers then rounded up all the females and forced them into one room of the house. The testimony recorded fails to describe when Miss Mews and McTier were raped, the charges and specifications seem to indicate it was on the night described. Mrs. Mew finally seized her young daughter and forced her way through the soldiers and out of the room into the hall where she was struck a severe blow on the head, which caused bleeding from her right ear (a usual indication of a skull fracture and rupture of the middle meningeal artery). Mrs. Mew and her daughter were ordered back into the room with the other women or she would have "her damned brains blown out." As she entered the dining room, on her way to the room ordered by her molesters, she noticed no one paying much attention to them and a window was open. She quickly had her daughter jump out the window, she followed and they successfully escaped.

They returned to the house later that night and found it completely ransacked, all clothing having been taken.

Dr. Hazle and Mr. Morgan managed to escape although they had been threatened to be killed by colored soldiers pointing loaded and bayoneted muskets at them.

A Mrs. Mary Heape testified that her house was attacked and burned on or about August 17, 1864 by colored soldiers. They entered her house between 10-11 PM and arrested a Mr. Youman and threatened to shoot him. They plundered the house offering severe threats and beat her young son severely. Mrs. Heape protested that she had "protection papers" issued by the Army Colonel. This enraged the looters who said the Colonel had nothing to do with them and if anyone set out to report this incident they would never reach their camp alive. Mrs. Heape's young daughter was raped twice during the attack on her home. Her house was burned a day or two after the attack. Throughout the testimony, Redding was cited as being present and the leader of the marauders and an active participant in most of the crimes.

The accused offered no witnesses in his behalf but did present a written statement prepared by his counsel to the Court.

"The Prisoner acknowledges that he was present at the house of Mrs. Mew: but denies that he had anything to do with the outrages. He knows that the things stated by Dr. Hazle were done, but he had nothing to do with them himself, Dr. Hazle is mistaken in the identity. The prisoner tried to prevent the outrages being committed. He was not the leader, but the leader was the Drum Major. The prisoner heard the screaming of the women, and ran to protect them, but was unable to do so. He solemnly and persistently protests his innocence."

The Judge Advocate filed a resume of the case with the Court.

"To the President and Gentlemen: Before submitting this case for your findings I would respectfully call your attention to the following matters to be considered. The prisoner is charged with having helped to attack and plunder the house of Mrs. Mew and of having belonged to the party that attacked and burned the house of Mrs. Heape, and of having ravished the person of Miss Eusebia Heape.

Does the evidence sustain the last charge and that immediately preceeding it? And would a conviction therefore be warranted by the testimony given? It is in evidence that the prisoner was present during the commission of each of the alleged crimes. It is also proven that by neither word nor deed did he attempt to prevent their perpetration. Mrs. Heape declares that during the foulest of them all, Viz: the rape of Miss Heape in her mother's presence, he was in the room quietly looking on.

It is an established principle that an accessory before or during any act, is as chargeable with the crime as the crime charged as the principal, in all respects. I do not deem it necessary, nor my province, at this stage of the proceedings to go over all the evidence, and show it's bearing toward the prisoner: but I merely desire to call the above quoted Maxim of Law to the attention of the Court, whether the weight of the evidence goes to prove the prisoner to be an accessory, before or during the infamous outrage laid to his charge, or to have aided and abetted others in it's commission, is a question entirely for your own judgements to decide. But I submit it to your understandings and judgements that if you believe such to be the case, the same justice and penalty should be meted out to the abetter or to the accessory, as to the Principal. If the prisoner was present during the perpetration of this outrage, aiding and abetting, he becomes *"ipso facto"* a principal. If he, knowing what was to be done, and being present when it was done, did not strive to prevent it or deter others from it's commission, as he being a United States Soldier should have done, he becomes *"ipso facto"*, an accessory. And if he is considered by you in either light, I hope I will not be considered as dictating to the Court when I press it upon their notice, that the prisoner should be held to account as a principal and treated accordingly.

While pressing this fact upon the attention of the Court, I would also, as the prisoner's life is at stake, call their attention to the necessity of carefully weighing the evidence as to the actual presence of the prisoner in the room during the ravishing of Miss Heape. The dim light from the fireplace, the confused struggle that must necessarily have taken place, and the natural terror of two helpless women among such a band of infuriated fiends, should all be very carefully considered in making a decision from the evidence as to the prisoners presence in the room.

Feeling assured that due and proper consideration will be extended by you to the case, both for the prosecution and the defense, I leave the case in your hands, without further action on my part."

Respectfully submitted,
Charles R. Pyne, Bvt. Capt.
1st Lt., Col'd. Infy.
Judge Advocate

The Court deliberated, found the prisoner guilty and sentenced him to be hung by the neck until dead.

The execution was carried out on November 20, 1865 at Hilton Head Island, South Carolina.

REFERENCES:
Military Personnel Records, RG-#94
Court Martial Proceedings, RG-#153 MM 3184

Case #258
Pvt. James Allen
Co. E, 3rd Inf Regt, USCT
Executed for Mutiny
December 1, 1865

DESCRIPTION:

23 years of age, 5 feet 11 inches tall, black eyes, black hair, black complexion, born at Knox, Indiana, occupation farmer, illiterate.

Allen enlisted and mustered into service at Philadelphia, Pennsylvania on July 7, 1863 and assigned to Company E, 3rd Infantry Regiment USCT. There is the standard notation of "Free on or before April 19, 1861" which qualified the individual for equal pay with white troops as well as retroactive payment of the difference between the original unequal pay rates prior to April 30, 1864. While the Regiment was in the Fernandina, Florida area, a mutiny took place in late 1865.

Private James Allen, Company E, 3rd USCT, charged with mutiny, Sunday, October 29, 1865.

A disturbance at the 3rd USCT camp near Fernandina, Florida was described as a riot. Allen is stated to have appeared on the Company Street with a musket in his hand, shouting, "Let me shoot the son of a bitch," referring to Lieutenant Colonel Brower who had been shot. The musket was wrested from him and discharged in the air by another member of the Regiment, Private Joseph Preston, of Company D. Allen then cursed Preston as "a son of a bitch" and Preston struck him.

One witness said several shots were fired and several other members of the Regiment, in addition to Lieutenant Colonel Brower, were wounded.

Lieutenant Colonel Brower was stated to have fired three shots at members of the Regiment (whether before or after he was shot was not stated).

Allen declared he protected his Company Commander by persuading him to return to his tent quarters and remained there after removing his weapons belt and sword. Allen further testified that he secured the tent flaps closed and remained as a guard at the tent entrance until the arrival of the Regiment C.O., Colonel F. W. Bardwell.

The Court found Allen guilty as charged and sentenced him to be executed by musketry at Fernandina, Florida on December 1, 1865.

Allen and five others were court martialed, found guilty and executed by shooting on December 1, 1865.

For details of the mutiny, see Case #260, Private Joseph Grien.

REFERENCES:
Military Personnel Records, RG-#94
Court Martial Proceedings, RG-#153 OO 1477

Case #259
Pvt. David Craig
Co. K, 3rd Regt, USC Infantry
Executed for Mutiny
December 1, 1865

DESCRIPTION:

21 years of age, 5 feet 7 inches tall, black eyes, black hair, black complexion, born in Pennsylvania, occupation laborer, literate, substitute.

Craig enlisted on July 16, 1863 at Pittsburg, Pennsylvania as a substitute and was mustered in for duty at Philadelphia. His regiment was on duty in northern Florida when he and several other members of his Regiment became involved in a mutiny. He was court martialed and sentenced to be executed on December 1, 1865.

While incarcerated Craig wrote to a friend, H. C. Marchand of Greensburg, Pennsylvania, a city about 20 miles southeast of Pittsburg, Pennsylvania. Marchand, in turn, immediately wrote to US Senator E. Cowan (from Pennsylvania). The letter read as follows: "Greensburgh, December 10/65, Hon. E. Cowan, Dear Sir, Yesterday I received a letter from David Craig (colored), Co K, 3, USCT dated 28 November in which he states that he was sentenced to be shot to death on the 1st day of December at Fort Clinch, Fernandina, Florida. I will be obliged if you make immediate inquiry at the War Department to ascertain the truth of this matter, and if this sentence has not been executed, to endeavor to have it postponed until I can get the necessary petition to Hon. V. showing his innocent and inoffensive character prior to his enlistment. Whoever raised the boy from his infancy our family has taken a deep interest in his welfare. The peacetime encumbrance under which he was induced to enlist by some of the white folks of Pittsburgh makes his fate the more unfortunate.

He was a minor at the time of enlistment without father or mother.

He wrote me that at the time of the mutiny he had been ordered to take the guns from some of the mutineers, and in doing so was involved, in the mutiny, the Colonel of the Regiment had his finger shot off.

Yours Truly,
H. C. Marchand"

A note scribbled on the margin of the letter directs, "Telegraph to Genl. Foster to suspend sentence and transmit records here."

A telegram in reply dated December 16, 1865, from Tallahassee, Florida, was received in Washington, D.C. on December 20, 1865.

"Your telegram in relation to David Craig, Company K, 3rd USCT is this day received. Private David Craig was executed on the first day of December, 1865. The proceedings in his case were forwarded on November 13, 1865, Maj Genl J. G. Foster."

A notation on the telegram states, "Senator Cowan informed December 20."

REFERENCES:

Military Personnel Records, RG-#94

Case #260
Pvt. Joseph Grien
NV: Green, Greene
Co. I, 3rd Infantry, USCT
Executed for Mutiny
December 1, 1865

DESCRIPTION:

18 years of age, 5 feet 4 inches tall, black eyes, black hair, black complexion, born in

Trenton, New Jersey, occupation farmer.

Grien had the pay qualifying statements in his file, V1Z: "Free on or before April 19, 1861," "Paid $7.00 per month from date of enlistment to the 31st of December 1863. Back pay due."

Grien enlisted in Company I, 3rd Infantry, USCT at Philadelphia, Pennsylvania on July 21, 1863 and was mustered into service on July 26, 1863. He may have served as a bugler as his records state he was charged for one bugle. He entered a hospital in Philadelphia, Pennsylvania on August 13, 1863. Grien was "in arrest" on April 26, 1864 and released from confinement on June 18, 1864. Grien was involved in a mutiny at Fernandina, Florida in November 1865 and was tried along with David Craig, James Allen, Jacob Plowden, Nathaniel Joseph, and Howard Thomas. They all were charged, court martialed and found guilty.

A General Court Martial was convened at Jacksonville, Florida and on November 3, 1865 began the trial of Private Joseph Grien (Green) Company I, 3rd Infantry Regiment, USCT on a charge of mutiny. Grien declined to have counsel assigned.

Testimony revealed that on October 29, 1865, a disturbance occurred in the camp of the 3rd Infantry Regiment of USCT. No explanation as to the cause of the disturbance is stated except that there was resistance offered to the authority of Lieutenant Colonel Brower during which event shots were fired and two enlisted men were wounded.

Lieutenant Colonel Brower testified that Grien, while loading and priming his musket advanced toward him, eventually leveling the weapon at Brower's chest. Brower advanced toward and fired at Grien, with a small caliber Smith & Wesson revolver and missed. He had hoped this would have halted Grien's advance but it did not. As Grien continued to approach, Brower said he fired several more shots at Grien for as he stated, "it was only a matter of a few seconds whether he shot me or I him." His last shot struck Grien and wounded him, as the surgeon testified "in the left elbow and left side of the chest," the bullet wounding him being of a very small size. The surgeon revealed that Grien told him he never advanced on Brower but stayed near a stove at the cook's tent and that Brower fired several shots at him.

Grien offered no defense but did made a brief statement as follows: "I did not lift the gun from the ground until I was struck I then threw it upon the wood pile. I did not attempt to shoot it off."

No further testimony being offered, the Court deliberated, found Grien guilty and sentenced him to death before a firing squad.

The execution was carried out at Fernandina, Florida on December 1, 1865.

REFERENCES:

Military Personnel Records, RG-#94
Court Martial Proceedings, RG-#153 OO 1477

Case #261
Pvt. Thomas Howard
Co. I, 3rd Inf Regt, USCT
Executed for Mutiny
December 1, 1865

DESCRIPTION:

19 years of age, no further data available.

Howard enlisted and mustered in at Philadelphia, Pennsylvania on July 20, 1863 and assigned to Company I, 3rd Infantry Regiment USCT. Howard served with the unit apparently untroubled until November/December, 1863 when he was fined by a Regimental Court Martial of one month's pay, $2.25 of which awarded to a Joseph A. Barbee, not further identified. Another notation states he is charged for a bugle, however, the meager information concerning Howard does not indicate that he was either a bugler or musician.

Howard was involved in a mutiny at the Quarters of the 3rd Regiment in or near Fernandina, Florida in 1865, with five other members of his Company.

A General Court Martial was convened at Jacksonville, Florida and on November 1, 1865 tried Private Thomas Howard, Company I, 3rd USCT on a charge of mutiny.

Howard declined to accept any counsel.

Testimony offered showed that a mutiny occurred on October 29, 1865 in the camp of the 3rd Regiment USCT. About 200-300 men of the Regiment were creating a disturbance on the Company streets. Lieutenant Colonel Brower was firing shots in the air which caused many of those who were unarmed to leave the area and return to their quarters. About 20-30 armed men remained and Lieutenant Colonel Brower and other officers fired at the remaining armed men.

It was said that Howard fired his weapon at Lieutenant Gray or Lieutenant Brown who was mounted on horseback.

Sergeant Handy of the 3rd Regiment USCT saw Howard with his rifle and he and another soldier went over and wrested the gun away from him.

The accused offered few convincing witnesses and then offered a statement in his defense.

"Statement of Thomas Howard, Private of Company I, 3rd USCT, I saw Lt. Colonel Brower firing. I was standing at the Cook house. As soon as I saw him hit a man I went and got my gun but I did not fire it at all."

The Court deliberated, found Howard guilty and sentenced him to death with musketry.

He was court martialed, found guilty and shot on December 1, 1865. The Regiment was mustered out of service on October 31,1865 at Jacksonville, Florida. For other details of the mutiny, see Case #260, Private Joseph Grien.

REFERENCES:
Military Personnel Records, RG-#94
Court Martial Proceedings, RG-#153 OO 1477

Case #262
Pvt. Joseph Nathaniel
Co. K, 3rd Inf Regt, USCT
Executed for Mutiny
December 1, 1865

DESCRIPTION:

20 years of age, 5 feet 7¾ inches tall, black eyes, black hair, black complexion, born in Kingston, Jamaica, occupation seaman, literacy undetermined.

Nathaniel enlisted and was mustered into service at Portsmouth, New Hampshire on September 10, 1864 and was assigned to Company K, 3rd Infantry Regiment USCT. The Regiment was on duty near Fernandina, Florida, when Nathaniel was involved in mutiny.

A General Court Martial was convened at Jacksonville, Florida and on October 31, 1865 tried Private Joseph Nathaniel, Company K, 3rd Regiment USCT on a charge of mutiny.

The accused stated he did not desire counsel.

Witnesses testified that on Sunday, October 31, 1863, a mutiny took place in the Camp of the 3rd Regiment, USCT. A prisoner was being punished in Camp by being strung up by his thumbs and groups of soldiers of the Regiment began to gather and finally to advance toward the site, within camp where the prisoner was undergoing punishment. Standing near the prisoner was Lieutenant Colonel Brower. The enlisted men advanced toward the Lieutenant Colonel and then retreated. They advanced a second time and

Lieutenant Colonel Brower fired three shots at them and one of the advancing group was seen to fall. The mob began to call out, "One of us is shot, get your muskets!" About fifteen or twenty responded to the cry coming with their muskets and began firing at the Lieutenant Colonel muttering "shoot the son of a bitch" and so forth and so on.

One officer went to Company K street and attempted to fall in the men. They did in fact only mill around and menace the officer and the accused in particular equipped with musket, bayonet and accouterments was about 8 paces away when he aimed his gun and fired at the Officer the ball passed close enough for the officer to hear it. The men called each other "cowards for being afraid of one man." A Sergeant and a Corporal of the regiment wrested the gun and accouterments from the accused while he shouted, "Let me go, I want to kill the damned son of a bitch."

Neither the defense or prosecution had more testimony to offer but the accused had a statement to present to the court.

Statement of Joseph Nathaniel the accused

"When the disturbance commenced I was down at the sink. I heard men yelling all along the line. And when I came up I saw the whole line was faced towards the Lieutenant Colonel where he was having a man tied up. I went then to the right of my cook house. I folded my arms. And the officer of the Day came along and told the men to go into their quarters and respect the Lieutenant Colonel. A few men only moved off. I went in and laid down and heard the shots fired. I ran out of my tent and saw a man was shot down. The Lieutenant Colonel and the Officer of the day ran towards me. I run into my tent and got my gun, and ran after the Officer of the day. And Sergeant Harry and Corporal Coffee saw me and took away my gun, etc. and put them in my tent. I then went into my own street with the rest of the fellows."

The Court deliberated, found the accused guilty and sentenced him to be shot to death with musketry.

The execution took place at Fernandina, Florida on December 1, 1865.

REFERENCES:

Military Personnel Records, RG-#94
Court Martial Proceedings, RG-#153 OO 1477

Case #263
Pvt. Jacob Plowden
NV: Plowder, Plowdin
Executed for Mutiny
Co. E, 3rd Inf Regt, USCT
December 1, 1865

DESCRIPTION:

44 years of age, 5 feet 7 inches tall, brown eyes, brown hair, brown complexion, born in Franklin, Tennessee, occupation farmer.

Plowden enlisted and was mustered into service at Philadelphia, Tennessee on July 8, 1863 and was assigned to Company E, 3rd Infantry Regiment USCT. He was promoted to Corporal September 29, 1863 and reduced back to ranks on December 7, 1863. He later was assigned as a teamster in the Quartermaster Department at Jacksonville, Florida. He was one of the six men of the 3rd Regiment USCT court martialed for mutiny at or near Fernandina, Florida in late 1865. Tried and found guilty, all six were hung for mutiny on December 1, 1865.

A General Court Martial was convened at Jacksonville, Florida on November 2, 1865 and tried Private Jacob Plowden, Company E, 3rd Infantry Regiment USCT on a charge of mutiny.

Plowden stated he did not desire any counsel.

Witnesses described the general course and tone of the disturbance that took place on Sunday, October 29, 1865 in the camp of the 3rd Regiment, USCT near Fernandina, Florida as well as Plowden's part therein. A member of the Regiment was being punished for an undisclosed offense by being tied up by his thumbs. The men of the Regiment strongly objected to this form of punishment and groups of soldiers gathered in the Regiment streets discussing and complaining about the matter. Plowden, who had apparently been drinking, emerged from his tent and began walking among the clusters of assembled soldiers talking very loudly. He urged them to cut down the soldier being punished and to resist any work or duty until this punishment was abolished. He said it was not used in White regiments nor in many colored regiments and their Regiment used it most. He cursed every officer from the Lieutenant/Colonel on down and urged the men not to perform drill or duty or work until this crime against the men was abolished. If this was not settled he would have revenge. In his harangues he shook his arms and body violently, like an orator or preacher.

Plowden then advanced with the crowd toward the prisoner being punished avowing to cut him down. The Lieutenant/Colonel fired. (It is not stated whether into the crowd or over their heads.) The mob then fell back and cries of "get your guns!" were heard. Plowden retreated with the rest and went into his tent and emerged with his musket and tried to load it but put it back in his tent when told to do so by a sergeant. Shots were fired at the officers, casualties of the disturbance were not entered in the record of the trial.

Plowden was described as a good soldier who was usually obedient.

There being no more testimony to be offered, the Court adjourned and deliberated. Plowden was found guilty and sentenced to be shot to death with musketry at Fernandina, Florida on December 1, 1865.

For more details on the mutiny, see Case #260, Private Joseph Grien.

REFERENCES:

Military Personnel Records, RG-#94

Court Martial Proceedings, RG-#153 OO 1477

1866
"The Last Executions of the Civil War Era"

Cases #264 - #267
(4 Executions)

Case #264
Pvt. Benjamin McCloud
Co. E, 37th Inf Regt, USCT
Never Executed Although Sentenced to be Shot for mutiny
February 9, 1866

DESCRIPTION:

32 years old, 5 feet 5 inches tall, black eyes, black hair, black complexion, born Pitt, North Carolina, occupation-farmer, illiterate.

McCloud enlisted at Washington, North Carolina on February 12, 1864 and was mustered into service at Norfolk, Virginia on April 7, 1864 in Company E, 37th Regiment Infantry, USCT. During his service, he deserted before Petersburg, Virginia, August 27, 1864 captured at Wilson's Landing, Virginia on August 30, 1864 and was reported sick on Hospital ship, December 1864, and sick in hospital through December 1864.

On the 23rd of September, 1865, at Camp Hilton (Hilton Head, North Carolina), McCloud was involved in a riot/mutiny and was arrested and charged with firing at his Regimental Commander, and missed him but is said to have wounded a Lt. Mellon instead. Arrested by the guard, he again escaped and deserted from Hilton Head, North Carolina September 25, 1865, was arrested at New Berne, North Carolina October 28, 1865, and court martialed on November 22, 1865.

A General Court Martial was convened at Wilmington, North Carolina and on November 22, 1865 tried Private Benjamin McCloud, Company E, 37th Infantry Regiment, USCT, on a charge of Mutiny with intent to kill.

Testimony revealed that a riot and mutiny occurred on September 23, 1865 at Camp Hilton, North Carolina in the quarters of the 37th Regiment of USCT. A Major Weinman of the 37th Regiment USCT was attempting to arrest some soldiers of Company D, 37th Regiment, USCT who had disobeyed his orders by breaking ranks and loading their rifles and McCloud appeared with his loaded rifle. Weinman ordered him to halt his actions, but McCloud turned and ran away. He was pursued by Weinman and several times during the chase McCloud halted his flight and turned toward the approaching Weinman, aiming his rifle at him. Weinman was too closely pursuing McCloud to permit him to have an opportunity to fire. McCloud finally re-entered Company D's street and was lost sight of amongst the agitated mob of rioters. Shortly thereafter shooting was commenced by the rioters and replied to by Officers and non-rioting troops. Weinman was a target of some shots but fortunately escaped unscathed. Not so fortunate was Lt. Millen of the 37th Regiment USCT and an enlisted man of Company A, 37th Regiment, USCT.

McCloud was arrested on the following day and while being escorted by a squad of guards en route to the Provost Marshall's guardhouse escaped. It is related that a large crowd of soldiers of the 37th Regiment crowded around the party, permitting McCloud to escape. McCloud was subsequently recaptured to stand trial.

McCloud offered several witnesses in his behalf who were ineffectual in establishing either the fact that his gun was not loaded or that he was not engaged in the Mutiny or attempt to shoot Major Weinman.

McCloud offered no statement in his defense. The court deliberated, found McCloud guilty and sentenced to be shot to death by musketry on February 9, 1866.

A notation in McCloud's personnel file dated April 13, 1893, issued by the Record and Pension Office of the War Department states the record of this man's execution is erroneous. He escaped from his guard, while awaiting execution of the sentence of the court and it does not appear he was ever retaken up to the date of his death in 1884.

He was found guilty and sentenced to be executed before a firing squad on February 9, 1866. Although his name is carried on the list of executed soldiers, he was never executed. The Record and Pension Office, War Department, in a Memorandum dated April 13, 1893 stated, "It has been determined by this Dept. from the records on file and from the testimony in the Pension Bureau that the record of this man's execution on Feb 9, 1866 in accordance with the sentence of a General Court Martial for mutiny is erroneous. He escaped from his guard while awaiting the execution of the sentence, on Dec. 15, 1865 at Wilmington, N.C. and it does not appear that he was ever retaken by the military authorities of the U.S. Army up to the date of his alleged death in Jan. 21, 1884."

Both McCloud and his widow applied for Army Pension Benefits but the Act of Congress, March 2, 1889 only authorized removal of charges of desertion from records of soldiers who: l) voluntarily returned to their units, and 2) served out the time lost during the desertion period. McCloud fulfilled neither of these requirements. Pension applications continued by his children are recorded as late as 1918 but all appear to have been fruitless.

McCloud was certainly never executed.

REFERENCES:

Military Personnel Records, RG-#94
Court Martial Proceedings, RG-#153 MM 3243
Military Pension Files, RG-#115

Case # 265
Pvt. Fortune Wright
Co. A, 96th Inf Regt, USCT
Executed for Murder
March 2, 1866

DESCRIPTION:

No official descriptive list was found in Wright's military personnel file.

Apparently Wright originally enlisted in Company A, 73rd Infantry Regiment, USCT on July 1, 1863 and was mustered into service on August 14, 1863 at Port Hudson, Louisiana. He was transferred to Company K, 73rd Infantry Regiment, USCT on November 30, 1863 and finally to Company A, 96th Infantry Regiment, USCT on September 23, 1865 which was stationed at Camp Parapet, New Orleans, Louisiana.

On October 25th, 1865, Wright was involved in an altercation with two white men on the street in New Orleans. Wright made the following statement to a W. R. Crane. "On the day of the killing, prisoner was approached and accosted by a colored woman, dissipated and unmoral, putting her hand upon my shoulder, and acting her willingness to prostitute her person. Said to me, give me a dime. Prisoner said, he had no dime. He have a wife and what dimes he get he give to her. The woman then said the prisoner was a God Damned liar, and had a dime in his pocket. Prisoner feeling angry with the woman for her insulting conduct and language to him, told her then if she did say to him or repeat that language he would slap her. She did immediately repeat more insulting language, and the prisoner did only slap her, just then two white men, one the deceased Doctor Octavius U. Tresgerant and Mr. W. F. Skott the main witness against prisoner at his trial came up. Prisoner had never seen either of them in his life before. They had no knowledge of the commencement of the difficulty with the woman and abused and roughly interfered with the prisoner, which he thought unjust and told them they had nothing to do with the business as he was not interfering with them and did not wish to as they were white men and he was a negro. Prisoner desiring to avoid difficulty with them started in the direction of his camp and did walk 3 or 4 paces when the deceased pursuing him struck him on the back of his head a very severe blow with a walking cane the deceased held in his hand. In self defense the prisoner wheeled round caught the cane or stick and said, "What have I done for you to strike me with this stick." And then deceased rushing on him in a most violent manner said, "Let go this stick you damned black son of a bitch" holding the stick in his grasp the prisoner retorted, "You are another son of a bitch." Deceased then violently grabbed hold of him by the collar of his coat. And prisoner still holding fast to one end of the stick. and deceased then drew back and struck Prisoner in the face violently with his fist, and then succeeded in jerking the stick out of Prisoner's hands. A tussle ensued between them and the *other* white man, being a little in the rear, came running up. And in a loud voice said to deceased, "Kill him. Kill the damned black yankee son of a bitch, there is no law for him, kill him." Causing a momentary separation of the tussle and struggle between the prisoner and deceased. Prisoner wishing to fall back, they both pressing upon him. Prisoner said to them. "If both of you jump on me I will cut one of you with this knife," which he had then drawn. They did both rush at and jump on him. Prisoner expecting instant death at their hands, in self defense and under these circumstances, the deceased again grabbing at his throat and coat collar, did strike and did cut deceased with the knife he carried and then had drawn and then got away from both of them and went straight to his quarters, hence his arrest, conviction and sentence of death but by exactly what means, he is ignorant, but most unjustly he does feel fully conscious."

General court martial was convened at New Orleans, Louisiana and on December 11, 1865 tried Private Fortune Wright, Company A, 96th Infantry Regiment, USCT on a charge of murder.

Wright requested the court to permit Captain Thomas F. McGowan, 78th Infantry Regiment, USCT to act as his counsel and permission was granted.

Wright was accused of the murder of Dr. Octavius Undecimen Trezgerant (Tresgerant), who eventually died of a stab wound inflicted by Wright in Carrollton, Jefferson Parish, Louisiana on October 23, 1865.

Autopsy Report:

"We the undersigned regular practicing physicians being duly sworn do depose and say that this day (October 26, 1865) having made a *Post Mortem* examination at the hour of 11AM upon the body of Dr. O.U. Trezgerant at his residence in Carrollton at the Brick House Station, made in presence of the Jurors at the Coroner's inquest, find that his death was caused by an incised wound made by a knife or dagger, the said knife passing through the middle of the 8th rib on the left side about 2 inches posteriorly to a perpendicular line through the nipple of that side, fracturing said rib, dividing the diaphragm and entering the cavity of the abdomen after dividing an intercostal artery, and then piercing the intestines producing fatal inflammation of the peritoneum from escape of fecal matter into the cavity and profuse hemorrhage into the said cavity, producing death."

Signed by: W. Hutchin, MD
H.P. Sauve, MD
Thomas Campbell, MD
James Purvance, Jr., MD

Testimony of witnesses revealed the following chain of events.

The accused offered witnesses on his behalf and questioned several of his witnesses as well as those of the prosecution. The accused also presented to the court a written defense in his behalf as follows.

"To the members of the Court, Gentlemen, Before submitting this case let us look at the charge and specifications on which the accused is charged in committing murder. The specification states that the accused (unreadable) with malice aforethought, and with intent to kill, willfully and feloniously assaulted with a knife, and stabbed Octavius Undecimen Trezgerant, thereby causing the death of the said Doctor Trezgerant.

Now gentlemen in order to prove against the accused the crime of murder, it is necessary for the prosecution to show that it was done with malice aforethought. This can be either expressed or implied.

Express malice, is when a person kills another in a sedate, deliberate state of mind and with a formed design. Implied malice is when a person kills another person, and the (consequences) of (such) killing will allow the law to imply malice, on the part of the offender.

Now the question to be considered is, did the accused hold malice against Doctor Trezgerant? Is there anything in the evidence adduced showing malice on the part of the accused either expressed or implied? Gentlemen, we think not. Not one witness brought before the court has testified that the accused stabbed deceased and Gentlemen this is too grave a matter to be decided against the accused without positive proof of his guilt.

We will state the circumstances of the occurrence, which the evidence will sustain. A Colored Soldier was assaulted with canes in the hands of two citizens, finding that he would be badly beaten, if not killed, did he not defend himself as best he could.

It is needless to go with a more lengthy defense. Gentlemen relying on your sound judgement and knowing that the accused is entitled to the benefit of all doubt we respectfully submit our case.

Thomas F. McGowan
Captain 78th Infantry, USCT
Counsel for Defense—"

The court deliberated, found the accused guilty of murder and sentenced him to be executed by hanging. The sentence was originally to be carried out on January 5, 1866 at New Orleans, Louisiana. The execution of the sentence was postponed a number of times. The first postponement date was advanced to February 9, 1866, then extended to February 23, 1866 and finally Wright was executed on March 2, 1866.

A number of petitions were gathered requesting the commutation of the sentence of death by officers of his Regiment, by citizens and lawyers of New Orleans and by Lt. Col. O. Fabriola, Wright's Regimental Commander. Most of the petitions cite similar grounds for clemency, among which are:

1. Wright acted only in self defense, fearing for his life.
2. There were a number of witnesses who could contradict the prosecution's witnesses but did not, for a variety of reasons, appear in court and testify.
3. Dr. Trezgerant's companion at the time of his stabbing was a W. F. Scott, referred to as a lawyer and sometimes as a judge, was the chief witness against Wright at the trial. It was said that Scott disguised himself as a Union Army Officer and interviewed Wright while he was imprisoned. Scott is accused of altering the statements made by Wright so as to indicate he (Wright) was the aggressor and intended to kill Dr. Trezgerant. The Jailer and Deputy Sheriff who were present at Scott's interview with Wright, refused to discuss the matter except "before a court of justice."
4. The Judge Advocate, at the trial of Wright, Lt. Thomas Day stated, "he would not have voted as the court did."
5. A conversation with a Father Lemarge, (a Roman Catholic priest) who attended to the religious needs of Dr. Trezgerant during his three terminal days and with Mrs. Trezgerant to the effect that Dr. Trezgerant expressed the desire that the assailant not be prosecuted. It is not known precisely whether this statement was based upon a spirit of forgiveness or the knowledge that he (Dr. Trezgerant) was the original assailant.
6. The following statement:

Hd. Quar. Bureau of Freedmen, State of Louisiana, New Orleans, January 10, 1866. "The prayer of the within petitioners is fully concurred in, I have not the least doubt that the prisoner acted in self defense in killing the deceased and that the person killed together with his friend, the chief witness, were his assailants. Reports come to me almost daily from quarters of the State telling of the murder of negroes by white men and I do not know of a single instance in which the murderer has been properly punished, if at all."

A. Baird
Bvt. Maj. Genl.
Asst. Comm. for LA

A plea for retention of the death sentence of Wright was also made by W. F. Scott the lawyer/Judge companion of Dr. Trezgerant at the time of his stabbing. Scott apparently was more concerned about how his professional reputation might suffer if Wright's sentence was commuted.

All the appeals were forwarded to the Judge Advocate General, J. J. Holt, by President Andrew Johnson for legal evaluation. After much study of the court martial proceedings and the various statements of petitioners, Judge Holt reported in a lengthy analysis of the entire trial and related facts, that "no evidence was found in it warranting a recommendation of clemency. Reference is respectfully made to that report the grounds of which are strengthened by the statements of W. F. Scott in the enclosed paper." Another excerpt recorded states, "and nothing therefore upon which this office can recommend commutation of sentence."

Wright's execution was set in motion by the following order for preparations. "The execution of Private Fortune Wright to take place on the 2nd of March, proximal, must be conducted in a quiet and solemn manner. Besides the usual escort, you will call upon the Cmdg. Officer at the Levie Steam Press Stables for two Companies of Infantry with field music, to be in attendance and under your direction. You will be present in person to conduct the execution and will see that the charge, sentence and order of Dept. Hdqs. are read aloud and distinct previous to the execution. That the Post Chaplain and two surgeons are present, to be ready to perform their respective offices. This does not prohibit the criminal from having any favorite Chaplain he may select, to officiate. But the Post Chaplain will be held responsible that the religious services are conducted in a satisfactory manner. The moment of the execution will be fixed upon by you, within the hours prescribed in the order. Precaution must be taken that the office of hangman be confided to a capable person so that no disagreeable results may ensue; and that the body be not disturbed until the surgeons have pronounced life to be extinct."

On February 7, 1866, the following message was sent from the Headquarters, Department of Louisiana, Office of the Provost Marshall General to a Lt. Combs: "You will not inform Fortune Wright of his execution if you have not already done so till the evening before his execution."

Wright, prior to his execution, was advised that his uncollected pay would not be forfeited, as no mention of same in his sentence. He then requested that the sum due him be paid to his father. No record indicates whether this was done.

On February 10, 1866, a memorandum was sent to Headquarters, New Orleans, Louisiana, Colonel:

"*Fortune Wright* of Co. A, 96th Colored Inf condemned to be executed has pay coming to him which his Captain informs me was not forfeited by the sentence of the court martial. He desires to collect it and pay the amount over to his father. Will the Genl Comdg. be kind enough to direct the paymaster to send the rolls to the prison to be signed or that the prisoner be brought out in order that the amount may be paid?

Please answer by bearer,
I am very respectfully
Your Obt. Servt
G. A. Pierce
48, Camp St."

On March 3, 1866, Major Jackson reported, "I have the honor to report that Fortune Wright Co A, 96th USCT was executed yesterday at 2 O'Clock PM.

I personally inspected the preparations yesterday morning taking with me persons who were well acquainted with such executions. Everything in connection with the gallows was thoroughly examined and pronounced by these parties in good condition and that the rope should be rubbed with soap to make it slip easily. This I ordered done and was afterwards informed on inquiry that it had been done.

The escort formed in front of the police jail at 12:45PM, the prisoner was brought out in charge of the Comdg officer of the jail and the prison guard accompanied by the chaplain in attendance and placed in the center of the escort. The column then marched to the place of execution in the Parish Prison."

The Daily True Delta, a morning New Orleans newspaper carried on Saturday, March 3, 1866, a long and detailed account of the execution of Private Fortune Wright on March 2, 1866.

The account as follows is edited for the sake of brevity, without materially affecting the facts.

"The streets around the jail were by this time crowded, thousands of persons, principally negroes, having been attracted to the spot by curiosity to see the prisoner, and many, as is always the case, by a superstitious desire to obtain a piece of the fatal cord (the hanging rope) as a charm against voudous."

Fortune Wright was a large and muscular negro, quite black, and with by no means a mild and gentle expression. His self possession was perfect, no traces of emotion being visible at any stage of the proceedings.

Wright was led out upon the drop (scaffold trap door) before the assembled troops and spectators, the prison windows being crowded with prisoners. Wright was cleanly attired in an undress United States uniform. The prisoner seated himself upon the stool on the drop, a stool which, by the way, has been the last seat of many strong men. Acting Provost Marshall Major Jackson then read the Court Martial order and the order for execution. Father Dufau, of the Jesuit church, placed a crucifix suspended on a chain about Wright's neck and offered a prayer for the condemned man as did the Rev. Elijah Guion, Chaplain of the 1st New Orleans Regiment. The prisoner, permitted last remarks, launched into a long rambling recitation of the trial and that he, Wright had always been a good man who obeyed orders.

Several Federal Army officers present commented that rather than a good man, Wright had always been regarded as extremely vicious when under the influence of liquor, having been suspected of a previous murder.

At the end of his message, a white cap was drawn over his face and the rope was adjusted. As the drop fell, Wright was shouting, "farewell friends." His body descended some six to eight feet, but the rope, not having been properly greased, the knot failed to slip, so that when the body rebounded, the knot twisted around to his forehead. Wright thus hung suspended by the loop passing around his forehead and under the very prominent developments of the head behind the ears (mastoid processes), hung by the head instead of the neck. A shudder of horror at the unfortunate occurrence passed through the witnesses; but the shock having been sufficient to render him insensible, Wright did not suffer by the accident. After hanging a few minutes, a copious perspiration occurred on his body, and soon his breathing became regular and natural. Surgeon Avery and Drs. Smith and Berthelot, having examined him, declared he could not die from the effects of this hanging. His body was lowered, taken off the rope and carried up a second time to the drop. The knot was retied and the rope again placed about his neck and his body propped into place. The drop fell (trap door sprung) and the noose again failed to slip, the rope being new and stiff, and not soaped, and the knot came around to the back of his head. The rope remained under the chin, however, immediately strangling the formerly unconscious man, and after a few convulsive throes, the soul of Fortune Wright had sped to its last account.

After hanging suspended for nearly an hour and being declared by the doctors "dead beyond doubt," the body was taken down and consigned to a coffin.

There were no friends or relatives to claim the corpse, but it was properly disposed of by the Government.

No blame can possibly be attached to any one for the accident which occurred, as the officers and their assistants were novices, and received no counsel or advice from the more experienced persons around them.

As the spectators left the jail, the negroes were crowding around the door begging everyone who came out for a piece of the rope.

Wright although having been found guilty by court martial and sentenced to be hung had a rather large number of petitions filed on his behalf requesting a complete reprieve or at least a commutation of the sentence to a term of imprisonment. In the petition filed by his Regimental Commander, Lt./Col. O. Fariola, it is stated that Dr. Tresgerant (who was stabbed by Wright and did not die immediately) on his death bed made the request that "the man who stabbed him should be unmolested." Other officers of the USCT command in the area either joined in common petitions or filed individual letters requesting clemency for Wright.

Citizens of New Orleans also joined in the effort on Wright's behalf filing a long letter asking for a pardon or sentence commutation to a prison term on December 30, 1865. Surprisingly enough, the Commander of Company A, Wright's Company, stated that "he would prefer not being called (to testify) as although he had known the prisoner about two years he did not think he could say anything in his favor." The statement was criticized by the Regimental Commander.

The various petitions forwarded on Wright's behalf resulted in a series of postponements of his execution until on February 24, 1866 his sentence was confirmed by the President and March 2, 1866 was set as the final date of execution. Wright having been held in close confinement in irons.

(One of the details of the preparation for hanging included a thorough soaping of the rope, to make it slip easily. Further, the Provost Marshall was to insure that the body be not disturbed until the Surgeon certified that life was extinct.)

REFERENCES:

Military Personnel Records, RG-#94
Court Martial Proceedings, RG-#153 OO 1494
Newspapers:
New Orleans Newspapers
The New Orleans Times, March 3, 1866
The Daily Picayune, March 3, 1866
The Daily Crescent, February 2, 3, 10, 16, 1866
The Daily True Delta, December 19, 1865; February 9, 16, and March 3, 1866
The New Orleans Tribune, March 3, 1866

Case # 266
Pvt. Lewis Wilson
NV: Louis
Co. L, 10th Heavy Arty. Regt - USCT
Executed for Murder
March 23, 1866

DESCRIPTION:

25 years of age, 5 feet 7 inches tall, black eyes, black hair, black complexion, born in Williamson, Tennessee, occupation laborer, married, illiterate.

Wilson enlisted on March 16, 1865 and was mustered into service on March 25, 1865 at Camp Parapet, Louisiana originally in Company E of the 77th Infantry Regiment, USCT and was transferred on October 1, 1865 to Company L, 10th Heavy Artillery Regiment, USCT. On January 14, 1866 Wilson murdered Private Thomas Kemper same Company and Regiment at Fort Pike, Louisiana.

General Court Martial was convened at New Orleans, Louisiana and on February 12, 1866 proceeded to the trial of Private Lewis Wilson, Company L, 10th Heavy Artillery Regt., USCT on a charge of murder.

Wilson applied to the court for permission to have Frederick Frye act as his counsel, which was granted.

Testimony of witnesses disclosed the following account of the events leading up to the shooting. About two weeks prior to the fatal event Wilson entered a room in the barracks where Kemper was lying on the floor before a fireplace fire. Wilson stepped over Kemper who vociferously objected to this. Wilson replied that he thought Kemper was asleep and wished only to avoid awakening him. The exchange of words continued for several minutes. At some time shortly after this encounter, Wilson complained to Captain Barstow, his Company Commander about Kemper. Captain Barstow ordered Kemper confined in the guardhouse for five days. On Sunday, January 14, 1866, Kemper encountered Wilson on a bridge near the boat house at Fort Pike and verbally attacked him saying, among other things, "Well Wilson, today me and you will go off and decide this business." Wilson replied, "I don't want to have anything more to do with you. The Captain punished you and I do not want anything more to do with you." Kemper continued, "Well, today is the day and one of us has got to die, and a soldier's life is no more than a hog's anyhow." Kemper than left to go the hospital at Fort Pike to receive medicine. Wilson left the scene of their encounter.

Not long after they parted, Kemper was near the entrance to the hospital, with a group of other soldiers, when Wilson arrived with his musket and walked up to Kemper. Wilson addressed Kemper, "Tom Kemper," "eh?" Kemper grunted. "You said you was going to kill me, and I want you to do it right now." Wilson then fired at Kemper, without putting the musket to his shoulder. Kemper was struck in both arms and the trunk of the body. Wilson, after firing the shot, ran to his Company Commanders quarters where he was arrested. Kemper was taken into the hospital where he died about 3-4 hours later.

The attending surgeon stated that "the ball entered the left arm between the wrist and elbow inflicting a flesh wound, and passing from that point through the abdominal walls immediately below the last rib; passing across the body, tearing on it's way the stomach, the arch of the large intestine and emerging at a corresponding point on the opposite side of the body; entering the right arm halfway between the elbow and wrist and emerging on the opposite side of the limb. These points are the result of a *Post Mortem examination.*"

The defense questioned witnesses and called witnesses on it's behalf. At the conclusion of the testimony at the trial it offered a defense statement.

"Gentlemen of the Court, The accused, Lewis Wilson is charged with the crime of murder in this, that he did, about the 14th day of January, 1866 at Fort Pike in the State of Louisiana, feloniously and with malice aforethought, shoot one Thomas Kemper with an Enfield Rifle musket and of which said Kemper died.

I respectfully urge, first that the offence is not now cognizable by Martial Law.

The Jurisdiction of Military tribunals is confined to those offenses which are made punishable by the Articles of War or Acts of Congress, so called, the Articles of War, are explicit in themselves, and do not confer jurisdiction in such cases, and the only Act of Congress conferring jurisdiction upon military tribunals for the crime of murder reads as follows, Section 30, page 541, Army Regulations, March 3, 1863, "and be it further enacted that in time of war, insurrection or *rebellion*, murder, etc. shall be punishable by the sentence of a general court martial or Military Commission, when committed by persons who are in the Military Service of the United States, and subject to the Articles of War."

At the present time, the court cannot say that either of the above contingencies exists. Neither War nor insurrection, *rebellion*, the only case which could confer jurisdiction then has ceased, Civil and criminal courts have been restored to their proper function in this, as in every State of the Union. No hostile cannon has been heard for months and the last armed Traitor to his Country surrendered nearly a year ago. It has needed no official Declaration to restore peace to the Country, as if in time of war with a foreign power for when the armed opposition to the government failed, Rebellion ceased to exist. Our army is reduced to a standard only proper for a Standing Army of so great a Republic and Martial Law no longer interferes with the due administration of justice in the several Courts of the state. These are facts of which this court is bound to take notice and this court is also bound to take official notice of the fact, as to whether a Rebellion is at present existing in the United States, if not, then the accused cannot be proceeded against by this tribunal, it is not whether *Martial Law even* still exists but whether *war, insurrection* or *rebellion* exists.

It cannot be said this plea comes too late, for in Criminal prosecutions want of jurisdiction is always a good plea, even after conviction, for if the Court have no jurisdiction, then proceedings are void absentia and in cases of this nature, *consent* can never confer *jurisdiction.*

If however the Court should come to the conclusion that it had jurisdiction in the case, I would then respectfully urge that here they can only convict of *Manslaughter.*

It appears that the deceased had a difficulty with the accused and for which upon investigation by the Captain Commanding the Post, the deceased had been punished by confinement in the Guardhouse for some 4 or 5 days, that upon the very morning of his release and meeting the accused, he was exasperated against him, that he attacked him (not with blows) but menaces and language, showing the old grudge was still alive within him, that he tells him, "Today must settle this matter, a soldier's life being no more than a hogs," that the accused endeavored to conciliate him and to avoid him when he saw the exasperation of the deceased, and that finally being wrought upon by the threats of the deceased, and actually fearing his life was in danger, he armed himself, with his every day weapon, no more offensive than defensive, and the only weapon, he as a good soldier knew, that he shortly after comes upon the deceased and after a few words showing he was still laboring under the fear of the threat to take his life in bringing down his gun it was discharged whether *accidentally* or not, the witness Henry Harrison could not say, but it would rather appear as if such was really the fact as the accused brought the gun to his side and not his shoulder, more in fact in the position of a charge bayonet, to defend, and from the description of the wound by the Surgeon where the ball entered and the course it traveled, it is evident that the gun when discharged was not at the shoulder of the accused, and might have accidentally gone off, if so then *Manslaughter* only can be charged, so again if the accused was really put in fear of his life and working upon his imagination made him believe his life in danger, all of which appears from the evidence, he then had a right to arm himself, and if in the excitement of the minute with this idea pressing upon his mind he shoots the deceased it is only *Manslaughter, no malice is shown.* The accused spoke in a calm manner, he is of a generally mild and peaceable nature, he shows no violence towards the deceased, endeavoring to pacify him and upon the impulse of the moment with no other object in view but self preservation the inflicts the wound of which the deceased died. Manslaughter is distinguishable from Murder in this that though the act which occasions the death is unlawful, yet the malice either expressed or implied which is the very essence of Murder is presumed to be wanting, in Manslaughter the act of Manslaughter is imputed to the infinity of human nature, and the *Law will not imply malice* where any reasonable provocation or excuse is shown for the commission of the act.

And lastly if the court should find the accused Guilty of Murder, they have still discretion in the sentence, the act of Congress previously referred to says "And the punishment for such offenses shall never *be less* than those inflicted by the Laws of the State, Territory or District in which they may have been committed." We have in this State a law which reads as follows, "In all cases where the punishment denounced by law is death it shall be lawful for the jury to qualify the verdict by adding thereto "Without Capital Punishment." Revised Stat. La. 1856, page 163, Section 26, So in this case the Court are the Jury to decide upon the facts and the Judges to decide upon the Law and as such have the right, though they should Convict the accused of Murder to add "Without Capital Punishment."

Frederick Frye
Counsel for Defense

The court deliberated, found the accused guilty and sentenced him to be executed by musketry. The execution took place in New Orleans, Louisiana, on March 28, 1866.

Issues of the "New Orleans True Delta" of February 11, March 18, March 23, March 24, 1866 provide details of the crime and Wilson's execution. Evidently Private Thomas

Kemper had a confrontation with Wilson on January 14, 1866 and threatened Wilson. Wilson, in a rage, went to his tent, loaded his rifle, returned to Kemper's presence and mortally shot him. Wilson was arrested, court martialed, found guilty and sentenced to be executed by a firing squad in the yard of the New Orleans Parish Police Jail. Wilson, described as a powerful and vicious fellow, appealed his sentence but the appeal was denied on the grounds that the shooting was a deliberate and willful act.

Wilson was attended, prior to execution by Father Dufau of the Jesuit Church of New Orleans and Chaplain Guion of the 1st New Orleans Regiment.

Wilson became very convinced he was going to Jesus but was more concerned that his hands would be bound too tight and he would fall too hard upon the ground. He begged the two clergymen to stand upon either side him as the execution squad fired and ease him to the ground when they fired. Understandably, both declined this request.

Seated upon his coffin, Wilson glanced down at this breast and said "shoot me here" indicating his heart. The execution squad fired and five balls passed through his chest in a compact pattern and a sixth passed through his head about the right ear.

A crucifix which hung upon the breast of Wilson was shattered into "a thousand pieces."

The fragments of the crucifix were gathered up, the body coffined and the spectators were dispersed.

Wilson was buried in Monument Cemetery, New Orleans, Louisiana on March 23, 1866.

Wilson is one of the very few executed soldiers who made a will. Wilson left everything to his wife, Sarah Wilson.

REFERENCES:

Military Personnel Records, RG-#94
Court Martial Proceedings, RG-#153   MM 3597
"New Orleans True Delta" issues of February 11, March 18, March 23, March 24, 1866.

Case # 267
Pvt. Robert Rogers
NV: Rodgers
Co B, 77th Ohio Infantry Regiment
Executed for Murder
June 8, 1866
(Last man executed during Civil War Service)

DESCRIPTION:

18 years of age (Note: U.S. Census report of 1860 gives Rogers age as 16 years, while the military records state 18 years.), 5 feet 6 inches tall, brown hair, dark eyes, dark complexion, born in Marietta, Ohio, occupation laborer.

Rogers enlisted at Marietta, Ohio on December 27, 1861. The Marietta Republican of January 10, 1862, reported: "Stealing and Stabbing Affray" - Two men, named Rogers, one a soldier, entered the store of Gerd Wendelken and attempted to steal a piece of cloth, but were detected as they passed out of the door, and the bystanders took the cloth from them. They then became boisterous, flourished knives, and made terrible threats, which were finally consummated by striking Wendelken in the mouth and stabbing him in the back. Wendelken will recover from his wounds, though they were considered, at first mortally dangerous. The two men have been arrested and are now in custody." Robert Rogers was sentenced to a jail term by civil authority, at Marietta, Ohio and was unable to present himself for duty with the Regiment and was dropped from the rolls. Upon his release from his jail sentence, Rogers promptly re-enlisted in Company B, 77th Ohio Infantry Regiment on October 9, 1862 and was forwarded to his regiment in the field. Rogers was discharged in 1863 and immediately reenlisted in the same Regiment as a Veteran Volunteer. On April 22, 1864, while in service in Arkansas, Rogers was assigned to duty as a guard on a supply wagon train to Pine Bluff, Arkansas. He was a participant in the battle of Mark's Mills, Arkansas on April 25, 1864 and was captured. He was taken to Prisoner of War Camp Ford, at Tyler, Texas and was released by exchange in February, 1865. The Regiment was than transferred to the Army of the Gulf and participated in campaigns in Alabama and Texas. The Regiment's last station was at Brownsville, Texas from August 1, 1865 until March 8, 1866 before being mustered out of service.

On February 21, 1865, between the hours of six and seven P.M. in the camp of the 77th Regiment near Brownsville, Texas, Rogers and a Dr. William A. Gardner had been drinking whiskey together. Gardner is described as a Sutler's clerk and ex-assistant Army Surgeon. Rogers and Gardner argued about some money paid for whiskey and custody of the bottle of same. Gardner is said to have begun to walk away from Rogers after being struck on the head with a whiskey bottle and Rogers ran to a tent and picked up a large tree branch fashioned into a club. Rogers, club in hand, staggered up the Company street in pursuit of Gardner, caught up with him and struck him a blow across his back which did not fell Gardner. Rogers then is reported to have struck Gardner several more times, the last blow crushing his skull and killing him. Rogers was immediately seized, arrested and confined in the Brownsville Military Prison awaiting trial by court martial.

On February 28, 1866, Major General G. W. Getty, Commanding the District of the Rio Grande, received the following letter.

"General, I have the honor to state that there is a soldier named Robert Rogers confined in the Military Prison at this post on a charge of homicide. Personally, he is utterly unknown to me. This afternoon he addressed me a note urgently requesting an interview, for the evident purpose of securing my services as counsel for his defense. I am in effect denied admittance to the prison in time to be of any use to this unfortunate man upon a question of mere form.The Provost Marshall of the Post and his Lieutenant are absent on business or pleasure; and the Acting Provost Marshall General, as a matter of Etiquette refuses to give an order which should properly emanate from the former! This man's trial, if it has not already commenced, will probably commence tomorrow. I respectfully submit for your consideration, General, whether under a wise administration, military or civil, Subordinates can thus be permitted to kill the spirit of the law by a pretended adherence to mere formula.

I should not have ventured to trouble you with a communication of this nature did I not feel that common justice and humanity demand it.

Previous to the recent changes, my relations with the Post and Provost Marshall General had been pleasant; but these positions, or at least the chief of them, appears to be now filled by gentlemen who are no less strangers to their official duties than to me. As this is a grave charge, I respectfully submit the following specifications.

Sometime before Major General Weitzel was relieved from Command of this District, I asked him for a general permit to visit the prison. This was in consequence of the reluctance manifested by Capt. Ayers Actg P.M.G. and Lieut. Potter, Prison Keeper, to accord me that privilege. A day or two after he had been relieved, I presented that order, and was refused admittance, on the ground that Genl. Weitzel was no longer in Command. I urged that Col. Wheeler, A.A.G., by whom it was so signed, still held the same position, and that his order entitled me to admittance without further question by a subordinate. On this argument I was admitted once as a *favor*, and requested to give up the order for the inspection of Captain Ayers, the new acting P.M.G. I did so, cheerfully, because in my previous intercourse with U. S. Officers, I had generally found them to be gentlemen. On my subsequent demand for the return of this paper, *as my property*, Capt. Ayers at first denied having received the paper at all, but afterwards declared it was *mislaid*! He however, agreed to give me a pass whenever I applied for one, and did so on two occasions. But to get a pass involves, 1st the necessity of finding the Captain and his clerk in the office at the same time, and disengaged; 2nd a delay of half an hour while the pass is being written out with due formality, and placed inside of an envelope, sealed and addressed to Lieutenant Potter; 3rd a long cautious and deliberate reading (perhaps spelling) of the pass by Lieut. Potter, which generally occupies a quarter of an hour or more.

I respectfully submit, General, that the paltry system of tergiversation is unworthy of any man, who, in the uniform of an Officer of the United States is permitted to represent them in even the meanest capacity. It is notorious that the prison is daily visited by many persons of more than questionable character without the slightest hindrance. Perhaps the fact of my *not* being the associate or partner of detectives, thieves or smugglers furnishes the real ground of my exclusion. If a more valid objection exists, if I am unfit to be trusted within the filthy Precincts of that den, it should be made known the cause of my exclusion or guarded admittance should be made public. Personally or peconiarcly I have no interest in going there, but it is the inalienable right of every American Citizen or Soldier accused of crime to be aided by counsel in making out his defense, and it is my *duty* to respond to this call.

Very respectfully, Your Obediant Servant
Frank E. McManus
Atty. at Law"

While we have been unable to locate a reply to McManus' letter, we know he did not, in fact, finally act as trial counsel for Rogers. Rogers was advised by Captain Robert Smithson, 77th Ohio Veteran Volunteers during the court martial.

Post Mortem Examination of the body of Dr. William A. Gardner by Dr. Ira Perry, Assistant Surgeon, 9th Regiment, USCT. "On the left side of the head just above the ear was a large contusion about four (4) inches in diameter at the outer angle of the eye. On the same side of the head there was another contusion. On opening the first contusion there was a large quantity of blood, beneath this blood the skull was found fractured. A piece of skull elliptical in form just above and in front of the ear two (2) inches in a horizontal direction and three (3) inches in a perpendicular direction was depressed about one fourth (1/4) of an inch, broken and driven in. On examining the Skull, a large clot of blood about three (3) inches in diameter and one (1) inch thick dropped out, this clot lay immediately under the Skull and below the fracture, the middle Meningeal artery was ruptured, the brain itself was uninjured except where depressed by the clot. The Membranes of the brain were also uninjured, and the fracture extended from the lower part of the first fracture to the outer angle of the eye on the same side extending then across the Orbital plate of the eye to the Median Line."

Asked if he had ever in his practice encountered similar injuries from which the patient recovered, Dr. Perry replied, "I have never seen one recover with so extensive an injury as that."

A General Court Martial was convened at the Headquarters of the 1st Separate Brigade, District of the Rio Grande, near Brownsville, Texas and on February 27, 1866 began the trial of Private Robert Rogers (Rodgers), Company B, 77th Ohio Veteran Volunteer Infantry on charges of Assault and Battery with Intent to Kill, Murder and Intent to Commit Murder.

The first charge listed resulted from Rogers' assault upon Private James Hazelton, Company C, 35th Regiment, USCT, at the prison guard room where Rogers was incarcerated awaiting trial. Rogers apparently acquired or fabricated a "Slungshot" (a cloth or leather bag filled with stones or leaden balls, much like a "Blackjack") and struck the guard several times severely injuring him.

During the course of the trial, testimony revealed that both Rogers and the deceased Dr. Gardner had been drinking heavily prior to the argument that precipitated Rogers' fatal attack on Dr. Gardner. Witnesses stated Rogers exclaimed after the attack, "When I strike a man, I strike to fetch him down" or "When I strike a man, I strike to kill." Either version tends to indicate intent to commit murder.

Other witnesses depicted Rogers as a mean and vicious individual even while sober.

Rogers was found not guilty of assault and battery with intent to kill, but guilty on the other two charges. He was sentenced to death by hanging on April 27, 1866.

When the trial proceedings were forwarded for approval, they were found to be faulty on certain legal points and were returned for correction. The court was required to be reassembled and correct the trial record. The order constituting the 1st Separate Brigade was to be attached to the proceedings to show jurisdiction. There was an omission of the appointment of the Judge Advocate in the order convening the court and the record did not show sufficiently clear that the court was sworn in presence of the accused.

These deficiencies were corrected and the proceedings and sentence were approved and confirmed.

Rogers was convicted of murder and sentenced to be executed by hanging on the 27th of April, 1866 in the prison yard at Brownsville, Texas. The Rio Grande Courier, April 20, 1866: "Sentenced to be hanged, Robert Rogers, Private, Co. B, 77th Ohio Infantry Vol. the murderer of Dr. W. A. Gardner was tried by General Court Martial and sentenced to be hanged. The sentence has been approved by the Dept Commander and will be carried out on Friday the 27th Inst. Between the hours of 12 and 4 o'clock pm."

Rogers apparently sought spiritual guidance and counsel as he was baptized in his cell at the Military Prison on April 19, 1866 by the Reverend D. Shaver, Church of the advent, Episcopal, Brownsville Texas.

On April 27, 1866, the date prescribed for Rogers' execution, a very serious flaw in the plan occurred, the principal performer, Rogers was nowhere to be found in the prison! A report of the escape was sent on April 27, 1866 by the local Provost Marshall, Captain Evans to Lieutenant Colonel D.D. Wheeler, Assistant Adjt. General.

"Colonel, I have the honor to report that the prisoner Rogers made his escape from the Military Prison last night.

As soon as I was notified of his escape I sent police up and down the river (Rio Grande) to search for him, but none of the police were able to find any trace of him.

I have since found that Rogers crossed the river last night, and that he is now in Matamoros (a Mexican town across the Rio Grande from Brownsville).

After a careful examination of the prison and finding the prisoner's chains in his room, it appears that Rogers filed or sawed off his irons, climbed over the partition of the room where he was confined, went into the yard of the prison where there were two (2) sentinels on duty, and made his escape over a brick wall about ten (10) feet high.

As one of the sentinels in the yard should have been walking his beat past the place where Rogers escaped over the wall it follows that Rogers could not have escaped as he did if the sentinel on duty at the time of the prisoner's escape had properly performed his duty.

As yet I have been unable to ascertain at what hour Rogers made his escape and consequently I am unable to ascertain which sentinel was on duty at the time when and place where Rogers made his escape.

I have arrested the three (3) sentinels on duty at the place where Rogers made his escape.

Very Respectfully, Your Obt. Servt.

Captain Evans (etc)

Needless to say, the newspapers did mention the event. The San Antonio Daily Herald, May 22, 1866, "From the Rio Grande —

Escape of a murderer, Robert Rogers, the murderer of Dr. Gardener, who was to be hanged yesterday* (April 27, 1866), escaped from the military jail night before last. It is hardly comprehensible how he could succeed in escaping from there, without outside help. He was in irons, they were found in his cell cut off: after cutting them, he climbed over a partition into another cell where four men were confined, walked down stairs where two sentinels were posted, scaled a wall some twenty feet high (sic) and landed in the yard of the residence of the Paymaster where there is also a guard, and no one heard or saw him. Vigilant guards they must have been. It was reported that he was seen in Matamoros and that he had joined the Contra Guerillas."

On April the 29th, 1866, "The Daily Ranchero" of Matamoros, Mexico printed a long poem on it's front page entitled "A Lyric of Brownsville" concerning justice and the soldier who killed a doctor. Excerpts from the lengthy poem include a few stanzas specifically referring to Rogers:

A soldier killed a doctor;
Justice gave a scream;
The soldier's capture shocked her
Like some unlikely dream.

Ah, Ha! they cried, the Varlet!
At once shall he be tried;
We'll stop these doings scarlet
On this our Texas side:

We'll make him an example
We'll hang him very high
And give the world a sample
of our law's majesty.

The soldier had his trial
Mid courts and prisons banged,
And was, beyond denial,
Ordered to be hanged.

But the day he is to dangle
So nicely in the air,
In jail just hear the wrangle
The soldier isn't there!

Rogers was becoming a local folk hero.

The mystery of Rogers' escape from the Military Prison was revealed in a letter dated May 24, 1866 from Bvt. Major General G. W. Getty to Bvt. Colonel C. C. Whittlesey, Assistant Adjt. General, Department of Texas.

"Colonel, I have the honor herewith to respectfully request that a day may be again fixed by the Dept. Comd. for the execution of Private Robert Rogers, Co. B, 77th Ohio Inf Regt. Veteran Volunteers, whose execution for murder was ordered by G. C. M. O. no. 12 Head Qrs. Dept. of Texas, Galveston, Texas March 27, 1866, to take place on Friday the 27th of April, 1866 at Brownsville.

On the night of the 26th of April 1866 Rogers was supposed to have made his escape from prison. In the morning of the day fixed for his execution he could not be found. It has just transpired that although he did escape from his room, he did not escape from the prison but concealed himself under the floor of one of the rooms of the prison and for the last month has been engaged in tunneling his way out. A plan for the escape of a very large number of men sentenced by the Civil Courts to the Penitentiary and to be hung was divulged by one of their number today, the escape was to take place tonight. This man moreover divulged the fact that Rogers was under the prison at work.

An examination of the prison disclosed where Rogers had been concealed, disclosed his implements of work and his tunnel not less than 80 feet long, leading through the prison wall, under two sidewalks, the street, a yard and a building. The tunnel was completed and Rogers, when discovered, had escaped from the tunnel which opened under the building and had attempted to secrete himself under the floor of the building, having crawled not less than thirty feet under the floor. There is no doubt about his identification. I therefore respectfully ask that another day may be appointed by the General

Commanding the Dept. for the carrying into execution the sentence of the Court which tried Private Rogers.

I have the honor to be Colonel

Your Obdt Servt.

G. W. Getty, Bvt Maj Genl

The Daily Ranchero of Matamoros, Mexico, Saturday, May 26, 1866 carried a long story on Rogers' disappearance and capture.

There are only a few details contained in the newspaper report which were unmentioned in the official communication previously quoted. The tunnel near its street termination was only 2-1/2 feet below the ground surface and of sufficient diameter to permit a large man to crawl easily through it. Rogers, while digging the tunnel, had food and water given him by other prisoners from their own scanty fare. He also received some help and obvious cooperation in his venture. His sole digging implement was one half of a metal canteen. The house which was over the termination of the tunnel was occupied by an American woman and her children. They noticed earth movements and noises as Rogers completed his exit. The woman and her children finally removed several floor boards and were astonished to see a man crawl out of the earth. They reported the matter and in a short while the mystery of Rogers' escape was solved. The tunnel was filled in by a work gang.

A new date was assigned for Rogers execution and he was hanged in Brownsville, Texas on June 8, 1866. His execution was the subject of a story in the Daily Ranchero of June 9, 1866.

A minister spoke, clearing Rogers of the crime and asserting the true murderer was the demon whiskey.

Rogers was dropped off the scaffold and fell four feet to his death at about 20 minutes past three o'clock. His demeanor before the execution was one of fear and appeared a cringing coward.

The execution of Private Robert Rogers on June 8, 1866 was the last of the 267 Union soldiers executed, as carried on the Official List, for crimes committed while in service.

REFERENCES:

Military Personnel Records, RG-#94
Court Martial Proceedings, RG-#153 MM 3768
The Daily Ranchero, Matamoros, Mexico, April 29, 1866, May 26, 1866, June 8, 1866.
San Antonio Daily Herald, May 22, May 11, 1866.
Official Roster of Ohio Soldiers, 1861-1866.
Ohio in the War, Whitelaw Reid, New York, 1868, Moore, Wilstack, and Baldwin.
Baptismal Record, Robert Rogers, "First Ledger of the Church of the Advent, Episcopal, Brownsville, Texas, 1851-1899.
The Marietta Republican - January 10, 1862
U.S. Census Report - 1860 - Washington County - Ohio
History of Washington County - Ohio
The Marietta Register - May 10-24, July 5-19, 1866.
The Marietta Times - May 10-24, 1866.
The Rio Grande Courier, April 20, 1866.

Appendix A

Photographs and Illustrations

Ante Bellum oil painting circa 1854 (attributed to itinerant Indiana artist R.B. Craft) of Minerva Hyner Cook (1828-1865) murdered in her plantation home near Vicksburg. Photo courtesy of descendant William C. Maute of New Orleans, Louisiana.

452
MICH.

4063
THOS. JOHNSON

Above: *Grave markers at Memphis National Cemetery for Jacob Snover (front) and rear marked unknown though believed to be for John Callaghan.* Left: *Grave markers at Memphis National Cemetery for Thomas Johnson (executed with Snover & Callahan) and Michael Flynn not on official list. Photos courtesy of Memphis National Cemetery.*

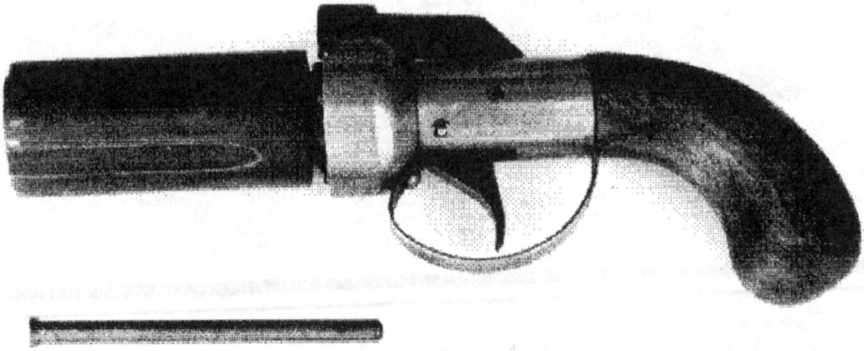

Ethan Allen Pepperbox Revolver (forerunner of colt revolver) similar to one used in Roger Johnson Case #134.

Photo of executed union soldier, believed to be Pvt. William Henry Johnson, Co. E, 23rd Regiment USCT. hung for attempted rape. He is not among those listed on "the Official List", but is mentioned in an Army of the Potomac dispatch dated June 20, 1864, which reads in part: "A negro named William Johnson was executed this morning in front of the Jordan house, in full view of the enemy, for an attempt to violate the person of a young lady at New Kent Court House (located between Old Church and White House). A battery close by had been shelling the rebels just previous to the execution, and they opened in reply, throwing a number of shells rather closer than desirable, one of which struck George Polley, Sgt. Maj. of the 10th Mass. Regiment who died in a few minutes." He had completed his term of military service and was to return to Mass. on the following day. Courtesy of Library of Congress.

Sketched scene of execution by Alfred Ward hanging of Pvt. Michael Lanahan in Washington, D.C., on Dec. 23, 1861, for the murder of Major Arnold Lewis of his Regiment. Courtesy of the Collection of Library of Congress.

Boyd County, Kentucky, Courthouse (left) and jail (right) where Civil War military arrestees were temporarily jailed. Rogers Case #267 among others was held here. Photo courtesy of Boyd County Historical Society.

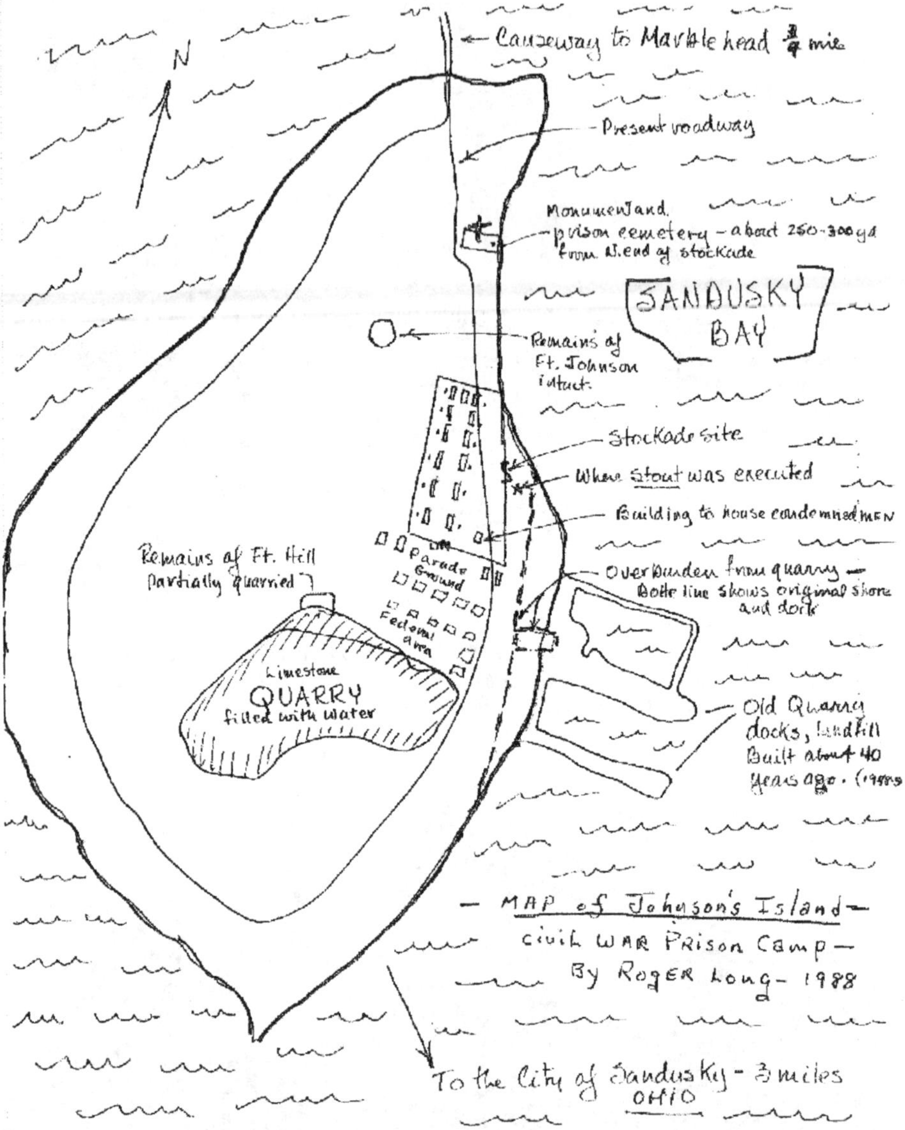

Map of Johnson's Island Civil War prisoner of war camp, 3 miles off shore of Sandusky, Ohio, where Reuben Stout was executed. Photo courtesy of Roger Long, authority on Johnson's Island.

Major General Marsena Rudolph Patrick, Provost Marshall of Army of the Potomac, at his quarters near City Point. Photo collection of Congressional Library.

Aerial view of Ft. Jefferson on Garden Key, the Dry Tortugas, 75 miles west of Miami, Florida used as a prison for some Union Army soldier convicts. Courtesy of the State Library of Florida, Dept. of State.

McRaven House in Vicksburg, Mississippi, home of Mr. John Bobb murdered by Union sol - diers. Photo courtesy of Vicksburg Evening Post.

Gloucester House, Home of George Washington Sargent, near Natchez, Mississippi where he was murdered on May 10, 1864. Sketch courtesy of Paula DeSmet.

Page from case book of embalming surgeon William J. Bunnell, 2 bottom entries are for Privates Geary and Gordon. Comment written vertically on right of entries states "these two men was hung for the rape of a lady." Courtesy of Mrs. Dorothy Bunnell.

Illustration from Frank Leslie's Illustrated Newspaper depicting January 4, 1862 scenes at exe - cution of deserter Pvt. H. Johnson. From E. C. Johnson family collection.

Unidentified scene of formation for an execution by hanging. Courtesy Library of Congress Collections.

Statue of the Reverend Father William Corby, C.S.C. chaplain of the Irish Brigade, at Gettysburg, Pennsylvania. Photo by Lane Studio, Gettysburg, Pennsylvania.

Execution scene (in period Aug.-Sept., 1864, not on official list). A clergyman praying with doomed man prior to execution. Courtesy Collection of Library of Congress.

Troops passing to view executed solider. Courtesy of Collection Library of Congress.

 # 1 Prisoner, "Mister, can you tell one how I can get out of this place. I want to fight the Ingins!" #2 on horseback, (Officer of the Day), "I don't know, you will have to see Captain Barnes." Prisoner wants to join US Volunteer Regiment to secure release from Point Lookout Prisoner of War Camp. From "Sketches From Prison", by a Confederate Artist, J.J. Omenhausser, 1863-65. Courtesy of Maryland State Park Foundation Inc.

Confederate prisoners of war taking oath of allegiance to United States before enlisting in U.S. Volunteer Regiments to serve in the western frontiers only. Courtesy Collections of Library of Congress.

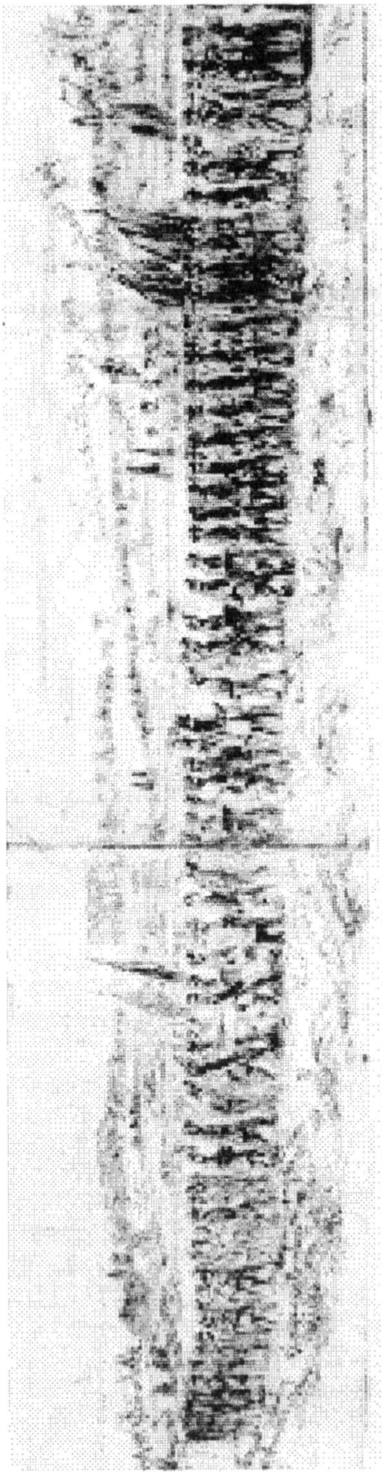

Sketch by Alfred Ward, for Leslie's illustrated Newspapers of the procession to execution site on Aug. 29, 1863, for 5 deserters, Privates Folancy, Kuhne, Lai, Rionese and Walter, recruits assigned to the 118th Penn. Regt. (cases #44-48). From right to left, Commander, band, color guard, firing party, details, carrying coffin, followed by future occupant and clergyman, pioneers with picks and shovels to bury coffined remains. Courtesy of Library of Congress.

Sketch of the actual execution, 5 firing squads firing simultaneously at men seated on their coffins. One did not fall over from seated position. The Surgeon present prevented the firing party commander from having to administer the coupe de grace by examining the man and proclaiming his death. Sketch by Alfred Ward, courtesy of Collections of Library of Congress.

Sign on embalming quarters of Wm. J. Bunnell, embalmer of Geary Case #127 and Gordon Case #128. Courtesy of Dorothy Bunnell.

Judge Advocate General Joseph Holt. Courtesy of the Collections of the Library of Congress.

Telegram

War Department.
Adjutant General's Office.
Washington. February 8. 1864.

Brig. General
B. F. Kelley.
Cumberland. Md.

The President has commuted the death sentence in the case of Private John Carter, Third Virginia Cavalry, to confinement during the war.
Acknowledge receipt.
E. D. Townsend.
Asst Adjt General

Official Copy.
C. A. Nichols
Asst Adjt General.

Acknowledgment receipt.

An example of President Lincoln's commuting the death sentence of a court martial. Courtesy of National Archives.

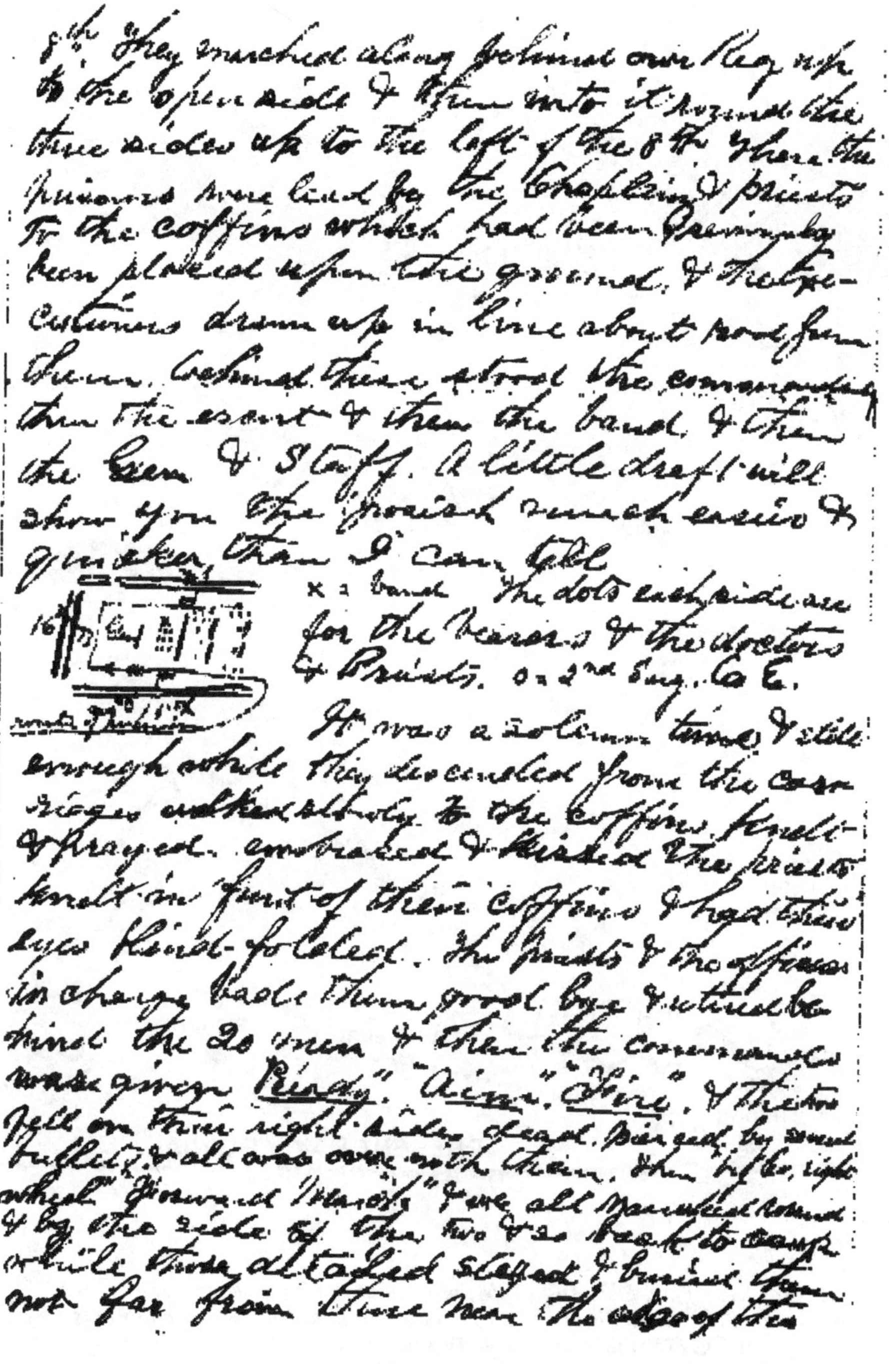

8th They marched along behind our Reg up to the open side & then into it round the three sides up to the left of the 8th. There the prisoners were led by the Chaplain & priests to the coffins which had been previously been placed upon the ground, & the executioners drawn up in line about 6 rods from them. behind these stood the commanding then the escort & then the band. & then the Gen & Staff. a little draft will show you the position much easier & quicker than I can tell

x = band The dots each side are for the bearers & the doctors & Priests. o = 2nd Brig. 6 C.

It was a solemn time & still enough while they descended from the carriages walked slowly to the coffins knelt & prayed. embraced & kissed the priests knelt in front of their coffins & had their eyes blind-folded. The priests & the officers in charge bade them good bye & retired behind the 20 men & then the command was given "Ready". "Aim". "Fire". & the two fell on their right sides dead. pierced by some bullets & all was over with them. then by the right wheel "Forward March" & we all marched round & by the side of the two & so back to camp while those detailed stayed & buried them not far from there near the edge of the

A letter from Civil War soldier, Henry Marshall includes a diagram of the military formation for an execution of Pvts. Wales and Vandall, cases #73 & 74, as well as description of the pro - cession. Courtesy of the Schoff Collection, Wm. L. Clements Library, University of Michigan, at Ann Arbor, Michigan.

Present day Pound Gap, Kentucky, 1997.

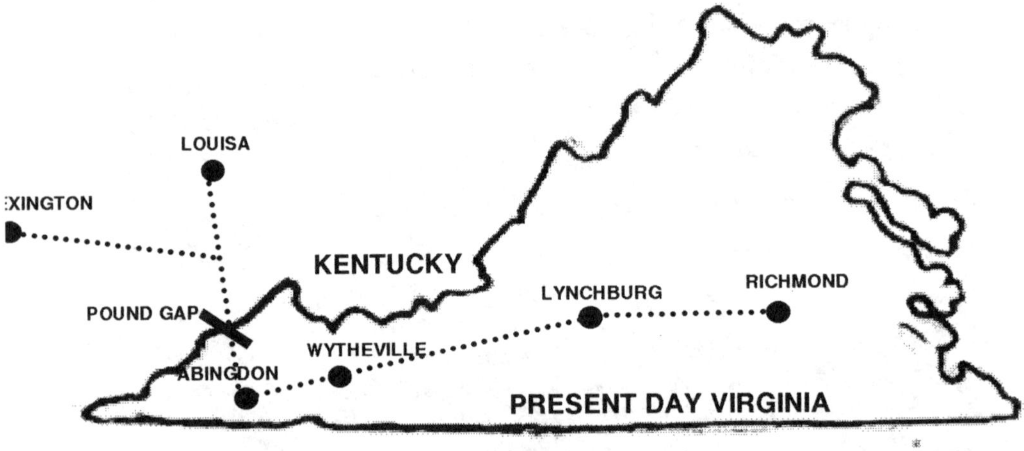

Confederate War Dept. G.O. #65, Aug., 1864, resulted in routing prisoners of war from Libby Prison and others in the Richmond area via the Virginia/Tennessee Ry. to Abingdon, Va. They were marched to Pound Gap and advised to head North to Louisa (due North) or Lexington, Ky. (Northwest) where Union forces were Hqd. and to report to the Provost Marshall as confederate deserters.

The execution of John T. Barnett on September 17, 1863, at Portsmouth, Virginia. Courtesy of Collections of Library of Congress.

FOR OFFICIAL USE ONLY

LIST OF

U.S. SOLDIERS EXECUTED

BY

UNITED STATES MILITARY AUTHORITIES

DURING

THE LATE WAR

Name	Rank	Co.	Regiment	Date of execution
ARKANSAS				
Keiffe, Peter	Private	B	2d Cavalry	Oct. 7, 1864
MeBroone, Alexander D.	do	B	1st Infantry	Apr. 21, 1865
CALIFORNIA				
Hudson, Frank	Private	I	2d Cavalry	June 16, 1865
Kerr, Robert	do	A	1st Cavalry	Mar. 20, 1864
Kleinkoff, Peter	do	E	4th Infantry	July 17, 1863
Smith, Charles	Corporal	K	1st Infantry	Nov. 26, 1862
COLORADO				
Lockman, Charles	Private	F	2d Cavalry	Nov. 10, 1864
Philbrooks, Darius A	1st sergt.	K	1st Cavalry	Apr. 8, 1862
CONNECTICUT				
Brown, John, 2d	Private	H	10th Infantry	Feb. 18, 1865
Collins, James	do	D	8th Infantry	Jan. 7, 1865
Cooper, William	do	E	10th Infantry	Mar. 11, 1865
Dix, Thomas	do	G	1st Heavy Artillery	Dec. 21, 1864
Dix, William	do	E	8th Infantry	Jan. 7, 1865
Elliott, Edward	do	I	14th Infantry	Sept. 18, 1863
Hall, John	do	G	1st Heavy Artillery	Dec. 21, 1864
Jackson, William	do	A	10th Infantry	Mar. 10, 1865
Jones, Thomas	do	H	do	Feb. 18, 1865
Landy, Michael	do	A	do	Feb. 17, 1865
Layton, George. alias Charles Eastman	do	K	14th Infantry	Sept. 18, 1863
Mahoney, John	do	K	10th Infantry	Mar. 10, 1865
McCurdy, Henry	do	G	1st Heavy Artillery	Dec. 21, 1864
Morgan, Jacob	do	D	8th Infantry	April 28, 1864
Newton, Frank L.	do	F	13th Infantry	June 16, 1862
Parker, John	do	G	10th Infantry	Feb. 24, 1865
Root, Newell W., *alias* George H. Harris	do	H	1st Heavy Artillery	Jan. 27, 1865
Rowley, John	do	D	7th Infantry	Sept. 3, 1864
Schumaker, Henry	do	C	6th Infantry	Apr. 17, 1864
Smith, John	do	G	1st Heavy Artillery	Dec. 21, 1864
Stark, Henry	do	E	6th Infantry	Apr. 17, 1864
Thompson, James	do	G	1st Heavy Artillery	Dec. 21, 1864
Vandall, Mitchell	do	K	8th Infantry	Nov. 9, 1863
Wales, Francis	do	D	do	do
DELAWARE				
Griffin, William T., *alias* George Bolter	Private	C	8th Infantry	Mar. 10, 1865
ILLINOIS				
Benjamin, Valentine	Private	C	44th Infantry	Nov. 13, 1863
Daily, Erastus C.	do	D	88th Infantry	do
Dickman, Robert	do	G	18th Infantry	Oct. 2, 1861
Geer, David	do	D	28th Infantry	Mar. 4, 1865
McLean, Henry	do	C	2d Light Artillery	Aug. 25, 1863
Myers, John	Sergeant	G	7th Infantry	Apr. 28, 1864
Wilson, William A.	Private	G	12th Cavalry	July 28, 1865
INDIANA				
Billingsby, Charles, *alias* Cooper, *alias* Roberts	Private		7th Battery	Dec. 23, 1864
Blazer, David	do		4th Battery	June 20, 1863
Gay, Robert	do	D	6th Cavalry	Mar. 27, 1863
Murray, John	do	Unas'd	11th Cavalry	Dec. 23, 1864
Reynolds, Hiram	do	H	82d Infantry	Aug. 17, 1863
Ryan, Thomas, *alias* Reagan	do	Unas'd	51st Infantry	Dec. 23, 1864
Stout, Reuben	do	K	60th Infantry	Oct. 23, 1863
Woods, John P.	do	F	19th Infantry	June 12, 1863
KANSAS				
Bell, John	Private	I	2d Cavalry	July 11, 1862
Cole, John W.	do	G	1st Infantry	July 14, 1861
Drescoll, Alexander	do	H	7th Cavalry	Mar. 18, 1862
Raymond, Joseph	do	C	do	Nov. 24, 1861
KENTUCKY				
Anderson, James	Private	H	27th Infantry	Sept. 4, 1863

military authorities during the late war.

Mode of execution	Offense	Authority
Shot	Murder	G.O., No. 168, Dept. of the Missouri, Sept. 14, 1864.
do	Desertion	G.O., No. 23, Dept. of Arkansas, Feb. 18, 1865.
Hanged	Murder	G.O., No. 40, Dept. of the Pacific, June 1, 1865
Shot	do	G.O., No. 4, Dept. of New Mexico, Feb. 29, 1864.
Do	Desertion and attempted murder	G.O., No. 149, War Dept., Adjt. Gen's Office, May 26, 1863.
Do	Mutiny	By order of Colonel J.R. West.
Hanged	Murder	By order of Lieutenant William Wise, 2d Colorado Cavalry.
Shot	Violation 9th Articles of War	G. O., No. 25, Dept. of New Mexico, Apr. 4, 1862.
Hanged	Desertion	G. C. M. O., No. 35, Dept. of Virginia, Feb. 17, 1865.
Shot	do	G. O., No. 179, Dept. Virginia and North Carolina, Dec. 30, 1864.
Do	do	G. C. M. O., No. 47, Dept. of Virginia, Mar. 9, 1865.
Do	do	G. O., No. 172, Army of the James, Dec. 20, 1864.
Do	do	G. O., No. 179, Dept. of Virginia and North Carolina, Dec. 30, 1864.
Do	do	G. O., No. 88, Army of the Potomac, Sept. 11, 1863.
Hanged	Murder	G. O., No. 172, Army of the James, Dec. 20, 1864.
Shot	Desertion	G. O., No. 44, Dept. of Virginia, Mar. 4, 1865.
Hanged	do	G. O., No. 35, Dept. of Virginia, Feb. 17, 1865.
Shot	do	G. O., No. 32, Dept. of Virginia, Feb. 16, 1865.
Do	do	G. O., No. 88, Army of the Potomac, Sept. 11, 1863.
Do	do	G. O., No. 44, Dept. of Virginia, Mar. 4, 1865
Do	do	G. O., No. 172, Army of the James, Dec. 20, 1864.
Do	do	G.O. No. 2, U.S. Forces Norfolk and Portsmoth, Apr. 27, 1864.
Hanged	Theft	S. O., No. 103, Dept. of the Gulf, June 14, 1862.
Shot	Desertion	G.O., No. 34, Dept. of Virginia, Feb. 17, 1865.
Hanged	do	G. C. M. O., No. 3, Army of the Potomac, Jan. 18, 1865.
Do	do	G. O., No. 97, Dept. of Virginia and North Carolina, Aug. 23, 1864.
Shot	do	G. O., No. 50, Dept. of the South, Apr. 15, 1864.
Do	do	G. O., No. 172, Army of the James, Dec. 20, 1864.
Do	do	G. O., No. 50, Dept. of the South, Apr. 15, 1864.
Do	do	G. O., No. 172, Army of the James, Dec. 20, 1864
Do	do	G.O., No. 24, Dept. of Virginia and North Carolina, Oct. 31, 1863.
Do	do	Do.
Shot	Desertion	G. C. M. O., No. 11, Army of the Potomac, Mar. 1, 1865.
Shot	Desertion	G. O., No. 244, Dept. of the Cumberland, Oct. 20, 1863.
Do	do	Do.
Hanged	Murder	Regimental court-martial.
Shot	do	G. C. M. O., No. 38, Army of the Tennessee, Oct. 31, 1864.
Do	Desertion	G. O., No. 105, Dept. of the Cumberland, May 9, 1863.
Hanged	Murder	G. C. M. O., No. 159, War Dept., Adjt. Gen's Office, Apr. 14, 1864.
Shot	desertion	G. O., No. 9, Headquarters Cavalry, Div. of the Gulf, July 25, 1865.
Shot	Desertion	G. O., No. 38, District of Indiana, Dec. 14, 1864.
Do	do	G. O., No. 108, Dept. of the Cumberland, June 19, 1863.
Do	do	G. O., No. 23, Dept. of the Ohio, Mar. 21, 1863.
Do	do	G. O., No. 38, Dist. of Indiana, Dec. 14, 1864.
Hanged	Murder	G. O., No. 188, Dept. of the Cumberland, Aug. 11, 1863.
Shot	Desertion	G. O., No. 38, District of Indiana, Dec. 14, 1864.
Do	Murder	G. O., No. 279, War Dept., Adjt. Gen's Office, Aug. 8, 1863.
Do	Desertion	G. O., No. 60, Army of the Potomac, June 8, 1863.
Hanged	Rape	G. O., No. 55, Headquarters 2d Kansas Cavalry, July 9, 1862.
Shot	Murder	Orders No. 8 Army of the West, July 12, 1861.
Do		
Do		
Shot	Desertion	G. O., No. 130, Dept. of the Ohio, Aug. 13, 1863.

Name	Rank	Co.	Regiment	Date of execution
KENTUCKY—Continued				
Calhoun, Samuel H.	Private	A	2d Infantry	Feb 5, 1862
Carmen, Frazier	do	F	27th Infantry	Sept. 4, 1863
Coffey, Christopher	do	C	do	do
Coffey, John W.	do	C	do	do
Gatewood, Richard	do	C	1st Infantry	Dec. 20, 1861
Minix, William	do	A	9th Infantry	June 16, 1863
Pointer, James A.	do	H	27th Infantry	Sept. 4, 1863
Rhea, Larkin D.	do	C	7th Infantry	Dec. 24, 1864
Roarch, Lewis	do	D	do	Jan. 6, 1865
Schockman, John	do	I	1st Infantry	June 21, 1863
Stivers, Lewis	do	B	7th Infantry	Sept. 21, 1862
LOUISIANA				
Scott, Francis	Private	F	1st Infantry	Aug. 14, 1863
MAINE				
Hunter, Cyrus H.	Private	G	3d Infantry	Dec. 4, 1863
Jewett, Thomas	do	D	5th Infantry	Aug. 14, 1863
Laird, William H.	do	G	17th Infantry	July 15, 1863
Lunt, William W	do	I	9th Infantry	Dec. 1, 1862
MARYLAND				
Downing, Samuel W., *alias* John W. Ball	Private	H	4th Infantry	Sept. 16, 1864
Jones, Albert	do	K	3d Infantry	Sept. 18, 1863
Kane, William, *alias* William Carter	do	A	8th Infantry	Dec. 16, 1864
Kuhnes, Joseph	do	I	2d Infantry	Mar. 7, 1862
McNealy, J.J., *alias* Joseph Johnson	do		1st Infantry	Mar. 18, 1865
McDonald, George W., *alias* M. M. Dunning	Sergeant	F	3d Cavalry	Sept. 21, 1864
Merling, Charles H.	Private	H	2d Infantry	Oct. 14, 1864
Sweney, John	do	C	1st Infantry	Sept. 20, 1864
Weaver, James, *alias* N. E. Baker	do	D	do	Mar. 26, 1865
Williams, Charles	do	D	4th Infantry	Sept. 25, 1863
MASSACHUSETTS				
Baker, Wallace	Private	I	55th Infantry (col'd)	June 18, 1864
Cook, John W.	do	B	do	Feb. 18, 1864
Dawson, Thomas R.	do	I	20th Infantry	Apr. 20, 1864
Dixon, John C.	do	H	1st Heavy Artillery	Dec. 23, 1864
Hill, William F.	do	K	20th Infantry	Aug. 28, 1863
Lloyd, Spencer	do	B	55th Infantry (col'd)	Feb. 18, 1864
Lynch, William	do	G	2d Cavalry	June 16, 1863
McElheny, Frank	do	F	24th Infantry	Aug. 8, 1864
Ormsley, William E.	do	E	2d Cavalry	Feb. 7, 1864
Roberts, John	do	H	15th Infantry	Oct. 30, 1863
Smith, John M	do	A	55th Infantry (col'd)	Feb. 18, 1864
Smith, John	do	1st Co.	Sharpshooters	Aug. 28, 1863
Starbird, John D.	do	K	19th Infantry	May 20, 1864
MICHIGAN				
Anderson, Henry	Private	D	9th Cavalry	May 13, 1865
Beardsley, Henry C	do	G	5th Infantry	Oct. 17, 1863
Milika, Julius	do	E	10th Infantry	May 15, 1863
MISSOURI				
Eastman, Edward	Private	B	2d Artillery	Nov. 25, 1864
Jackson, Jefferson	do	B	9th M. S. M. Cavalry	Oct. 28, 1864
Kingston, Paul	do	M	1st Cavalry	Nov. 27, 1863
Purvis, Abraham	do	C	21st Infantry	Jan. 13, 1865
Reily, John, Jr.	do	L	2d Artillery	Apr. 29, 1864
Richardson, Ephraim	do	C	21st Infantry	Jan. 13, 1865
NEW HAMPSHIRE				
Benson, John		Unas'd	5th Infantry	Jan. 6, 1865
Bradley, George, *alias* George W. Bates	Private	H	do	Dec. 23, 1864
Brown, James F.	do	G	3d Infantry	Dec. 26, 1864
Burnham, Henry A.	do	E	5th Infantry	May 9, 1864
Eagen, John	do	A	2d Infantry	Apr. 15, 1864
Genan or Jenos, Michael, *alias* John Martin	do	B	5th Infantry	Dec. 30, 1864
Holt, Henry	do	F	2d Infantry	Apr. 15, 1864

military authorities during the late war.

Mode of execution	Offense	Authority
Shot	Murder	G. O., No. 7, Dept. of the Ohio, Feb. 4, 1862
do	Desertion	G. O., No. 130 Dept. of the Ohio, Aug. 13, 1863.
do	do	Do.
do	do	Do.
do	do	G. O., No. 13, Dept. of Western Virginia, Nov. 15, 1861.
do	do	G. O., No. 140, Dept. of the Cumberland, June 12, 1863.
do	do	G. O., No. 130, Dept. of the Ohio, Aug. 13, 1863.
Hanged	Murder	G. O., No. 178, Dept. of the Gulf, Dec. 20, 1864.
do	do	G. O., No. 180, Dept. of the Gulf, Dec. 29, 1864.
Shot	Desertion	G. O., No. 153, Dept. of the Cumberland, June 22, 1863.
do	Murder	
Shot	Murder	G. O., No. 58, Dept. of the Gulf, Aug. 10, 1863.
Shot	Desertion	G. O., No. 103, Army of the Potomac, Nov. 20, 1863.
do	do	G. O., No. 73, Army of the Potomac, Aug. 7, 1863.
do	do	G. O., No. 57, Dept. of the East, July 7, 1863.
do	do	G. O., No. 171, War Dept., Adjt. Gen's Office, Oct. 29, 1862.
Shot	Desertion	G. O., No. 83, Dept. of Washington, Sept. 14, 1864.
do	do	G. O., No. 88 Army of the Potomac, Sept. 11, 1863.
Hanged	do	G. C. M. O., No. 50 Army of the Potomac, Dec. 12, 1864.
do	Murder	G. O., No. 87, Army of the Potomac, Mar. 4, 1862.
Shot	Desertion	G. O., No. 12, Army of the Potomac, Mar. 11, 1865.
do	Desertion and attempted murder	G.O. N. 74, Middle Department, Sept. 19, 1864.
do	Desertion	G. C. M. O., No. 36, Army of the Potomac, Sept. 18, 1864.
do	do	G. C. M. O., No. 32, Army of the Potomac, Aug. 31, 1864.
do	do	G. O., No. 12, Army of the Potomac, Mar. 11, 1865.
do	do	G. O., No. 90, Army of the Potomac, Sept. 17, 1863.
Shot	Mutiny	G.O., No. 90, Dept. of the South, June 16, 1864.
Hanged	Rape	G. O., No. 6, Dist. of Florida, Feb. 17, 1864.
do	Desertion and rape	G. C. M. O., No. 40, War Dept., Adjt. Gen's Office, Mar. 15, 1864.
shot	Desertion and rape	G. C. M. O., No. 51, Army of the Potomac, Dec. 17, 1864.
do	do	G. O., No. 86, Army of the Potomac, Aug. 24, 1863.
Hanged	Rape	G. O., No. 6, Dist. of Florida, Feb. 17, 1864.
Shot	Mutiny	G. O., No. 46, Dept. of the East, June 6, 1863.
do	Desertion	G. O., No. 91, Dept. Virginia and North Carolina, Aug. 6, 1864.
do	do	G. O., No. 10, Cavalry Camp, Vienna, Feb. 7, 1864.
do	do	G. O., No. 98 Army of the Potomac, Oct. 24, 1863.
Hanged	Rape	G. O., No. 6, Dist. of Florida, Feb. 17, 1864.
Shot	Desertion	G. O., No. 86, Army of the Potomac, Aug. 24, 1863.
do	do	G. C. M. O., No. 18, Army of the Potomac, May—, 1864.
Shot	Murder	Military Commission, General Kilpatrick.
do	Desertion	G. O., No. 95, Army of the Potomac, Oct. 8, 1863.
do	do	G O., No. 100, Dept. of the Cumberland, May 4, 1863.
Shot	Desertion and pillage	G. O., No. 174, Dept. of the Missouri, Sept. 23, 1864.
do	Murder	G. O., No. 190, Dept. of the MIssouri, Oct. 6, 1864.
Hanged	do	G. O., No. 122, Dept. of the Missouri, Oct. 21, 1863.
do	do	G. O., No. 3, Dept. of the MIssouri, Jan. 9, 1865.
Shot	do	G. O., No. 41, Dept. of the Missouri, Mar. 19, 1864.
Hanged	do	G. O., No. 3, Dept. of the Missouri, Jan. 9, 1865.
Shot	Desertion	G. C. M. O., No. 1, Army of the Potomac, Jan 2, 1865.
Hanged	do	G. C. M. O., No. 51, Army of the Potomac, Dec. 17, 1864.
Shot	do	G. O., No. 173, Army of the James, Dec. 24, 1864.
do	do	G. O., No. 56, Dept. Virginia and North Carolina, May 4, 1864.
do	do	G. O., No. 43, Dept. Virginia and North Carolina, Apr. 14, 1864.
Hanged	do	G. C. M. O., No. 52, Army of the Potomac, Dec. 24, 1864.
Shot	do	G. O., No. 43, Dept. Virginia and North Carolina, Apr. 14, 1864.

Name	Rank	Co.	Regiment	Date of execution
NEW HAMPSHIRE—continued				
Kendall, John	Private	G	2d Infantry	Dec. 17, 1863
Lynch, John, *alias* John Wood	do	F	5th Infantry	Dec. 23, 1864
McDonough, Owen	do	K	2d Infantry	Apr. 29, 1864
Miller, Henry	do	F	3d Infantry	Apr. 16, 1864
Miller, Williams, *alias* James Craig	do	F	5th Infantry	Dec. 23, 1864
Murray, William F.	do	F	2d Infantry	Aug. 2, 1861
James, Scott	do	G	do	Apr. 29, 1864
Sharp, Joseph H., *alias* Samuel Trangler	do	A	12th Infantry	Feb. 9, 1865
Thompson, John	do	H	5th Infantry	Dec. 16, 1864
Velon, John	do	G	do	Oct. 28, 1864
NEW JERSEY				
Callaghan, John	Private	H	2d Cavalry	June 10, 1864
Connelly, Joseph	do	H	4th Infantry	Oct. 9, 1863
Cox, Peter	do	A	do	Jan. 6, 1865
Johnson, Thomas	do	D	2d Cavalry	June 10, 1864
King, Charles	do	L	3d Cavalry	Jan. 6, 1865
Krubert, Christopher	do	B	13th Infantry	June 19, 1863
Regley, Henry	do	L	3d Cavalry	Jan. 6, 1865
Smith, John	do	H	8th Infantry	Mar. 18, 1865
Snover, John	do	M	2d Cavalry	June 10, 1864
NEW MEXICO				
Coffield, Joseph	Private	K	1st Cavalry	Jan. 19, 1864
Carrabojal, Homoboma	do	D	do	Nov. 27, 1863
Madrid, Juan	do	C	do	Sept. 8, 1865
NEW YORK				
Abraham, Thomas	Private	G	139th Infantry	Mar. 7, 1864
Aierdain, Jacob	Corporal	G	119th Infantry	Sept. 17, 1863
Allen, Winslow N.	Private	H	76th Infantry	Dec. 18, 1863
Brandt, Frederick W.	do	E	81st Infantry	Mar. 26, 1865
Butler, Bradford	do	I	157th Infantry	Aug. 1, 1863
Devlin, Jas., *alias* Pat, Diamond, *alias* Fr'k Tully		E	43d Infantry	Feb. 3, 1865
Devoe, William H.	Private	B	57th Infantry	Dec. 18, 1863
Flood, John, *alias* John Smith	do	E	41st Infantry	June 19, 1864
Geary, Daniel	do	E	72d Infantry	July 15, 1864
Gillespie, Francis	do	B	15th Cavalry	July 11, 1864
Gordon, Ransom S.	do	E	72d Infantry	July 15, 1864
Hamill, Henry	do	D	131st Infantry	Apr. 25, 1863
Hoefler, John	do	E	124th Infantry	Feb. 17, 1865
Hummel, Charles	do	E	7th Infantry	Dec. 16, 1864
Jangrow, Newal	do	H	64th Infantry	Mar. 3, 1865
Johnston, William H.	do	D	1st Cavalry	Dec. 13, 1861
Kessler, John	do	K	103d Infantry	Dec. 5, 1862
Lynch, William I.	do	B	63d Infantry	Sept. 30, 1864
McMahon, John	do	F	99th Infantry	June 13, 1862
McNamara, Patrick	do	K	132d Infantry	June 30, 1863
Nichols, John	do	A	69th Infantry	Mar. 14, 1865
Preble, James	do	K	12th Cavalry	Mar. 31, 1865
Prevost, Joseph	do	A	1st Lin. Cavalry	Nov. 10, 1864
Raymond, Anthony	do	B	64th Infantry	Mar. 3, 1865
Rowe, Edward	do	C	179th Infantry	Dec. 10, 1864
Smalz, Adam	do	E	66th Infantry	Oct. 2, 1863
Smith, Daniel C.	do	C	179th Infantry	Dec. 10, 1864
Smith, William	do	E	78th Infantry	Sept. 18, 1863
Sperry, Charles	Sergeant	E	13th Cavalry	Mar. 3, 1865
Suhr, Christopher	Private	E	7th Infantry	Dec. 16, 1864
Thornton, Waterman	do	E	179th Infantry	Jan. 6, 1865
Timlin, John	do	D	145th Infantry	Sept. 25, 1863
Treece, Cornelius	do	K	78th Infantry	do
Turner, Charles	do	C	114th Infantry	Dec. 28, 1863
Van, George	do	D	12th Infantry	Sept. 18, 1863
OHIO				
Connel, Michael	Private	E	24th Infantry	Mar. 5, 1862
Hardup, John W.	do	A	43d Infantry	Sept. 6, 1865
Prince, George W.	do	B	22d Infantry	Dec. 16, 1864
Rodgers, Robert	do	B	77th Infantry	June 8, 1866
Thompson, John H.	do	C	1st Cavalry	Apr. 29, 1864
Whitlow, Isaac B., *alias* John Hall	do	D	23d Infantry	Aug. 5, 1864

Mode of execution	Offense	Authority
Shot	Desertion	G.O., No. 111 Dept. of the South, Dec. 14, 1863
Hanged	do	G.C.M.O., No. 51, Army of the Potomac, Dec. 17, 1864
Shot	do	G.O., No. 45, Dept. Virginia and North Carolina, Apr. 18, 1864
do	do	Drum-head court-martial, Apr. 16, 1864
Hanged	do	G.C.M.O., No. 51, Army of the Potomac, Dec. 17, 1864
do	Murder	G.O., No. 25, Dept. Northeast Virginia, Aug. 1, 1861
Shot	Desertion	G.O., No. 45, Dept. Virginia and North Carolina, Apr. 18, 1864
do	do	G.O., No. 26, Dept. of Virginia, Feb. 4, 1865
Hanged	do	G.C.M.O., No. 50, Army of the Potomac, Dec. 12, 1864
Shot	do	G.C.M.O., No. 39, Army of the Potomac, Oct. 15, 1864
Shot	Rape and theft	G.C.M.O., No. 119, War Dept., Adjt. Gen's Office, May 26, 1864
do	Desertion	G.O., No. 91, Army of the Potomac, Oct. 2, 1863
do	do	G.C.M.O., No. 1 Army of the Potomac, Jan. 2, 1865
do	Rape and theft	G.C.M.O., No. 119, War Dept., Adjt. Gen's Office, May 26, 1864
do	Spy	By order of General Sheridan
do	Desertion	G.O., No. 63, Army of the Potomac, June 13, 1863
do	Spy	By order of General Sheridan
do	Desertion	G.C.M.O., No. 12 Army of the Potomac, March 11, 1865
do	Rape and theft	G.C.M.O., No. 119, War Dept., Adjt. Gen's Office, May 26, 1864
Shot	Murder	G.O., No. 33, Dept. of New Mexico, Dec. 31, 1863
Hanged	do	G.O., No. 104, Dept. of New Mexico, Sept. 30, 1863
do	do	G.O., No. 23, Dept. of New Mexico, Sept. 2, 1865
Shot	Acting as a spy	G.C.M.O., No. 26, Dept. Virginia and N. Carolina, Feb. 29, 1864
do	Desertion	G.O., No. 88, Army of the Potomac, Sept. 11, 1863
do	do	G.O., No. 104, Army of the Potomac, Dec. 5, 1863
do	do	G.C.M.O., No. 51, Dept. of Virginia, Mar. 25, 1865
do	do	G.O., No. 71, Army of the Potomac, July 21, 1863
do	do	G.O., No. 9, Dept. of the East, Feb. 1, 1865
do	do	G.O., No. 104, Army of the Potomac, Dec. 5, 1863
do	do	G.O., No. 91, Dept. of the South, June 17, 1864
Hanged	Rape	G.C.M.O., No. 194, War Dept., Adjt. Gen's Office, July 8, 1864
do	Murder	G.O., No. 44, Dept. of West Virginia, July 10, 1864
do	Rape	G.C.M.O., No. 194, War Dept., Adjt. Gen's Office, July 8, 1864
Shot	Pillaging	S.O., No. 37, Advanced Brig. on Bayou Boeuff, La., Apr. 25, 1863
do	Desertion	G.C.M.O., No. 7, Army of the Potomac, Feb. 9, 1865
Hanged	do	S.C.M.O., No. 50, Army of the Potomac, Dec. 12, 1864
Shot	do	G.C.M.O., No. 9, Army of the Potomac, Feb. 20, 1865
do	do	G.O., No. 52, Army of the Potomac, Dec. 11, 1861
Hanged	Murder	G.O., No. 186, War Dept., Adjt. Gen's Office, Nov. 15, 1862
Shot	Desertion	G.C.M.O., No. 35, Army of the Potomac, Sept. 15, 1864
Hanged	Murder	G.O., No. 54, Dept. of Virginia, June 1, 1862
do	do	G.O., No. 71, Dept. of North Carolina, May 31, 1865
do	Desertion	G.C.M.O., No. 11, Army of the Potomac, Mar. 1, 1865
Shot	Rape	G.O., No. 22, Dept. of North Carolina, Mar. 26, 1865
hanged	Murder	G.O., No. 72, Dept. of West Virginia, Sept. 10, 1864
Shot	Desertion	G.C.M.O., No. 9, Army of the Potomac, Feb. 20, 1865
Hanged	do	G.C.M.O., 49, Army of the Potomac, Dec. 6, 1864
Shot	do	G.O., No. 92, Army of the Potomac, Sept, 27, 1863
Hanged	do	G.C.M.O., No. 49, Army of the Potomac, Dec. 6, 1864
Shot	do	G.O., No. 88, Army of the Potomac, Sept. 11, 1863
do	Rape	G.O., No. 31, Dept. of Washington, Feb. 27, 1865
Hanged	Desertion	G.C.M.O., No. 50, Army of the Potomac, Dec. 12, 1864
do	do	G.C.M.O., No. 1, Army of the Potomac, Jan. 2, 1865
Shot	do	G.O., No. 90, Army of the Potomac, Sept. 17, 1863
do	do	G.O., No. 88, Army of the Potomac, Sept. 11, 1863
do	do	G.O. No. 80, Dept. of the Gulf, Dec. 7, 1863
do	do	G.O., No. 88, Army of the Potomac, Sept. 11, 1863
....	....	..
Hanged	Murder	G.C.M.O., No. 8, Dept. of the Ohio, Aug. 4, 1865
Shot		Desertion G.O., No. 74, Dept. of Arkansas, Nov. 8, 1864
Hanged	Murder	G.C.M.O., No. 21, Dept. of Texas, May 28, 1866
Shot	Desertion and theft	G.C.M.O., No. 170, War Dept., Ajt. Gen's Office, Apr. 21, 1864
do	Desertion	S.O., No. 30, U.S. Forces in the Field, Dept. of West Virginia, Aug. 4, 1864

Name	Rank	Co.	Regiment	Date of execution
OREGON				
Ely, Francis	Private	A	1st Cavalry	Mar. 11, 1864
PENNSYLVANIA				
Barnett, John T.	Private	A	11th Cavalry	Sept. 18, 1863
Clark, Charles	do	H	1st Light Artillery	Mar. 2, 1863
Dormady, William	do	H	do	do
Folancy, John, *alias* Geacinto Lerchzie	do	I	118th Infantry	Aug. 29, 1863
Foster, John	do	Unas'd	58th Infantry	Jan. 3, 1865
Goodrich, Peter	do	I	97th Infantry	Feb. 27, 1864
Grover, William	do	A	46th Infantry	June 19, 1863
Haley, James	do	B	116th Infantry	Oct. 16, 1863
Howe, William H.	do	A	do	Aug. 25, 1864
Kelley, James	do	Unas'd	67th Infantry	Mar. 9, 1865
Kuhne, George, *alias* G. Week	do	Unas'd	118th Infantry	Aug. 29, 1863
Lai, Emil, *alias* E. Duffie	do	Unas'd	do	do
Lanahan, John	do	I	46th Infantry	Dec. 23, 1861
McKee, William	do	A	do	Jan. 6, 1864
Murphy, James	do	I	55th Infantry	Jan. 6, 1864
Oliver, Hiram	do	Not given		Sept. 6, 1865
Rionese, John, *alias* George Rionese	do	I	118th Infantry	Aug. 29, 1863
Roberts, Jeremiah—Richards	do	D	55th Infantry	Mar. 27, 1865
Smitz, William	do	F	90th Infantry	Oct. 2, 1865
Thompson, James	do	K	97th Infantry	Feb. 7, 1864
Walter, Charles, *alias* C. Zene	do	Unas'd	118th Infantry	Aug. 20, 1863
Wert, Michael	do	G	184th Infantry	Jan. 6, 1865
Wilson, James	do	B	97th Infantry	Feb. 7, 1864
RHODE ISLAND				
Davis, William	Private	G	2d Cavalry	Aug. 30, 1863
Smith, Richard	do	F	do	do
TEXAS				
Garcia, Pedro	Private	E	1st Cavalry	June 27, 1864
VERMONT				
Blowers, George E.	Private	A	2d Infantry	Dec. 18, 1863
Carpenter, Charles	Unassigned Recruit			Apr. 22, 1864
Riley, Matthew, *alias* John Roach	Unassigned Recruit			do
Tague, John	Private	A	5th Infantry	Dec. 18, 1863
WEST VIRGINIA				
Marcum, John	Sergeant	F	5th Infantry	Jan. 19, 1864
Raber, Phillip	Private	K	9th Infantry	Nov. 27, 1863
WISCONSIN				
Carroll, John	Private	D	20th Infantry	Nov. 11, 1864
U.S. VOLUNTEERS				
Dowdy, William C.	Private	E	1st Regiment	Sept. 9, 1864
Smith, William M	do	C	4th Regiment	Dec. 22, 1864
VETERAN RESERVE CORPS.				
Johnson, William G.	Sergeant	F	21st Regiment	Jan. 3, 1865
U.S. COLORED TROOPS				
Allen, James	Private	do	3d Infantry	Dec. 1, 1865
Brooks, Dandridge	do	G	38th Infantry	July 30, 1865
Catlett, Alfred	do	E	1st Heavy Artillery	May 6, 1865
Collins, Aaron	do	H	6th Cavalry	Aug. 18, 1865
Colwell, Alexander	do	E	1st Heavy Artillery	May 6, 1865
Cowell, Willis	do	F	1st Cavalry	May 26, 1865
Craig, David	do	K	3d Infantry	Dec. 1, 1865
Davis, Emanuel	do	A	48th Infantry	Aug. 31, 1864
Dixon, George	do	K	79th Infantry	July 21, 1865
Four, Thomas	do	D	52d Infantry	May 26, 1865
Grant, Simon	do	H	21st Infantry	June 23, 1865
Grien, Joseph	do	I	3d Infantry	Dec. 1, 1865

military authorities during the late war.

Mode of execution	Offense	Authority
Shot	Desertion	G.O., No. 8, Dept. of the Pacific, Feb. 2, 1864
Shot	Desertion and highway robbery	G.O., No. 256 War Dept., Adj. Gen's Office, Aug. 1, 1863
Hanged	Murder	G.O., No. 10, Dept. of Virginia, Feb. 18, 1863
do	do	do
Shot	Desertion	G.O., No. 84, Army of the Potomac, Aug. 23, 1863
do	do	G.O., No. 181, Dept. Virginia and North Carolina, Dec. 31, 1864
do	do	G.O., No. 17, Dept. of the South, Feb. 2, 1864
do	do	G.O., No. 63, Army of the Potomac, June 13, 1865
do	do	G.O., No. 95, Army of the Potomac, Oct. 8, 1863
Hanged	Desertion and murder	G.O., No. 26, Dept. of the Susquehana, Apr. 9, 1864
Shot	Desertion	G.C.M.O., No. 11, Army of the Potomac, Mar. 1, 1865
do	do	G.O., No. 84, Army of the Potomac, Aug. 23, 1863
do	do	do
Hanged	Murder	G.O., No. 54, Army of the Potomac, Dec. 13, 1861
Shot	Desertion	G.O., No. 63, Army of the Potomac, June 13, 1863
do	do	G.O., No. 1, Dept. of the South, Jan 1, 1864
Hanged	Murder	G.C.M.O., No. 8, Dept. of the Ohio, Aug. 4, 1865
Shot	Desertion	G.O., No. 84, Army of the Potomac, Aug. 23, 1863
do	do	G.C.M.O., No. 53, Dept. of Virginia, Mar. 26, 1865
do	do	G.O., No. 92, Army of the Potomac, Sept. 27, 1863
do	do	G.O., No. 17, Dept. of the South, Feb. 2, 1864
do	do	G.O., No. 84, Army of the Potomac, Aug. 23, 1863
do	do	G.C.M.O., No. 1, Army of the Potomac, Jan. 2, 1865
do	do	G.O., No. 17, Dept. of the South, Feb. 2, 1864
Shot	Mutiny	Order of Colonel H. Robinson, 1st Louisiana Cavalry
do	do	do
Shot	Desertion	G.O., No. 44, U.S. Forces on the Rio Grande, June 21, 1864
Shot	Desertion	G.O., No. 104, Army of the Potomac, Dec. 5, 1863
do	do	G.O. No. 28, Dept. of the East, Apr. 12, 1864
do	do	do
do	do	G.O., No. 104, Army of the Potomac, Dec. 5, 1863
Hanged	Murder	G.O., No. 20, Dept. of West Virginia, Dec. 9, 1863
Shot	Desertion	G.O. No. 14, Dept. of West Virginia, Oct. 15, 1863
Shot	Rape	G.C.M.O., No. 263, War Dept., Adjt. Gen's Office, Aug. 30, 1864
Shot	Violation 7th and 21st Art of War	G.O. No. 64, Headquarters 1st U.S. Volunteers, Sept. 8, 1864
do	Desertion	G.O., No. 166, Dept. Virginia and North Carolina, Dec. 9, 1864
Shot	Aiding desertion	G.O., No. 181, Dept. Virginia and North Carolina, Dec. 31, 1864
Shot	Mutiny	G.C.M.O., No. 39, Dept. of Florida, Nov. 13, 1865
Hanged	Rape	G.C.M.O., No. 268, War Dept., Adjt. Gen's Office, June 7, 1865
Shot	do	Drum-head court-martial, S.O., No. 43, May 4, 1865
Hanged	Murder	G.C.M.O., No. 62, Dept. of Kentucky, July 31, 1865
Shot	Rape	Drum-Head court-martial, S.O., No. 43, May 4, 1865
Hanged	Murder	G.C.M.O., No. 60, Dept. of Virginia, May 19, 1865
Shot	Mutiny	G.C.M.O., No. 39, Dept. of Florida, Nov. 13, 1865
Hanged	Murder	G.O., No. 15, Dept. and Army of the Tennessee, July 14, 1864
do	do	G.O., No. 73, Dept. of Arkansas, July 14, 1865
do	do	G.C.M.O., No. 18, Dept. of the Mississippi, May 10, 1865
do	do	G.O., No. 92, Dept. of the South, June 14, 1865
Shot	Murder	G.C.M.O., No. 39, Dept. of Florida, Nov. 13, 1865

Name	Rank	Co.	Regiment	Date of execution
Gripen, James	Private	F	104th Infantry	Nov. 20, 1865
Hamilton, Henry	do	I	2d Infantry	Nov. 4, 1864
Harrison, William H.	do	A	69th Infantry	May 12, 1865
Henderson, William	do	B	66th Infantry	Dec. 7, 1864
Howard, Thomas	do	I	3d Infantry	Dec. 1, 1865
Jackson, Washington	do	E	1st Heavy Artillery	May 6, 1865
Jackson, William	do	G	38th Infantry	July 30, 1865
Jay, Henry	do	I	57th Infantry	June 21, 1865
Johnson, Henry	do	D	52d Infantry	May 26, 1865
Kease, William	1st sergt.	I	116th Infantry	Aug. 11, 1865
Kemp, Lawson	Private	A	55th Infantry	Nov. 19, 1863
Lewis, John	do	E	13th Heavy Artillery	June 13, 1865
Mapp, Samuel	do	D	10th Infantry	Apr. 20, 1865
McCloud, Benjamin	do	E	37th Infantry	Feb. 9, 1866
McDowell, Ephraim	do	D	52d Infantry	May 26, 1865
Mitchell, John	do	B	53d Infantry	Sept. 15, 1864
Moore, Doctor	Sergeant	I	116th Infantry	Aug. 11, 1865
Moore, Peter	Private	D	52d Infantry	May 26, 1865
Morrison, James	Corporal	D	do	do
Nathaniel, Joseph	Private	K	3d Infantry	Dec. 1, 1865
Pierce, Otto	do	L	5th Heavy Artillery	May 26, 1865
Plowder, Jacob	do	E	3d Infantry	Dec.1, 1865
Quinn, James	do	A	11th Heavy Artillery	Nov. 25, 1864
Rawling, Mose	do	D	52d Infantry	May 26, 1865
Roger, Johnson	do	H	6th Heavy Artillery	Sept. 1, 1864
Rudding, Benjamin	do	D	104th Infantry	Nov. 20, 1865
Sheppard, John	do	I	38th Infantry	Oct. 13, 1865
Simms, Giles	Sergeant	F	49th Infantry	Sept. 25, 1864
Stokes, Darius	Private	I	2d Infantry	Dec. 16, 1861
Thompson, Cornelius	do	A	48th Infantry	June 24, 1864
Tontine, Washington	do	F	49th Infantry	Sept. 25, 1864
Turner, Charles	do	E	1st Heavy Artillery	May 6, 1865
Vess, Alexander	do	E	3d Heavy Artillery	Dec. 16, 1864
Walker, William	do	E	21st Infantry	Mar. 1, 1864
Wallace, William	do	D	52d Infantry	May 26, 1865
Williams, Charles	Unassigned recruit			Nov. 25, 1864
Williams, James	Private	G	6th Heavy Artillery	Sept. 1, 1864
Willis, John	do	D	52d Infantry	May 26, 1865
Wilson, Lewis	do	L	10th Heavy Artillery	Mar. 23, 1866
Wright, Fortune	do	A	96th Infantry	Mar. 2, 1866
REGULAR				
Chandler, Seldon S	Private	K	4th Artillery	Sept. 2, 1864
Gibbons, Barney	do	A	7th Infantry	Aug. 12, 1864
Lanahan, Michael	do	A	2d Infantry	Jan. 6, 1863
McMann, John	do	B	11th Infantry	Dec. 18, 1863
Murphy, Frederick *alias* James Powers	do	F	6th Cavalry	Mar. 3, 1865
Tansey, John	do	K	3d Cavalry	Apr. 6, 1862
MISCELLANEOUS				
Loge, William, *alias* French, Bill				Dec. 2, 1864

military authorities during the late war.

Mode of execution	Offense	Authority
Hanged	Rape	G.O., No. 63, Dept. of South Carolina, Nov. 17, 1865
Shot	Mutiny	G.O., No. 132, Dept., of the Gulf, Sept. 18, 1864
Hanged	Murder	G.O., No. 39, Dept. of Arkansas, May 6, 1865
Shot	do	G.O., No. 81, Dept. of Arkansas, Dec. 3, 1864
do	Mutiny	G.C.M.O., No. 39, Dept. of Florida, Nov. 13, 1865
do	Rape	Drum-head court-martial, S.O., No. 43, May 4, 1865
Hanged	do	G.C.M.O., No. 208, War Dept., Adjt. Gen's Office, June 7, 1865
Shot	do	Drum-head court-martial
Hanged	Murder	G.C.M.O., No. 18, Dept. of the Mississippi, May 10, 1865
Shot	Mutiny	G.C.M.O., No. 1, Military Div. of the Southwest, July 14, 1865
do	Rape	Drum-head Court-martial
Hanged	Murder	G.C.M.O., No. 35, Dept. of Kentucky, June 4, 1865
Shot	Mutiny	G.C.M.O., No. 55, Dept. of Virginia, Apr. 9, 1865
do	do	G.C.M.O., No. 9, Dept. of North Carolina, Feb. 1, 1866
Hanged	Murder	G.C.M.O., No. 18, Dept. of the Mississippi, May 10, 1865
Shot	Desertion	G.O., No. 20, Army of the Tennessee, Aug. 4, 1864
do	Mutiny	G.C.M.O., No. 1, Military Div. of the Southwest, July 14, 1865
Hanged	Murder	G.C.M.O., No. 18, Dept. of the Mississippi, May 10, 1865
do	do	do
Shot	Mutiny	G.C.M.O., No. 30, Dept. of Florida, Nov. 13, 1865
Hanged	Murder	G.C.M.O., No. 18, Dept. of the Mississippi, May 10, 1865
Shot	Mutiny	G.C.M.O., No. 39, Dept. of Florida, Nov. 13, 1865
do	Murder	G.O., No. 119, Dept. of the Gulf, Oct. 15, 1864
Hanged	do	G.C.M.O., No. 18, Dept. of the Mississippi, May 10, 1865
Shot	do	G.C.M.O., No. 15, Dept., Virginia and N. Carolina, July 14, 1864
Hanged	Rape	G.O., No. 63, Dept. of South Carolina, Nov. 17, 1865
do	Rape and Murder	G.,C.M.O., No. 268, War Dept., Adjt. Gen's Office, June 7, 1865
Shot	Mutiny	G.O., No. 20, Army of the Tennessee, Aug. 4, 1864
Hanged	Murder	G.O., No. 149, Dept. of the Gulf, Oct. 15, 1864
Shot	do	G.O., No. 9, Dist. of Vicksburg, June 20, 1864
do	Mutiny	G.O., No. 20, Army of the Tennessee, Aug. 4, 1864
do	Rape	Drum-head court-martial, S.O., No. 43, May 4, 1865
Hanged	Murder	G.C.M.O., No. 250, War Dept., Adjt. Gen's Office, July 9, 1864
Shot	Mutiny	G.O., No. 8, Dist. of Florida, Feb. 28, 1864
Hanged	Murder	G.C.M.O., No. 18, Dept. of the Mississippi, May 10, 1865
do	do	G.O., No. 109 Dept. of Washington, Nov. 16, 1864
Shot	do	G.C.M.O., No. 15, Dept. Virginia and N. Carolina, July 14, 1864
Hanged	do	G.C.M.O., No. 18, Dept. of the Mississippi, May 10, 1865
Shot	do	G.C.M.O., No. 20, Dept. of Louisiana, Mar. 6, 1866
Hanged	do	G.O., No. 74, Dept. of Louisiana, Dec. 16, 1865
Shot	Desertion	G.C.M.O., No. 31, Army of the Potomac, Aug. 26, 1864
do	do	G.O., No. 124, Dept. of the Missouri, July 19, 1864
Hanged	Murder	G.O., No. 1, Army of the Potomac, Jan. 2, 1862
Shot	Desertion	G.O., No. 104, Army of the Potomac, Dec. 5, 1863
do	do	G.O., No. 20, Middle Military Division, Feb. 22, 1865
do	Murder	G.O., No. 26, Dept. of New Mexico, Apr. 5, 1862
Hanged	Desertion and murder	S.O., No. 107, Military District of Harper's Ferry, Dec. 2, 1864

INDEX

INDEX

Key to Crime Index
A = Attempted
B = Burglary
D = Desertion
M = Murder
MU = Mutiny
NCL = No cause listed
P = Pillaging
R = Rape
RO = Robbery
S = Spying
Th = Theft

To The Reader

Note: The original manuscript of "All Were Not Heroes" ran upward of 1000 pages which made it difficult to secure a publisher. After much thought we settled for publishing of the present volume of "All Were Not Heroes" which contains the available individual records of the 267 men executed. This was achieved by cutting out a number of relevant chapters which allow the reader to better understand the Civil War laws, rules and regulations as well as military procedures. A companion volume being published contains the following chapters: Military and legal terminology and abbreviations, Articles of War, complete listing of the rules for military conduct and punishments for their violation in force during the Civil War, military court martial procedure, President Lincoln and his decisions on court martial decisions, the colored troops and their problems, the Draft Act during the Civil War bounties for enlistment and bounty jumping. Some cases we discovered which are not included on "The Official List", the trial and identity of the 6 Andersonville Raiders hung in the prison. Some unusual cases uncovered during our research and a list of some military forms and documents and illustrations.

Please notify me when the companion volume to "All Were Not Heroes" is available for purchase. I understand this does not imply an order for purchase.

Name ______________________________

Address ______________________________

City, State, Zip ______________________________

Phone ______________________________

Mail to: E. C. Johnson, 5033 W. Gunnison, Chicago, Illinois 60630